CHOICE & CHANGE

The Psychology of Personal Growth and Interpersonal Relationships

Seventh Edition

April O'Connell

Vincent O'Connell

Santa Fe Community College
University of Florida
University of Maine
at Machias

Lois-Ann Kuntz

PEARSON
Prentice
Hall

Upper Saddle River, New Jersey 07458

Library of Congress Cataloging-in-Publication Data

O'Connell, April.
    Choice and change: the psychology of personal growth and interpersonal relationships /
April O'Connell, Vincent O'Connell, Lois-Ann Kuntz—7th ed.
        p. cm.
    Includes bibliographical references and index.
    ISBN 0-13-189170-7
        1. Personality—Textbooks. 2. Maturation (Psychology)—Textbooks.
    3. Adjustment (Psychology)—Textbooks. I. O'Connell, Vincent, II. Title.

BF698.O27 2004
155.2′5—dc22

2004049276

Sr. Acquisitions Editor: Jeff Marshall
VP/Editor in Chief: Leah Jewell
Editorial Assistant: Jill Liebowitz
Director of Marketing: Beth Mejia
Marketing Assistant: Irene Fraga
Managing Editor (Production): Joanne Riker
Asst. Managing Editor (Production): Maureen Richardson

Manufacturing Buyer: Tricia Kenny
Cover Design: Bruce Kenselaar
Cover Illustration/Photo: Photodisc, Inc.
Composition: GGS Book Services, Atlantic Highlands
Full-Service Project Management: GGS Book Services, Atlantic Highlands
Printer/Binder: Phoenix/BookTech

This book was set in 10/12 Times Roman. The cover was printed by Phoenix Color Corp.

Pearson Education Ltd.
Pearson Education Australia PTY, Limited
Pearson Education Singapore, Pte. Ltd
Pearson Education North Asia Ltd
Pearson Education, Canada, Ltd
Pearson Educación de Mexico, S.A. de C.V.
Pearson Education–Japan
Pearson Education Malaysia, Pte. Ltd

10 9 8 7 6 5 4

ISBN 0-13-189170-7

Contents

7 THE COLLEGE EXPERIENCE TODAY: Whether Fifteen or Fifty, Traditional or Nontraditional, College Is for Everyone 165

8 ADULTHOOD THROUGH THE SECOND HALF OF LIFE: Marriage, Divorce and Child Custody, Remarriage, and Stepfamilies 191

9   CONDITIONING AND LEARNING: How We Have Been Conditioned and How We Can Use Conditioning to Build Constructive Habits   220

10   THE PSYCHOTHERAPIES: Many Approaches, Many Applications   238

11   PSYCHOLOGICAL DISORDERS: Trying to Function in Dysfunctional Ways   263

12   STRATEGIES FOR STAYING HEALTHY: Coping with the Stresses and Strains of Modern Life   291

Preface

To Our Readers: Welcome to the 7th edition of *Choice and Change*.[1] You are an extraordinary generation of college students and we are honored to be the authors of your psychology textbook. Your generation is the most multiculturally diverse college population ever. You are also the most psychologically self-aware and the most intelligent generation of students that has ever existed.[2] You are forging new paths toward your personal, educational, and vocational life-careers. Whether male or female, whatever your age or ethnic background, whatever walk of life you come from, and whatever path you take toward your future life, we are looking to you to be tomorrow's leaders. This is one of the continuing themes of *Choice and Change*.

Another theme of this book is that human existence is not simple. It requires all the courage, stamina, and integrity that we can muster to face the day-to-day challenges that come our way. You may find yourselves in difficult situations that are not of your choosing. To live authentically, you may have to "stand up and be counted" for unpopular causes and for what you believe to be truly right and just. You may even have to be a "minority of one" to live with your conscience. In which case, you will have joined those scholars and scientists, saints and sages who, down through the centuries and across cultures, helped this world to be a better place in which to live.

A third theme of this text is embedded in the title of this text, *Choice and Change*; to help you to discover that there are always many possible *choices* open to you. Perceiving those choices is the first major step to *changing* your life for the better. A good example, although a tragic one, is what a young lad cried after he shot the classmates who had been bullying him. After giving himself up to the authorities, he crumpled on the ground, and kept repeating, "I had no choice. I had no choice." The high school shooters at Columbine left tapes that indicate the only thing they could think to do was to shoot the students that bullied them, and then kill themselves. Then there are those people who continue to lead lives of "quiet desperation" because they do not know what else they can do. We hope that by the time you have finished this book, you will be better able to perceive the many *choices* always available to you, and to be able to make the *changes* necessary for a happier, healthier, and more creative life-career.

---

[1]To be accurate, this is the 8th edition, because the second edition was called a "revised edition."
[2]You'll learn about that "intelligent" bit in Chapter 5, when we discuss the Flynn effect.

Acknowledgments

We must thank our editors, in particular Jeff Marshall and Jill Liebowitz for sharing our vision of this edition and for having patience with us. We thank those people in our personal lives who did not get upset when the pressure of writing had to precede our usual phone calls and get-togethers, including Sheila and Josie Lescarbeare, Beatrice Shafer, Lia Norstrand, Joan Quay, Helen Parramore, and Jean Baney. We also want to acknowledge the help and support of Shannon Rivera, the Kuntz and Mellerup families, and, most especially, Loie Mellerup and Sheffia and Aaron Fulmer.

In the educational environment, we particularly want to acknowledge the following persons who have inspired us by their honesty, by their courage, and by always being willing to be exactly who they are: Michael Reiner, Barbara Oberlander, Patricia Grunder, Carolyn Woods, and Donna Waller of Santa Fe Community College; Larry Tyree of the University of Florida; and our long-time friends, Annie Kollisch and George Barton. Thanks also to a special friend, Brian Carnahan at Auburn University. At the University of Maine at Machias, we wish to acknowledge the kindness of Cyrene Wells, Linda Willey, Cynthia Huggins, and—in memoriam—John Joseph.

Many thanks to our reviewers: Peggy Norwood, Metropolitan State College of Denver; Cheryl McFadden, York Technical College; Mark Harmon, Reedley College; Vicki Dretchen, Volunteer State; Sam Gaft, Macomb Community College; and Kimble Richardson, University of Indianapolis. We haven't the faintest idea which review belongs to which of the six of you, but we do want to thank you for your detailed and cogent comments. They were the very finest reviews we have ever received because of the time and trouble you took to make your thoughtful suggestions. We couldn't adopt all the suggestions of all the reviewers (six reviewers sometimes have six different opinions) but you may be surprised by how many we did take very much to heart.

Again, thank you from your authors.

April O'Connell
Vincent F. O'Connell
Lois-Ann Kuntz

We dedicate this book
to
all the workers in the vineyard:
those who came before us,
those we have worked with,
and
those who will come after us.

The Psychology of the Self
Self-Concept, Self-Esteem, and Self-Actualizing

BOX 1.1 SCENARIO
One Identical Letter, Six Very Different Reactions

On a bright, sunny day in May, six people each received the following formal letter from the Admissions Office of the college to which they had all applied.

Dear Prospective Student,

With regard to your application to be admitted as a freshman to State College, we are sorry to inform you that we cannot process your application officially at this time. You passed the math examination, but your scores on the reading and composition portions are below the cutoff level for immediate acceptance.

We can, however, admit you to our pre-college program. The pre-college program is designed to bring students up to passing levels in these courses. You have already passed your math, so you need register only for the reading and composition classes. Your scores were just below the established cutoff scores, so we are confident that you will have little trouble in passing the two exams within one term. Since you only have to take two pre-college classes, you can also take an actual college course. We suggest a psychology course, which will help you make some decisions about your educational/vocational objectives and your life-career in general.

Please call us to schedule an interview with one of our academic counselors at your earliest opportunity, so we can register you and plan for your further education.

Very sincerely yours,

I. L. Andrews
Dean of Admissions and Records.

Eduardo Sanangelo (22 years, Hispanic-American) was elated! He threw his cap into the air, caught it, and rushed into the house shouting, "I'm in! I'm in! Well, sort of in. I can't register as a freshman right away but I have been admitted on the pre-college level. They have these courses you can take to bring you up to level and then you get in! I knew my English wasn't good enough. But I passed the math so all I have to do is take two English courses, and I'm in!"

Jonnimae Jones (30 years, African-American, single working mother of two teenagers) read the letter, and then clutched the letter to her heart. Her eyes were misty but she was smiling as she whispered to herself, "I can do it. I know I can. I've come this far. It won't be easy, but I'm going to make it."

Shannon McCrory (17 years, Caucasian, and just graduated from high school) leaned her head on her father's shoulders and wailed, "Oh, Pa, does this mean I got to go to college? They'll laugh at me. I don't have nice clothes and I sound like the hillbillies on TV." Shannon didn't give voice to her most troubling anxiety, but her father knew what it was. He put his arm around her. "Girl, there ain't nothing you need be ashamed of. Folks know you're the prettiest and smartest girl hereabouts. But, honey, you ain't gotta do nothin' you don't want."

Dan Westwind (38 years, Navajo Native American) had been working on an old truck until he saw the Chief walk toward him with a letter in his hand. The old man handed Dan the letter. After reading the letter, Dan turned to the Chief and said, "For me to go an extra term will cost more money." The old man shrugged. Dan understood the shrug: He was to go no matter what the cost. Dan nodded, folded the letter, and put it in his pocket. Neither man said anything

BOX **1.1**   SCENARIO (continued)
One Identical Letter, Six Very Different Reactions

more. Dan waited respectfully until the old chief left and then resumed working on the truck.

Natasha Petrovicc (24 years, Caucasian and a newly arrived refugee from the Balkans) put her hand to her mouth in astonishment. She had only applied to the college at her husband's urging. And now she was accepted. This was not the way things happened in the old country. There you had to be one of the rich elite. Or know somebody in the Politburo. It was all too new,

too wonderful . . . and too scary all at the same time. Waves of dizziness overcame her and her legs gave way from under her. She found herself sitting on the ground quite faint and frightened.

Nat Bernstein (19 years, Caucasian, Jewish, son of Dr. Ellen Bernstein and Dr. Harry Bernstein) walked into his parents' bedroom, took a gun from the bottom drawer of his father's bureau, and put a bullet through his head. He was pronounced dead-on-arrival (DOA) at the hospital.

HOW WE COPE WITH LIFE EVENTS DEPENDS ON OUR PERSONALITY STYLE

The introductory scenario describes an identical event in the lives of six people. How each of those six people reacted to this identical event was dramatically different. Given the encouragement of the Dean's letter, what could account for Nat Bernstein's suicide? What accounts for the exuberant response of Eduardo Sanangelo and the unemotional response of Dan Westwind? Given the burdens that Jonnimae Jones is carrying—member of a depressed minority, single working mother of two teenagers—what gives her the self-confidence that she can "make it"? What are the factors behind Shannon's lack of confidence and Natasha's dizziness? The answers to these questions, of course, involve what we call "personality" or personality style (see Tip 1.1).

Defining Personality: It Includes Every Dimension of Human Experience

The general public tends to think of personality as our "public image"—what we show to others when we put our "best foot forward." But the psychological definition of personality involves much more than our public image (see Tip 1.2). Our personality involves our physical characteristics and general health. (When we are feeling sick, we may become irritable and pessimistic whereas we are ordinarily cheerful and optimistic.) Personality also involves our **cognition** or mental abilities. (If a brilliant individual suddenly develops a brain tumor, not only is his intellectual ability severely hampered, his personality will undergo a dramatic change as he struggles with his impairment.) Our personality also includes our **worldview**,

---

Tip 1.1 Why Did These Six People React As They Did? At the end of this chapter, we look into some of the possible reasons why each of these peoples reacted as they did. (If you would like to know immediately, turn to pp. 18–23.)

Tip 1.2 Defining Personality: Unique, Dynamic, Consistent. Most professional definitions of personality include three characteristics: uniqueness, dynamic organization, and consistency. *Uniqueness* means that no two personalities are exactly alike (not even those of identical twins). *Dynamic* means that our personalities are not static but fluid and changeable in mood and intensity from moment-to-moment. Yet despite these moment-by-moment changes, most of us develop a fairly *consistent* personality patterning that is recognizable to others.

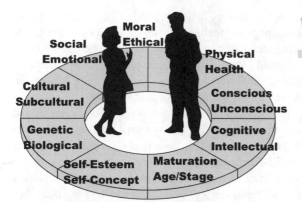

Figure 1.1 Personality consists of every dimension of human existence.

which is how we perceive the possibilities for living and which also partly determines our moral/ethical values. (A person who believes the "world is a maggot hill" will interact with others quite differently from a person who believes, as Will Rogers did, that "a stranger is a friend I haven't met yet.") Our personalities are also influenced by our **culture** (Caucasian, Hispanic, African-American, Mid-Eastern, etc.) and by all the **subcultures** of our profession, place of work, religious affiliation, and clubs and recreations. In short, personality includes just about everything we know about ourselves (see Figure 1.1).

In addition to what we know about ourselves, personality also includes many things we don't know about ourselves, called the **unconscious** parts of personality (Freud, 1900). Even though we may be unaware of the unconscious aspects of our personality, they influence our personality style throughout our lifetime. Two core dimensions of personality have to do with self-concept and self-esteem.

Self-Concept: How We *Think* of Ourselves

Self-concept and self-esteem are sometimes used interchangeably as if they mean the same thing; but while these two terms are closely related, their meanings are somewhat different. Our **self-concept** has largely to do with factual information—how we *think* about ourselves in terms of our gender, sibling rank, race, nationality, religion, etc. When we are young, our self-concept is a matter of destiny—we are born into it. As a child, we may say, "There are four of us children—I'm the oldest." As we get older, we may identify ourselves in terms of our family's religion. We say, "In our house, we're Baptist/Catholic/Jewish/Muslim." Still later, our self-concept enlarges to include the region of the world we come from. A man smiles as he says, "Ma'am, ah'm from TEXAS" and that tells us that his self-concept includes a very strong identification as a Texan. Very often, our self-concept is the way we introduce ourselves to others: "I'm Doris Davidson, your neighbor three doors down from you, and I'm organizing a crime-watch organization in our neighborhood." Or the way others introduce us: "This is Jim Delericio. He's your son's Little League coach."

Self-Esteem: How We *Feel* About Ourselves

If our self-concept is how we *think* about ourselves, our **self-esteem** is how we *feel* about ourselves. Other terms that mean almost the same thing are *self-respect, self-liking, self-confidence, self-worth, self-regard*. There have been hundreds, perhaps thousands, of studies done on self-esteem. The findings have been remarkably consistent; namely, that our self-esteem affects every area of our life—for good or for ill (Rogne, 1991). Some of these findings are summarized next. In general, self-esteem has to do with a) how we believe others value us, and b) how competent we believe ourselves to be in managing our lives (Roberts, 2002).

The Consequences of Positive Self-Esteem. When we have positive self-esteem, we generally feel joyous, exuberant, happy. We will enter into new situations with optimism. We will make constructive goals for our life-careers and we will be proud of ourselves when we accomplish those goals! We will accept our negative feelings as well as our positive feelings without being ashamed of them or denying them. We will not be overly dismayed by those moments of confusion and worry that visit us all. We will understand that everyone—no matter how successful—has periods of heartache and despair as well as joy and happiness. We will look forward to learning new skills and knowledge or to taking on new job responsibilities. We will be more open about the problems in our lives, and we will seek counsel and advice from others. If we run into frustrating situations, we will not give up after one or two attempts. We will maintain the attitude that most problems can be solved—if not by us, then by someone else whom we can consult. We will accept the responsibility for our lives and make decisions with confidence. If our decisions result in negative situations, we won't tell ourselves that "nothing we do comes out right!" Instead, we'll simply "go back to the drawing board."

The Consequences of Poor (or Negative) Self-Esteem. When we have negative self-esteem, we feel alternately depressed, helpless, unable to cope, and inferior to others in our personal, social, and vocational arenas. We will have an exaggeratedly low estimate of our abilities and believe we are of little worth to anyone. Even when people compliment us on our special skills and talents, we will tend to minimize them and describe them as "really nothing." We will tend to hang back from entering new situations and think "I can't do this . . . " or "I could never learn to do that . . . " When we feel unable to cope with a situation, we will reject the help of others (parents, siblings, close friends, coworkers) because we are ashamed to let others know how inadequate we feel. In fact, we may act "tough" to cover up our sense of inferiority. We may be very defensive (hurt, upset, angry) if someone offers friendly suggestions or constructive criticism. People who have extremely low self-esteem tend to blame other persons for what is going wrong in their lives because that is the only way they know how to manage their overwhelming feelings of inadequacy and failure (Baumeister, 1991).

Sometimes Our Self-Concept and Our Self-Esteem Can Be Diametrically Opposed

Although our self-concept and our self-esteem are usually positively correlated, in some people they may be diametrically opposed to each other. An example will illustrate. A colleague of ours has earned a national reputation as a medical researcher. We were surprised, therefore, when she came to our office one day, fell into a chair, and blurted out something as follows:

> I'm a sham. I've been playing a game all my life. People come up to me and compliment me on my research and all I want to say at that point is, "Oh, shut up! I don't want your compliments." But of course I don't. I just smile and say "thank you." But inside I feel so angry. I really want to say to them, "I'm not as great as you think I am." I may be good at research, but that's because I spend so much time at it. If the truth be known, I'm just a lonely person with no one to love and no one to love me. I spend a lot of time at my research lab because I have no other place to spend it. I have no friends, only colleagues. I haven't had a romantic involvement in years. In fact, I think I signal men to stay away. It's easier to reject them than to suffer the fear that eventually they'll reject me.

This woman had a positive self-concept as a competent medical researcher but her self-esteem was negative. Deep within her was a hurt and bewildered child that she kept hidden from others and even from herself. The hurt and bewildered "child within" has been the subject

BOX **1.2** STUDENTS VERBATIM
How My Self-Esteem Got Battered

Female: When I was in grade school, no one knew I had a hearing problem. They thought I was mentally retarded and I was put into a class for special education.

Female: In the fifth grade, I had buck teeth and I was fat. No one knows how awful it is to be called "fatty" and "rabbit." My teeth got fixed and I lost my baby fat. I think I look nice now, but I have to watch my weight all the time.

Male: I didn't have a lot of friends when I was in second and third grade so I became a bully. Boy! Was that dumb! That just made everybody hate me even more. I didn't get friends until I won some athletic awards in high school. Then I became a better person.

Male: My dad was a drunk. I hated to bring anyone home because I never knew how he would be. When he was drinking, he would call my girlfriends awful names, and then he and I would get into fights.

Male: My mother was always dating jerks who would treat her extremely bad, but I wasn't old enough to do anything about it for years. This made me feel really low.

Male: In eleventh grade, I didn't make the first string on the football team. I had to sit out almost every game on the benches watching our team. It was humiliating.

Female: In my senior year, my boyfriend (we were intimate for many months) suddenly dropped me for my best friend. I felt betrayed. It was hard to face my friends because I felt so small. I cried for weeks.

Male: When I was in the fourth grade, I was held back by my parents—they held me back, not the school. So there I was left back and all my friends went on to the next grade. Boy, did I feel dumb.

Female: In high school once, I was not dressed for cheerleading because I didn't know we were going to cheer. I just happened to have my cheerleading outfit in my car. So I went there to change into it, and suddenly a policeman was looking in at me. I almost got arrested for indecent exposure.

Female: I'll never forget this. In kindergarten, a boy pushed me down and knocked out one of my front teeth. I didn't realize then that another tooth would grow in. I didn't smile for weeks, I was so embarrassed by my looks.

Male: Here's one for the books: In high school, my dad let me have a car, which I wrecked. I had to take my date to the Senior Prom so he let me rent a car. I had an accident with that one too.

Reflective Writing: Now describe how your self-esteem has gotten battered in the last year.

of many books, articles, and now even on Internet Web sites (Dunn & Soasey, 1988). In fact (as the reader will discover in Chapter 11) an entire therapeutic approach, called **transactional analysis (TA)**, was developed involving the way all of us still act out our "child ego-state" (Berne 1961, 1978; Harris, 1969; Newell & Jeffrey, 2002). Frequently, the very people who seem the most "successful" on the outside are the very people who are the most shy of revealing how lost and hurt is the child that still resides in their emotional memory (Cappachine, 1991). (For other examples of battered self-esteem, see Box 1.2.)

Most of Us, However, Are Combinations of Positive and Negative Self-Esteem. Generally speaking, most of us are combinations of both positive and negative self-esteem. If we have been strong and athletic all our lives, we will have positive self-esteem in regard to sports. On the other hand, if we were so good at sports that we neglected our studies in high school, we may now have low self-esteem regarding our academic skills. College professors frequently hear students say, "I do well in English, but I'm terrible in math. I just can't do it." Or "I'm really dumb in English. I like science and math, but writing comes hard to me, and I always get poor marks in composition." Even celebrities who seem "to have it all" have areas in which they feel limited or insecure or inferior to others! No one feels adequate every day in every way in every area of their lives (Sanders, 1991).

Unlike Our Self-Concept, Our Self-Esteem Gets Battered Throughout Our Lives.
Our self-esteem is not easily enhanced. If anything, our self-esteem is battered almost every day of
our lives. From our earliest years onward, our society has been constantly calling attention to our
errors. If we didn't get good marks in school, our parents may have berated us for our "failure" to
live up to their expectations. Our playmates often said mean things to us. When we wrote a composition in high school, the paper may have come back with a passing grade that didn't seem to
compensate for all those red markings all over it. Society has developed many ways to communicate its displeasure with us. By contrast, we don't get as many positive "strokes" (Berne, 1978).

Does It Get Any Better When We Become Adults? Not on Your Life! As adults we
may be yelled at by the boss, which doesn't enhance anyone's self-esteem one whit. We get
into a fierce quarrel with friends and family, and we get assaulted with name-calling and accusations of misbehavior. We're driving along a sunny highway and suddenly we become aware
of a siren shrieking and a blue light that tells us a policeman wants us to pull over. There we
are with a ticket for speeding, which deflates both our pockets and our self-esteem. It is no
different for celebrities. If a movie star begins to lose box office ratings, they find themselves
no longer esteemed by the public or movie producers. And what do you think a political figure
feels when the election results suggest that he or she has lost the public confidence? The continual battering at our self-esteem is simply part of "the human condition" (Arendt, 1970).

The Time of Lowest Self-Esteem: High School. Most adults report that their self-esteem
was at its lowest ebb during high school, more than at any other time of their lives. Furthermore,
the low self-esteem we probably all experienced in high school was not something we could
easily talk about—if at all. If we tried to tell our parents how "unpopular" we believed ourselves
to be, they generally tried to buck us up with remarks like, *Oh, that's silly, you've nothing to be
ashamed of*, or they didn't listen to us at all. We couldn't share our feelings of misery with our
friends because it would have been generally too embarrassing. Ironically, at no time in our lives
do we long to be accepted by our peers as we do in high school. Ironically, that is the time that
acceptance by our peers is the hardest to achieve. Adolescent groups demand strict conformity to
group standards of behavior and mete out harsh punishment to those who don't comply with
their rigid codes of dress, language, dating, etc. The slightest deviation from the "in-group" standards results in jeers, sarcasm, and eventual outright rejection. If the reader doubts these studies,
we have only to point to the figures on absenteeism, truancy, and dropouts from high school. If
the high school years were not so unhappy, there would not be as much delinquency and teenage
violence (including the carrying of knives and guns to school) at ever younger ages. Nor would
there be as much suicide and attempted suicide in the adolescent years (Woods, 1990).

**But the Good News Is . . . There Is No Better Time to Enhance Self-Esteem Than in
College!** If the high school years are the years of lowest self-esteem for most people, the good
news is that the adult years are the time when we can consciously develop more positive self-
esteem. You can begin to discover your areas of interest and what you are "good at." You can
find others who share the same interests as you, whether these interests are sports, journalism,
art, auto mechanics, computers, electronics, drama, politics, or the human service professions.
Sharing common interests becomes the basis of friendship rather than what people look like or
what they wear. The college experience enables students to discover and acknowledge their
skills and competencies and to enhance their self-esteem. Furthermore, our self-esteem
increases as we mature. It is now fairly well established that for most of us (aside from people

with severe mental disorders), the older we grow, the happier we get. And why? Because the more we have lived through and resolved the problematic situations in our lives, the more confident we become that we can manage future crises. Moreover, the more experiences we have, the more insight we gain into what makes for a successful life-career (Vaillant, 2000).

But Is It Really Possible to Raise Our Self-Esteem?   Yes, but it ain't easy. We would be lying to you if we said it was. So the real answer is YES . . . It can be done IF . . . we are willing to believe we can, and IF . . . we are willing to consider alternate choices, and IF . . . we are willing to make changes. Unfortunately, many people believe they are doomed to live the life they are leading. Like the people of ancient times, they feel they are the pawns of demons and gods that rule the universe. The Ancients believed that they had little control over their lives. It is the kind of thinking that assigns the control of one's life to external (and usually demonic) forces. The language of this worldview includes such terms as *fate, kismet, karma, predestination, the will of the gods*, and *"It is written in the wind."* Psychologists today call it an **external locus of control**. People who hold this worldview see little possibility of changing their lives (Rotter, 1990).

But developing new behavior patterns is not easy because change does not come easily to the human personality. Call it habit or conditioning or "fear of the unknown," we tend to cling to our present circumstances, no matter how difficult they are. Listen to people describe their difficult life situations: abusive relationships, jobs they hate, families that are dysfunctional in which everyone is driving everyone else "crazy." When you suggest to them they might do something to change their situation, their responses often sound something like this:

> I know my boyfriend/father/husband is abusive but I can't survive financially without him.
> I have no choice in this matter. My hands are tied.
> It's no use trying to get out of this situation. I just don't see anyway out.
> I hate my job but everyone says I'd be a fool to leave, so I guess I gotta stay where I am.

So they remain where they are, leading lives of quiet desperation.

People who have an **internal locus of control** believe they are able to direct their lives (at least in part) and change their circumstances for the better. The fact that you are reading this text means that you believe education will improve your life. If that is so, you have an internal locus of control, in that you set goals for yourself, and accomplish them to the best of your ability. Now this does not mean that you always will accomplish them as soon as you want. From time to time, all of us are beset with obstacles and problems that may disrupt our projected time line. But with an internal locus of control we know that, with a little patience and fortitude, most obstacles can be overcome and most problems can be resolved.

How to raise your self-esteem and take control of your life is one of the major themes of this text. Although there have been many books written on this topic, with titles such as *Ten Secrets for Being Happy* or *How to Succeed in Business* or *Finding Your Soul Mate*, many of them come under the heading of "pop psychology," described as "self-help books that are filled with half-truths and myths" (Peterson, 2004). The suggestions and guidelines you will read in this text are not "pop psychology" but are based on actual research findings about healthy and happy people. One consistent finding, for example, is that living happily and healthily does not mean living for one's own selfish pleasures alone. What the research has shown is that living happily and healthily involves having a sense of purpose that, in some way, benefits others as well as ourselves. It means a dedication to being truthful with ourselves and with others; being true to our convictions; and being willing to stand up for

what we know to be right and just. It may not always be easy to do. But those who do live with these values report an enduring sense of well-being. Their heart-felt conviction is that their life *is* worth living and meaningful. No matter how big or small our contributions may be, we know we have made a difference—somewhere, somehow—with our family and friends perhaps, or in our line of work, and within our larger community. But before we get to these research findings (and others) in more detail, turn to Box 1.3 and take the opportunity to assess whether you have an internal or external locus of control.

BOX **1.3** SELF-EXPLORATION
Do You Have an Internal or External Locus-of-Control?

Respond to the following items as follows:

Circle A if you feel it to be Always or Almost Always True;
Circle S if you feel it to be Sometimes True;
Circle R if you feel it to be Rarely True.

1. When I give a job enough time, attention, and effort, I generally do well .... (A) S R
2. When people get ahead, it wasn't because of *what* they knew but *who* they knew .... A (S) R
3. When a day starts off badly, I know nothing else is going to go right that day .... A (S) R
4. Trouble always comes in threes .... A S (R)
5. When good things happen to me, I think "Somebody up there likes me" .... (A) S R
6. I believe in the saying, "Where there's a will, there's a way." .... (A) S R
7. Hard work is rewarded by teachers and employers .... (A) S R
8. Generally, I know how to handle problems that come along in my life .... (A) S R
9. No matter what I have tried to do in my life, something or somebody has interfered .... (A) S R
10. If I am friendly and courteous to other people, they are generally friendly and courteous to me ... A (S) R

☐+☐+☐

Scoring: Score 2 for every S you circled. For items 2, 3, 4, 5, and 9, score 1 if you circled A and 3 if you circled R. For items, 1, 6, 7, 8, and 10, score 3 if you circled A and 1 if you circled R. Then count up the scores for each column and add the three columns for your total score. Write down your total score in the large box.

My Total Score is ☐

Now look at the Scoring Key below and read what it says.

Scoring Key for Box 1.3:
  15 and below. If you scored below 15, you tend toward having an external locus-of-control. You probably feel timid and unsure of yourself. You need to develop more confidence in your ability to take charge of your life. But take heart! Your college education will help you to do just that. As you learn to be competent in your chosen vocational field and in computer skills, you will find yourself becoming more sure of your abilities and more self-confident.
  16–20. If you scored in this range, you probably underestimate your abilities. Nevertheless, you have a good balance of internal and external LOC. You do the best you can in pursuit of a goal, but you also realize that there will be times when life events may result in having to postpone your goals due to events you had no control over. But you also know that if you just "hang in there," you can get back on track and go on from there.
  21–24. You have a strong internal LOC. You probably have had a lot of success in your past endeavors so that now you feel competent and confident that you are going to succeed in whatever you choose to do. One caution: If you don't always rate yourself as A+ in what you did, don't berate yourself that you didn't do your best. Example: Students who generally get straight A's in their exams often get unduly upset if they receive a lower grade. There is nothing wrong with an occasional B or C.

BOX 1.3 SELF-EXPLORATION (continued)
Do You Have an Internal or External Locus-of-Control?

25–30. Well, well! You certainly have a strong locus-of-control. Congratulations! You probably have a very high positive self-esteem, which will stand you in good stead in most situations. Do be cautious, however, in taking on jobs or responsibilities that are beyond your present competencies. You may need to develop a little more caution before jumping to conclusions. When a task seems larger or more complicated than you expected, don't be shy about consulting others who can help you.

*[handwritten: Two forces that dominate psych:
→ Studying rats (reductionist theory)
→ Studying the bad in ppl.]*

HOW THE STUDY OF WHAT MAKES FOR HAPPY AND HEALTHY PEOPLE CAME ABOUT

Humanistic Psychology as the "Third Force" Movement

Prior to World War II, most of our knowledge about human nature was derived from two major "forces" that dominated psychology at that time. The first force was focused on the experimental studies of animals in laboratories. These studies were valuable because they provided us with much information about basic biological drives (our need for food, water, safety and security, etc.). Unfortunately, this type of research led to the **reductionist theory** (or **mechanistic theory**) of human nature. According to reductionist theory, human beings are not much more than intelligent rats. A good example of the reductionist point-of-view was provided by Desmond Morris, a noted ethnologist (a scientist who studies animal behavior). According to Morris, human beings are simply sophisticated "naked apes" who live in "human zoos" (Morris, 1970). (See Figure 1.2.)

Figure 1.2 The Reductionist Theory.
Desmond Morris views human personality as not much more than intelligent apes who live in human zoos.

The second force that was dominating psychology was the study of abnormal personalities, usually patients in hospitals or criminals incarcerated in prisons. This approach told us quite a bit about people who were not functioning well in society, but it did not tell us much about people who were functioning very well, even admirably, in the everyday world of family and work. Even Sigmund Freud, who did much to help us understand human personality was unable to describe the creative and productive person. Freud was once asked this question: *You have told us a lot about the unhealthy person. What can you tell us about the healthy person?* Freud could only answer: *Arbeiten und Lieben,* which can be roughly translated from the German as "someone who is able *to work* and *to love others.*" He could not say anything more. He did not know.

Then after World War II, psychologists began to object to such reductionist theories. Gordon Allport, a president of the American Psychological Association (APA), gave official voice to these objections. He insisted that we are not just human *beings*, we are human *becomings*, capable of growth and change throughout our lifetime. Said Allport, we are certainly more than conditioned rats, more than just naked apes, and certainly more than intelligent robots (Allport, 1955). We are a species always in the process of self-discovery and evolution.

[handwritten: after WWII Allport said we are not human beings but becomings? We are able to grow & change]

Abraham Maslow's Study of Highly Self-Actualizing Subjects. Allport's push to study humanity from the premise that we are human beings always evolving to more intelligent and creative expression was quickly followed by research studies of artists, writers, executives, and other fully functioning personalities. But it was Abraham Maslow who put these sporadic investigations into a coherent framework that psychologists and educators still find useful today. In his classic book, entitled *Motivation and Personality* (1954), he described what he called "highly self-actualizing" personalities.

What Maslow was saying was this: As we grow in age and maturity, our needs and motivations change. That should not be surprising since we all know that the wishes and joys of childhood no longer satisfy us when we become adults (*"When I was a child, I thought as a child . . ."*). But Maslow also pointed out that until our basic *deficiency needs* are satisfied (hunger, thirst, warmth, shelter), we cannot reach the higher human *meta-needs* involving love and belongingness, esteem, cognition, aesthetic, and self-actualizing needs. Maslow's model of the hierarchy of needs involves seven levels (see Figure 1.3).

In deriving his hierarchy of needs, Maslow described highly self-actualizing persons as the "shining lights" of any society. Early on, he said, they set goals for themselves and achieve

Figure 1.3 Hierarchy of Needs. Created by Abraham Maslow.

Table 1.1   Maslow's Seven-Level Hierarchy of Needs

Physiological Needs.   Physiological needs are the basic needs to survive, such as air, food, water, and clothing for warmth. People deprived of these needs will seek to satisfy them by any possible means including working for "slave wages," begging, prostitution, and stealing. A sound mind needs a sound body for functioning fully at every level. Globally, we are becoming aware of the need for good nutrition, pure water, and a nontoxic environment.

Safety and Stability Needs.   Our many homeless people wandering the streets and running from the police have no protective shelter and, in times of freezing temperatures, are sometimes found frozen to death on the streets. But simple shelter is not enough. Our home should be a place of sanctuary. If our domicile is a place of constant turmoil, physical violence, alcoholism, etc., we are living in a kind of hell. If we are having trouble with a roommate, we may hate to return to our apartment. Be it ever so humble, all of us need our home to be a stable sanctuary of safe retreat.

Love and Belonging Needs.   When we are children, our needs for love and belonging are fulfilled by a close and caring family. As we transit into adolescence, we long for acceptance by other teenagers. As adults, these needs are met in our own family grouping. But what if we did not have such an ideal growing up? Some men and women, whose home life was marked by divorce or death, may search for a life-partner to fulfill their longing for the absent father or absent mother. Or suppose our life-partner turns out to be alcoholic or drug addicted. In that case, our love and belonging needs will not be fulfilled very often—unless we enjoy the caretaking role of co-dependency. Belonging needs are also met by affiliating with a club, a profession, a church, a political party—or simply a group of friends.

Esteem Needs.   In addition to being loved and cared for by others, human becomings have a need to give as well as to receive. We need to make a contribution to our society. For some, this will come through great political, scientific, or artistic achievement. But we do not have to become public figures to achieve our esteem needs. We can contribute also by working with charitable organizations. Or we can take a leadership role in one of the many civic groups in any city, town, or village. One of the most significant avenues for achieving our esteem needs is through a work of our liking, one we believe to be valuable and of service to others. We study hard for a profession we can pour our hearts into, whether it be in teaching, in auto electronics, in law enforcement, or in the many human service areas.

Cognitive Needs.   Our need for knowledge may lead us to become research scientists. Or we may have a "nose for news" and become investigative reporters. Formal education, of course, is the most direct route to satisfy our cognitive needs, but we keep learning in other ways as well. We read the morning newspapers and listen to the nightly newscasts to keep up with "what's been going on" or with the latest athletic standings. We patronize the local library because we are "history buffs" or find biographies to be of more interest than fiction. We take adult education classes to enlarge our leisure recreations or technical skills. In fact, the more technological our society becomes, the more driving becomes our need to know more about our world. We are a curious species with an unquenchable thirst for knowledge.

Aesthetic Needs.   The aesthetic needs involve a quest for creating beauty in our lives. This need is so intense in some people that they devote their entire lives to creating works of art and music. Others will satisfy their aesthetic needs by designing clothes, automobiles, planes, or household goods. Profit-oriented corporations know that "a thing of beauty" is "good business." Community planners are careful to preserve the natural beauty of the earth along with planning new traffic routes. All of us express our aesthetic needs in some way or other, whether it be arranging the furniture in our homes or offices, tending our gardens, or sending our children off to school as neatly and attractively as possible.

Self-Actualizing Needs.   Maslow described self-actualizing as the need to express the highest potential that we are capable of reaching. People who have become self-actualizing live according "to their own lights," pursuing their goals and dreams throughout their lives. But they are not hedonistically self-serving. As Maslow's subjects developed and evolved larger worldviews, they also enabled others in their society to evolve larger perspectives as well, and to be truly caring for all humankind.

what they have wanted to achieve in their lifetimes (Maslow, 1954). Moreover, their achievements are not for themselves alone but for the betterment of humankind. They may be writers struggling to alert us to the ills of our society. They may be scientists looking for a cure for some dread disease. They may be artists and musicians who break through to new illuminations of color and sound. They may be humanitarians spending their life in service for others. Maslow used the **case study** method (see Box 1.4) with subjects that included living persons (Albert Einstein and Eleanor Roosevelt) and historical figures (Abraham Lincoln), all of whom achieved their personal dreams and hopes for society.

BOX **1.4** RESEARCH METHODOLOGY
The Case Study

The case study applied to a physically ill person. The case study method, which had its origins thousands of years ago in the physician/patient relationship, is a summary record of many observations of one subject—the patient. When we are ill, the physician makes the following kinds of observations:

Observation 1: Interviews us and listens to our symptoms.
Observation 2: Does a cursory clinical exam with stethoscope; looks in our mouth and has us say "Ah-h-h."
Observation 3: Secures analysis of our bodily fluids, such as blood and urine.
Observation 4: Sends us to a laboratory for other exams, such as a chest X-ray and EKG.

One subject: Many observations. The physician then makes a diagnosis and prescribes treatment.

The case study applied to an educationally disadvantaged child. A psychologist gets a referral from a teacher about a child who is failing in his subjects. She will then compile as much data on this child from the following kinds of observations:

Observation 1: Perusal of the child's cumulative folder.
Observations 2, 3, and 4: Observe the child in class, in the lunchroom, and on the playground.
Observation 5: Interview the parents of the child.
Observation 6: Interview the child through a battery of tests, such as IQ and achievement tests.

One subject: Many observations. The psychologist summarizes the data into a report for the school and inaugurates a plan of action to help the child.

The case study applied to an event. The case study approach can be applied to events as well as to persons.

When there has been a major accident, various kinds of research teams study every available bit of data to learn the nature and cause(s) of the accident. In the famous case of the crash of the Boeing 747 over Lockabie, Scotland, thousands of persons collected the bits and pieces of the airplane over many miles of ground. The "black box" recordings were analyzed by specialists in that area. The CIA and the European Interpol network examined passenger lists, freight lists, passports, etc. Intelligence agencies of every nation pooled their findings to discover who and what had blown up the airplane.

One subject: Many observations. The investigators make a judgment about the cause of the crash.

PRO: Advantages of the Case Study Method. A case study is a comprehensive picture of one subject and very necessary in order to diagnose the person's problem and to develop a treatment or action plan. No other method analyzes a single person or event so profoundly. In the healing arts particularly, the case study is an essential method to uncover the underlying etiology of a problem. By healing arts, we mean not only medicine, but also psychotherapy, special education, physical therapy, speech and hearing therapy, etc.

CON: Limitations of the Case Study Method. On the other hand, we have to be cautious about applying the case study findings about a single person to other people. Discoveries from one subject cannot be generalized to a population without corroboration. Scientists feel much more secure when they study larger samples of (say) one hundred, or a thousand persons, or even several thousand persons. Another problem of case study work is that it is very, very expensive in terms of time, professional staff, and financial resources. Nevertheless, problems of expense are disregarded when what is being studied is an epidemic, a plane or auto accident, or a homicide investigation.

Self-actualizing persons, said Maslow, have a strong belief that they have some control over their lives (an internal LOC). Despite the setbacks and tragedies they endure, they recover and they continue with their life-careers. They do not blame others for their limitations. They do not fob off their inadequacies on "an unhappy childhood" or "second-class citizenship." They know that while the "blaming game" may comfort us, it isn't very productive. They know we will all be visited occasionally with heart-breaking life situations but they keep going, unwilling to be overcome by obstacles or tragedy. Self-actualizing personalities strive always toward the "farthest reaches of personality," and by their insights and achievements enable their societies to evolve as well. They know too that the older we get, the more times we will have to mourn the death of those we dearly love. That is part of "the human condition" (Arendt, 1970). (They know that the only way to avoid these experiences is to die young.) But they are determined to live as courageously and authentically as possible. They know also that the responsibility for our lives is squarely on our own shoulders and ours alone. In fact, the only person any of us can change is first person singular—the person we refer to as "I." Notice also that the term Maslow preferred is "self-actualizing," not "self-actualized." Maslow said we should always use the progressive present tense (the -ing ending). He explained that we are never completely self-actualized. Self-actualizing is a never-ending process. There is always more to know, more to do, and more to become.

But What About Our Responsibility to Raise Moral/Ethical Children? You may feel some concern about your children—present and future. Aren't we responsible for them? Yes, of course, we are! Especially when they are young. The socialization process of the child (teaching the child to live according to the standards of society) is one of the primary functions of the family. We do our best to raise our children to be morally responsible adults. But as they get older, we must be careful that in our sincere desire to raise morally responsible children we do not become domineering, over-demanding, and insist on absolute conformity to *our* ideas of how *they* should be. Our children, like ourselves, are also *human becomings* (Allport, 1955) and they also need some life-space to evolve according to "their lights" as well.

Maslow's pioneering work stimulated professionals in many fields to humanize our societal institutions. For example, today we understand the educational setting not only as a place to learn to read and write and compute numbers, but also as a place to make friends, fulfilling our *love and belonging* needs. We recognize now that the workplace is not just where we earn a living, but where we can have our *esteem* needs met when we produce things others appreciate. Understanding that slums foster delinquency and criminality, city planners and architects are doing their best to replace "the concrete jungle" of our cities with a "greening of America," helping to meet the *aesthetic needs* of our poorest people. So as not to become slums, architects are designing multifamily residences to include shrubs and trees and neighborhood parks for children to play in (Clay, 2001; Reich, 1970). But as valuable as Maslow's work was, psychologists were left with some very tough questions; for example:

- **How exactly can any one of us reach a highly self-actualizing level?**   Maslow's subjects were already the "brightest lights" of our society when he studied them. How can the rest of us reach a higher level of self-actualizing?
- **If we have a higher standard of living than ever before, why aren't we happier?** Presumably, a higher standard of living means that many more of our human needs are being met. Yet studies of **subjective well-being** (SWB) indicate that people in affluent countries worldwide are not any happier than they were 10 or 20 or 50 years

ago. In fact, the World Health Organization (WHO) has been reporting a slight decrease in the "happiness factor" (Diener, 2000; Inglehart, 1990; Peterson, 2000).

• **What is "happiness" anyway?**   Can it even be defined? Are the emotions we describe as *happiness, joy, exuberance, contentment*, or a general feeling of *well-being* all the same or are they different? Is "happiness" different for different individuals, for different cultures, or even for different eras of history? (See Box 1.5 to assess

---

BOX **1.5** SELF-EXPLORATION
What is Your Concept of Happiness?

Instructions: *From time immemorial, writers, philosophers and sages have defined the essence of happiness. Before reading the quotations below, write down your definition of happiness.*_____

Now read over the following quotations and answer the items at the bottom of the page.

A man's happiness lies in doing a man's true work. —Marcus Aurelius: *Meditations* VIII.xxvi.

Happiness and Beauty are by-products. —G. B. Shaw: *Maxims for Revolutionists.*

It is neither wealth nor splendor, but tranquility and occupation, which give happiness. —Thomas Jefferson: *Letter to Mrs. A. S. Marks* (1788).

Happiness depends, as Nature shows.

Less on exterior things than most suppose. —William Cowper. *Table Talk* [1782],

I believe in one God and no more, and I hope for happiness beyond this life. I believe in the equality of man; and I believe that religious duties consist in doing justice, loving mercy, and endeavoring to make our fellow creatures happy. —Thomas Paine. *The Age of Reason* [1793].

The happiness of life is made up of minute fractions—the little soon forgotten charities of a kiss or smile, a kind look, a heartfelt compliment, and the countless infinitesimals of pleasurable and genial feeling. —Samuel Taylor Coleridge. *The Friend. The Improvisatore* [1833].

Morality is not properly the doctrine of how we may make ourselves happy, but how we may make ourselves worthy of happiness. —Immanuel Kant. *Critique of Practical Reason* [1788].

Happiness Makes Up in Height for What it Lacks in Length. —Robert Frost. Title of poem [1942].

No man chooses evil because it is evil; he only mistakes it for happiness and the good he seeks. —Mary Wollstonecraft Godwin. *A Vindication of the Rights of Men* [1790].

Instructions: Respond to the following items:

  a. Read the definitions over again and pick out at least two common themes, and write them on the lines below.

  1. _____

  2. _____

  b. Now compare your definition with the definitions you read.

  1. Which definition do you like the best?_____

  2. Which definition comes closest to yours?_____

Common themes. 1. Happiness has less to do with external possessions, as it has to do with internal understanding. *The secret of happiness is within us.* **2.** Happiness is less the accomplishment of fame, success and wealth as it is in simple, everyday events. **3.** An essential ingredient for happiness is the warmth of friendship. **4.** Happiness lies not in self-gratification so much as it is a by-product of a good work and a life well-lived.

your definition of happiness and how your definition compares to literary scholars down through the ages.)

- **However we define happiness, how can we foster it in children and adults?**   Is the state of well-being something that is inherited or is it learned? In either event, could we teach it in our public school system? Would it be possible to require it as a college course along with English composition and elementary algebra?
- **And the most vital question of all—how can we achieve peace in our time?**   This most vital of questions involves not only discovering the *causes* of prejudice, discrimination, and war, but also how to *eradicate* them.

A Further Humanistic Thrust: Positive Psychology. In 1998, Martin Seligman became the president of the American Psychological Association (APA). In his official capacity as president, he spearheaded a further thrust of the humanistic approach, which he called **positive psychology**. Picking up where Allport and Maslow had left off, positive psychologists are focusing on not just what is *wrong* with human nature, but also on what is *right* with human nature. They want to identify what is *noble, uplifting, transcending, even inspiring* in human personality (Seligman & Csikszentimihalyi, 2000). In his presidential address, Seligman called for "coconspirators" from any and all professions and walks-of-life to join in the work. Since that time, there have come eager responses from many areas of society and from many countries. Positive psychology has become interdisciplinary and international.

Characteristics of Positive, Happy, and Transcending Personalities. Positive psychologists have been hard at work for well over two decades now. Have they discovered some personality factors that can benefit the rest of us? Well, yes, at least a few—some of which may be quite surprising to a few readers. However they have been called (happy, self-actualizing, fully-functioning, fully-realized, or transcending), people who have a long-lasting sense of subjective well-being (SWB) (Peterson, 2000), exhibit the following characteristics:

They Are Generally Optimistic, Friendly, and Outgoing. They describe themselves as generally positive and outgoing. Their friends, families, and neighbors agree by saying they are friendly, welcoming, and extroverted. They seem to exude a sense of confidence and joy that is inspiring to others (Peterson, 2000). All of these qualities have been long observed by other **personality theorists** (psychologists who study human nature in its entirety). Alfred Adler, an associate of Freud, described them as having a strong *gemeinschaftsgefuhl*—a strong sense of loving-kindness toward others (Adler, 1954). Carl Rogers described them as more accepting of people they work with, and more loving toward members of their family (Rogers, 1961). Carl Jung described them as more spiritually evolved (1955). And so on. They are the kind of people we can go to when we are in need of a friend. Maslow had also noticed their strong qualities of optimism and good cheer. His highly self-actualizing people were not immune to the misfortunes that visit all of us from time-to-time, but he observed how quickly and how well they could rebound from what disaster or loss they had to endure. Today, this quality is called **resilience**, which we discuss in more detail in Chapter 5.

They Can Distinguish Happiness from Pleasure. Positive psychologists differentiate *happiness* from *pleasure*. **Happiness** is a *long-lasting* feeling of well-being. **Pleasure**, on the other hand, is a *temporary* feeling that quickly dissipates after the pleasurable activity is over. For example, a child gets much pleasure from sucking on a lollypop, but as soon as the lollypop is all gone, so also is the pleasure. Temporary pleasures include alcohol, gambling, drugs, or any other addiction. They are distractions from our anxieties and unhappiness. When the pleasure is gone, we need another "fix." By contrast, we achieve a long-lasting feeling of well-being when we are engaged in activities that renew us, that give us energy, and are inspirational. It may be a vocational calling, such as the ministry or the health professions, or the mission "to serve and protect" as it is with police, firefighting, and other social agencies. But it can also be other careers that involve creating beautiful things (airplane or car design); growing beautiful things (flowers or vineyards); fostering the healthy growth of others (as in the teaching and medical professions); or the fascination of solving problems (such as how to bring a polluted river back to its former pristine state). It is not just *the achievement* of these activities that provides a state of well-being and happiness, it is also the *process of achieving* them. An enduring feeling of satisfaction comes also from the knowledge that we are investing our body, mind, and spiritual energy in something that will benefit others (Seligman & Csikszentimihalyi, 2000; Strizke, Lang & Patrick, 1996).

They Do Not Confuse Happiness with Materialism. Studies of people who are rich (such as the Forbes list of the 100 richest Americans) reveal they are not much happier than people with average incomes. Once we have a modicum of financial security so that we have a dry roof over our heads, food on the table, and dependable transportation, buying more and more objects doesn't make us much happier. There is even some evidence that the need to buy a new car every year or so or to shop endlessly for clothes and jewelry indicates a lack of self-esteem. Nor does winning the lottery (or inheriting a sizeable amount of money) lead to permanent happiness. After an ecstatic shopping spree and perhaps taking a cruise or two, the euphoria slowly recedes and the fortunate recipient's emotional level returns to its previous "set point" of happiness, or in some cases, even further down into depression (Arken & Chang, 2002; Petersen, 2000).

Their Sense of Well-Being Is Deeply Rooted in Moral/Ethical Values. Grounded in a strong moral/ethical philosophy, they eschew a life of unbridled **hedonism**; *i.e.*, chasing pleasure endlessly for its own sake. The Italians call a life devoted solely to pleasure *la dolce vita* (the sweet life). In English, it is sometimes called "the good life" of wine, women, and song. Positive and transcending persons know, almost instinctively, that the achievement of a more permanent state of well-being comes not from living the "good life," but from "living a life that is good." They are quite often "religiously active people" who derive emotional nourishment in finding ways to help others less fortunate.

We have to be very careful here, however, to note that certain types of strong religious affiliation can engender prejudice, cult membership, and hate groups. But these aberrant affiliations aside, studies have shown that "religiously active people" are happier, have better health records, have children who are less liable to get into trouble with the law, and better able to cope with distressing events. And they live longer!

Being "religiously active" does not necessarily mean church-going. Such persons may not have a specific religious affiliation but they do have a spiritual orientation that is expressed in some kind of service to others, such as raising money for charitable organizations, working for the betterment of the community, or being strong advocates for world ecology. They can also be identified as those attorneys who engage in **pro bono** work (working for the common good without pay) and who spend many nights representing prisoners who cannot afford lawyers. They can be identified as that weary government official flying to yet another corner of the world to heal a conflict between two warring nations. Or as the health professionals who spend several weeks a year, both here and overseas, to provide free eye-glasses to the aged, or vaccines for babies and young children, or to provide crutches and wooden legs for amputees (Inglehart, 1990; Diener, 2000).

A Call for Positive and Transcending Persons. The last two decades, with their religious conflicts and terror events, have been deeply distressing to Americans as well as to other nations around the world. We have been shocked by the tragic high school shootings here, in Canada, in Europe, and elsewhere. Teachers and professors have been shot by disgruntled and depressed students. Deranged postal employees have killed their coworkers en mass. Here, in the United States, we have been devastated by Americans who have exploded bombs in large office buildings where people work, and in schools and parks where children play. Then on September 11, 2001, Americans finally experienced the devastation of war on their own grounds, when international terrorists managed to dive bomb the World Trade Center, the Pentagon, and cause the collapse of five other skyscrapers in New York City. On television, we watched the terrible fires that caused people to jump out of upper story windows rather than be burned to death. In the wake of the devastation, we kept count of the dead and missing. And we mourned.

It was a sobering event. If we believed in the fairytale that nothing that bad could happen to us in the United States as has happened so often in war-torn areas elsewhere on the globe, we learned differently. We have become a more realistic nation. And what we realize is that disturbed adolescents can shoot their classmates; that hate groups can kill members of minority groups; and that terrorists here and abroad can strike at the very heart of our democracy.

In light of these events, we need people of spirit and courage to join the positive psychologists, educators, clerics, and others to work toward a better world. We need professionals dedicated to diminishing spouse abuse, child abuse, and the abuse of the elderly. We need teachers, recreation leaders, and city planners to provide activities for our youth so that delinquent adolescents do not become career criminals. We need people who are willing to support organizations seeking to clean up our rivers and lakes and oceans, and to renew and preserve our precious heritage of woodland and forest. We need people who are willing to be activists against those contaminates that poison the food we eat, the water we drink, and the air we breathe. We need people of all religions, all races, all ethnic backgrounds, who are willing to come together and work for more understanding of our multicultural diversity. We need people dedicated to help starving populations here and elsewhere—not just by giving them food but by teaching them how to farm. *If we give people food, they can eat for a day; if we teach them to grow their own food, they can eat for a lifetime.*

Positive psychology has sent out a call for people who have the virtues of altruism and all those qualities we call "good, old-fashioned character," people who are willing to help others less fortunate and to work toward a more peaceful world. There are rewards for being such a person. You will gain that sense of well-being and happiness that comes from a life lived well. You may think that, at the present time, working hard at getting an education and having a part- or full-time job, you do not have time to engage in such noble activities as we have been describing. We understand, especially those of you who also have families to support! But the time will come when you will be able, at least in part, to join the other coconspirators working around the globe.

In the meantime, there are things you can do as a human *becoming*. You can learn the causes of prejudice and discrimination and what can be done about them. You can become a role model for others in your family, friendship, and work communities. You can develop interpersonal skills that make for long-term relationships and a loving and supportive family life. You can take to heart the strategies that make for a *rewarding* as well as a *successful* life-career and, particularly, how to balance work, family, and personal leisure. We do not promise you absolute solutions. To paraphrase the remarkable Gordon Allport who called us *human becomings*, ". . . there is no master key. Rather, what we have at our disposal is a ring of keys, each of which opens one gate of understanding" (Allport, 1954, p. 204).

Studying Human Personality Via the Case Study Method

Using the case study method as a means of investigation, let's reconsider the six people described in Box 1.1. All six people received the same identical letter, but each reacted quite differently. By providing more information about their personality style and their life experiences, we may be better able to understand their dramatically different responses. The case study approach is a good place to begin our understanding of research methodology.

Case Study: Eduardo Sanangelo. Eduardo was the youngest child of the Sanangelo family. Moreover, he was the first son. Eduardo's parents had despaired they would ever have a male child to carry on the family name, so Eduardo seemed an answer to their earnest prayers. Little Eduardo was welcomed into the world with much celebration in his large extended family in rural New Mexico.

Little Eduardo became the center of family life, and the joy of his parents. For his four older sisters, it was like having a wonderful baby doll that could walk and talk and play with them. When it came time for Eduardo to begin school, his parents lectured him repeatedly about the importance of working hard at school and "doing everything the teacher tells you to do!" His sisters were given the job of making sure he did his homework correctly. All the importance placed on "learning" and being personally tutored at home by one or the other of his sisters proved to be of lasting value. Eduardo proved himself not only on the playing fields but also in the classroom. His grades were excellent, and it was the family's high expectation to send him to the big university in Albuquerque. His high school math and science grades gave him the confidence to go for an engineering degree. He would be the first in his family to go to college!

He was also a little nervous about his English language competency exam, since English was his second language. Nevertheless, he applied to the local college and took the entrance exams. Does his exuberant response to the letter surprise anyone?

Case Study: Jonnimae Jones. Jonnimae was born into a large migrant family in which poverty and hunger were the rule. When Jonnimae's father could not find employment, he took his drunken despair (and loss of manly self-esteem) out on his wife and children. Jonnimae learned to stay very still and not call attention to herself so she escaped most of the brutality, but her mother's bruised face and the screaming of her brothers and sisters would remain forever in her memory. Schooling was always a hit-and-miss affair, but somehow Jonnimae managed to learn to read (fairly well) and write (with many misspellings) and to do elementary sums. In fact, when her illiterate parents discovered her ability to add numbers, they made her the money manager of the family so as to stave off the creditors. Eventually, the other illiterate migrants began asking for her help in interpreting letters or official documents. "Miss Jonnimae," they would say holding up a piece of paper, "Can you tell me what this says?" It made Jonnimae feel good.

As is the case with so many below-poverty-level adolescents, Jonnimae was pregnant and married by the time she was 16. When they were first married, her husband was proud of being "the man Jonnimae married," but his pride turned to resentment (about the hours she spent helping other people) and jealousy (of their respect and awe of her). Within a few months, her husband began to exhibit the same abusive pattern as her father: bouts of drunken despair and rage, which he took out on Jonnimae, followed by abject guilt and sorrow and promises to her that he would "be better" to her in the future. By the time Jonnimae was 20, she was the mother of a girl and boy. Still, the physical and verbal abuse became more and more frequent and more and more intense. After one particularly violent beating, Jonnimae ended up in the hospital with a shattered face and several broken bones. With a social worker's help, Jonnimae initiated both a court restraining order and divorce proceedings. But Jonnimae knew that neither a court restraint nor a divorce decree would prevent her husband from "claiming his rights" as husband and father. Quietly (and telling only her parents where she was going), she took herself and her children off to the city where she found a room for rent and a job as a dishwasher.

She was a hard worker—and honest. When the manager discovered her ability to do sums and make accurate change, he made her permanent cashier. The additional pay enabled her to get a tiny three-room apartment for herself and the children. For a few years, Jonnimae was happier than she had ever been. But something kept nagging at her. She could hear her mother's voice urging her to get an education: "You're good with people, Jonnimae. You can make something of yourself." It seemed such an impossible dream. Nevertheless, one day, with a lump in her throat and a queasy stomach, Jonnimae walked into the college's administration offices. She waited quietly in the corner until her turn came. The fact that the counselor turned out to be an African-American like herself made the words easier to say, "I want to be a nurse." The counselor was startled. She had seldom heard such a clear statement of vocational aspiration.

"Well, do have a seat," replied the counselor, "and let's see what we have to do to get you there." That had been the beginning. Now this letter! Nothing could stop her now, nothing!

Case Study: Shannon McCrory. Even as a baby, passersby would stop to gasp at the beautiful child with silver-blonde hair and sky-blue eyes. So what could be so anxiety-provoking for Shannon that she was scared to go to college? Just this! Shannon had been born with a club foot. Shannon's mother stated later, "She was not a 'blessed event' at all." In the hospital, she refused to have anything to do with the baby. The attending physician diagnosed her mother as having a "post-partum depression." Shannon's young father turned to his mother for help. Although now in her forties, Shannon's grandmother was glad to take care of the child since

her own three children had all "left the nest." The arrangement was supposed to be temporary—only until Shannon's mother came back "to her senses" again. But, as fate would have it, Shannon's mother became pregnant again, and a prenatal exam revealed she was carrying twins. Everyone now agreed that it would be best to keep Shannon with her grandmother—for just a little longer. Weeks turned into months and months into years. Eventually, there was not even any more talk about Shannon going back to the family.

Although Shannon had looked forward eagerly to "making friends" with children of her own age, the reality was otherwise. Her club foot and ungainly walk produced aversion in the other children. And although only one or two of her classmates made fun of her openly, the other children tended to avoid her. For the first time in her life, Shannon began to see herself as an "ugly cripple." By the time other children got used to her club foot and tried to approach her, she kept them at a distance. She loved the learning activities, but by the end of the day she waited eagerly for the bus to take her back to the warm safety of her grandmother's house.

On the way to the college to take her admissions exam, Shannon became sick to her stomach. Her father had to stop the car so she could "upchuck" on the side of the road. She managed to get through the exams, but her head ached all day and when she turned her paper in she knew she had not done well. The test results that came were no surprise to her. Shannon was relieved. Now maybe she didn't have to go to college. She could stay home and take care of her grandmother (who was quite old now). Furthermore, now that she could be of help in the house, even her mother seemed more accepting of her in a distant way. When her mother was having "one of her spells," it was Shannon who cooked the evening meal for her father and "the boys." If she was scared to go out into the world, she knew that at least she could be useful to her family and that made her feel valued.

Case Study: Dan Westwind. Dan knew the extra money needed to go to college was not the issue. The basic issue was that the tribe needed him to be their representative to the Bureau of Indian Affairs. Dan had been given a grave responsibility and he would undertake whatever was necessary on behalf of his people. But he did not look forward to going through years of schooling to get the necessary degree. Still, in the ways of his people, Dan stoically accepted whatever came his way and did not question the designated path that was chosen for him. *¡Que sera, sera!*

Like some other traditional societies, Dan's life-career had been chosen by the tribal elders. When the tribal elders had decided to send one of their own people to the white man's college to become a lawyer, Dan had been the obvious first choice. Of all their people, Daniel had spent more time than anyone else in the white man's world, even graduating from their high school. He also had a trade, having worked as a car mechanic in Albuquerque for several years.

But there were several problems connected with Dan as a choice. He was already near 30 years of age. He would be close to 40 before he could call himself a lawyer. Furthermore, they knew he hated the white man's world because of what had happened to him in the city. What the Elders knew went like this: While having coffee one day at a diner, Dan had discovered that his waitress was half Native American. They found themselves *simpatico* and were married. Soon they had two sons. Daniel seemed to be making the transition from mountains and desert to life in the city. In actuality, Daniel hated living in the city. He hated listening to the white men "joking around" with their "squaw waitress," asking her whether she thought there would be another Indian uprising. He resented the way the white car owners spoke to him as though he was just a "dumb Indian." Still, he kept his peace. Then disaster hit. While crossing the street one day, his wife was killed by a white hit-and-run driver. Shocked and grief-stricken, he brought his sons back to his mother's house. He then went on an alcoholic binge that lasted for three months. He woke one morning to find himself in City Hospital full of tubes leading to hanging bags of intravenous fluids. He had been in the hospital for one week. His mother and the Navajo governor were sitting across from him.

Through the pain he could hear the nurse speaking to him, "If you tried to kill yourself with alcohol, you were almost successful." Daniel knew it was true.

The Governor waited until the nurse had left the room before he spoke: "Mourning time is over. It is time to live. If you don't want to live for yourself, then you can live for your people. There is much work for you to do."

His mother said simply, "The boys need you. They need their father. Come home."

So Dan went home. That was three years ago. He picked up the pieces of his life and went to work as a mechanic for a service station in the village, and in his spare time served as a maintenance person for the Navajo community. If there was a chance for personal happiness (a concept he only dimly understood), Dan knew it could only be where he could see his beloved mountains. Nevertheless, when the elders told Dan of their decision, Dan would do what he had to do. But the only relief he could envision to the bleak future of the next few years of his life were the times he could allow himself to journey back to the Navajo reservation.

Case Study: Natasha Petrovicc. Natasha Petrovicc is not just an immigrant to the United States. She and her husband, Gregori, and their two children are actually refugees from a former communist bloc country. Gregori had no English at all when they came to the United States, so he got work as a custodian in the local elementary school. It was he who persuaded Natasha to go back to school so she could get a good job that would help them all.

"You speak good English," Gregori said to her one day. "You are the one to get an American education so you can get a good job. Me, what can I do? I am no good at speaking English. No one understands me. I cannot read the English. As janitor, I know what I must do and Mister Evans, the principal, he likes that I am nice to the children so I get on. But I can't get a better job until I know more how to speak English. So you must be the one to go to the college and become educated."

"But what about the children? Who will take care of them? Who will cook the food? Who will clean the house?" cried Natasha.

Gregori said, "I will take care of everything here. We will put Nikki and Reza in the nursery school near my school. I will take them there. I will bring them home. I will cook the meals. I will keep the house clean. You must not concern yourself with these things. You must concern yourself with your classes at the college. You must make good marks. You must find something good to work at. You must do these things for all of us. You can teach all of us to speak good English. You can help the children with their homework to get good grades. We have not come to this country to live like peasants forever. We have come to make a good life for ourselves."

So Natasha applied to the college. She had not expected to be accepted. It was all happening so fast. While she was happy to be far from the violence that seems never to end in the "old country," she was having difficulty getting used to the newness of everything in the "new world." At times, she would experience dizzy spells. Sometimes, she even felt wistful for the "old country"—horrors at the thought! She sometimes felt depressed—all this while being grateful to be in a country free of brutal political violence, free of state police, free of prying neighbors ready to report your every word or action.

Case Study: Nat Bernstein. Receiving the Dean's letter was only the trigger-point for what happened. Nat's whole life seems to have been a disaster. Nathan was born to a Jewish family in which education and academic achievement were valued and fostered. Both parents were college professors. Nat's older brother, Aaron, graduated from Princeton with a Ph.D. in physics. By 36 years of age, Aaron was well on his way to a successful academic career.

If Aaron was the "model son," Nathan was the "problem child." By 10, he was smoking cigarettes and then grass with the gang. He stole his father's liquor and money enough to buy drugs. He dropped out of school at 16, watching TV during the day and skipping out at night with his friends, doing "God-knows-what," said his parents in despair. Eventually, petty crimes followed, and from then on, he was in and out of juvenile detention centers. Nothing seemed to help Nat; not counseling sessions or halfway houses for his drug abuse. He always ascribed his difficulties with the law on the "lousy police" or "the system." He screamed four-letter words at his parents.

To begin with, Nathan was two months premature. Furthermore, it had been a complicated "breech birth," and the baby had to be isolated with a life-support system for several weeks before his parents were allowed to take him home. Even the pregnancy had been difficult, according to Nathan's mother. At various times during her pregnancy, she had experienced nausea, anoxia, swelling of the ankles, and high blood pressure. Nathan's problems continued throughout infancy. He was colicky. Strange faces would start him crying. He would scream for fifteen or more minutes when he was left at the nursery school, according to the caretakers. He did not initiate play with other children. In grade school, he showed extremes of behavior. When he wanted to, said his teachers, he could do better than anyone else in the class. But he was "moody." He would sometimes sit staring. Or he might suddenly hit one of his classmates "for no reason."

Eventually, the school counselor recommended that he be given a complete psychological and physical evaluation. Diagnosis: epilepsy of the "petit mal" type. Petit mal epilepsy does not result in "fits" or "convulsions." The epileptic episodes last only for a few seconds, not even long enough to fall down. Nathan's particular type of petit mal epilepsy was

---

BOX **1.6** APPLICATION
Applying the Case Study Method

After you have read all the previous brief case studies, respond to the following items:

Eduardo Sanangelo:
1. Name three factors in his background that could account for Eduardo's cheerful and optimistic nature? _____
2. What do you think his chances are for doing well in college? Support your answer.
   _____

Jonnimae Jones:
1. Identify three factors in her childhood and adulthood that contributed to her positive self-esteem in regard to her ability to "make something" of herself._____
2. List three character traits that make her a good prospect for becoming a nurse._____

Shannon McRory:
1. Suggest three possible motivations for Shannon's lack of self-esteem and reluctance to go to college despite her brilliance as a student.
   _____

Dan Westwind:
1. What are Dan Westwind's chances for success in terms of coping skills and purpose?
   _____
2. Describe his self-concept and personality style.
   _____

Natasha Petrovicc:
1. Although she is happy to be away from the violence of the old country, why does she sometimes yearn to go back? _____
2. What might be happening that results in her occasional dizziness?_____

Nathan Bernstein:
1. How do you evaluate Nat's self-esteem?
   _____
2. Name four factors that could be involved in his self-destructive behavior._____
3. What evidence is there that Nat does not understand his problems?_____

preceded by noises (sometimes even bits of speech), called an epileptic aura. The bits of speech he would hear were similar to what he had heard at home. "Why aren't you more like your brother, Aaron!" "You'll be the death of me." Not realizing these comments were coming from his own brain memories, he thought his classmates were ridiculing him. With angry "knee-jerk" responses, he would turn around and hit them.

When he was 18, Nat took off. For eighteen months, no one knew where he was until he showed up at his parents' home again, looking somewhat better than he had for some time. He had a young woman with him whom Nat introduced as Amber, his "soul mate." Amber seems to have been a good influence on him, so his parents allowed them to share a room in their house, although an intimate relationship without marriage was painful for them. At mealtimes, the two young people would introduce the family to "New Age" concepts. Things seemed to be working out better for Nat. With Amber's encouragement, he finished high school at night. He even contemplated enrolling in the local college and took the necessary entrance exams. Little by little, however, Nat's previous behaviors returned: drug addiction, petty theft, drunken sprees, and obscenities toward his parents and even Amber.

One night, Amber left quietly without even writing a note. Nat got drunk, cried a lot, and called her obscene names. That night he had a bad trip on drugs. The Dean's letter came in the morning mail. He dropped the letter, went into the house, and shot himself.

Important Terms and Concepts to Know

- abnormal
- abuse
- becomings
- belongingness
- control
- case study
- discrimination
- experimental
- genetics

- happiness
- hedonism
- high
- high school
- hierarchy
- internal
- life-careers
- locus of control
- materialism

- meaning
- moral/ethical
- negative
- optimistic
- personality
- physiological
- pleasure
- positive
- psychology

- rats
- reductionist
- self-actualizing
- self-concept
- self-esteem
- shootings
- unconscious
- world

Create Your Own Chapter Summary by Filling in the Blanks

Use the "Important Terms and Concepts to Know" to fill in the blanks.

Personality. How we cope with life events depends on our _____ [personality] style. Personality includes every dimension of the human experience, such as _____ [self-esteem] (how we *feel* about ourselves), our age and health, our _____ [culture] (what we inherit), our life experiences, conscious factors and _____ [unconscious] factors (things we don't know about ourselves).

Self-concept Versus Self-Esteem.   As compared to self-esteem _____ [self-concept] is how we *think* about ourselves, in terms of sibling rank, religion, and subculture, etc. We can have a positive self-concept but a low or _____ [unhealthy/negative] self-esteem. Most of us have a combination of

~~LOC~~ and negative self-esteem. People who believe that what happens to them is their fate or believe in "lucky/unlucky days," have an external ___. People who have an internal LOC believe they have at least some control over their lives and what happens to them. Our self-esteem is generally lowest during the ___ years. The good news is that as we get older and become experienced in our ___, most people become more self-confident and happier.

Personality Theory.   Before World War II, most of what we knew about human nature was derived from two sources: from ___ studies of rats and other animals in the laboratory and from ___ people who were so dysfunctional they had to be institutionalized. Some social scientists even posited that we are nothing more than intelligent apes, called the ___ theory. Then after WW II, psychologists objected to this type of thinking. Gordon Allport, for example, said we are not just intelligent robots or conditioned ___. He said we should think of ourselves, not as human beings, but as human ___, always growing, changing, and evolving.

Abraham Maslow.   Maslow focused our attention on highly ___ persons, and provided us with a seven level ___ of needs model for human personality. An example is having enough food, water, and air constitutes the most basic level, called the ___ needs. Another example is: Having friends and a close-knit family constitute the love-and-___ needs. Maslow studied his subjects via the ___ method of research. While Maslow's pioneering

work was ground-breaking, psychologists were left with some difficult questions, such as *How can anyone of us attain a ___ level of self-actualizing* and *Can self-actualizing be taught?*

On Being Happy and Healthy.   A further humanistic thrust came about by way of positive ___, which is trying to answer these questions. These psychologists have discovered several important factors about ___. For example, happy people are generally ___ and outgoing. They can distinguish happiness (which is an enduring emotion) from ___ (which is a distraction that is short-lived). They realize that happiness is not the same as unbridled ___. They do not mistake making money and other kinds of ___ for genuine happiness. Their well-being and happiness is grounded in a strong ___ philosophy of life.

The Positive Psychology Call to Action. Americans have been understandably shocked by the events of the last three decades, including the tragic high school ___ and the terror attacks of 9/11. Positive psychologists are calling upon people from every walk-of-life to join them in working for a better ___. There are many avenues of endeavor that people, such as ourselves can do, including diminishing spouse, child, and elderly ___; and by bringing peoples from different races, ethnic background, and religion together toward diminishing prejudice and ___ in our society. The rewards are great, including a sense of well-being, energy, and inspiration that comes from living a life that has ___ and value for others as well as ourselves.

The Self in Society
How Groups Affect Our Attitudes and Behaviors

BOX 2.1 SCENARIO
What Makes for Human Prejudice, Cults, and Hate Groups?

Professor Wietzman: We have been discussing the various factors of personality such as self-concept and self-esteem. But we can never really understand human behavior until we include the cultural context in which the person exists. That's a fancy way of saying that many of our attitudes and behaviors are the result of societal influences—the person's racial, ethnic, religious affiliations, and other groups to which he or she belongs. Prejudice, hate-crimes, and genocide can all be viewed from the perspective of the person's group membership.

Alec: I'm glad we're getting into this, Professor. Why is there so much hate crime? I have a personal reason for asking this. I come from a really prejudiced family. It was only in the last two years of high school that I learned how prejudiced they are. I moved out as soon as I could.

Professor Wietzman: First of all, Alec, I have to tell you that there isn't anyone entirely free of prejudice. We are all of us prejudiced to some degree.

Eduardo: Hey, I resent that, Professor! I don't think I'm prejudiced. I accept everybody as being equal to me.

Professor Wietzman: Eduardo, what vocational area are you aiming for?

Eduardo: I'm going to be an engineer.

Professor Wietzman: Would you employ a woman as an engineer?

Eduardo: A woman! Why would a woman want to be an engineer when she'd be so much better at being a teacher or social worker maybe.

Martha: Talk about prejudice!

Professor Wietzman: To be specific, that's called *gender bias.*

Eduardo: (*now a little rattled*) I thought prejudice meant thinking that a certain ethnic group has . . . bad traits.

Professor Wietzman: Prejudice simply means *prejudgment*, making assumptions about someone without knowing them. One example is called *stereotyping*, assuming that somebody has certain characteristics because they are members of a certain group.

Alec: But just what makes us stereotype people?

Professor Wietzman: To answer that, we need to understand the terms, *cognitions* or *cognitive schemas*, which are thoughts, ideas, or perceptions about the way things are or should be. We have cognitive schemas for just about everything in our social world and these cognitive schemas guide our actions.

Martha: Eduardo has a cognitive schema that women shouldn't try to be engineers.

Alec: So racial and ethnic prejudice has to do with rejecting anyone who doesn't fit our cognitions about what it is to be a good person or a good American?

Professor Wietzman: Very good, Alec. That's part of it. Cognitive schemas are the result of many factors—past experiences, our defense mechanisms, our age—just about everything. Anything that threatens to disrupt our cognitive schemas makes us uncomfortable, and we have an innate tendency to reject it. Cognitive schemas are the way we make judgments.

Martha: Like parents who object to their son's choice of a wife because "she isn't our kind"? That's what my in-laws said when they met me. I'm Italian and they didn't think I was good enough for Rodney. I guess I didn't fit into their cognitive schema about what kind of wife would be right for Rod. Fortunately, Rod didn't feel the same way.

Jonnimae: I listened to Alec describing his prejudiced family and how he got outside of the . . . prejudicial cognitive schema of his family. I think that's amazing. I've heard that it is very difficult to get beyond prejudice.

Professor Wietzman: It is difficult because many of the prejudices and attitudes we have as adults were

BOX 2.1　SCENARIO (continued)
What Makes for Human Prejudice, Cults, and Hate Groups?

learned so early in our lives that they seem built into the very fabric of our personality structure. Nevertheless, by learning how groups influence our behavior, we can begin to develop wider cognitive schemas and enlarge our own worldviews. As well, there is another explanation for why we react to people unlike ourselves. This explanation stems from a relatively new approach to understanding human behavior, called "evolutionary psychology." It has to do with our inherited behaviors.

Alec: Evolutionary psychology? Is that like genetics and DNA and all that?

Professor Wietzman: Well, not exactly. Genetics has to do with what each individual has inherited directly from his or her parents. Evolutionary psychology has

to do with what the entire human race has inherited from earliest times. But it's a very controversial theory at the present time and the arguments pro and con are raging.

Alec: Why do scientists argue so much? I hear this word *controversy* over and over in my physical science class too.

Professor Wietzman: All theories are controversial, Alec, particularly in the social sciences. It is the task of scientists to try to spot flaws in any theory and then develop a wider, more comprehensive theory. That's how any science makes progress. Science doesn't proceed by agreement and consensus. Science proceeds by disagreement, argument, and debate.

THE POWERFUL FORCES OF OUR GROUP MEMBERSHIP

Social psychologists focus on the very questions we ask ourselves when we learn about tragic events via the public media:

> *What makes people participate in the atrocities of war and genocide?*
> *Why do some people not help in an emergency, whereas others are "good Samaritans"?*
> *Why do people choose to become gangsters and live outside the law?*
> *Why do people give up their liberties and even their lives to follow a cult leader?*

Whereas social psychologists have not discovered all the answers to these questions, they have discovered a few of them. For example, if we have grown up in an affluent family that believes the making and spending of money is the ultimate value in life, then we may very likely grow up to think of money as the basis of "the good life." If we have grown up in a home where the adults express fear or hatred and prejudice toward other ethnic groups, then we may very likely become fearful or hateful toward these groups.

Our attitudes are also shaped by the groups we admire and would like to belong to, called **referent groups**. In fact, throughout our life time we are learning continually to conform to the behavioral expectations of our professions, our political affiliations, and our civic and religious associations. Group membership makes us feel stronger and more secure. We feel we belong somewhere, which seems to fulfill Maslow's third hierarchical level of love and belongingness. That's the bright side of the coin; the other side of the coin is darker. By definition, *in-groups* make for *out-groups*. Once we become an in-group member, those who are not part of this group are, by definition, members of the out-group.

Research in social psychology had its beginnings at the end of the nineteenth century when a French scientist, by the name of Émile Durkheim (1884), studied the social factors involved in suicide. While his research parameters are somewhat primitive (when compared to research today), many of Durkheim's basic findings are still valid. He discovered that many people who committed or attempted to commit suicide were isolated from their **primary groups** (the families they were born into) and their **secondary groups** (their friends and close associates). At the time of their suicide, they had left their homes in other parts of France and were living in Paris; had not yet established new relationships or friends; nor a way to make a secure living for themselves. Far from home, lost, bewildered, and running out of funds, they fell into despair. Feelings of failure and having no one to turn to for help prompted them to end their miserable existences.

Adorno's Study of the Authoritarian Personality

After Durkheim, there followed some sporadic investigations, but the great impetus came with the rise of Nazi Germany and the atrocities of that era. One of the earliest of these studies was that conducted by Theodor Adorno and his associates (1973), and it is still noteworthy because it defined the "authoritarian" personality type. The authoritarian personality is considered so valid a personality type that it has been incorporated into (literally) thousands of research studies ever since.

Adorno was himself German-born. Horrified by the takeover of the Nazi regime, he emigrated to the United States in 1934. After World War II, Adorno organized a research team at Berkeley, California, to investigate whether Americans could become as fanatic and Fascist as the Germans and Italians under the regimes of Hitler and Mussolini. The specific questions posed by Adorno and his research team were as follows:

> *How could the German people have been induced to follow such despotic leaders?*
> *What is the personality style of people who blindly obey terrible orders such as happened in the Holocaust?*
> *How could the nation that produced some of the greatest musicians, philosophers, scientists, and humanitarians the world has ever known also produce the atrocities of the Nazi regime?*

And most compelling of all their questions:

> *Could the atrocities that happened in a Fascist state also happen in a democracy?*
> *Could Americans, who have been brought up in a democracy, be as easily regimented as the Germans?*

The research findings of Adorno and his team were shocking even to them. Their conclusion was that even here, in the bastions of democracy, a large percentage of people had attitudes that were consistent with the Fascists of Italy and Germany.

The F-Scale. Because of some faulty design errors, Adorno's work fell into some disrepute. Later, however, other researchers corrected the flaws of the original **F-Scale** (short for Fascist Scale) instrument and, since the 1980s, there has been a resurgence of interest into authoritarianism because of the cults, hate groups, and other extremist groups that have arisen in the last three decades. We present next the general findings of Adorno along with the findings of those who have extended and refined his original studies (Altmeyer, 1996; Duncan,

Peterson, & Winter, 1997; Jones, 2002). Some of the statements that highly authoritarian personalities would agree with are:

- Obedience and respect for authority are the most important virtues children should have.
- Our country would be better off if we got rid of the immoral, crooked, and feeble-minded.
- People can be divided into two distinct classes: the weak and the strong.
- Homosexuals are hardly better than criminals and ought to be severely punished.
- Lawbreakers should have harsher penalties.
- There is more delinquency these days because working mothers are not staying at home and taking care of their children.
- We have too many immigrants in this country, particularly, Latinos, Japanese, Chinese, Filipinos, Africans, Arabs, Hispanics, and Jews.
- AIDS is God's punishment for homosexuality.

Characteristic Traits of the Highly Authoritarian Personality. Adorno's research and more recent studies have resulted in a fairly consistent profile of those who rank high on the F-Scale. The major characteristics are as follows:

- They blindly follow authority without question (as did the Germans during the Hitler regime).
- They have a lack of positive self-esteem. In fact, they tend to feel vulnerable and defenseless. Belonging to an authoritarian organization provides them with some measure of security and self-esteem.
- Although they are dominant and authoritarian and expect unquestioning obedience from their children and employees, they are nevertheless very submissive to those who are their superiors in authority. In other words, said the researchers, they could have made "good Nazi soldiers."
- They are harshly judgmental about others, particularly minority groups. They tend to view racial, ethnic, religious, and other minorities as "enemies of democracy." By contrast, low-authoritarian subjects (defined as more open-minded and democratic) were more egalitarian and were willing to accept all ethnic groups as equal to the WASP (White Anglo-Saxon Protestant) dominant population group of that time (the late 1940s and early 1950s).
- Their cognitive schemas are *dogmatic*, *stereotypic*, and exemplify *rigid either/or thinking*.

Authoritarian Cognitions: Dogmatic, Stereotypic, Rigid Either/Or Thinking. **Dogma** refers to a set of beliefs held to be true and absolute without evidence of proof. *Dogmatic* individuals not only subscribe to a prescribed set of beliefs, they often behave in an "arrogant" fashion toward those who believe otherwise. In our personal lives, we all know dogmatic people who are absolutely convinced that what they believe is right and that other people are wrong. They do not like to listen to others who have a different opinion, particularly if that opinion comes from a minority group they dislike or from a person younger than themselves. You may know such a person who says, "Until you're my age, keep your opinions to yourself."

Not only were Adorno's authoritarian subjects dogmatic, they also fell prey to stereotypic thinking and all-or-nothing thinking. **Stereotypes** are the cultural assumptions that people who belong to a certain group all share the same personality characteristics. Stereotyping people is a normal cognitive process. It is sometimes called a **cognitive shortcut**—how we clump events together in chunks to make sense of our world. If we had to cogitate (think deeply) about the thousands of objects and people we encounter over the course of the day, we would hardly be able to function at all. Cognitive shortcuts make life simpler and easier to manage when it comes to objects and events, but when these shortcuts are applied to people, they can be the basis of much of our prejudicial thinking. **Gender stereotyping** seems to be the most common, but all segments of our population get their fair share of stereotyping.

Women are emotional, illogical, and passive.
Men are macho, logical, and aggressive.
Jews are clever in business affairs.
Blacks have rhythm.
Italians are passionate.
Germans are methodical.
The British are reserved.

Lawyers are manipulative.
Artists are uninhibited.
Old people are feeble-minded.
The Scots are tight with money.
Blondes are airheads.
Computer programmers are nerds.
Accountants are conformists.

Now there may be some truth to the perception that accountants are more conforming than (say) artists and entertainers—after all, accountants have to understand thousands of IRS rules and conform to them. But there are always exceptions to any stereotype, and we miss the real person when we view him through stereotypic glasses: *I may be a woman and a blonde, BUT I AM NOT AN AIRHEAD!*

Either/or thinking is the tendency to think in terms of black and white. When adults indulge in either/or thinking, they tend to see a few people as "good guys" but almost everyone else as "bums" or "SOBs." They view people like the heros and bad guys of Hollywood Westerns—as wearing white hats and black hats. The democratic personality tends to view almost all people as having some good in them (see Box 2.2).

BOX **2.2** STUDENTS VERBATIM
Identifying an Authoritarian Personality

Male Student, 18 years: That's my father. He's a retired colonel. There's five of us in the family, all guys. I'm the next to the oldest. None of us can ever disagree with him. If we want to do something he doesn't like, he just says, "My way or the highway!" which means if we don't do what he wants, we are free to leave. And if we don't do what he wants us to do (like mow the lawn) exactly when he wants us to, he starts his damn (excuse me for cussing) yelling. I don't know how my mother has stood his yelling all these years. I still live there because it's cheaper than getting my own place while I'm going to school. But my older brother and I are talking about getting a place to live, like an apartment or house, as soon as we've saved enough money.

Female Student, 19 years: Does that ever describe my brother! He's only two years older than me, but he thinks he knows everything. You can't have a discussion with him. If he's made his mind up, he won't even listen to what I have to say. It's infuriating. Not only am I younger than him, as far as he is concerned, I'm just a "stupid broad"!

Female Student, 37 years: My uncle! He and my dad were country folks and I guess it was still traditional for some country folks to say "Children should be seen, and not heard." I remember my uncle saying that to us whenever we spoke up at the table when he was there or a family picnic. Then he'd turn to my father and say something like, "How can you let them talk to you like that." My dad isn't that way at

BOX **2.2** STUDENTS VERBATIM (continued)
Identifying an Authoritarian Personality

all. My dad is really neat! I'm sure glad my dad isn't like his brother. My uncle was so strict with his kids that they all hated him. Funny thing, though, one of his kids turned out just like him.

Male Student, 42 years: You may not believe this, but it's the God's honest truth. Most of the professors here are really decent, but this term, I just ran up against a really crazy professor. I signed up for this math course with this lady teacher and the first day in class, she tells us she's really mean! She gives ten "pop" quizzes during the term (along with the midterm and final exams). If we are absent, we get a zero. OK, I figure she's trying to motivate us to study everyday. So here's the real kicker! On the second day of class, she gives the first pop quiz. That was kind of shocking, but OK. But this other guy in class raises his hand and says, "This is my first day in class. I didn't know we were going to have a quiz." So, get this! She says, "If you don't know it you get a zero." He says, "But I just registered this morning." She says, "Too bad, you should have registered on time." I was shocked! I guess everybody was. You could have heard a pin drop.

After I got out of class, I went right over to the add-drop counselor, and dropped the course. When I told the counselor about what happened in class, she said, "I don't blame you." I'm not great in math and I've been doing all right so far, at least getting by with B's, but I don't need to have her as a teacher. Talk about an Authoritarian Personality. Whew!

—Author's note: Our college prides itself on being student-oriented, and we were as shocked as the student. We checked with the drop-add counselor and she verified this student's story. Several students had complained about the instructor and almost one-third of the students had dropped her class. The counselor said she was a graduate student from the university and hired just to teach this one course. She felt sure that, with all the complaints coming in, she would not teach again.

Reflective Writing: Write a short paragraph describing someone you know whose personality seems to fit the Authoritarian Personality.

How Can We Know Whether We Are Holding a Dogmatic Position on an Issue? Ends versus Means. One way to know is to examine ourselves: Do we justify the *means* in pursuit of the *ends*? Many terrible deeds have been committed by **dogmatic** people out of their conviction that since they know what is right, others are not only wrong—they must be purged of their misbeliefs or simply wiped out. The Inquisition came into being to root out not only the Devil but also to discover anyone suspected of "heretical thinking." The purpose of the Inquisitors was to save the heretic's soul through any means, including torture—even if the body died in the process (see Tip 2.1). Two centuries later, the very Puritans who sailed to the New World for reasons of religious freedom became, in turn, equally dogmatic—resulting eventually in the witch trials and witch burnings in Salem, Massachusetts.

In a democracy, the *ends* may never justify the **means**. We are involved with the "due process of law" as much as we are involved with "law-and-order." That is why our Supreme Court defends our liberties of free speech and free assembly even to those who are political adversaries of democracy. Sometimes, for example, we may become horrified that permission to march has been granted to white supremacist groups. But, unless these groups are conspiring to overthrow our constitutional government or commit a crime, the Supreme Court has

---

Tip 2.1 The Devil's Advocate. Even during the time of the Inquisition, the Catholic Church allowed for the defense of accused persons by appointing a cleric to defend them. For, said the Church, even the Devil deserves to be heard, and the defense counsel-cleric became known as the "Devil's Advocate."

declared that they have as much right to assemble and to speak as does anyone else (see Figure 2.1).

Figure 2.1 Ends versus Means. The Supreme Court has declared that even white supremacy groups can assemble and march as long as they do not advocate overthrowing the government.

Prejudice versus Discrimination. Prejudice and discrimination are often confused, so let's make sure we understand the difference between these two terms. **Prejudice** involves an immediate emotional pre-judgment about others in *stereotypic* ways (such as being untrustworthy, greedy, dirty, crippled, deformed, retarded, and so forth). According to **evolutionary psychology** (theories pertaining to traits we have inherited as a member of the human species), we are all prejudiced. According to evolutionary theory, suspicion of others unlike ourselves is built right into the very fabric of human nature. The ability to detect dangerous situations—ferocious animals and human aggressors—is what helped the human species to survive. Fear and suspicion of people who are different may be as instinctive as running from fire: *Is that person friend or foe?* This instinct is not just for people who differ from us in terms of color, ethnic background, or language. Upon first encountering a man who is dwarfed or a woman who is obese or a child with Down's syndrome, we may jump back with an instantaneous negative response. That is the nature of **negative prejudice** (Fishbein, 1996; Jones, 2002).

We can also have **positive prejudice**. Millions of dollars have been spent to determine what makes a jury decide the innocence or guilt of the defendant. What has been discovered is that we tend to be *positively* prejudiced toward those who are similar to ourselves as compared to those who are different from ourselves. For example, a middle-aged, white businessman on a jury will tend to be positively prejudiced toward a witness who is also a white, middle-aged businessman (Jussim, Nelson, Manis, & Soffin, 1995).

Whereas prejudice can be positive or negative, discrimination can only be negative. **Discrimination** is *acting* upon our prejudicial feelings in *negative* ways (Allport, 1954; Mackie & Smith, 1998). Discrimination manifests as acts of violence against the individual, including verbal slurs, beatings, house burnings, and even murder.

Scapegoating is a particularly horrible example of violent discrimination. Hitler projected the economic disaster of Germany onto the Jews and used that distortion to carry out the horrors of the Holocaust. In the United States, scapegoating resulted in the near genocide of our Native American population and the horrors of lynchings of our African-Americans. We now are facing an upsurge in **hate crimes**—the brutal violence of one group against innocent victims. These crimes are receiving harsher penalties from the courts. Sadly, too, scapegoating can sometimes be observed in the dynamics of a family or classroom. If a child in a family tended to "act up" and got caught at it a few times, the other siblings soon catch on that they can blame the miscreant and escape the "heat" themselves.

But it can also manifest in social ways, such as preventing people from living in certain areas or refusing to hire them to fill certain jobs. There are even more subtle methods to discriminate against a certain group. By requiring police officers to be 5′ 9″ or taller, we may be discriminating against women. By having a voting machine on the third floor of a building without an elevator, we may be discriminating against people who can only get about in wheelchairs (Jones, 2002).

So What Can We Do about Our Innate Prejudicial Thinking? Well, if we can't get rid of our instant prejudicial cognitions, is there nothing we can do? Well, yes, social psychologists have suggested several things we can do:

1. **Don't try to suppress the undesirable thought or feeling.** Trying to rid ourselves of a prejudicial thought from our consciousness just doesn't work. In fact, there is some research evidence that trying to suppress stereotypic cognitions may rebound again and again and flood the subject's consciousness. This **rebound effect** may actually reinforce the unwanted prejudice and discriminatory behavior (Macrae, Bodenhausen, & Milne, 1998). But if we can't get rid of our instant prejudicial cognitions, there are other responses that will neutralize them.

2. **Realize that we all have prejudices so we need not feel guilty.** If our prejudices are built right into our cognitive structure, as evolutionary psychologists tell us, then we need not feel guilty. Everyone has some kind of prejudice. We need to acknowledge them without remorse or guilt and then neutralize them by getting around them with more rational cognitions.

3. **To avoid either/or thinking, develop several perspectives.** If you catch yourself thinking in terms of *right versus wrong* ("That's right and this is wrong"), develop the skill to perceive a situation from several points of view with *who, when, where,* and *under what circumstances* as your guidelines. *Who might it be right for and when might it be wrong? Under what kind of circumstances would the same action be right for you and wrong for you?* The Ancient Greeks were fond of saying *there is always a third alternative.* Look for a third alternative . . . and a fourth one . . . and a fifth one . . . and so on.

4. **To know if you are holding a dogmatic position, employ the means versus ends test.** The acid test for knowing if you are holding a dogmatic position is to check out which you are making more important: the *ends* or the *means.*

There seems to be a positive correlation between authoritarianism and education. One social scientist identified the authoritarian cognitive style (dogmatic, stereotypic, and rigid either/or thinking) as more prevalent among those who come from lower educational levels. We become more open-minded and democratic in our thinking as we become more and more educated (Leung, Lau, & Lam, 1998).

Solomon Asch's Studies of Conformity: Giving into Social Pressure

Another burning question for social psychologists of the post–World War II decade went something like this: *Just how were the German people made to conform to the racist philosophy and brutal tactics of the Nazi war machine?* Much research has been undertaken to answer this question and social psychologists have come up with a few insights for us. One line of investigation, under the direction of Solomon Asch (1951), demonstrated just how easily people can be made to conform even when conforming went contrary to their beliefs or perceptions.

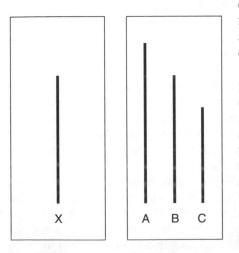

Figure 2.2 Asch's Study of Conformity.

Social conformity

A typical experiment would be set up as follows. Asch would invite about six to eight college subjects (the number varied according to the particular study) to a classroom to judge the comparative length of similar lines (see Figure 2.2). It's important to understand that of all the students in each experimental session, *only one student was a real subject*. All the others were confederates of the experimenter—but of course the real subject (let's call him Student S) did not know that. As far as Student S was concerned, they were all real subjects like himself.

In the beginning of the experiment, all is rather hum-drum. All the students agree that Line X is most similar to Line B. But after a few rounds, something seems to go wrong. The first five students state that Line X is most similar to Line A or Line C. Movies of this experiment clearly show that Student S is obviously puzzled. He looks at the lines again. He squints at them. Sometimes he even wriggles nervously in his seat. What will he do because of his difference of opinion? Will he go along with the crowd? Or will he candidly express his opinion in the face of overwhelming public opinion? About 35 percent of the time, Student S conformed to public opinion and agreed with the other students. But that was only the beginning.

Asch then concerned himself with the 65 percent who were able to diverge from public opinion. He wondered what would happen if he increased the public pressure on them. Would they be able to maintain an independent stance? This is how Asch increased the social pressure: He instructed the other students that if Student S turned out to be an independent type, they were to laugh at him and make derisive remarks about his intelligence, etc. The public pressure was effective. Now 75 percent caved in under this increased public pressure.

When all the real subjects were asked later why they gave in to public opinion, they offered two major responses. The first was that in light of what everyone was saying, they began to doubt themselves and their own senses. They thought that maybe there was something wrong with their eyes or the lights in the room. The second common response was that they knew their own perceptions were right but they "didn't want to make waves." So what Asch did was to change the experimental conditions. Student S continued to listen to the other students but was allowed to give his own answer in private. Without the public condemnation, Student S did not change his own belief that he was mistaken.

Asch was dismayed by the results of his studies, not just because people will give in to public pressure but for the fact that his particular subjects were college students—presumably, the nation's most intelligent young people. Subjected to enough social pressure, the majority could not resist the pressure of social conformity. They just kept still. *Is that what happened to the Germans who said nothing while their friends and relatives were dragged off to concentration camps? They just kept still?*

But there are also some brighter results in these generally dismal findings. No matter how much pressure was applied, 25 percent of the subjects did not conform, not when they were questioned privately, nor when they were ridiculed publicly. They were able to remain a "minority of one." Another finding: If Student S had at least one ally, someone who agreed with him, he was much more able to stand up against the social pressure. In fact, he was unlikely to conform. It reminds us of the saying: *A good friend is a strong defense.*

Milgram's Experiments in Obedience: *Blindly Obeying Authority*

Stanley Milgram, a former student of Asch, was so concerned by the massacre of villages of men, women, and children during the Vietnam War that he undertook a project to determine just how far Americans would go to obey orders, no matter what might result. His research in this area is now known as the "obedience experiments" (Milgram, 1974).

What Milgram did was to post an advertisement in the local newspaper for volunteers to take part in a university experiment. The volunteer would receive $4.50 an hour (a good hourly rate at that time). When the subject appeared at the office, he was introduced to another person who apparently had also answered the advertisement. The Experimenter appeared and told the two men that the experiment was to discover the effects of punishment on learning and that one of the subjects would be the Teacher and the other would be the Learner. These roles were drawn from slips of paper in a hat in a seemingly random manner. Both the Teacher and the Learner were conducted to a booth where the Learner was strapped into a chair. The straps, explained the Experimenter, were merely to prevent excessive movement, but then an electrode was placed on the Learner's wrist and some electrode paste was applied in order "to avoid blisters and burns." The Learner asked if the shocks would be painful. The Experimenter replied that while the shocks might be a little painful, they would not do any permanent damage.

The Teacher was then conducted to a second booth from which he could not see the Learner and where he was shown an apparatus that registered the voltage of electric shock in units from 15 to 450 volts. The Teacher was then given a booklet full of questions. He was told to ask the Learner a question through an intercom. If the Learner answered correctly, the Teacher was to go on to the next question. If the Learner answered incorrectly, however, he was to be punished with a shock, starting at 15 volts and going up to the highest volt level, 450 volts.

As you may have already guessed, the Learner was really part of the experiment. (Both slips in the hat read "Teacher.") All the Teacher knows is that as the shocks increase in intensity, the Learner begins to cry out that he is in pain and pleads to be let out of the experiment—at least in the beginning. The Learner's protests get louder and louder. Then he yells out, "I can't stand the pain," and he begins to scream in agony. At a certain point, he screams out that he has a heart condition. At 300 volts the Learner begins to pound on the wall. Still the testing goes on. The reader should not get the idea that the Teacher is impervious to the cries of the Learner. Movies of this experiment clearly show that the Teacher is perspiring and visibly shaken. He turns frequently to the Experimenter (who is dressed in a pristine white lab coat) and questions the Experimenter anxiously about the Learner's welfare. *Perhaps they should stop?* But in a cool and unemotional tone of voice, the Experimenter merely replies that "the experiment must continue." The Teacher continues asking questions and administering shocks (he thinks).

Eventually there is no more screaming—just silence. No matter how many times the Teacher tries to get a response from the Learner, there is only this ominous silence. As far as the Teacher knows, the Learner could be dead. Yet approximately 66 percent of the Teachers obeyed "the Authority" right up to the 450 volt level. Whenever this happened, the Teachers often behaved in strange ways. One man giggled every time he heard a scream. A few of the people who truly believed that the Learner was dead were asked how they felt. They replied in a variety of ways. One man replied, "So he's dead. I did my job." A few even placed the blame for the Learner's death on the Learner himself. *It was his own fault for being so dumb.* When Milgram's experiment was **replicated** (repeated) in Australia, South Africa, and in several European countries, the results were similar or even more dramatic. In one German study, 85 percent of the subjects were found to be obedient to the end.

Disturbed that Americans, born and bred in the very country that has been so concerned with "human rights," would obey authority to this extent, Milgram wondered if college students would show more resistance to such inhumane orders. But a replication of the study

with Yale undergraduates yielded similar results. *What about women who are supposed to be the "gentler sex"?* But women Teachers also administered heavy shocks to the Learners. Perhaps the subjects were influenced by the impressive environment of Yale University where the experiment was taking place. So the experiment was tried in a dingy store in a nearby town—and still the same results. Milgram came to some dismal conclusions:

- Independent thinking and moral/ethical judgment are not built-in attributes of a free society. Evidently, some people will do things simply because some more powerful authority tells them to do so.
- When faced with the painful dilemma of hurting someone or disobeying some authority, most people will obey "the authority." Milgram wondered if comparisons could be made with the Nazi concentration camp officers who complied with orders to murder millions of people.
- An implication from this comparison was that the Nazi murderers were merely average bureaucrats following orders and trying to do their jobs as well as they could.

Zimbardo's Prison Experiment: *The Powerful Effect of Our Social Roles*

Figure 2.3 Zimbardo's Prison Experiment. The students who were selected as prisoners were picked up by the police, handcuffed and taken to the city jail, where they were fingerprinted, photographed, and given prisoner uniforms before being "jailed" at the college.

Another classic experiment was carried out by Philip Zimbardo (1976) of Stanford University, who provided more information about group membership and how it defines our roles. Zimbardo's purpose for running the experiment was "to understand just what it means psychologically to be a prisoner or a prison guard" (Zimbardo, 1976, p. 277). The pay was advertised as $15.00 per day—quite a decent rate for college students at that time. Of more than 70 students who answered the ad, they ended up with "about two dozen" young men who were "*mature, emotionally stable, normal, intelligent college students from middle-class families*." We have taken pains to describe the subjects because of what ensued. As far as Zimbardo and his team were concerned, their subjects were the "*cream of the crop of this generation*" and none had any criminal record or had been in any serious difficulties growing up.

The next step was to select the college students who would be the prisoners and those who would be the prison guards. (By the way, all students were actual subjects.) The selection was made by a genuine flip of a coin. The prisoners were picked up unexpectedly at their homes by an actual city policeman in his squad car, handcuffed, taken to the city jail where they were fingerprinted, stripped, searched, deloused, given a prison number, and put into a prison cell.

In the meantime, the "prison guards" were made aware of the dangers of guarding prisoners (as is done in actual prisons) and were told they could make up their own rules to maintain law and order with one exception—they could not physically hurt the prisoners. The events that happened next horrified the research team. The behavior of the guards became increasingly "cruel and inhumane." Some guards treated the prisoners like "despicable animals," who took pleasure in making the prisoners perform senseless and demeaning actions. The research team watched with amazement as the prisoners became not just docile but servile. Although the prisoners were free to leave at any time, none asked to leave. In fact, Zimbardo had to forcibly insist that three prisoners leave because of the severe emotional symptoms they were exhibiting, such as hysterical crying, confusion in thinking, and severe depression. Eventually, Zimbardo had to stop the experiment and release all the prisoners after only six days.

WHAT MAKES DECENT HUMAN BEINGS MAKE MORALLY WRONG CHOICES? SOME THEORIES AND EXPLANATIONS

When we discussed the findings of Adorno's investigation into the *authoritarian* personality, it was shown that those people who are the most likely candidates for joining antidemocratic hate groups are from less-educated groups, even prison groups. But in the experiments by Asch, Milgram, and Zimbardo, the subjects were often college students, professional people, and perfectly decent citizens judged to be morally upstanding and mentally healthy. The question then arises: What are the dynamics that underlie the willingness of people to behave in such reprehensible ways, without regard for human existence? Overall, these studies point to the following factors:

- Power as a corrupting force of human personality;
- The dehumanizing effect of a demeaning environment;
- The human tendency to conform to membership in a group;
- The inability to resist overwhelming public group pressure;
- The powerful influence of social roles, such as *authority, prison guard*, and *prisoner*.

Even when we enter the workplace, the pressure to conform continues. The pressure may come from the corporations we work for, the professions we go into, and the political parties we belong to. Simply put, like other gregarious species, we follow the herd. In the political arena, it is called "getting on the band wagon." Milgram's experiments in obedience suggest that our societal structure has such a built-in awe, fear, or reverence for those in authority that we will obey orders even when they endanger human life. Zimbardo's prison experiment has helped us understand the power of our social roles. The simple act of donning a uniform may cause human beings to take on, with extraordinary swiftness, the psychological attributes that the uniform represents. In the Zimbardo experiment, the prison guards became authoritarian, punitive, harsh, abusive, and inhumane. The prisoners became passive, submissive, and psychologically demeaned. Indeed, we are reminded that "*power corrupts and absolute power corrupts absolutely*" (see Tip 2.2).

These social psychology studies provided us with much information about what makes people conform to public pressure, blindly obey authority, and the powerful effect of our social roles. But these experiments may never be **replicated** (repeated), as they would violate the updated APA code of ethics (see Box 2.3).

Tip 2.2 On the Corrupting Effect of Power. This theme has been repeated by many persons down through the ages. The phrase we have used comes from a letter written by Lord Acton to Bishop Mandell Creighton (1887). Tacitus, the Roman philosopher born in A.D. 55, wrote that "lust for power, for dominating others, inflames the heart more than any other passion." William Pitt in a speech to the House of Lords in 1770 said, "Unlimited power is apt to corrupt the minds of those who possess it." Edmund Burke repeated this a few years later when he wrote in his essay on "A Vindication of Natural Society" the following words: "Power gradually extirpates from the mind every humane and gentle virtue."

BOX **2.3** **Ethics in Psychological Research**

Asch, Milgram, and Zimbardo all received many honors and awards for their work, but they also received strong criticism for putting their subjects through such stressful situations. These experiments and others resulted in additions to the code of ethics of the American Psychological Association. The additions prohibit social scientists from performing such psychologically painful experiments. Even though the Teachers in Zimbardo's experiments were later debriefed by explaining the nature of the experiment and by actually seeing that the "dead Learner" was really alive and unharmed, the APA said that debriefing the subjects later does not justify the agony they initially went through. *Even for the sake of discovering more knowledge, the ends do not justify the means.* The APA guidelines are extensive and cover many professional topics. We present some of the guidelines that pertain to ethics in research methodology. The APA code of ethics is phrased in professional language, so we have paraphrased them in simpler terms for the sake of clarity.

1. **Concern and care for all experimental subjects must be maintained in the design of the research and in the carrying out of the research design.** The researchers must take steps to ensure the physical safety and health of both human and animal subjects. For human subjects, care includes "due concern" for the person's dignity along with his or her physical welfare. In other words, the subjects must not be put into situations that demean them in any way.

2. **The research must be carried out with approval from the host institution. No psychological research can be conducted in any institution without prior approval.** A description of the research must contain clear disclosure. In other words, the host institution may not be deceived.

3. **The people who are to be used as subjects must give their informed consent.** Informed consent means that the researchers provide a general description of the study in clear and simple language. There is to be no deception of any kind, although in order to prevent bias on the part of the subjects, certain details can be left out until after the research is over.

4. **All subjects are free to participate or not.** The researcher will provide the subjects with the clear message that they have a right to refuse to participate. If they do participate, they may withdraw at any time.

5. **Informed consent also involves the use of filming or recording of any kind.** All citizens are protected by what the U.S. Supreme Court has called "expectation of privacy," which means that we do not record activities in places that are supposed to be private, such as our homes, public bathrooms, and store dressing rooms. In environments where there is no "expectation of privacy," the researcher is free to record such behaviors, for example, as observing how people go through customs or line up at a ticket counter, etc.

6. **Information about the nature of the research should be made available to the subjects as soon as the opportunity permits.** If for reasons of mitigating bias, the subjects are not told about the precise nature of the research but have given their informed consent, the researcher has a responsibility to disclose this information to them at the earliest possible time. This information includes the purpose of the research, the results, and conclusions.

7. **The subjects' anonymity and privacy must remain intact.** Under no circumstances is any information to be made public that would disclose the identification of the subject, the purpose of the subject's inclusion in the research, or any personal information about the subject.

Carl Jung: Deindividuation

Another theory that fits very neatly into Zimbardo's experiment is the phenomenon of *deindividuation*. Carl Jung was at one time a student and then a colleague of Sigmund Freud. It was he who formulated the concepts of *individuation* and *deindividuation* (Jung, 1955). *Deindividuation* is what happens when people are taken over by what is sometimes called "mob psychology." It is what makes perfectly decent people do terrible things in the frenzy of a crowd that they would not do alone and "in their right mind"—such as yelling "Jump! Jump!" to a potential suicide victim fourteen flights up. Fraternities have hazed a pledge to death. Posses have lynched a person without trial. At such times, these people are not acting as individuals. **Deindividuation** is what happens when people lose their individual identities and behave in accordance with the actions of a mob. Deindividuation is augmented under conditions of anonymity, when wearing uniforms, and in the dead of night. Under just such conditions the Ku Klux Klan would meet and carry out its dark and dreadful deeds. **Individuated persons** have the courage and the ability to stand up and be counted. It takes a person firmly rooted from his or her "center" to resist the pressure of conforming to public opinion. We describe individuated persons later in this chapter.

Some political leaders have been expert in techniques of deindividuation. Significant in Hitler's rise to power were the techniques by which the Nazis transformed huge assemblies of people into a mass of deindividuated and mindless robots. Movies taken at the huge coliseum at Nuremberg record the dramatic rites and rituals used to orchestrate human emotions and human behavior. Against the darkness of increasing night and against a backdrop of flaming torches, there would begin a hypnotic beat of drums. Then someone would begin the chanting of the two words "Heil Hitler" over and over again. The drum beats and the chanting were kept up for some minutes until the assembled Germans had become mesmerized—now a mass of deindividuated and mindless beings ready to follow their leaders without question. Deindividuated behaviors have been described as "emotional, impulsive, irrational, regressive, or atypical for the person in a given situation" (Forsyth, 1983, p. 322).

When Will People Help? The Bystander Effect

On March 13, 1964, around 3:00 A.M., something so shocking took place on the streets of New York City that it spawned a line of investigations ultimately called the *bystander effect*. The event was the murder of a young woman. But it wasn't simply the murder itself that shocked the nation but the circumstances of her death.

Detectives investigating Kitty Genovese's murder discovered that at least 38 of her neighbors had heard her screams for help over the course of 30 minutes and some had witnessed at least one of the attacks on her. Except for one man who had shouted "Leave that girl alone," no one had come to her aid, not even by calling the police. The police who investigated the murder were shocked by the apparent indifference of the apartment dwellers who were her neighbors. These decent New Yorkers turned off their lights and some went back to sleep after the first attack. They were awakened again by the second and third assaults. When questioned as to why they didn't intervene in this nightmarish and brutal event, they replied that "We didn't want to get involved." The murderer himself said he knew no one would do anything (Dorman, 1999). The term **Genovese Syndrome** was coined to describe this do-nothing-to-help attitude and behavior.

The Genovese murder gave rise to many questions: *Are New Yorkers simply too selfish and self-absorbed to help another human being in dire trouble? Are big city dwellers really so alienated from their neighbors that they avoid getting involved when someone needs help? Are there special circumstances that determine whether or not we will help our neighbor? Part of the answer lies in what is called the diffusion of responsibility.*

Diffusion of Responsibility. Two of the people shocked by the murder were two young psychologists working in the New York area at the time. They decided to investigate the Genovese Syndrome. The first of these research investigations (Darley & Latané, 1986) revealed that one variable in whether someone will help or not help another individual is the number of people in the vicinity. In effect, the more people in the vicinity, the less likely one will stop to help. When there are many persons in the vicinity, passersby assume that there are enough people to help already. In fact, in staged experiments, subjects who thought there was no one else around to help were much more responsive and willing to help (75 percent on average) than those who were aware of other people in the vicinity (53 percent on average). The staged experiments involved many different apparent emergencies, such as fire, asthma attacks, flat tires, faintings, etc. Another reason for diffusion of responsibility is that people tend to hang back if they are not sure how to help and assume that other people in the vicinity know more what to do.

Cultural Differences. Cultures that are small, rural, and traditional (such as those found in Latin America and the Pacific Rim) are more likely to go to the aid of someone in trouble than highly technological cultures (such as the United States, Great Britain, and Germany). Traditional societies, such as Thailand, Peru, Malaysia, and Guatemala, tend to value group membership, group achievement, and group productivity. Loyalty and concern for each other are valued more than individual achievement. These traditional cultures were also more willing to help other people. Even in the United States, people in small towns are more likely to help than people in large cities (Amato, 1981). This difference may be accounted for by the fact that people in a smaller town have a better chance of knowing each other. In a large city, a person can walk for miles without meeting anyone they know. In a world of strangers, we are less likely to be a "good Samaritan."

Social Loafing: Another Variation of Diffusion of Responsibility. The phenomenon we discuss now is no doubt familiar to all of you reading this book. In either your high school or college classes, or in your job, or anywhere you have to work with others to achieve a goal, have you ever noticed that some do very little work? In fact, they seem to be expert in doing virtually nothing and (as if that isn't disagreeable enough) happy to share the credit for work done by others. This phenomenon is called **social loafing** and is defined as reduction in effort by individuals when they work in groups as compared to when they work alone. In fact, the more people in a group, the less productive it is (Kravitz & Martin, 1986). And why? Because with more people, there is more duplication of services, or group members may work at cross purposes. If the reader has heard people bemoaning the inefficiency of large bureaucratic organizations, the cause may be, in large measure, attributed to diffusion of responsibility and social loafing (Latané, Williams, & Harkins, 1979).

Attribution Bias Theory: *The Tendency to Cast Blame* One of the distinguishing characteristics of the human species is our need to discover reasons for things. In psychology, the answers we derive are called *attributions*. Attributions consist of judgments we make about what has caused a situation. There are two types of attributions: internal and external. When we believe the cause of an event is due to a person or a group of people, it is called *internal attribution* or **character attribution**. When we believe the cause of an event to be something in the environment, it is called *external attribution* or **situational attribution** (Jones, 1990). Example: Suppose we give a friend a very important letter to mail and the letter doesn't arrive at its destination on time. Naturally, we will try to determine what happened. We may decide that our friend never mailed the letter (because he was lazy or forgetful), which would be a *character* attribution. Or we may decide that the letter got lost in the mail, which would be a *situational* attribution. So far, so good.

[handwritten marginal notes:] attribution bias ex: parents. good we take credit. when bad circuit → blame someone else.

But the problem is that we tend to indulge in self-serving **attribution bias**. If we experience good fortune (such as a raise in salary or being selected as "salesperson of the year," we will attribute our good fortune to our character (we worked hard, we had the best sales record, etc.). But what if someone else in the company gets the raise or is selected "sales person of the year"? We are apt to attribute that person's selection as the result of the situation—he or she was in the "right place at the right time" or that the person was "buddy-buddy" with the guys in the front office—not because he or she did a good job.

Attribution bias may also account for why we tend to assign negative qualities to groups different from ourselves. Thus racial and ethnic groups will attribute negative qualities to each other: black versus white; Jews versus Arabs; Turks versus Greeks, and so on. Attribution bias also works along a geographical variable. Northern Americans will tend to judge Southern Americans more harshly than themselves. Northerners are apt to label Southerners as "rednecks" and Southerners still talk (only somewhat kiddingly) of the "damyankees" (Little, Sterling & Tingstrom, 1996).

CHARACTERISTICS OF HIGHLY SELF-ACTUALIZING, INTEGRATED, AND CREATIVE HUMAN BECOMINGS

It is far easier for social scientists and commentators to describe the evils of any society than it is to describe what is good and noble. Thus, it is that most textbooks tend to emphasize the negative side of human nature. We do not want to leave this chapter on such a negative note and, indeed, positive psychologists are urging us to look for what is noble and inspiring in human nature, and so we shall. As we noted in Chapter 1, Gordon Allport described the human *becoming* as always growing and evolving. In Chapter 1 we also spent several pages describing Abraham Maslow's subjects who not only evolved to a higher level of self-actualizing themselves, but who enabled their societies to evolve as well. We noted also Carl Jung's description of the individuated person, the person who is able to resist public pressure and act according to his or her conscience. Finally, we noted the descriptions of people whom positive psychologists have described as optimistic, outgoing, and friendly—who emanate joy and well-being despite the crises and hardships that we all experience from time to time.

A Metastudy Approach

Now let's put all of these studies together and derive some common characteristics. Our purpose is to discover the psychological processes by which they are able to utilize everything in their personality in order to achieve their life career goals. In describing the characteristics of these highly-evolved persons, we are using a metastudy approach, which is to say that we have analyzed many research studies and have drawn overall conclusions from overlapping data. Such an undertaking, however, involves inherent research difficulties (see Box 2.4).

1. They are more open-minded in their cognitive processes and democratic in behavior. Philosophically, they have a multicultural worldview. In a nutshell: they are democratic (Sumerlin & Bundrick, 1996). Because they are less narrowly dogmatic, they are more accepting of other traditions and other ways of life. While they respect multicultural differences, they tend to see the underlying universal principles of other faiths, other religions, other philosophies, and other political persuasions. They view these diverse cultural traditions

Maslow → H of needs
Allport → human becoming
Jung → individuated pp.?

as expressing a fundamental human quest, the quest to understand the meaning of life, and to live according to the highest possible moral/ethical values. They are not impressed by status or degrees or appearance. While others may think "clothes make the man," Maslow said, his self-actualizing subjects knew that character cannot always be judged by how a person appears on the outside. (Some of our most successful white-collar criminals are dressed immaculately, speak articulately and come from the "best schools.") As Martin Luther King, Jr. said so eloquently, "I have a dream that my four children will one day live in a nation where they will not be judged by the color of their skin but by the content of their character."

2. Socially, they are less conforming, highly individuated, and more willing to be themselves. Being more individuated, they have less need of a mask or "persona" (Jung, 1955) or "public image" (see Figure 2.4). Enmeshed in our conditioned habits, it is very difficult for us to break with ingrained ideas. Yet Maslow discovered his highly self-actualizing persons could embrace new ideas. This ability involves shaking themselves loose from outmoded traditions and "conventional wisdom" (Galbraith, 1985) and breaking through to new ideas. As difficult as it may be, the ability to go against the tide of public opinion has been the distinctive quality of every great reformer. Sometimes, they

Figure 2.4 Authenticity. Highly individuated persons are more willing to be themselves and so have less of a mask.

BOX **2.4** RESEARCH METHODOLOGY
The Metastudy Approach

For almost one hundred years now, there have been literally thousands of studies in the area of personality. Hundreds of these studies have been done on the same topic. For example, by 1985, there were well over 3,000 studies done on "job satisfaction." Meta-analysis is a specific analytic technique for averaging the results of many studies or drawing out commonalities.

PRO
1. **Summarizes many research studies and draws out commonalities and differences.** A metastudy elicits data from a multitude of studies and draws some overall conclusions. A person can review one single metastudy instead of the hundreds that have been done.
2. **Provides a jumping-off place for other studies.** Other investigators can then use the metastudy data and conclusions as a starting place, rather than having to go back and review all the studies for the last 90 years.
3. **Valuable for pointing out needed research areas.** If well done, a metastudy can make needed

recommendations for future investigations by pointing out the limitations of previous studies, as well as by noting promising lines of investigation.

CON
1. **The terms and definitions may differ.** *The terms may sound similar, but they may actually cover somewhat different areas.* The result may be nothing more than comparing oranges and apples.
2. **The target populations may not be synonymous.** If the samples and populations of the research studies are not carefully defined, the conclusions drawn may not be warranted. Commonalities may appear where there are none. Or there may seem to be no commonalities because the dissimilar samples and populations have canceled out their respective research findings.
3. **Earlier research findings may be outmoded.** In this era of great social and technological change, studies done a few years apart may reflect changes in the attitudes and the cognitive schemas of the sample subjects.

BOX **2.5** STUDENTS VERBATIM
Student Choices for Transcending Personalities

The following persons were chosen by students as transcending personalities because they challenged the worldview of their time and era and broke through to larger cognitive structures of what it means to be a man, or a woman, or a citizen of the world.

Abraham Lincoln (1809–1865) rose from log-cabin poverty to become the sixteenth president of the United States. He is known not only as the president who fought to save the Union, but also as the writer of the *Emancipation Proclamation*, which freed the slaves. At the end of the Civil War, Lincoln pleaded with Congress not to take revenge on the South but to have "malice toward none" and "charity toward all." Alas, he was assassinated before he could carry out his mission.

Emile Zola (1840–1902), a famous scholar and novelist, was already internationally famous before taking on the entire French government (including the French army) in the so-called "Dreyfus affair." Alfred Dreyfus, a Jewish officer, had been falsely accused as a traitor, convicted of treason, and sent to the infamous prison of Devil's Island. Zola sacrificed his health and his safety through his outspoken document *J'accuse* (I accuse), written to clear Dreyfus. He had to flee to Great Britain for his life, dying only a year after Dreyfus' release.

Mahatma Gandhi (1869–1948) challenged the entire British empire by breaking Britain's hold on India. He did this by organizing India's people of color to resist the oppressive colonial regime through nonviolent and peaceful means. Ultimately, he won his country's freedom. He was assassinated by an Indian who differed from him politically.

Eleanor Roosevelt (1882–1945), an extremely shy person as a child, broke through the traditional mold of the silent First Lady of the White House and became one of the greatest humanitarians of her day. When opera star Marian Anderson was refused permission to sing by the DAR (Daughters of the American Revolution) because of her color, the First Lady brought the issue of discrimination to national attention by resigning from the DAR and inviting Marian Anderson to sing on the steps of the Lincoln Memorial. A crowd of 75,000 white and black persons gathered on Easter Sunday, April 9, 1939, an event that made international news. Later, as a representative to the United Nations, she became an international spokesperson for women, children, and all oppressed peoples.

Martin Luther King, Jr. (1929–1968), a minister who had modeled his passive (and peaceful) resistance movement on the principles outlined by Mahatma Ghandi, organized the year-long black boycott of the local bus company in Montgomery, Alabama. He won significant civil rights for African-Americans—and, like his role model, he too was assassinated. He is famous for his "I Have a Dream" speech given before 200,000 demonstrators in Washington, DC.

Nelson Mandela (1918–) became a lawyer through a correspondence school. He spent most of his life working and fighting for the cause of the oppressed peoples of color of South Africa. He was condemned to prison for many years. In the face of world criticism, the government of South Africa offered Mandela the opportunity of release if he would cease his political agitation. He refused and spent more years in prison. Finally released in 1990 and an old man, he still maintained his stance in favor of a government for *all* peoples. He was awarded the Nobel Prize for his humanitarianism in 1991 and elected as president of South Africa from 1994 until 1999.

Andrei Sakharov (1921–1989) was a Russian physicist who opposed the building of atomic weapons. He supported East–West cooperation and human rights. Along with his wife, Yelena Bonner, he became a leading dissident of the oppressive Soviet regime in power. In 1975, he was awarded the Nobel Peace Prize, but he was exiled to Gorky five years later, where he lived under terrible conditions. He was restored to favor in 1986, and elected to a high official position in 1989.

Albert Einstein (1879–1955) was awarded the Nobel Prize for physics in 1921. He was removed from his teaching post by the Nazis because of his antiwar politics and his Jewish background. He emigrated to the United States when he was offered a teaching post at Princeton University. His theories helped develop the atomic bomb. Nevertheless, he continued to speak out against war and the use of atomic weapons and in support of world peace for the rest of his life.

Mother Theresa (1910–1997), born in Macedonia, became an Irish nun and then worked as a missionary in India. Seeing the poverty and degradation of people dying on the streets, she organized an Indian order of sisters to shelter and administer to the sick and dying. She received the Nobel Prize for humanitarianism in 1979.

BOX **2.5** STUDENTS VERBATIM (continued)
Student Choices for Transcending Personalities

Dian Fossey (1932–1966), supported by the National Geographic Society, studied the mountain gorillas of Rwanda, Africa, and became an activist to save the last 250 surviving animals from extinction. Because she openly confronted those who were killing the gorillas for money, she was murdered in her sleep. Her book *Gorillas in the Mist* became a best seller, and was then made into a movie. Today there is an institute and fund to carry on her work for the survival of the mountain gorillas.

Florence Nightingale (1820–1910), born to an aristocratic family, gave up thoughts of a comfortable life by becoming a nurse and organizing the first army nurse corps ever. With 38 women, she sailed for the Crimea, and there she and her nurses cared for the wounded and dying soldiers in terribly primitive and filthy conditions. She returned to England with only a handful of surviving nurse volunteers and suffered physically for the rest of her life. Nevertheless, she continued actively supporting the improvement of hospitals, nurse's training, and the care of the ill.

Harriet Tubman (1829–1913) was born a slave, but escaped and became an abolitionist. She returned to the South time and time again, each time at risk to her own life, to help African-Americans travel to the North via the Underground Railway. She is sometimes called the "Moses of her People."

Rachel Carson (1907–1964), a naturalist who worked as marine biologist for the U.S. Fish and Wildlife Service, wrote the classic book *Silent Spring* to alert the world to the ecological dangers of agricultural pesticides. She worked intensely all her life toward protecting the ecology of the earth. She pioneered the conservation movement of the 1960s just before her death.

Reflective Writing: From your studies or your own personal reading, whom would you nominate as a transcending person? State your reasons. When you have described the qualities you would like to emulate, see Tip 2.3, below.

---

have had to suffer the consequences of their courage by being publicly ostracized, or imprisoned, or put to death. Regardless of the consequences, however, they are people willing to "stand up and be counted." They live authentically, which means *they have an internal locus of control*. In study after study of the highly integrated and self-actualizing person, one theme is particularly dominant—that of self-determination. Highly self-actualizing persons, said Maslow, take responsibility for their lives, for their actions, and for their destinies. They are determined to carry on despite crises, setbacks, tragedy. There are situations and events over which we have little or no influence: death of the people we love, natural catastrophes, accidents, and all the chance events of the natural world. No matter how hard we work to achieve position, esteem, security, and prestige, and to deal honorably with the world, there is always the possibility that our dreams and plans may go awry. There is, then, a reality to the Greek description of the Fates.

The Fates notwithstanding, however, highly integrated persons do not give up in the face of hardship or tragedy. They can have moments of loss of confidence and discouragement. But they refuse to wallow in their negative emotions. They make mistakes as do the rest of us, but they acknowledge them and learn from them. Despite moments of anxiety, guilt, shame, sorrow, and grief, Maslow's subjects did not allow themselves to get entrapped in self-pity and self-blame. William Ernest Henley, the crippled poet, exemplified this

---

Tip 2.3 On the Qualities You Admire About Your Role-Model. We emulate what we admire. Whatever qualities you stated you admired in Box 2.5 are the qualities you are developing within yourself. You may add those qualities to your self-esteem.

attitude when he wrote that he was determined to be "the master of my fate . . . the captain of my soul. . . . "

3. They comprehend personality integration is a life-long process. One of the questions that young people are often heard to say goes something like "I wish I knew who I was. If I only knew who I was, I wouldn't have as many problems." Such a question indicates that they believe personality integration is something that is achieved once and for all as if it is a medal or a diploma.

Nothing could be further from the truth. Personality integration is a life-long process. Suppose, for a moment, you had a mirror like Snow White's evil Stepmother. Suppose you could pose this question: *Mirror, Mirror on the wall, tell me who I am once-and-for-all.* Suppose, further, that the mirror could answer you. Would the answer the mirror gave you at fifteen suffice for you when you were twenty? Or would the answer at twenty suffice for you at thirty? Or would the answer at thirty suffice for you at fifty?

Obviously not, because as we grow through our lives we add stature to ourselves. We become more knowledgeable year by year. As we get older we become more able to cope with things that would have devastated us earlier. We develop more of our gifts and talents. We become wiser over the years. Abraham Maslow made this very telling point. We may be born intelligent, but wisdom is something that happens as a result of many years of living. Not necessarily everybody becomes wiser—only those committed to understanding themselves and the world around them: They are life-long learners.

4. They often become activists for human rights. Transcending personalities are not content with understanding others, they become activists in their striving for human rights for all persons, regardless of their religion, race, age, ethnic affiliation, sexual orientation, or socioeconomic status. Transcending persons rail against the evils of society and strive for the benefit of humankind. The German religious leader, Martin Luther, nailed his ninety-nine theses on the doors of a corrupt church and spoke the words that still ring across the centuries. "Here stand I—I can do no other. God help me! Amen." His namesake, Martin Luther King, Jr., was able to stand up for his people and be counted. In South Africa, Nelson Mandela was offered release from prison if he would cease agitating for freedom for all South Africans—he refused. When he was finally released from prison, he spoke for acceptance of all people of color, including the white oppressive regime which had kept him captive for so many years.

5. Spiritually, they live their lives with meaning. Agreeing with Jung, Viktor Frankl urged humankind to live their lives with meaning or they shall surely suffer from **noogenic neurosis**, by which he meant a state of apathy, aimlessness, and boredom. At the age of 37 years, Viktor Frankl was a practicing physician and psychiatrist who was sent to the Nazi concentration camps because he was a Jew. He survived and when released wrote of his experiences and the meaning he had derived from it. Said Frankl: *A life lived solely for pleasure is not true happiness. The pursuit of pleasure and living solely for ourselves eventually leaves us feeling empty and unsatisfied—or with the taste of bitter ashes—and so we fill it up with more pleasure, a cycle that never ends* (Frankl, 1962). Maslow noted that his subjects had a deep and abiding feeling of identification with all of humankind and a general desire to help others however they could. The positive psychologists have confirmed Maslow's observation that highly self-actualizing people want to live a life of meaning and purpose (Sumerlin & Bundrick, 1996).

Transcending personalities have a steady love of humankind (even when humankind is disappointing), which in Latin is called *caritas*. In Greek, it is called *agape*. Today, we may call it *compassion* or *loving-kindness* or *good will toward all*. Whatever it is called, this quality is the dominant personality characteristic of the great saints and reformers of the world. In other times, said Maslow, they might have been men and women "of the cloth," that is, priests, ministers, rabbis, monks, nuns, etc. Today, they can be found in every segment of our secular world as well. Instead of becoming a minister or priest, the spiritually oriented person may be a diplomat who wearily boards yet another jetliner to fly to yet another far-off place to forestall yet another intertribal war. Or it may be a judge in a courtroom doing her best to mete out justice and mercy within the parameters of obsolete laws. But such persons do not have to be prominent. It may simply be our next door neighbor knocking on our door for the sake of some charitable organization. One sociologist has made a memorable statement: *The idea that everybody wants money is propagated by wealthy addicts to make themselves feel better about their addiction to money* (Slater, 1980, p. 25). Certainly, Frankl would have agreed to that. *Happiness*, said Frankl, *is not achieved by pursuing it: happiness is a by-product of giving ourselves to a transcending purpose*. It was also Frankl who said that we should live so that the meaning of our lives outlasts us (Frankl, 1962).

Important Terms and Concepts to Know

- Allport
- authoritarian
- authority
- bad
- becomings
- bias
- bystander
- character
- conformity

- cults
- deindividuated
- diffusion
- discrimination
- dogmatic
- ends
- ethics
- evolutionary
- Frankl

- genetics
- good
- Maslow
- means
- noogenic
- obedience
- prejudice
- psychologists
- rebound

- referent
- replicated
- roles
- situation
- stereotyping
- submissive
- trait

Make Your Own Chapter Summary by Filling in the Blanks

Use the "Important Terms and Concepts to Know" to fill in the blanks.

Inherited personality traits. _____ has to do with the specific traits we inherit from our parents while _____ theory has to do with what we have inherited as a member of the human species. Our attitudes are shaped by our primary group membership and our ~~sub primary~~ groups (the groups we would like to belong to).

Prejudice versus discrimination. According to evolutionary theory, prejudice is a built-in personality _____. Attempts to suppress our prejudices seem only to make them flood the consciousness, called the _____ effect. Prejudice can be either negative or positive, but discrimination is always negative. Judging a person according to the person's group membership is called _____. Adhering to a set of beliefs blindly
stereotyped / e.g. shcut.

and without question leads to a _____ position in which the ends precedes the _____. In a democracy, the means must always precede the _____.

The classic studies of social psychology. Adorno and others investigated highly _____ personalities, people who would have made good Nazis. These personalities are _____ toward their superiors and demand _____ from subordinates and family members. Asch's studies of _____ demonstrated how easily people cave in to public pressure. Milgram's research reveals the extent to which people will obey _____. Zimbardo's prison experiment demonstrated how quickly our social _____ affect our behavior. Carl Jung described the person who falls in with mob psychology as the _____ person. These classic studies help us to understand why people who are born into a democratic society are so willing to give up their personal freedoms when they join _____, but these studies may never now be _____ (repeated) because of the APA code of _____.

Other influences on behavior. The _____ effect helps explain when and where we are willing to be "good Samaritans." _____ of responsibility is part of the reason for the inefficiency of bureaucracy. Attribution _____ reveals that we attribute our good fortune to our good _____, and our bad fortune to the _____. Conversely, we tend to attribute some one else's _____ fortune to the situation and their _____ fortune to their character.

Although positive _____ are urging us to lead a life of meaning and value, they aren't the first to do so. Other psychologists who have done so include Gordon _____, who called us human _____; Abraham _____, who studied highly self-actualizing persons; and Viktor _____ who said that the modern "neurosis" is _____; i.e., that we are living for pleasure when we should be living with meaning.

3 Personality Theory
Emotional/Social Influences Throughout the Life Span

For his theories of personality development, Freud drew on biblical history, and all the great mythologies, literature, and folklore of the Western world.

He was not always right. Some of his theories have fallen by the wayside, but he changed our understanding of the nature of humankind. His genius is shown by the sheer number of concepts we still use today of which the following are only a few:

anxiety	Freudian slips	reaction formation
castration complex	id	reality principle
catharsis	introjection	regression
conversion hysteria	obsessive-compulsive	repression
defense mechanism	Oedipal complex	sibling rivalry
displacement	pleasure-pain principle	sublimation
dream interpretation	preconscious	superego
ego	projection	suppression
Elektra complex	psychotherapy	unconscious
free association	rationalization	

BOX 3.1 SCENARIO
My Daughter Is So Bad! What Can I Do with Her?

Jonnimae and her sister, Sarakate, are in Jonnimae's apartment, catching up on the events of the last two years while keeping an eye on Sarakate's two children. Four-year-old Janie is busily devouring her cookies, and the baby is holding on tightly to his bottle. The two women continue talking until the baby begins to whimper. His bottle is now in the hands of four-year-old Janie.

Sarakate: Janie, did you take the baby's bottle?

Janie: No! He dropped it! I was just picking it up.

Sarakate: No, he didn't! You took it from him! (*Sarakate grabs the bottle from the little girl, slaps her hand, and gives the bottle back to the baby.*) That's for hitting him! (*She slaps the little girl again.*) And that's for lying to me! (*Howling, Janie crawls away from the group, lies down on the floor, and begins to suck her thumb.*) She's why I've come,

Jonnimae! I don't know what's gotten into her, I swear I don't. She has temper tantrums. She's sucking her thumb again. She steals the baby's bottle and actually drinks from it. Four years of age and still drinking from a bottle! It just shames me. I've spanked her till her back side is red. (*A scream from the baby interrupts the conversation. There is an angry-looking red spot on the baby's arm. Sarakate picks up the little girl and shakes her.*) Jonnimae, what am I gonna do with her? She's so mean to the baby! She's got a mean streak in her, I swear she does! And she used to be so good. What's the matter with her?

Jonnimae: In my psychology class, I learned it's a natural thing to be jealous of a baby brother. It's called sibling rivalry.

Sarakate: Oh, I know children can be jealous of each other. I was jealous of you, Jonnimae, because you

47

BOX **3.1** SCENARIO (continued)
My Daughter Is So Bad! What Can I Do with Her?

were so smart and everybody admired you. But I wasn't mean like Janie.

Jonnimae: Oh, yes! You pulled some lies on me, telling Mama that I hit you! Then I'd get whipped.

Sarakate: I'm sorry! I don't remember that, but I know you wouldn't lie to me. Only isn't there anything

I can do to stop Janie from being so mean to the baby?

Jonnimae: There must be, for sure. But first we have to understand what's going on inside Janie. Then maybe we can figure out what we can do about her.

SIGMUND FREUD: REVEALING THE "DARKER SIDE OF HUMAN NATURE"

It is difficult for young people growing up today (with our more open attitudes toward human sexuality) to imagine the sexual repression of a hundred and fifty years ago. Called the Victorian Era in Great Britain, it was a society that gave legitimacy to the double standard, that what is right for men is not right for women. While middle- and upper-class women were expected to remain virginal until marriage, men were encouraged to "sow their wild oats" before settling down into marriage. Their "wild oats" were generally the offspring of the *demimonde* of Europe (see Tip 3.1). It gave tacit permission for aristocratic men to lead double lives. Overtly, these men assumed the posture of respectable husbands and fathers. Covertly, their evenings were often spent in brothels in the company of prostitutes or with their paid mistresses who came from the *demimonde* of Europe. Aristocratic men married "good" women in order to have children and carry on the family line, but they often turned elsewhere to "have fun" with sexually permissive women. It was not unusual for these men to introduce their pubescent sons to their first sexual experience by escorting them personally to the brothels or to an obliging maid servant (who received a payment of money for their services).

Figure 3.1 Sigmund Freud. Pioneer into the "dark side" of human nature.

No such equivalent behavior was permitted of "good women." Women were expected to remain virginal until introduced to the sexual act by their husbands. It was not unusual for mothers to teach their daughters that sex was something women had to endure "in order to have children." Women wore clothing that hid every part of their bodies except their face and hands. We say words now that once would have caused a woman to "swoon" in public. So careful were the Victorians to refrain from using the words "breast" and "thigh," they began to refer to these parts of the chicken as "light meat" and "dark meat," terms we still use today (Mencken, 1963).

It was also generally believed that personality and character were the result of heredity. Marriages were made between families of "good stock" rather than "bad blood." Royalty and nobility married into similar classes so as not to contaminate

---

Tip 3.1 The *Demimonde* of Europe *Demimonde* is a French word having the connotation of what we might call "not quite respectable people," particularly women who were actresses, ballet dancers, and cabaret singers. Readers who have had humanities or art courses may be familiar with paintings that depict the turn-of-the-century *demimonde*. Toulouse-Lautrec made posters of the famous can-can girls. Degas painted ballet girls in their tutus. Whistler and other artists painted Lily Langtry, a society beauty who became Prince Edward's mistress and later an actress.

their blood lines with that of "commoners," who were considered inferior. Running rampant also was a political philosophy called **social Darwinism**, which attributed one's membership in the "ruling classes" to their superior character. *Cream rises to the top.* Now into all this smug self-satisfaction of the wealthy elite, a book appeared on the publishing scene, entitled *The Interpretation of Dreams.* The author was an unknown neurologist by the name of Sigmund Freud (Freud, 1900). What he wrote shook up that wealthy elite: that the way they were raising their children was producing serious mental illness. It was the first real introduction to the concept that heredity was not the sole factor of personality, but that *environment* also had a great deal to do with it. In a very real sense, his theories of personality triggered the enduring question psychology has been concerned with ever since: *How much of human nature is due to our heredity and how much is due to our environment?* Psychologists generally use the shortcut phrase: the **nature/nurture controversy**.

Ever since the publication of his first book, Freud has been idolized, vilified, lionized, and demonized. He was sometimes called a sex-fiend by polite society and the "Anti-Christ" by the Church (see Tip 3.2). He rather foresaw this and made this statement to a friend that *They only mutter about me now; tomorrow they may stone me in the streets* (Jones, 1961). He drew his theories not only from his patients, his friends, and his family, but also from history; from European and American literature; from theology and religion; from mythology, folklore and fairytale; as well as from what today we would call cultural anthropology from around the world. He could also speak and write in several languages, including German, French, and English, and the total number of his books, essays, and journal articles still inspires awe in scholars and social scientists who have studied them. Freud was not always right, and some of his theories have fallen by the wayside, but his genius can be illustrated by the sheer number of the terms and concepts he originated and which we still use today (see p. 47).

Freud's Theory of Psychosexual Development

Figure 3.2 Freud's Metaphor of the Iceberg.

Freud likened the human personality to an iceberg (see Figure 3.2). Only 10 percent of an iceberg is visible above water. The other 90 percent is hidden beneath the surface. In like manner, said Freud, only 10 percent of our personality is conscious. Most of our motivation is hidden—even from ourselves—in what he called the **unconscious** part of the personality. This unconscious aspect is composed of the **id** (our biological urges and drives) and the **superego** (what society has taught us we must and must not do). The id and the superego wage war throughout our lifetime. Out of this eternal warfare, said Freud, the third part of the personality emerges—the **ego**, which is the only part of the personality that is conscious. It is the task of the *ego* to keep a balance between the pleasure-seeking *id* and the prohibitions of the *superego*. It is not easy for the beleaguered ego to keep the unruly *id* in check and, at the same time, to prevent the *superego* from becoming overly punitive. Instead of the metaphor of an iceberg, Freud might better have used the metaphor of an active volcano, because the unconscious aspects of personality, like molten magma, are in constant

Tip 3.2 Freud as a Proper "Victorian Era" Gentleman. He was not a sex fiend at all; in fact, he admits in several of his books and writings that what he discovered in his patients and the insights that he gained into his own personality structure so filled him with anxiety, that he occasionally fainted.

(*dynamic*) turmoil. Furthermore, every so often, bits and pieces of these unconscious urges and anxieties erupt into our everyday consciousness as slips of the tongue and pen, dreams, fantasies, defense mechanisms, and physical symptoms. How these three parts of our personality (id, superego, and ego) develop, said Freud, comes about through five stages of growth, which he called the **psychosexual development** of the person.

Five Stages of the Libidinal Drive

From his studies of human nature, Freud arrived at this conclusion: Human sexual development does not suddenly manifest at puberty. He believed that we are all born with a strong sexual drive, which he called the **libido**. If that sounds shocking, it is because we need to understand how Freud conceived of the libidinal drive. In its narrowest sense, the **libidinal drive** is the drive toward sex and procreation, but in its widest sense, it is the drive toward pleasure and caring and all those emotional satisfactions that make life worth living. Without this libidinal drive for pleasure, there would be no desire to live—a state of being we sadly observe in suicidally depressed people. According to Freud, the libidinal drive normally develops in five stages from birth to puberty. Each of these stages has a psychological aspect as well as a sexual aspect, which is why Freud called it the *psycho*sexual theory of development of the individual (Freud, 1900).

 1. **The Oral Stage and the biological urges of the id.** Freud explained that in this first stage of psychosexual development, the libidinal drive is centered around the mouth. We only have to observe a baby happily sucking on bottle, breast, thumb, or pacifier to witness the intensity of the libidinal drive. Just try taking the nipple away from a baby and the result may be a "force twelve" howling. Today we are not shocked by this concept because we know that if the baby doesn't find pleasure in sucking and swallowing, or if these reflexes are poorly developed, the baby may "fail to thrive." But in Freud's day, the idea that a baby could have a libidinal drive was anathema! But Freud further observed that even as adults, we find pleasure in many kinds of oral activities. We love to eat. We nibble when we are bored or anxious. In the absence of something to eat, we may chew on a pencil, on our fingernails, on a stick of gum, or even (like an author of your text) on our eyeglasses. Finally, expressions of love, tenderness, and caring often begin with kissing the child or adult we love. (We might mention also that Freud was sometimes teased by his colleagues for his own oral habit—the cigar he was almost never without—and which eventually killed him.) This baby id is dominated by what Freud called the **pleasure/pain principle**, which means simply that the baby seeks only pleasure and avoids pain. Now most of us try to avoid pain and pursue pleasure, but we have learned that in our pursuit of our pleasure we must avoid causing pain to others. Since the baby is not aware of other people, his pursuit of pleasure may cause pain to others (see Box 3.2).

 2. **The Anal Stage and the development of the superego.** According to Freud, the baby is the center of family life. In a healthy family, the baby is loved and cared for in a paradise where all his needs and wants are fulfilled. But he will not be permitted to exist forever in this Garden of Eden. Eventually, his teeth will break through his gums and nursing will become too painful for Mother to continue. Moreover, Mommie (or whoever is the chief caregiver) will get tired of constantly changing his diapers and will decide that it is time for toilet training. He is expelled from his Garden of Eden by being weaned away from the breast and seated on the

BOX **3.2** HELEN KELLER

The Unbridled Id (Before the Child Is Socialized)

We can get some insight into a child's primitive psychology (before the child is socialized) from Helen Keller's autobiography. Helen was blind and deaf from about six months of age. Her family loved her but did nothing to socialize her. She lived in a sightless, soundless chaos and was allowed to do whatever she wanted, even grabbing food off everyone's plate. Eventually she was socialized and taught sign language. She even went on to graduate from college. She was obviously a brilliant person, and when she was eighteen, she wrote her autobiography, describing her lack of conscience and fierce sibling rivalry with her baby sister.

. . . I think I knew I was naughty, for I knew it hurt Ella, my nurse, to kick her, and when my fit of temper was over, I had a feeling akin to regret. But I cannot remember any instance in which this feeling prevented me from repeating the naughtiness when I failed to get what I wanted. . . . After my teacher, Miss Sullivan came, I sought an early opportunity to lock her in her room. I went upstairs with something which my mother made me understand I was to give to Miss Sullivan, but no sooner had I given it to her than I slammed the door to, locked it, and hid the key under the wardrobe in the hall. I could not be induced to tell where the key was. My father was obliged to get

a ladder and take Miss Sullivan out through the window— much to my delight. Months after I produced the key . . .

. . . For a long time I regarded my little sister as an intruder. I knew that I had ceased to be my mother's only darling, and the thought filled me with jealousy. She sat in my mother's lap constantly, where I used to sit, and seemed to take up all her care and time. . . . One day I discovered my little sister sleeping peacefully in [my doll's cradle] . . . I rushed upon the cradle and overturned it, and the baby might have been killed had my mother not caught her as she fell."

Source: Helen Keller, *The Story of My Life* (New York: Globe Books, 1962), pp. 24–29.

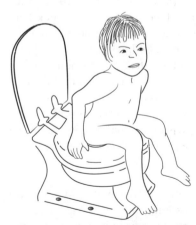

Figure 3.3 Toilet Training Initiates the Socialization Process. Toilet training is a major part of the socialization process and initiates the second stage of psychosexual development.

"potty." The **socialization** process (of weaning and toilet training) is the impetus for the next stage of psychosexual development (see Figure 3.3). But there is more going on at this stage than just weaning and toilet training. The baby is learning that he cannot do *whatever* he wants *whenever* he wants and *wherever* he wants. He cannot have the breast or bottle any more; he must learn to drink from a cup. He cannot hurt other people— even innocently. If he pulls Mommie's hair, she will get annoyed. Nor can he hurt his baby sister or brother. The pleasure/pain principle is giving way to the **reality principle**; i.e., the baby is learning that if he continues to do these things, some dire consequence will follow.

Although the baby railed against toilet training in the beginning, the toilet-training process eventually becomes quite pleasurable. There are rewards for "doing his duty." People praise him and caress him and kiss him! He also discovers certain pleasurable feelings result by controlling his bladder and bowel. His libido is becoming focused on the anus and the child comes to associate being loved with being clean; i.e., making "doo-doo in the potty." ("Doodoo" in his diapers means he is not a good boy and is not loved.) Feces or any kind of dirt comes to be associated with "being bad." He has entered the **anal stage** of psychosexual development.

Keep in mind, also, that while the child is being weaned and toilet trained, he is also being taught all the rules and commandments of five thousand years of civilization—the *do's* and *don'ts* of his society: *Thou shalt do this! Thou shalt not do that! Thou must do this! Thou must not do that! Thou should do this! Thou should not do that!* It is a lot to learn, but if the socialization process is successful, learn it he does. All these do's and don'ts become introjected (absorbed) into the baby's unconscious as the superego. We should not break things. We should say "please" and "thank you." We shouldn't say "bad things." The **superego** (which means "over I" in Latin) contains all the "voices" of the child's society and makes up the second part of the unconscious aspect of personality. In fact, *Freud equated the superego with the conscience.*

3. The Phallic Stage and the development of the ego.   At about the age of three or four, the male child discovers that if he manipulates his penis in a certain way, he experiences paroxysms of pleasure. The libidinal drive now becomes focused on the penis, and the psychosexual development of the child enters the third or **phallic stage** (*phallus* is Latin for penis). In Freud's day, the little boy was given dire threats that if he continued "to play with himself" his penis may get diseased or even wither and break off! To validate these threats, he discovers to his horror that little girls have lost their penises! Freud thought these threats led to the **castration complex** in little boys—the fear of losing the penis or having it destroyed in some manner or other. More modern research indicates that the castration complex may exist in little boys even in homes where the parents are permissive and understand that masturbation is a "normal" development phase of children (Conn & Kanner, 1947). Freud also thought that girls must have a penis envy because they do not have such a pleasurable organ. (Ah, well, we'll forgive Freud for his lack of understanding of female psychology.) (See Tip 3.3.)

The Oedipus Complex and the Elektra Complex.   During the phallic stage, the child begins to develop a special attachment to the parent of the opposite sex. Freud called the special mother–son attachment the **Oedipal complex.** Oedipus was the Greek hero who (unwittingly) killed his own father and married his own mother. Little boys frequently resent their fathers, who take so much of their mothers' time, and boys may, in fact, wish their fathers dead. Of course, "dead" to a little boy does not have the same connotation as it does to an adult. The little boy simply wants to get rid of this male giant who grabs his mother's attention. He wants her all to himself. Little girls and their fathers often develop a strong father–daughter attachment, which Freud called the **Elektra complex** after another Greek myth. In fact, Freud came to believe that ancient mythologies represent the primitive worldview of ancient humanity and also the primitive psychology of the young child today.

Sibling Rivalry.   Not only are small children resentful of the parent of the same sex, they are also resentful of anyone who takes their parents' time and attention. A three- or four-year-old child who has been the "baby" of the family may become quite jealous of a new baby in the house. Even if the older child has been looking forward to a brother or sister "to

---

Tip 3.3 Karen Horney on Penis Envy. A female psychoanalyst, Karen Horney (pronounced HORN-eye) interpreted penis envy in another way. What Horney said was that it wasn't so much the penis that women envied, but the freedom and power that came with being born a male.

BOX **3.3** STUDENTS VERBATIM
On Sibling Rivalry

Read the paragraphs below and then respond to the question at the bottom of this box.

Female: I was the older child, but a lot of times I would be punished for upsetting my little sister, even when it was she who had been the aggressor. I remember many times when she would beat on me and then cry and pretend I hit her. I would promptly be either spanked or severely reprimanded and it wasn't even me.

Male: I love my kid brother now, but I remember the day my parents brought him home. There they were at the doorway, my mother holding the baby. I remember how furious and jealous I was. (I was three years old at the time.) When my mother held the baby down for me to kiss, I bit him instead. I don't remember what happened after that, but it couldn't have been pleasant.

Female: I was the youngest of three girls, each two years apart. I would always meddle with my sisters'

toys or tear them up as soon as they would get them. They would have to take care of me when both my parents worked. I was the dominator of the house, and my sisters didn't like me. I don't blame them. I knew I was getting away with murder. My parents always blamed them instead of me.

Male: My three brothers and I get along OK now, but when we were growing up I can't remember anything good that we did together. We didn't just quarrel—we physically fought all the time. The funny thing is I think my Dad actually encouraged our fighting with each other, but I don't know exactly how he did that. The only time we got along was when somebody outside the family tried to pick a fight with one of us or bully us. Then we all hopped on him.

Reflective Writing: Now reflect on your own experience with your siblings.

---

play with," the actual event is a big let-down. Instead of a brother or sister to play with, the new baby turns out to be a rival, stealing the attention he or she used to get. Listen in on the quarrels older children engage in. "You're Mama's favorite, you always have been!" and the retort: "Well, Daddy always gives in to you!" (see Box 3.3). Parents are always hopeful that sisters and brothers will develop loving relationships with each other, but Freud pointed out that, in fact, history has not proved that hope to be borne out very often. Cain killed his brother Abel out of jealousy, and the Biblical Joseph was sold into slavery by his ten older jealous brothers. History is replete with examples of bitter rivalries of brothers such as the famous King John who was willing to let his brother, Richard the Lionhearted, languish in a prison rather than raise the money to ransom him out and regain his throne. In a conscious or unconscious attempt to regain some of the attention he used to have, the older child may start having "accidents" again, begin thumb sucking again, and even ask for a bottle. Freud called this behavior **regression**.

4. The Latency Stage: The libidinal drive becomes dormant. At the age of six or seven, the child's psychosexual development enters the fourth stage. At this time, the strong libidinal drive seems to lose some of its power and becomes quiescent, which is why Freud called it the **latency stage**. Freud observed another phenomenon associated with this stage. Children begin to pair off with members of their own gender. Up until now, children have been happy to have anyone to play with: young, old, male, or female. Now, the boys develop a strong gender bias; in fact, they regard girls as "the enemy." On their part, girls begin to show disgust for the boys they used to play with and wholeheartedly agree that "snips and snails and puppy dog tails, that's what little boys are made of!"

5. The Genital Stage: The beginning of adult heterosexuality. The latency stage comes to an end at puberty. Not only does the libidinal drive come to the fore again, it does so with even greater intensity and strength than ever before. The "enemy gender" now becomes the object of the young man's sexual interest. In order for normal heterosexual development to be achieved, the young man must withdraw some of the emotional attachment from his mother and redirect it to a younger person of the opposite gender. Similarly, the young girl must also withdraw some of her emotional attachment from her father and direct it toward younger males. This process is, according to Freud, the resolution of the Oedipus and Elektra complexes.

But What Happens When Normal Psychosexual Development Goes Awry? Fixations and Neuroses. Until this point, we have been describing what Freud considered as normal development. However, society places so many taboos and prohibitions on sexual expression that the course of psychosexual development hardly ever runs smoothly. But if the socialization process has gone awry, the person develops fixations of behavior that are primitive expressions of emotional development. Freud called these fixated behaviors by the term **neurosis** (see Tip 3.4).

1. Fixation at the Oral Stage: The passive-dependent personality. If the socialization procedure is not successful, the person becomes fixated at the *oral stage* of psychosexual development, and for that reason, the person is sometimes said to have an **oral** or **passive-dependent personality**. Either the caregiver didn't insist on the child becoming toilet trained and picking up his toys and clothes, or the child's refusal to do so was too strong for the caregiver. Freud explained that these personality types may appear to be grown up, but underneath their adult clothing they are still emotional infants who expect others to take care of them. Their fixation at the oral level may include overeating to the point of obesity, drinking to the point of being alcoholic (they are still on the bottle), and the seeming inability to do anything by themselves including making decisions. They sometimes expect others to "pick up" after them and wash their dishes. Passive-dependent personalities frequently marry a "Mommie" or "Daddy" type to take care of them, and are amazingly successful in manipulating other people "to do" for them. Students sometimes identify such a person as their roommate. "What can we do?" they often ask us, to which we can only answer (somewhat sadly), "You alone probably can't do anything except to set limits and boundaries to areas that are yours that your roommate may not transgress."

2. Fixation at the Anal Stage: The obsessive-compulsive personality. This person's socialization was overdone, or at least that's what Freud believed, and the person is fixated at the anal stage of development. He may have been made so anxious about making a "mess" in his pants that he became obsessively fearful of anything resembling feces, dirt, germs, or even just untidiness (see Tip 3.5). The reader may recognize this person as the

---

Tip 3.4 Neurosis as a Professional Term Is No Longer Used. Mental health professionals have agreed to eliminate the term "neurosis" from professional use because of its lack of definitional preciseness. However, since this term has been used for over one hundred years, it behooves the student to be familiar with it.

Tip 3.5 On the Obsessive-Compulsive Disorder. While Freud accurately described this personality type, we no longer attribute this disorder solely to an overly strict toilet training. While an overly demanding socialization process may be involved, the genetic evidence is strong that it "runs in families."

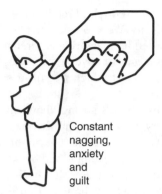

Constant
nagging,
anxiety
and
guilt

Figure 3.4 The Superego. If the superego is overdominant, the person will be vulnerable to continual anxiety and guilt no matter how hard he or she tries to be "good" (clean, neat, perfect).

"eternal housekeeper" who is constantly washing, dusting, sweeping, and cleaning everything in sight. Even if this person has just finished cleaning, she can see specks of dirt everywhere she looks. Up she must go and clean again. To visit this person may be a very uncomfortable event, since no sooner do we finish drinking from a cup or glass than she has whisked it away, cleaned it, and returned it to the cupboard. Sometimes this anxiety about dirt gets transformed into an obsession about money. The person exhibits miserliness and the tendency to focus on unimportant details. At the office, he may make a good bookkeeper because he will know just where every cent (the smallest of details) has gone. But because he is so preoccupied with the pennies, he loses sight of the dollars (the big picture) and so does not make a very good accountant. An over-active superego, said Freud, is not a person with a good conscience but a person who is so laden with guilt that he is tormented all his life with feelings that his best is never good enough (see Figure 3.4).

3. Fixation before the Genital Stage: The Oedipal complex is not resolved. Freud explained that the resolution of the Oedipal complex occurs after puberty when the adolescent male withdraws his emotional attachment from his mother and redirects this libidinal drive toward other females. This resolution must be achieved if the young boy is not to remain under his mother's domination the rest of his life. The reader may, in fact, know of a man who is still so attached to his mother that he puts her wishes and her desires and her needs before those of his wife and children. They also may marry someone who takes the place of "Mother" and who will play the dominant role in the house. In like manner, a young woman who has not resolved her Elektra complex may remain "Daddy's little girl" the rest of her life. Or she may marry someone "just like Daddy."

Freud also thought that **homosexuality** was another result of the unresolved Oedipal complex. Since the mother has such a dominant hold on the young boy, he is unable to disengage from her emotionally. Freud theorized that in order to stay "loyal" to his mother, the young lad does not form attachments to women, but forms attachments to men instead. In that way, he does not betray his mother by loving other women. Freud's explanation of homosexuality does not hold up today. More and more evidence has been gathered concerning the biological underpinnings of homosexuality. Freud's explanation might possibly account for a percentage of homosexuality, but it would seem to be a small percentage.

The Repetitive Nature of "Neurosis." How serious does a behavior have to be to qualify as a "fixation" or "neurosis?" All of us have leftover behaviors of the oral stage or anal stage. We chew gum or smoke a pipe, for example, but does that make us an "oral personality"? We may enjoy a clean house, but does that make us an "obsessive-compulsive personality"? If we clean our house or car and then relax and enjoy ourselves, we are not displaying obsessive-compulsive behavior. If, on the other hand, we have to get up several times in the night to check that all the doors and windows are locked, then we may have an obsessive-compulsive reaction to our anxieties. Mental hospitals frequently have patients who have scrubbed their hands with a harsh abrasive hundreds of times a day until they have patches of raw skin up to their elbows. These patients are extreme cases of obsessive-compulsive disorder.

Freud's "Long Shadow" on the Twentieth Century. Almost overnight, Freudian theory changed our understanding about the nature of human personality. We know now not "to beat the devil" out of a child. Nor do we shame a little boy when he masturbates. Freud brought to light the significance of dreams and instituted the whole area of psychotherapy as we know it today. He created a lexicon of psychological terms, most of which we still use today (see page 47).

If the scientific and medical communities were put off by Freud's strong views on human sexuality, there was one group, at least, that responded very positively to his theories; namely, the creative artists and writers of both Europe and America. Almost overnight, authors such as Eugene O'Neill, Henry Miller, and E. M. Forster were writing erotic books revealing the libidinal behaviors and fantasies of modern men and women. The Irish novelist, James Joyce, created an extraordinary novel, *Finnegan's Wake*, in which the narration is almost solely the protagonist's stream of conscious and unconscious thoughts. Salvador Dali painted dream-like landscapes where clocks ooze over tables and fences. Marc Chagall actually painted his dreams and his childlike memories of growing up in Russia. T. S. Eliot's poem "The Love Song of J. Alfred Prufrock" is a complex flow of free associations of an aging man who acknowledges the urges of his libidinal drive and is repulsed by them.

Another spin-off from Freud's theory of personality is the technique frequently used in movies and TV in which psychological motivation is revealed through flashbacks. In the midst of the story-line, the action of the hero or villain is suddenly interrupted, and we see instead some event in the life of a little boy or girl. All of us recognize what is going on. We are being let in on some incident of the person's past, some conscious or unconscious memory. But the most literate person of the nineteenth century, if he or she were to watch the movie with us, would be utterly baffled by these interruptions and flashbacks. Such has been the influence of Sigmund Freud on artistic and literary expression. He was not always right, and we can find many errors and limitations in his theories of human psychology (see Box 3.4). And on this side of the Atlantic, we oversubscribed to some of his theories. Nevertheless, he was a giant, and we midgets who stand on his shoulders and criticize him are not taller than he.

The NeoFreudians: Modifying and Adding to Freudian Theory. Despite public condemnation, Freud's theories about the "dark side of human nature" began to attract men and women from various professions. Many of the people who came to study with him were already well-known psychologists, psychiatrists, physicians, philosophers, or merely very educated laypersons. Eventually, they formalized their association into what ultimately became known as the International Psychoanalytic Congress of Vienna. The president was (of course) Sigmund Freud. The association's expressed purpose was to continue to investigate human personality using Freud's new methods of free association, psychoanalysis, dream interpretation, and so on. For a while, the group members worked amicably together, but eventually conflicts began to splinter the group. Eventually, some of the members of the group were forced to form their own "schools of analysis" in order to pursue their particular insights. Together, they are called the neoFreudians and include many names the reader will encounter from time to time if he or she pursues further study in psychology, counseling, education, social work, and other mental health professions. The neoFreudians were not opposed to Freud's theory of a powerful libidinal drive as a motivator of human behavior—not at all. However, the neoFreudians believed that there are also other factors to account for what we do and why, such as the desire for *self-esteem, competency*, and *power*. The

BOX **3.4** EVALUATING FREUD
How Well Do His Theories Stand Up Today?

It is more than a hundred years since Freud's first major writings appeared on the publishing scene. Under the scrutiny of modern scientific research, some of his theories still stand up and some have fallen by the wayside. We list below only a few of the positive and negative criticisms.

On the Minus Side

1. **Limitations of the case study method.** Freud's major method of investigation was through the (retroactive) case study. It is particularly apt for diagnosing disease, but when we apply this method to psychological disorders, we are on dangerous ground. We can read anything we want into a person's past history and assign erroneous reasons for a person's problems.
2. **Lack of empirical evidence for his theories.** Freud's division of the personality into the id, the superego, and the ego has probably met with the most severe criticism because empirical proof of these concepts is impossible. Science demands that empirical proof should be more concrete than "inner" material such as dreams and fantasies.
3. **Overlooked the influence of genetics and culture.** Freud was almost completely in the environmental camp of the nature/nurture debate. Convinced as he was that adult personality is formed by a child's experiences in the first six years of life, he ignored the area of genetics, neurobiological pathology, and cultural and subcultural differences. We know now that human nature is multidetermined and multivariate.

4. **Little understanding of female psychology.** As an example, we only have to mention his concept of "penis envy."

On the Plus Side

1. **Positive influence on child rearing.** He changed our assumptions in the area of child rearing, parenting, and education. Example: We no longer advocate punishing children for masturbating or "beat the devil" out of them.
2. **Women given back their right to full sexuality.** Instead, frigidity became the twentieth century "neurosis."
3. **Formulation of the psychotherapeutic approach.** His greatest achievement may be the beginning of psychotherapy as we know it. He demonstrated that physical symptoms could be eliminated through the "talking cure."
4. **Dream interpretation.** He helped us to understand that dreams are another expression of the person and meaningful indeed (discussed in Chapter 13).
5. **Formulation of anxiety and defense mechanisms.** He formulated many of the defensive behaviors that we still consider valid today.
6. **Concept of unconscious forces on personality.** The concept of the unconscious had been discussed for a hundred years prior to Freud, but it was he who gave it sum-and-substance through the evidence of dreams, repressed memories, slips of the tongue, etc.

neoFreudians we discuss in this chapter are Alfred Adler, Carl Jung, and Erik Erikson (who is sometimes called a "second generation neoFreudian").

ALFRED ADLER: THE STRIVING FOR COMPETENCE AND POWER

Life Style

In English, we use the term *life style* to mean financial status or the leisure and recreational activities we prefer and can afford. But Alfred Adler, who originated the term, meant something quite different. Adler defined his concept of **life style** as the unique underlying theme (or themes) that motivates each individual throughout the life span (Adler, 1954). He likened each human life to a river that bubbles up from its source, twisting and turning as

Figure 3.5 Alfred Adler. He added the drive for competence and power to our understanding of personality.

it travels—sometimes with calm passages and sometimes through rapids—before it reaches its final destination. To catch hold of the person's theme, we must consider everything about that person: the person's values, attitudes, goals, aspirations, as well as the person's seemingly strange choices at times. In some people, this theme is easy to identify. A career politician wants to reach a level of power so as to effect change in government. An artist wants to produce works of beauty and may even be willing to live a life of poverty to do so. A scientist is searching for some kind of truth. These are easy life styles to understand.

Living a Life Lie

Other persons, however, seem to lead such confused chaotic, even self-destructive life styles, they appear to have no unifying theme. To continue Adler's metaphor, the flow of their lives seems not like rivers that have a direction but like churning whirlpools going nowhere or dark pools of stagnant water. That is where we are mistaken, said Adler. Each person is seeking to express his or her underlying life theme, no matter how bewildering and contradictory their life styles may seem to us. The reason for their unhappy or destructive life styles is that they are living a **life lie**. A woman may be working successfully but really wants to live a more traditional wife-and-mother life as a homemaker. A man may want to enter the arts, but instead he is working in the family business (for which he has no liking). The therapist's job is to help the person discover his and her unique life theme and to develop a life style that is more harmonious with that theme (see Box 3.5). How is it that human beings have such different life themes leading to such different life styles? Adler's answer: A person's life style develops from two principal sources: first, from the person's sense of inferiority and the need for power; and second, from what he called *gemeinschaftsgefühl* (Adler, 1954).

The Inferiority-Superiority Complex

Small children live in a world of tall and powerful giant adults who control their lives and tell them what to do. These giants are superior to them in every way—in strength, in everyday skills, in language—and particularly, in power. This superiority of their parents (and older siblings) is overwhelming and intimidating for the child, leading to intense feelings of *inferiority*. The more inferior (incompetent) the child feels, the more he strives for *superiority* (so as to have some kind of power and control in life). This desire to overcome our inferiority and become competent and powerful leads to what Adler called the **inferiority-superiority complex**. We make up for our weaknesses and limitations by achieving superiority in other areas of our personality, which Adler called **compensation**. All of us compensate, said Adler, which means that we try to overcome our limitations by developing other areas of our personality. In that respect compensation is a healthy defense mechanism. In fact, Adler believed that if we didn't feel inferior to some degree, we would not strive to achieve anything at all. Adler attributed his own personality to his childhood frailty (and subsequent feelings of inferiority) and his academic brilliance to his striving for superiority.

BOX **3.5** STUDENTS VERBATIM
Living a Life Lie

Students often feel confused because they are not sure what they want to do with their lives or what vocation they should enter. If they are living a life lie, their anxiety and confusion is often phrased as the following: Who am I really? If I could understand who I really am, I would not feel so confused and anxious all the time. Why do I feel so different from the other members of my family? Why do I feel like a phoney? What kind of work do I want to do? Why did I do such a stupid and crazy thing? Fortunately, college is the "golden opportunity" to discover more authentic ways to live.

Female (22 years): My mother has always told me to study to become a nurse. My mother is a single parent who has had a tough time raising the two of us. So she wanted us to have the security of a good job "to fall back on." I got accepted at the nursing school, but after two terms I know I have made the wrong choice. I just don't want to be a nurse. I'm living a life lie. Shall I just quit? What do I say to my mother—after all she's the one who paid for all this? Yet I know I don't want to do this.

Male (21 years): I thought to get on at college, I had to do everything my roommates and their friends did. I went out drinking and smoking grass and doing really dumb stuff. My grades began to suffer but I didn't care. I thought I was being real cool. When I got put on academic probation, I had to look at what I was doing. I had to stay with my roommates until the lease was up and then I moved out. I have some serious roommates now and I'm doing better in school.

Female (18 years): I didn't realize what a life lie I was living when I was in high school. I wanted to be accepted by the "popular" group so I did everything like them, using a lot of makeup and very sexy clothing. I dropped my previous friends and hung around the popular crowd. I let myself become intimate with the popular boys because that was part of the game—even boys I didn't like. Then I came to college and realized that I didn't want to be like them anymore. I wanted to be myself. I'm really glad I came to that realization. I feel so much freer now and able to live the way I should live.

Reflective Writing: Reflect upon some time you were living a life lie and what enabled you to live more authentically.

Compensation versus Overcompensation. Some persons, however, *overcompensate* for their low self-esteem. The reader may have noticed that tall, strong men often seem very gentle in their dealings with others. They move and talk quietly. Since they know they are superior in height and strength, they don't have to "throw their weight around." By way of contrast, Adler described the **Napoleonic complex**: How very short men need constantly to prove themselves superior in one way or another. Napoleon Bonaparte was very short, and Adler suggested that his drive to conquer all of Europe was his unconscious attempt to overcompensate for his short stature. We cannot know, of course, if this was actually the case, but it is interesting to note that another world conqueror, Alexander the Great, was also small in stature in comparison to the Greeks of his time. A second example: A little girl who feels unloved because her sister was her father's "favorite" may spend a lifetime proving herself attractive to men. She spends exorbitant amounts of time, energy, and money on clothes, makeup, and hair styling. She engages in flirtations or love affair and may even become a breaker of men's hearts—the French *femme fatale*. To love her is to suffer heartbreak. Another example: The little boy who feels outstripped by his siblings may pursue a vocation in business in which he seeks to outstrip others through aggressive—even ruthless—competitive methods. Sometimes the drive for superiority can be hidden under a camouflage of virtue. For example, the person may strive to become superior in "goodness" in a way others may not appreciate. The person may not be so much "good" as either a "martyr" trying to make others feel guilty or "holier than thou," indicating that the rest of us are "sinners."

Gemeinschaftsgefühl: The Development of Character

If human nature were nothing but this striving for power and superiority, we would exist only in a dog-eat-dog world in which everyone is seeking to overcome others. Fortunately, that is only half the story. There is, said Adler, another very powerful drive within the human heart—not one that seeks to overcome others—but one which seeks to cooperate with others and bring out the best in them. Ideal mother love is an example of this drive. He called this drive to be of service to others *gemeinschaftsgefühl*. Our German-speaking colleagues tell us that this word is impossible to translate precisely into English but that it has overtones of *love, caring, loving-kindness*, and *compassion*. Persons who have a highly developed *gemeinschaftsgefühl* have a compassionate love of all humankind despite our human foibles and follies and apparent madnesses at times. So taken was Abraham Maslow by this quality in his self-actualizing persons that he included *gemeinschaftsgefühl* as one of their personality characteristics.

Persons with a highly developed *gemeinschaftsgefühl* manifest a goodness that we instantly recognize, but not of the "holier than thou" kind that makes us feel inferior. They arouse in us a sense of happiness and joy. We are glad to be in their company. Across cultures and down through the ages, there have always been those whom biographers have described as "saint-like" or "enlightened" or as representing a highly evolved moral/ethical orientation. They continue to manifest joy and spirituality despite the setbacks, obstacles, and tragedies in their lives. The person with a highly developed *gemeinschaftsgefühl* may be described as growing always in wisdom and in grace (see Box 3.6).

BOX **3.6** **Alfred Adler's Description of Highly Developed**
            Gemeinschaftsgefühl

Note how Adler describes people with highly developed Gemeinschaftsgefühl (pronounced ga-MINE-shofts-ga-full). Note also how he contrasts these people with two other groups of people: people who remain distant and aloof from the rest of us and the group that actually spreads gloom (Adler, 1959).

. . . We can easily measure anyone's *gemeinschaftsgefühl* by learning to what degree he is prepared to serve, to help, and to give pleasure to others. The talent for bringing pleasure to others makes a man more interesting. Happy people approach us more easily and we judge them emotionally as being more sympathetic. They are the people who appear cheerful, who do not go about forever oppressed and solicitous, who do not unload their worries upon every stranger. They are quite capable, when in the company of others, to radiate this cheerfulness and make life more beautiful and meaningful. One can sense they are good human beings, not only in their actions, but in the manner in which . . . they speak, in which they pay attention to our

interests, as well as in their entire external aspect, their clothes, their gestures, their happy emotional state, and their laughter. . .

[By way of contrast] . . . There are some people who are absolutely unable to laugh because they stand so far from the innate bond that connects human beings that their ability to give pleasure or to appear happy is absent.

There is also another little group of people who are utterly incapable of giving anyone else joy since they are concerned only in embittering life in every situation which they may enter. They walk around as if they wish to extinguish every light. They do not laugh at all, or only when forced to do so, or when they wish to give the semblance of a joy-giver.

Reflective Writing: From your own association with other people, describe a) someone who seems to you to have a highly developed gemeinschaftsgefühl; b) someone who is distant and aloof from others; and c) someone who actually spreads gloom.

Birth Order

It is not just the giant-sized adults that make a child feel inferior or superior. It also happens through rank and gender of birth order. Much has been researched on birth order and many books have been written on the subject in the last fifty years, but it was Alfred Adler who first called our attention to the child's place in the family constellation (Adler, 1929, 1959). Adler hypothesized many effects of birth order. More recent research has added to and modified his original observations, but most of his insights into the effects of birth order have been somewhat validated by empirical research (Sulloway, 1998). Consider the following hard data.

Firstborn children go on to college and graduate school and become university professors more often than their younger siblings. They also make up the majority of doctors, lawyers, accountants—in fact—they more frequently go into all the professions. They are also "overrepresented" in corporate leadership, political office, and even in the field of aerodynamics—almost all the famous astronauts were first born. Does this mean that firstborn children have more intelligent genes? Of course not. But it does mean their parents were more motivated to help them succeed. Whether it is writing a school report, or playing in Little League, or taking private lessons in music or dance, parents of firstborn children were willing to chauffeur them, pay for what they needed, and encourage their skills and talents. By the time the younger siblings come along, parents begin to run out of energy, time, and money, with the result that later-born children are not so closely supervised. Oldest siblings often accuse their parents of letting their younger sibling "get away" with things the oldest child could not. "Boy! I wasn't allowed to do the things he's allowed to do!"

Being closer to their parents, firstborn children *introject* (observe and imitate) more of their values and behaviors. Consequently, when firstborns become adults, they fit more comfortably into adult society and, consequently, are more at ease in the corporate structure. Furthermore, their parents have often given them the job of taking care of their younger brothers and sisters and so first-borns develop more responsibility toward "the family good" and later "the corporate good." But a sense of responsibility also results in guilt when they do not live up to what they think they should do or should be. Consequently, first-borns tend to be more guilt-ridden and more anxious generally with a tendency to worry more than later-born children (see Box 3.7).

Younger children often accuse their oldest sibling of being "bossy" and abusive. Since younger siblings do not have the physical or verbal power of the older siblings, they develop crafty strategies to get even. As younger children, we may have screamed to make our parents think we were being hurt by our older sibling. We may have become expert in blackmail and extortion, "I won't tell Mom what you said if you won't tattle on me about the cake." Being born later, we were not pushed to make good grades so we probably put more emphasis on having fun than on our studies. We grew up to be much more spontaneous and popular with our friends, more interested in physical sports, or expressing ourselves in the arts. We are not nearly so responsible as our firstborn siblings; nor are we as burdened with guilt as they are. The youngest child often expresses this sentiment (sometimes quite vehemently): "I don't have anyone I can boss around."

The "lost" middle child needs special attention. The reason for this special notation is that the middle-born child (or several middle-born children) tends to get lost, particularly in a large family. Studies indicate that the middle child is less verbal. It may have been simply too difficult for the middle-born to get a word in edgewise at the dinner table because of the superior verbal skills of the oldest child and the demands for attention by the youngest child. In

BOX **3.7** SELF-EXPLORATION
Is This True of Your Sibling Experience?

This self-exploration can be answered in either of two ways: as if applied to yourself or a sibling. But remember to use your judgment about the sibling rank. For example, a third child born seven or eight years later than the second born may very well be like another firstborn child. A middle child, but the first son in a family, may be treated like a firstborn. Add up each column then circle the column that has the most points.

Firstborn Children: Are these statements true or false of your own experience?

1. Tends to be more conforming to parental values and societal status quo.	T	F	?
2. More supervised in educational and extracurricular activities by parents.	T	F	?
3. More motivated to go on to college and/or professional school.	T	F	?
4. More willing to assume responsibility.	T	F	?
5. More emotionally identified with parents.	T	F	?
6. More communicative and verbal than later born.	T	F	?
7. More apt to seek help from parent, friend, or physician when hurt or puzzled.	T	F	?
8. More apt to be bossy and verbally assertive or aggressive.	T	F	?
9. More willing to be concerned and caring about other members of the family.	T	F	?
10. More tendency toward introverted, quiet leisure activities (reading, gardening, running).	T	F	?

Totals

Middle-Born Children: Are these statements true or false of your own experience?

1. More distant from parents, hostile and suspicious of authority and rebellious of rules.	T	F	?
2. Less inclined to study and make good grades.	T	F	?
3. Tends to be more popular in school and have more friends.	T	F	?
4. More willing to take time to have spontaneous fun.	T	F	?
5. More engaged in sports and action-oriented activities.	T	F	?
6. More aggressive and acting-out behavior (temper tantrums, crying, fighting).	T	F	?
7. More apt to go into positions that allow independent action (dentist, forester, truck-driver, artist, writer).	T	F	?
8. More apt to keep problems to self rather than confide in parents or other adults.	T	F	?
9. More democratic in group decision-making process.	T	F	?
10. Gets into more trouble than other members of the family.	T	F	?

Totals

other ways, too, the middle child gets lost. Because of the soon-after arrival of a newborn baby (or babies), parental attention to middle-born children may have been skimpy at times. The middle-born child's lower grades in school is well documented. When the middle-born child started school, there may have been a lack of supervision of homework. How to overcome this problem? In a nutshell: by parent and teacher diligence. Parents need to make special time with middle-born children, and not with other siblings around. It can be a special storytelling time. It can be shopping trips all by themselves—and no one else. It can be through parent-teacher conferences on ways to provide opportunities for middle-born children to shine in the classroom. And let's make sure that if middle-born children do come home with a good grade or "happy face," that it gets put up on the proverbial refrigerator door, alongside the youngest child's kindergarten drawings.

Only children are much like first-born children with these exceptions: Not having had to vie for parental attention or having experienced sibling rivalry in the nursery, only children tend to have more open, trusting, and optimistic attitudes toward life. While some only children become the traditional "spoiled rotten" stereotype, most only children are generous in

BOX **3.7** SELF-EXPLORATION (continued)
Is This True of Your Sibling Experience?

Youngest Children: Are these statements true or false of your own experience?

1. More willing to play the comic and make people laugh.	T	F	?
2. More eager to make a name for yourself and show up your older siblings.	T	F	?
3. More able to negotiate with people in a friendly way.	T	F	?
4. More willing to consult others when in trouble or confused.	T	F	?
5. Enjoy other people so long as they treat you as an equal.	T	F	?
6. More willing to get help when hurt physically.	T	F	?
7. More willing to let others "have their way."	T	F	?
8. Learned crafty ways to get back at your older siblings.	T	F	?
9. Tend to watch others to discover what mood they are in.	T	F	?
10. Still feel you are not taken seriously enough at times.	T	F	?

Totals

Only Children: Are these statements true or false of your own experience?

1. Apt to be very verbal.	T	F	?
2. Feel close to adults.	T	F	?
3. Apt to be bewildered by fighting and jealousy of other children.	T	F	?
4. Tend to be fairly self-confident about self and abilities.	T	F	?
5. Tend to be easy going in temperament and trusting of other persons.	T	F	?
6. Tend to be more oriented towards professional school and graduate degrees.	T	F	?
7. Tend to be trusting of others and bewildered when others betray that trust.	T	F	?
8. Not so able to deal with direct confrontation, oversensitive, and hurt when bawled out.	T	F	?
9. Generally have an optimistic attitude towards life.	T	F	?
10. More able to draw on "inner resources" so as to develop the imagination and talents (art, writing, etc.).	T	F	?

Totals

Reflective Writing: If any of these sibling categories accurately reflects your experience, state how. If your responses do not reflect your experience, explain how.

dealing with other children because they have not had to fight for time, attention, or material things. Unfortunately their lack of experience of sibling rivalry results in a certain naiveté. Not having witnessed the hair-pulling, tattling, jealousy, lying, and betrayal that goes on in the nursery, they tend to be surprised, even astonished, by what they observe in others. They are continually asking others, "Why are they doing that? Why did she say that? Do all people do that? Do others feel that way?" Unfortunately, because they are quite naive about the ways of the world, they are also more likely to be "taken in" by schemers and scoundrels.

Adler's Creative Self versus Freud's Conflicted Self. Although both Adler and Freud placed heavy emphasis on early environment as a major factor of personality, there were several major differences. While Freud attempted to describe personality in terms of the libidinal drive, Adler added the need for competence and power. Another difference is that Freud's model of the personality is a conflict model (the id versus the superego) while Adler's model involves a *creative self* that guides the person along and through the shoals and rapids of life. This creative self uses the raw material of both his heredity and his experiences in life to interpret and give meaning to his life. Adler likened the person's creative self to an artist who conceptualizes a portrait of himself and then works to live up to this self-portrait. In short, this creative self drives us to do what we do. In most of us, the self-portrait we have imaged for ourselves is healthy, but some people create an unhealthy one, which accounts for what seems to be destructive behaviors. Today we would perhaps call these self-portraits by terms introduced in Chapter 1: *self-concept* and *self-esteem*.

CARL JUNG'S TRANSPERSONAL MODEL OF HUMAN EXISTENCE

A Four-Stage Model of the Life Span

Carl Jung was another personality theorist who had to break with Freud. He did not believe (as Freud did) that the human personality was fully formed by age six. Jung's model of personality described four great chapters, or eras, covering the whole life span, each of which has unique characteristics, needs, and motivations (Jung, 1955). The four eras include *childhood*, *youth*, *maturity*, and *old age* (see Figure 3.6). He was also responsible for originating and describing a concept that we have taken much to heart—the *midlife crisis*. The midlife crisis became a focal point of Jung's theories about human existence since he considered this juncture in our lives a time when we can become truly, authentically ourselves—a process he called **individuation** (Jung, 1955).

     Stage I. Childhood (From Birth to About 20/25 Years). Many of the readers may be surprised to discover that Jung would regard them as still in the stage of childhood. According to Jung, childhood is roughly that stage from birth to the late teens and early twenties. It is the

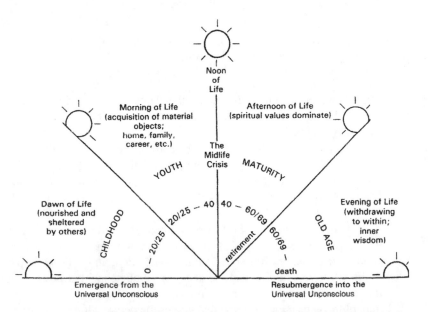

Figure 3.6 Jung's Four Stages of the Life Span. Where Freud believed adult personality to be fully formed by age six, Jung posited four age/stages, each of which has needs and values different from the others and which influences our personality and character.

"dawn of life" in which the person is emerging out of the "Universal Unconscious" into an individual self-identity distinct from the other family members. But until a person is financially self-supporting, Jung regarded the person as being protected and harbored within the safety of the family unit.

Stage II. Youth (About 20/25 Years to 37/38 Years). Jung described the second stage of youth as "the morning of life" in which the young adult is setting out on his independent life-career. The tasks of youth are twofold. The first is the development of an *ego complex*, by which Jung meant a level of consciousness characterized by a "high degree of self-identity and continuity of personality." We seem to know who we are and what we want from life. The second task is *acquisition*: the acquisition of whatever we think to be essential to our happiness and well-being. From our early twenties to just before age 40, we go about the job of acquiring job and career, spouse and children, house and furnishings, and, of course, always a bigger and better automobile—all those material objects we believe will bring us satisfaction and happiness. It is at this time that we define our life goals in terms of family, money, position, and success in our life-career. It is a time of competition, struggle, hard-work, and task-directed behavior.

Figure 3.7 Carl Jung. The psychologist who reintroduced the terms *soul* and *spiritual* into psychology.

The Midlife Crisis (From 37/38 Years to About 42/43 Years). In contrast to Freud's "neurotic" patients who were so emotionally disabled they were unable to work or live harmoniously with others, Jung's patients were often the great and near-great of Europe. When they came to Jung, they were unable to put into words just what was troubling them. In fact, they sometimes described themselves as having "everything that life has to offer." Yet, as they approached their fortieth year, they had become aware of "an emptiness" or "void" or some "lack" in their lives. Somehow, life had ceased to have any meaning. Jung described their problem as **spiritual bankruptcy**. In their pursuit of worldly "success," they had neglected the spiritual dimension. By *spiritual dimension*, Jung was referring to all those nonmaterialistic values we all need in our lives: tenderness and caring within the family grouping; intimate friendship and challenging companions; moments of deep conversation and quiet intimacy; and the appreciation of nature, whether awesome or beautiful. What had been neglected were the needs of the Soul. In fact, Jung entitled one of his books *Modern Man in Search of a Soul*. The therapy, of course, was to enable them to get in touch with their **transpersonal** *needs*: more time with their family and friends, more time for the contemplation of nature, and ways they could be of service to those now living or to those who come after us.

Stage III. Maturity (About 42/43 Years to Retirement). If men understand what is happening to them and if they process the midlife crisis successfully, they now devote themselves to these suprapersonal values during the "second half" of their lives. They make friends with their children, who are becoming young adults. With their adult children "leaving the nest," husbands may seek ways to share activities with wives, something they have not done in many years. Now they have time to take the vacations they have longed for and to visit with relatives and friends they haven't seen in many years. They value leisure time over the need "to make money" and begin to "throttle back" at work. If a man is a physician, he may now take Wednesdays off to join some friends on the golf greens. Or he may decide he needs to make a major midlife vocational change. He may leave his "fast track," super-competitive job and buy that small bookstore he has always wanted. He looks for ways to give of his time, energy, and money to charitable organizations. Unlike the "do-gooder," he does so because he finds joy in the giving.

Successful processing of the midlife crisis leads to what Jung called **individuation**. The man after 40 truly has a chance of becoming "his own person." He is unshackled from the compulsion to live up to someone else's standards of behavior. He need not be who *they* think he should be or do what *they* think he should do with his life. Unlike adolescents (who are living through the most *unindividuated* time of their lives), people in their maturity are now free to be who they are and to pursue their own needs and the values *they themselves* want to express (Jung & Aniela, 1964).

On the other hand, if he misconstrues the changes he needs to make to resolve his midlife crisis, he may destroy everything he has built up for the last two decades. He may suddenly divorce his wife, abandon his children, buy a sports car, and take up with a woman half his age. His adult children may tell their friends, "Dad's gone completely crazy." Jung would say that he really isn't going crazy. He is misconstruing his midlife crisis. The changes he needs to make are not so much external as *internal*. Instead of making a transition to the next level of conscious maturity, he is trying to turn back the clock, what people call "chasing his youth."

Stage IV. Old Age (From Retirement to Death). If we have processed the midlife crisis successfully and evolved to a more transpersonal life style during the stage of maturity, we will be able to live out the "evening of life" in dignity and peace. Our spiritual values now allow us to confront the last part of our lives with acceptance and grace. We do not regret the ending of existence, because we know that we have lived our lives as well as we could. We know our lives have been worthwhile and that we have touched the bodies, minds, and hearts of others when we could. The older person is preparing to reemerge into the Universal Unconscious again. Time now to focus on the inner world and "things of the spirit." But, not just yet! There is one more task left to do. If the task of youth was acquiring an ego complex and the task of maturity was individuation, the task of old age is to inspire in the younger generation the understanding that renunciation of worldly goods leads to luminous wisdom. Then: *Consumatum est.*

But What About Women? At this point, female readers must be wondering if Jung ever wrote anything about women and the midlife crisis. Well, yes, he did. As a matter-of-fact, he was one of the first social scientists to champion career women. What he said went as follows. In their striving for career, money, status, power, and all those material goods men believe make for happiness, men miss out on the opportunities to have warm, close relationships with others. If they were successful businessmen, they hardly took time out to enjoy nature. They also didn't have the opportunity to connect intimately with their children as they grew up. So all of these lacks in their lives is what men need for the "second half" of their lives.

Women, on the other hand, have spent almost their entire existence in just those areas that men lack; nurturing others, and enjoying intimate conversations with other women. If she didn't have a garden, she generally had indoor plants placed in sunny windows and often took

BOX **3.8** EVALUATING JUNG
Psychologist or Mystic?

The Minus Side. If Freudian psychology was attacked as being nonverifiable in the laboratory, Jungian psychology has been even more heavily criticized in this direction. Freud himself thought that Jung's emphasis on the transpersonal and spiritual dimension of human existence was delving into nonscientific areas. As we investigate more of Jung's theoretical concepts, we may find ourselves agreeing with his critics. Furthermore, his writing is sometimes so obscure that it is difficult for psychologists to agree just what he means by certain terms. What did he mean, for example, by the *Universal Unconscious*? It is difficult sometimes to know whether he is talking psychology or theology (he came from a long line of ministers).

The Plus Side. Despite these harsh criticisms, we cannot lightly dismiss Jung—too many of his concepts have touched a genuine chord in the general population. Although Jung's transpersonal view is one of the reasons that experimental psychologists have tended to avoid Jung's theories of personality, but developmental and social psychologists have found validity in many of Jung's theoretical formulations, particularly concerning the midlife crisis and the process of individuation. In fact, the midlife crisis has become one of the most popular underlying themes for movies, TV dramatizations, and books. In classes, students readily volunteer real-life examples of the midlife crisis from their own families. As a term, the *midlife crisis* has even passed into popular usage in the media and in everyday conversation. Since Jung's death, the midlife crisis has been verified by many other studies (Levinson, D., Darrow, C. N., Klein, E. B., Levinson, M. H., & McKee, B., 1978; Lim, J. K., 2000; Sadler, 2000).

walks with the children on pleasant afternoons. But in all their nurturing and caring for others, the women of Jung's day had little encouragement to develop their intellectual abilities and, with children and husband to care for, not much opportunity to work outside the house. If they were now content to take on a grandmotherly role, all well and good. But some women, he observed, had a desire now to do something just for themselves. If they wanted to have a career in business, Jung was all for it. Or they might try their hand at writing or painting if they had such an inclination. He supported women doing whatever it took for the successful resolution of their midlife crisis.

We add just a personal note here. We have observed that those older nontraditional women students who have come back to college for their own purposes are some of the best students we have ever had. They are not only highly motivated to get good grades (and they often skew the grade curves) but with so many years of real life experience behind them, they appreciate what they learn in psychology. And why? Because they've been "out there" in the so-called "real world" and have experienced much of what the text is discussing. They are always most welcome in our classes.

ERIK ERIKSON'S EIGHT-STAGE PSYCHOSOCIAL THEORY OF PERSONALITY

In the years between World War I and World War II, thousands of studies literally were done on various aspects of human development. These piecemeal studies seemed a jumble of chaotic, confusing, and seemingly contradictory investigations. Then, in 1950, a psychologist by the name of Erik Erikson pulled many of these theories and research studies together in an eight-stage model he called a psycho*social* theory of human development. Each stage has a specific **life crisis** that must be confronted and successfully resolved in order to achieve the **life task** of that age/stage. Successful achievement results in a positive *personality trait*, and an achievement

Table 3.1   Erikson's Psychosocial Model of Development

	Age/Stage		Life Task	vs.	Failure	Character Outcomes
I	(0–1 yrs.)	Infancy	Basic trust		Mistrust	Hope and drive
II	(1–3 yrs.)	Toddler years	Autonomy		Shame	Self-concept and willpower
III	(4–5 yrs.)	Play years	Initiative		Guilt	Direction and purpose
IV	(6–12 yrs.)	School years	Industry		Inferiority	Method and competence
V	(10–22?)	Adolescence	Identity		Role confusion	Devotion and fidelity
VI	(to 40?)	Early adulthood	Intimacy		Isolation	Affiliation and love
VII	(40–65?)	Middle adulthood	Generativity		Stagnation	Production and love
VIII	(65–?)	Old age	Ego integrity		Despair	Renunciation and wisdom

of *character*. Failure to achieve it results in a negative personality trait (see Table 3.1). Psychologists have found Erikson's model so useful in describing the life span experience that it has been included in almost every textbook dealing with any aspect of psychology.

Stage I. Basic Trust versus Mistrust (Infancy). Noting that the human infant comes into the world a helpless entity, Erikson said that the child needs to develop **basic trust** in people to love him and to care for him physically and emotionally. This special kind of "mothering" provides the child with the emotional security that he is wanted and loved. If the infant is neglected, abused, or rejected by the caretakers, he or she will become sickly or retarded physically, intellectually, and emotionally—if the child survives at all. We know that children left in orphanages and hospitals for too long can become emotionally withdrawn. They may even "fail to thrive." Or they may develop a severe personality disorder that lasts all their lives (Bowlby, 1969; Provence & Lipton, 1963).

Stage II. Autonomy versus Doubt and Shame (Toddler Years). Somewhere between seven months and two years, infants are accomplishing the life task of autonomy. **Autonomy** is the desire for self-control and the willpower to accomplish it. They are beginning to feed themselves, to crawl, and eventually to walk by themselves. In fact, they struggle for independence; wiggling out of their parents' arms to go where they want to go. They are gaining control of the bodily functions of bladder and bowel. They are learning to use language that gets them what they want ("Cookie!" will get them something good to eat). But it is equally important that children learn that the world can say NO to them too! No, they are not to hit their mommies. No, they may not throw food on the floor. If children do not learn to abide by the rules and regulations of society, they may remain aggressive and rebellious, always side-stepping the law and always a little bit "shady."

Figure 3.8 Erik Erikson. Constructed an 8-stage model of the life span.

Stage III. Initiative versus Guilt (Play Years). At about three years of age, children are acquiring initiative. **Initiative** means children are being able to organize the chaos of everyday events into meaningful organization. In contrast to the toddlers of Stage II who live in an eternal *here-and-now*, children in this stage are beginning to understand the concepts of morning, noon, and night. They are getting a sense of their immediate geography and can play outdoors unsupervised (but "only on this side of the street—and don't cross the road!"). They are also learning to play cooperatively with others, and to share toys. If the child does not learn to be cooperative, he will remain forever at odds with his peers, trying to win out over them competitively and always aggressively "on the make."

Stage IV. Industry versus Inferiority (School Years). Until children go to school, they are involved in the serious task of playing. Then around age six, they are sent to school. Their life task from six to adolescence, said Erikson, is **industry** (learning to work) to prepare them for adulthood. To achieve adult competency in Alaska, children must learn to build igloos. In the South Pacific, they must learn to fish. In our technological society, children must become literate. They must learn to read and write and do arithmetic so that as adults they can become employable and manage their personal affairs. Failure to achieve this life task of industry results in inferiority. If that sounds harsh, consider the plight of illiterate adults. They are unable to fill out a job application. They cannot read directions on a label or instructions on the simplest gadget. They cannot read a map. They cannot order meals from a restaurant menu. They may be intelligent people, but they are functioning at the level of mental retardation.

Stage V. Identity versus Role Confusion (Adolescent Years). Erikson characterized adolescence as "the big crisis" in complex technological societies. One reason is that while young men and women may be biologically ready for sexual cohabitation, the rules of our society say they must not "give in" to this drive, and so they live in suspended psychobiological tension, sometimes for many years. A second reason is that while adolescents have the power and drives of an adult, they often still have the emotions of a child. The sweeping psychobiological changes that come about at puberty result in alternating bouts of giddy elation to crashing loss of self-confidence. Teenagers deem themselves to be "fat" or "stupid" or "unattractive" or "unathletic" or "unpopular" (or whatever). The slightest negative comment or rejection will confirm that sense of unworthiness. In the hunt for their own identity, adolescents often reject their families and their families' values. But their newly developing adolescent self-identity is not yet very secure. They cannot stand alone. They cling to each other, copying each other's clothes, slang, musical preferences, hair styles, and so on. In the struggle to find their identity, they may try on many roles, adopting other people's mannerisms until they find a life style that fits their unique temperament.

Stage VI. Intimacy versus Isolation (Young Adulthood). Adolescents think in terms of "I" and "me." The task for young people entering adulthood is learning to think in terms of "we," "ours," and "us," pronouns that have to do with spouses, children, and all our "significant others." **Intimacy** involves sexual intimacy, of course, but it also involves psychological intimacy. We learn to share our hearts and minds and souls with other human beings. Intimacy makes possible genuine partnership in interpersonal relationships: friendships, life-partners, and warm relationships with coworkers. The lasting character traits are those of altruistic love and affiliation with others.

If adults retreat from intimacy, they are subject to an alienating sense of isolation and the inability to relate to others. They may develop protective devices to keep others at a distance. They may be described by others as snobbish, cold, rude, or even arrogant. They feel alienated from others and do not take part in community affairs, church, or social gatherings. They may even become reclusive, hiding in their houses away from society. They are also vulnerable to the lure of cults and hate groups.

Stage VII. Generativity versus Stagnation (After the Midlife Passage). After the midlife passage, the adult experiences the need to give something back to the community and to be of service to others. Erikson called this need **generativity**, helping younger persons become productive and creative. For some, it may be the simple task of enabling their adult children to buy a home and get started on their life-careers. It may take the form of fostering the creativity of younger persons at work and mentoring their leadership skills. Generativity prevents the stagnation of personality. The identification being accomplished in this life task is that of being a *transpersonal* human being. We are fostering others to be productive citizens and leaders who will be the caretakers of the next generation.

Stage VIII. Ego Integrity versus Despair (Aging Years). The identification to be acquired in this last stage of the life span is that of being a spiritually integrated human being. We all know people who, as they got older, became wizened not only in body but also in mind and spirit. We are not talking here about the ravages of Alzheimer's disease. We are talking about those persons who became mean-spirited, grasping, bitter. Charles Dickens depicted such a person in his well-loved *A Christmas Carol* in the personage of Scrooge. It is not a small achievement to live out our lives with *ego integrity*; i.e., maintaining a sense of joy and peace despite the ending of life. Erikson calls the successful outcomes of this awareness *renunciation* and *wisdom*. When we meet older people who have achieved this understanding, we are awed by the way they are living out their lives. They have let go of the anxieties and strivings that mark the rest of the human life span. They have gone beyond the plane of our common human foibles.

Are there any such older persons? Some of the readers may know such a person in their own lives and can affirm that such ego integrity is possible. Students often tell us that this person has been a guiding light for their own development. To those readers who do not know such a person, we point to some of the extraordinary figures of history who achieved this transpersonal level of awareness even in their final years: Socrates, Diogenes, Plato, Einstein, Albertus Magnus, Blaise Pascal, Benjamin Franklin, Carl Jung, Albert Schweitzer, Jean Piaget, all of whom worked joyfully into their eighties and nineties. We can also point to Mother Teresa of India; the American artists Grandma Moses and Georgia O'Keefe; Margaret Kuhn, who founded the Gray Panthers in her sixties and worked for the organization until well into her nineties; the Delaney sisters, two African-American women, an attorney and a physician, who wrote their joint autobiography around their one hundredth birthday; as well as two remarkable women who worked internationally from their sixties on, Eleanor Roosevelt and Margaret Albright.

ANXIETY AND THE DEFENSE MECHANISMS

Before we end this chapter on personality theories of human development, we need to add a final topic, that of defense mechanisms. It was Freud who first formulated the defense mechanisms, but other psychoanalysts, psychiatrists, and psychologists have been adding many others, until now there are a list of 30 official such mechanisms. We certainly don't want you

Figure 3.9 On Anxiety.
When physical pain over-
whelms us, we lose
consciousness; when psy-
chological pain threatens to
overwhelm us, we escape
via our defense mechanisms.

to memorize all of them; some of them are infrequently used. So what we are
listing are only the most common. As you read each defense mechanism
described, think about examples you have observed either in others or in
yourself.

Symptoms of Anxiety: Their Many Shapes and Forms

It was Freud who first defined our present understanding of anxiety. He differentiated *anxiety* from *fear*. We generally know what we are afraid of, be it
another person or a test we don't think we'll pass or not having enough
money to pay our bills. Anxiety, on the other hand, is a more diffuse emotion,
which cannot always be easily identified. Anxiety can be felt psychologically
as "nervousness," without knowing why, or expressed as "knots in the stomach" or "weak in the knees." The symptoms and complications of anxiety are
legion! (See Table 3.2.)

To truly understand the phenomenon of anxiety, we must comprehend
this basic fact: *Anxiety is painful.* The pain of anxiety may come from a sense
of guilt, from a secret shame, from the memory of an abusive past, from fear
of the future, and so on. But wherever it comes from or however it is experienced, anxiety is painful. When we experience overwhelming physical pain,
our body defends itself by losing consciousness. We faint. We pass out. In
like manner, when the pain of anxiety becomes overwhelming, we defend
against that pain by losing conscious awareness of it. We may lose the conscious awareness of the pain but the anxiety manifests in other behaviors, which Freud called
defense mechanisms.

Physical and Verbal Aggression. One of the most primitive forms of defense is physical aggression, in which the person tries to inflict pain on another person. It can be seen in
young, upset children who hit each other or their parents. In high school, the formation of
gangs actually legitimizes the physical aggression of "gang wars" and vandalism. In some
people, alcohol seems to unleash a tendency toward physical aggression whether in a barroom
brawl or domestic violence: spouse abuse, sibling abuse, and elderly abuse. Acting out behaviors are reported in the media quite frequently. Example: The Olympic ice skater who hired
two accomplices to injure her chief competitor. Example: The adolescent girl who shot the

Table 3.2   Common Symptoms of Anxiety: Their Number is Legion!

Alcoholism	Grinding teeth	Minor acne	Picking off lint
Allergies	Headaches	Mouth clucking	Procrastinating
Anger (excessive)	Heart palpitations	Muscle cramps	Puckering lips
Clammy hands	Heartburn	Muscle spasms	Rocking
Crying (excessive)	Hyperactivity	Nightmares	Rubbing hands
Drug addiction	Insomnia	Night terrors	Sighing (constant)
Facial tics	Junk food eating	Oversleeping	Stuttering
Fainting	Lip biting	Perspiring	Sweating (profuse)
Fatigue (constant)	"Lump" in throat	Phobias	Tongue clicking

Figure 3.10 Verbal Aggression: A frequent defense mechanism.

wife of her alleged lover. The high school shootings of the last few years are causing Americans to reevaluate the roots of our violent society and determine what can be done to instigate more peaceful interaction among our young people. Also getting attention in recent years is the form of aggression called *road rage*. Frustrated by red lights, stop signs, school zones, expressway tie-ups, and bumper-to-bumper driving, aggressive drivers react by forcing other drivers off the road, shouting obscenities at passing cars, and even shooting at other drivers. So rampant has this form of aggression become that Americans sometimes say they are more afraid of road rage than drunk drivers (Sleek, 1999).

Verbal aggression can be heard whenever children call each other names, but it reaches its apex in high school where it becomes the adolescent way of relating to each other. They either make biting remarks to each other, or they tear themselves apart before others do it for them. One of the most damaging of all verbal aggression is what an abusive parent screams at a child. The pain caused by a physical beating can fade over time, but the brutal things a parent screams at a child may be indelibly imprinted on the child's memory forever.

"I wish you had never been born!"
"How can you be so stupid?"
"You're a whore just like your mother!"
"You're to blame for my headache. Go away! I can't stand the sight of you!"

Denial. We can observe denial quite easily in children. Ask three children, "Who ate the cookies?" and all three children will probably answer, "Not me!" And they are not lying! They have heard themselves say they didn't eat the cookies so it must be true. Denial is quite "normal" in children. It is often our first reaction to painful news. Kubler-Ross (1975) lists the shock and denial response as the first stage of a person's reaction to being told he or she has a terminal illness. Upon being told of the prognosis, the patient often disclaims it with such remarks as, "No, it can't be true. There must be some mistake." Another example: When told that their son has been sexually abusing their grandchild, parents can steadfastly refuse to believe it is true—their son would not do such terrible things!

Autistic Fantasy. Sometimes the person simply withdraws into a world of fantasy. Instead of dealing with the everyday world in which they feel inadequate and unable to cope, they use fantasy to fill the emptiness and loneliness of their lives. Unlike the homeless or runaways, people who use autistic fantasy as their major defense may go to their school or job each day and carry out their tasks as best they can. But they will hurry home to watch TV, which is the only reality they can relate to without fear. Or they may bury themselves in a romantic novel in which the hero and heroine get married at the end and live (presumably) "happily ever after." Or they may indulge in fantasies whereby they fulfill some of their dreams without real physical involvement. Children who are failing in school are no longer psychologically present in the classroom. Instead of listening to the teacher, they are tuning in to a better world where they are being successful and admired.

Projective Identification (Blaming Others for Our Behaviors). Projective identification provides the person with an excuse to aggress against others. Listen to a spouse abuser explain the reasons that he beat his wife. "She drove me to it!" (In actuality, the woman did everything she could to prevent his abuse.) "All she does is nag, nag, nag. I couldn't help myself." (In actuality, the woman has become a very submissive and silent individual.) Notice how the abusing husband is distorting what happened by placing the blame for his actions onto his wife. Men who molest or rape the young girls in a family grouping sometimes say something like, "She asked for it. She was all the time cozying up to me." Delinquent teenagers use projective identification as a way of excusing their actions. When confronted with their behaviors of truancy, drinking, vandalism, dope addiction, or shoplifting, they defend themselves by blaming their parents, or their teachers, or the shop owners, or "the system." Their conflicts with society are never their fault—not in the least. Somebody else is always to blame.

Rationalization. Rationalization is the concealment of the real reason for thoughts, feelings, actions, and events by proffering an elaborate or self-serving explanation. Some examples of rationalization can be quite amusing because it is so easy to see through them. The sour-grapes rationalization was taken from the fable by Aesop. In that story, a hot and weary fox spies a bunch of cool and delicious grapes hanging from a tree—just the thing to quench his thirst. But despite many jumping attempts, he is unable to reach them. Frustrated and weary, he stalks off saying to himself, "They were probably sour anyhow." Rationalization is a frequent defense for all of us when we experience what we perceive as "failure." Here is a real-life example observed by the authors on the beach one day. Several young men were gazing at a lovely young lady in the distance. They all acknowledged her attractiveness in a bathing suit and were fantasizing about how they might approach her without her taking offense. One young man finally approached her and "made a pass." We could not hear her answer at that distance, but whatever she said resulted in his backing off rather quickly. By the time he returned to the group of boys who were now laughing and making sarcastic comments, he had his rationalization ready: "Yeah, she turned me down and was I glad. She looks good from here, but when you get up close, she's really 'a dog.' "

Reaction Formation. In the **reaction formation** defense, the person's thoughts and feelings seem to go in reverse. The little girl who is jealous of her baby brother gets punished when she shows any overt dislike of him. Eventually, she becomes so guilty whenever she experiences any negative feelings toward her little brother that she represses these feeling and begins to behave in positive ways toward him. In fact, she becomes a little "second mother" by asking to wheel him in the baby carriage or give him his bottle. However, the negative feelings that have been repressed may surface in ways that are dangerous to the baby. The baby carriage tips over "by accident" or the baby's milk bottle begins to choke him. The readers may remember the motion picture *Throw Mamma From the Train* in which Danny DeVito hires someone to kill his mother. At the end of the film, he has become so guilty about his murderous thoughts that he plies her with flowers and candy and tells her how much he loves her, surely one of the most repulsive creatures ever depicted in film history.

Omnipotence. People using this defense are protecting themselves against feelings of inferiority by ascribing to themselves superior attributes or powers that set them above others. Omnipotent thinking and behavior can be very easily observed in small children who pretend they are Superman flying through the air. Adolescents who have a negative self-esteem will try to bolster their self-confidence by displaying a know-it-all exterior; flashy clothes, souped-up cars, the adoption of an aggressive posture, and a "tough" personality style. Anyone recognize these adolescents? Generally speaking, they are not doing well academically. Nor have they found much recognition in sports or other high-school activities.

Devaluation. Some people deal with their sense of inferiority by devaluating the talent, attractiveness, or abilities of others. Most readers will remember how academically bright students in high school were devaluated as "nerds." The athletically talented student was devaluated as a "stupid jock." Students who develop a good relationship with a teacher or who contribute to class discussions were devaluated as "brown-noses" or as "trying to earn brownie points." Listen to workers talk about a person who got a significant raise or promotion. Only the most mature individuals will admit the person deserved it. Less mature workers will attribute the raise or promotion to "favoritism," "sucking up," or "she probably got her promotion in bed."

Displacement. If someone is threatening us and we are unable to "strike back" at that person, we may transfer our wishes and actions onto a substitute person or object. Generally, the substitute person or object has less power and cannot retaliate and so is "safe" to aggress against. The classic example in most textbooks goes something like this: The boss shouts his anger at his employee. When the employee goes home, he snaps at his wife. His wife doesn't want to further upset him so she "keeps the peace" by not retorting. But at home, she becomes "fault-finding" toward her children. One of the children displaces his hurt feelings by kicking the dog.

BUT AREN'T THERE ANY HEALTHY DEFENSE MECHANISMS?

By this time, the reader may be wondering if there are any *healthy* defense mechanisms. That's a touchy question because as long as we are reacting to pain, we are on the defensive, and it is difficult to respond to situations in creative ways if we are on the defensive. What makes them more constructive is that a) they do not do injury to others; b) they are not destructive to ourselves; and c) they may even promote our psychological growth.

Self-Observation. Basic to all higher-level defenses is the ability to examine our own feelings and thoughts through the process variously called self-examination, introspection, meditation, meditative prayer, and so forth. It is not easy to penetrate our defenses since they were erected in order to prevent us from insight. To be truly self-observing takes honesty, stamina, and courage. We have to be willing to see our faults and our own culpability in any situation. We must strive to determine how we participated, no matter how innocently, in the event. *What did we do to hurt someone's feelings so that they have gotten angry with us or refuse to talk to us? How did we phrase a sentence so that we hurt someone else unintentionally? How did we actually invite a behavior that was injurious to us?*

Suppression. Suppression is confused with repression, so let's make the distinction clear. Repression inhibits the *conscious* knowledge of the wish, thought, or event, while suppression inhibits only the *behavior*. *Suppression* means we remain *conscious* of the impulse, but we do not act it out. The classic textbook example goes like this: Our spouse yells at us for no apparent reason. We may want to hit our spouse in return. If we repress our feelings, we no longer remain aware of that urge to hit. If we remain aware that we would really like to sock our spouse, but refrain from doing it, then we are using the defense of suppression. We are in control of our behaviors.

Affiliation. Affiliation means turning for help to people who can help us sort out our feelings and suggest alternative actions. We do not drop our problems into their laps. What we do is to share our concerns and problems and get their feedback. Obviously, the therapeutic situation is a very appropriate environment for this kind of sharing and feedback, but it is not the only one. We may have close friends who hold what we say in absolute confidence. If our concerns or problems are work-oriented, we may be able to find a **mentor**, an older person who can counsel us. If we are affiliated with a church, we may be able to discuss the situation with our minister, rabbi, or priest.

Altruism. One way to cope with our conflicts is through altruistic service to others. Do not confuse *altruism* with the self-sacrificing behavior of the *martyrdom syndrome*. The family and friends of a martyr may eventually realize that the person's self-sacrificing is a type of control. She has succeeded in making others feel guilty in order to get them "to do" for her. By contrast, altruism is not self-sacrificing. Truly altruistic persons experience joy when they are able to help others become more self-supporting or help them over a crisis in their lives. Good examples of altruistic behaviors can be observed when persons who have suffered trauma help others who are in a similar situation. The father of Adam Walsh, a little boy who was kidnapped and murdered, formed an organization to help other parents search for their missing children.

Humor. What humor does is to drain some of the negative charge out of a painful situation. When we are able to see the sheer idiocy of an offensive person's behavior, we can smile (to ourselves) instead of getting angry. Or if we can reply to an angry criticism by a humorous retort, we not only save face, but enable the other person to see the irony of the situation. Abraham Lincoln was a master of this kind of humor. Lincoln was a very tall man with long, gangly legs. His appearance was often ridiculed by the opposition party. To a critic who asked him how long should a man's legs be, he replied, "Just long enough to reach the ground." Such humorous retorts can defuse even the most self-righteous criticism.

Sublimation. We can also channel socially unacceptable motivations into behaviors that are socially acceptable and that may even gain the approval of our society. Sports may be a way for channeling aggressive behavior into behaviors that provide public entertainment and in which no one (it is hoped) gets seriously hurt. Voyeurs (peeping Toms) may sublimate their desire to look at naked bodies by becoming artists who paint nudes. A pyromaniac may sublimate his desire to play with fire by becoming . . . (what else?) a fireman. Incidentally, psychologists have been called voyeurs as well, since we seem to like to peek inside peoples' private worlds.

Anticipation. A highly adaptive coping style to perceived threats is to consider possible consequences or emotional reactions in advance of the event. Professionals refer to this type of anticipation as "worse case scenarios." To be forewarned is to be forearmed! But it is not enough to simply imagine serious consequences. That is only the first step. The second step is to plan alternate courses of action. Let's take a very real-life example close to the hearts of most students. Let us suppose the readers are going to have to enroll in a course in which they believe themselves to be at "high risk" for failure. If they use anticipation to contend with their anxiety, they first acknowledge their anxieties: they won't do well or may even receive a failing grade. They then devise alternative educational plans for themselves. They may take a pre–college-level course to bolster their academic skills. They can participate in a tutorial lab situation to get extra practice in the assignments. They could get themselves an individual tutor to help them get through the course. But supposing their worst fears are being realized and they are in danger of failing, another alternate plan would be to withdraw from the course before the drop deadline. These are all constructive ways to use anticipatory coping strategies.

Self-Assertion. Self-assertion is dealing with an emotional conflict by expressing our feelings to another, not in anger or by trying to "cast blame." True self-assertion is not easily acquired for a number of reasons. Many of us have become afraid of hurting other people's feelings and prefer to "suffer in silence." Others of us are so used to being verbally aggressive that it is difficult to learn more respectful communication methods. Self-assertiveness is a fine line between verbal aggression and submissiveness. It is such a subtle skill that courses in self-assertiveness abound in colleges, universities, and professional workshops.

Suppose a person asks us to do something we don't want to do. It may not be illegal, but there is something "unsavory" about the request. If we don't have positive self-esteem, we may comply with their request—even though it goes against our moral/ethical grain. On the other hand, if we respond with verbal aggression, we may shout derisive comments, such as, "Are you crazy? How dare you!" A self-assertive response might be, "Doing that would make me uncomfortable so I think I have to say no this time."

BOX **3.9** STUDENTS VERBATIM
On Their Defense Mechanisms

Male (17 years): I'm taller now but when I was in grade school, I was pretty short, shorter than the other guys. So I used to get called names like "Short Stop" and "Shorty" and "Pip Squeak" and "Mighty Mouse." It wasn't that the guys didn't like me. They did like me and I got along good with everybody until they called me these names. It was just a tease, like, but it used to make me so mad, I'd fight them. Honest. Just haul off and let them have it. I got taken to the office a lot of times. It was like I couldn't help myself. Talk about physical aggression. That was me. No more. Anyway, I've grown taller since then.

BOX **3.9** STUDENTS VERBATIM (continued)
On Their Defense Mechanisms

Female (19 years): When I was in high school, I was fat. So I would just sit in the house and wouldn't go anywhere. I felt sluggish and I used to take so many naps, my mother thought I was sick and took me to the doctor. He said I must be hypothyroid or something. I knew I wasn't sick. I was just depressed only I couldn't tell anyone. I got out of my depression by going on a diet and walking three miles a day. As I began to lose weight, I began to feel better. I didn't sleep as much. I got to feel energetic, especially when I got into size 10 clothes. Today I feel great.

Female (20 years): When I was in high school, I was going with this good-looking jock who was on the football team. I felt so lucky he chose me to go to the Junior Prom with him. It didn't take long for us to get intimate. I was nuts about him. Then some of my girlfriends kept telling me he was cheating on me. I didn't want to believe it. When I asked him about it, he said they were making up stories because they were jealous. I chose to believe him. I kind of knew my girlfriends were telling me the truth. I was just in denial, I guess. Finally, I caught him and this other girl in bed together in my apartment. Can you imagine? In my apartment. In my bed!!!

Male (28 years): I'd been trying to quit smoking for years. But I kept making up excuses why I couldn't.

I was studying for a test. I'd quit after my exams. I had to go to my summer reserve unit for a month. I couldn't quit until I got out because you had to smoke with all the guys. I would think up one excuse after another why I couldn't quit just then. Rationalizations one after the other. By the way, I finally quit. Glad I did.

Male (24 years): When I was in high school, I used to make fun of the guys who were making good grades. I used to call them "nerds" and (excuse the expression) "brown nosers." Now that I'm in college and getting pretty good grades, I can see how childish I was by devaluating the guys who got good grades.

Female (28 years): This is not about me but I was the cause of someone else's denial. When I was 14 years I finally admitted to myself I was lesbian. I went in to tell my mother. I said, "Mom, I'm lesbian." She said, "No, you're not. Go make me a cup of coffee." And that was it. She just was not going to accept the fact that I am lesbian. I didn't mention it to her again for years.

Reflection Writing: Recall an incident in which you used a defense mechanism and describe how you used it. Then look over the more constructive defenses, and describe how you could use one of them today, given the same situation.

Important Terms and Concepts to Know

• aggression	• Elektra	• material	• rationalization
• altruism	• five	• midlife	• reality
• anxiety	• four	• neoFreudians	• spiritual
• autonomy	• generativity	• neurosis	• superego
• character	• genitals	• nurturing	• task
• compensation	• humor	• obsessive-compulsive	• theme(s)
• competence	• id	• Oedipal	• theorist
• conscience	• individuated	• oral	• trait
• crisis	• inferiority	• order	• trust
• devaluation	• injurious	• passive-dependent	
• displacement	• libidinal	• penis	
• eight	• lie	• psychosexual	

Make Your Own Chapter Summary by Filling in the Blanks

Use the "Important Terms and Concepts to Know" to fill in the blanks.

Sigmund Freud. Freud was the first personality _____, which means he provided us with the first comprehensive analysis of how we grow and develop as human beings. He posited _____ stages of the _____ drive, the drive for pleasure. He divided human personality into three aspects: the _____, which is what we are born as; the _____, which is composed of all the "voices of society" and which Freud equated with the _____; and finally the ego, which mediates between the other two. In the _____ stage, the libido is centered around the mouth; in the anal stage, it is centered on the anus; and in the phallic stage, it is focused on the _____. In the anal stage, the pleasure-pain principle is replaced with the _____ principle, which means that the baby's drive for pleasure is mediated by the possibility of dire consequences. During the phallic stage, the little boy develops an ardent love for his mother, called the _____ complex. The little girl develops an ardent love for her father, called the _____ complex. This "normal" development of the _____ stages sometimes goes awry and the child is emotionally fixated at an earlier level, which Freud called _____. An example of the _____ neurosis is the inability or refusal to clean up after oneself. The _____ neurosis is marked by fear of dirt and germs, and incessant cleaning. The _____ agreed with Freud's concept of

the strong libido as a drive, but posited other motivations that determine human personality as well.

Alfred Adler. Adler posited the need for _____ and power. At the same time, he described the neurosis of over-_____, which is a desire to win out over others. He is best known for his _____-superiority complex. He believed that to become integrated personalities, we must stop living a life _____, and get in touch with the underlying _____ of our lives. It was Adler, also, who first called our attention to the effects of birth _____.

Carl Jung. Jung brought back the _____ dimension of human personality into psychology. He developed _____ age/stages of the life span. In and around age 40, men and women may experience a _____ crisis. If this crisis is resolved successfully, men in Western society have a chance to become more _____ because it is in the "second half" of life that they can acquire transpersonal (spiritual) values in place of their previous _____ values during the first half of life. Women who have spent their lives _____ others, may choose to develop their cognitive and creative abilities.

Erik Erikson. Erikson expanded Jung's four stages into _____ psychosocial stages. Each of these stages has a life _____ to be resolved, and a life _____ to be achieved. Each successful resolution achieves a positive personality _____. The first life task is that of basic _____. The next stage is called _____, which develops about the time the child is beginning to walk and be toilet trained. And so it goes. The life task after the midlife crisis is _____ when we value fostering the growth and creativity of younger people who will take our place in society.

The Defense Mechanisms. It was Freud who explained that our defense mechanisms help protect us from the pain of _____ but, unfortunately, they are barriers to our emotional growth and can be _____ to others. The most primitive defense mechanism is physical _____ when we try to hurt someone else. When we invent excuses, we are using the defense of _____. Teenagers in high school typically use the defense of _____ when others prove to be superior in some way. Taking out our pain on someone who can not retaliate is called _____. Two constructive defenses are the use of _____, a mechanism often used by Abraham Lincoln, and _____, turning our own hurtful experience into helping others in a similar circumstance.

4

Parenting Babies and Young Children
From Conception to Preschool

BOX **4.1** SCENARIO
What's the Right Way to Raise Children?

The instructor has been discussing the many problems that parents face in raising children.

Martha: So what's the right way to raise children?

Professor Weitzman: (laughing) You have just asked the traditional American question.

Jonnimae: A baby doesn't come with a manual of instructions.

Professor Weitzman: That aphorism sums it up rather neatly. We know a lot of things that are *not* good to do but there are few hard and fast rules about what is right to do. It depends on so many other variables: The child's genetic structure, the child's personality "type," sibling rank order, gender, and even the traditions the parents have come from.

Li Ho: I'm going to pick up on what you just mentioned—traditions. My families on both sides are very tradition-oriented—like filial piety, meaning they want us to respect them and use their wisdom in guiding our lives. Their traditions differ somewhat and I respect both of their traditions—a lot. But their traditions don't always fit into what's going on today. Here I am living in the computer age and still trying to please my parents who don't even understand what is meant by the "information society." They still believe that children should listen and I have had to contend with that. But what will happen when I present them with grandchildren who are loud and rowdy and haven't been taught to be so respectful?

Professor Weitzman: What Li has just said applies to our society in general. In previous eras, young parents could rely on centuries-old traditions to guide them—a kind of tribal parenting. Today we are being influenced by a mix of cultural models, subcultural models—even TV family sitcom models. We are living in a time when each new set of parents has to make parenting decisions on their own. That's not easy. We're all beginning at Square One again.

Martha: In other words, there is no right way to raise kids . . . only "wrong" ways.

Professor Weitzman: Well, I wouldn't put it quite that way. But I do say modern parenting is a paradoxical situation. Most young people genuinely assume that the job of parenting "comes naturally." The trouble is that what comes naturally is that we generally imitate how our parents raised us. They are the role models that have been "hard wired" in us—without our even being aware of it.

Alec: If that's true, I sure don't want to have children. My father beat the hell out of us when we didn't jump at his commands.

Professor Weitzman: In that case, Alec, your parents may be role models of a different sort—negative role models.

Li Ho: Negative role models? What's that?

Professor Weitzman: It's trying to do things in reverse from the role models we have inherited. Alec, for example, shudders when he thinks how his father raised him—which may lead him to try to do everything quite oppositely from the way he was raised.

Alec: You bet I will!

Eduardo: But, Alec, that may just lead you into doing things that may not really be good either. You would be just reacting and not thinking about what you are doing—if you can understand what I'm saying—like playing defensively instead of offensively. I'm not sure how to express it.

Professor Weitzman: Parenting is probably more difficult today in our society than it has ever been before. Yet when things go wrong, others in our society are too willing to point a blaming finger at the parents who have done everything as well as they have known how to do. In fact, so difficult is it to raise children that it is high on the list of reasons for divorce. Parents fight continually over each other's treatment of the child and what the children are expected or not expected to do. We all want to raise our children to be loving, intelligent, authentic,

BOX **4.1** SCENARIO (continued)
What's the Right Way to Raise Children

assertive, morally responsible adults. How to do that . . . is the question.

Martha: A lot of things my parents did with us I wouldn't want to do with my kids. Yelling was part of our family environment. But, gosh, the love that was all around. It poured out like the spaghetti sauce on pasta—that was something marvelous. That feeling of being loved is something I do want to hang on to. But I truly don't want to yell at them any more like my

family does, and they don't even realize they are yelling. I love my Italian heritage. It is warm and family-oriented, and secure, but I do want to stop the yelling.

Professor Weitzman: Martha, all I can say is that if we truly let our children know we love them genuinely and sincerely, and admit to them when we have made mistakes, they will forgive us. When we can say, "I'm sorry," to them, children are remarkably forgiving.

THE CHILD'S PERSONALITY DEVELOPMENT: *A MIX OF MANY FACTORS*

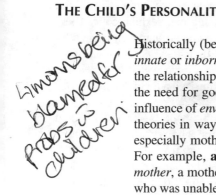

Historically (before the publication of Freud's works), the child's personality was attributed to *innate* or *inborn* causes, what today we would call *genetics* or *nature*. When Freud discovered the relationship of a person's personality to early childhood experiences, we became aware of the need for good nurturing, particularly for the baby and young child. Today we call that the influence of *environment* or *nurture*. However, American psychology oversubscribed to Freud's theories in ways that Freud himself would probably never have approved. American parents, especially mothers, were blamed for almost everything that was "wrong" with their children. For example, **autism**, characterized by a lack of language, was attributed to a *schizogenic mother*, a mother who had so severely neglected or rejected her baby that it resulted in a child who was unable to relate to human beings. We know now that autism is the result of damage to the brain (Rodier, 2003). The damage can occur during pregnancy (nurture) or it can be the result of the child's genetics (nature). One of the basic questions of the science of psychology is just this: *How much of human personality is the result of genetics and how much is the result of environment?* Psychologists call it the **nature/nurture controversy** (see Tip 4.1).

Children Come Into the World with Different Personality Temperaments

Disgusted by the way mothers were being blamed for everything that was wrong with their children, a research team, composed of a pediatrician, a physician, and a psychologist, decided to investigate this assumption (Chess, Thomas, & Birch, 1976). They undertook a large empirical study to compare "families with problem children" with "families of children growing well." What they concluded from their investigation was something that parents had been saying for years: *Children are just born differently.*

Tip 4.1 On the Basic Questions of Science. Every science has basic questions it seeks to answer. For example, physics is attempting to answer such questions as: *What is the nature of the universe? Is it expanding or contracting? Did it have a beginning and will it have an ending?* Biology attempts to answer questions like: *What is life? How is all life related?* Psychology has its basic questions as well. The nature/nurture question is one. Another is called the mind/body problem: *How do the "mind" and "body" interact or are they one and the same thing?* A third burning issue, at the present time, concerns the question of intelligence; namely, *just what is intelligence and how should it be defined?*

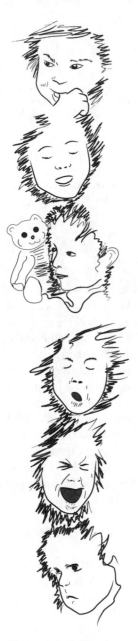

As far as the team of researchers were concerned, the differences in personality style had little, if anything, to do with the family environment. They did discern that there were four distinctly different kinds of baby temperaments, which they described as the *easy* child, the *slow-to-warm* child, the *difficult* child, and the *changeable* child. The researchers concluded that parents have been blamed "too much" and "too long" for the difficulties their children may have.

The **easy child**, which made up 40 percent of the sample, has a generally moderate activity level, is generally positive and cheerful in mood, has a low or moderate intensity of reaction, is adaptable, and quickly establishes regular sleeping and feeding schedules. Later this child participates easily in school routines. The **slow-to-warm child**, 15 percent of the sample, has a moderate activity level, but, unlike the easy child, tends to withdraw from new situations and is slow to adapt. These children are somewhat negative in mood and need some time to get used to new routines. Once they do become familiar with the routine, they do what is asked of them. They just need a little time to adapt. The **difficult child**, 10 percent of the sample, is difficult from birth. This child has difficulty eating and sleeping; many exhibit colic. These children find it hard to adapt to new situations and cry a great deal in their later childhood. Their crying has a characteristic quality that their parents find unnerving. Finally, there is the **changeable child**, 35 percent of the sample, who doesn't seem to fit very neatly into any category and who seems to go through a lot of "phases."

The Genetics of Personality. There is no doubt about it: Much of who and what we are, we have inherited from our forebears. The research evidence is becoming more and more evident as studies have come in from all over the world. That is not to say that we are completely determined by our heredity, but it does substantiate the conclusions of Chess, Thomas, and Birch that babies come into this world with definite personality traits. We have long known that physical traits, such as color blindness, baldness, diabetes, and alcoholism run in families. But it is only in the last fifty or so years that we have become aware of the many mental disorders that have a strong genetic component. The evidence for the nature side of the nature/nurture question comes from many statistical studies from world-wide sources. These studies include the following types of research methodologies:

- Twin studies: identical twins separated at birth and raised in different environments.
- Studies of genetic defects among relatives: parents, siblings, cousins, children, etc.
- Comparisons of adopted children with their biological versus adoptive families.
- Molecular biology: the study of DNA material and personality traits.

Figure 4.1 Babies Are Born Different. The Chess, Thomas, and Birch team discovered four distinct personalities in babies.

One of the most famous of these "twin studies" is that initiated by psychologist Thomas Bouchard in 1970, at the University of Minnesota. Bouchard reported that when he started his study he was clearly in the *nurture* camp rather than in the *nature* camp. But after bringing together some adult identical twins who had been separated at birth and raised in different environments, he and his team of researchers found themselves absolutely "spooked" by the extraordinary similarities. The University of Minnesota has continued this line of research studies ever since, and publishes updates of their findings every so often. At the present time, the **concordance rate** (the percentage of twins who exhibit the same trait) hovers between 50 and 75 percent, depending on the specific trait. The thumbnail sketches of some of the identical twins are absolutely astonishing (see Box 4.2).

Ethnically and Racially Distinct Characteristics

When a population remains stable over a period of centuries (does not move to other areas of the globe and does not interbreed with other populations), certain genes increase in frequency in that gene pool—for good and for ill! Africans have a deficient gene in their genetic

---

BOX **4.2** RESEARCH METHODOLOGY
The Twin Studies (Genetics Are Constant and Environment Varies)

For almost 40 years, the University of Minnesota has been the site of an investigation on the characteristics of identical twins. Some of these twins, who were separated at birth and brought together for the first time; showed such extraordinary similarities that the researchers were actually "spooked" by their similarities, despite the enormous differences of their adoptive family environments. Some of the outstanding examples will illuminate this finding.

The Jim Twins. The research study began with the study of identical twins who, by some strange token, were both named "Jim." They were both adopted into working-class Ohio families, but never knew each other before the study. Both were good in math but poor in spelling. Both had worked as part-time deputy sheriffs. Both vacationed in Florida. Both preferred Chevrolets. Both like the same brands of liquor and cigarettes. And as if that were not enough, when they got anxious, they both chewed their fingernails to the nub.

The Ring Twins. Bridget and Dorothy were 39 years old when they met for the first time. Both twins had an extraordinary fondness for beautiful hands. Not only did they both have manicured nails, they both wore seven rings on their hands and three bracelets.

Roger and Tony Twins. Roger was raised in Florida by highly educated Jewish parents and Tony by an Italian family in Philadelphia. They were found to have identical IQ scores and similar jobs. They liked the same toothpaste, aftershave lotion, and cigarettes, and the same type of women . . . , and (get this!) they had similar giftgiving preferences. After they met, they gave each other a surprise gift: identical shirt-and-tie sets.

The German/Jewish Twins. But perhaps the most extraordinary example is that of two boys, one raised by a German Nazi mother, the other by his Jewish Hispanic father in the Caribbean. Besides looking very much alike, both wore pin-striped suits, a small mustache, and rimless glasses. Considering the extreme differences of their growing up, the investigators were amazed at their similarities.

The strong personality genetics of twin studies have been confirmed by a massive Swedish study involving five hundred pairs of Swedish twins, both identical and fraternal. So far, the personality factors listed below have been established as having a strong genetic component and the list keeps growing!

Mental Factors	Anxiety/Emotional Factors	Worldview	Work and Leisure
Intelligence (IQ)	Alcohol & drug addiction	Optimism	Television viewing
Mental speed	Self-esteem & shyness	Alienation	Leadership
	Crime & violence	Religiosity	Job satisfaction
	Depression & "neuroticism"	Authoritarianism	Thrill-seeking
	Extraversion & dominance	Traditionalism	

Sources: Blonigen et al., 2003; Bouchard et al., 1990.

BOX **4.2** RESEARCH METHODOLOGY (continued)
The Twin Studies (Genetics Are Constant and Environment Varies)

Criticism of the Twin Studies

1. **Concordance Rate Is Only 50–75 Percent.** If genetics were the sole causative factor of personality traits, the concordance rate would be 100 percent or very close.
2. **Environment Plays Equal Part.** Critics have warned us not to fall into the nature camp too wholeheartedly. If the heritability traits hover around 50 percent, it still leaves 50 percent to the environment.

3. **Blaming the Victim.** By focusing on the genetic aspect of personality, we are ignoring the real causes of violence and crime; namely, poverty, racism, illiteracy, and unemployment. Biology may contribute to violence but environment tips the balance.

---

pool that makes them susceptible to sickle-cell anemia. Northern Europeans are susceptible to phenylketonuria (PKU), which, if not treated, can result in mental and physical retardation. Mediterranean peoples, such as Italians, Greeks, and North African Arabs, are susceptible to thalassemia anemia. East European Jews are susceptible to Tay-Sach's Disease. Both Jews and Africans have higher-than-average allergic reactions to milk products. The genetic differences of these populations do not mean they are inferior. Despite the pride that the royal families of Europe take in their "royal blood," their inbreeding has produced a high frequency of hemophilia. So much for the superiority of royal blood!

On the other hand, stable genetic pools can produce other characteristics that are not so unfavorable. The Scandinavians and Highland Scots of Europe, the Masai of Africa, and the Sioux Nation of America are genetically tall. Does that mean that they are superior? No, only that they are taller. We are finally getting over our nervousness about racial and ethnic differences and are able to celebrate our multicultural diversity. In addition to physical characteristics, research has even revealed that "emotionality" differs significantly in different racial and ethnic groups (Freedman, 1974). For example: When a loose, tented handkerchief is placed over the faces of neonates, Native American and Chinese American babies adjust their heads slightly, but go on sleeping. Caucasian children, on the other hand, raise a hue and cry until the tented handkerchiefs are removed.

Environmental Influences

What we used to think was that the developing baby in the womb was safely ensconced in its watery environment and, more-or-less, protected by the placenta from environmental toxins. We had debunked the old wives' tale that if a pregnant woman suffered a severe shock, her child would be deformed. Oh, yes, we knew that certain infectious diseases, such as scarlet fever and *rubella* (German measles) might penetrate the placenta and cause severe damage to the growing child (blindness and deafness, for example), even death. But it was thought that these were just unusually virulent diseases.

Toxic Penetrance Factors. But then physicians began to observe that other toxins were definitely penetrating the placenta. For example, if some pregnant women, perhaps ten percent, imbibed in alcohol—even as little as three ounces a week—it could result in **fetal alcohol syndrome (FAS)**, a serious birth defect that results in physical deformities and mental retardation. Three ounces of alcohol is only a glass or two of wine per week, or perhaps two bottles of beer. Almost coincidentally, physicians were observing the birth of "crack babies," the result of the mother's use of cocaine and other drugs. It was becoming apparent that the placenta wasn't the protective shield against toxins as was previously believed.

Perhaps the wake-up call for the medical and pharmaceutical professions came with the appearance of the **thalidomide babies**. In the late 1950s, European and Canadian physicians were prescribing thalidomide for morning sickness of pregnant women. We don't know how many babies were actually affected because thousands were still born or died before they were one year old. But finally, in 1961, the medical profession finally realized that the thalidomide drug was producing babies born, not with normal hands, arms, feet, or legs, but with flipper-like appendages. These birth defects were particularly great when the drug was given during the **embryo** stage of development (the first three months of pregnancy). Upon this discovery, the drug was immediately withdrawn from the world market. Fortunately, thalidomide had *not* been approved by the American Food and Drug Administration (FDA), and only a few thalidomide babies were born to pregnant American women living in other countries. At the present time, there are approximately 5,000 adults who are survivors of that catastrophe. We can be justly proud of our Food and Drug Administration because it refused to release it to the medical profession until stringent tests had been performed.

Poor Nutrition: Low Birth-Weight and Obese Babies. Physicians also became concerned about the consequences of *low birth-weight* babies (5.5 pounds or under). Not only are these babies born with underdeveloped lungs and severe respiratory problems, they may have other health problems later in life, such as breast cancer, diabetes, and even heart disease (Abel, 1997; Begley, 2003). Poor nutrition is generally associated with poor families, but low birth-weight babies are not only found among economically deprived populations. In middle- and upper-socioeconomic classes, the desire of women to stay as slim as possible during and after pregnancy has also led to the birth of low-weight babies.

Today, physicians are becoming more and more concerned, not only about how much food pregnant women eat, but also what kind of food they are eating. French fries and greasy hamburgers are not only poor in nutritive value, but the grease may result in a child whose metabolism turns much of what they eat into fat, resulting not just in fat babies but in obese babies. Longitudinal studies have revealed that obese babies become obese adults. So concerned is the American Medical Association (AMA) about obesity in babies, that it has alerted all the social science and health organizations to do what they can by way of public awareness and prevention. Chubby babies may look cute and healthy, but they may, in fact, be already showing signs of life-long obesity, leading to serious illnesses and a shorter life-span.

A New View of Life-in-the-Womb: Amazing Fetal Sensitivity

Despite our deepening awareness of the many penetrance factors that can affect the growing child, until the last ten years, we really didn't know how truly sensitive the fetus is to environmental factors. In the last two decades, we have gained an entirely new understanding of what the child-in-the-womb is experiencing. Let's take hearing, for example. By four months the **fetus** (the growing child from four months to birth) can react to loud noises, such as the slam of a door or car backfiring. (We know this because mothers report a sudden fetal jerk.) By six months, it can hear much quieter sounds, such as people speaking. Even more intriguing, it seems the unborn child can distinguish its mother's voice toward the eighth month of prenatal development, because its heart beat will slow down when its mother is talking. Some believe that the sound of mother's pleasant voice has a calming influence on the fetus (Begley, 2003; Pekkanen, 2001).

Would you be surprised (as we were) to learn that, toward the end of pregnancy, the child seems to be able to taste and smell? Physicians have long observed that the **amniotic fluid** (the fluid in which the baby floats) can have a distinct odor of food, such as curry or garlic or onion. Perhaps that is why children have distinct food preferences. Born to a Hispanic mother, the Hispanic baby may already have a taste for chili and hot tamales. As well, it appears that, although the womb is dark, the unborn child may react to—and be damaged by—strong external light shining directly on the mother's stomach, precisely the kind of bright lights of an examining room or a delivery room (Begley, 2003; Pekkanen, 2001).

Prenatal Factors and Personality Development. Social scientists are now investigating the relationship of prenatal factors and personality factors. For example, we know that every time a pregnant woman takes a puff off her cigarette, her unborn child's heart beats faster. There is also evidence that smoking during pregnancy does increase the risk of premature birth, hyperactivity, and diminished "IQ." *If this is true, can learning problems, such as attention deficit/hyperactive disorder (AD/HD) be traced to prenatal factors?* Another example: Some prescribed medications (such as tranquilizers) are **depressants**, that is, they slow down the action of the nervous system. Even many over-the-counter drugs that we generally believe to be safe (such as cough medicines) contain nervous system depressants. *Do tranquilizers and cough suppressants contribute to a depressive personality later in life?*

As yet, the research is unclear about this connection, but it is just as well if pregnant mothers avoid any kind of medication without consulting their gynecologist. Because some drugs take a few days, even a few weeks, to be completely flushed out of the body, the medical professions advise eliminating all drugs the moment the woman begins to think about having a child–long before conception!

The medical profession has also become very concerned about the many toxic ingredients in our food, in our drinking water, and in our air; for example, polychlorinated biphenyls (PCBs). Known to have a detrimental effect on the neurological and intellectual development of the fetus, PCBs have been found in fish (particularly bottom feeders), fatty meats such as cold cuts, and even in many dairy products (Pekkanen, 2001). We are not trying to worry the reader unduly. We are alerting you to the need for social concern about the worldwide use of both chemical fertilizers and pesticides.

Unwanted Children and Their Later Lack of Self-Esteem. Whether because there are already too many children, not enough money to pay the bills, or because the mother is an unwed teenager, the pregnant woman may not want her child. We already know that if a woman is depressed about her pregnancy in any way, it may alter her hormones which, in turn, will adversely affect her child. Some of this theory is still speculative, but the relationship between one prenatal factor and a child's later personality has been clearly established—the unwanted child. Expectant mothers were interviewed during their pregnancy as to whether their pregnancies were wanted or not. The children born to them were interviewed several times during their childhood, as well as when they were 18 years and 23 years. What the researchers discovered was that the unwanted children had significantly poorer self-esteem and poorer academic grades than children who were wanted (Ainsworth, 1979; Axin, Barber, & Thornton, 1998).

Maternal Stress. Finally, we come to the possible effects of maternal stress. If there are problems in the mother's environment, if there is spouse abuse, too many children to care for, or not enough money to pay bills, she is experiencing environmental stress. We have been aware for some time that the hormones of the pregnant woman are continually bathing the developing fetus. *Since stress changes the hormonal balance of her body, can it be that the mother's own anger or fear can produce an aggressive or fearful child?* There is a hint of such a relationship now, and it may not be too many years in the future that researchers will be able to provide us with some definitive answers.

How other influences of the uterine environment affects the unborn child remains to be seen. In the meantime, it might be wise to take to heart that old folk's tale in specific ways. To avoid contagious diseases, the health professions are suggesting that pregnant women should avoid crowds, particularly at the holiday seasons. The more people you come into contact with, the higher the chance of rubbing shoulders with someone who is ill. If possible, the pregnant woman should avoid contact with people who have "just a cold." That could might be a virus and a virus can penetrate the placenta. Finally, and above all, the pregnant woman surely needs a home environment that is secure, peaceful, and free from worry and strife.

BIRTHING AND PARENTING THE NEW BABY: WELCOMING THE "NEW IMMIGRANT" INTO OUR WORLD

Gentle Birthing

Physicians used to bring forth the baby in the bright lights and cold temperature of the operating room, cut the umbilical cord as soon as possible, wipe the baby's eyes with silver nitrate, turn him upside down, and spank the baby's bottom to encourage breathing (see Figure 4.2). Such were the birthing procedures even as recently as thirty to forty years ago. Then the **gentle birth** philosophy and procedures of the French physician, Dr. Frederick Leboyer (1975) were introduced into this country. It took a while for the medical professions to appreciate what Leboyer was saying; namely, that Western birthing procedures, with its poking and jabbing and spanking, was not a welcoming into the extrauterine world, but a vicious introduction.

Leboyer's intent was to make the baby's first experience in our world more welcoming and more loving. He redesigned the birthing procedures. Leboyer's babies were ushered into a dimly lit, very hushed, and very warm room—an environment as similar as possible to the dark, warm, quiet environment of the womb. Right after birth, the baby was placed on the mother's abdomen (close to where he had been growing for nine months) and where he could feel his mother's familiar heart beat. The umbilical cord was not severed until it stopped pulsating (about six minutes after birth) and then the baby was lowered into a basin of warm water. The warm water was not just to clean the baby, but also to allow him to rest for a few

Figure 4.2 Gentle Birth. Frederick Leboyer took birth trauma seriously and campaigned against "violent birth."

minutes in a womb-like fluid that has less gravitational pressure. Leboyer made the assumption that this gentle birth must reduce the birth trauma and have a positive effect on the baby's personality.

There have been precious few research studies on the Leboyer babies, but to the list of amazing fetal sensitivities must be added the experience of being born. Today, the obstetrics profession has adopted most, if not all, of Leboyer's birthing procedures. As well, natural birthing places, such as midwifery homes, have sprung up throughout Western society. The intent is to use as many of Leboyer's gentle birth procedures, including making the delivery room as much like a home place as possible rather than as a hospital operating room.

Bonding and Attachment in Early Infancy

Another classic study that fits very neatly into the study of unwanted children described previously was that done by Ainsworth and her research team (Ainsworth, 1979). In the first part of the twentieth century, the newborn baby was whisked off to the nursery, sometimes for as long as six to twelve hours. The intention was well-meaning—so that the mother could rest from her labors—but the consequences were not good. The very important *mother-baby bonding* could be severely damaged. The child may have refused to breast-feed and cried at any attempt to have it do so. The mother may have then felt inadequate about her mothering skills. Or she may have developed *post-partum depression* ("the blues" that can occur after she births a child). If the mother-baby bonding is disrupted, the child may never develop a strong **attachment** to its mother. Strong attachment in infancy is associated with **separation anxiety** from the mother; i.e., the child cries or shows other distressed behaviors when the mother leaves, and goes to her eagerly on her return.

Children with weak attachment do not show the same kind of distress. Instead, they seem to be indifferent, confused, or angry at her departure, and they do not go to her easily when she returns. An earlier study had already revealed that when children in war-torn countries were left too long in orphanages or hospitals, they began to withdraw from human contact (Bowlby, 1980). Ainsworth's study was significant in that it was also longitudinal. The quality and strength of the attachment, strong or weak, proved to have long-lasting effects. At 11 years of age, the children with strong attachment had closer friendship ties and better social skills. As adolescents and adults, they were more able to form more intimate love relationships. Because they were comfortable with new situations, they enjoyed learning new things, and that proved to be significant for successful academic achievement (Shulman, Elicker & Stroufe, 1994; Weiss, 1986).

Positive Parenting of the Infant: Birth to Two Years

Repeating again our concern that textbooks tend to emphasize the negative aspects of living, we turn our attention to some guidelines for positive parenting. Notice that we use the term "guidelines." What may work for one child may not work for another child. A good example is a child's response to taking naps. Most babies and young children do not fuss about being tucked into their cribs at nap time and, in fact, you may discover they have already fallen asleep on couch or floor when nap time is approaching. But not all children. There are some children who resist nap time strenuously. They just seem to go and go and go, causing mothers to be anxious that their toddlers are not getting enough sleep. If this is true of the reader's toddler, check with a pediatrician, and if the pediatrician says the child is healthy, you can relax. Some children are "just born that way" (a theme you've read before and will, very likely, read again).

But aside from these unusual individual differences, there are many ways to foster healthy personalities in children. These activities are generally what used to be called old-fashioned "mothering" skills. Today, we acknowledge the ability of fathers to care for their young babies and children, so we use the term *caregiving* instead. Parenting and baby books provide many such caregiving skills and the reader can look over the vast array now available from booksellers or in your public library. Employ the caregiving skills you feel comfortable with and that seem to fit both you and the baby. The caregiving skills we are focusing on here have to do with communicating love and tenderness via all the child's senses.

Communicating Through the Sense of Touch. The sense of touch is the most basic sense we have. Only a few hours old, the newborn infants exhibit the *rooting response*. They will turn their heads in the direction of the slightest pressure on their cheeks. The pressure can be a soft nipple, or a finger, or even an eraser at the end of a pencil. Later, the sense of touch is utilized when the baby sucks on a pacifier. This basic sense of touch communication remains with us all our lives. We shake hands to augment a greeting, and human sex begins with kissing and tactile stroking. When we need comforting, even as adults, we hold one another. Affection is demonstrated by hugging, even man-to-man, as demonstrated by a sports team that has achieved a victory. The primary caregiving skill, then has to do with the sense of touch: cuddling and rocking the baby, even in that old-fashioned rocking chair. Bathing the baby is a magnificent opportunity to caress the baby with soap and water. Gently toweling the baby dry is another pleasurable tactile sensation for the baby. Even burping the baby while holding the baby against one's shoulder can be a loving communication that all is well even if he has a little gas that needs to come up.

Communicating Through the Visual and Taste Senses. The baby's vision is one of the least developed senses at birth, and it takes time for the baby to recognize objects that pass in front of her visual field. One of the first objects she will recognize is Mommie's face, as well as the milk bottle or breast that will start her sucking response even before Mommie puts the nipple in her mouth. She will engage in a fierce type of eye contact with Mommie, while sucking strenuously on bottle or breast nipple. (Try to take the nipple out of her mouth and you will discover just how hard that sucking response can be!) In fact, the baby seems to be hard-wired to look at face-type images and even primitive symbols of a face will hold a baby's attention longer than other visual objects. Repeated smiles from Mommie-face-object (the visual sense), along with being held (the tactile sense) while nursing (the taste sense), will convey love, affection, and comfort. Later as the baby can focus on other objects, being able to play with a hanging crib toy provides the baby with practice for coordinating her visual skill with her motor responses. But perhaps the visual activity that is the most intellectually stimulating for the baby is the "peek-a-boo" game comprising, as it does, a nonverbal but highly significant caregiver–child communication. When the baby is playing peek-a-boo, she is not just mimicking the adult, she is discovering that she can be in control of the communication. There is not much the baby is control of as she is picked up, laid down, has food pushed in her mouth, diapers changed, and is washed and dried without her permission. If she protests by crying in the middle of having her diapers changed, too bad. It's got to be done! Peek-a-boo allows the baby to be in control of the communication. When she hides her eyes and peeks through her fingers, she sees that the caregiver did the same. When she takes her hands away from her eyes, she watches with delight that the caregiver follows her example. The peek-a-boo game may be her first conscious experience of internal locus-of-control. At the same time, she is developing her hand–eye cognition and coordination.

Communicating Through the Sense of Hearing. One of the most significant correlates of whatever it is we call "intelligence" is verbal ability—being able to speak our native tongue. In fact, the ability to use language is so intimately related to "IQ" scores, that on some tests of intelligence, they are almost one-and-the-same. It follows then that anything that increases a child's verbal ability is also increasing the child's "IQ." Starting out with a newborn in our arms, we speak what is called *motherese*; all those coos and baby sounds adults use when communicating with infants. While you are rocking the child in her cradle or in your arms (the tactile sense), singing a few lullabies is another way to develop the child's language ability. It doesn't matter that lullabies have little real meaning. Just hearing the lullaby sounds will stimulate the baby's sensitivity to language. There is a *critical time* for learning language, any language, somewhere between birth and three years of age (more specific time hasn't quite been pinned down as yet). After this critical time, it is much harder to learn language, as most college students can testify when they struggle to learn another language. Later, when the child can sit up and eat in a high chair or crawl around the floor, the caregiver can promote language development simply by talking out loud while doing household chores or when shopping. It doesn't matter that the toddler does not understand everything you are saying as you talk to yourself. Little by little, the toddler will pick up words and phrases without your awareness. Reading baby books to the child, reciting nursery rhymes over and over again (to your boredom sometimes), and singing "Teensy Weensy Spider" are a few of the many ways we can foster her language development.

Figure 4.3 Comforting the Immigrant to Our World. Picking up the baby when he cries does not "spoil" him; in fact, it makes him more secure so that he is more independent and cries less after six months of age.

But the Bottom Line Is: Have Fun with Baby. Baby books will provide you with many more suggestions than we have discussed. Don't get overwhelmed by all their suggestions. Make use of those suggestions that seem to fit your personalities as parents. You will know you are parenting *positively* if you find yourself having fun with the baby. You will know that you have a happy baby if the baby gurgles and coos and laughs when you play all those peek-a-boo and patty-cake games that have come down to us through countless generations. (Unhappy and unhealthy babies don't gurgle and coo and giggle.) You will know that you have a healthy baby when the baby eats well and sleeps well and learns easily to control bladder and bowels. If the baby cries, don't be afraid to pick the baby up. Studies have shown that picking up the baby when the baby cries in the first six months of life results in much less crying after six months than babies who have not been picked up for fear of "spoiling" the baby. In fact, by picking up the child when he cries and comforting him (see Figure 4.3), you will be providing a loving welcome to this new "immigrant" to our world by which he learns to trust and feel safe (Solter, 1998).

PLAY AS PREPARATION FOR LIFE

In previous centuries, a child's playing was viewed as something children did when they didn't have anything better to do. Amusing to watch, yes, but before the twentieth century most philosopher-psychologists thought of play as not much more than the drain of excessive energy. Twentieth-century psychologists have taken children's play a lot more seriously. Freud's theory of play was that a child uses play as catharsis for his anxieties, his resentments, and his confusions through play (Freud, 1926). Watch a child play with her dolls after she has been disciplined. She may scold them, make them stand in a corner, or even spank them. She is displacing her hurt onto her dolls. Erik Erikson (1950) viewed play as part of the child's whole psychosocial development. If children are allowed "free play," they learn the tasks of *autonomy* and *initiative*. The pretend games of childhood are ways children learn their gender roles: "I'll be Daddy and you be Mommie and Jimmy can be the baby!"

Jean Piaget, the Swiss psychologist who pioneered the study of how children learn to think, placed even more importance on the activity of play. For him, play was essential to cognitive development and even moral–ethical development. In play, explained Piaget, the child is learning many perceptual skills, hand–eye coordination, physical dexterity and balance. He is learning to cooperate with others and to share things. Play allows the child to invent rules and abide by them (Piaget, 1973). Modern child psychologists generally confirm Piaget's theories, and agree with Piaget in all but one respect. Piaget did not think children younger than ten years of age have any internalized sense of morality. Psychologists today believe that while young children may not be able to verbalize their concern for others, they often act it out (Lillard & Curenton, 2003). An example: Consider the little boy whose mother begins to cry. He runs to the bathroom and brings back a box of Band-Aids to his mother. In another example, a little girl pretends her baby doll is sick or crying and she picks it up to hug it, rock it in her arms, and console it. Today, no one doubts that play is the serious business of childhood before the children go to school.

Positive Parenting for the Preschooler

For the child beyond the baby stage, we are about to describe some of the activities for the child from two years old to preschool. They include:

- Allowing free out-of-doors play;
- Encouraging indoor art play;
- Reading to the child;
- Helping the child deal with common childhood fears;
- Choosing an appropriate parenting style;
- Encouraging psychological androgyny;
- Teaching simple indoor rules and out-of-door rules.

All of these activities will enable the child to make a successful passage through Erikson's second and third stages of psychosocial development involving the tasks of *autonomy* and *initiative*. Moreover, these activities will develop the child's understanding of when and where certain activities are appropriate when he begins school. Free out-of-doors play is a recess activity. Quieter activities, such art play and listening at story time are what children do in the classroom. The simple rules the child learns at home will go a long way to helping the child adapt to school rules. In the following pages, we discuss these suggestions in more detail.

Play-Deprived Children. There are many types of play. There is physical play where children can run, jump, and even engage in rough-and-tumble play (hopefully on areas of grass or sand). There is cooperative play such as skip-rope or hide-and-seek. There is exploration of nature play, such as provided by baby pools and sandboxes. There is "let's pretend" play in which the children act out "mommy, daddy and baby" activities. What is important in all these types of play is that, once the safety rules have been established and there is safe supervision, it should be **free play**, even free enough to have an occasional tumble from a tricycle or a jungle jim or from a swing. Free recess play helps little boys settle down later for independent seat work or group activities in preschool, kindergarten, and the early primary grades. Free rough-and-tumble play even seems to calm the lad with attention deficit/hyperactive disorder (ADHD). The developmental and therapeutic power of play is so strong that we are about to describe how free play literally changed a child's life. When children are deprived of play, it can affect the child-becoming-adult in many ways (see Box 4.3).

If you have never seen a **play-deprived child**, it is an awesome experience. In kindergarten or first grade, the child will not know how to join in the fun and games of the other children. Instead, the child will simply sit or stand and watch. If the teacher tries to draw the child into the play activities, the child will draw back and any more attempts to coax the child

---

BOX **4.3** A Play-Deprived Child

It so happens that your authors know a woman who was a play-deprived child. Let us call her Patricia. Today, at 50 years of age, Patricia is a competent and much appreciated nurse, both by the hospital staff and her patients. We have known her for almost 30 years, but it took a long time before we began to understand her lack of ability just to "have fun." As far back as we can ever remember, Patricia's life has always been full of woe and pain. As her friends, we struggled for years to get her to discard some of the responsibilities she has assumed, let loose a little, and enjoy a few hours of just plain "fun." But to no avail! We puzzled over her inability to play a little until she told us about her life.

Patricia's mother was married very young to her father, then a handsome sailor. For a few years, the couple enjoyed cruising on his motorcycle all over their section of the country. All seemed to go well until Patricia's mother became pregnant and was unable to go sightseeing with her husband anymore since she now had a baby to take care of, our friend Patricia. Evidently that's when things began to go wrong. Patricia's father blamed the little girl for his wife's inability to go places with him. When Patricia was little, her father was not physically abusive, but he treated her quite strangely. For example, he would not allow her to play with other children. When the children in the neighborhood played games, he made her sit on the stoop by herself. All she could do was watch. Her mother, who became sickly after the birth

of Patricia, remained an invalid for the rest of her life. She could no longer cook, clean the house, and take care of her husband's needs. So little Patricia, even as a child of five, had to learn to cook for the family, see to the washing, and generally do the household chores.

Never having been allowed to play with other children, Patricia prayed for a little brother or sister she could have as a playmate. She was overjoyed then when, at 15 years of age, a baby sister (whom we shall call Ernestine) was born. Because her mother was still an invalid, Patricia became Ernestine's "second mother." She fed the child, bathed and dressed her, got her off to school when it came time, and took care of her after school along with all her other duties. But Patricia's life grew even harder when their father became alcoholic and turned abusive. When their father was in one of his abusive rages, Patricia would grab her little sister and run for the woods. Her mother, lying helplessly in bed, could do nothing.

But one thing Patricia's mother did do was to constantly encourage Patricia to get good grades in school so she could go to college and get a good life-career for herself. Patricia was always a good student and, ultimately, Patricia became a nurse. Then when her father became so alcoholic that he couldn't keep a job, Patricia became, not only the family cook, housekeeper and general caregiver, she was now the sole wager earner for her entire family of four. To this day, she has never learned how to look out for herself or to play a little.

to play may very well end in tears or a frozen rigidity. The developmental and therapeutic power of play is so strong that it can literally change a child's life.

The Therapeutic Power of Play

Freud may have considered play as the child's way to purge his anxiety, but it was Freud's daughter, Anna Freud, and Melanie Klein (another member of the Psychoanalytic Congress of Vienna) who between them developed therapeutic play techniques (Freud, 1926; Klein, 1960). In this country, **play therapy** was popularized by Virginia Axline. The fictionalized account she wrote of her play therapy with one little boy, *Dibs in Search of Self* (Axline, 1964), electrified the psychological and educational worlds.

Dibs was the only child of two very brilliant parents, who gave him physical care but were emotionally cold and rejecting and regarded Dibs as interfering with their careers. Dibs was referred for psychological assessment by his nursery school teachers, who were concerned about his strange, silent, and autistic behavior. He avoided others and kept to himself; crawled under the tables, desks, and chairs; and acted more like a cornered and wounded animal than a little boy in nursery school. Indeed, his teachers wondered if he was perhaps mentally retarded. Axline was called in for consultation. She undertook play therapy with Dibs for an hour a week in the play therapy room. A play therapy room has many toys and paints and even sand and running water. The child is allowed to do anything he wants, including marking on the walls with crayons and splashing water all over the floor. The only things he is not allowed to do is to hurt himself or hurt the play therapist. The therapist simply observes the child and makes quiet reflective comments: "Oh, you are throwing the father doll down and stamping on it! You must be very angry at the father doll."

In the hours that Dibs spent with Axline, the child played with small dolls to act out the fury, the confusion, the cold meaninglessness and profound sadness of his life at home. An absorbing part of the book is the chapter in which Dibs creates a play fire into which he throws the mother doll and the father doll, cremating with joy the symbolic representations of his parents. In psychoanalytic language, fire is equated with overpowering rage and thoughts of destruction. But fire can also be cleansing and purifying—a transforming act of pure creation. It is through the fires of self-examination that we learn to become more self-aware. It is in the fire of purification that heroes are transfigured. It was through the fire drama that Dibs began to purge his inner torments. The fire scene was the crisis and crescendo of Axline's work with Dibs. After that, bit by bit, Dibs made his way back to the world of people. The unexpressed fears and guilts and hatreds were dissolved in hour after hour of play therapy, until at last his appearance, so woebegone before, began to brighten, and he was able to smile, to laugh, to talk, and to develop interactions with others in his world.

Art Play as Preparation for School. Although there have been many studies of children's drawings, it was Rhoda Kellogg (1970), who has "made sense" of the scribblings of nursery school children's stick figures and all-head people (which she has called "tadpole" people). She says that she studied literally "thousands of scribbles" until she began to see a steady progression of design and representation (see Figure 4.4). She concluded that what seem to be merely scribbles show a definite developmental sequence, a sequence that reflects the child's cognitive growth. She believes that children should be allowed full freedom to scribble, draw, and paint as they like without having any adult interference or supervision.

Figure 4.4 Rhoda Kellogg: Stages in Children's Art. As Kellogg analyzes children's art, it has clearly recognizable stages as follows:

Stage 1 (before 2 years of age). Simple marks or scribbles on the paper. Although the scribbles on the page may seem to be stray hit-and-miss marks, those marks represent a magnificent achievement on the part of the infant. The child is learning to focus on a small area (the paper) and make a mark on it. In other words, he is learning eye/hand coordination and direction: up/down, center, and around and around.	
Stage 2 (between 2 and 3 years). Geometric shapes. The child is developing shape awareness, making crosses, circles, even squares and triangles, which someday will be reflected as part of a reading readiness program in the early grades.	
Stage 3 (after 3 years). Combining shapes. For example, a circle and some straight lines make a person. Kellogg was also fascinated by the child's obsession at this stage with creating circles and then the tadpole people that emerge at this stage. It was Kellogg's theory that this circle can be equated with Jung's concept of the **mandala,** the Eastern symbol that represents wholeness, health, and harmony. Jung had noticed that his patients began to dream and draw these symbols when they were reaching new levels of personality integration. Kellogg believes the circles of this stage denote a new level of cognitive and personality achievement. Eventually, the circle-head clones a circle-torso, and the body becomes more and more refined with hands and fingers, feet, and so on. As children become better able to integrate their physical coordination and to orient themselves in space, their figures become more complex, complete, and "human." In other words, their drawings reflect their own cognitive and emotional self-concept.	  A typical "tadpole" person.
Stage 4 (beginning at 4 to 5 years). Pictorial objects. Children are attempting to make representations of their world, those familiar pictures they draw of houses, people, trees, and animals. She cautions parents and teachers *not* to tell them how to draw but to allow them to develop their understanding of "reality" through free art play.	

Their self-directed artistic constructions will stand them in good stead later in school when they are beginning to learn to read and write. Spontaneous art is a preparation for "reading readiness."

Art Play Often Reveals What Children Cannot Verbalize

After World War II, children's art also became a diagnostic tool in cases of alleged or suspected physical or sexual abuse. Unfortunately, many times people who are not qualified to make diagnoses interpret what they want to see in children's art. Nevertheless, children's art can sometimes reveal what is going on in the house. For example, Drawing A in Figure 4.5 was a shock to the teacher who collected the papers. The little boy who drew the picture (whom we shall call Tommy) was six years old, the youngest sibling of three children. The

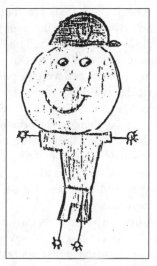

Drawing A. The six-year-old boy who drew this said, "This man is kissing her and they are laying on the bed with the pillow over their heads, and clothes off. But their shoes are still on."

Drawing B. This first-grader complained of headaches, but no one took him seriously until an alert art therapist noticed that she had drawn huge heads on all her figures. The mother consulted the family physician and the diagnosis was "migraines."

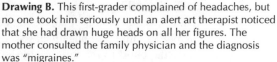

Drawing C. Drawn by a 10-year-old boy. A generally happy household including grandparents, mother, and himself. But who is the stick figure on the right? Said the boy, "That's my father. He's divorced from us. But I don't know how to draw him. But notice how well drawn all the other figures are.

Drawing D. Another 10-year-old-boy. What struck the teacher was the strange elbows and knees. He drew all the other figures in the same way. The art teacher said, "This would seem to me to be a pretty good description of how the boy feels about his body. He is very awkward and un-coordinated. Very immature physically.

Figure 4.5 Children's Drawings. Children often express in their drawings what they cannot verbalize.

immediate family consisted of mother, older brother (11 years), and older sister (8 years). The mother had divorced the father, a physician, two years prior to the drawing. Although very neat and clean in appearance and physically healthy, the boy was not doing well in school.

Tommy described this Drawing A in the following way: "This man is kissing her and they are laying on the bed with the pillow over their heads, and clothes off. But their shoes are still on." He described the boy as "Danny," who is 7 years old, and the girl as "Ginny," who is 6 years old. Alarmed, the teacher wisely refrained from saying anything more to the child. She took the child's drawing to the principal and school counselor who referred the matter to the proper authority. From the drawing itself we cannot infer whom Tommy may have seen. Is it the mother and a "friend"? Is it his older brother and sister? The latter seems the more likely, but we cannot make any valid judgment. We can say, with a good deal of certainty, that this bright six-year-old witnessed something that he could not comprehend and that was causing him considerable anxiety.

Sensitive art therapists can pick up on other kinds of physical or psychological problems. No one realized the severity of a little girl's headaches until she drew figures with huge heads on top of tiny figures (Figure 4.5, Drawing B). Ordinarily, a huge head is typical of a child emerging from the "tadpole people" stage, around five years of age. But this child was quite intellectually advanced for her age and her figures show sophisticated details. Why then are these huge heads so out of proportion to the rest of the drawing? The mother took the child to the family physician, who diagnosed the child as having, not occasional headaches, but severe and lasting migraines. It is a wonder that the child was doing as well as she was.

But a child's art can also be representations of happy scenes. When we see a sun shining and a rainbow in the sky and smiles on the faces of the people, we may infer that—no matter how serious a child's present problems may be—the child still has an optimistic worldview. When the child depicts flowering plants and tall trees growing straight, we can presume that the child feels that she too is blooming and growing tall and straight and being productive—at least to some degree.

HELPING CHILDREN COPE WITH THEIR FEARS

Except for falling, loud noises, or the sudden introduction of unfamiliar objects within their visual field, infants have few real fears. Babies have an "experimental" approach to exploring their environment (Piaget, 1970). Given a reasonably healthy infancy, babies are relatively unafraid of the dark or new territory. In the words of a first-grade child, "Babies are just too dumb to know any better." As children grow older, around two to three years of age, they develop a distinctly human cognitive ability, which we can call imagination. Imagination allows children to make up pretend games and to invent a world of their own. But this very same ability leads also to imagining frightening possibilities. What are they afraid of? Lots of things. For example, they are afraid of getting hurt.

Fear of Bodily Injury.   Sometime in their year of life, children become aware that they are vulnerable to injury. The little girl who has scratched herself yells, "Mommie, my blood is running out!" The little boy becomes panic-stricken when he watches his sun-burned skin begin to peel off. The best thing a caretaker can do is to apply a Band-Aid to the child's scratch, no matter how small it is, and top it off with a kiss "to get better." The Band-Aid's curative effect owes as much to its magical powers as to its healing properties. For the little boy whose sunburned skin is beginning to peel off, other magical remedies can be used (such as calamine lotion), even if the medication is only a psychological placebo.

Fear of Castration: Yes, It's Real!   Yes, Freud was right in this respect. Little boys do develop a fear that their penis may wither away, die, and fall off! Freud assumed this anxiety occurred only in children who are threatened in this manner when they masturbate, causing castration anxiety. But more recent research indicates that this is a normal anxiety for most or all male children, even in the most permissive of homes (Conn & Kanner, 1947). When little boys observe that little girls don't have such a magnificent organ, they develop secret fears that they might lose theirs as well.

Fear of Monsters That Lurk in the Dark.   Somewhere between age two and three, children begin to develop fears about the dark, about kidnappers that might steal them, or about monsters lurking under the bed or in the closet. They may even wet the bed out of fear of going to the bathroom by themselves at night. As for the monsters under the bed, several college students have volunteered that they still get nervous when they step off their beds and onto the floor in the middle of the night. A night light is a wonderful protection against "things that go bump in the night."

Fear of the Monsters in Their Nightmares.   Children may also start having bad dreams from which they wake up screaming. The frightening dream symbols may actually be big animals or monsters or "bad men" who will kidnap them. When a child has such a frightening dream, the important thing is not to say something like "there are no such things as monsters." The child knows there are! He has just dreamed them! A child has very little ability, as yet, to distinguish between what we adults call "reality" and the dream state (Piaget, 1962).

What can we do to help the child get over a frightening dream?   We can let the child talk and talk about "the monster" or "bad men" until the child quiets down (see Box 4.4). Talking is just as cathartic to children as it is to adults. Furthermore, you are building the child's trust in you. You are someone who believes him. He feels safer. Don't start impressing on the child that "it was only a dream." Save that until the next day. Then in front of the child, say to anyone in hearing, "Lucy had a bad dream last night." A discussion about scary dreams that other members in the family have had will not only be therapeutic, it will be the first step in Lucy's understanding that dreams are not the same as "real life."

Children's Literature: Moral/Ethical Instruction in a Language Children Can Understand

By the late 1800s, there had grown up in Europe and Great Britain a field of study that investigated legends as a way to study the psychology of ancient peoples and tribal societies. Certain of these nineteenth-century scholars became especially interested in myth and fairytales as keys to the phenomenology of children—a Rosetta Stone by which we could discover how children think and what they believe. Freud drew from these studies in his formulation of a child's psychosexual development. The Oedipus legend, for example, formed the basis for his Oedipal complex theory. But fairy tales also fascinated him.

BOX **4.4**   **Helping a Child Cope With a Nightmare**

A colleague of ours reported a conversation with his four-year-old daughter following a nightmare that had awakened her. The remarkable aspect of this conversation was that her father refrained from denying her reality and enabled her to purge her fear of the monster. Although he had come to us to ask what he should have done, there was nothing we could suggest to improve how he handled the situation. All we could do was to congratulate him for his parental intuition.

Child: It was a monster. A big monster. He was after me. Big! Big!

Father: A very big monster?

Child: Yes! Big! Big!

Father: As big as me?

Child: Bigger!

Father: As big as a horse?

Child: Yes!

Father: As big as this house? *(The child has become a little quieter. The question-and-answers have become gamelike.)*

Child: Yes!

Father: Where is the monster now?

Child: Under the bed!

Father: Under the bed?

Child: Yes. Under the bed.

Father: How can a monster as big as a house get under the bed?

Child: I don't know. But he's there just the same!

Father: Can I look and see if he's there?

Child: *(after a moment)* Yes.

(Her father pretended to look under the bed. He remained "looking" for several moments not saying anything. At last the child's curiosity got the better of her and she broke the silence.)

Child: Do you see him?

Father: Nope.

Child: Are you sure, Daddy?

Father: I'm sure. Just your old teddy bear.

Child: Let me see! *(The girl maneuvers herself so that she can hang her head down and peer under the bed.)* I want my teddy bear!

Judging that the child was calmed down now, he helped her settle back into bed.

The Fairytale as Metaphor of the Child's Worldview. Why do fairytales have such appeal for young children? Because the characters in the typical fairytale represent the child's phenomenological world. As fairytales evolved over the centuries, handed down from generation to generation in oral tradition, they developed stock characters. A typical fairytale involves a Good King and a Beautiful Queen and either a Princess or a Prince, and one more very important character—the Wicked Witch or the Wicked Stepmother. The King and the Queen obviously represent our parents who, after all, were the King and Queen of our young world. The little boy identifies, of course, with the Prince and the little girl identifies with the Princess. But who can the Wicked Witch or Wicked Stepmother be? Ah! Therein lies the value of the fairytale!

As young children, we adored our mothers. She was the giver of all good and all pleasure. She comforted us when we were hurt or scared. She provided us with all kinds of goodies to eat. She was indeed the Beautiful Queen of our small world. But she was not always a Good Queen. Sometimes she did not give in to our demands for more candy—"Not until after supper." Sometimes she frustrated our desires—"No, you can't stay up. It's bedtime!" Sometimes she could be outright mean—"You threw your food on the floor? You clean that up right now!" We didn't love them then. In fact, we have even hated them then. But we are taught we aren't supposed to hate our Mommies—we are supposed to love them. Besides, Mommies are only mean sometimes. A serious dilemma of our child psychology! Fairytales solve this dilemma very nicely. Fairytales devised two mothers: A Beautiful Queen, who died

Figure 4.6 Fairytales. A type of moral/ethical instruction in a language children can understand where the bad are punished and good wins out.

when the baby was born, and the Wicked Stepmother who married the Good King after the Beautiful Queen died. Oh, she is so nice to us when the Good King is around. When he is gone, she becomes her old mean self!

Or take, for example, the problems of the youngest child in the family who generally feels shoved around by his or her older siblings and can be actually heard to complain of having nobody "to boss around." Such resentments and desires are wonderfully portrayed in fairytales in which the youngest child is the hero or the heroine. A typical tale begins: "There once was a miller who had three sons, and the youngest of them went out to seek his fortune . . . " Now the youngest son is frequently referred to as a "simpleton" or "dolt." But who winds up with the fortune? Who slays the dragon? Who is it that marries the princess? The older, more intelligent and capable brothers? Not at all! It is the youngest child, the child called a "dolt and simpleton," of course. Which just goes to show that younger siblings will some day outdo their scornful and more powerful older brothers, so there!

Purging Childhood Fears and Anxieties: Particularly, the "Beast Within."
Fairytales are not sweet "Dick and Jane" type of stories. They may start off with an innocent

"Once upon a time long, long ago . . . " and they may end with an optimistic ". . . and they all lived happily ever after," but in between that innocent beginning and optimistic ending, fairytale plots involve all the evils of the world. In fairytales, the hero or heroine suffer from a variety of injustices: insults, calumny, kidnapping, child abuse, rape, or—like Hansel and Gretel—the threat of cannibalism. The child experiences all of these kinds of anxieties and fears. For example, her older brother has said he will flush her down the toilet! But the worst fear and the worst anxiety the child must confront each day is, wrote Bruno Bettelheim, a noted child psychiatrist, the child's own inner self (the baby **id**) that urges him to do things he shouldn't. A child's worst anxiety is the "Beast Within" himself (Bettelheim, 1987).

Freud and other psychologists have noted the fierceness of children's sibling jealousy when they have been displaced by a baby brother or sister. Their sibling rivalry stems from their desire to be the only object of their parents' love and devotion—particularly from their mother. Children would like to do away with the father and siblings who grab mother's attention. As Freud explained it, the socialization process takes many years, so the desires and urges of the ferocious "id" will make itself felt from time to time. Despite the violence and brutality of fairytale plots, Bettelheim says fairytales actually provide children with hope that they will someday be able to conquer the "Monster Within." The Prince who slays the Dragon provides that hope—for the Dragon is a wonderful representation of the "Beast Within." Bettelheim's thesis is that we should not deny fairytales to our children because they are violent. Their very violence helps children have a cathartic experience over their inner torments and frights.

Fairytales As Moral/Ethical Instruction. Erich Fromm, another noted psychologist, explained it this way. Just as we read adult fiction to catharsize the woes of our lives, so too do children love to listen to fairytales for precisely the same reasons. Furthermore, fairytales deal with morality at a level the child can understand. The real themes of fairytales are good versus evil, the poor versus the rich, the weak and the helpless versus the strong and the mighty. Ultimately, fairytales are teaching children about crime and punishment and the existential problems of death, injustice, and despair. Fairytales hold out the promise of ultimate justice and ultimate success. Evil is eventually punished, the good are eventually rewarded, and all who deserve it live "happily ever after."

They also teach lessons in parable form. In the words of one writer of children's fiction, "Beauty and the Beast" should be ready by every pretty girl who places too high a value on masculine good looks, and also by every unfortunate boy with acne who knows that he's a prince "down deep" (Hornyansky, 1969). We add the note that a little introspection into the favorite fairytales and stories of our own childhood may give us an insight into our struggle for personality integration as we were growing up (see Box 4.5).

PARENTING THE CHILD FOR SCHOOL READINESS

Parenting Styles: Authoritarian, Permissive, and Authoritative

One of the tasks that children encounter when going to school for the first time is discovering they are not the center of the adult's world. They have to learn to share their toys. They have to learn that they must stay seated sometimes and "do independent seat work." They have to learn how to raise their hands to talk. They need permission to go to the bathroom. They can't run in the halls. They have to learn to write the letters and numbers between two lines at a time

The Significance of My Fairytale

The following are the responses of college students regarding a significant fairytale, folklore, or story of their own childhood.

Female: The story of "The Three Billy Goats Gruff" was a very important story to me. I guess because the three goats gruff all were aspects of me. I am usually very shy and quiet and can only make a little noise like the littlest goat gruff, and I am kind of defenseless. The middle-size goat is like me when I have enough courage to assert myself a little more. And the large billy goat gruff is me when I'm angry and can make a really loud noise. But I can't do that very often.

Male: My favorite fairytale was the "Three Little Pigs." The story was about three little pig brothers who all built houses. Two of the baby pigs built theirs with straw or something. So when the big, bad, ugly wolf came along, he just blew those straw houses away. But the third pig had built his house with bricks and the wolf couldn't blow his house away. After reading this chapter, I realized the wolf was my father. He was usually nice until he got drunk and then he used to beat us all up. I used to hide and stay very

still when he came home drunk and I didn't get beaten up as bad as my brothers. This has all been very strange for me to realize.

Female: I think the story of "Snow White and Rose Red" meant a lot to me. Although my sister and I were very close, I always felt like Rose Red. For some reason, Snow White is the main person in the story, and she gets the prince, and Rose Red only gets to marry the prince's friend. My sister was fair and I was dark, just like Snow White and Rose Red, and I always thought she was much prettier than me and had more boyfriends than me somehow.

Male: I was the youngest of four children and came late in my parents' life. I had three sisters who were all in their teens when I was born, which made it seem like I was living with five big grownups, all of whom were always telling me what to do. My favorite story was "Jack and the Beanstalk." I used to get a charge out of the fact that he outwitted the giant and brought him down. I can see that I identified with Jack, and the giant was all the grownups in my family. And I also have a sneaking suspicion that I get a charge still out of outwitting my boss, or my father, or anyone in authority. I'll have to look into this.

when their fine motor coordination is not yet developed. They have to learn to read despite the fact that the English language, being as unphonetic and huge as it is, may be *the* most difficult language to learn to read. At this early age, children have to learn endless rules and, at the same time, to acquire many language and computing skills. What parents can do is to foster the child's adaptation to the school environment, suggested by the classic Baumrind studies (1973) on styles of parenting.

Authoritarian Parenting. This is the traditional and historical parenting style and is based on the use of power. The parents assume the responsibility for their children's welfare and upbringing. The assumption underlying this style is that "parents know best" and what is good for the child. Since parents are the adults and have more experience of the world, they feel they must take charge of the child's education and experiences. The parents make the rules, and the children are expected to obey them without question. If they disobey, physical force or punishment may be used. When the children are little and question why they should do something, the answer goes, "Because I say so." These families are adult-centered and adults make the rules of the house. When the children reach their adolescence and want to kick over the traces, the answer goes, "As long as you're under my roof and I am paying the bills, you follow my rules." This style of parenting is still the predominant style of the working class. It is also consistent with the type of jobs working class people have where there is a boss who says what should be done and when. No excuses! No alibis! Just do it! Period!

Some of these parents have never experienced any other way of relating to authority, and this is the way they relate to their children.

Permissive Parenting. This style emerged in the 1960s as the result of our changing views about personality development. It was based on Rogers' model of self-discovery and nondirective counseling style. Rogers (1950) had posited that each of us has a **center-of-growth** that is uniquely our own. When we are in touch with our center, we act appropriately. When we are always being told how we should be and how we should think, we grow up confused and alienated from this center-of-growth. Rogers' therapy was to listen reflectively to clients but not to interpret for them or tell them what to do. Permissive parents applied Rogers' theories to raising their children. These parents believed that in a democratic society, it is more appropriate to raise children, not in an authoritarian style, but in a more "democratic" style. Their homes were "children-centered" and freer in atmosphere. In child-centered homes, children were given as few rules as possible. Permissive parents wanted their children to discover the world for themselves without adult "interference." They would then grow up more in touch with their center-of-growth, and therefore more spontaneous, more authentic, and more creative.

Authoritative Parenting. This style evolved out of the criticism leveled at permissive parenting. Critics were particularly concerned about allowing children to have complete freedom of choice, such as what time they wanted to go to bed. Children, they said, are simply not yet capable of making mature judgments. Another criticism: Permissive parenting sometimes led to such loud and unrestrained attention-getting behavior on the part of the children that visiting these homes was often a nightmare. The most serious criticism was that children had so much "center stage," they were growing up to be attention-demanding adults with little respect for the needs of others.

Authoritative parenting is based on Skinner's **operant conditioning**, which stresses positive reinforcement for constructive behavior (discussed in more detail in Chapter 9). **Environmental engineering** is used instead of ordering or physical force. Instead of rules there are guidelines. Parents use themselves as role models. If a child leaves a tricycle in the driveway, parents may remind the child several times to put it away. If the child continues to leave the tricycle on the driveway, the parent simply puts it away until the child demonstrates the required behavior. Punishment is used but only rarely since parents are aware that punishment only raises hostility in the child and the behavior doesn't cease—it merely goes underground. Authoritative homes are not adult-centered but neither are they child-centered. They are family-centered.

Adaptation to School. Baumrind's objective was to discover how these three parenting styles affected the child's adaptation to school. The results clearly revealed the children's parental upbringing. As we might have guessed, children from authoritarian homes were belligerent and aggressive with other children. They tended to regard teachers and other adults somewhat suspiciously and to keep their distance from them. Adults mean "trouble" so stay away from them! They fought with other children more often on the playground and more often were verbally abusive toward other children in the classroom. While a minority of these children remained antisocial, however, the majority eventually adapted quite well to the classroom situation. After all, they were used to rules in their home; they simply had to learn new rules. The negative side, however, was that they had a hard time doing "independent seat work" or working creatively with others in joint projects.

Children from the authoritative home were clearly the most at ease in the new classroom situation. They conformed easily to the school rules and responded well to praise and direction, particularly if the teachers used the same kinds of positive reinforcements as the parents. But these children also demonstrated socially responsible and self-controlled behavior. All in all, the child from the authoritative family was the best adapted to the new school environment.

BOX **4.6** SELF-EXPLORATION
Parenting Styles and Adjustment to School

Parenting Style	Assumptions	Values	Behavioral Consequences
Authoritarian Adult-centered *Based on authority and power.*	Parents have responsibility for child's welfare.	Obedience to rules. Respect for authority. Parents supervise and punish transgressions.	Initially belligerent but makes quick adaptation to school. Avoids adults. Some remain belligerant but most settle down. Not motivated to do "seat work" or creative projects.
Permissive Child-centered *Based on Rogers' client-centered counseling.*	Freedom from rules or parental interference enables child to actualize center-of-growth.	Children encouraged to discover the world and to express themselves.	Lost in new environment. Lacked self-reliance and unable to adapt to not being center of attention. Good at creative projects, but difficulty in sharing.
Authoritative Family-centered *Based on Skinner's operant conditioning.*	Children acquire responsible behavior through observational learning and adult role-modeling.	Parents set guidelines. Child's autonomy is respected.	Adapted quickly to school routine. Able to play cooperatively with other children. Good "inner resources."

Reflective Writing: What Kind of Parenting Did You Have? Response to the following items.

1. What kind of ethnic or cultural background do you come from? _____
2. If your ethnic background is not "mainstream America," how did it affect your ability to cope in school?
   _____
3. In your family, who had the supreme authority or was it democratically equal? _____
4. Were your parents authoritarian, permissive, or authoritative? _____
5. Describe your family environment in terms of health and harmony. _____
6. Were you raised androgynously? Whatever your answer, describe how it affected your personality.

7. Reflecting on your own upbringing, describe:
   a. one thing you would keep the same _____
   b. one thing you might change as you bring up your children _____

Surprisingly, the poorest adaptation was displayed by the children from the permissive home. They seemed at a total loss in the new environment. They lacked the very self-reliance that permissive parents were trying to foster. From an environment in which they were the center of attention, they were now only one child in a classroom full of thirty other children. It took these children a lot longer to get their "sea legs" and learn what was expected of them.

Teaching a Few Simple Outside and Inside Rules. So how should we parent? Perhaps there is a place for all 3 parenting styles. If a child runs into a street full of cars, this is not the time to be permissive. That kind of situation calls for a loud *Get out of the street!* In times of danger or crisis, we may need to be very authoritarian indeed! When the situation is dangerous, as in playing near water, there are certain restrictions and rules the child must learn to obey. If the children are playing safely on the beach making sand castles, parents can afford to be very permissive indeed (while keeping one eye out). At other times, we can do our best to be authoritative, which means that while we keep an eye on their safety, we foster their own exploration of the world.

As children approach kindergarten age, they need to have learned to obey a few simple house and neighborhood rules, such as:

- No running in the house.
- No playing in the street.
- No crossing the street unless accompanied by an adult.
- Washing hands before each meal.
- Washing hands after a trip to the bathroom.
- After dinner, putting their dishes on the kitchen counter.
- Putting their toys away before going out to play.
- Coming in when called for meals or bedtime.

Figure 4.7 The Androgynous Child. This type of child will have a broader range of interests and abilities and therefore will have higher intellectual and emotional intelligence.

These rules may seem obvious and absurdly simple but the point is that the child does not have a choice in these matters—the child is simply learning to mind a few simple do's and don'ts. If the child learns to follow the house rules, learning to follow school rules will come easier and problems of discipline will be less liable to rise. Learning to pick up their toys before going out to play will enable them to follow the teacher's instructions to put away their paste and coloring tools before they line up for recess.

Psychological Androgyny: A Larger Worldview and Expanded Capabilities

Originally, the term **androgyny** meant a person who had both male and female sexual characteristics. The social sciences borrowed the term and applied it to psychological characteristics. As a medical term, it indicates a difficult condition, but as a psychological term, it connotes something quite beneficial. **Psychological**

androgyny refers to children who have developed skills, interests, and abilities of both genders. The androgynous girl-child has not been severely punished for being a "tomboy" or for showing interest in competitive sports, mechanics, math, science, or business. The androgynous boy-child has not been severely punished for his interests in art, music, reading, nurturing, and other pursuits that our culture has labeled "feminine." Androgynous children show a wider range of intellectual pursuits and a more sophisticated palette of emotional responses. They can be both competitive and cooperative, and they have a larger worldview. By contrast, all-girl families tend to foster "ladylike" behaviors such as politeness, courtesy, and an interest limited mainly to domestic affairs. All-boy families tend to encourage sports, aggressiveness, and competition. In mixed-gender families, however, boys grow up interested not only in athletics and cars but also in their sisters' games and puzzles and reading material. Likewise, girls who grow up in mixed-gender families show an interest not only in dolls and games, but also in their brothers' sports, science projects, and mechanical pursuits. Bem (1975) pioneered studies of androgyny. Studies indicate that psychologically androgynous children have higher IQ scores, get better academic grades, and have higher educational/vocational goals. Furthermore, the boys have healthier interpersonal relationships since they are able to express tenderness and are more comfortable with intimate relationships. Their psychological androgyny does not make them confused about their sexual identity. In fact, they are more sure of their gender roles and secure in who they are as male or female. Most important of all, they have better coping mechanisms to survive the stresses and strains of adult life (Bem, 1985).

Important Terms and Concepts to Know

• androgyny	• Dibs	• id	• play
• art	• disabilities	• injury	• rules
• attachment	• fairytales	• nightmare	• self-esteem
• authoritative	• family	• nurture	• senses
• bonding	• fertilizers	• obese	• stress
• castration	• fun	• penetrance	• thalidomide
• deprived	• gentle	• permissive	• "twin studies"

Make Your Own Chapter Summary by Filling in the Blanks

Use the "Important Terms and Concepts to Know" to fill in the blanks.

The Developing Embryo Fetus. Many difficulties that children have were once blamed on poor parenting. Now we know that many of these difficulties have to do with genetics and _____ factors during pregnancy. The _____ support the nature side of the nature/nurture issue, while problems as the result of the mother's illness, smoking, drugs, and medications during pregnancy would come under the _____ side of the issue. Perhaps the final "wake up" call came with the _____ babies, whose mothers were given that drug for their morning sickness. The health professions are also concerned about poor nutrition, low birth-weight babies as well as _____ babies, and toxins in our environment, such as chemical _____ and pesticides. Finally, health officials warn against maternal _____ as it is very possible that the hormones of anger and fear are being transmitted to the growing baby. Lower _____ is associated with the unwanted child.

Birthing and Parenting the New Baby. Much has changed about the way we birth new babies, thanks to the _____ birthing procedures of Dr. Leboyer. As well, we have discovered the great importance of mother-baby _____ immediately after birth, so that the child can develop a strong _____ to the mother or other caregiver.

Positive Parenting. Positive parenting for the infant up to two years includes communicating through the five _____, fostering language development, and just having _____ with the child. Positive parenting for the toddler and preschooler includes many types of indoor and outdoor _____. Play-_____ children may even suffer learning _____ and other neurological problems. Play therapy was devised for children who have been unwanted and neglected, such as the little boy, called _____. Free _____ play often

reveals the anxieties and confusions children cannot verbalize. Children have many fears, such as the fear of something happening to their penis, which Freud called the _____ complex. They are also afraid of bodily _____ and of monsters that lurk in the dark. According to Bruno Bettelheim, a noted child psychoanalyst, the monster the child is most afraid of is the powerful "Beast Within" that Freud called the _____. Bettelheim advised reading _____ to children because they are a type of moral/ethical instruction in a form children can understand. If a child has a _____, don't tell the child it is not real (it is to him or her) but allow the child to talk about it.

Parenting Styles. Baumrind and her associates studied three types of parenting. The authoritarian parenting style involves many _____ and punishment. The _____ parenting style emphasizes self-discovery with few rules and regulations. The _____ parenting style is based on conditioning in which the child's desirable behavior is reinforced by praise. Baumrind compared the three parenting styles with adjustment in the first grade. The child who made the best adaptation overall was the child from the _____-centered home. There are times when all three parenting styles are appropriate. Psychological _____ fosters higher "IQ" scores, more social skills, and greater creativity.

5

Fostering Caring, Conscientious, and Creative Children

From School Entrance to Puberty

The Child's Entrance Into the Great Big, New, Wonderful, Scary World of School

Jill Smith is once again leading a small group discussion.

Jill Smith: The chapter we are going to be studying this week has to do with how children develop intellectually and morally during the grade school years. To start us off, I'm going to ask each of you to remember something about your very first day of school.

Martha: I remember I wore a pretty new dress and shiny patent leather shoes. I sure thought I was "big stuff."

Ernesto: I had a new pencil box with pencils and erasers and a ruler, and I was so proud of it.

Shannon: I was scared to death. I think I cried. I remember I wouldn't let go of my father's hand and he had to carry me into school.

Dan: What I remember was having to ride the school bus for an hour to school and an hour back. I remember the bus driver had to stop sometimes because the kids were making so much noise and acting up. I hated that bus ride. In fact, I hated that school. Mostly white kids who thought us Injuns still wore feathers and war paint.

Alec: I didn't like school either. (To Dan) Did you get in trouble?

Dan: No, I just stayed quiet and kept my distance.

Alec: Not me! I used to fight the other guys and then I'd get sent to the counselor's office. I didn't want to get in trouble, but the other kids used to call me "dummy." I just couldn't seem to learn what the other kids were learning. I couldn't even sit still at my desk. Later they told me I had a learning disability, they called it AD/HD. (*To the rest of the class*) That stands for attention deficit/hyperactive disorder.

They'd call my parents and I'd get a beating when I got home. Except for physical education and recess, school was hell on earth, let me tell you.

Li Ho: I got hit, too, if I didn't pay attention when my father was correcting my math homework, I'd get a "bop" on the head. It wasn't a hard "bop" though, and I knew he did it out of caring for me that I would get good grades and make something of myself.

Natasha: Miss Professor, I listen to all these students. I am very . . . what is word? . . . ah . . . ah . . . ah . . . stonished. Most say bad things about school. I ask my two children "What you do today? What you learn?" They say they *play*. I have conference with teacher and room is like playroom. Pictures on walls and toys in corner. In my country, it is more serious. If children not serious, they must stay home. My grandmother tell me in her day, they beat child right there in classroom. So why everybody complaining?

Jill Smith: That's a big question, one that has a multitude of answers. I can only sum it up for you by saying that a large part of the problem stems from our multicultural society, and what we call the individual differences of each child.

Natasha: What means that . . . in .di. . vid ual differences?

Jill Smith: What that means is that each and every child comes to school with vastly different abilities, different skills, different ethnic backgrounds, and different learning problems. In a single classroom, one child may not even speak English yet. Another child's family is below the poverty level, and she comes to school hungry. Another child, like Alec,

BOX **5.1**   SCENARIO (continued)
The Child's Entrance Into the Great Big, New, Wonderful, Scary World of School

has a learning disability. Let me tell you about one little girl who was just adorable and whom everybody liked, including her classmates. One day she came to my office where I was interning as a school counselor, and broke into tears. I asked her if she was hurt. She shook her head and, between sobs, the story came out bit by bit. She was being molested and she was scared to tell her mother. Public school teachers have the responsibility of trying to meet the learning needs of each and every one of these children, especially with the federally mandated mission now, entitled *No Child Left Behind* Act. Teachers are doing the best they can but it's a tall order. We're doing fairly well with the majority of our young children, but there are still many children who are having problems in school, being retained, and dropping out completely as soon as they can. They need our help.

THE GRADE SCHOOL YEARS: THE DEVELOPMENT OF INDUSTRY, COMPETENCE, AND MORAL/ETHICAL VALUES

Acquiring the Task of Industry

When we see grade-school children working busily on their "independent seat work" or out at recess playing gleefully with their friends, we tend to view them as healthy and doing well. And for the most part, they are. In terms of health, the childhood diseases are over, and the mortality rate is lower than it will be at any other time of life. Even the accident and injury rate is lower than either the preschool years or the adolescent years. The grade school years are generally regarded as the easiest and happiest years of childhood. The children are meeting and mixing with others of their own age. They are acquiring new competencies, the well-known "three R's" of reading, writing, and 'rithmetic. The ability to read will open the doors to exciting literature—even if, in the beginning, it is just the comic strips. Mathematical skills will give them the power to understand the economics of an allowance and to buy things at the store with their "own money." The ability to write will allow them to compose birthday cards for their mommies and Father's Day cards for their dads. All of these competencies will add to their self-esteem as members of the classroom and the family. Furthermore, they have not yet entered the teen years with their confusing biological changes, intense interpersonal problems, and adolescent–parent conflicts. In fact, children between six and puberty are still quite conforming to parental expectations and school regulations. Most of our grade-school children are accomplishing what Erik Erikson said was the life task of this stage, acquiring the task of *industry* (1950).

The Most Intelligent Generation of Children Ever—The Flynn Effect!

Besides being the happiest and healthiest generation that has ever been, this generation of children is the most intelligent generation ever, if we are to believe the Flynn effect. The Flynn effect has been making headlines throughout the scientific world! Because of the Flynn effect, social scientists everywhere are having to reevaluate all the "conventional wisdom" of so-called "IQ" tests. So profound is the impact that the Flynn effect is having, it is almost like starting from Ground Zero about just what comprises "intelligence." To appreciate what all the excitement is about, we have to understand how the Flynn effect has upended all our previous assumptions about "IQ" tests.

The So-Called "IQ" Tests. In 1916, Lewis Terman of Stanford University published the first American "IQ" test, called the *Stanford-Binet Test of Intelligence*. The Stanford-Binet and the *Wechsler Intelligence Scale for Children* (WISC), which came later, became the standard measurements of children's intelligence. The assumption underlying these two "IQ" tests (and all others) was that intelligence is mostly *genetic* and more-or-less *permanent*. On the basis of these "IQ" tests, children were admitted into advanced scholastic programs or put into institutions for mental retardation, etc. (see Tip 5.1).

Over the eight decades of their use, professionals in many areas of social science objected to the wholesale use of "IQ" tests that were disadvantageous to children from certain populations who were being rated as lower in intelligence. These populations included Native American children on reservations, city children in slum ghettos, children of coal miners in Appalachia, and any child who was not white, middle class, or living in and around San Francisco, New York City, and other urban centers of this country. These objections to the abuses of the so-called intelligence tests led to the use of quotation marks in the term "IQ" to remind everyone that the scores on these tests may not reflect the child's true intelligence. Even though these two tests were revised, from time to time, to meet these objections, it was becoming painfully apparent that what was often being measured was not a child's *intelligence*, but the culture from which the child came—Hispanic, African-American, poor Appalachian white, Native American, and so on. By the mid-1980s, many psychologists were protesting the use of "intelligence" (as defined by "IQ" tests) as being as useful as a corrupted computer disk. The final blow to "IQ" tests as some kind of permanent and genetic personality trait may come about now by way of the Flynn effect.

Now Back to the Flynn Effect! For the last 30 years, a remarkable and enterprising psychologist by the name of James Flynn has been gathering data on "IQ" tests from technological nations all around the world, including Great Britain, the Netherlands, Germany, Scandinavia, Belgium, Israel, Germany, as well as the United States. His findings have astonished the psychological world agog! For what he has concluded from these statistical data is that there has been a steady rise of "IQ" scores, generation after generation, for the last fifty years. Furthermore, on **culture-reduced tests** (less biased in favor of white, middle-class, well-educated youth), this rise approximates 18 points per generation, totally demolishing the concept of the "IQ" as something that is fixed, genetic, and unalterable (Flynn, 1999). Many reasons have been given for this rise in "IQ" points: better health of our children, more enlightened teaching methods, integrated schools, Head Start programs, the information children are acquiring from television and the Internet, and better communication between children and adults (Flynn, 1999; Neisser, 1998; Goleman, 1995).

Tip 5.1 Abuses of the "IQ" Tests. Some of the abuses of these "IQ" tests seem to us now as being absolutely imbecilic. For example, several of the tasks of these "IQ" tests involve verbal ability; yet a few untrained test administrators used them with children who stuttered. Other tasks involve visual acuity, yet they were administered to children with poor eyesight. A few scandalous cases involved children who were put into institutions of mental retardation but who were actually severely hard-of-hearing or deaf.

So What Is Going Wrong? Some Dilemmas

But if it is true, as the Flynn effect suggests, that we are producing the smartest generation ever, we are faced with several dilemmas. For instance, *in spite of the fact that modern educators know a lot about what makes for good teaching and good learning, why are so many of our children failing in the first three primary grades?* Or consider that *if this generation is the most intelligent generation ever, why are so many of our adolescents unhappy enough to drop out of high school as soon as they can?* Additionally, *in a nation with as high a standard of living as we have, why are so many of our adolescents falling prey to alcohol, drugs, truancy, and delinquency?* Social scientists have proposed many answers to these dilemmas. A few are discussed in this chapter and other answers will be discussed in later chapters.

Social scientists on the cutting edge of research are saying that we are going to have to redefine our entire concept of intelligence. They reason that superior intelligence is not simply a matter of a high "IQ" score, high academic achievement, or the right to put a few initials after our names (M.A., M.S., M.D., or Ph.D.). Superior intelligence, say these psychologists, is something more than "book learning." They believe that we can no longer separate cognitive abilities (reasoning, logic, computational skills, etc.) from the other aspects of human personality. We all know people who have been described in the following ways:

> *She's really very smart but she just lacks good, old "common sense."*
> *He's so intelligent but he's always in trouble with the law. If he would just use his intelligence and stay on this side of the law, he could be a real success in business.*
> *People call her a genius. Too bad she spends so much time in a mental institution.*
> *He may be intelligent but he's not a very nice person. He's always bickering with someone. If he tried to smile, his face would crack.*

These psychologists theorize that any definition of intelligence must also include the person's moral/ethical character and the person's mental health (Flynn, 1999; Neisser, 1998; Sternberg, 2003). If any one of these personality factors—*cognitive abilities, mental health*, and *moral/ethical development*—is obstructed or disrupted in any way, the individual may be functioning at a lower level than his "IQ" scores indicate. To understand how these three personality factors relate to "intelligence," we take the reader back almost a century to the work of one of our most famous and revered psychologists, Jean Piaget.

JEAN PIAGET: THE PIONEER OF COGNITIVE AND MORAL/ETHICAL DEVELOPMENT IN CHILDREN

A Qualitative Model of Cognitive (Thinking) Development

The beginning of any new field of science seems to need an intellectual giant to pioneer a foothold. Astronomy had its Galileo. Physics had its Isaac Newton. Emotional development had its Sigmund Freud. In the area of **cognition** (the professional term for thinking), that giant turned out to be a Swiss psychologist by the name of Jean Piaget. Today every textbook in psychology, education, philosophy, and theology includes Piaget's contributions to our understanding of human growth. The basic theme that underlies his immense number of books and essays is precisely this: *Cognitive development and moral/ethical development go hand-in-hand.*

Piaget was already established as a brilliant investigator long before he began his studies of children. His genius showed up so early in his life that he had his first scientific paper published when he was only 11 years of age (on the discovery of an albino sparrow). Then as a young man, he was part of the French team that put together the first test of "mental abilities" of children, and which ultimately led to the first American test of "IQ," called the *Stanford-Binet Test of Intelligence.* Later, and this is not generally known, he also studied psychoanalysis, becoming acquainted with the science of personality theory. He was therefore admirably suited to the scientific observation and recording of children's behavior in their natural habitats of home, classroom, and free play (see Box 5.2).

BOX **5.2** RESEARCH METHODOLOGY
Piaget's Naturalistic Observation Studies

On the Plus Side

1. **The pioneer of the cognitive and moral development of children.** Just as Freud was the pioneer of the emotional development of personality, so was Piaget the pioneer of the cognitive and moral/ethical development of children.
2. **Much prior scientific experience in naturalistic observation of animals and children.** Piaget had a brilliant and wide-ranging background in observing and recording the behavior of animals and children. He was therefore admirably suited to the scientific observation and recording of children in their natural habitats.
3. **The method of naturalistic observation.** The study of organisms in their natural environment is called *naturalistic observation.* The advantage of this research method is that behaviors can be observed that are not observed in an artificial situation. By observing the wild chimpanzees in their natural jungle habitat, the extraordinary Jane Goodall discovered that they were tool-making and that, although they were generally peaceable and cooperative, certain "aberrant" chimps could kill baby chimps and commit cannibalism.
4. **His theories have engendered much research and application.** The acid test of the importance and validity of a scientist's work is the amount and quality of further research it inspires. Piaget's work has engendered literally thousands of studies world-wide, and has become an essential topic of philosophy, theology, psychology and education.

On the Minus Side

1. **The disadvantages of naturalistic observation.** Although this method of research escapes the artificiality of the laboratory, it is impossible to assign cause-and-effect absolutely to natural observations. For example, millions of dollars are being spent in observing courtrooms to discern what factor (or factors) influence a jury's verdict. Is it the demeanor of the defendant? Is it the testimony of the "experts"? The eloquence of the attorneys in their summing up? Perhaps it is the demographic variables of the jury members. Or is it the fact that the defendant has already been convicted by the media? We can make good guesses but, without corroborating evidence, we may never be absolutely sure.
2. **We know now that some children can demonstrate some stages at younger ages than Piaget posited.** It has been reliably validated that toddlers can exhibit what might be called compassionate behavior to others. Also object permanence seems to develop several weeks earlier in some babies. This finding is not a criticism of Piaget's powers as an observer but as a consequence of better research technologies which Piaget did not have at his disposal (Dunn, 1988; Hoffler, 1991).
3. **Like Freud, Piaget did not take into account the demographic variables of gender, socioeconomic status, and multicultural background.** Although he invited scholars and researchers from all over the world to participate in his work at his Geneva summer institutes, he was unacquainted with the broader cultural influences on a child's personality development.

Piaget's Four-Stage Model of Cognitive Development

His work, involving the mental abilities of young children, led Piaget to an interesting theory about their worldview, which he said was vastly different from that of adults. He explained that children do not have the same cognitive processes as grownups. They may use the same words that we do, but they do not think like us. In point of fact, Piaget said that until children reach approximately 12 or 13 years of age, their entire worldview is alien to ours. According to Piaget, the development of a child's cognitive ability develops in four stages, which he called four **organizations of mind**. He described these stages as **qualitative changes**; which is to say that they are more like quantum leaps of evolution, than like the gradual development of height and weight (Piaget, 1929). (See Table 5.1.)

Stage 1. The Sensory-Motor Stage (Birth to 2 Years). Like Freud, Piaget regarded the newborn baby as a rather unorganized complex of primitive but very strong reflexes. During this stage, the baby has no **mediation**; i.e., the baby does not have any perceptions, ideas, or thoughts in his head. Well, if the baby does not have any mediation, what does it have? It has a **sensory-motor organization** of "mind," which means that it *must* respond *motorically* (physically) to whatever stimulus breaks through to its sensory awareness. Sensory stimuli can be internal (coldness, wetness, hunger, pain) or external (light, sound, or a caretaker's face moving across its visual field). An example should help clarify the term *sensory-motor*.

Let us suppose that we are dangling a string in front of a four-month-old kitten so as to catch its (sensory) visual attention. Can that kitten just watch that string? No, that kitten must respond (motorically) by trying to catch it with its paws. It is a natural animal instinct or reflex—call it what you like. Similarly, if we dangle a set of keys in front of a four-month-old baby so as to catch her (sensory) visual awareness, the baby must respond (motorically) by reaching-grabbing-and-putting-them-in-her-mouth (if she can). Neither the kitten nor the baby has any choice in the matter—no choice but to respond. That is what is meant by a sensory motor organization of mind. The child has no **mediation** (thoughts, concepts or ideas). However, during the sensory-motor stage, the baby will be developing many sensory/perceptual abilities that will make mediation possible by two years of age. These abilities include the development of the *constancies, object permanence*, the ability to make *symbolic connections*, and, finally, the beginning of *memory*.

The Development of the Constancies, Object Permanence and Stranger Anxiety. In their first few weeks of life, objects enter and leave a baby's visual field without any meaning. As the weeks go by, certain face-objects (bottle-object and Mommie-face-object) will come to have meaning (*MMMMMmmmmm . . . milk*). Then, little by little, sights and sounds become connected and other objects, colors, shapes, and size take on meaning. These are called **object constancies** (see Tip 5.2). Then, Piaget observed that somewhere between the sixth and

---

Tip 5.2 The Constancies Are Not Necessarily A Permanent Achievement: They Can Be Lost! Just because we achieve the constancies of size, shape, color, etc., in infancy, does not mean they are permanent achievements. People who are in the midst of an acute schizophrenic episode can lose these constancies. People and objects can become distorted, magnified, or shrunken. People who suffer from diseases of the nervous system, as in Alzheimer's disease, can also suffer loss of their constancies and lose their perceptions of time and space. Furthermore, in times of great distress, any of us can have visual hallucinations in which objects and people become distorted and unreal. High fever and hallucinogenic drugs can also cause disturbance of the constancies.

Table 5.1   Piaget's Age/Stage Model of Cognitive and Moral Development

Cognitive Age/Stage	Cognitive Limitations	Cognitive Achievements	Moral Age/Stage	Morality
Stage 1. **Sensory-Motor** (Birth to 2 yrs.)	No mediation. Only reflexive schemas (ex: see-reach-grab-put-in-mouth). *[handwritten: is no self aware-ness]*	Object permanence. *[handwritten: is beginning to comprehend]* Constancies of: *[handwritten: objects th... dont see.]* size, shape, color. Beginning of time: past (memory) and future (imagination). Symbolic function is beginning that will lead to language.	Amoral.	No conscious awareness of any sort.
Stage 2. **Preoperations** (2 to 7/8 yrs.)	Cognitions are concrete, functional, egocentric, animistic Cannot decentrate. Worldview is magical. Metaphors are not understood.	Can mediate one idea but one idea only. Can make choices. Symbolic function makes language possible. "A puddle is to jump in."	**Stage 1.** **Moral realism or moral restraint**	No real morality. A "good" child has learned obedience. Does not understand why rules exist. Justice without mercy. Centrated on effect.
Stage 3. **Concrete Operations** (7/8 to 10/12 yrs.)	Thinking is concrete and many abstract concepts (terms like freedom, democracy, allegiance) will not be understood.	Can mediate two ideas, making possible mathematical operations. Child can decentrate. Worldview is less magical, more realistic.		
Stage 4. **Formal Operations** (11/12 yrs. to adulthood)	Can invent solutions to mechanical problems and think scientifically.	Able to perform hypothetical reasoning, which makes possible true creativity and scientific thinking. Comprehension of abstractions, such as democracy, politics, government, *due process*).	**Stage 2. (begins at 10 yrs.)** **Moral relativity or moral cooperation**	Ushered in by rule-making. Children are learning that people make rules for good of all. Centrated on fair/not fair. Can consider causation and motivation. Morality is becoming internalized. Can now temper justice with mercy.

eighth month, the baby develops a dim awareness that objects exist even if they cannot be seen, a cognitive skill that Piaget called **object permanence**. Babies will engage in searching behavior for an object they cannot see any more. For example: If you take away the keys that they have been playing with, babies will continue to look for them, at least for a few seconds. (More recent investigations have shown that object permanence comes earlier than Piaget could determine—not because Piaget was inaccurate, but because we have more sophisticated technology with which to measure a baby's visual focus.)

An interesting consequence of object permanence is the development of **stranger anxiety**. Since infants can now recognize the *familiar* face-objects of their immediate family, they are also able to recognize *unfamiliar* face-objects. Furthermore, if these unfamiliar face-objects come too close, small babies may get frightened and begin to cry. It is a good idea to introduce new people slowly to help the baby get used to the new face-objects.

The Beginning of Memory. Object permanence is demonstrated by the baby's *searching behavior*. But this same searching behavior for a hidden object, said Piaget, also demonstrates the development of *past memory*—even if it only lasts for a few seconds duration. By eleven months of age, Piaget noted, infants are also developing a sense of *future* time. By way of illustration, Piaget provided this real-life observation: One day, his youngest child, Lucienne, was watching her mother put on her hat. Suddenly Lucienne began to cry. Lucienne was now capable of recognizing that *Mommy is here now but she will soon be gone*— a demonstration of her ability to construct a future time, if only for a few moments. This ability to think in future tense may be the single most important distinction between human beings and other life forms. Why so? Because this cognitive skill leads eventually to the abilities we call *imagination, planning, logic, creativity, inductive reasoning, and hypothesis-making*, etc. (Piaget, 1970).

The Development of the Symbolic (Semiotic) Ability. Lucienne's crying behavior also indicates another development; that is, the beginning of the *symbolic (semiotic) function*: "Mother-putting-on-her-hat" has become the symbol for "Mommy-is-leaving." The development of the symbolic function is another achievement of *homo sapiens* and will ultimately lead to the "miracle of language." The infant is acquiring many symbolic sight-and-sound connections over the next two years, like "Mommy" and "Daddy" and "All gone" and "Cookie." In fact, the average two year old will have developed up to a hundred symbolic connections for speech and be able to comprehend several hundred more (Clark, 1991). By two years of age, so many of these symbolic connections will have occurred that the infant will undergo an evolutionary leap to the second organization of mind—the **preoperational stage**. Why did Piaget believe this transition to be an evolution in the child's consciousness? Because, said Piaget, it is at this second stage that the human species is capable of mediation (ideas, concepts, and other thought processes).

Stage 2. The Stage of Preoperations: The Ability to Mediate One Idea in Mind (2 Years to 7–8 Years). By two years of age, the child is capable of **mediation**, which is to say that the child can now hold one idea in mind. This new ability allows children finally to have some choices in their lives, at least to the extent of agreeing or disagreeing with what is going on. (*Do you want a cookie? Yes! Do you want to take a nap? NO!*). Before this stage, the child could only cry if unhappy; now the child can agree or refuse to do something. This ability to make a choice is significant. *Piaget equates choice with intelligence.* According to Piaget, the more choices a life-form has, the more intelligent it is (see Tip 5.3). *But the preoperative child can hold one idea in mind and one idea only.* Don't try to give a three year old two commands at the same time (*Sally, go get your other shoe and pick out a pair of socks to wear*). By the time Sally has found her other shoe under the bed, she may run and give it to you. Picking out a pair of socks has faded from mind.

By four years of age, the child may have as many as several thousand words in his speaking vocabulary. Because he has become such a grand conversationalist, adults may think he is capable of adult reasoning. Such is not the case, said Piaget. Although the four year old has an astonishingly good grasp of language, he has a very different **phenomenology** (thought process and worldview) from adults. Among other properties, the child's thinking is concrete, functional, egocentric, and animistic (Piaget, 1970). Let's consider these properties one at a time.

Concrete Thinking. A child's concrete thinking means that children have a very literal phenomenology. For example, suppose you take your eight-year-old little boy and your four-year-old preoperative little girl to the supermarket with you. If you are like many parents, you may say, "If you are good in the store and don't whine and fuss, you may each have a quarter to spend." Unthinkingly, you give your only quarter to your four-year-old little girl and two dimes and a nickel to your eight-year-old little boy. You explain to your preoperative four-year-old that her quarter is worth the same as her brother's two dimes and a nickel. Does she understand that concept? No, she very probably does not! Very soon, tears may be streaming down her face. After all, her brother got three monies and she got only one!

The preoperative child's concrete thinking also means they will not "catch on" to jokes or understand metaphors. "Oh, dear," said a lady to her husband, "The sewing machine has developed a birdie. We'll have to take it to the repair shop." Of course, what the lady meant was that the sewing machine had developed a loud, shrill whining noise. A few minutes later, she discovered her five-year-old son staring sadly at the sewing machine. Realizing that her son had taken her words at their literal meaning, she quickly explained that there wasn't really a bird in the sewing machine, but that "a birdie" was simply another way of saying "noise like a bird." (For other examples of a child's thinking, see Box 5.3).

Functional Thinking. Functional thinking means that children understand the objects in their world in ways that make sense to them. The function of a bed is to sleep on it. The function of a glass is to drink from it. The function of a spoon is to eat with it. All well and good. But now ask a little boy what a mud puddle is for, and he answers, "To splash in." And what are rocks for? To throw of course. Ask a little girl what sand is for and she answers, "To make sand castles." At this age, children are making sense of objects in their world in the best way they can.

Tip 5.3 Piaget: Intelligence as Availability of Choices. Piaget posited that the more choices we can make, the more "intelligent" we are. A baby can only cry if it is in pain. A two year old who gets hurt can either cry *or* run to someone for help. A ten-year-old can cry *or* run to someone for help *or* apply a Band-Aid. An adult can cry *or* go to someone for help *or* apply medicine *or* go to the emergency room. Intelligence for Piaget is simply the number of other possibilities and alternatives we are capable of pursuing.

BOX 5.3   STUDENTS VERBATIM
The Concrete (Literal) Thinking of Preoperational Children

Male (17 years): I'll never forget this because I got spanked for it. Once I called my father a "smart Alec." I thought I was saying something nice, like he was really very smart.

Female (20 years): When I was young, I was really confused by the term "turning over a new leaf." I knew it meant something good so whenever I was outside with my mother, I kept turning over leaves. She thought I was looking for bugs.

Male (24 years): I had no idea what people meant when they said they had a "frog in their throat." I really used to imagine a frog and I hoped it wouldn't happen to me.

Male (24 years): When I was in kindergarten, I didn't understand the difference between "on accident" and "on purpose," which really got me into trouble. One day, I knocked a kid down while we were at recess. When the teacher asked me if I did it *on accident* or *on purpose,* I said "on purpose." I got sent to the corner for the rest of the day.

Female (42 years): When I was between four and seven, they still used radios a lot. I believed that radios actually had people in them talking and singing. It was always a mystery how all those people could fit into such a small box.

Male (22 years): I misunderstood the word *divorce* when I was about five. That was when my parents got a divorce. I must have asked why Daddy was leaving, because I remember my mother saying, "Because of the divorce." I thought it was some type of monster that was driving my daddy away from me.

Male (19 years): When my little brother went out to play and came back in, my mother would ask him, "And where have you been, pray tell?" But one day, he got really angry when she asked him and shouted, "Nowhere! And stop calling me *Praytell!* My name is *Joey.*"

Figure 5.1 The Preoperative Child's Egocentric Worldview. When asked what is closest to the teddy bear the adult is holding, the child will point to the ball. He can only see the world from his perspective.

Egocentric Thinking. Be careful of Piaget's use of the term, **egocentric**. He does not mean it as we generally use it; that is, someone who is so self-centered that he thinks only of himself and rarely of other people. What Piaget means by *egocentrism* is the special worldview of the child that Piaget phrased as follows: *A child is only able to understand his own perspective and not the perspective of other people.*

The common Piagetian example goes like this: Suppose you place a four-year-old child in front of a table with several objects on it, such as a ball, a book, and a toy car. Ask him to hold the teddy bear while you arrange the objects so that the ball is nearest to him and the toy car is nearest to you. If you ask the child which object is nearest to him and his teddy bear, he will correctly say "the ball." So far, so good. But let's take this example a bit further. Ask him to let you hold the teddy bear. When he gives you the teddy bear, you ask the child what is nearest to his teddy bear *now*. He will still say "the ball." Unlike adults, he cannot perceive the world from any perspective but this own (see Figure 5.1). Here is a real-life example you may have had. A four year old runs in excitedly with a picture she has drawn and holds it up for you to see. But she is holding the blank side toward you and the picture side toward herself. So you say, "Hold the picture so we can see it." What does she do now? She doesn't turn it around; she simply holds it higher, the blank side still facing you (see Tip 5.4).

Animistic Thinking. Primitive peoples of the past (and some traditional societies even today) held an *animistic* view of life. **Animism** is defined as the belief that *natural phenomena have supernatural causation.* Rivers, mountains, and clouds have special gods or demons that cause floods or landslides or thunderstorms. Cause-and-effect is magical and inanimate objects have animate life. For example, in the nineteenth century, when the Easter Islanders were asked how their 40-ton long-eared statues got to the seashore so many miles from the quarry, the Easter Islanders replied, "They walked there of their own accord." Children demonstrate this same animistic thinking: *Q: How did the cookies get into your room? A: I dunno. I guess they just got there.* It is a world where the witches and ghosts of Halloween make a lot of sense and where things "go bump in the night." Or consider this example of animistic thinking: A little girl gets her hand caught between the door and the jamb. After the screaming and tears are over, what does she do? She goes over to the door and kicks it! *There, you bad door, take that and that and that!*

Stage 3. Concrete Operations (From 7–8 Years to About 11–12 Years). In this third stage of cognition, children are losing their magical view of the world and their understanding of *cause-and-effect* is becoming more realistic. They are also able to hold two ideas in mind now. For example: A child at this stage will be able to enjoy jokes (primitive ones at least) that depend on the double images of puns. *Q: Why is Goofy standing on the corner with bread in his hand? A: He's waiting for a traffic jam.* (The child can now hold in mind both the image of the *jam* we eat and the image of a *traffic jam* at the same time.)

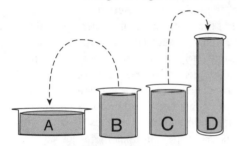

Figure 5.2 Conservation of Liquid Amount. The preoperative child is centrated on height and length. If we show a four year old that beakers marked B and C have the same amount of liquid in it, she will understand that. But if we pour beakers B and C into beakers A and D to the brim right in front of her and ask which has more, the child will answer D. Because D is taller it seems to the child to have more than the short, fat beaker A. The child in the stage of preoperations cannot remember the previous image of two beakers (B and C) as having had an equal volume of liquid.

The Achievement of the Conservations. The ability to hold two concrete ideas or images in mind also results in the achievement of the conservations. **Conservation** is the recognition that although *something may change in form, its essence remains the same*; that is to say, that the certain properties are retained (conserved). For example, even though water, ice, and steam appear to be different, they are different only in form, not in the essential aspect of H_2O.

Let's apply conservation to the psychology of a four-year-old preoperative little girl and her eight-year-old brother who is now firmly in the stage of concrete operations. Suppose you have two beakers of orange juice that are identical and you want to divide them equally into a tall, thin glass and into a short, fat glass (see Figure 5.2). Right in front of your two children, you

---

Tip 5.4 Why Children Seem to Say Cruel Things to Each Other. We have already described the preoperative child's egocentric thinking, the inability to view the world from any other perspective but his or her own. This self-centered perspective is one of the reasons children sometimes seem to say cruel things to each other. The preoperative child may say to a little girl with crossed eyes, "Boy, are you funny looking!" Children of this age cannot yet comprehend how they would feel if someone said the same thing to them. In other words, children have not yet developed the capacity to understand another's feelings.

pour the two equal beakers into the tall, thin glass and the short fat glass right up to the brim of both glasses. If you give your four-year-old little girl the short, fat glass, she will think you have given her brother more orange juice because his is the taller glass. Preoperative children, said Piaget, are **centrated** on the two properties of *height* and *length*. Your eight year old has now achieved the ability to **decentrate** and to remember the previous image of the two beakers containing equal volumes of orange juice, but your four year old cannot understand this. She has not yet achieved *conservation of liquid amount*. **Centration** is the term Piaget used for concentrating (centering or focusing) on one property to the exclusion of others.

Here's another example. Let us suppose you have two clay balls of equal mass. You give one clay ball to your little preoperative girl and you keep one clay ball. Now ask your little girl: *Whose clay ball is bigger? Yours or mine? Or are they both the same?* Your four year old will probably answer quite correctly: *Both the same.* So far so good. But now you take your clay ball and roll it out into a long, thin snake and ask the same questions. What does she answer? You've got it! She answers that *your* clay is larger because it is longer. She has not yet achieved *conservation of substance*. There are many conservations to be achieved in the stage of concrete operations, but eventually the child will achieve them.

Achievement of the Conservations and the Ability to Do Arithmetic. There are many other conservations to be learned during this stage, including the conservations of number, length, area, weight, volume. They do not all arrive at the same time, but rather are achieved one-by-one at different ages between 7 and 11 to 12 years of age. The importance of understanding the development of these conservations is this: Until the child achieves these conservations, she will not be able to understand even the simplest mathematical processes. If we insist on having her learn a mathematical process before she achieves the necessary conservation, she will simply get discouraged at her failure to understand. Furthermore, her discouragement will *generalize* (spread) to everything having to do with mathematics. Textbooks on education are now urging teachers-in-training to make sure the child has the necessary conservations before demanding that he understand, for example, the logic of number sets and beginning algebraic equations. If we do attempt to teach these processes, we will be setting the child up to hate math (see Tip 5.5).

Stage 4. The Stage of Formal Operations. The big leap to adult consciousness is the ability to think abstractedly, a powerful property of the stage of **formal operations**. With this ability, adolescents will be able to make deductive and inductive hypotheses from observations they have made. They will be able to make repairs on their bikes or cars that they have never had to handle before. They will be able to think up new ideas and demonstrate true creativity. In fact, they are becoming problem solvers. Piaget described this new ability as being able to derive new operations from previous ones. With their developing abstract abilities, adolescents can appreciate the similes and metaphors of literature (especially those of love poetry when they develop a crush on a school mate). Adolescents are also developing the

---

Tip 5.5 Who Hates Math? As a case in point, have the teacher ask members of the class to raise their hands if they "hate math." We bet the majority of the class will raise their hands. And why? Piaget would say we insisted on teaching certain mathematical concepts before these students had achieved the necessary conservation. Piaget would ask: *Why must we hurry the child by pushing him to learn when he is just not ready?* In three, four, or five months time, the child will have achieved the necessary conservation and solve the arithmetic problem with ease and liking.

ability to see themselves more objectively in terms of society. They can identify themselves according to their gender, their ethnic roots, and their religious orientation, quite apart from the orientation of their family. (*My family is racist but I think that's wrong!*) They are beginning to make independent judgments in terms of their own identity and independent choices in terms of their own life (*My dad wants me to go into business, but I think I'd rather teach*).

Piaget's Theory of Moral/Ethical Development: A Two-Stage Theory

After his monumental work on cognitive development, Piaget could have spent the rest of his scientific career continuing to fine-tune his cognitive model. But he was concerned about something we are all concerned about now: How children develop their moral/ethical character, which is to say, how they develop their ideas of "right" and "wrong." Freud had attributed our "character" to our emotional development. Piaget approached the area of moral/ethical development from another perspective altogether. One of the notations we made earlier in this chapter was that Piaget became firmly convinced that cognitive development and moral development go hand-in-hand. In other words, *children cannot reach a certain level of moral/ethical development until they have attained a certain level of intellectual functioning*. For example, we can't expect a child of five to have the same kind of compassion as we adults do for people who are physically disabled. In fact, a person with a disfigurement of some sort may even frighten them. As a result of his research, Piaget proposed a two-stage theory of moral/ethical development.

Stage 1. The Stage of Moral Realism (Also Called the Stage of Restraint). Before the age of ten, said Piaget, the child has no real morality. Children as young as three years of age can learn the rules of the house. But children obey these rules simply because they must, not because they understand the reasons for the rules. Why should he not go out into the street? Because he might be hit by a car? Well, he doesn't really believe that can happen to him. If he obeys the injunction not to play in the street, it is because Mama said so! Besides, he might get caught—and that means trouble! Before the age of ten, said Piaget, children have not developed any real internalized code of ethical principles. If children are "good," it is because they have developed **obedience**.

Centrated on Effect, Not Cause. An interesting difference between adults and children is this: While adults focus on **causation**, young children are centrated on **effect**. What that means is that adults want to know *why* a person did something while young children look at *what was done*. For example, consider the following dialogue between an adult and a five year old. Consideration of motivation and extenuating circumstances are cognitive skills that children have not yet developed.

Q: A poor boy and a rich boy both stole bread. What should happen to them?
A: They should go to jail.
Q: But the rich boy had money and the poor boy didn't.
A: Then he should ask his mommy for it.

Justice, Not Mercy. A child's moral/ethical judgments are based on justice without mercy, and the young child's sense of justice is harsh, grim, and uncompromising. If punishment is meted out, it is meted out to all and to all alike—no exceptions for extenuating circumstances. If the eight-year-old boy is going to be punished for stealing a toy from the toy store, so should his two-year-old sister who also picked up a toy. He does not understand yet that she was not "stealing," but simply copying his behavior. If we tell him that his baby sister "didn't know any better" and was only following his example, he will think we are "favoring" her. If we punish him and not his baby sister, he will be angry and think he is not being treated "fairly." Nor should we, as teachers or coaches, turn a miscreant's fate over to his classmates. Their justice will be more like the Old Testament's "an eye for an eye and a tooth for a tooth," and worse. The young child's worldview understands only black-and-white morality, the morality of folklore, fairytales, and fables. When Hansel and Gretel are rescued from the cannibalistic witch, do they show any mercy? Not on her life! They push her into her own oven to burn to death.

Stage 2. Moral Relativity (Also Called the Stage of Cooperation). It took humankind a millennia to evolve from the just God of *Leviticus* to the compassionate God of *Amos* to the merciful God of *Micah*, and to the loving God of the *New Testament*. Today, if a person has committed a crime out of extreme provocation, the law no longer demands "an eye for an eye and a tooth for a tooth." Today, the law considers *mercy* as well as *justice*. After years of physical brutality, a woman takes a shotgun one night and murders her husband. A brother and sister kill their father because he has sexually molested them for years. Justice versus mercy has become a dominant theme not only in the courts of law, but also in theology, religion, psychology, education, and literature. One of the most beautiful speeches in all Shakespeare has to do with the difference between justice and mercy. In *The Merchant of Venice*, the lovely and intelligent protagonist, Portia, describes justice as "an attribute of Kings," but mercy as an "attribute of God himself" (see Box 5.4). Piaget says that children transit from justice to mercy in the second stage of moral/ethical development, the stage he called *moral relativity*. Moral relativity has to do with consideration of individual situations and extenuating circumstances. Even then it will be many years before most of us can truly appreciate the profound maxim of Native Americans: *Never judge a person until you have walked a mile in his moccasins.*

Centrated on Rules. The stage of relativity is ushered in with an intense preoccupation with rules—to the point of obsession. Using the investigative technique called naturalistic observation (see Box 5.2), Piaget concluded that children will spend as much time arguing

---

BOX **5.4** Portia's Speech on the Quality of Mercy

The quality of mercy is not strain'd,
It droppeth as the gentle rain from heaven
Upon the place beneath: it is twice bless'd;
It blesseth him that gives and him that takes;
'Tis mightiest in the mightiest; it becomes
The throned monarch better than his crown;
His scepter shows the force of temporal power,
The attribute to awe and majesty,
Wherein doth sit the dread and fear of kings;
But mercy is above this sceptered sway,

It is enthroned in the hearts of kings,
It is an attribute to God himself,
And earthly power doth then show likest God's
When mercy season's justice. . . .
Though justice be thy plea, consider this,
That in the course of justice none of us
Should see salvation: we do pray for mercy,
And that same prayer doth teach us all to render
The deeds of mercy.
—*The Merchant of Venice*, IV, i, 184

about the rules of a game as playing it. Piaget gives the following wonderful illustration. A group of boys were let out for recess in his native Switzerland. It was winter, and the boys, delighted at the snow that had fallen overnight, made preparations for a snowball fight. But before they started making the snowballs, they got into a heated discussion over the "rules of the game." They decided, for example, how the two teams would be chosen and how they would elect the captain of each team. Then they argued over what would be "fair" and "not fair," and what the forfeit would be if someone broke a rule. (Snowballs made with stones and rocks would not "be fair.") This discussion lasted so long that the boys hardly had a chance to play before they were called in from recess. But that was of little importance, according to Piaget, their play was making "the rules."

Higher Applications of "Fair" and "Not Fair." Piaget explained that the centration on rule-making is not just play. The social fabric of our society is composed of house rules, school rules, club regulations, community ordinances, federal laws, and of course our religious commandments. All of these injunctions are the gears by which the whole machinery of our society can function and people can live together in (fairly) peaceable ways. What children are really learning at this ten- to twelve-year-old stage is how to be *rule-abiding* so that later they can be *law-abiding*. In the earlier stage, children do not consider the reasons for rules, only that they have to obey them. Rules exist because God or Mama or Daddy made them. Now children are learning that *people* make rules, people like themselves, in order for everyone to get "fair play." In fact, our civil law is just such a matter of deciding what is "fair." While most local judges and juries decide on this question for individual cases, it is the purpose of our higher courts to decide what is "fair" for groups of people. The only real difference is the terms being used: The higher courts use more sophisticated terms, terms like *human rights, equal rights*, and *civil rights*, but both the courts and children are considering issues of "fair play."

HARTSHORNE AND MAY: MORALITY IS A DEVELOPMENTAL PROCESS . . . AND SITUATIONAL

A study that fits very nicely into Piaget's moral/ethical theories is a study carried out in the late 1920s by the New York City public schools, from grade 1 through grade 8 (Hartshorne & May, 1930). The psychologists defined morality by such terms as honesty, trustworthiness, and self-control. What they observed was that all the children in grade 1 cheated (looked at answers on the teacher's desk) and stole (took cookies from another desk) when they had an opportunity and if they thought they would not get caught. Little by little, as the children progressed from grade 1 through grade 8, fewer and fewer children engaged in stealing or cheating when the opportunity arose. The researchers concluded that, more often than not, children develop honesty and self-control by getting caught, or by observing others getting caught, or by admonitions of what can happen if they do get caught. *Morality*, the researchers concluded, *is a process that develops over time, bit-by-bit*.

The researchers also discovered that this developmental process is *situational*. A child might do something "wrong" at home that he wouldn't dream of doing in school. Somehow it's okay to take money from Mom's purse, but he would never take money from the teacher's purse. Another example: The 12-year-old child might think it wrong to steal something from

BOX **5.5** **Can Very Young Children Empathize? It Looks Like They Can**

One of the limitations of the work done by Piaget and Kohlberg was dependence on the child's language ability. Until the children are three years of age, their verbal ability is quite primitive. In order to take advantage of good language skills, Piaget began with six-year-olds. Kohlberg reached down to the three-year-old level, which is the age that most children have enough linguistic ability to engage in a question-and-answer dialog if it is kept simple. But if we discover that very young children seem to be able to demonstrate empathy completely without words of any sort, would that indicate that very young children demonstrate an *empathetic morality*? That is what developmental psychologists asked and tried to find out.

Observational studies have confirmed that very young children do indeed demonstrate a well-developed sense of empathy—particularly, if it is someone they know and identify with. For example, children who were present when their parents are hurt either physically (father having a bad headache) or emotionally (mother having received bad news and crying) react with discernible empathy and comfort. They wanted to help the parent or to "fix" the problem. For example, after one mother had an argument with her husband and broke down crying, her

not-quite-two-year-old daughter climbed on her lap and became physically affectionate.

But the ability to be empathetic may begin even earlier than two years. Some years ago, Martin Hoffler began observing infants and babies right from birth. Several researchers have traced evidence of empathy to early infancy. They hypothesize that empathy evolves along with the concept of a Self in babies. Newborn babies do not have a sense of Self; they cannot distinguish between themselves and other people. For example, when neonates hear other infants cry, they themselves begin to cry—and they cry more fiercely than when they hear any other loud noise. Sometime later in their first year (the studies do not agree on just when), infants begin to get a sense of themselves as distinct from other persons. Now when they hear other babies crying, they may not themselves cry. Instead, they may turn in the direction of the crying. Or if they are toddlers, they may run to their mothers and climb on her lap, very unhappy until the crying ceases. Sometime during their second year, they may even try to help the crying child by offering their teddy bear or comforting them. As they get older, their repertoire of helpful, comforting behaviors increases.

Sources: Dunn, 1988; Hoffler, 1991.

"old Mr. Swenson" who owns the neighborhood convenience store "because he's nice and he doesn't have a lot of money." But somehow it's okay to steal from a large department store "because they're rich and have insurance."

LAWRENCE KOHLBERG AND CAROLE GILLIGAN: IS MORALITY GENDER SPECIFIC?

A fascinating controversy is going on at the present time that centers on the work of two formidable psychologists: Lawrence Kohlberg and Carole Gilligan. To appreciate how this controversy came about, we will provide a bit of background on both psychologists in turn.

Lawrence Kohlberg

Although he came from a wealthy family and could have had a life of complete leisure, Lawrence Kohlberg wanted to make a difference in the world in some highly altruistic way, to do something for the common good. As a graduate student at the University of Chicago, he came across Piaget's work at a time when Piaget's theories were not yet accepted in the United States. So impressed was Kohlberg by Piaget's stage theory of moral/ethical development, that Kohlberg decided to devote his entire academic career toward investigating its **validity** (the professional word for its truthfulness and accuracy). In particular, he wanted to determine if Piaget's model of moral/ethical development, which was predicated on French-speaking children in Switzerland in the first half of the Twentieth Century, could also be applied to English-speaking children living in America in the second half of the Twentieth Century.

Kohlberg's Three-Level, Six-Stage Model of Moral/Ethical Development

Piaget had only studied school-age children from seven years to thirteen years. Kohlberg started with three-year-old children (when they can understand simple questions and reply to them) and went up to 16 years. Despite the differences in time, culture, and age, Kohlberg validated some of Piaget's basic findings (for example, that children younger than the age of ten do not have any internalized sense of morality). He also validated another of Piaget's findings; namely, that a young child's judgment of right and wrong is not based on *causation* but on *effect*. Not only did Kohlberg substantiate Piaget's basic stage theory, he extended it considerably, to three levels and six stages (see Tip 5.6).

Level One: Preconventional Morality (3–10 Years). Agreeing essentially with Piaget, Kohlberg maintained that young children before the age of ten have no real internal morality. They are at the preconventional level of moral development. Kohlberg also validated Piaget's observation that a young child's judgment is based on the tendency to centrate on *effect* rather than on *cause*. Let us suppose, for example, that Allen has been sent to the cupboard by his mother to get one plate and accidentally breaks five plates. Bobbie, on the other hand, sneaks into the cupboard to get a cookie and accidentally breaks one plate. Adults will look at motivation and judge Bobbie to have been naughtier than Allen. Children, however, are centrated on effect and will say that Allen was naughtier. Consideration of causation will not emerge, generally, until the conventional level of moral/ethical development.

Stage 1: The Stage of Obedience/Disobedience: Avoiding Punishment. At the first stage of the preconventional level, the child's morality is based on obedience (just as Piaget had said). The child refrains from doing wrong things because he wants to avoid punishment.

Q: Why should children not do bad things?
A: So they don't get into trouble.

Stage 2: Hedonistic Self-Interest: Looking Out for Number One. The morality of the second stage of the preconventional level (starting around seven years) is based on self-interest. Although the child may seem to be a little more considerate of other children, he is motivated by what he will get out of it. If he is generous toward others, it is because he may reap rewards later.

Q: Why should you let Johnie play with your toys?
A: If I let him play with my toys now, he'll let me play with his toys.

Tip 5.6 On the Titles of Kohlberg's Stages. Over the decades that Kohlberg developed his stage theory of moral/ethical development, he changed some of the titles of his stages. If the readers come upon different titles than those in this chapter, they will be easy enough to identify.

Kohlberg noted that this preconventional level can be applied to the general population as well as to young children. Ask career criminals in prison what they did wrong and, more frequently than not, the answer will be "I got caught." Other adults who are at the preconventional level are the "con man" who scams us out of our money and the Internet "identity thief."

Level Two: The Conventional Level (10–13 Years).   At around ten years of age, children begin to exhibit a morality based on the standards of society. It is also the morality of most Americans, said Kohlberg. It is a conventional morality in which there is a right/wrong dichotomy. Certain things are right and everything else is wrong in black and white, having no shades of gray.

Stage 3: Good Girl/Good Guy Reputation: Wanting Others to Think Well of Them.   In stage 3 (about ten years of age), the child's moral reasoning is based on what others will think of him or her. He wants his parents to be proud of him. He wants others to like him. He acts in ways that will earn their trust and liking.

Q: Why should you be good?
A: So Mommie and Daddy will be proud of me.
Q: Why should you not tattle?
A: So the other kids will like me.

Stage 4: Respect for Law, Duty, and Authority: Conforming to Rules, Regulations, and Laws.   At about twelve or thirteen, the child enters the fourth stage of morality, a stage that is characterized by a respect for society at large. They are beginning to understand the concepts behind the solemn oaths we take, such as the *Scout's Oath* and the *Pledge of Allegiance*.

Q: Why should we obey laws?
A: (12 years) If we didn't have laws, some people would get more. That isn't fair.
Q: Why do we have laws?
A: (16 years) If we didn't have laws, there would be anarchy, and that would be awful.

Level Three: Postconventional Morality (Age 13 and Up).   Well, is there anything beyond conventional morality? Yes, said Kohlberg, there is another level. Some people develop a personal conscience that is so strong that they are willing to follow their own higher ethical standards rather than the standards of conventional morality. It is not an easy task to follow one's conscience rather than societal standards. It requires "taking thought." It requires recognizing that societal rules and laws sometimes lag behind the moral issues of the day. It requires a recognition that if we always go "by the book," we may be committing a *legal* right but a *moral* wrong. Their inner direction leads these people to see beyond the "letter of the law" to the "spirit of the law."

Stage 5: Contractual/Legalistic: Respect Our Laws or Change Them.   This stage involves being committed to upholding rules whenever possible, but being willing to bend them a bit when needed in individual cases. For example, health-care procedures in hospitals frequently require a multitude of official procedures and paperwork that are very time consuming, sometimes involving delays for days. In certain life-and-death situations, health-care workers develop "shortcuts" so as to save the patient's life. They do the procedures first, and fill out the required paperwork after the fact.

Q: Have you ever "broken" the law?
A: Not really, although sometimes I have had to be very liberal in my interpretation.

Stage 6: Individual Conscience. People who have reached this sixth stage of postconventional morality are willing to disobey "unjust laws." They are following their individual conscience. An example of this, of course, are those civil rights workers who broke the unjust laws of desegregation before the Civil Rights Act of 1954. The idea of disobeying unjust laws brought down condemnation upon Kohlberg from many critics. They accused Kohlberg of encouraging delinquency, perhaps even anarchy. His answer to these critics came by way of quoting Socrates, Ralph Waldo Emerson, Chief Justice Louis Brandeis, and Martin Luther King, Jr.

Mark Twain provides a literary example in *Huckleberry Finn*. In the early part of the story, Huck runs into Jim, who is an escaped slave on the run. Huck has been taught by the "good people" of Hannibal, Missouri, that slaves are the property of their masters. To help a slave run away is the same as stealing the master's property. A person can go to Hell for stealing! But Huck regards Jim as a friend. He thinks about the beatings Jim will get if he, Huck, returns Jim to his master which is a heart-wrenching thought for Huck. At this point, Huck engages in a monologue just as soul-searching as Hamlet's "To be or not to be" (a speech in which Hamlet ponders the issue of suicide). Huck makes his choice based on his own individual conscience rather than on the societal standards of Hannibal, Missouri. Although he imagines the gates of Hell are opening wide in front of him, and he knows he will never to able to return to Hannibal, he chooses to befriend Jim. He shrugs and guesses he will "just have to go to Hell," after which, Huck and Jim sail to freedom on that famous raft down the Mississippi.

Carole Gilligan: A Feminine Perspective

Let's listen now to "a different voice," one that bespeaks of a feminine point-of-view of moral/ethical development in women. Carol Gilligan began teaching at Harvard with the renowned psychologist, Erik Erikson, whom you met in Chapter 3. Later, she became a research assistant for Lawrence Kohlberg. It was Kohlberg's thesis that only ten percent of the American population ever reached the highest stage 6, and that few, very few, of them were women. This conclusion, particularly as it related to women, led Gilligan to investigate the moral/ethical development of women. As a result of her research, she came to the conclusion that it is *not* that women do not reach the highest levels of morality but that women have a *distinctly different* kind of morality, one based on caring and concern for others. To really appreciate Gilligan's thesis, we make note that her book, *In a Different Voice: Psychological Theory and Women's Development*, was published 1982, just at the time when many feminists were insisting that there are no essential differences between males and females. Yet Gilligan was saying that there *is* a difference between male and female moral/ethical orientation, and a huge one at that.

Male versus Female: Justice Orientation versus Care and Responsibility Orientation. First of all, said Gilligan, men are more concerned with abstract *principles* of equality and fairness (*We hold these truths to be self-evident: that all men are created equal . . .*). It is the type of moral/ethical problem solving that befits the legal system, courts of law, political governance, and business contracts. Women, on the other hand, are concerned with people first, and the care and responsibility we all have toward others. Given the same moral/ethical dilemmas that men encounter, women respond first to the person who needs help immediately, and only later considers what rules and regulations are involved. Men tend to be more narrow and self-first focused whereas women are more willing to be self-sacrificing in order to help others. Men build hierarchies of status and clearly established pecking orders that distance people from each other. Women's orientation is connecting with others, which precludes dominance and power.

A Three-Stage Moral/Ethical Model for Women. Gilligan outlined the moral/ethical growth of women in three stages: first, a preconventional selfish stage; then a belief in conventional morality; and finally, a post-conventional morality. The three stages sound similar to Kohlberg's three levels, but the descriptions diverge considerably.

Stage 1: Preconventional Morality or Selfish Stage. Like little boys, little girls begin with a selfish stage, which may last right up to adolescence. (Is there anyone as selfish as the adolescent girl in full bloom?)

Stage 2: The Belief in Conventional Morality: Taking Care of Others. Even as selfish little girls, they are taught to care for others. Ultimately, as they grow up, their care for others takes precedence over care for themselves. In fact, they come to equate concern for themselves with selfishness and typically sacrifice themselves for those they love and care for.

Stage 3: The Post-Conventional Stage: Taking Care of Self. Eventually, women come to recognize that it is wrong to always put others ahead of self. Women begin to understand that it is just as important to take care of themselves as it is to take care of others. In a difficult relationship with another person (male or female), someone is going to get hurt, but that doesn't mean that it has to be the caring and responsible woman that gets hurt. As far as Gilligan is concerned, women perceive the injustice that can be done by the male preference for rules and regulations, and by sticking to the *letter* of the law rather than to the *spirit* of it. Gilligan provides examples of male and female morality at the highest levels as follows:

At the highest levels, men operate according to:
An ethics of justice
Out of concern for principles and logic
A concern not to have our freedoms restricted
Feel safer when there is an orderly hierarchy
Prefer to remain distant and separate on a personal level

Men were more apt to choose these choices:
We ought to worry about our own country first and let the rest of the world take care of itself.
I find it hard to be sympathetic toward starving people in foreign lands when we have so many in our country.
It's not my problem if others are in trouble and need help.

At the highest levels, women operate according to:
An ethics of care
Out of concern for personal responsibility
An imperative to alleviate the sufferings of others
Make connections by diminishing power and status
Prefer personal warm relationships and intimacy

Women were more apt to choose these choices:
I would agree to a good plan to make a better life for the poor, even if it causes me to have less money.
Americans should change their eating habits so as to provide food for the hungry elsewhere in the world.
I get very upset when I see people treated unfairly.

What Can We Do Now to Foster More Care— Orientation in Our Children?

Many social scientists are investigating this question, both nationally and worldwide. Of course, it takes many years to discern whether or not certain parenting and school practices in early childhood through to high school result in the successful attainment of the care mode of personality in both genders. We await the results of these longitudinal studies with a great deal of anticipation. In the meantime, we can provide the reader with some recommendations presented by the American Psychological Association to offset the external influences of violence, such as daily violence on TV, a generally hostile neighborhood, and a culture that exalts "heroes" who are violent and even criminal.

- Treat children with the same kind of respect and dignity you would like them to show others: *Thank you for getting the newspaper this morning, when I was so sick, and bringing it to me.*
- Let them know how highly you regard their kind behaviors: *I saw you help that little girl up on the playground. That was so kind of you. It makes me very proud of you.*
- Let them know how strongly you feel about their unkind acts: *When you punched your sister, it made her cry. We don't like behavior like that. Treat your sister more kindly. If you are upset with her, talk to her first; and if that doesn't work, talk to me.*
- Provide them with books that promote compassionate behavior, but not the kind that have "goody two-shoes" characters. Look for books that show ordinary people who perform acts of caring and concern.
- Find out about movies your children want to see. If they are excessively violent or if they glamorize criminals, do not sit down to watch these movies with your children. As they get older and can watch these kinds of movies themselves, have discussions with your children that deal with other ways the characters could have acted. A little discussion goes a long way in having teenagers reflect on the movie. Reflective critiquing will partially negate an accepting attitude to everything they view.
- Educate your children about famous altruists. Local museums and your public library will be very helpful in finding books and other materials that foster appreciation of outstanding historical or living persons. Ask them who they admire and why.

Who Reaches the Highest Levels of Moral/Ethical Development? College Students Like You!

Kohlberg concluded from his research that only 10 percent of the American population ever reach this sixth stage of moral development. Who are these persons? Kohlberg described them as mostly male, middle class, college-educated people. It is the middle class, college-educated young people of any country who not only develop the highest levels of morality and ethics, but who are willing "to stand up and be counted." They have the ideals and physical energy to move their society to new levels of justice, mercy, and "fair play." In other words, they may very well be each of you, the readers of this book. We also believe that many more of you, men and women both, will reach those levels than did Kohlberg's subjects. Your generation is a much more sophisticated and "savvy" generation than the generations of Kohlberg's research studies. You are a post-Watergate, post-Vietnam, post-Kennedy/Martin Luther King Jr. assassinations, post-Berlin wall, post-Chernobyl, post-9/11 generation. You pay more attention to news broadcasts. You are more attentive to newspaper editorials. You tune in to presidential debates on TV. You are more apt to make your voices heard. You keep an eye on your governmental officials. You know and understand the need for freedom of the press and all media. As such, all of you are potential candidates for the highest levels of moral/ethical development.

BOX **5.6**   EVALUATING THE KOHLBERG–GILLIGAN CONTROVERSY
Different Research Methodologies

Lawrence Kohlberg

On the Plus Side

1. **Validation of Piaget's stage theory.** Although Piaget's observations were carried out in the first half of the twentieth century and on his specific French–Swiss culture compatriots, Kohlberg's work demonstrated that Piaget's stage theory can be applied to English-speaking children living in a highly technological society in the second half of the twentieth century.
2. **Extension of Piaget's stage theory.** Not only did Kohlberg validate Piaget's stage theory of moral development with American children, he also extended it. By studying children as young as 3 years of age and upward to 16 years of age, he was able to fine-tune and extend Piaget's work to three levels and six stages.
3. **A framework for parenting and education.** Kohlberg also validated Piaget's theory that moral/ethical development has a natural progression. The consequence of this process thesis is that we can perceive "disruptive" children or "naughty" children, not as "just plain bad," but as being at a lower stage of moral/ethical development. That being so, it follows that we can foster higher levels of moral/ethical development at home, in

the classroom, and on the playground. Kohlberg's theoretical formations have become a significant part of philosophy, theology, education, sociology, psychology, and education, etc.

On the Minus Side

1. **Sample bias.** Kohlberg's study was sample biased because his subjects came mainly from white, affluent, and well-educated families. His research findings cannot be generalized to minorities and to other socioeconomic levels without more research on these other subcultures.
2. **Gender bias.** Gilligan pointed out that Kohlberg's sample was also gender biased. Because he did not take into account the possibility of gender difference, he believed that far fewer females than males reached the highest stages of moral/ethical development.
3. **Social desirability bias of the interview method of research.** Social desirability is the desire to provide acceptable answers to an interviewer. What children acknowledge to be the right thing to do is not necessarily what they actually do. Children may be able to say what is the right thing to do but, under the pressure of the peer group at the moment of decision making, they may make a choice of going along with

BOX **5.6** EVALUATING THE KOHLBERG–GILLIGAN CONTROVERSY (continued)
Different Research Methodologies

the crowd and make the wrong moral/ethical choice.

Carole Gilligan

On the Plus Side

1. **Research based on both men and women facing *actual* moral dilemmas.** Noting the social desirability of Kohlberg's studies, Gilligan approached the study of female moral/ethical development with a different research approach. Many of her conclusions were the result of interviewing men and women *in the middle of an actual moral dilemma*. The men were considering enlisting during the Vietnam war; the women were having to make decisions about abortion. Follow-up on these interviews of what the subjects actually did narrowed the social desirability bias.
2. **A care and responsibility model for women.** She proposed the thesis that men have a *justice* orientation and that women have a *care and responsibility* orientation that develops in three stages. The three stages are the result of how women have been brought up to be caring and responsible for others.
3. **The care and responsibility orientation of traditional societies.** Gilligan also posited the theory that this orientation will be found among smaller, more traditional cultures, a thesis that looks promising but needs to be considerably researched.

4. **A stage theory of feminine self-actualizing?** If Gilligan's model proves to be valid, she may have constructed a stage theory for women's self-actualizing, as distinct from that of men.

On the Minus Side

1. **Creating a woman-as-victim industry.** Some critics have said that Gilligan has exploited the myth of "girls as victims" in our educational system. These critics point out that, at the present time, girls are out-performing boys in every area of school except in sports. Girls are more motivated to study, get higher grades, and are more likely to go to college from the middle and working socioeconomic classes. At the same time, these same critics say that Gilligan's model denigrates young boys and men that is disrespectful and harmful (Sommers, 2000).
2. **Validation of her findings has been notably lacking.** A more serious charge has been the lack of verification of Gilligan's findings. This lack of validation may simply be flaws of the replicated studies, but it may be due to a more serious problem. Gilligan used anecdotal evidence and has not allowed other researchers to look at the data. Gilligan has defended this lack of openness about her interviews on the basis of confidentiality but, by using pseudonyms, that confidentiality would not be violated.

SOME ANSWERS TO WHAT IS GOING WRONG?

Learning the "Three R's" Involves Learning a Whole New Set of Behaviors

What we need to understand is that learning the "three R's"—reading, writing, and 'rithmetic—is not easy for many children (see Tip 5.7). In kindergarten and first grade, they have to learn to do things they have never had to do before. For example, in first grade, they have to

---

Tip 5.7 On the "Three R's." Over many years of teaching we have discovered that some students have no idea what the traditional "three R's" refers to, either because they are international students or simply have not come across this term before. The term can be confusing. The traditional "three R's" refer to *reading, writing, and arithmetic*. Why are these three terms called the "three R's" when only one of the terms begins with R? Sometime in the distant past, someone coined the phrase for the skills of reading and writing (which though it begins with W, is pronounced as an R) and 'Rithmetic (a contraction of the word *arithmetic*).

learn to sit quietly in chairs at their desks to do their "independent seat work" for what seems to them long stretches at a time. Moreover, they aren't supposed to talk to their neighbors, and since that is very hard for them to do, they get reprimanded. They have to learn to raise their hands before they answer questions, and sometimes they forget and yell the answer (which may be wrong) and get reprimanded again, even if ever so gently. At home, they were taught to go the bathroom as fast as possible to avoid "accidents." Now they have to learn to raise their hand to go to the bathroom. And hardest of all, for the little boys in the class, they have to learn to write letters and words between two lines, which takes a lot of fine finger–hand coordination, skills in which boys lag far behind the girls. After a few minutes of this tiring work, they can be seen to lay their heads on their desks, not because they are lazy, but because they are tired out from all that hard "writing stuff."

Environmental Deprivation

Some children come highly prepared for learning their "A B C's," in fact, some children may already be reading and writing to some degree. These children generally come from homes where they were read to, where books and magazines abound, where the parents esteem education and foster their children's language skills early on. Many of these parents are professional people who make sure that their children have a "good start" at home, with proper nutrition, who make sure their children brush their teeth, take daily baths, and wear clean clothes.

But not all children have these advantages. Some children may live in isolated areas where poverty and illiteracy abound, as many of our Native Americans still do in their sometimes very inhospitable reservation environments. Children of migrant workers have to move from school to school, sometimes several times in the same school year. Some children have families who do not speak English, and so come to school having to learn English as a second language. Or they may have parents who are alcohol- and drug-addicted and are suffering from parental neglect. Or there may be several sets of parents, by reason of divorce and remarriage, and the children are continually shuttling from one set of parents to the other set. Or there may be a mother and many "uncles" who come and go in swift succession. Or they may live in single parent homes (usually with mothers), who are doing their best to be both mother and father. Then there are the terrible living conditions of slums and ghettos and barrios where ten- and eleven-year-old children learn to survive by carrying knives and guns, and become the "mules" for dope for their older siblings. These streetwise children learn, early on, to disrespect school. The respect they crave is from the older members of the street gang.

For those whose families live under the poverty level, or in the ghettos and slums of the big cities, the school systems have instituted Head Start programs for children from three to five years of age. These programs try to provide those kinds of experiences and learnings that will catch them up, a little at least, with those children who have come from better home environments.

But even children who come from a good environmental background can also have problems of a different kind. For example, they may have physical disabilities, such as being visually impaired or hard-of-hearing, or they might have a debilitating disease that drains the child of the energy needed for learning. Or they may have a disability of another sort, a learning disability such as **dyslexia** (difficulty in learning to read) or **hyperactive/attention disorder** (**ADHD**) (unable to sit quietly and focus on their studies). In this chapter, we are going to discuss two other damaging environmental influences that impede a child's ability to learn: first, the shameful and terrible topic of child abuse; and second, the emotional consequences that come from school failure and grade retention in the primary grades.

BOX **5.7** STUDENTS VERBATIM
Moral/Ethical Development

Immature Moral/Ethical Behavior

Male, 6 yrs: In first grade, I cut up the school bus seat with a razor blade and blamed someone else.

Male, 8 yrs: I stole $2.00 from a student's desk. I have never stopped feeling bad about it. It wasn't that I wanted the money. I just wanted to see if I could get away with it.

Male, 8 yrs: I found out where all the Christmas presents were. So I looked for the ones that had my name on it. After I opened them to see what was inside, I wrapped them all up again. Obviously, my mother knew it was me. I didn't know how she knew because I thought I had done a good job wrapping them back up. Of course, I know now.

Female, 9 yrs: I roomed with my sister who was two years older than me and I knew she had this diary. So I took it one day to school and me and my friends sat around and read all her secrets about who she had a crush on and all that. It got back to her though and she went home crying.

Female, 10 yrs: I picked up a small bottle of perfume from my friend's dresser when she went out. I was going to put some on myself but I dropped it and it broke. When my friend came back to the room, she saw it on the floor. I pretended I didn't know anything about it.

Female, 12 yrs: I stole some items from a store for Mother's Day.

Male, 12 yrs: I had a paper route. Once when I threw the newspaper, it hit a potted plant and broke it. I didn't want to get blamed so I switched my paper with my competitor's paper from the next house over. I guess he got blamed. I still feel sorry about that.

Male, 13 yrs: My friend's father was my teacher for biology. I talked my friend into getting me the answers to a test.

Female, 15 yrs: I wasn't doing well in Spanish so I told the teacher that I had been very ill with mononucleosis. I guess she believed me because I got a C for that six weeks.

Mature Moral/Ethical Behavior

Female, 9 yrs: When I was in the fourth grade, we used to bring in cupcakes for a birthday. This one time, I brought the cupcakes in but when I put them out on the plates, I realized we were short by one. I didn't tell anybody. I just went without, and they were chocolate, too!

Female, 11 yrs: In sixth grade, the kids used to make fun of a girl who had acne, and I stood up for her. I still feel good about that.

Male, 15 yrs: When I was a senior in high school, all my friends were going to "egg" this popular girl's house, but I backed out at the last minute. When they got caught later, I was sure glad I had.

Female, 15 yrs: When I was a sophomore, I started visiting the area hospitals after school on Fridays, seeing the patients and sitting with them, and giving them a copy of whatever newspapers I had with me. It made me grow up a lot and feel good too.

Male, 16 yrs: My friends and I were going tubing down the Ichetucknee River, and we rented tubes. My friends felt like we had gotten ripped off (in price). So they wanted to steal the tubes, but I talked them out of it.

Male, 17 yrs: I was working as a cashier for a hardware store. A customer accidentally gave me a $50.00 bill, thinking it was a $5.00 bill. It was tempting, but I pointed out to her what she had done.

Reflecting Writing: After you read the examples, describe an immature behavior of yours when you were younger than you are now. State the age of the misbehavior.

Now describe something you did, either when you were younger or only recently, that reflects a more mature moral/ethical behavior.

Sexual Abuse of Children

Statistics on child abuse in all its forms—sexual, physical, emotional, and neglectful—are difficult to come by: First, because these abuses are difficult to define; second, because of their **comorbidity** (two or more kinds of abuses with the same child); third, because the abuse is very much underreported; and fourth, because different states have different systems of reporting. Let's take sexual abuse as an example. We all could probably agree that if an adult has actual intercourse with a ten-year-old child that sexual abuse has been perpetrated. But when the situation is less clear, researchers are confronted with the question of just what constitutes child sexual abuse. For example: If bathing a baby girl up to two years of age is an act of a caring father, is it still OK for that father to be bathing his eight-year-old daughter? Or if a father is massaging his daughter's thighs and calves because they are painfully cramped after a soccer game, is that to be considered as molestation? Considering all of these difficulties, as well as the fact that different states have different definitions of sexual abuse (or any kind of child abuse), estimates vary from 30 percent to as high as 60–70 percent (Haugaard, 2000).

Consequences of Sexual Abuse. The effects on the child are variable. Some children seem to recover quite quickly and with little long-lasting consequences, partly because of their own innate **resilience** (inner strength and ability to rebound from stressful conditions), and partly because of the type of molestation or abuse. **Prognosis** (prediction) for swift recovery is positive if:

1. The molestation was a single event and not violent (exhibiting in front of the child);
2. External to the family grouping (such as a stranger masturbating in front of the child);
3. The child is given emotional support by other family members; and
4. It is kept confidential so that her schoolmates and neighbors do not learn of it.

The prognosis is much poorer if the molestation does become public—in spite of the combined efforts of family, police, health officials, and other agencies to keep it confidential. The child is then confronted with whispers and curious looks of neighbors and classmates, which intensify the child's trauma. An even more serious and grievous situation occurs if the child is not believed. The child may be accused of lying to get back at the offending parent, or of wanting special attention by pretending to be a victim.

Presuming that the perpetrator is a relative or male friend of the family, the effect on the child may be even worse. Family members may accuse the child of bringing shame on the family name. They may even tell the child she should have kept her mouth shut. Even if these accusations are never spoken aloud, the child senses the unspoken hostility within the house. Along with the shame of what happened to her, the child now has a heavy burden of guilt for revealing her dark secret. The child now feels friendless and abandoned, which may prove even worse than the sexual abuse itself. If the abuser was the father or father surrogate, the consequences of a court trial and incarceration of the perpetrator results in diminished income without the father's salary, which may be blamed on the victimized child by other family members. If the child is temporarily placed in a foster home, the alienation from everything she has known and everyone she has loved is complete.

We need to add this note. Sexual abuse is not limited to girls. We are beginning to become aware of the number of boys who also have been sexually abused by family members, by Boy Scout and church leaders, and by pedophiles who have kidnapped them.

Physical Abuse of Children

Physical and sexual abuse are often perpetrated on the same children. There are times, however, when the child is not sexually abused but only physically abused. As a nation, we have been shocked by reports of children who have been burdened, beaten, and even killed by parents, stepparents, or parent surrogates. Like sexual abuse, it is difficult to secure accurate statistics on physical abuse, but the following reported statistics may provide some insight into the enormity of it, underestimated as it surely is (Emery & Laumann-Billings, 1998):

- Approximately three million allegations of child abuse and neglect are reported every year.
- Homicide is one of the five leading causes of death of children under 12 years.
- Over half of these homicides are perpetrated by a family member.
- Estimates of 1,200 to 1,500 children are killed each year by a parent or parent figure.
- A shocking estimate of 80 percent of the aggression against children occurs by sibling abuse. It should be noted, however, that a child can be injured by siblings through seemingly "normal" sibling behaviors such as pushing, grabbing, or hitting their younger siblings.

If the child does not die, the tragedy of this kind of abuse is not just the visible physical scars that remain but the invisible emotional scars. The little girl or boy remains a psychologically "wounded child" that takes abuse from others or fights viciously with them (Teicher, 2002). In homes where there is a stepparent or unattached male, the risk of physical abuse is about eight times higher than with a biological father. When confronted with their actions, the perpetrators often rationalize their abusiveness that the child "had it coming." (When the abuse is sexual, the perpetrator often rationalizes that the child was "coming on to them.") Whatever may be the "causes" of child abuse, the number of reported cases of physically abused children has been steadily increasing year by year. Whether this increase is actual or more a matter of public awareness of the problem is still unknown (Teicher, 2002), but the problem is immense.

The Emotional Consequences of School Failure and Retention

We come now to a problem that as many as 5 to 10 percent of American children face and which we, as a nation, *can* and *must* do something about; the problem of children who experience the humiliating and debilitating effects of school failure and retention. Retention in the primary grades is supposed to help a child "learn the basics." But a meta-analysis of studies was carried out during the decade of the 1990s (Jimerson, 2001). Of the 20 studies analyzed, only four showed positive results; all the other 16 studies showed negative results for the child. Factually, what these research studies indicate can be summarized as follows:

- Most children do not "catch up" on their basic skills when held back.
- Although some children seem to do better at first, they often lag behind again in later grades.
- Students who are held back tend to get into more trouble at school and with the law.
- They tend to drop out of high school as soon as they reach sixteen.
- They have a higher dislike of school.

- They show a lowered self-esteem.
- They have poorer interpersonal skills.
- They have a higher tendency to become alcohol and drug addicted.

It is hardly surprising that, instead of helping children do better in school, retention only discourages them. Consider what it means to the children to be "left back." All their friends and classmates have gone on and here they are sitting with younger and smaller children, most of whom are doing better than they are. They may try to do the required seat work and struggle with their reading but they now hate school. Their bodies are at school but their hearts and minds are elsewhere. When the recess bell finally rings, they are the first to line up, eager to get away and out of the classroom. Consider this also: If these retained children hate to be in school, then school has become their prison. If school is their prison, then they are prisoners and we, their teachers, have become their prison guards. This situation is hardly a psychological state of mind that fosters learning.

We add one more fact for your consideration. Most of the retentions in the public school system over the last one hundred years occur either in Kindergarten or in the first three primary grades (Sakowicz, 1996). What we are doing then, as a society, is to convey to children who are only five, six, seven, or eight, that they are failures in life, which is an emotional blow that most children never recover from. Research has shown that even academically able children view retention in school to be as terrible as the death of a parent or blindness (Sevener, 1990). Factor in this information as well: The preponderance of children who are retained are children who:

- Come from poorer minorities and families who do not have much education themselves;
- Are mostly boys who are generally conceded to develop cognitive skills later than girls;
- Come from large families with parents who do not have time to supervise homework;
- Have been moved from one school to another;
- Come from a bilingual background; and
- Have learning disabilities that need to be identified earlier and offered remedial services by the school.

So Do We Have To Socially Promote Children Who Can't Read and Write? No, we don't, provided the school system has been given the funds to provide alternatives. The National Association of School Psychologists (NASP) has advocated the following measures:

- Provide mixed-age classes for the first three grades (where most of the retentions occur) and let the children learn at their own rate. Children come to school wanting to learn, but when we push them beyond their age/stage readiness (as Piaget pointed out so early on), they fail and they grow to hate school.
- Lower the number of students in the early primary grade classes so that the teacher has time to spend with each and every child.
- Assign our *best* teachers to these early grades because that is where they are needed to prevent student failure.
- Send instructional aides to the homes of high-risk children to provide the parents with specific, structured ways to set up study times for their children, to help their child

with homework; and to act as part of the child's learning team along with the child's teachers.

- In addition, we can and should provide individual tutoring for the children who need special help. One-on-one tutoring is the best type of instruction in academic subjects just as it is the best type of coaching in voice and music lessons, in boxing, golf and other sports, and in computer science.

If "IQ" Scores Are Highly Suspect, How About Multiple Intelligences?

Back in the early 1980s, when professionals in the field of psychology and education were getting rather fed up with the uses and abuses of "IQ" tests, a psychologist–educator by the name of Howard Gardner suggested we stop thinking and talking in terms of "IQ" entirely. Since "IQ" scores are predicted solely on academic aptitude, he said, we are overlooking many other kinds of intelligence. We all probably have known very high "IQ people" who are academically smart, but are quite inadequate in other areas of living, such as in social skills, and who seem to lack plain old common sense, and, in general, live a very constricted existence. On the other hand, we have all known (or read about) people who never got very far in school but were such great salesmen that they climbed the organizational ladder swiftly and easily. Other people may have a real talent in music and dropped out of school to join a rock-and-roll band and made good. Gardner knew of these types of people, too. He proposed that we start considering **multiple intelligences** (MI) (1983). As other professionals suggested other kinds of abilities, MI theory came to include *musical* intelligence, *linguistic* intelligence (writing a poem or reading a book), *spatial* intelligence (ability to put things together), *bodily-kinesthetic* intelligence (athletic and dance, etc.), *interpersonal* intelligence (getting along with others), *intrapersonal* intelligence (insight and understanding of oneself), *natural* intelligence (ability to discern patterns in nature), *spiritual* intelligence (concern for cosmic understanding), and *existential* intelligence (concerned about the meaning of life). But of all the multiple intelligences suggested, the one kind of intelligence that took the strongest hold of the psychological and educational communities in the 1990s was *emotional* intelligence.

NEW DEFINITIONS FOR INTELLIGENCE

Defining Emotional Intelligence (EQ)

The two psychologists who first used the term **emotional intelligence** (**EQ**) defined it as a set of skills involving the ability *to understand our own feelings and the feelings of others and to use this information to guide one's thinking and actions* (Salovey & Mayer, 1989). Social intelligence is what enables us to deal with difficult situations without panic. However it is defined, emotional intelligence or EQ has become recognized as far more important than "IQ" scores for academic achievement, vocational success, and family relationships (Goleman, 1995). The definition of emotional intelligence has not yet stabilized. But most psychologists agree that the following traits and abilities are included:

- Empathy
- Understanding one's feelings
- Expressing feelings
- Respect for others
- Adaptability
- Ability to get along with others

- Controlling one's temper
- Independence of thought
- Independence of action
- Persistence
- Friendliness

- Sensitivity to the feelings of others
- Optimistic and smiling demeanor
- Kindness
- Self-awareness and desire to improve
- Ability to understand other people's feelings

And Still Another Definition of Intelligence: The "New Three R's"

Here's another definition of intelligence, almost hot off the press, so to speak. Each year, the American Psychological Association (APA) honors an outstanding psychologist by electing him or her as president. We have already referred to the work of several of these presidents: Gordon Allport, who called us "human becomings"; Martin Seligman, who inaugurated the focus on "positive psychology"; and Phil Zimbardo, who is best known for his prison experiment. Whereas the position is largely honorary, it is customary for each president to initiate a specific mission for his or her year of office. In 2003, newly elected president, Robert Sternberg, initiated a thrust toward eradicating violence, intolerance, and hate groups, and working for civic tolerance, understanding of others, and peaceful interaction of all our citizens. Sound familiar? Of course. But of special interest to this chapter, is that much of this effort is being directed toward educating our children in what is now being called the "**New Three R's**" of *reasoning, resilience, and responsibility* (DeAngelis, 2003; Dodgen, 2003; Sternberg, 2003).

Defining the "New Three R's." In defining the educational "New Three R's," Sternberg believes that **reasoning** (the first of the three R's) is what school systems typically view as "intelligence." Sternberg's research findings, however, reveal that reasoning (or what is sometimes called analytic intelligence) cannot be isolated from the other two R's of responsibility and resilience. High-school students, for example, who scored high in responsibility and resilience along with reasoning, were more likely to succeed in college than those who tested high solely in *reasoning*. The second of the three R's, **resilience**, is the ability to confront challenges and resolve problems. All of us, says Sternberg, at sometime in our lives, will encounter periods of "staggering defeat" or at least times of extended discouragement. To quote Sternberg, "The question is not whether you will go through [such periods]; it is how you will come out of [them]" (DeAngelis, 2003, p. 46). The third R, **responsibility**, makes our achievements worthwhile by benefiting other people. Sternberg's Center for the Psychology of Abilities, Competencies and Expertise at Yale University is attempting to discover ways to actually teach principles of wisdom so that their graduates will not make poor choices, like the executives and accountants of Enron and other corporate "white-collar gangsters."

Implications of the "New Three R's." The implications of the "new three R's" of intelligence are staggering. It means that good mental health is a significant aspect of intelligence. It means that we can no longer describe a career criminal as "highly intelligent." It means that a person with high moral/ethical values is manifesting more "intelligence" than those who think greedily only for themselves no matter what their "IQ" score is. It implies that members of hate groups and cults must be considered as less intelligent than those who are open-minded and accepting of others who are different in race, religion, ethnic background, and language.

The major thrust of the "New Three R's" is educational. They need to be the central focus for parents, teachers, athletic coaches, church and civic leaders, and, indeed, for anyone whose work involves children and adolescents (Kersting, 2003). Fostering the "New Three R's" has become a major mission for psychology and education, not just to make "good people," but to foster people's creative intelligence. To Piaget's thesis that cognitive development (reasoning) and moral/ethical development (responsibility) go "hand-in-hand," has been added what the "New Three R's" is calling resilience, a personality trait that is indicative of good mental health.

BOX **5.8** THE "NEW THREE R'S"

Fostering Resilience and Responsibility for Truly Creative and Intelligent Children

Raising emotionally intelligent children means fostering their resilience and responsibility. The following are suggestions only and not hard-and-fast rules. Each child is unique and what may work for one child may not work for another child. These suggestions, therefore, are guidelines only.

Resilience

1. Keep communication open. Be the kind of parents that your children are not afraid to come to with problems. Let them know that if they tell the truth, they will not be punished by you. That does not mean that they get away "scot free" for a mean or very inappropriate behavior. (See suggestion #2 under Responsibility.)

2. Act as role models in problem solving. You have probably heard this before but what we are suggesting here is not to appear perfect. Share problems you have with children of the appropriate age, small problems with young children and more serious problems with adolescents. Then allow them to observe how you resolve the problems. What you are doing is providing them with insight that problems are solvable.

3. Demonstrate interest in them. Be actively interested in what is going on at school, at home, and with friends. More and more, parents are becoming out-of-touch with their children, whether because of working or having to be out-of-town on assignment, or being intimidated by children's computer Internet skills. We need to know more about what our children and adolescents are doing. They will be glad that you are interested enough in them to know what they are doing and why.

4. Start early to educate them about alcohol and other drugs. Don't wait until they are in their teens to talk about drugs. A large part of being vulnerable to

drugs is peer pressure. Children younger than teenagers are still parent-oriented rather than peer-oriented. Get them involved in question-and-answer games, such as *How would you go about resisting someone who offers you cigarettes/alcohol/drugs? What would you say to your best friend who tells you he won't like you if you don't join in?* Don't tell them they are right or wrong. What you want is for them to think about it and derive answers for themselves. You are fostering resilience to temptation.

5. Encourage the child's self-competence. Resilience is built by making objectives and achieving them. The child's goal may be competency in sports or one of the arts, or attaining badges in the Scouts. Whatever the child's goal is, do what you can to enable the child to achive them. Goal attainment in childhood will encourage later goals as a teenager. One success fosters the child's confidence in being successful in other goals.

Responsibility

1. Establish gentle but firm discipline. Don't be afraid of setting house rules for young children and appropriate "night out" curfews for teenagers. Let them know that if they keep the rules and curfews responsibly for (say) six weeks, they will be given more possibilities for self-direction. If it is possible among other parents, establish common guidelines. It will help you and your child to know that the rules they need to abide by are shared by other families.

2. Allow them to make amends for errors. What you really want is to teach your child that errors need to be corrected. If you punish them physically, they will only think of the pain you caused them. If you punish them in other ways, such as grounding them for a month, they may feel you are being unfair. So allow

BOX 5.8 THE "NEW THREE R'S" (continued)

Fostering Resilience and Responsibility for Truly Creative and Intelligent Children

them to think of ways to make amends. Example: If they broke someone's window, they can help pay for it. Example: If they were mean to a young sibling, they can think of some way to be good to the child.

3. Apologize to the child when you make a mistake. No one's perfect. We all make mistakes. When you apologize to a child or teenager, you are doing good things. First, you are making amends for your error. Second, you are teaching him how to apologize, a great skill that many people are unable to do for any number of reasons: poor self-esteem, emotional immaturity, or a mental disorder.

4. Encourage "random acts of kindness and senseless acts of beauty." Allow the child to witness your own acts of kindness and beauty. While walking, pick up litter and encourage the child to help you. If an older child has a sick friend, encourage visits, talk to the friend on the phone, or volunteer to bring home school assignments from the teacher.

5. Foster school responsibility. Don't be afraid to expect good grades. In his/her hardest subjects, help the child with homework or get a tutor. In easier subjects, set up study time, but don't interfere with the child's own competence and creativity. If the child proves to have a learning disability, confer with the teacher about ways to enable the child to learn. It is a good idea to have a child with you in the teacher conference so he/she is participating in the remediation plan. The child also may need special learning disability assistance.

Important Terms and Concepts to Remember

• animistic	• emotional	• moral/ethical	• responsibility
• care	• Flynn	• morality	• retention
• causation	• formal	• multiple	• rule-making
• centrated	• functional	• negative	• sexual
• cognitive	• hand-in-hand	• obedient	• situational
• concrete	• justice	• object	• social
• constancies	• levels	• post-conventional	• Three R's
• conventional	• male	• preconventional	
• developmental	• mediation	• preoperative	
• effect	• morality	• resilience	

Make Your Own Chapter Summary by Filling in the Blanks

Use the "Important Terms and Concepts to Know" to fill in the blanks.

Jean Piaget. Piaget was the pioneer of cognitive and _____ development. _____ development has to do with the way children learn to think. Piaget outlined four organizations of mind, starting with the sensory-motor stage in which children have no _____, which means they do not have ideas or thoughts in their head. During this stage, children develop _____ permanence (the understanding that things exist even if they aren't seen) and the _____ of color, shape, and size.

The second stage is called the _____ stage, characterized by _____ thinking, which means that children perceive the world in ways that make sense to them; for example, a puddle is "to jump in." _____ thinking is defined as imbuing inanimate objects with life. The third stage is called the stage of _____ operations, in which the child can mediate two ideas or concepts at the same time, making possible the understanding of simple mathematical facts and figures of speech. During this third stage, children are no longer _____ on height and length. The stage of _____ operations is the beginning of adult thinking, which means that the individual can truly think creatively and scientifically. Piaget hypothesized that before the age of ten, a child has no real _____. If a young child is "good," he has simply learned to be _____. Adults seek to understand the reasons for human behavior, thus they are concerned with _____. Young children, however, are centrated on _____. The beginning of true morality begins with an obsession with _____. Hartshorne and May discovered that morality is a _____ process over time and is _____.

Lawrence Kohlberg and Carol Gilligan. Kohlberg validated Piaget's moral/ethical developmental stages but extended it to three _____ and six stages. Most American adults are at the _____ level, while children and career criminals are at the _____ level. Kohlberg believed that only ten percent of American male adults reach the highest _____ level, and females even fewer.

Gilligan, on the other hand, posited a gender difference in that men have a _____ orientation while women have a _____ and _____ orientation.

Moral/ethical considerations. The _____ effect has upended our understanding of intelligence by positing a continual rise in "IQ" over the last 50 years. If Piaget was right that cognitive development and moral/ethical development go _____, why are so many of our children becoming delinquent and using drugs at earlier and earlier ages? The answer lies, in good measure, in the environmental variables of _____ abuse, physical abuse, and emotional abuse, which retard the child's normal development. High risk for abuse is a household with an unattached _____. Another obstacle to cognitive development is _____ in the primary grades. Most research studies indicate that retaining children has _____ consequences and is not supported by the National Association of School Psychologists. Nor is _____ promotion advocated; other alternatives are provided in the text.

We no longer put as much credence in "IQ" tests today and we are considering the thesis of intelligences, of which _____ intelligence has taken the strongest hold. Most recently, there has been proposed another definition of intelligence; that it is not simply reasoning; it must also include _____ and _____. Guidelines for teaching the "New _____" are suggested.

6

The Agonizing Journey Through Adolescence

Teaching Our Children How to Avoid the Perils of the Teenage Years

---

Shannon Confides in Her Friend, Jonnimae

Shannon and Jonnimae are having lunch together in the cafeteria.

Shannon: There's somebody I like a lot and I think he likes me. How can you tell if a person is interested in you, I mean *really* interested?

Jonnimae: Bless your heart, Honey, I think I know who it is! Eduardo, right?

Shannon: (*blushing*) How did you guess?

Jonnimae: I got eyes. You got a king-size crush.

Shannon: Is it that obvious? (*Jonnimae nods.*) Oh, dear, I hope everybody hasn't noticed. I hope Eduardo hasn't noticed.

Jonnimae: Why don't you want him to know, for heavens' sake!

Shannon: Because maybe he doesn't feel that way about me.

Jonnimae: Of course he does! How come you don't know he's got a crush on you too?

Shannon: Does he really? How come he hasn't said anything to me?

Jonnimae: Honey, he's probably just as scared as you to make the first move. You gotta let him know.

Shannon: How do I do that?

Jonnimae: Well, the first thing you can do is when he looks at you, don't look away like I see you do. Smile at him. Let him know you like him.

Shannon: What will he think of me if I smile like that? My mother would call that being "brazen."

Jonnimae: These are things girls learn how to do naturally when they reach about thirteen.

Shannon: Gosh, I'm so ignorant about guys. You see, I've never been on a date—not a real one. We used to go on church picnics and we got paired, sort of, by the organizers. Girls brought the picnic and guys brought things to sit on and games to play. I hated those picnics because I never really knew if the guy liked me or just felt sorry for me because . . . well, you know . . . because of my club foot.

Jonnimae: A pretty girl like you afraid of boys? You just got to let them know you like them. Boys aren't nearly as tough as they put on. They can brave eleven other men out on the football field, but make a speech in front of a class or approach a girl they like, and their knees turn to sand and they get tongue-tied. I guess I'm going to have to tell you about how girls and boys go about getting to know each other and dating. I've been talking to my teenagers about sex and dating and all that. I might as well talk to you, too—if you wouldn't mind, that is.

Shannon: Mind! I've been dying to have someone talk to me. I'm just plain ignorant. Compared to all the boy–girl movies I see on TV, I'm so backwards about sex, I could cry. I never had any girlfriends in high school. Please talk to me about dating and sex—if it wouldn't embarrass you. My mother never talks to me about anything except what she wants me to do in the house. And it's the one subject my daddy and I never talked about. I guess it would have been too embarrassing for him—and me too, I guess.

UNDER A CALM EXTERIOR: ANXIETIES, FEARS, EMOTIONAL MOOD SWINGS

When we watch teenagers walking across a high school or college campus, the landscape seems to be one of busy but unexciting clusters of students. When we ask them what they have been doing or learning, their verbal replies seem to corroborate the scene we are watching: *Nothing much. You know, school, homework, hanging out with friends—the usual.* But our observations and their answers do not match the roller coaster of moods and emotions of their interior landscape. Studies of teenagers reveal that their moods and emotions swing from ecstatic satisfaction to the depths of depression several times a day, particularly in the first two years of high school (Fischman, 1987). Both their ecstatic elations and their dejections revolve around peer acceptance or rejection and a lack of meaning in their lives. They attempt to fill up the void they feel by socializing with their peers, talking on the telephone with their friends, watching TV, and—when all else fails to alleviate their feelings of emptiness—by sleeping. Their parents, who are nagging them to do their chores or trying to get them involved in family affairs (which they mostly hate) wonder (as do we all): *Just what are teenagers troubled about?* From the point-of-view of their bewildered parents, teenagers today have more money in their pockets, more "advantages," than they had, and more leisure activities to get involved in than any previous generation. So what is ailing them? A lot of things!

Puberty versus Adolescence

Before we go any further, we need to define two commonly misused terms, *puberty* and *adolescence*. **Puberty** refers to all the sweeping physical changes that turn a girl into a woman and that turn a boy into a man. In the female, these changes include the development of breasts, rounded hips, pubic hair, and the **menarche** (the first menstrual period). In the male, these changes include the development of a muscular body, broadening of the shoulders, enlargement of the scrotum, deepening of the voice, and facial and pubic hair, etc. **Adolescence** refers to all the psychosocial changes that accompany puberty (see Figure 6.1). These changes include a sudden and strong attraction to the opposite gender, anxiety and confusion about how to achieve peer acceptance, and an intense desire to be rid of parental control and manage their own lives.

Figure 6.1 Puberty versus Adolescence. Puberty refers to the physical changes and adolescence refers to the psychosocial changes.

THE TROUBLED ADOLESCENT: MORE FRIGHTENED AND INSECURE THAN ADULTS REALIZE

It was an early American psychologist, by the name of G. Stanley Hall, who called our attention to the turbulence of this time of life by coining the term **adolescence**, from Latin root words meaning "to grow up" (Hall, 1904). He described this age/stage as a period of *sturm-und-drang* (German for storm-and-strife). It will come as no great surprise to the readers that adolescence is an even more difficult age/stage today than a century ago (see Tip 6.1). Parents of this age group freely admit adolescence to be the most trying time of parenting. High school teachers not infrequently get "burned out" by trying to teach classes of students who have intense adolescent problems. Nor do adolescents themselves experience this time of life as a happy one. Studies reveal that the self-esteem of adolescence is lower in high school than at any other time of the life span (Beane & Lipka, 1986.) If the readers are still in their late teens and early twenties, they can probably still remember some of the confusions, anxieties, and problems of their own high school years. The pressure to perform, to excel, to be pretty, to be thin, to be an athlete, to be a "jock," to dress, to drive a car, to be just accepted by one's peers—in short, to compete with others in every dimension of high school life—all make the years of junior and senior high school a misery for most young people.

For many years, Hall's metaphor was quite accepted, but as the decades passed, his metaphor of the teenage years as being a time of turmoil was largely discarded as not typical of the "average" teenager. Psychologists and educators began to describe "most adolescents" as quite well adjusted and growing well. And then in the decade of the 1990s, the nation was rocked by news of violence among the nation's 10 to 18 population, particularly by the high-school shootings of Littleton, Colorado, and Conyers, Georgia, and elsewhere. What was also startling to the middle- and upper-socioeconomic classes, these shootings were not committed by teenagers in the slums and ghettos of our major cities. The shootings were being perpetrated by middle- and upper-middle-class white youths in the suburbs that seemed the epitome of "a good place to live and raise your children." Americans are now asking themselves: *What is going wrong?*

Their Struggle for Identity: More Difficult Than During Past Eras

Erik Erikson (1950) posited the life task of adolescence as *identity*; that is, to know who they are as contrasted with their families. Up until adolescence, children identify strongly with their families. The eight-year-old boy will say proudly, "We're Rebublicans/Democrats in our family." The ten-year-old girl comments to her new best friend, "We're Protestants. What are you?"

By contrast, the adolescent is trying to find an identity of his/her own. In our society, it is not easy. The adolescent may now say, "My parents think I should go to church every Sunday. I don't think that's right. I would rather go to church because I want to and not because I have to!" So difficult is it for adolescents in our time to discover who they are and where they are going, that Erikson described this time of life as the "big crisis" (Erikson, 1950). A large part of this problem can be attributed to the changes in our society during the past century.

Tip 6.1 On the Term, *Sturm-und-Drang*. Hall saw a correlation between the emotionally expressive poetry and life styles of the Romantics of the eighteenth century (Byron, Shelly and Keats, for example) and the adolescent's emotional turmoil. He compared the Romantics' struggling for freedom with the adolescent struggle for freedom—with this essential difference: Where the Romantics were struggling for the freedom from Europe's oppressive governments, today's adolescents are struggling for their own personal freedom. In the worldview of today's adolescents, the rest of us are a supporting cast, either helping them to achieve their quest for self-expression or interfering with their freedom to do so. Generally speaking, the people who are hindering them the most are their parents, but others in the supporting cast of their romantic drama are their teachers, principals, officers of the law, etc.

We regard teenagers, not as adults, but as youngsters who are still not prepared for life and we require them to remain in school, at least until the age of 16 and (hopefully) into their twenties. So here they are, the adolescents of our time, feeling like adults but viewed by society as children, neither fish nor fowl, struggling to understand who they are. To achieve the task of identity, they may reject their family values and even their families. Moreover, their self-esteem at this time of life is as fragile as a bubble, easily punctured by verbal jeers, snubs, and bullying by their peers. To be accepted by some clique or crowd, they may indulge in alcohol and drugs, engage in shoplifting, burglary, and worse. We then may send them to a juvenile detention center, half-way house, or even prison, still keeping them under our supervision. By way of contrast, let's consider previous eras.

In previous centuries, once young boys and girls got past the age of 11 or 12 years of age, they were no longer viewed as children to be taken care of, but as working members of the family, particularly in the middle and lower socioeconomic classes. Sons of farmers worked with the adults in the fields. Sons of shoemakers learned the trade of shoemaking alongside their fathers. Other young lads might be apprenticed to a baker, a bricklayer, or an iron monger—and their fathers paid well for the apprenticeship. Girls began to learn their adult roles even earlier, helping their mothers to cook, bake, and take care of the little ones. The Industrial Revolution brought with it sweat houses where both adults and children might labor twelve hours a day, six days a week. Nevertheless, young adolescents were learning their adult roles alongside their parents and other adults.

Young lads, who got in trouble or wanted to rebel from the standards of their parents and community, could become a cabin boy on an oceangoing vessel at fourteen years of age. Or he could follow the advice of Horace Greely, the newspaper editor, who said "Go West, Young Man," and become a cowboy, a gunslinger, or a hobo. Sometimes, after the young man had enough of this kind of adventurous life, he might settle down and become a "respectable citizen," if he was lucky enough to live that long. But the point is that if he ran away at 13 years of age to join the circus, he wasn't taken into custody as a truant from school as he would be today (Hine, 2000). There are no such options for today's adolescents who want to leave the nest and try their wings. They cannot legally escape from a society that tells them they have to remain where they are, no matter how miserable they are feeling. And many of them are feeling miserable. If it were not so, we wouldn't have as many school drop-outs, suicides and attempted suicides, runaways, and violence in the schools as we do. (The National Incidence Studies of Missing, Abducted, Runaway and Thrownaway Children (NISMART 2), released October 2002, for example, estimates that more than 800,000 children are reported missing each year, the largest percentage of them are runaways.)

We have to be very careful to emphasize that the teenage years in previous centuries were never idyllic. Not at all. Besides the sweat houses noted, young men who ran away to become sailors discovered that life on the sea was brutal, particularly if the

Figure 6.2 Adolescents in a Sexual Vise. Caught as they are between their maturing biological drives and society's social prohibitions, teenagers run the gamut of emotions from anxiety and confusion to embarrassment, shame, and guilt.

captain was sadistic. Life on the open range involved riding horseback from sunup to sundown in heat, cold, rain, or snow, with not much to show for it except chapped thighs, body aches and pains, and exhaustion. Many youngsters never survived their first cattle drive. Nevertheless, the problems that our present adolescents face, while not as physically fierce, are psychologically more intense.

Consider also that in smaller traditional tribes, young people could (and still can) marry and mate as soon as they pass puberty. In our society, we frown on early teenage marriage (and rightly so) because teenagers are so unready for the responsibilities of modern family life. Still, it is a difficult task for adolescents to abide by societal standards on the one hand and on the other hand to cope with their "raging hormones" (to employ a popular expression). Adolescents find themselves in a sexual vice (see Figure 6.2), they are in a constant flux of emotions that confuse them and cause them anxiety.

THREE PERSPECTIVES: THE ADOLESCENT GIRL; THE ADOLESCENT BOY; AND THEIR PARENTS

From the Perspective of the Adolescent Girl

The Need to Be Attractive, Slim, and "Sexy." The teenage girl is obsessed with her appearance. Having developed two years (on the average) earlier than boys, she has been waiting for them to show an interest in her (see Tip 6.2). She studies the young movie stars and what they look like. She rips through fashion magazines and spends hours at the shopping malls to find clothes that will make her look slim, smart, and "sexy." Often, there is also a subtle and covert campaign going on with mothers and their daughters. While mothers do not want to see their daughters engage in destructive premarital sex, many mothers apply subtle pressure on their daughters to demonstrate their sexual attractiveness. She outfits her daughter with bras, guides her in selection of clothes, and instructs her in the subtleties of makeup. When the daughter is besieged with requests for dates, both mother and daughter feel validated. The mother can be reassured that she has brought up her daughter to be poised, socially graceful, and able to handle herself in the "dating game," which is tantamount to saying: *Be attractive to the boys but don't let them engage in sexual exploration.*

Teenage girls are gaining fat in their breasts and hips and thighs as a result of puberty. These changes are in direct opposition to what our society (as portrayed in the media) finds attractive. Even when she is slim, she misperceives herself as fat when she looks in the mirror. If she is overweight, she goes on a diet. Or she may avoid most food at all costs and may become a victim of **anorexia nervosa**; that is, eating so little that she has not the required 85 percent of the average weight for her height and frame. Since a certain amount of weight is necessary for a normal menstruation, she may even experience **amenorrhea**, the absence of

---

Tip 6.2 Why Girls Become "Boy Chasers." Girls mature, on the average, about two years earlier than boys. For example, it is not unusual for their skeletal growth to begin as early as the fourth grade and their breasts may bud out by the sixth grade, while boys can be as late as high school before their bodies begin the pubertal process. Nature has made her eager to pair up with a boy she likes. He, on the other hand, remains disinterested. The result is that she pursues him and he runs the other way. She is labeled a "boy chaser" and her behavior is thought of as aberrant. Actually, she is simply responding to Nature's prodding. What she has not yet learned to do is to be subtle about her attraction to the young man. Over time, she will develop these subtle sexual cues so as not to appear "on the make."

her monthly periods. Amenorrhea is a frequent situation for female runners, for models, for gymnasts, and for ballet dancers. Other consequences of amenorrhea are anemia, dry skin, brittle hair and nails, sensitivity to heat and cold and changes in temperature, and cognitive deficits. Sometimes girls even develop growth of downy hair on their legs and cheeks. If she is hungry and cannot resist food and is afraid she is getting fat, the teen may become bulimic. **Bulimia** is binge eating followed by vomiting and regurgitating the food she has binged on. She may even use diuretics, laxatives, and enemas to keep her weight down. Whether anorexic or bulimic, these thin-obsessed girls will develop strategies to avoid treatment and recovery. They will mouth what family and physicians want to hear—that they need to gain a few pounds and are working on it. They will even prepare food for the family as a way of camouflage and then pretend to eat it (Wolf, 1992).

The Ever-pressing Question for the Girl-in-love: *Shall I or Shan't I?* Having proved themselves dateable, girls are now troubled about what to do with their boyfriends who are pressing them for sex. Their boyfriends are no longer content with simple "necking," and they pressure their girlfriends to "give in": *If you really loved me, you would!* If the girl chooses to remain virginal, she may find that she has lost her boyfriend to someone who has been willing to comply with his demands. On the other hand, if she continues to date him and wants to restrict their sexual involvement, she may discover one afternoon or evening that she has gotten herself into a situation from which she cannot escape and falls victim to "date rape." It is difficult to obtain statistics on premarital sex, teenage pregnancy, and rape, and the estimates vary widely.

Problems of the Sexually Active Girl. If the girl has become sexually active, she lives with the fear, not that she will get a sexually transmitted disease (that really doesn't occur to her), but that she may get unexpectedly pregnant. If her period is late, she lives through anxious day after anxious day until her period does arrive. If she discovers she is pregnant, she has the anxiety of deciding what to do now. As well, a girl's reputation suffers if she is sexually active in high school. If she gets a reputation that she is sexually promiscuous, she may discover that she suddenly has a lot of bids "for a date." This sudden popularity may make her feel good about herself for a while, but she may discover, alas, that her popularity is the result of "locker room bragging." Having gained a reputation for **promiscuity**, she is now the open target for any adolescent male eager to have a sexual experience (see Box 6.2). In certain adolescent crowds, a sexual "conquest" may be one of the "rites of passage" to membership. He may use any manipulative device to win her compliance.

From the Perspective of the Adolescent Boy

Teenage Boys Are Even More Frightened of the Physical Changes They Are Experiencing. Their emotional makeup has undergone a remarkable change, and they find themselves having feelings they have never had before. Their sexuality, which has been more-or-less dormant for some years now, is emerging in daytime fantasies and in nighttime dreams. At times, biological urges seem to take over their everyday consciousness. If we do not accept this one basic fact, say the social scientists who research this area, we will simply not understand the young boy-becoming-man (Goedert, 1991; Rice, 1989). If the young man does have **erotic dreams**, they may interrupt his sleeping and he wakes up to discover he has

BOX **6.2** STUDENTS VERBATIM
On Their Adolescent Sexual Experiences

Female (23 years): I was one of those who got "used" by my boyfriend. I really was. I believed everything he said to me. He kept saying how much he loved me and how he couldn't wait till we got married—that the other girls were doing it for their guys and if I really really loved him, I'd let him. My head told me "no" but it got to the point in our necking, I couldn't say no anymore. It may have been puppy love, but it was love. Then I began to notice looks I was getting from girls and boys I knew. Boys began calling me for dates, guys who wouldn't have looked at me twice. I kind of suspected a little, but he had promised me faithfully that he would keep it a secret. So I kept fooling myself until suddenly he dropped me for one of the "good girls" in the school. I know it sounds like an old story. The funny part is I laughed at my mother when she used to warn me about the guys. Besides the fact that I had gotten a "bad reputation," . . . what hurt me the most was how he had used me to make himself big.

Male (18 years): I am eighteen years old and I've been involved with Anne for three years. I really love her. We are both freshmen in college and living together. But Anne wants us to get married. She says that if I don't make up my mind soon, she's going home after the term ends. I really don't know what to do. I feel too young to take on the responsibility of marriage. But I don't want to lose Anne either. Also, this is the first serious relationship I've ever had, and I don't know if I want to tie myself down with Anne for the rest of my life. I'm just too young to know what I really want.

Female (27 years): There's something about me I guess that just attracts real "losers." I could go on and on but I'll just tell you about my first guy. When I first met him, I was almost fifteen and he was nineteen, just kicked out of the Marines. He had been mixed up with drugs and disowned by his family even. Yet, there was a certain magic in his touch that quickly made me fall head over heels in love with him. One night in a drunken stupor, he made me do seven different positions and told me he didn't love me in the middle of it. That was the worst night of my life. When I started to cry he told me to shut up. All I wanted was to be held, but he wouldn't even do that. Instead he told me that I should go out, meet more guys, and practice. After this, my eyes were opened and I never saw him again. I wouldn't even

speak to him when he phoned. It took me a long time to trust any man again.

Male (22 years): I have been secretive about my affairs but I'm going to level with you right now. I've been pretending that all the affairs I have had are with girls. Well, some of them have been, but I've come to believe I'm gay. Don't get me wrong, I'm still attracted to girls occasionally and I think maybe my attraction to men is just a "phase" I'm going through, although I can remember playing doctor with a boy across the street. I couldn't have been more than four or five at the time. For years I played it "straight." I went with girls even, but none of them were serious episodes. I enjoyed petting with them but I never went the "whole way" with them. After high school, I went into the army. I hoped that would "straighten me out," being with a lot of other men. It did keep me busy, too busy to think about sex. But when I came out of the army, I had the same old problem. Being gay doesn't bother me so much. It's all the rest of it that I hate—the gay bars, the one-night stands, the coded dialog with its innuendos. I want a relationship that has meaning. I sometimes just get depressed because I don't know what to do with my life.

Female (22 years): When I discovered that I was a lesbian I was terrified. In Korean families, it is a bad shame. I was terrified that my mother would find out. I was only twelve years old when I first knew I loved another person like myself. She was my first and only girlfriend for many years. Then my parents received notice that we could come to the United States. I was so disheartened. So was my friend. We cried in each other's arms many times together. So now I am here and very alone. I like all my friends in college but I can never forget my girlfriend who lives on the other side of the world. We write but little by little, the letters take longer and longer to be answered. Will I ever find anyone else that I can love? Then there is my mother who is always asking me when will I settle down and get married. She wants to see her grandchildren before she dies. She introduces me to many Korean men and I pretend to be interested. But I tell her I cannot get married until I finish my college and graduate, which will take a long time because I am going into pharmacy. What will I tell her after I am graduated and have a job and still not have a boyfriend? I do not know.

had **nocturnal emissions**, known popularly as "wet dreams." During the day, he may have **spontaneous erections**, which embarrass him. If he has not masturbated since his early child-hood, he may now discover he has the urge to do so again. But whereas masturbation came easily as a child, he is older now and the desire to masturbate is masked with shame and fear. He is caught between the twin furies of desire and guilt. He yearns to talk to someone about his awakened sexuality but does not dare. Instead, he joins the boys in locker room bragging, which he knows is mostly "sound and fury signifying nothing."

Boys, Too, Are Worried about Their Appearance. Like girls, boys are tremendously worried about their appearance. If he is late-maturing and sees himself in the mirror as gangly, thin, and undersized or as the fat boy everyone calls names, he is stricken with low self-esteem. He wants girls to find him attractive but they obviously prefer the jocks. He must endure the insulting names he is called by the other boys: Skinny, Fatso, String Bean, Shortie, Half-Pint, Peanut, Pee-Wee, Noodle-Head, etc. He dresses in a far corner of the locker room so his lack of sexual maturity is not obvious. To compensate for his lack of "manliness," he watches for signs of beard growing. He works out in the gym to develop muscles in order to look more virile. Nothing seems to work. Some of our young adolescent males resort to using steroids in pursuit of the advertised image of a muscular male body. Unfortunately, use of steroids can lead to increased aggression, severe acne, sexual impotence, and (if needles are shared) to AIDS. Life seems mean, and he hasn't found many activities he can do that will bolster his self-esteem. If he's good at his school subjects, the "jocks" will call him a "nerd"—so getting good grades doesn't give him any pleasure. In fact, if he's smart, he'll make sure no one finds out the high grades he has been getting (Hall, 1999).

They Are Afraid of Being Bullied. Bullying is rampant. Investigations into the possible causes of the Littleton shooting (and there have been many), reveal that one variable appeared, time and time again: the bullying that was going on by the larger, macho boys against the smaller more vulnerable boys. Teachers, say high schoolers, turn a blind eye on anything that doesn't occur in their classrooms. Yet the bullying is going on all the time in the halls, in the boys' bathrooms, in the locker rooms, on the playground, and on the school bus (Fitzpatrick, 1999).

The Former Enemy Has Become Objects of Desire and He Has No Idea How to Approach Them. The young man's awakened sexuality not only astonishes him, it puts him into an embarrassing position. Since the first grade, young boys have regarded the opposite sex as "the enemy." Whereas girls between six and puberty have been willing to share confidences about which boys in class they like, boys of the same age have been only sharing their mutual dislike and disgust of the female gender. They smirked at the romantic affairs of their older brothers, and while they may have poured over a magazine of female nudes, their interest in breasts and buttocks was mostly academic. In their worldview, they considered girls to be inferior in every way. They can't play football or baseball! They like to play stupid games! And all they talk about is movie stars and clothes. *What do older guys see in girls anyway?* Now, almost overnight, their feelings about the opposite sex have undergone a dramatic change. The very personages they have been disparaging for so long are now the focus of their eager interest. They are bewildered by their realization that their former enemies have turned into objects of desire.

The young teenage boy has no idea how to institute diplomatic relations with the former enemy. Girls are different! They talk differently. They act differently. They seem to giggle over things that boys can't fathom. And they seem so . . . soft, ah that's not right. *So delicate, yeah, delicate, that's the word.* How do you get to talk to one of them? He doesn't know how to make an approach and he is too embarrassed to ask someone who could advise him. Unable to solve this dilemma, he does nothing. Well, not exactly nothing. He engages in a lot of covert girl-watching. He listens to the guys brag in the locker room. He peruses those magazines filled with girls in bathing suits (or less), and hides them where he thinks his mother or sister won't find them.

On Moving to a New School, They Are Afraid of Not Being Able to Make Friends. As traumatic as it is to move for the entire family, it is probably hardest on teenagers. Moreover, since the cliques and groups of the high school hierarchy have been firmly established by the sophomore year, both adolescent girls and boys are daunted by the prospect that they may not be able to find a group with whom to relate. Teenage boys, in particular, need the support and strength of friends in order to fend off the bullying that goes on. Or else they have to learn to endure insults or develop protective devices by which to fend off the insults and the bullying—in short, to accept being on outcast. To be an outcast boy is to be a "nonboy," to be feminine, to be weak. The outcasts are accustomed to the daily onslaught of bullying. Outcasts survive by their stamina, sometimes by their fists, but mainly, if they're lucky, with the help of the "family" they've created among their outcast friends (LeBlanc, 1999).

Homosexual Adolescents: "High Risk" for Suicide

Another problem that some adolescents will have to deal with is homosexuality. No one can imagine the utter bewilderment and loneliness, or the guilt and despair of adolescents who wonder, as they are growing up, if there is "something wrong" with them. They know they are not experiencing the same reactions as other girls and guys in their peer group. They may even have inklings that they might be homosexual but are not quite sure (many desperately hope they are not). Their growing self-awareness is accompanied by anxiety and guilt since it is so overtly condemned by so many in society. In the meantime, they have to withstand the onslaught of jokes and slurs about "gays," "fags," and "fruits," all through the day. It has been estimated that the high-school male hears about 25 antigay remarks in the course of a day. Not only do adolescents fear their own differences and being "found out" by their peers, they also do not want to hurt their parents if their parents are **homophobic** (an exaggerated fear and dislike of homosexuality).

The DSM: Homosexuality Is No Longer Listed as a "Disorder." In the 1980s, the *DSM-III* removed homosexuality from the list of abnormal disorders "to be cured." Mental health professionals have also rejected many other fallacies concerning homosexuality. For example, we know that homosexuality does not come about generally as the result of seduction by an older person. As well, the evidence of a genetic and biological basis is mounting. In the "soft revolution" of the 1960s and 1970s, homosexual men and women organized themselves into activist communities and called themselves gay. They came out of the closet not only in America but all over the world. They revealed themselves not as the stereotypic "drag queen" but as responsible men and women in many endeavors: as scientists, as military officers, and as some of our most notable writers, artists, entertainers, and athletes. Furthermore, the Supreme Court upheld the right of American homosexuals to have the same civil rights as other minorities in our society; i.e., they may not be fired from a job solely on the basis of being gay. Our society was becoming more realistic in its understanding of homosexuality, and we began to acknowledge their creative contributions to our culture and civilization (see Tip 6.3). Gradually, more enlightened attitudes were taking over the prevailing homophobia in the United States.

Then something happened that resulted in a sudden whiplash of intolerance: the discovery of AIDS in the early 1980s. Because it was first detected among the homosexual population, the disease itself was blamed on homosexuals. In Africa where it originated, however, AIDS is a heterosexual disease. Then a number of terrible abuses of adults on children came to light. Ministers, priests, Sunday school teachers, and boy scout leaders were brought to trial as child molesters. Once again, homosexuality was indicted as being an aberration and in terms of children (pederasty)—it certainly is! (What we were ignoring was that a much higher percentage of heterosexual adults have been child molesters than homosexual adults.) The courts had ruled that what occurs between two consenting adults is a private situation. Nevertheless, homophobia began to increase again.

Self-Awareness for Males Generally Comes about in Adolescence. If that is so, then what these youngsters-becoming-adults need is education, including sex education, just as all our young people do. They need the kind of education that will enable them to become responsible and moral individuals, as all our adolescent youngsters need. They need to understand the stresses and strains that go along with being homosexual that must still be covert in many areas. They need to be even more aware of the danger of sexually transmitted diseases (STDs) in general and AIDS in particular. They need not just education but counseling about what it means to be a sexual minority. They need effective education to build their self-esteem. They need vocational counseling to enable them to find work that leads to responsible citizenship. If they do not get this kind of intervention, they are at high risk for suicide. In a health survey carried out on 35,000 students in Minnesota public schools, homosexuals have a much higher rate of suicide than the general population. Fully 28 percent of the bisexual and homosexual boys reported a suicide attempt compared with 4 percent of the heterosexual boys (Remafedi, French, & Story, 1998). Clearly, they need adult understanding, adult acceptance, and adult support.

Tip 6.3 Famous Homosexuals and Bisexuals in History

Alexander "the Great," world conqueror
Julius Caesar, emperor and world conqueror
Ellen DeGeneres, comedienne
Melissa Ethridge, singer
E. M. Forster, writer
John Maynard Keynes, economist
Leonardo da Vinci, Renaissance painter and inventor
Frederick "the Great," Prussian king

Richard Lionheart, King of England and crusader
Erasmus, Medieval cleric and philosopher
Michelangelo, Renaissance sculptor and painter
Sappho, ancient Greek poet
Richard Turin, scientist and British Intelligence Officer
Peter Tchaikovsky, musician and composer
Tennessee Williams, playwright
Virginia Woolf, writer

FROM THE PERSPECTIVE OF THEIR PARENTS

Sudden Personality Changes in Their Adolescents

After congratulating themselves for having raised decent human beings at about age eight through ten, parents suddenly find that their "decent human beings" have become over-emotional, unreasonable, hyper-critical, victims of wild mood swings, and selfish to the extreme. *What has happened to our "decent human beings?"* Their adolescents have developed several personality traits their parents haven't seen before. On the surface they can strike us as amusing or simply irritating. But these characteristics can also prove to be dangerous—even lethal! (Elkind, 1984).

An Exaggerated Belief in Their Abilities. First, adolescents begin to have an exaggerated idea about what they can do and accomplish. They consider themselves now as adults who do not need or want parental guidance. Question teenagers who have run off (and perhaps gotten into drugs, prostitution, and other destructive life styles) as to how they thought they were going to survive without money, without a high school diploma, or a way to make a decent income, and the typical answers are: "I thought I could handle it. I thought I could make it on my own." They do not yet know what they don't know—that kind of understanding comes with more experience of the world and is the benchmark of creative philosophers, writers, and scientists, and generally all mature adults.

Adolescent Egocentrism. Adolescents are developing a social conscience for people in far-off corners of the world but it does not seem to apply to people closest to them. Tammy "hogs" the bathroom despite the fact that other family members have been pounding on the bathroom door for some time. When Tommy gets permission to use the car, he returns it with so little gasoline in the tank that Mom can't get it started the next morning. Tammy "borrows" her mother's best blouse without asking, although she would be outraged if her mother invaded her closet. Tommy "forgets" to return his father's tools after using them and they are now rusted. When confronted with their behaviors, they storm upstairs and slam their bedroom doors. But even behind closed doors, they can be heard all over the house.

> *"No matter what I say or do, I'm always wrong."*
> *"Why does EVERYONE keep treating me like a child. I know what I'm doing."*
> *"Nobody in this house cares about my feelings."*

They have "retrograded" into what Elkind (1984) has termed **adolescent egocentrism**, unable to appreciate the situation from any point-of-view but their own. They probably regard their parents as "old fogies" or "really dumb" and "behind the times." They are already making plans to avoid all their parents' "mistakes." They are going to be "perfect" parents and have "perfect" children. In the words of Mark Twain, "When I was fourteen, my father was so ignorant I could hardly stand to be around him. When I reached my twenty-first year, I was amazed at how much the old man had learned in seven years."

The Personal Fable. As the hero and heroines of their life stories, they are prepared to set forth on crusades to help feed the poor, to aid the victims of hurricanes and earthquakes, and to set forth on missions of peace. The are John Glenn, Joan of Arc, Robin Hood, Florence Nightingale, young Tom Edison, and James Bond. They see themselves as special and are sure that what applies to other people should not apply to them. Their failure to get a term paper or term project in on time should not result in points being taken off for lateness because . . . because their little sister had to go to the hospital last night. Because the family car broke down two days ago. Because they had to help clean the house this past weekend. The term paper deadline was set six weeks ago but *their situation is different.*

The personal fable refers not just to the hero and heroine role they are acting out; it refers to their belief that they are invincible. The accidents and tragedies that touch the lives of other people will never happen to them. Waking up in the hospital, their parents ask them what on earth induced them to drink and drive. *Didn't they know they could have an accident that way?* The usual answer: "I didn't think it would happen to me." When they become pregnant, and are asked why they didn't take precautions: "I didn't think it would happen to me." And tragically, when they practice unsafe sex and contract AIDS, the answer is still "I didn't think it would happen to me."

The Imaginary Audience. The adolescents' heightened self-importance gives rise to a phenomenon Elkind calls the **imaginary audience**. Preoccupied with themselves as the "star" of their personal fable, they are constantly concerned how they appear to others, and they are desperate for acceptance. In fact, the lower the self-esteem they feel, the more they will engage in **social conformity**. They adopt the same dress, the same slang, the same taste in music and entertainment, etc. as everyone else. But no matter how much they ape their peers, they are never sure of their acceptance by others. They alternate between bouts of self-aggrandizement and self-abasement, from elation to depression during the course of the day. The agony of being unaccepted may end in vandalism of their high school or even violence as in the tragic high-school shootings.

Adolescents: Caught in a Sexual Vise. Parents are also concerned about adolescent sexuality. While they want their teenagers to be "popular," they are nervous about the dating game and the initiation into active sexuality. They are worried about the teenagers going "too far," about possible pregnancy, about teenage parenthood, about the possibility of sexually transmitted diseases—and most dreaded of all their fears—about the possibility of AIDS. They try to warn their adolescents of these possibilities. But teenagers are listening only with their heads. Their bodies are not listening.

Although the beginning of "going steady" may involve walking close together, holding hands, and sharing experiences, as the two young people become more and more involved with each other, they find themselves drawn biologically to each other. Were they being raised in more traditional societies in Asia, in Africa, or in the Middle East, they would now be married and having children. This earlier timetable is more in the natural "order of things." But technological societies require longer and longer periods of schooling to prepare young people for adulthood, which prevents the young people from following their biological inclinations to cohabit and to begin a family. They find themselves in a sexual vise (see Figure 6.2). Their psychophysical readiness and urgings are opposed to the prohibitions of society. Added to the prohibitions of society is the ever-present specter of sexually transmitted diseases that hovers over the sexual act. If the young couple engage in sexual activity and do not use some method of birth control, they may end up getting married when the girl becomes pregnant. Or the young girl or her parents may decide on an abortion. While abortion may seem the easy solution, it may have a lasting emotional toll of remorse and guilt. If they do not get married, their passionate attachment may soon wear itself out and one or both of the partners may want OUT. The couple then separates from their commitment to each other.

Rape: The Reported Figures Are Rising

Parents have every right to be worried about their adolescents. Along with the many other topics that are confronting their children, so are the issues of stranger rape, date rape, and sexually transmitted diseases. They are also fearful of their children becoming parents and being married far too young. Adolescents who find themselves as parents-to-be may actually believe it will be fun to "get away from the home" and set up housekeeping for themselves. But their parents know only too well the difficulties inherent in teenage marriage.

Although the definition of rape is different from state to state, **rape** is generally defined as *forcible sexual intercourse with a person who does not give consent.* Let there be no misunderstanding. No matter what fallacies and fantasies have been generated about rape, rape is a violent and horrible act that leaves the victims with many physiological and psychological symptoms. Besides the possibility of an unwanted pregnancy or a sexually transmitted disease (STD), the victim is often injured by the brutality of the act. Psychologically, the victims can suffer from symptoms of anxiety and panic attacks, a sense of shame, feelings of being "spoiled" or "dirtied," insomnia and nightmares, and a sense of distrust and fear of the sexual act, which may affect future sexual activity in adverse ways.

Only a percentage of rape crimes are reported—somewhere in the vicinity of 200,000 annually, but this figure may be only one-fourth of the total rape crimes, which means that more than a million persons (women and men) are raped every year. When surveyed, college students report that in the period between 14 years of age and entry into college, as many as 28 percent have had experiences that can be defined as rape (Caron & Carter, 1987). This figure does not, of course, reflect rape reported by women after college age. Victims are naturally reluctant to report rape for many reasons. First, the victim does not want to go through the humiliation of exposure. Second, there is still, even yet, a popular fallacy that if a person is raped, the victim somehow "asked for it." (That is the equivalent of saying that if a man beats his wife, she somehow must have "deserved it.") Third, it is very difficult to prove the crime of rape (unless there are witnesses) and to get a verdict of guilty in the courts. Fourth, the victim may be scared that the rapist will come back and get revenge by another rape attack. Fifth, the victims may fear family members will abandon them if they make the crime public (and this is sometimes the case). And at the base of all her fears, she may wonder guiltily if she really was to blame for the crime against her (see Box 6.3). We should note that although most victims are women, men are also raped—particularly in prison—and generally by heterosexual men. In this case, the rape is a means whereby the prisoner establishes his power and domination over others (see Tip 6.4).

Date and Acquaintance Rape. One of the disturbing features of rape is the high percentage of **date rape**, which is rape by someone with whom the individual is at least casually acquainted. The figures on college date rape keep increasing. A survey of college men

---

Tip 6.4 Gang Rape as a Rite of Passage of Street Gangs. In contrast to rape by an individual, gang rape is perpetrated on the victim by two or more persons. This brutal act is often a "rite of passage" for admittance to gang membership. Even an unwilling rapist may not be able to oppose the group standards in this situation.

BOX **6.3** **Facts of Adolescent Sexuality**

1. **Age of First Average Intercourse.** About 16, regardless of gender, education, social class and other factors.
2. **Proportion of Sexually Active Youngsters, Age 15–17.** The proportion of sexually active youngsters of this age period increased by 18 percent in the 1980s—with increases mostly among white teens in high-income families.
3. **Teenage Pregnancy.** Every year, one out of every ten adolescent girls in the United States becomes pregnant, which amounts to 1 million adolescent females every year. Eighty percent of these pregnancies are unintentional. Our rate of teenage pregnancy is the highest among the world powers, exceeded only by Chile, Hungary, Romania, Cuba, and Bulgaria. About 500,000 of these pregnancies result in birth. Of the other half million, 13 percent end in miscarriage or stillbirth and the rest in abortion.
4. **Rape.** As of the early 1990s, only about 200,000 rapes were being reported each year, but the estimate is that this figure represents only a small percentage of the cases. It is probable that over a million rapes occur every year if we include date rape and marital rape. Reported rape has increased to four times the rate of reported overall crime in the last decade. It is not clear whether that means the actual crime of rape has increased or the willingness of women to report the crime has increased. From the statistics we do have, 36 percent of victims were raped in their own home.
5. **AIDS.** The best estimate at the present time about the number of cases of AIDS in this country is about 1.5 million. Reported deaths from AIDS is about 60,000 per year. Although it is difficult to get a true cross section of a community's adolescents, we know that the two fastest growing rates of AIDS are among teenagers and heterosexual women. Surveys in Washington, DC, of 13 to 20-year-olds over a three-year period revealed that the infection rate had risen from one in 250 teenagers to one in every 90 teenagers. The prediction is that the rate will soon rise to one in every 30 in the next few years. The number of AIDS cases is rising at a more rapid rate among women than men and, in certain urban centers, has become the leading cause of death among women.
6. **Other Sexually Transmitted Diseases (STD).** These diseases are on the rise and include gonorrhea, syphilis, human papilloma virus, chlamydia, and herpes of the genitals. For example, in 1988, there were 720,000 new cases of gonorrhea reported to the National Center for Health Statistics. After the 20 to 24-year-old group, the next highest "at-risk" group are the 15 to 19-year-olds.

Sources: The University of California at Berkeley Wellness Letter, 7(7). School of Public Health; Newsweek 116 (4), 46–53; Newsweek 128 (5); Amaro, H., American Psychologist 50 (6), 437–441.

revealed that two-thirds of them admitted to fondling women against their will and over one-half of them admitted to forcing women into coitus (Bohmer & Parrot, 1993). College men give the following kinds of rationale to defend their behavior:

> "If she didn't want sex, why did she come to my room?"
> "When she invited me in for a drink, I took that as an invitation to have sex."
> "Girls say 'yes' when they really mean 'no.' "
> "I was tired of her playing 'hard to get.' "
> "I thought she really wanted it but didn't want to admit it."
> "I was so worked up, I couldn't control myself."

Rape in Other Countries. In the Middle East countries, women are kept in seclusion before and after marriage. If a young woman is raped by a relative, she still bears the brunt of the blame and, though illegal, it is still tradition that the males of the family kill the young woman to get rid of the shame, hence rape is under-reported. In the predominantly Catholic countries of Europe and Central and South America, females are strictly chaperoned even when in the presence of their fiancés. In societies that are made up of small tribes and clans, fear of discovery prevents the pubescent male from forced sexual entry. Discovery would mean expulsion of both parties from the only community they have ever known, or possibly they may even be put to death. But we cannot lay the blame solely on the freedom of women in our nation. Other nations who have evolved more gender equality do not have nearly as many rape crimes (see Tip 6.5). Countries such as Denmark and Sweden have far fewer sex crimes than in our country, fewer unwanted pregnancies, fewer teenage pregnancies, and fewer abortions (Walker, 1999). At the same time, both of these countries have extensive sex education programs and governmental counseling for adolescents. We need more enlightened attitudes about the rights of women to consent to or refrain from sexual intercourse, and we need more frank and open sex education to keep our adolescents safe from AIDS and other sexually transmitted diseases (see Box 6.3).

Sexually Transmitted Diseases (STD)

Diseases that are contracted primarily through sexual intercourse used to be called *venereal diseases* but that term has been replaced professionally by the term **sexually transmitted diseases** (**STDs**). The most common STDs include gonorrhea, syphilis, chlamydia, herpes genitalia, and AIDS. We have to understand that when the term sexual transmission is used, it does not necessarily mean genital-genital contact. These diseases can also be contracted through oral-genital and anal-genital contact. These diseases have become an increasing health problem in the United States, and particularly among adolescents. The highest numbers of STDs are among the 10 to 14 age group but the next highest is the 15 to 19 age group. Our adolescents are engaging in the most unsafe-sex possible despite the urges of public health officials and the public media. In fact, in some locales, the Boards of Education still refuse to consider teaching their high schoolers—the use of condoms—in their sex education programs (see Boxes 6.3 & 6.4).

The most feared of STDs, of course, is **AIDS**, because of its death-sentence. AIDS stands for **acquired immune deficiency syndrome**. People do not die of AIDS; they die of AIDS-related diseases. What happens is that the body's natural ability defense system breaks down. The person dies from cancer, pneumonia, heart disease, leukemia, and so on.

From the Harvard Medical School Comes a Warning! There Is No Such Thing as "Safe Sex." When queried, a high percentage of people admit they lied about their state of health or the number of sexual partners they have had to their new partners (Cochran & Mays, 1990). That adolescent phenomenon of the personal fable (discussed earlier in the chapter) hinders them from realizing that AIDS *can* happen to them. A typical attitude is: *He can't possibly have AIDS. He comes from a good family and he's a nice guy.* (Some of the nicest people we know have died of AIDS.) Another typical attitude is: *I can't have been exposed to AIDS. I've only had sex once.* (But once is all it takes.) Finally: *He's so sweet and kind. He'd have told me if he had AIDS.* (Maybe he doesn't even know it himself.) Despite the advances

---

Tip 6.5 Prime Minister Golda Meier's Retort. Under the leadership of Israel's first woman prime minister, the Israeli Cabinet was discussing the rise of reported rape in Jerusalem. When one of her cabinet members suggested establishing a 10:00 P.M. curfew for women, Meier responded, "Why should the women have a curfew? It is men who are committing rape."

BOX **6.4**) **What To Tell Young Adolescent Girls About Rape and How to Protect Themselves**

Facts about Rape

1. **Rape is the number one crime against women.** In the years between 1973 and 1982, 1.5 million rapes or attempted rapes were reported on telephone hot lines. The actual number far exceeds that, of course, because many victims do not want to go through the humiliating procedures of police and hospital reporting.
2. **Most rapes are perpetrated by people the victim knows.** We teach our children about strangers who want to gives us candy or go with them somewhere. We should teach our girls that rape is perpetrated by people they know so they must be on the alert at all times.
3. **The crime of rape is difficult to prove unless there are witnesses.** This fact makes it even more uncomfortable for women to report rape and prosecute.
4. **Rapists seem like respectable men until the rape.** And so they are. They are not borderline personalities who go on rampages. Tell your daughter that most rapists can be "good citizens" of the community, good fathers, and (seemingly) good husbands—another factor inhibiting reporting of the crime.
5. **Rapists usually blame the victim.** If the young woman tries to escape the rape, the man will say something like, "You're a big girl. You came up here on your own. You must want it."
6. **The average age of victims of reported rapes is 18 years.** But victims have ranged from babies to 80-year-old women.
7. **Half of the known perpetrators were dates.** The victims were shocked by the fact that their dates raped them. They did not expect it.
8. **The rape may last for a long time.** Sometimes for hours.
9. **The rape may be accompanied by other brutality.** Knifing, mutilation, and death are not infrequent with stranger rape, but they may also accompany rape by a person the victim knows.
10. **Rape trauma syndrome follows most victims.** Phobias, flashbacks, general distrust of men, sexual dysfunctioning, and a lasting feeling of shame and lowered self-esteem are the consequences.

Sources: Dizon, Dorian, "Hidden Rape: The Shocking Truth Behind the Statistics." *Redbook* (July, 1988) 92–93; "This Pamphlet is About Rape," Santa Fe Community College, 1990.

How to Protect Herself

1. **Acquaintance rape occurs most often between 10:00 P.M. and 2:00 A.M.** Be particularly careful about late-night dating after the football game, the dance, the fraternity party, etc.
2. **Rapes often occur on the man's turf.** Be very alert to invitations to his apartment, house, office, fraternity.
3. **Rapes also occur in secluded areas.** In your first several dates with the man, and until you get to know him and can trust him, carefully plan dates that are *not* secluded.
4. **Most date rapes occur on the first several dates.** Most rapes occur early in the "dating game"— generally in the first, second, or third dates. Be especially careful when first dating someone new. It is a good idea to double date with another couple several times.
5. **The perpetrator has often been drinking or is on drugs.** Be wary if your date shows up obviously tipsy or drunk or seems to be "high." He may want you to drink. Girls who have been drinking are more vulnerable to rape. Be wary about date rape drugs.
6. **Most rape victims were slow on-the-uptake.** No matter how well you think you know the man, stay alert and be aware to possible signals that the man wants more than you want to give. If he feels he has been "short-changed" or "led on," he may resort to revenge by rape.
7. **Don't be afraid to say No.** You don't owe him anything, no matter what kind of a nice time he has given you or how much money he has spent.
8. **Call a designated other adult for a bailout.** If you feel in anyway unsure of the situation, call someone to come and get you.
9. **If you can't call someone you know, approach someone in the vicinity to help get you to a police station.** Obviously, we recommend approaching a woman, but in an emergency approach a couple or a man. Most people will respond immediately to a distress call.
10. **If the worst should happen, tell someone.** You need to get medical attention ASAP and psychological counseling—whatever it takes to help you to get over the trauma.

being made concerning the detection and prevention of AIDS, it should be emphasized to our young people that neither condoms nor the new simplified AIDS test is 100 percent safe. The moral of our discussion of sexually transmitted diseases is that, barring abstinence, there is no "safe sex." There is only "safer sex."

> **And Now Another Warning to Women: Promiscuity Is a High-Risk Factor for Cervical Cancer.** Studies of women with cervical cancer have led to the discovery of the **human papilloma virus** (**HPV**), a sexually transmitted disease. Since this cancer is caused by a virus, the more sexual contacts a woman has, the higher risk the woman has for contracting it—just as the more people we kiss during a flu epidemic increases our chances for catching the flu. Fortunately, the so-called pap test can detect this virus, which can be treated and "nipped in the bud," so to speak. Untreated, HPV not only leads to cervical cancer but also death. In other words, a simple pap smear test every other year could save your life.

EARLY AND LATE-MATURING ADOLESCENTS: A SURPRISING REVERSAL OF SELF-ESTEEM

We have been discussing several difficult and unpleasant topics; namely all the problems that our adolescents may encounter in their growing up. We prefer not to end this chapter on such a "down note." So we turn the reader's attention to another adolescent problem, but one that often, very often, has a happier ending. The problem we are discussing has to do with those adolescents who are slower-than-average in their pubertal growth and are called "late maturers."

Advantages of Early Maturation

It becomes obvious that early pubertal maturation has definite advantages for the adolescent. All of a sudden, the young girl has become a young woman and the young lad has become a young man. Their status within the peer group rises considerably. She has been transformed into the fairytale princess for whom brave young men compete. His early maturation results in a more muscular body, which results in superior athletic prowess, which leads to heroic achievement on the playing field. He has become the "Alpha Male" that attracts the females of the group. In addition, their maturation brings about higher (Piagetian) cognitive skills and heightened social awareness. In addition to their heightened status within the peer group, the adults in their society begin to treat them with more respect and equity. Mom will ask her daughter which blouse looks better on her—this one or that one? Instead of telling his son to stay out of the way, Dad will ask his help while adjusting the points on the family car or holding the end of a board while he makes a cut on it. Teachers at school will give the obviously more mature students those jobs that require responsibility. Thus, their early physical and psychological maturity will result in heightened self-esteem. So our early maturing teenagers have the advantage of being treated as more adult, which leads them to act more adult, a phenomenon known as the **self-fulfilling prophecy** (we become how others treat us or think of us).

Disadvantages of Late Maturation

We have discussed some of the problems of late-maturing teenagers. But let's just enumerate a few other disadvantages. She does not get those looks of admiration from the boys in the class. He does not get chosen for team sports until the end because he lags behind in physical prowess. They don't have the prestige, generally, to get nominated and elected to school office. They lag behind in the "dating game." All-in-all, their self-esteem gets dented fairly regularly and they yearn earnestly for signs of maturation. He begins to shave before he needs to. She asks her mother for a bra even though it won't make much difference to her silhouette.

So Where Is the Happy Ending?

Well, here it is. Early maturers are given the gift of "popularity" by virtue of their physical attractiveness. Members of their peer group court their favors. They reign supreme without having to make too much effort to "make friends." People (both male and female) gravitate to them as if attracted by a magnet. Late maturers who do not get elected to student government, who are not chosen as cheerleaders, who do not get to play first string on the school teams— all these late maturers have to do something else. What do they do? They join the band or glee club, take part in school theatrics or special interest clubs, write for the school newspaper or work on the school yearbook. In point of fact, they frequently become the "movers and shak- ers" of the high school, the ones who "get things done." Through these extracurricular activi- ties, they are developing their talents, skills, and interests, which will prove valuable in col- lege and also later in their adult vocational and avocational arenas. It will stand them in good stead to speak in front of a group of people or to work with others to create a publication or to develop their artistic talents. They are, in effect, developing what teachers call their "inner resources." After all, there is really not much opportunity to be cheerleaders and football play- ers after high school or college.

Furthermore, whereas the early maturers have not had to work hard to attract friends and dates, late maturers recognize that they must develop personality traits that attract others. What kinds of traits make them attractive? For starters, a cheerful nature, a ready smile, and a willingness to help others. They may be developing into "good listeners," which is an attribute everyone appreciates. They may have a natural "sense of humor," which they discover causes other people to want to add them to a party or to an outing.

How do we know all this? Because longitudinal studies have revealed that early matur- ers who have higher self-esteem in high school and college did not always hold on to that level of self-esteem throughout the life span. As the years creep on and their initial good looks and attractiveness begin to wane, their self-esteem begins to diminish. So much of their self- value was vested in their attractiveness, that they did not develop their other gifts and talents. In contrast, late-maturers had a better chance of gaining self-esteem throughout the life span just because of those "inner resources" they were forced to develop in high school if they wanted to make friends. As they get older, they are valued precisely for being the interesting persons they are and for their generosity in using their skills and talents for the general good (Santrock, 2001). In other words, they have a better chance to develop as a truly authentic, creative, and self-actualizing human being.

But Why Do Adolescents Make Wrong Choices? Many Environmental Explanations

This question is an issue for professionals in every field of endeavor, as well as for concerned parents. How is it that today, in the most affluent of societies such as ours, that there is so much drug addiction, delinquency, suicide, and violence? There are a multitude of possible answers, some of which we have discussed in previous chapters, and some in this chapter, which we recap here briefly:

- They may have a genetic inheritance that predisposes them to personality disorders, making them "high risks" for alcohol and other drug addictions.
- They may have been subjected to **antigens** (toxic substances) and trauma while still in the womb.
- As babies, they may have been those unwanted children who suffer later in life from lack of self-esteem.
- They may have been sexually and/or physically abused.
- They may have been retained in the early primary grades and/or may have dropped out of school at an early age.
- They may be at "high risks" for delinquency because of the social values of their street gangs.

To this list of possibilities, other factors have been indicted to account for poor judgment:

- They lack wholesome communication with parents and other adults at home and school.
- They may not be getting enough sleep, which is affecting their ability to make sound judgments (Dahl, 2001).
- They are watching more and more violence from TV movies that glamorize violence and war.
- They are lacking the guidance of missing fathers. Whether through abandonment, separation, death, divorce, or lack of fathering is being recognized as more important than previously thought, particularly for adolescent males (Beaty, 1995; Coley, 2001).
- They are spending increasingly more time on the Internet, playing war games and "first person shooter" (FPS) games that erode their sense of compassion for others (Leland, 2002).

In their search for identity, adolescents are pulling away from parental control but, as yet, haven't got enough self-confidence to stand alone. They are desperate to fit in with some group, somewhere, somehow, including street gangs, cults, and hate groups. Jung described this age group as the most deindividuated time of life (Jung, 1955). But we also have to add one more theory to account for why even the most secure and well-adjusted adolescents can make poor judgments, an explanation that has to do with the adolescent brain.

A Neurological Explanation: Still a Very Immature Brain. For most of the twentieth century, it was generally assumed that the three-pound organ we call the brain was more-or-less fully developed by the time the growing child reached the early primary grades. Neuroscientists have reversed that opinion. They now believe that just as the rest of the body is undergoing pubertal growth changes (such as muscle and skeleton, hormones, and facial characteristics), so also is the brain. In retrospect, it seems obvious to us now that *if the rest of the body was undergoing sweeping transformation during adolescence, why not the brain?* (Brownlee, 2001).

The brain seems to have evolved in three evolutionary stages (MacLean, 1993). The first stage is called the **old brain** (or hindbrain) and is more-or-less an extension of the spinal cord as can be observed in primitive vertebrates (such as lizards and snakes). The human old brain contains most of the organ systems essential for existence. The second stage evolved into what is called the **midbrain** (or mammalian brain). The midbrain in humans is the seat of primitive emotions, such as the **fight-flight-freeze response**. This response enables mammals *to fight* an aggressor, or to *take flight*, or *to freeze* so as not to be observed. For example: Suppose you are walking on a street late at night and you hear something that sounds like footsteps behind you. You stop to listen and the footsteps stop. So you continue on your way and so do the footsteps. You walk faster. So do the footsteps. Convinced there is someone following you, your midbrain is now pumping fear hormones through your body. You can decide to turn and *fight* the person following you. Or you can decide that your best defense is to try *flight*. Or you decide to turn into a doorway and *freeze*, hoping in that way, the person behind you will walk right by and you will escape detection. Any of those three responses are the primitive responses of the midbrain's fight-flight-freeze response reaction (see Tip 6.6).

Again, in the course of evolution, the body developed the third part of the brain we call the **new brain** (or forebrain). In human beings, the new brain is much larger and more wrinkled than in all other mammals and contains millions upon millions of neurons (which we can call "brain cells"). This new brain with its wrinkled **cortex** is the most "intelligent" part of the brain, particularly the quarter-inch outer surface of the brain, called the **neocortex**. So important is this narrow strip of neocortex, that if there is even the slightest injury to this area, the individual can suffer serious consequences, such as numbness in a leg or paralysis of an arm, the inability to speak, and so forth. It is in the ***frontal neocortex*** where our most intelligent judgments and cool decision-making take place. (If you put your hand just above your forehead, you can locate your frontal lobe.)

What neuroscientists have discovered in the last two decades is that the *neocortex is not fully mature, but keeps developing until well into the twenties.* They account for the adolescent's violent mood swings in this way. Sometimes adolescents act from their maturing neocortex and then they make calm, thoughtful decisions. However, if adolescents feel threatened in any way, they may suddenly revert to acting from their midbrain with its primitive fight-flight-freeze response. Moreover, the adolescent midbrain is not as good at interpreting facial expressions or social verbal interchange as the mature neocortical brain. What

The more mature frontal cortex reacts with calmer, more rational decision making

The midbrain reacts with the primitive emotions of the fight-flight-freeze response

Figure 6.3 The Adolescent Brain. When threatened, the adolescent reacts from the primitive midbrain.

Tip 6.6 Two More F's? Some wit has ventured the idea that the fight-flight-freeze response should be extended to two more F's: *faint* and *fumble* because when human beings get overly stressed out, they can "fumble the ball" (as we say) or just faint away.

adults recognize as surprise may be perceived by the adolescent as anger. What adults recognize as an innocent joke may be perceived by the adolescent as an insult. What adults recognize as mild annoyance may be perceived by the adolescent as aggression. If the adolescent's response is *fight*, the "Incredible Hulk" has been released, and he will aggress, physically or verbally, against others. If the adolescent's response is *flight*, it may take the form of tears and crying, isolating themselves in the bedroom, and staying away from others. If the *freeze* response occurs, it may come in the form of a deep depression or depressed sleep (see Figure 6.3).

What amazes adults is to watch these mood swings come and go, one upon the other in quick succession, in the course of the day to the most innocent of looks or remarks. Acting from the still immature midbrain may be the reason some adolescents run away from home. Or why the high school shootings occurred. It may be the reason that there is date rape or why adolescents do not engage in "safe sex." With their immature brain development, their sexual passion is not under the control of their frontal neocortex but under the control of their primitive midbrain arousal.

FOSTERING HIGHER EMOTIONAL INTELLIGENCE AND THE "NEW THREE R's"

Guidelines for Young Adolescents

We've been discussing the many problems and crises of the teenage years. That's all well and good, but what adults want to know is: *Whatever it is called, whether high emotional intelligence or the "New Three R's," how can we foster this kind of decision-making in our adolescents?* These following guidelines are appropriate for the early teen years:

- Keep the adolescent in school any way possible. Emotional intelligence is increased with every year of schooling.
- Provide more time for positive social interaction with peers and adults at home, in school, and after school.
- In school and elsewhere, find areas in which every adolescent can excel.
- In discussions with the adolescent, structure certain times for studying, sleeping, spending time with friends and what is allowed regarding sleepovers, parties, and dating.
- Share with the adolescent the information you have read in this chapter regarding sex, date rape, "safer sex," and sexually transmitted diseases. If you watch a documentary about these topics, invite your adolescent to watch it. Don't make watching the documentary an ultra-serious situation. Keep the mood light by providing snacks (for example) or folding laundry or fixing a drawer that sticks while watching.
- Make sure the adolescent gets enough sleep. Bedtime during the school week should be early enough to get between 7 to 9 hours of sleep. Some catch-up sleep can happen over the weekend or by napping but all of the missed hours of sleep cannot be "made up" by napping. Nothing takes the place of a good eight to nine hours of sleep (Dahl, 2001).
- Make sure there are family activities in which everyone participates, such as school functions, athletic competitions, holiday picnics and celebrations, and special events for birthdays. Ask the adolescent what kind of special event he or she would like (if

affordable and achievable). They will be much more motivated to participate if they have had a hand in the planning.

- If the young adolescent pushes too hard against these limits, discuss the situation with the adolescent and keep the discussion going. One time is not enough. If the adolescent continues to break agreed upon limits, instead of "coming down" on the adolescent yourself, change the locus of responsibility. Ask the adolescent what should be the consequence. It will require the adolescent to do some thinking about the situation. And that's what you want them to do, to think about their actions and their consequences.

- While you may have to "come down" on your adolescent at times when he or she doesn't live up to an agreement, make sure also to comment positively when they do live up to their agreements. "Thanks for returning those tools on time just as you promised." "I appreciate how courteous you were to our guests last night." "Congratulations for cleaning up your room without having been told. I really appreciate that."

- Finally, if the adolescent does make a mistake, ask the adolescent "What have learned?" "Given the same situation, what would you do next time? That's really what you want them to learn to do—to act from their more mature prefrontal neocortical level.

For More Mature Adolescents: Replace Rules and Regulations with Guidelines and Principles

As adolescents get older and showing more maturity, it is time, said Lawrence Kohlberg (1984), to replace rules and restrictions with guidelines and principles. Rules and restrictions tell us what we should or should not do. Guidelines and principles, on the other hand, are suggestions that we have to think about and interpret according to the situation. To make an intelligent decision, adolescents need experience. Much of adolescent experience happens by way of negative events: an automobile accident, getting caught shoplifting, or by catching a sexually transmitted disease. What we need to do is to provide adolescents with experience in decision making *before* they get tempted to drink-and-drive or join their friends in experimenting with controlled substances. The kind of experience we are suggesting can only happen in an environment where adolescents are not just preached at, but are listened to, in a free and friendly atmosphere. The following are suggestions for providing just this kind of experience.

Engage them in friendly family talk (perhaps at the dinner table, when the family is in the car going somewhere, or other relaxed atmosphere) with moral/ethical dilemmas. One such technique involves the "What would you do if . . . " game. The questions you might ask are:

- What would you do if your best friend wanted to copy your test answers?
- What would you do if you knew your sister was invited on a date by a guy who has a bad reputation with girls?
- What would you do if you meet a nice-looking guy at a party and he volunteers to drive you home alone in his car?
- What would you do if the crowd has been drinking, but you don't drive and there is no one else sober enough to be the "designated driver"?
- What would you do if you know you've done something wrong or poor in judgment?

These kinds of questions are not like test items that have a "right" or "wrong" answer. Whatever they answer is listened to and debated perhaps, but under no circumstances do we indicate the answer was not what you were expecting. Comments such as "That's an interesting response but what if . . . " and give them a further dilemma to think about. Taking the first dilemma, for example, the dialog might go as follows:

Q. What would you do if your best friend wanted to copy your test answers?
A. I'd pretend I didn't hear him.
Q. But what if he whispers louder?
A. I'd say "Shhh. The teacher will hear you."
Q. But what if he said that the teacher was busy talking to another student? . . . And so on. Eventually, the adolescent may say something like:
A. I'd just tell him I don't want to cheat.

Realistically under the pressure of the actual situation, the adolescent may in fact give in and let his friend copy. But with more and more practice in responding to the simulated dilemmas, the adolescent will begin to perceive how to respond to real-life dilemmas. If there are younger children listening, they may not fully understand the issues. But they will derive benefit from the give-and-take of the adults and adolescents. They may even make suggestions on their own. If their answers are funny, making everyone laugh, so much the better. A bit of humor will keep the atmosphere from getting tense.

Another technique to provide them with experience is to ask adolescents the meaning of the traditional maxims, sayings, proverbs and parables that can have multiple interpretations. These questions range from simple to ones that take more thinking:

- What does it mean that "a stitch in time saves nine"? After reasonable interpretations have been offered, ask for examples.
- Why should you "look before you leap"? Ask for an example when they leaped before they looked, but give an example out of your life first. Make sure you state what you learned from that experience, and ask them what they learned from their experience.
- One man who was a journalist said, "Never do anything you don't want published in the paper." What do you think he meant by that?
- An Hungarian friend of ours always told his children, "Always tell the truth. That way you don't have to have a good memory." What did he mean by that?
- It is said that "Pride goeth before a fall." What does that mean?
- "It's not a beautiful face that counts but a beautiful heart." What do you think of that statement, especially when Hollywood puts so much emphasis on beauty?

Adolescents who are provided with these metaphors may not have an in-depth understanding of them. They may not even think about them consciously when they are with their peer groups. But when they are repeated again and again, these metaphors will be woven into the adolescent's emotional memory. Then in situations that call for cool judgment, these sayings, proverbs, and parables will echo and resound at some level of themselves, and have an influence on their decision-making process in those times when peer pressure is strong.

Important Terms and Concepts to Know

• AIDS	• date rape	• friends	• responsibility
• amenorrhea	• dating	• gender	• safer sex
• anorexia	• *DSM*	• give in	• spontaneous
• anxious	• egocentrism	• homosexual	• storm-and-strife
• audience	• emissions	• late-maturing	• suicide
• brain	• erotic	• mood	• traits
• bulimia	• euphoria	• promiscuous	• violent
• bullied	• fable	• puberty	
• communicate	• fight-flight-freeze	• resilience	

Make Your Own Chapter Summary by Filling in the Blanks

Use the "Important Terms and Concepts to Know" to fill in the blanks.

Adolescence.   As a term, adolescence was coined by an American psychologist, G. Stanley Hall, who saw it as a period of *sturm-und-drang* or _____. Although this term fell into disfavor in the second half of the 20th century, the _____ events in our high schools of the last two decades have caused us to reevaluate the problems of this age period. Under their seemingly calm exteriors, adolescents are more _____ than adults realize, signified by their emotional _____ swings. They alternate between _____ and depression as they try to find acceptance by their peers.

Problematic Issues for Adolescent Girls.   The girls are walking a subtle line of being poised, socially, gracefully, and sexy but, at the same time, to be able to handle herself in the "_____ game." So concerned is the adolescent girl with being slim, that she may find herself becoming a victim of _____ nervosa or _____ (alternately binge eating and throwing up). If she gets too thin, she may also experience _____, which is the cessation of her menstrual periods. The adolescent girl is confronted with the ever-pressing question of whether she should "_____" to her boyfriend or take a chance of losing him to a more compliant female. If she continues to refuse, she may discover she has gotten herself into a _____ situation and doesn't know how to get out. On the other hand, if she is sexually active in high school, she may find herself with a reputation of being _____.

Problematic Issues for Adolescent Boys.   Boys are also bewildered by the physical changes they are experiencing, such as _____ dreams, which are often accompanied by nocturnal _____, and the embarrassing _____ erections they may have during the day. Boys may be even more concerned about their physical appearance, particularly the _____ boy. They are afraid of being _____ by larger, stronger, aggressive males. Finally, they are confused by their new attraction for the opposite _____, which up to now they have treated like the enemy. They are uncertain how to approach girls and _____ with them. If they have moved to a new school, they are afraid they may not be able to make new _____. A boy who suspects he has _____ inclinations is high risk for _____. The _____ or "Psychiatric Bible" no longer lists sexual preference as a mental disorder, unless he is suffering great guilt, anxiety, or depression because of it.

Problematic Issues for Parents of Adolescents. Parents are rightly concerned about their adolescent's welfare, including some of the personality _____ they observe in them, such as an exaggerated belief in their abilities. They also believe in a personal _____, in which they are the heros of their own stories and they often dress and behave for an imaginary _____. They also exhibit adolescent _____, which means that it is difficult for them to consider the perspective of other people. Parents are deeply concerned also about adolescent sexuality in terms of pregnancy, rape, and sexually transmitted diseases, the most deadly of which is _____. From the Harvard Medical School comes a warning: There is no such thing as "safe sex," only "_____."

Why Do Adolescents Make Wrong Choices? There are several possible answers, one of which has to do with the adolescent's still immature _____. Neuroscientists now believe that the brain is not fully mature until the early twenties, which means that the adolescent's reactions may waffle between the midbrain with its _____ response and the frontal neocortex with its more logical and calmer decision-making process. The chapter ends with a list of suggestions and guidelines for fostering _____ and _____ in the teenage years. Since _____ is happening earlier, even as young as ten years of age, these suggestions and guidelines should be employed as soon as children show signs of early physical maturation.

7

The College Experience Today

Whether Fifteen or Fifty, Traditional or Nontraditional, College Is for Everyone

BOX 7.1 SCENARIO
Our Multicultural Differences in Communication

As the students file into the classroom, Professor Weitzman is writing the following question on the blackboard: Who do you have difficulty communicating with?

Professor Weitzman: For starters on today's topic, interpersonal communications, I'm asking for volunteers to respond to the question I've written on the board.

Jill Smith: I'll start. I find it very hard to have a friendly discussion with my mother. Every time I visit her, she starts in criticizing everything I am wearing. I get back to my own apartment and I'm utterly ashamed of myself. It only takes 10 minutes and we're bickering!

Alec: Ten minutes! What's your secret! I can't talk to my father for two minutes without us getting into the same old arguments. I know what's coming! He wants to know what crazy new-fangled idea I've learned at school! "Filling your head with all that liberal trash!" I can't stand that man!

Eduardo: Gosh, Professor. I don't find it hard to talk with my family at all. They are always eager to listen to me and find out what I'm learning in school.

Li Ho: I feel a little like Eduardo except for one thing. My Japanese family is holding on to a lot of their traditions. They think I've become too "Americanized." Don't get me wrong. I love some of their traditions. But when I bring home a Haoli girl who's used to speaking up, they're too polite to say anything but I know they think she is too forward. They want me to bring home nice Japanese girls who are respectful toward their elders and keep quiet.

Jill Smith: They should only speak when spoken to?

Li Ho: Not quite that bad. My family has been living in Hawaii for three generations. Once, though, my family went back to Japan to visit the relatives. I was just a teenager and was used to talking up in school. My father gave me a stern dressing-down once when I talked up without being addressed. That was kind of a shocker. I loved Japan but I was glad to get back to Hawaii.

Martha: Tell me how to communicate with my mother-in-law. We have to go to dinner there every other Sunday, kids and all. (The in-between Sundays we go to my parents.) Everything is so polite and stilted and, of course, that's just when the kids start acting up. Dinners at my parents' house are much different. Rod says it's so chaotic and noisy he can't hear himself think. And it's true. There are usually ten or twelve people for dinner and we argue about everything under the sun. Wow! Talk about not understanding another culture right here in this country (*class laughter*).

Professor Weitzman: How about you, Dan? We haven't heard from you for quite some time now.

Dan: Native American's don't do as much talking as the rest of you. It's not like what Li Ho was describing—a matter of respect. I mean we do respect the Elders and all that but it really has more to do with not speaking unless you have something important to say. It's just part of us.

Shannon: I talk with my dad and brothers OK and we get along fine, but outside of my family, I'm so shy I can hardly talk sometimes. Sometimes people think I'm just dumb.

Natasha: I would like to say that at home we get along OK. Sometimes Georgie gets a little . . . I think the word is maybe irrr . . . irr . . . ?

Professor Weitzman: Irritable?

Natasha: Yes, irritable, but I understand that. We have no family here but ourselves. He was very much

BOX **7.1** SCENARIO (continued)
Our Multicultural Differences in Communication

important in the old country because he was auto mechanic—very good. People have much respect for him. Here he is only custodian at the school. He hurts inside.

Professor Weitzman: Very understandable.

Jennimae: I used to have wonderful communication with my kids. Now they are teenagers and we are always at each other's throats.

Professor Weitzman: Communicating with those closest to us, the people in our family, can be the most difficult type of interpersonal communication of all. We may both be psychologists, but occasionally my wife and I can get into it pretty hot and heavy. What we have going for us though is our determination to resolve the situation for both of us. That doesn't happen overnight. It may take a day or two, or even longer.

WHAT IT MEANS TO BE A COLLEGE STUDENT TODAY

College was once considered a **moratorium** (time out) between graduation from high school and taking on adult responsibilities for the economic and social elite (Erikson, 1950). In the years before World War II, college was modeled after the great universities of Europe, which were intended for the affluent and social elite. There were very few scholarships and even fewer opportunities to earn money while attending classes for those who were not financially supported by their families. Consequently, the student populations of prestigious colleges (for example, Harvard, Yale, and Princeton for the men, and Radcliffe and Bryn Mawr for the women) came from the upper social classes; namely, the dominant cultural group of that era; the White Anglo-Saxon, Protestant elite. In those days, college wasn't exactly a playground, but it was the era when the Greek fraternity and sorority dances were at their apex, where young men and women could meet the opposite gender, and choose an acceptable life mate of their own social class (see Tip 7.1). In this socially stratified higher educational situation, the college experience was viewed as a "lock-step" four-year program. Students right out of high school were expected to finish their four-year undergraduate education exactly in "lock-step" with all those they began with as freshmen. If a student dropped out or somehow failed to get a degree in the four-year time period, it wasn't exactly a failure, but it was something a little bit dishonorable.

World War II and all the sweeping social transformations that have gone on since then have radically changed the philosophy of higher education. Today, college is no longer considered a moratorium for the economic and social elite. Nor do we hold the "lock-step" four-year model of education as valid for today's generation of students. What changed the philosophy

---

Tip 7.1 On the Teacher Colleges and the State Universities. At this time, there were also the smaller colleges and state universities (such as the agricultural and mechanical colleges and teacher colleges) which provided practical education for those who would have to work for a living: teaching, farming, engineering, nursing, and so on. These institutions, however, were not generally considered to be a "real" college education, but more as vocational schools. Also they did not require as much schooling. For example, a student could get a teaching degree in only two years. Today, even the professional schools (law, medicine, psychology, etc.) can be considered as vocational schools that simply require more years of education.

of higher education was the return of World War II veterans. For the first time in history, the United States made available to its 11 million returning veterans a wide offering of benefits, known as the G.I. Bill. One of these benefits was money for some kind of schooling. Millions of the ex-GIs registered for college. These veterans were rarely from the social elite. In fact, they came from every segment of society. War-weary and anxious to make a better life for themselves, the veterans were not at all interested in pledging to Greek fraternities or working on floats at the homecoming game. Many of these veterans were already in their late twenties and early thirties and their motivation for college was to get good jobs.

In addition to their studies, most of them had adult responsibilities. The financial aid they were getting did provide for their tuition and books with some money for living expenses, but with families to support the veterans also had to work at part- or full-time jobs. Sometimes they had to take fewer classes because of the requirements of their work or even drop out for a term or two before completing their degree. The four-year "lock-step" tradition was forever broken. Colleges and universities all over America changed their educational philosophy to adapt to this new breed of students.

Today: A Multivariate Approach to Education to Fit Our Multicultural College Population

Today, college administrations encourage students to complete their degrees any way they can, by taking fewer classes if they need to, or by dropping out and back in when they are able. Colleges also made it possible for students who hold full-time day jobs to attend classes in the evening and on weekends, a situation almost unheard of before WW II. Today there is a multivariate approach to education to meet the needs of our multicultural college population. Students are being offered an ever wider menu of educational opportunities, such as miniterms, 45 semester-hour courses over an extended four-day weekend, and even full-time courses online. Moreover, whether we are technicians or professionals, most careers require us to keep updated through further on-site training, taking more classes, attending workshops and conferences, and so on. We now consider education as a life-long process (Maehl, 1997). Today men and women of all ages are returning to school whether single or married, fresh out of high school or after some years of working. College no longer suffers from agism.

Nor is the student population restricted to any one dominant cultural group. College students today reflect a wide diversity of ethnic background and financial status. Multicultural diversity has become the educational theme across the nation. Some of you may be just out of high school but are having to work in addition to going to school. Some of you have been out there "in the real world" working for a few years, and now are back to earn more marketable credentials. Some of you have had to wait until your kids were of an age when you felt you finally could get that education you always longed for. So whether you are 15 or 50, whether you are single, married, divorced or remarried, you will find something of value in this chapter on how to make friends, how to maintain friendships, and how to repair broken friendship ties. In this chapter too, we discuss such topics as how to meet other people, how people become attracted to each other, romance and love, and what happens when a long-term relationship dissolves. In the next chapter, we discuss the topics of marriage and children, infidelity and what happens when it is discovered, divorce, and reintegrating oneself in society. Whoever you are and whatever diversity you represent, this chapter and the next are focused on helping you discover more about who you are and how to establish more rewarding interpersonal relationships.

YOUR PERSONALITY "TYPE"

Learning More about Your Personal Identity. To start us off on this topic of developing rewarding interpersonal relations, we invite you to take a personality "Type" inventory that tells you something about yourself. Students report that it is fun to take and easy to score themselves. You don't have to worry about what you may discover about yourself as none of the traits have anything to do with being abnormal or with having "good" or "bad" personalities, any more than it is "good" or "bad" to have brown eyes, blue eyes, or green eyes. Then we'll apply what you have discovered about yourself to your friendship needs and how to interact with other people according to their personality "Type."

"Type" psychology is based on the work of Carl Jung, the Swiss psychiatrist, and two Americans, Isabel Myers and Katharine Briggs (Jung, 1955; Pearman & Fleenor, 1996). Type psychology is based on the assumption that we come into the world with different "types" of personality. It is not our environment that has determined our personality patterning but something innate and inborn. College students enjoy assessing themselves through this test because it does not stick you into an "abnormal" category. On the contrary, it provides you with some appreciation of your strengths and natural gifts. What it does also is to provide us with insight into people we have difficulty understanding because their personality "type" is so different from our own. Discovering the way others function naturally will enable us to communicate in ways that will have meaning for them. According to Type psychology, there are 16 basic personality types consisting of four dimensions:

> Extroversion-Introversion (E-I)
> Sensing-Intuition (S-N) (Since the letter "I" is already used for Introversion, "N" is
>   used for Intuition.)
> Thinking-Feeling (T-F)
> Judging-Perceiving (J-P)

It is important to remember that we all have some measure of these eight functions or we couldn't survive. But generally speaking, we favor one function or the other. You may already know which side of these four dimensions defines you best. If not, check out the descriptions in Box 7.2 to get an idea of your personality "type." Even though we usually are dominant on one side or the other on the four dimensions, it may be that you find yourself exhibiting a little bit of both sides. In that case, accept whatever seems to be true of you, but in any case, accept only what you think is true of you.

The Extroversion-Introversion Dimension. Most Americans are familiar now with this first dimension—our orientation in the world and where we get our energy from. **Extroverts** are turned toward society. They get their energy from other people. They find delight in social situations and enjoy people-related tasks. Because they are interested in others, they make delightful hosts, friendly companions, and good committee chairs. Generally speaking, they are adaptable and affable and can get people to work together on projects and tasks with comparative ease. That is why they make such good managers. They can make good counselors and grade school teachers because they like people. However, they have a desire to be liked, so they may pursue popularity and adopt whatever fads are going around. They may vote for government officials, not because they have truly examined the issues, but because they want to join "the band wagon."

BOX **7.2** SELF-EXPLORATION

Which Personality "Type" Are You?

Read each pair of statements for each dimension. Mark the box that is more true of you. Then add up the marked boxes under each dimension. Example: If you have seven boxes marked under Extroverts and three boxes under Introverts, put an E in the first of the four boxes at the end of the self-exploration box. Do the same for the other dimensions.

EXTROVERSION-INTROVERSION DIMENSION

Extroverts

Enjoy social events, "party animals." ☐
Enjoy work teams even with a few
   incompetents. ☐
Good hosts who make people feel at home. ☐

Don't mind interruptions by phone calls. ☐
Need some social contact each day to
   feel good. ☐
Have many friends and casual
   acquaintances. ☐
Communicate freely, often first to talk in class. ☐

Like to hear what others think of movies, politics. ☐
Not afraid of revealing inner ideas and feelings. ☐
It's 5:00 P.M. on Friday. What they would
   prefer to do is meet friends for a TGIF
   drink or meal. ☐
☐

Introverts

Prefer peaceful and quiet atmospheres. ☐
Prefer working alone, especially if team has
   incompetents. ☐
Trouble remembering names and faces of casual
   acquaintances. ☐
Dislike unexpected interruptions while working. ☐
Need some private time each day "to think own
   thoughts." ☐
Prefer a few intimate friends rather than many
   casual friends. ☐
Prefer to keep thoughts private until feeling
   comfortable. ☐
Trust own judgments over the judgments of others. ☐
Prefer maintaining privacy as "nobody's business." ☐
It's 5:00 P.M. on Friday. They look forward to
   going home, kicking off shoes, and having a
   drink while reading or watching TV. ☐
☐

THINKING-FEELING DIMENSION

Thinkers

Prefer cool logic to emotional arguments. ☐
Prefer to treat people fairly but firmly. ☐
May be accused of ignoring people's
   feelings. ☐
Like organization and logical discussions. ☐
Concerned first about justice and principles. ☐

Firm-minded and objective about others. ☐

Prefer to discuss issues rather than people. ☐
Able to reprimand or fire people when
   needed. ☐
Dislike emotional scenes and arguments. ☐
On trips and vacations, like to plan out ahead
   of time where they are going, where they will
   stay, and what they will be doing. ☐
☐

Feelers

Prefer to evaluate situations on basis of their feelings. ☐
Prefer to treat people kindly. ☐
Often a "soft shoulder" for people to confide
   their problems. ☐
Prefer harmony; dislike confrontation with others. ☐
More concerned for people than principles
   of justice. ☐
Empathetic toward others; accused of being a
   soft touch. ☐
Prefer to discuss people rather than issues. ☐
Dislike hurting others by reprimanding or
   firing them. ☐
Prefer "gut" reactions to logical argument. ☐
May have a general idea of where they would
   like to vacation, but prefer to be able to do
   something spontaneous from time to time
   and not be restricted to a definite schedule. ☐
☐

BOX 7.2 SELF-EXPLORATION (continued)
Which Personality "Type" Are You?

SENSING-FEELING DIMENSION

Sensors		*Intuitives*	
Prefer to stay rooted to reality and known facts.	☐	Like to propose new ideas, even if ideas are "far out."	☐
Prefer the "tried and true" over risking new ideas.	☐	Like to think about what "could be" rather than "what is."	☐
Patient with details; aim for "zero mistakes."	☐	Work in bursts of inspiration; then slack off for a time.	☐
Firm footing in physical world of objects and tools.	☐	Enjoy contemplating the universe; solving mysteries.	☐
Highly practical; distrust inspiration and hunches.	☐	Rely on inspiration, hunches, and sudden insights.	☐
Rely on numbers, figures in decision making.	☐	Ideas come so fast, they are not sure how they got them.	☐
Good with names, faces, directions, maps.	☐	Not attached to material objects; lose keys, glasses, etc.	☐
Like to finish a job meticulously.	☐	Prefer to "rough-in" ideas, let others finish job.	☐
Think others sloppy on details.	☐	Avoid nitty-gritty details; prefer working on "big picture."	☐
Enjoy learning new technological skills.	☐	Insights can be brilliant, but may also be "crackpot" ideas.	☐
They like to look their best when they step out of the house, even if just going to the store.	☐	They care more about what they are doing than how they look when they are doing it.	☐
	☐		☐

JUDGING-PERCEIVING DIMENSION

Judgers		*Perceivers*	
Like to get a job done as quickly as possible.	☐	Prefer to take time to plan a project before doing it.	☐
Make decisions in an instant and act on them.	☐	Prefer to mull over a decision from different perspectives.	☐
Like fast action and plenty of it.	☐	Prefer calm atmospheres to too many things going on.	☐
On tests, finish quickly; among first to leave.	☐	Don't like to rush through tests; among the last to leave.	☐
Dislike too much talk about job—"let's just do it!"	☐	Do not like to be pushed into making a quick decision.	☐
Like to do something rather than nothing.	☐	Tend to procrastinate on finalizing a project and turning it in.	☐
Often told that they leap before they look.	☐	Often told to make up their minds and do something.	☐
Fast acting in an emergency.	☐	Procrastinate so long, some decisions made by indecision.	☐
Often finish jobs ahead of deadlines.	☐	Finish projects at last minute; may stay up all night to do so.	☐
Opinions of others made quickly.	☐	Take time to form an opinion of others.	☐
	☐		☐

BOX **7.2** SELF-EXPLORATION (continued)
Which Personality "Type" Are You?

Scoring: Count each column of boxes below each dimension. Then mark the boxes below whether you are E or I, S or N, F or T, J or P. (Examples E S F P or I N T J)

My "Type" is

Reflective Writing: Describe your Type traits according to the Boxes. Does it accord with your understanding of yourself? Ask someone who knows you well, if it accords with his/her opinion of your personality style? Write your conclusions as to what fits or does not fit how you think of yourself. _____

In contrast, **introverts** are turned inward, toward their own thoughts and feelings. They dislike crowds and prefer activities that involve introspection and concentration. They are less interested in public opinion than in their own opinions. They are independent in judgment and, when necessary, can be a "minority of one" when everyone else is caving in to popular opinion. They are, therefore, less impressed by status or the material wealth of a person, and they do not judge a book by its cover. Introverts are capable of working on projects that require long, isolated stretches of time. People may sometimes get the impression that they don't have feelings for other people. They do, but they keep their feelings, for the most part, to themselves. However, persons who are *extremely* introverted may be so out-of-touch with other people as to be difficult to get to know and hard to work with. But once they make a friend, they will keep that friendship for life. An absolute "must" for introverts is some private time to themselves each and every day (see Figure 7.1).

The Sensing-Intuition Dimension. There are two ways of "making sense" of the many events that are taking place from moment to moment—through our senses or by intuition. **Sensing** is using our physical senses to derive information and conclusions about the world we live in. When we walk into a room we observe its size and shape. We make a map "in our heads" when we drive around a city. People with a strong sensing function can remember a route even though they haven't traveled it for years. *Sensors* like to make order out of chaos and enjoy

Figure 7.1 Extroversion versus Introversion. It's the end of the workweek. Given the opportunity to rest and relax, extroverts would relish the chance to socialize with others. Introverts would probably prefer to read the day's mail, watch TV, or curl up with a good book.

figures and tools that take measurements. They are eminently practical in their approach to living in the world. They perform well as engineers, construction foremen, carpenters, bookkeepers, and managers in any area that requires accurate perception of environmental details. They may be good also at remembering names and faces and be able to describe what a person was wearing a day later. They also like to keep order in the world. Their houses tend to be neat, their cars washed, and the lawns manicured nicely. Their clothes are well matched in color and accessories, and somehow they generally manage to keep spotless no matter the temperature or terrain.

The second way to derive understanding about the world is through what is called intuition. **Intuition** is much harder to pin down and define. It is the function that is operating when we do not know how we arrived at the answer or conclusion we came up with. It has been called "a hunch" or a "lucky guess" or even quantum leaps of cognition. Whatever intuition may be (and there are lots of theories), intuitive persons are sometimes capable of such new and creative perception as to astonish others. But strong intuitives are not as sure-footed in the physical world as strong sensors. They can get lost while driving, forget where they've parked their cars, and lose their wallets. The reason for their "absent-mindedness" is that they are often so absorbed in what they are working on "in their heads," they forget to pay attention to what is going on "outside." Sometimes they can come up with ideas that prove impractical or even wildly inaccurate. Nevertheless, when a group of people have a hard time solving a problem, the intuitive person can cut through the "Gordion Knot" with an incisive shortcut or a brand-new concept no one has thought of. Since intuitives cannot detail how they came up with their conclusion or idea, they can drive sensors to distraction. Sensors may accuse intuitives of "not sticking to the facts." Intuitives, on the other hand, may think that sensors "can't see the forest for the trees" and lack imagination (see Figure 7.2).

The Thinking-Feeling Dimension. All of us think, and all of us feel. But most people lean in one direction or another. Strong **thinking** types like facts and figures before coming to a conclusion. They distrust emotion and prefer "logic." They want to evaluate the pros and cons, the plus and minus factors of any situation, and to weigh them all with a cool, level head. They try to account for all the pertinent data and to present it in as clear and objective way as possible. For that reason, they often make excellent executives and administrators. They enjoy research

Figure 7.2 Sensing versus Intuition. The woman is a good sensor. A mistake in a pharmaceutical could be deadly. The composer is playing out the melodic structures within his psyche. He is strong in intuition.

and knowledge for its own sake. If they go into education, they prefer to teach higher grades—high school or college. If they go into medicine, they prefer research to patient care. The limitation in their style is that they do not recognize the nonintellectual aspects of working with people. Unintentionally, they may seem uncaring, if not downright cruel, in their executive style.

By contrast, people who are strong **feeling** types have a genuine regard for the feelings of other people. Furthermore, they can sense a person's feelings even when the person is unable to express concerns and anxieties. For that reason, feeling types make good therapists, counselors, nurses, and physical therapists. They also make good grade school teachers because their hearts go out to the children who are having problems of one sort or another. They are particularly good at reading body language and other nonverbal clues. They are "heart people" and rush to the aid of others in distress. Their limitation is that their feelings can become so overdominant as to overwhelm them. Parents will say of feeling children that they "don't use their heads." As adults, Feelers may get so overinvolved with other people's problems that they wear themselves out. Strong Thinkers will say people with a strong feeling function are overly sensitive and get their feelings hurt too easily. Strong Feelers will say that strong Thinkers don't consider a person's feelings (see Figure 7.3).

The Judging-Perceiving Dimension. This dimension has to do with how we act upon the conclusion we have drawn from our sensing-intuitive and thinking-feeling processes. Having drawn some conclusions and made some decisions, what action do we now take? And how quickly? A popular misconception is that judging means judging others, as in stereotyping, but that is incorrect. Judging refers to the quality and swiftness of the decision-making. Strong Judging types will keep their eyes firmly fixed on the target and the target date. If there is a paper due, the strong Judger will prepare it well in advance and get it in on time. Strong Judgers are capable of sizing up a situation quickly and accurately, seeming to be able to take in enough details of a situation for swift action. Consequently, they are the type of people that are valued in occupations that need that kind of instant decision-making and fast action, such as

Figure 7.3 Thinking versus Feeling. Strong Thinkers are interested in principles and theories. Judges need to be strong Thinkers so as to decide the principles of law. Grade school teachers need to be strong Feelers to enhance the child's self-esteem along with their academic skills.

Figure 7.4 Judging versus Perceiving. For occupations such as piloting airplanes, the person should be strong in the judging (action) function. For an occupation such as building large buildings, the architect needs a strong perceiving function so as to consider the many various factors and possible problems.

S.W.A.T. team members, fire-fighters, emergency room attendants, and courtroom attorneys—anywhere immediate action is needed. On the downside, they may jump to conclusions without knowing all the facts, make too-hasty decisions, and leap before they look.

Perceivers like to take their time making decisions and taking action. They want to get all the facts possible. They want to keep their options open and to be very thoughtful before coming to conclusions. They are not as time-conscious as strong Judgers and they dislike being hurried. They are the kind of people you want on a committee when an issue needs to be looked at from many angles before deciding what to do. If they are given one perspective, they will immediately consider the situation from another one, which can be infuriating; but this makes people stop and think about what they are doing. If they are too far extended on the perceiving side, they may postpone making decisions until it is too late to make a conscious choice at all, causing decisions to be made by indecision—by default. Judgers accuse Perceivers of never being able to make up their mind. Perceivers say of Judgers that they don't give enough thought before taking action (see Figure 7.4). As you continue on in this book, you will discover more about how your personality "Type" affects how you interact with other people—what you do well and what you need to become aware of and practice as you develop your "people skills."

MAKING FRIENDS, MAINTAINING FRIENDSHIPS, AND MAKING AMENDS

Proxemics: Interpersonal Distance

A much studied dimension of interpersonal communication is the distance at which we communicate. Results of the seminal research of Edward T. Hall (1959) still provides the classification we use today for categorizing how close or how far apart we sit and stand when interacting with others:

Intimate space, from 0 to 1 $\frac{1}{2}$ feet. This is the zone of intimacy, reserved for our most dearly loved persons, generally our families, our sexual partners, and closest friends, but only at times of intimate situations, many times involving touching, embracing, and kissing.

Personal space, from 1 ½ to 4 feet. This is the zone of most of our conversations with families and close friends. Interactions here are informal and friendly.

Social space, from 4 to 12 feet. This zone involves most group and working relationships. These interactions can be quite friendly, but leans in the direction of formality.

Public space, from 12 feet and beyond. Interpersonal communication is formal. Some communication can occur toward the 12 foot end but as the distance increases, the amount of interpersonal communication diminishes and becomes a matter of public speaking before an audience.

Cultural Differences. These spaces vary according to gender, age, size, and cultural affiliation—and yes, personality type again. Children under ten years of age can invade the personal space of strangers without offending them, but if an adult stranger moves into our personal space, our instinct is to back away. Larger people like to have more space around them than smaller people. Women tend to cluster closer together than men. Mediterraneans (Greeks, Arabs, Italians, Spaniards) cluster closer than Nordic types. Japanese and Chinese adults tend to keep respectful distances from even their closest family members (Harris & Moran, 1991). Learn about the cultural context of other ethnic groups. You don't want to startle them with a cultural *faux pas*. To the males reading this text: Consider how you would feel if you were embraced by another man. Yet this is part of the friendly paralanguage of the Italians, the French, and the Russians. French officers, by the way, not only shake the hands of soldiers receiving the *croix de guerre* (a very high medal of honor), they also embrace and kiss them on both cheeks (Ivy & Backlund, 1994).

While Westerners regard eye contact as a sign of friendship and honesty, the Japanese regard it as rude staring. Northern Europeans avoid personal questions until they have gotten to know each other fairly well. Greeks, on the other hand, will ask personal questions upon meeting you as a way of indicating their interest in you. Conventional wisdom in the United States is to avoid discussing politics and religion if we want to establish a friendly relationship. The French will avoid personal questions on first getting to know you, but they find argument over the political situation as a delightful way of establishing a relationship right from the get-go.

How we approach someone we would like to get to know has a lot to do with their cultural background and our ability to time our overtures in accordance to the person's cultural rhythm. Americans generally move in fairly quickly in making friendships. Perhaps we do this because we are living our lives in the fast lane, particularly in the cities where the pace is simply faster. We do everything fast, including establishing friendships. Or perhaps it is because we move so often—about 20 percent of Americans move yearly, many times hundreds or even thousands of miles across this vast country. But other cultures are not so quick to make friendships. Family members are considered the primary source of friendships, and it is not easy to be admitted into their circle of family-and-friendship. A British family may invite the reader to tea but that invitation may not include an invitation for friendship. As they are wont to say: *We open our houses but not our homes to other people*. To be invited to their house for tea is not unusual; to be admitted to their home (their circle of friends) may take months and years. On the other hand, Mediterraneans and Hispanics on this side of the Atlantic tend to be inclusive rather than exclusive. They open both their houses and their homes to strangers and treat them as "family": *Mi casa es su casa* (Alba, 1990).

Personality "Type" and Proxemics. In terms of personality types, Extroverts and Feelers can both be approached very quickly. But we may offend the sensibilities of introverted types or perceiving types if we move in too closely and too fast. Introverts only admit a few people into their circle of close friendships, so give them plenty of time as well as space. And never rush Perceivers! They take their time in deciding if they want to make a commitment to an acquaintance. They are well aware that friendships take time and energy, and they weigh the cost-benefits carefully.

Conversation Openers. Conversation openers are the slow and gentle way of initiating friendships. Conversation openers may not mean much in terms of information exchange but they serve as subtle yet powerful indicators of interest or friendship. They are also an invitation to respond. The following are some examples of conversation openers.

Hi! Were you here yesterday? I'm missing some notes.
Gosh! It's raining again! Is it ever going to stop?
This lecture is so boring, I'm going to sleep.
Is it just me or are you finding it hot in here? I'm stifling.
Do you have the date of the next exam? I left my notebook in the car.
What's happened to all the students in this course? Have a lot dropped out?

It really doesn't much matter what kind of a conversation opener you use, as long as you remember to let it be neutral in tone until the person signals she is ready for the next step. If the person indicates a willingness to respond, then you can take the next steps. In a classroom setting, you can indicate that you are having a hard time settling on a major. If the person responds with any degree of interest, you might want to ask him what his or her choice of major is. If the person responds to that question, you may want to follow it up with: *How did you decide on that as a major?* Or, *You must be pretty good at that. I hear it's a really hard major.* Or, *What do you intend to do after graduation?* Notice that you are showing interest in the person but you also are keeping to fairly neutral territory. At this stage of the relationship, you are proceeding slowly and easily, testing the water at all times. After two or three such conversation openers, you might just introduce yourself: *By the way, I'm Tony Smith.* Or, *My name is Sally Jefferson.* Don't ask for the other person's name. One of the clues that a relationship is developing is that the person will state his or her name as well. From now on, each small conversational remark is establishing a bond between you. You and the other person are becoming familiar with each other and at ease with each other. In a classroom full of strangers, he or she will look forward to each new exchange with you. Again! Don't rush things. Take your time.

Self-Disclose S-l-o-w-l-y. In 1964, a psychologist by the name of Sydney Jourard wrote a book entitled *The Transparent Self* (1964). In this book, Jourard explained that deep friendships are the result of self-disclosure, and that the more we self-reveal, the more transparent we become. The more transparent we become, the more authentic we are. What Jourard meant by **transparent** was that we should not hide parts of our personality from others. He meant that when we are "an open book" and reveal intimate parts of our life, we engender trust in others and they in turn engage in self-disclosure. Jourard's book caused a sensation and readers by the thousands began to self-reveal. Many times, the self-disclosure did make for openness and trust in others and encouraged their own self-disclosure. But not always. Sometimes the self-disclosure backfired in negative ways. Some people were put off by the information they received so suddenly and so early in a relationship.

Later studies of self-disclosure confirmed that *timing* and *rhythm* is all important. When appropriately used, self-disclosure does engender trust in another person and a willingness to reciprocate. When we are at the initial stages of a relationship, we can disclose low-risk information. When the other person reciprocates, we can then move to disclosing more high-risk information. Finally, as we reach more and more openness and trust with each other, we can disclose our most intimate life-events. But at every level of disclosure, it is wise to wait until the other person reciprocates with self-disclosure on his or her part. Men do not find it as easy as women to self-disclose so it will take longer for two men to reach a high level of intimacy.

Maintaining Relationships

The sensitive and skillful use of paralanguage is also involved in maintaining relationships. Keeping friendships requires as much attention as establishing them. Although some friendships come to a nightmarish end because one or the other feels betrayed, lied to, and "used," most friendships that end have simply faded away from lack of frequency contact (Duck, 1994). One or the other friends may get a change of job so that frequent contact is no longer available. One or the other of the friends may move away or go back to school, which limits the time available for social events. Or the intense pace of our lives has left little room for intimate dialog. In any of these situations, a major facet of maintaining a friendship has to do with how we use the paralanguage of communication. In this very common situation, we utilize a paralanguage technique that has been described as "stroking."

Mutual Stroking. Some years ago, Eric Berne described what he called "strokes" (1978). "Strokes" are the little verbal or nonverbal interactions between two people that do not seem to contain much cognitive information but which are powerful emotional transmissions. These strokes include smiles, hand greetings, a "Hello" or "Hi," remarks about the weather, and nonquestions such as "How are you?" which should be answered with a conventional, "Fine, thanks and you?" These seemingly insignificant remarks are actually sending powerful affirming messages. Berne called them "strokes" and are conversational exchanges that tell each person that the other still acknowledges him as worthy of a greeting. After a few strokes, each person continues on their way. No real news has been exchanged, but the stroking has validated that they are still friends.

Staying in Touch. Friendships can quite literally simply wear away from disuse when they are not renewed occasionally. If the circumstances of your lives prevents you from frequent contact, then you need to be very creative in finding ways to keep the relationship alive and nourished. It will take effort to maintain but friendships that have been full of growth for both parties are well worth the effort and creativity it takes to maintain them. As people get older, they often discover that the friends they value the most are those they have known the longest.

One way to maintain a long-distance friendship is by phone or writing. At the suggestion of maintaining a correspondence with friends who move away, some readers may groan and say something like: *But I'm no good at writing letters. I hate writing.* At which point, we retort that, in this day-and-age, e-mail technology has changed the way people communicate

BOX **7.3** **Some Electronic Emoticons**

Electronic mail has adopted a short-hand system for indicating the emotional subtext of the written message. Below are some of the more frequent symbols presently in use:

:-)	Smile face	:-&	Tongue-tied	((()))	Lots of hugs
:-l)	Smiley with a mustache	:-J	Joking	l-)	Giggle ("hee-hee")
D	Big smile	:P	Sticking out tongue or raspberry	:/	Not funny
;-	Wink	:*	Kiss	>:-<	Angry
:-@	Scream	:**:	Returning kiss	:-(	Sad
:X	Keeping mouth shut	()	Hug	:'(	Really sad; crying

Source: Charles Bowen. (January, 1995) *Home PC*, p. 109.

with each other. For almost the entire twentieth century, literary commentators had been decrying the lost art of letter writing—an endangered people skill on its way to extinction. But correspondence between people has had a resurgence thanks to electronic correspondence. Literally, millions of people worldwide are e-mailing messages to each other. They have discovered they don't have to go in for lengthy letters. Short e-mail notes do just fine. In fact, e-mail is replacing "snail mail" all over the world. Since the single most important consideration for maintaining relationships is frequent contact, e-mail provides us with the opportunity for doing so. However, since electronic mail is much shorter than letters, it is more difficult to express emotion. Furthermore, e-mail lacks the warm expressiveness of body language and voice quality so that jokes and kidding can be misunderstood. In order to place the words within a context, there has been developed a whole lexicon of **emoticons**, keyboard symbols used to convey emotional subtext (Duck, 1994). (See Box 7.3.) There are also some conventions that need to be adhered to when we use electronic mail. Unless it is an emergency or a real plea for help, SHOUTING, by using capital letters, is considered impolite. Do we need say that off-color language and jokes are prohibited and the person that uses them may find themselves off-line?

Making Amends. In all relationships, there are bound to be some occasional squalls. If you believe that there is something amiss in the friendship, ask the other person if the two of you can straighten it out. What we would like you to understand here is how important is the setting you choose in which to iron out your difficulty. Most people choose their home or their office to discuss a problem. We suggest not doing this. The person's home or office is one person's turf, demoting the other person to the diminished status of being a guest. Choose a neutral environment, where both of you are on an equal footing. And (if possible) choose a friendly environment. You want to keep the discussion of what is wrong in as friendly a manner as you can. If the difficulty seems to be something fairly minor, suggest the friendly atmosphere of a pub or restaurant. This suggestion already communicates a friendly overture. Furthermore, when two people are having drinks or sharing their mealtime in a pleasant environment, such as at a public restaurant, they have already made a head start in conflict resolution. The para-communication taking place is that you are still good enough friends to eat together.

If the problem seems to be the sort that cannot be discussed easily during a meal, there are several other settings that are conducive to conflict resolution. Try taking a walk together while talking. Walking involves movement and movement allows us to deal with hurt or angry emotions. Walking also provides the opportunity to be occasionally silent. Sitting together face-to-face while discussing a problem increases the intensity of an emotional discussion. Silences are embarrassing for many people and they tend to want to fill it with words—and unless we are careful, these words may be negative in content, which only increases the problem. Walking allows the two people the opportunity of talking, and it allows them to be sometimes silent without embarrassment while they reflect on what has been said and how they would like to respond. Discussing a problem can then be done with much more ease and comfort.

Another idea is working on a task together. There is nothing like helping a person wash and wax his or her car to "wash and wax" the relationship. Washing and waxing takes considerable effort and the physical exercise involved is another way of draining the negative emotions. Further, the other person cannot help but be appreciative of your willingness to help. The same applies for other jobs such as window washing, grocery shopping, and leaf raking—any job that allows for verbal interchange (mowing the lawn is out). So how do you offer to help? Listen to the person's answer when you suggest discussing the problem. The person may provide you with the very lead you need as in the following interchanges:

> **You:** *I'd really like it if we could take some time to straighten this out.*
> **Friend:** *I'd like to but I've got to wash and wax the car this afternoon.*
> **You:** *Great! I'll come over and help you, and we can talk while we're washing and waxing your car.*
>
> **You:** *What do you say to discussing the problem?*
> **Friend:** *I'm so busy right now. I've got to go to the mall to return something.*
> **You:** *I've got an errand I'd like to do at the mall myself. How about we meet there? What time do you want to meet?*

Finally, one of the friendliest things a person can say when dealing with a problem is "I'm sorry." Those two words, perhaps followed by an explanation has a tremendous healing effect for both parties concerned. There are many different ways to express regret.

> *Hey, I was way out-of-line. Sorry.*
> *Can you find it in your heart to forgive my insensitivity?*
> *I can't imagine why I said that. It is blatantly untrue of you.*
> *How could I have been so forgetful as to not remember our anniversary/your birthday!*
> *I can imagine how you feel. I'd be pretty upset if you had done that to me.*

Personality Type and the Art of Making Amends. The ability to make amends with sincere apologies does not imply a weak person. On the contrary, only people with a good deal of **ego strength** (a professional term for positive self-esteem and emotional stamina) can make sincere apologies. For those who find it difficult to make apologies, we suggest you read this section carefully and practice. Making apologies will be easiest for Extroverts and strong Feeling types. They know that, in most situations, sincere apologies can quickly mend a wounded heart or an indignant ego. Sensing types will be willing to mend fences if you can demonstrate the facts and figures of where you went wrong. Thinking types are usually willing to mend fences if you stay away from an emotional scene and provide a rational and logical explanation. Don't get weepy with either sensors or thinkers. *Just the facts, ma'am, just the facts.* Introverts will be a little harder to get through to. Introverts don't easily open up to other people, so if you offend them in some way, don't confront them head on. Simply explain your mistake and request a time when you can straighten it out with them. It might be a good idea to leave them a message on their telephone or e-mail them so they can mull over the proposed meeting. Another hint: Leave the time and place of the meeting up to them. That gives them a chance to take a cautious step and they will feel more secure. This hint applies for the Perceiving type too. Just ask for a chance to straighten things out; when and where is up to them. Judging types can take offense easily. What you need to do with them is to convey as quickly and tersely as possible that you are sorry. They react quickly to humor so you might want to make a sign and hold it up: *Let's Kiss and Make Up* or *I Don't Want to be in the Dog House Any More*. Strike their funny bone and they will be just as quick to laugh as they were to take offense.

What If Someone Is Attacking Us with Irritation, Anger, Hurt Feelings, or Accusations? Do we still apologize and try to make amends as we do when we've made a mistake? No, not necessarily. This kind of attack (for that is what it is) is another situation entirely. For whatever reason the other person is upset and "coming at you," what you need to know is just what has triggered his or her intense emotions. What is needed now is to stay calm, collected, and avoid any remarks that will only intensify the other person's feelings. We may need to apologize if we really have committed a grievous error, but right now what we need to know is just *exactly what the person is angry or hurt about*, and that can only come about by listening to that person's complaint. We know it is difficult to stay calm and collected when someone is screaming, raging, crying, or accusing us of some misdemeanor or other. When we are in this kind of a situation, it will take all our ego strength not to retaliate or respond in ways sure to intensify the person's emotions. Difficult to do at times? Absolutely. Impossible? No. It is tempting to retaliate when someone is being verbally aggressive with us, but retaliation only leads to more screaming and verbal aggression. What is necessary is to learn how to speak softly even when someone is being verbally aggressive with us. How do you do that? If it is a friend, colleague, or your employer, just listen quietly and calmly to the person until he or she has finished shouting. Then feed back whatever you believe to be the person's concern.

> *You're saying somebody didn't lock up last night and you think it was me?*
> *I understand. You're irritated because I should have called in yesterday that I was sick.*
> *I understand why you are upset. You thought I was coming to the meeting.*

You will be surprised by the other person's response. When the person realizes that you have put the issue into accurate terms in an easy voice without anger, the person's outrage will diminish in a most amazing way. He or she may either nod (almost speechless that you have phrased his concern so well) or quietly reply affirmatively.

> *Well, yes, as a matter of fact.*
> *Exactly! That's exactly what I feel.*

Now it is your turn to respond. If you are innocent of the charge, you just say (very quietly) something as follows:

> *I would have locked the door but I wasn't the last to leave. Harry was still here.*
> *I did call in sick. I told the receptionist. I guess she forget to tell you.*
> *I was going but we had an emergency in the machine shop. I've been waiting to tell you about it.*

It may sound like a very simple recipe, but we assure you that this way of responding will work like magic. What you did was to stay calm; to let the person know you understood the cause of the irritation; and (very importantly) you didn't get upset because you were innocently accused. Your calm responses will raise the person's respect for you and, in the future, he or she will probably check with you before getting irritated.

But what if the charge is accurate? How do you respond now? Again, by staying calm and saying something as follows:

> *Yes, I should have locked the door. I thought Harry was still here. I'll check hereafter.
> I had to go to the emergency room, but I should have called no matter how sick I was.
> If an emergency happens, I'll send the secretary with a note to where the meeting is. You
> have a right to know what happened that I wasn't there.*

Again, you may be surprised (and quite gratified) by the other person's response. He or she may then just go on to discuss the next bit of business with you. Or simply nod and walk away, satisfied that you are sincere and will mend your ways. Why? Think what you have accomplished so graciously. You have been honest. You did not make up a transparently poor excuse. You indicated that you were sorry for the error. And you have assured the other person that it will not happen again. And you did all that in a sentence or two without groveling or getting up on your "high horse."

PREMARITAL RELATIONSHIPS: ATTRACTION, DATING, AND FALLING IN AND OUT OF LOVE

Some individuals enjoy pursuing the "bachelor" or "heartbreaker" life. These individuals love the chase-and-conquest game of pursuing (or attracting) the opposite gender and then dropping them. "Love 'em and leave 'em" is their motto. But these individuals aside, most of us want to find that special someone with whom we can build a permanent life structure. So, for the last several decades, social scientists have been taking a close-up look at what makes people fall in and out of love, and what makes for long-lasting and happy relationships. While no two relationships are identical, researchers have discovered some fairly common patterns in premarital and postmarital relationships (Baxter, 1984; Brown & Amatea, 2000; Sternberg, 1985). To summarize these studies, there is emerging a stage model of what happens from initial attraction, to friendship, to romantic love, to a long-lasting commitment (living together or marriage), and, also, what makes for the dissolution of these relationships. In this chapter, we discuss their findings of *premarital* relationships. *Marriage* and *postmarital relationships* are discussed in the next chapter.

> **Stages of Premarital Relationships** (discussed in this chapter)
> Initiating attraction
> Casual dating
> Being in love
> Deepening of the relationship
> Decay of premarital relationships
> Terminating premarital relationships

Stages of Marital and Postmarital Relationships (discussed in the next chapter)
    Becoming (permanent) partners
    Divorce, adjustment, and remarriage

The Initiating Stage

This stage has to do with becoming interested and attracted to another person. Meeting and becoming interested in another person doesn't happen the way it is sometimes shown in the movies—by accidentally being knocked down by another person on the sidewalk or by sharing a taxi in a big city. Nor does it happen generally as the result of a "one-night stand," which may actually result in lowered self-esteem afterwards. It may happen through a "blind date" (33 percent). But where it generally happens is among groups of people having fun together or working together (Knox & Wilson, 1983). Almost half of the college students met their future love relationship at places where people gather for a good time, at parties and special events, or at work or college classes. If a person is "still looking," going with friends to a football game, to a movie or play, to a church group, or to a "Happy Hour," provides a good opportunity to meet someone interesting. But it doesn't happen overnight. Finding the "just right" attractive partner takes time. (We caution those of you who are strong Judging types to take your time and not jump. We know such a strong judging person who has had three short-lived marriages and, in the last two years, has been engaged and disengaged to three different women.)

But What Arouses the Interest of One Person in Another? Social scientists have discovered significant **gender** differences in mate selection. In a cross-cultural study of 33 nations, men were more enticed by physical attraction while women were more interested in the man's financial situation, ambition, and prospects (Brown & Amatea, 2000; Buss, 1994). Evolutionary theory explains a man's initial attraction to younger, more attractive women as a sign of their fertility. Fertility means the survival of the species, and particularly a man's own genes. Evolutionary theory explains the attraction of women to the man's financial status as her need for good providers for her and for their children (Buss, 1994). But after that first initial attraction, both men and women ranked personality characteristics, such as being kind, understanding and intelligent, more important than physical attractiveness or earning power. Personality, it seems, plays an all-important role in our choice for a partner.

Similarity of Background. We also know that we are attracted to people who are similar to ourselves in terms of status and wealth, in terms of educational level, in terms of physical attractiveness, and in terms of intelligence. (This last factor, intelligence, has a modifier: Men tend to be attracted to women who are *less* intelligent, and women tend to be attracted to men who are *more* intelligent.) Why is this so? Simply, because we feel more comfortable with people who are similar to ourselves. Echoes of this phenomenon can be heard in young people who are ecstatically in love.

Oh, we're so alike. It's like we've grown up together.
We have so many things in common. We like to do the same things.
We are so similar, I know I've found my soul mate.

At this juncture, the reader may want to ask: *But what about the saying that opposites attract?* Well, it depends on what we mean by "opposites"? It probably doesn't mean differences in social status, educational level, or physical attractiveness. It probably means certain personality traits. If one person is introverted and quiet, this Introvert may be attracted to the bubbly, outgoing nature of an Extrovert. An Extrovert, with all those friends and social activities, can easily become overextended and so may value the calm steadiness of an Introvert who acts as a stabilizing anchor. Yes, in that way, opposites do attract.

But if there are too many personality differences in the two people, they may not have enough "glue" to keep them together. Using "Type" personality dimensions again, suppose one partner is an ESTJ (Extroverted, Sensing, Thinking, Judging) and the other is an INFP (Introverted, Intuitive, Feeling, Perceiving) type. They may be attracted to each other in the beginning, but eventually their overwhelming personality differences can erode their relationship. Ideally, we need to have some differences of personality to keep our time together interesting and exciting, but we need enough similarity to make for common ground so that the relationship will endure. If you are both introverted and enjoy reading, you will look forward to Sunday morning brunch and think that reading the Sunday papers is a wonderful way to relax after a hectic week. If you are both extroverted and enjoy sports, you will be only too glad to take your turn on the weekends to host a group of other sports fans. Are you both hikers and enjoy marathon walks or nature trails? These common interests and values and activities will keep you together much longer than physical passion.

The Casual Dating Stage

There are many reasons for casual dating in college. For one thing, there is a long-standing traditional attitude that it isn't a good idea to "get serious until after college." Presumably, falling in love will be detrimental to studying and getting good grades. Actually, there is probably no better place to find a suitable prospective partner than in college. But there are also other reasons for casual dating. Some college students may be recovering from a breakup of a previous relationship, and cautious about "getting serious" again.

> *I'm not ready for another relationship. The last one was too painful.*
> *I don't want to get so emotionally involved again.*
> *My boyfriend/girlfriend was so possessive, I just need some freedom for a while.*

In this casual dating stage, mutual attitudes toward sex may be explored.

> *I don't think it's right to kiss on the first date.*
> *I like to get to know a person well before we have sex. What about you?*
> *What's your opinion of casual sex?*
> *I've got to tell you right now that I am more traditional than a lot of my friends.*

The two people are developing a mutual comfort zone. Other topics they will explore are future goals, attitudes about having children (and how many), and their attitude about the "sacred nature" of monogamy versus infidelity. One topic that looms large these days is the possibility of AIDS and other STDs, as well as the use of condoms. Dating couples may feel a powerful attraction for each other but they are trying to maintain control of their emotions until they feel sure they are both feeling similarly about their relationship. The stage of casual dating generally lasts between three or four months (Loyer-Carlson, 1989).

The Being-in-Love Stage

For the most part, animals mate as a biological imperative not much different from eating, defecating, or giving birth. By contrast, human love is a dizzy, palpitating, overwhelming experience, unlike anything that other species experience. People in love are changed beings. They may feel radiant, exuberant, joyous, full of energy. As well, they may feel astonished by the emotions they may be feeling for the first time. These emotions trigger a transformation of their perceptions of the entire world, which now suddenly seems wonderful and luminous. But until they know their passion is reciprocated, they may also feel unstable, giddy, shy, sleepless, and out of control. They may even find themselves unable to concentrate, riddled with obsessional thoughts, jealous of other people, and afraid of being rejected (Fisher, 1998). Small wonder that we use such expressions in English as:

> *I never knew what hit me. I was crazy in love with her.*
> *I was so in love with him, I lost my head.*
> *I was head-over-heels in love.*

So strange are the behaviors and obsessions that can afflict the person in love, that Shakespeare concluded "the lunatic, the lover, and the poet" are all alike (and all obviously quite mad). As passionate intimacy develops, the two people may experience enhanced self-esteem, emotional closeness that invites physical closeness, and a feeling of self-actualizing. If they decide they are truly "in love," they may now make a commitment to each other and begin by making the relationship exclusive.

The Deepening Stage

Now committed to each other, the two people are "seriously dating" in a way that does not include the rest of the world. Since just being together makes them feel good, they turn down invitations to join their friends for a social gathering, much to the amusement of their friends. During this stage, the couple engage in deeper self-disclosure of their problems with their families or their past relationships, for instance. They begin to build a common ground of what they like or dislike in other people, what they enjoy doing, and their happiness with each other. It is at this stage that the couple have to deal with important issues involving priorities of time, loyalty, other friends, and family ties.

> *You're playing softball on Saturday? You said you'd go shopping with me.*
> *Why must we spend Thanksgiving with your parents? My parents are expecting us.*
> *You're being jealous for nothing. We were just talking.*
> *I don't care if he/she is just a casual friend. You spent a lot of time together just talking.*

It is at this time that serious issues have to be resolved if the relationship is to avoid decay. Possessiveness is the most frequently cited reason for the breakup of college relationships. Surprisingly, it is deemed to be a more important issue for women (44 percent) as compared to 27 percent for men (Baxter, 1986). Another important issue is the right to say *no* to sex without jeopardizing the relationship, a situation particularly difficult for women because men may interpret that as rejecting their advances when it may be a matter of religious conviction, or not feeling well, or simply "not in the mood."

The Decay of Premarital Relationships

If the issues noted are not resolved satisfactorily, the couple's relationship may founder and begin to deteriorate. The absolute end can come about within a month as the result of a verbal fight during which such terrible things are said, they cannot be taken back. Or it may take up to a year (or even longer) if the two partners are hanging on to the hope that the relationship will somehow improve. If one of the issues is alcoholism or infidelity, it may be that one partner is hoping desperately that the other will mend his/her ways. For example, if one partner has been "fooling around" with other people, but keeps promising to be faithful, the other may be willing to believe it until the painful truth can no longer be denied. Or it may be as simple a reason that the intense feelings they have had for each other have been petering out, bit by bit, but the two people have not acknowledged (even to themselves) that they have been growing apart. One of the problems of passionate and romantic love is that it can fade very quickly as compared to *companionate love* (Sternberg & Barnes, 1988).

Terminating Premarital Relationships

Even when the two people have acknowledged that their relationship has somehow petered out, it may take the couple as long as six months before deciding to end the relationship for good and all. They avoid the need to end the relationship for several reasons. It may be that breaking up is simply too emotional for them to deal with (Baxter, 1984). Sometimes the reason for postponing the official end of the relationship is simply out of fear of never finding someone else to love. It may be that the breakup is wanted by one person but resisted by the other. Or their attempts to mend the relationship only end in bitter accusations of what the other did that was wrong.

> *You used to be thoughtful. You've become selfish and self-centered.*
> *I'm tired of talking to you. You just don't listen to anything I say.*
> *We've been over this and over this, and you still won't change.*
> *You say you still love me and then act like a bitch/bastard.*

For whatever reason, the relationship may drag out as an on-again, off-again arrangement until both partners realize it is just a no-win situation for either of them. Now the couple begins to discuss and quarrel over *who* came into the relationship with *what*. Instead of the "we" and "ours" that marked the stages of *being in love* and *deepening*, they are now using the pronouns "I" and "mine."

If the breakup happens suddenly when one partner "dumps" the other, seemingly "out of the blue," the person who was dumped is generally traumatized, and recovery may take as long as two to four years or even longer. When college students report being dumped and have not yet recovered from the shock, they genuinely believe that they had only "one great love" and will never be able to love anyone again with that kind of trust, passion, and intensity. Whatever the reasons for the final breakup, either partner or both may experience anger, depression, and loneliness. They may feel out of control and revert to behaviors that shock others in the vicinity, such as public displays of grief, destroying things, or even harassing the lost loved one.

But How Can We Know If Our Particular Relationship Will Last?

Can we truly predict what makes for long-term relationships? Well, certainly not precisely. Despite all that we have learned, human love transcends anything we know about it. But we do have some clues about what makes for what social scientists call "successful long-term relationships."

Deep Regard for the Other's Well-Being. One such clue is how Robert Sternberg (1985) defined *mature love*, as distinct from *sexual passion*. What he did was to list some of the components that make up what he called mature love. Altogether, these components add up to being concerned for the other person's welfare and happiness. Specifically, a genuinely mature love involves something more than viewing each other as exciting and convenient sexual objects. Sternberg defined **mature love** as a relationship in which each gives and receives emotional support from each other. It involves the ability to have intimate conversations, being loyal to the other, and valuing the loved one's safety and well-being even more than one's own. To determine whether you and your partner have a mature loving relationship, ask and answer the following type of questions:

> *Can I count on him/her when I need support? Or does he/she desert me when I need him/her the most?*
> *Does he/she enjoy being alone with me? Or does he/she prefer going out with his/her friends?*
> *Is he/she understanding and supportive when something is troubling me? Or is he/she a little girl/boy in some ways so that I always have to be "the strong one" and keep my problems to myself?*
> *After I have been with him/her, is my self-esteem deflated as if there is something wrong with me? Or do I feel good about myself and know that he/she values me?*

Love, Yes, But Also Mutual Liking. Another strong indication is whether the two people not only *love* each other but *like* each other. Liking each other seems to be even more important for a long-lasting relationship than the romantic passion you feel for each other (Sternberg, 1985). After some of the ardent sexual passion begins to abate, without mutual regard for each other, a romantic relationship can disintegrate quickly under the pressure of the realities of living together. On the other hand, if the two people have interests in common, have respect for each other, and just like doing things together, the relationship has a chance to develop into an even deeper and more profound intimacy. It is this mutual liking and regard that can help the relationship survive the end of the "honeymoon" period, and steer the couple through the shoals and rapids of long-term relationships. Many people believe they like each other when, actually, they only *think* they do. To test your liking for the other person, ask yourself the following questions:

> *Am I proud of him/her when we are out together? Or does he/she embarrass me?*
> *Do I approve of his/her general behavior? Or do I try to control his/her drinking/smoking/drug addiction?*

Does he/she make constructive decisions? Or do I have to tell him/her what to do?
Do I like him/her just the way he/she is? Or do I think his/her dress/language/behavior
*   needs a little improving?*

The "Ideal Partner" versus the "Real Partner." Most of us carry around an "ideal" image of the person we want as a partner. The more realistic we are about our **Significant Other**, as compared to the ideal person we may have imagined, the more likely is the relationship to endure. If we have been influenced by romantic movies with their fairytale endings at the altar and the expectation that everyone "lived happily ever after," we are not prepared for the reality of living with another person. It has been said, many times, that *we never really know a person until we have lived with him or her.* And so it is. An occasional argument may actually make the relationship better because it can clear the air and resolve problems. But if you find yourself feeling badly after being together, time after time, you need to ask yourself if this relationship is a healthy one for you. There is a tendency for students to condone the verbal abuse or unacceptable behavior of their partner. Students may provide excuses for the person's behavior.

She never lets me out of her sight, but that's just because she had such an unhappy
*   childhood.*
It isn't really his fault that he doesn't trust me. His former girlfriend was cheating on him.
She tends to be a little jealous but it's because her father was so unfaithful to her mother.

And the statement we dread hearing most of all:

Sometimes he/she is hard to get along with, but I'm sure that will change after we're
*   married.*

The Acid Test of a Healthy Relationship: Being Your Authentic "Real Selves" with Each Other. Being your "real self" comes about by being with each other in a variety of situations over a period of time. As we get to know each other in these different situations over a few weeks and months, we become more comfortable with each other and allow our "true selves" to emerge. It is not that we have been pretending to be a certain way, but that in our eagerness to please the other person, we submerge our own identities (see Tip 7.2). If we enjoy doing the dishes and cleaning up the garage just to be together, it's a good sign. If after seeing each other without makeup or grimy after working underneath the car and still think each other attractive, it's a very good sign. If one of you gets irritated occasionally (but only occasionally), but apologizes later, you're doing fine. Apologies after an unfair accusation, a flare-up of temper, or a missed appointment is one of the best signs of a person easy to live with—as long as the undesirable behavior is not repeated and repeated. In that case, the apologies don't mean much. The more you are together in real-life situations, the better the chances that living together will be successful.

Tip 7.2 On Long-Distance Relationships. One of the problems of being in a long-distance relationship is that when the couple finally can get together, they try to make it as romantic as possible. That's very understandable. The problem with that, however, is that the couple never get a chance to see each other in more normal circumstances being their authentic selves. If they do decide to get married or live together, they may discover they do not know each other well at all.

Homosexual Relationships. Gay and lesbian relationships are similar to heterosexual relationships in their attraction and esteem needs. Like heterosexual men, homosexual men are attracted by physical good looks and obvious sexuality. Not only are they attracted to the physical looks of other men, homosexual men also devote a lot of time on their own physical attractiveness. Homosexual women, just like heterosexual women, place more emphasis on personality. Homosexual men, like heterosexual men, engage in more "one-night stands," while homosexual women, like heterosexual women, commit themselves to more permanent relationships much more swiftly. There is, however, a vast difference in how homosexual couples behave in public as compared to homosexual couples.

Because of societal sanctions, homosexuals do not behave similarly in public. Heterosexual couples are allowed to touch each other affectionately, display pictures of their family at the office, show wedding photos and take calls from their spouses at work. Because sexual minorities are still not widely supported by society, these common heterosexual traditions are not often exhibited by sexual minority couples. They have learned to refrain from these public displays out of fear of antigay prejudice and violent discrimination. This kind of prejudice and discrimination is still so strong in our society that there is, at the time of this writing, a hate group Web site entitled <*godhatesfags.com*>, with membership increasing monthly.

Concerning On-Line Relationships. There is much concern these days about the dangers of online relationships. While the Internet stretches the geographical boundaries so as to "meet" a wider range of new people, make new friends, and discover potential lovers, it lays the person open to **sexual predators**. It is imperative that online subscribers keep their wits about them. Because of the seeming "anonymity" of the communication, it is relatively easy for the clever sexual predator to entice more and more personal information from unsuspecting victims. The ordinary protective restraints of social behavior have been removed. There are no lie detectors to protect you from "little white lies" about who they are, their marital status, or if they have been in prison. For your protection, keep the Ten Online Commandments in Box 7.4 close-at-hand if you are using the Internet to widen your social horizons (Heart, 2003).

BOX **7.4** **Ten Commandments for Online Communication**

1. **Keep your first communication brief.** If you are initiating the Internet communication or answering an advertisement, make your first communication a good first impression—you don't have a second chance. Don't write a "saga," keep your response interesting but brief.
2. **If the response is a "saga," move on.** Similarly, if someone writes you a lot, say in the first or second message, interpret that as too personal, too eager, too self-revealing. Do not respond.
3. **Expect a picture.** If you have submitted a picture but the Other User has not, ask yourself "Why?" What is he/she hiding? What is it that the Other User does not want you to know until maybe later when, presumably, this hidden element would not matter so much?
4. **Be careful of seductive messages.** When receiving a message that says, "It seems we have a lot in common," be a little cautious as you continue the communication. But messages such as "I think we are perfect for each other!" or "I love you!" should act as red lights or STOP signs, particularly if these messages come very early on. The Other User does not know you. You don't know the Other User. E-mail communication is too anonymous to be valid. Don't be flattered. Be nervous.
5. **Make your first offline contact a phone call.** If you are interested enough to consider meeting the Other User, make a phone contact first. You may be able to get more accurate information concerning gender, age, and personality.

BOX **7.4** (continued)
Ten Commandments for Online Communication

6. **Make the first meeting a public one.** If you have become comfortable enough to meet, make the first meeting in a public place. Stay near other people in a lighted area. Don't make it a glamorous setting where drinks are served. Getting together for coffee or lunch is a pleasant, casual way to meet someone but also safer. If it turns out that the Other is far different from the image presented to you, walk away. You have no obligation to hang around. Simply say something like, "Thank you for meeting me, but you are different from what I expected. It isn't any use to continue this meeting for your sake or mine."

7. **Take a friend with you.** In a group of three or more persons, you have a chance to assess his/her social manners in public. Do we have to add that it is also a safer way to meet a person who is still a stranger? There is less likelihood of the other person being a sexual predator if other people know his/her identity.

8. **Do not bring your date back to your house with you after this first meeting.** Even though you may have had what seems to be very intimate online conversations, you still do not know this person. Use the same kind of common sense and guidelines that you would use after any first meeting.

9. **Don't ever allow being picked up at your house UNTIL . . .** you know the person better. Until the Other knows that other people are aware of your relationship. Until he/she knows that these other people have his/her online address, telephone number, etc. Perhaps it would be even more wise to let the Other know they all have a copy of his/her photograph.

10. **Final tip for getting out of trouble.** If you are starting to feel the least insecure with your date, remove yourself from the situation immediately. If alone, do not hesitate to ask for help from anyone nearby. Ask them to call the police if you feel the situation is getting out of hand. Trust your instincts!

Important Terms and Concepts to Know

- age
- authentically
- casual
- conflict
- cultural
- decay
- deepening
- disclose
- education
- e-mail
- emotional
- Extroverts
- feed
- feeling
- in love
- Internet
- Introverts
- Intuitives
- Judgers
- moratorium
- multicultural
- openers
- Perceivers
- personality
- predators
- proxemics
- recover
- romantic
- Sensors
- similar
- social
- stroking
- terminating
- Thinkers

Make Your Own Chapter Summary by Filling in the Blanks

Use the "Important Terms and Concepts to Know" to fill in the blanks.

The college experience: yesterday and today. College today can no longer be considered as a _____ for the social elite. Today's generation of students are a hard-working and _____ population, representing a wide range of _____, gender, ethnic background, etc. We recognize too that the institution of _____ has become a life-long process, and today's college student has a wide menu of educational opportunities.

Personality "Type." _____ get their energy from the external world and the enjoyment of friends while _____ need private time each day for themselves. In comparison to strong _____ who acquire information from facts, figures, and the physical world, _____ are never quite sure how they acquire information but can come up with new ideas and solutions. Strong _____ types can sense the unspoken anxieties and concerns of other people. _____ evaluate situations according to rational logic and are suspicious of emotional scenes. _____ act quickly in emergencies but sometimes too quickly, while strong _____ like to take their time in decision making, but may procrastinate.

Making and maintaining friendships. _____ has to do with interpersonal distance. There are distinct _____ differences in how close people stand to talk. Making friends can be initiated through conversation _____, but we must self-_____ slowly. Mutual _____ does not contain much cognitive information but does send powerful _____ transmissions. Friendships can dissolve simply from disuse and must be renewed occasionally by phone, letters, or _____. _____ resolution can be more easily accomplished by meeting at a neutral setting or helping the other person with a task. When other people shout at us, we can diminish their upset by remaining calm and then _____ back what we believe is the person's concern.

Premarital relationships. We tend to be attracted to people _____ to ourselves. We are initially attracted to the person's physical appearance, but after that _____ traits rate high. _____ dating stems from a long-standing tradition that it is not a good idea to "get serious until after college." The person _____ is a changed being who is astonished by feelings never before experienced. The _____ stage is characterized by discussing important issues such as priorities of time, loyalty, family ties, etc. If these issues are not resolved satisfactorily, it may result in the _____ of the relationship. _____ the relationship may take many months for many reasons, including the fear of not finding another permanent relationship. If a person has recently broken up with someone, or been "dumped" unexpectedly, it may take a lot of time to _____ from the previous relationship.

Various kinds of relationships. A good way to test whether a relationship will be enduring is to be _____ yourself in a variety of situations rather than always meeting in a _____ setting. Homosexual couples are similar to heterosexual couples but are not permitted the same public displays of love and affection because of _____ sanctions. Guidelines are provided for meeting someone through the _____ and the reader is warned about sexual _____.

8

Adulthood Through the Second Half of Life

Marriage, Divorce and Child Custody, Remarriage, and Stepfamilies

BOX 8.1 SCENARIO

A Heated Discussion Over Marriage—and—Family!

Professor Weitzman: How many of you are married or intend to get married? (*Many hands are raised.*) OK, that's almost all of you. Now, let me ask this question: How many think your marriage will end in divorce? (*No hands are raised.*) But we know that at least one out of every two marriages will end in divorce. What makes you think yours will be different?

Eduardo: My parents had a good marriage. I never heard them quarrel. That would mean they were good role models, yes? Now my sister, she has not such a good marriage. Her husband beats her sometimes. I would never do that. I would be like my father.

Professor Weitzman: But your father went to work and your mother stayed at home. Is that what you are expecting from your marriage—you'll work and your wife will stay at home? Yes? Do you plan to have children?

Eduardo: Of course. Lots. I love kids. I want a houseful.

Professor Weitzman: Do you want them to go to college?

Eduardo: Yes, even the girls. I want the best for all of them.

Professor Weitzman: If you want this house full of children to go to college, how will you finance it? At the present time, it costs more than $500,000 to raise a child and finance him or her through four years of college. Think of it! A half million dollars for each child. Are you going to be able to do all that on your single salary with a house full of kids?

Eduardo: I didn't think of that.

Jonnimae: I'll never get remarried. My father beat my mother and the kids. And then I married young just to get out of the house. I discovered I had married a man as abusive as my father. I got out and I'm glad I'm not married anymore. Single parenting is hard,

let me tell you, but it's better than an abusive husband.

Alec: I don't blame Jonnimae. I never want a marriage like my parents. That wasn't a home we lived in. It was a battleground! I used to ask my mother why she stayed with my father. Why didn't they just get a divorce! And you know what she said? She said they were staying together for the sake of the kids!

Natasha: I've been listening to you all and I am . . . surprised! Aren't there any happy marriages in America? When I see American movies, Americans seem to all have happy lives, mostly.

Alec: You mean like the TV sitcoms, where there is this happy little family with perfect parents and almost perfect children. And whatever problems they have get solved in 30 minutes and they live happily ever after. What a joke!

Shannon: I think our family was pretty happy . . . except for Mom. I mean my grandmother and Dad and the twins, we all got along. We just learned to watch out for Mom's moods.

Professor Weitzman: This discussion points out what we are going to be talking about throughout the next few days. Marriage is not a "crib" course. It's probably the most difficult relationship we will ever form.

Jonnimae: But is it really worse now than in past times? With the divorce rate so high, is it really true that our society is in "moral decay"?

Professor Weitzman: That's a good question, Jonnimae. There are two schools of thought on this. Traditionalists call attention to all the problems of modern family life—the high divorce rate, the difficult task of single-parenting, "latch-key" kids, and children being raised with several sets of parents and stepparents. Nontraditionalists argue that what

191

BOX **8.1** SCENARIO (continued)
A Heated Discussion Over Marriage—and—Family!

is really going on today is not moral decay but a renunciation of all the abuses that "traditional marriage" covered up, such as incest, child and spouse abuse, and screaming conflict-ridden homes where the weapon of choice is verbal abuse or worse.

Eduardo: Are you saying we can't go back to the old traditional marriage like my parents had?

Professor Weitzman: We can never turn back the clock. We are living in a different society from that of our grandparents and even our parents. We can only forge ahead. What is needed is to forge a new type of family, a family that retains traditional values of love and respect and commitment but without the hypocrisies and abuses of previous generations.

DEVELOPING HEALTHY AND HAPPY MARRIAGES AND OTHER LONG-TERM RELATIONSHIPS: TO RECAP THE STAGES OF LOVE

In the last chapter, the text described the first five stages of long-term premarital relationships. To refresh the reader's memory, the first four stages are initiating attraction, casual dating, being "in love," deepening and terminating premarital relationships. In this chapter, we continue with permanent relationships, including marriage and raising a family, problems of family relationships, and aspects of terminating the relationship such as divorce, custody of children, and remarriage.

The Sweeping Sociological Changes of the Last Fifty Years

There is no doubt about it—in the last 50 years, our society has undergone enormous changes in our attitudes and behaviors of love, sex, and marriage. In this past half century, we have witnessed experimental ways of bonding, childbearing, and living together. We have learned about open marriage, gay marriage, adoption by single parents, increased teenage pregnancy, surrogate mothers, conception *in vitro* (test-tube babies), children divorcing their parents, and the cloning of animals. A few decades ago, this dizzy onslaught of the new and unexpected was called **future shock** by Alvin Toffler (1970). Future shock is even more intense today. Some traditionalists view these events as a sign of moral decay and point to the fact that about 50 percent of all marriages end in divorce (see Tip 8.1). To nontraditionalists, these changes herald a "brave new world" that refuses to cover up hypocrisy, infidelity, spouse and child abuse, and incest.

Can Marriage as an Institution Even Survive These Winds of Change? Oh, yes, undoubtedly—marriage as an institution has stood the test of thousands of centuries. Yes, it will survive but in what kinds of models and varieties remains to be seen. What we are struggling with, at the present time, is how to update our traditional model of an enduring

Tip 8.1 Caution in Interpreting This Statistic. The fact that 50 percent of all marriages end in divorce does not mean that one out of every two people will experience divorce. Included in this statistic are those people who marry more than once, even twice, and even many more times than that. To cite a well-known example: The movie star, Elizabeth Taylor, over the course of her life has married eight times.

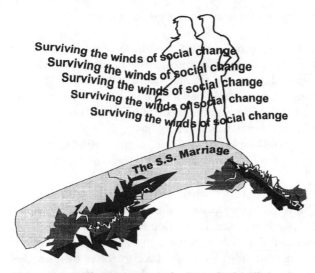

Figure 8.1 Will Marriage Survive? Undoubtedly! Although it may change in unexpected ways.

family, but a family that is not based on power and abuse, but rather on the loving support of all the family members with each other. A tall order? Undoubtedly. There are many obstacles in the way of this ideal family model. We need to understand what these obstacles are before we can propose healthier and happier marital relationships (see Figure 8.1).

One of the chief obstacles is that young people, who have had little experience of the "real world," discover that marriage based solely on romantic passion does not survive the harsh realities of living with another person. If those romantic but star-crossed teenagers, Romeo and Juliet, had managed to live together for any length of time, they would have discovered that romantic passion does not long survive the problem of each other's frailties. As they say, *If love is blind, marriage is an eye opener!* What is needed then are more realistic models of long-term relationships in a society that is unlike anything that has gone before and includes:

- More and more dual-income families;
- More and more burdens of the nuclear family;
- More and more parental activities that drain our time and energy;
- More and more time spent working outside the home place by both adults;
- More and more demands of our jobs, such as earning more CEU credits, learning more sophisticated computer skills, professional conferences, etc.

So What Is Going Wrong with Modern Marriage? Romantic Love versus the Realities of Living

What is going wrong may well be that modern men and women have greater expectations from their long-term relationships than ever before in history. We want a life-partner who is not only an ardent lover, faithful spouse, and devoted parent, but who is also an astute financial manager, a homework supervisor and athletic coach for our children, an able car maintenance mechanic, a lively recreational partner, a competent host or hostess, an outstanding cook and . . . (whew!) need we go on? Not only do we want all this from our single life partner, but we also want that person to be someone with whom we can always be in harmony, with whom we can grow, and with whom we can develop a more creative lifestyle. How can one person live up to so many expectations? Romantic love is too fragile a vessel to carry all those expectations and demands. When the realities of living overwhelm two young people just setting out on their voyage of marriage, romantic love capsizes very easily.

Romantic love has to do with sexual attraction. It has to do with the arousal of the physical senses. It has to do with the euphoria two people experience when they discover each other. It has to do with the sheer wonder of finding intimate companionship in a world of strangers. Romantic love is so compelling an experience that poets have spent their lives try-ing to express it in words and song.

But romantic love does not have much to do with the realities of everyday living together. The realities of everyday living have to do with cooking meals and washing clothes day after day. The realities of life have to do with cleaning the house and changing diapers. They have to do with paying bills, fixing plumbing leaks and mowing the lawn, taking care of a sick spouse and ailing children. Reality has to do with the shock of being laid off from a job and not knowing where the next dollar will come from. Reality has to do with those times when an adolescent runs into trouble with the law. Reality has to do with debilitating diseases that occasionally strike down the hardiest family member or an accident that derails a care-fully planned future.

Young people do not anticipate these realities when they set sail so optimistically into marriage. The two persons begin to feel inadequate to the problems they are facing, disappointed in each other, and disillusioned by the destruction of their romantic dream. Damaged self-esteem arouses hostile and destructive defense mechanisms. They blame each other for the problems they are encountering. They may take solace in extra-marital affairs or one-night infidelities. If alcohol enters the picture, abuse is likely. The couple may become so alienated from each other that divorce follows quickly. If they do not divorce, the relationship that was once so joyful devitalizes into tiresome routine, or becomes **conflict-habituated**, or is reduced to a cold atmosphere of strangers living under the same roof (Cholst, 1991).

If marriage relies solely on romantic love, chances for its survival are slim. We have only to keep up with the romantic courtship and marriage of Hollywood celebrities, followed by quick and bitter divorce, to realize just how short is the shelf-life of romantic love. The question that follows, of course, is: *If romantic love does not survive, what kind of love does survive?* The answer has to do with the transcending values of respect and equality. Have such partnerships ever existed? Yes, particularly, when people have had to build a genuine partner-ship to survive adverse circumstances. A good example: The evolution of the American family during colonial times.

THE EVOLUTION OF A NEW BREED OF PEOPLE: THE AMERICAN FAMILY

In our early history, first as colonies and then as an independent nation, we developed a dif-ferent kind of family from what was traditional in Europe. America was settled by many groups seeking religious and political freedom to worship and live according to the dictates of their conscience. They found the freedom they wanted, but they had to wrest their survival out of a wild and forested land. They had come from countries that had been cultivated and farmed for centuries. In the new land they had to ax down trees, to shape logs for cabins to live in, to drag tree roots from the earth, and fish the dangerous rock-bound coasts of New England. It was backbreaking work. Fierce winters brought illness and death. When spring came late and plantings were delayed, vegetables and fruit were scarce. To prevent starvation, the men had to take to the woods for days and weeks at a time to hunt for rabbit, turkey, veni-son, and anything else that could be eaten. At these times, their wives and daughters had to become head of their households, managing the financial affairs of the homestead and edu-cating the children.

A New World Personality Style for Women

It may have been the duty of New World fathers to *read* the Scriptures at family devotions, but it was the duty of New World mothers to *teach* their children to read the Scriptures. Fortunately, their women folk were equal to these tasks for they were not like the women of the Old World. They were not the illiterate peasant women who walked humbly behind their husbands. They were a different breed of woman largely unknown in the history of Western civilization, who had been raised to be literate, intelligent, independent, and assertive. This new world required women who were firm in their convictions, courageous in trying times, and who had strength of character. The frontier needed women who could do more than tend the hearth. Frontier women had to help clear the wilderness, sometimes with shovel, ax, and plough. When the men were called upon to leave for weeks at a time on scouting parties or on hunting-and-trading trips, they needed women who could manage the homestead intelligently, who could buy and sell products with financial acumen, and who could defend the homestead from raiding parties or the unscrupulous. The New World man needed a New World woman—a true helpmeet. So strong and assertive was the New World woman that Abigail Adams (wife of President John Adams) could entreat him to make laws to free women from the tyranny of men:

> Remember the Ladies and be more generous and favourable to them than your ancestors. Do not put such unlimited power into the hands of the Husbands. Remember all men would be tyrants if they could. If particular care and attention is not paid to the Ladies, we are determined to foment a Rebellion, and will not hold ourselves bound by any Laws in which we have no voice, or Representation.

While Abigail was protesting the tyranny of men, she could not have done so had women of that period not gained a certain amount of stature and equality. So sure is she of herself, she even threatens a woman's revolution.

A New World Personality Style for Men

The men of the New World were also developing a different personality style. The Old World with its class society had bred obsequiousness among working-class men and an intricate formality among upper-class men. Old World youngsters were taught to bow to their elders and "to be seen and not heard." But the New World settlers did not have time (or desire) for either obsequious manners or ritualized formality. New World men addressed each other by first names or as "Brother." They addressed neighbor women by their first names preceded by a respectful "Sister" or "Mistress." "Good day, Sister Prudence." Or, "You're up bright and early, Mistress Rachel." When Alexis deTocqueville came over here in 1830 to see what kind of people the New World was producing, he was amazed by the informality and friendliness of everybody (see Box 8.2). In fact, the American family was based, not on class distinction and power, but on a community of equality and cooperation. It was a family style in which every adult—even the hired hands—had a say in the management of the homestead. While we are extolling the early American settlers, however, we must be careful not to over-romanticize them. There were deep pockets of prejudice, intolerance, and superstition even in the New World. The Salem witch hunts testify all too well to that. But the ideals of "town hall democracy" were reflected in community-based family life.

BOX **8.2** Alexis deTocqueville Describes the New World Family

Alexis deTocqueville was the remarkable Frenchman who came to the United States in the early part of the nineteenth century (1830) to discover for himself what kind of people the "American experiment" in democracy was producing. He was similar to anthropologists who travel the globe today studying indigenous cultures. DeTocqueville was studying the Americans of the New World. His expedition took him from Canada to Florida and from the Eastern Seaboard to the frontiers of the Mississippi. He went back to France and wrote his classic treatise, *Democracy in America*. He had lots to say about us, and not all of it was complimentary. Some of what he had to say, however, was quite glowing.

He described Americans and Canadians as the friendliest peoples he had ever come across. He noted how everyone called each other by their first names: husbands and wives, parents and children, employers and employees, even village acquaintances, which he found remarkable. He found warm-hearted hospitality that he (a visiting stranger) received from everyone he met unusual. He was also deeply impressed by how educated everyone seemed to be, even humble hired hands could read the Bible, Shakespeare's plays, and the works of such poets as Robert Burns. And he was particularly impressed by the women he met.

When asked to what the prosperity and growing strength of the American people ought mainly to be attributed, he replied without hesitation, "The superiority of their women." In contrast to the women of his country, he described them as literate, educated, and assertive. His description of the New World woman was a radical departure from the European tradition that "A woman is to be from her house three times: When she is christened, married, and buried."

MARRIAGE PRESENT: THE EXHAUSTED NUCLEAR FAMILY

The Extended Rural Family

How then did we lose this sense of community within the family? Why are so many modern marriages ending in alienation, conflict, and divorce? These questions have been the earnest study of many social scientists, and they have identified a myriad of causal factors. They point out that we are still trailing obsolete and destructive traditional models of marriage based on *power* and *dominance*. They point to our increasing anxiety to survive and to achieve in our complex and competitive society. In particular, they point to the pressure of the many roles each partner has to play—which is exhausting them. By contrast, the rural **extended family** (more than two generations living under one roof) provided both physical, emotional, and social support for all members of the family.

In addition to Mom and Pop and the children, the extended rural family might also include one or both grandparents, widowed Uncle Will, young orphaned Cousin Hester, and maybe a "hired hand." There was a sense of community to these family groupings. The housekeeping tasks, the farm tasks, and the tasks of child raising were shared among the several adult members of the extended family. We hope that no one believes the extended rural family lived in idyllic harmony as portrayed in Norman Rockwell magazine covers. There will always be some dissension among a group of people living in close proximity over a long period of time. And the more people that live together, the more issues there will be to argue over. But at least there were people to share the tasks and responsibilities. If Mom fell ill, Grandmother could take over the cooking and Cousin Hester, though young, was a built-in babysitter. If Father hurt his back, Uncle Will or Grandfather could take over farm chores, and even the women could help out.

Consider now the **nuclear family** composed only of one generation of adults. They have to play a multitude of roles, some of which were shared by others in the extended family

Figure 8.2 Role Overload. The multi-roles of the modern nuclear family.

(Figure 8.2). So when Mother falls ill with the flu, she can expect very little help with the children or household tasks. Her husband can't afford to take off more than a day or two from his job to help out. Often the grandparents live too far to come and help her or are themselves working at full-time jobs (Steinberg & Silverberg, 1987).

The Plight of the Modern Husband-and-Father

Consider also the plight of the modern husband/father. He finds himself working a full-time job and maybe "moonlighting" as well. When he is not working, he may have to take more courses or attend conferences on the weekends, coach his son for his Little League participation, become the house maintenance engineer, and "pick up" a few things on the way home from work. He has to acquire the skills of plumber, carpenter, electrician, garage mechanic, mason, gardener, and roofing expert. Modern life has not allowed us to have more leisure. What modern life has done is to raise our desire for a higher and higher standard of living, which in turn demands that many people are having to work two jobs to pay the bills. We are overwhelmed by the number of roles we have to play and the number of skills we have to learn. In working conferences of the 1980s and 1990s, the one overwhelming problem employers and employees alike discussed was being overworked to the point of continual fatigue (Davidson, 1995).

Men also have lost that sense of belonging to the home place. It seems to the man that his work place is his domain and the home place is "her" domain. *She* buys the things for the house. *She* is in charge of the food. Even if father and children have a good relationship, the children run to Mom when they are hurt or scared or need help with something. *She* tells him what they need in the way of house and family needs. *She* has become the social chairperson and has control of their social schedules. *She* pays the bills and controls the cash flow. His sense of powerlessness makes him feel like "a wimp." At work he feels competent. At home, he is not sure of himself and what his role is. In short, the "man of the house" has been replaced by a "lost soul" (Bly, 1992; Faludi, 1999).

The Plight of the Modern "Super Mom"

From her point-of-view, he has turned over the responsibility of the house to her completely, and she is overwhelmed by the number of things she has to do: the shopping, the cooking, the meal planning, seeing to it that the kids take baths and are clean when they go to school, supervising their homework, trying to keep the house clean, worrying about who needs what in the way of clothes or other supplies and how to balance the budget. All this while, in addition, working part- or full-time. There is not enough time in the day to do everything she is "supposed to do." She, too, is exhausted. She feels that she gives and gives and gives and gets less and less in return. Even when she asks him to do something simple, such as take the garbage out or fix the living room lamp, he exudes resentment (Glass, 1998; Gray, 1992).

The Stresses and Strains of Modern Parenting

Huge Demands on Our Time and Energy. There is a centuries-old tradition that the more children that are produced, the more advantages to the family—and the more marital satisfaction. This may have been true of previous traditional societies when children were an economic advantage. Children were free labor. There were also deemed to be the staffs who would care for an aging parent. In an agrarian economy even today, children can help with the planting, weeding, harvesting, etc. But today studies of marital satisfaction actually show a reduction in happiness with every child that comes along. Why so? Because we want our children to have "every advantage," and we devote our time, our energies, and our financial resources to that end. We urge our children to go on for further education after high school and further education means additional financial support of them. Moreover, all those music, dance, and swimming lessons cost money. So do athletic uniforms, band uniforms, and cheerleading uniforms. The more we want for our children, the more it costs. If a child with a debilitating disease needs extended medical help, only a portion of it will be paid by insurance benefits. We can afford this kind of physical and emotional energy with one or two children. By the time the third and fourth child come along, our energies (both financial and emotional) are exhausted. As children come, one by one, and grow into their teens, the sad truth is that marital satisfaction declines, as shown in study after study over the last 50 years (See Figure 8.3).

Financial Stress. The research data in this area are unequivocal. Financial security and adequate income are basic indicators of marital success. It is more truth than poetry that *when bills fly in the window, love flies out.* When credit card balances climb and debts pile up, the normal stresses and strains of married life are compounded by anxiety and despair. Small tensions become large ones. Quarrels about how to spend the available money and accusations about each other's wastefulness become hot and explosive. She may vent her anger and despair on her husband with unjustified accusations that he is an inadequate breadwinner. His feelings of inadequacy and failure may lead to drinking or a night out to "have a little fun." That "fun"

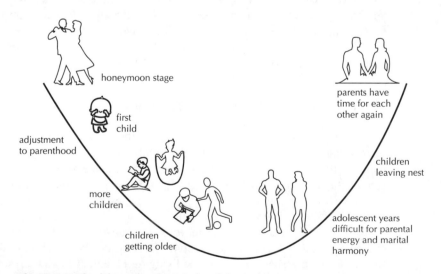

honeymoon stage

first child

adjustment to parenthood

more children

children getting older

parents have time for each other again

children leaving nest

adolescent years difficult for parental energy and marital harmony

Figure 8.3 The life cycle of marital satisfaction.

may involve other women who seem to restore in him his sense of adequacy and masculinity. The drinking may result in abuse of his wife and children (Gelles & Straus, 1989).

Parental Responsibilities. Because we want to give our children "every possible advantage," American parents have become chauffeurs to band practice, play practice, athletic games, boy and girl clubs. We attend teacher conferences and PTA meetings. We squire them to their doctor appointments, dentist appointments, to their music lessons or gymnastic lessons. We are on the run to do whatever we can for them. But all that running, all those errands, all that quality time we make for our children means less time we have to spend with our life-partner. If the catch phrase for parenting in the 1980s and 1990s was quality time with our children, the catch phrase for the present decade might need to be quality time with every member of our family, and that includes our **Significant Other**. Moments of intimacy between two persons cannot be expressed when other people are in the immediate vicinity. Maintaining the glow of intimacy requires privacy—without friends, without relatives, without business associates, and without children present. Privacy and quality time was what the two people who fell in love valued most dearly. The problem is that the older we grow and the more responsibilities we take on, the harder it is to find that kind of time for intimacy. Guidelines for maintaining intimacy are discussed at the end of this chapter.

Domestic Violence. The statistics on reported domestic violence is shocking (see Box 8.3). Statistics indicate that the spouse murder rate in this country is the fifth highest in the world, ten times higher than in England and 25 times higher than in Spain (Wallach, 1995). Our most recent information indicates that one out of eight husbands is physically

---

BOX **8.3**) **Signs of an Abusive Relationship**

Separation: The batterer isolates his victim from her support system of friends and family. He insists that they are making her unhappy or interfering in their marital relationship. He may move her to an isolated area so that she has little opportunity to see other people.

Surveillance: He wants to know where she is at all times. He convinces her that he needs her presence constantly. If he cannot force her to quit her job, he may drive her to work, meet her for lunch, and pick her up at closing time to drive her home.

Verbal abuse: He may accuse her of infidelity with others when that is what he is involved in. He may tell her she is sexually incompetent in one way or another. He will criticize her constantly. He complains continually that she is a "lousy" cook and a "lazy" housekeeper.

Exhaustion and hunger: He may deprive her of sleep by keeping her up late and making her wake up early in the morning while he sleeps late. He makes her work on projects that are overwhelming for her, like

helping to build a new home or starting a new business in addition to her other responsibilities.

Hostility and paranoia: He may throw food, break furniture, burn or tear her clothing, threaten her life, or the life of the children. She often describes him as a Dr. Jekyll and Mr. Hyde, charming in public but brutal in private. He can be so convincing that she questions her own sanity.

Chemical dependence: Batterers will often encourage a woman to become dependent on drugs or alcohol as a way to control her and make her totally dependent on him.

Financial dependence: He will try to make her financially dependent on him. If she works, he will make her give him her paycheck and spend it on things he wants. Or he will convince her not to work so that she will be dependent on him for money.

Financial deprivation: When she is totally financially dependent on him, he will mete out money to her

BOX (**8.3**) **Signs of an Abusive Relationship (continued)**

penny by penny. Then he will accuse her of not managing the budget competently, even though he does not give her enough money to pay the bills. He may prevent her from having transportation to get around, so that she becomes a prisoner in her own home. She then stops buying clothes, begins to look bedraggled, and may even cut her own hair rather than go to the beauty shop.

Battering: Once she is isolated from her emotional support system and becomes convinced that she is an incompetent adult who cannot survive without him emotionally and financially, the battering increases. It starts with irrational arguments followed by mild threats, and then escalates to shoving, pushing, hitting, and slapping, and ultimately to the use of objects and dangerous weapons.

Cycle of violence: After the violence, he convinces her that he just couldn't control himself and that it will never happen again. After the battering, he may apologize, shower her with gifts, love, and swear he'll never do it again. Or he may convince her that she was responsible for the beating. In either case, she is expected to conceal her bruises and cuts and lie about what really happened. She is then the one who feels guilty. He has convinced her that she "drove him to it." The perpetrator has transformed himself into the victim.

Sources: Lenore Walker, *Terrifying Love: Why Battered Women Kill and How Society Responds* (New York: Harper & Row, 1999).

aggressive at least once toward his wife each year. Think of it! In 12 percent of marriages, a woman has been physically assaulted by the very man who once declared his love for her and promised to cherish her (see Table 8.1). Students frequently ask: *Why doesn't the battered woman just walk away from the marriage?* Her friends and family usually cannot understand why she just does not walk out the door. They get her to escape to a shelter for abused women, only to discover she has returned to the abuser's domicile. Angry and frustrated, they assume she must want to be abused. But those who have done case studies of battered women explain

Table 8.1 Domestic Violence: Its Pandemic

- Every year at least 1.6 million U.S. women are beaten by their husbands.
- Being a woman is the single most powerful predictor of becoming a victim of violence.
- Being exposed to violence at home during childhood is the most powerful predictor for a man to use violence against his wife and child.
- Alcohol is a contributing factor in more than 75% of the cases of abuse.
- In the United States, battered women are four to five times more likely to attempt suicide.
- Women who have been abused earn up to 20% less than women who have not been abused.
- Women in the United States are more likely to be assaulted, injured, raped, or murdered by a current or former male partner than by all other types of attackers combined.
- In the United States, it has been suggested that between 30–70% of women have been victims of rapes during their lifetimes.
- In Colombia, Canada, and the United States an estimated 33% of the women have been physically assaulted by an intimate male partner.
- In Latin America, Asia, and Africa this abuse may be as high as 75%.
- In Norway, the United States, Canada, New Zealand, Barbados and the Netherlands 33% of women were sexually abused during childhood.
- It is estimated that 28% of gay males and 25% of lesbians experience domestic violence.

Sources: Bailey, 1996; Jacobson & Gottman, 1998; Nelson, 1996; and Walker, 1999.

it this way. She has been brainwashed. Her image of herself has been virtually destroyed. She has been taught that she is ugly, incapable, and incompetent. Her self-esteem and self-confidence have been eroded. Her will has been paralyzed. Her perceptions of reality are seriously skewed. If she has been a "homemaker," the battered woman may have no vocational skills. She may have two or more preschool children and no one to leave them with so she can find some kind of job, no matter how menial. Family members who do not believe in divorce may even tell her that she *made her bed so she has to lie in it.*

Some abusers apologize for their abuse and promise never to do it again. Some abusers live up to their promise, but, unfortunately, most abusers simply repeat the cycle of (1) romantic involvement, (2) irritation, jealousy, etc., (3) violent abuse, then (4) apologies and promises to do better in the future. And then back to (1) romantic involvement. But when the abuse is repeated over and over and trips to the emergency room are repeated, eventually the abused spouse will be forced to leave or the "next time she'll be dead." Another disturbing fact is that it is known that the abuse may not stop even if the woman leaves the batterer. Many batterers continue to harass, stalk, and harm the woman who has left him. If she hides out in a "safe house" with her children, he may even use his charming wiles to connive the location of the safe house out of a relative, friend, or even an unsuspecting worker at the Family Protective Services (Jones, 1999).

Let's Not Go In for Man-Bashing: Women Have Also Been Violent. Even though the majority of victims are women, too many books have presented a one-sided picture. Men, too, have been insulted, humiliated, and assaulted by women. While discussing this subject one day in one of our classes, we said something like this: *No physical violence is allowed by either party. Just as men should not sock their women, women should not think it permissible to slap their men.* A few of the female students expressed surprise. Evidently, they were assuming that somehow a "slap in the face" by a woman was acceptable even though they railed against being slapped in the face by a man. Counting acts by both men and women, more than 10 million Americans experience physical violence every year. Violence is a hangover from previous power-dominated relationships and is not limited to our nation. It is pandemic worldwide.

DEVELOPING BETTER INTERPERSONAL COMMUNICATION

Men and Women Develop Different Communication Styles

Men and Women Come from Different Cultures. Men are goal-oriented. Men value power, competency, efficiency, and achievements. Their sense of self is defined through their ability to get results. They are fulfilled through achievement, such as building skyscrapers and super highways. Women, on the other hand, are relationship-oriented. Women value tenderness, communication, beauty, and intimate interpersonal relationships. They spend a lot of time supporting, helping, and nurturing one another. Their sense of self is defined through sharing and caring. Rather than building structures and highways, women are concerned with building relationships.

Boys-becoming-men are taught to be tough, to be self-reliant, not to show weakness, to do what has to be done, and to bite-the-bullet when they are hurt. Girls-becoming-women are taught to be gentle, to comfort and care for others, to be of service whenever possible (Gilligan,

1982). He is taught to "stand up for himself." If he can't fight the other guy, he can at least yell at him. So while she is learning to be polite and soft-voiced, he is learning to argue and shout. Let's not blame our parents for this. These values have been sanctioned everywhere in almost every society for thousands of years. Men can argue and cuss at each other one minute and in the very next minute go off and have a drink together. This is true on the athletic field, on the job site, or in the office. A man does not understand that when he shouts at a woman, she gets hurt. He thinks: *Doesn't she realize he was just blowing off steam?* No, she doesn't. Brought up to be soft-spoken, those words and names he has shouted at her are daggers in her heart (Kipnis & Heron, 1995). The problem with verbal abuse is that it can never be truly erased, no matter how sincere an apology is offered. It remains in the person's verbal memory.

Developing a Common Communication Style by Changing Our Pronouns. It makes us feel good to blame others for problems. We tell ourselves: *It was his fault—not mine*. Or how about: *She started the argument, but I'm going to finish it*. Finding other people to blame absolves us from guilt and the responsibility to make amends. The blaming game comes out in accusations and the use of the pronoun *you. You did this!* Or *You did that!* What we need to do is exchange the pronoun *You* with the pronoun *I*, and the pronouns *I, me, mine* with the pronouns for *we, us, ours*. When we use first person plural pronouns, we do not send accusing statements. We send the message that no one person is to blame for problems. We send the message that all problems are to be shared. We send the message that solutions must be arrived at jointly. Avoiding the "blame game" is easy to learn but hard to remember to do in the heat of raging emotions. Like skill on the athletic field or in the concert hall, it takes determination and much practice to develop a supportive communication style. Compare, for example, the emotional impact of the accusing pronouns "you" and "your" with the pronouns "we" and "us" in Box 8.4.

BOX **8.4** APPLICATION
The Emotional Impact of Pronouns

This is an activity you can do in class or by yourselves. Compare the emotional impact of the pronouns "you and your" with the pronouns "we and our" in otherwise similar statements as shown.

Accusing "You" Statements	Cooperative "We" Statements
Why didn't **you** remember to pick up the cleaning?	Why do **we** forget who's supposed to pick up the cleaning?
Your son misbehaved in school again. What are **you** going to do about it.	**Our** son misbehaved in school again. What should **we** do about it?
You never want to go anywhere with me.	**We** need to find things to do we can both enjoy.
You didn't tell me you were going to work late.	**We** need a better system of keeping each other informed when one of us is going to be late.
The minute I sit down, **you** want me to do something.	**We** need to figure out when each of us needs to let the other know we want to relax a bit.
You left me high-and-dry at the party so I didn't know what to do with myself all evening.	If that happens again, **we** need to work out a signal between **us** to stay with each other.

Reflective Writing: What is the emotional effect of using "you" and "your" as compared to using "we" and "our"? What is the subtle difference of the second column of sentences?

If a Quarrel Does Break Out, We Can Quarrel Intelligently and Constructively. A few psychologists have suggested that if we follow certain guidelines for domestic harmony and peace, the couple may never again have another argument. With that premise we disagree. Whenever people live together in close contact over a period of time, friction happens. It happens in the office; it happens on the athletic field; it even happens at social functions. Arguments will break out despite all our attempts to stay cool and rational. That is the nature of things—human nature. But quarreling does not have to be a knife to the jugular if both parties understand that even a quarrel can have several legitimate purposes; namely, to give vent to unexpressed feelings and needs, to get problems out in the open, and to work through to solutions.

We can quarrel constructively if we follow a few simple rules. If this comes as a surprise, remember that wrestling matches, Olympic competitions, and football games all have rules. Even warring nations are supposed to abide by the Geneva Convention. If we have never tried to argue within a framework of guidelines, it will not be an easy habit to learn, but it *can* be learned. It is also a skill that couples develop in successful long-standing relationships. We suggest our set of guidelines, but each couple may want to work out adaptations of their own (see Tip 8.2 and Box 8.5).

BOX 8.5 When Arguments Break Out, Guidelines for Constructive Quarreling

Guideline 1: Quarrel about one thing at a time. Perhaps you have known couples who, when they argue, drag out every conflict they have had since Day One. When this happens, there are so many tangled threads to the argument, the result is one huge knot that can never be untangled. Problems can only be resolved when a single issue is under discussion. This is a basic tenet of Robert's Rules of Order. It is a basic tenet of most guidelines for intelligent argument.

Guideline 2: "Hit-and-run" drivers not allowed under any circumstances. You probably know what we are talking about even before we explain it. It's saying or doing something that really hurts the other person and then storming out, getting into the car, and leaving. That's not just a cheap shot—leaving the scene of a crime is a criminal act. If you find yourself running off, turn around and come back. Apologize for the terrible thing you said and for leaving. (It's OK to still be angry—just not OK to be a reckless driver.)

Guideline 3: Keep your voice as calm as possible. Don't start shouting. Keep your voice down and as normal as possible. When we shout at people, we are deafening them. They cannot hear the words because they are defending themselves against the noise of shouts and screaming. Furthermore, if one person shouts, the other has to shout louder in self-defense. Neither person is listening anymore. They are simply screaming. It has become a madhouse.

Guideline 4: Keep to the truth. People who are quarreling tend to exaggerate their complaints or to throw a red-herring lie into the argument. Not allowed! Lies are neither intelligent nor constructive. It's tempting to exaggerate, but it only confuses the issue. What is needed is clarity about where things are going wrong.

Guideline 5: Don't go in for the blaming game. Just remember that in a problematic situation, everybody is involved. All problems are shared. Use "we" instead of "you."

Guideline 6: Don't play the silent game. Say openly and honestly what is upsetting you. Here's the scenario: The husband comes home and knows right away something is wrong. His wife does not have her usual smile on. In fact, she goes on with what she has been doing and hardly seems to notice his presence. "OK," he says, preparing for an all-out encounter,

---

Tip 8.2 On Agreeing to Your Quarrel Guidelines. Be sure to make up your guidelines after you have had one or two quarrels but are now feeling good with each other. After you have had some serious conflicts, you are now in a position to identify what upsets each of you.

BOX **8.5** **When Arguments Break Out, Guidelines for Constructive Quarreling (continued)**

"What's wrong?" Does she tell him? Not on your life! "Nothing," she says in a tone that says "There's plenty wrong, but I'll be damned if I'll tell you." This script could be entitled "Guess What I'm Annoyed About." There will be times when you don't feel able to talk about it rationally. Simply say so. "Yes, there's something I'm disturbed about, but I just can't discuss it now. I need to wait until I'm calmer."

Guideline 7: When the argument is reaching "critical mass," call for "time out." Sometimes even the calmest persons can begin to feel that the argument is getting out of hand. If so, call for "time out" so that both of you can collect your thoughts and feelings and return to a calmer place. Simply say, "Look, this argument is getting too much for me, and I can't handle it rationally any more. Let's talk later when we are both cooled down."

Guideline 8: Look for win-win solutions. We can win a battle, but no one really wins in a war. The defeated party may acquiesce or surrender but the hurt, the anger, the bitterness will come out in covert ways. Therefore do no look for anyone to lose. Instead of looking for whose to blame, look for solutions. Instead of concentrating on win-lose solutions, seek win-win solutions.

Guideline 9: Avoid acts of terrorism. Don't bomb the other with catastrophic statements. When some couples argue, they begin to threaten each other.

> *If you do that again, I'll leave you.*
> *If you walk out that door, don't bother to come back.*
> *I'll never forgive you for that! Never!*
> *I guess you want a divorce. Call the lawyer in the morning.*

Whatever you were quarreling about has now been blasted out of memory by the bomb you have just tossed into the argument. If the other person calls the lawyer, remember that you asked for it.

Guideline 10: No violence. Not any! Not of any sort! No pushing, shoving, hitting, beating, slapping. No throwing things even if you know you aren't going to hit the person. A person we know once threw all the food the other had just finished preparing on the floor. That is violence. Throwing a cup or a glass is violence. Slamming cabinet doors or bedroom doors is violence.

Reflective Writing: Think of a rule or guideline that is appropriate for you and your significant other.

When Romantic Love Ebbs, Compassionate Love Endures

In Chapter 7, we described the phenomenon of romantic love as so intense that the couple are swept into heights of emotional and physical passion. Romantic love is the stuff that songs and poems and the great love stories of all time are made of. Unfortunately, Americans have been propagandized by Hollywood movies that the fierce sexual attraction lovers feel for each other during their courtship days will remain as intense long after their passion is consummated. Such is not the case. The thirst for physical intimacy eventually becomes somewhat quenched over time.

This is not to say that marriage becomes sexless. On the contrary, long-lasting relationships includes sex, but passion waxes and wanes over the course of a committed relationship. Many factors contribute to the ebb tide of physical sex. Either one or both of the couple may have physical health problems. The pressures and deadlines of job and career, from time to time, may have to take precedence. The demands of college classes may force one or both to study far into the night. Conscientious supervision of the children's homework after toiling all day at work and home depletes whatever emotional and physical energy the couple have left. Prolonged illness or death of a child, parent, or sibling may exhaust the emotional and physical energy of one or both of the couple. When such events intervene, sexual passion wanes dramatically. In fact, some studies have found that 15 to 20 percent of double-income marriages may have sex ten times a year or less (Deveny, 2003). What may be needed at these times is not physical intimacy but **compassionate love**, respect for what the other is going through and strong emotional support (Sternberg, 1985). If both persons are capable of compassionate love, their relationship can endure and become stronger. But if one partner becomes frustrated or angered by the lack of sex, infidelity may follow.

When Vows Are Broken

Defining Infidelity. There are relationships in which one or both partners tolerate affairs of one sort or another, sometimes called an **open marriage**. We are not speaking here of those situations. As generally defined, **infidelity** is a *secret* relationship outside of the committed relationship. When the infidelity is discovered, the Betrayed Person experiences a range of traumatic emotions: shock at having been lied to and deceived; loss of trust in the other, humiliation at having been cheated on; outrage that money and time was spent on the Other Person; and grief and despair that what was special to the two of them no longer exists. People frequently ask: *Is it possible for people to have an intense attraction to someone else, even if they believe they have a good marriage?* Yes, it is possible, and with more and more women entering the workplace, the opportunity for infidelity by both partners is increasing (Glass, 1998). But when infidelity is discovered by the other partner, divorce is frequently the result. If we are interested in maintaining the commitment with our partner, *can we predict what leads to an affair so as to avoid falling into one? If an affair does occur, what are the consequences? Does the other partner simply submit to the situation, as painful as it may be? Is divorce inevitable? Can the relationship, in some way, be mended?* These are the questions that both partners in the relationship must address (Pittman, 1989).

Marital Unhappiness. Obviously, marital unhappiness is one absolute predictor for falling into an affair, particularly for the woman. When she begins to feel unhappy, she will try to let her partner know there is a problem in the marriage. She is trying to improve their relationship as best she can. Believing that her husband will understand her unhappiness, she expects that he will endeavor to improve their situation by responding more to her needs.

Ironically, the effect of her confrontation on the man is just the opposite. For example, while she feels better for having told him about the lack of communication between them, he interprets her complaints as being something wrong with him. He doesn't know how to respond to her desire for more intimate talk between them, so he responds by clamming up even more. *He doesn't know what she wants him to talk about.* If her complaints involve all her exhaustion for trying to do everything she is "supposed to do" with the management of the household and discipline of the children, he doesn't know how to help her (or feels it's none of his affair). So he retreats even more from any kind of authentic communication. *After all, what's the use? With all that he has to do, she is expecting too much from him.* When she struggles to express her loneliness and lack of appreciation for all that she is doing both at work and at home, he feels put down. If she goes so far as to express her deepest feelings—that she sometimes feels like the "family drudge," seeing to everyone else's needs while her own needs always take a back seat to everyone else's—he feels so helpless to respond to her misery that he retreats even further from any more such discussions. The woman keeps trying to get him to listen to her, which he interprets as "nagging," and the cycle continues: The more she brings up her unhappiness, the more he retreats.

Finally, when she realizes that it's just no use to try to reach him, she finally gives up even trying. If that happens, the marriage is dangerously down the road to dissolution. Because she doesn't complain any more, her husband thinks things are better. He doesn't notice that she has detached herself from the marriage. She is now emotionally available for an affair. Since he has retreated from any genuine interaction between them, so does she (Glass, 1998). She may even ask for a divorce. After infidelity, abuse, and alcoholism, the next most frequent reason women give for wanting a divorce is lack of communication. At the lawyer's office, the following exchange is quite frequent:

Husband: I didn't know she was unhappy. I thought everything was fine.
Wife: He just wouldn't listen. I've been telling him for years our marriage was in trouble.

Other Predictors of Affairs. If we are in a work setting where many people are having affairs and the general work environment has a permissive attitude toward extramarital situations, we're more likely to have an affair. If we come from a family where it is known that our parents have had affairs, we're more likely to have an affair. In some cultures, men believe affairs and mistresses are their entitlement, and these relationships are right out in the open. In American culture, there is a tacit belief among some men that it is OK to have an affair as long as it is kept secret (Glass, 1998). These men separate sex and affection: *There are nice girls you marry and have children with, and then there are the other women with whom you can have a dalliance and add spice to your life.* Men who score high on traits of authoritarianism such as military officers fall into this category of separating sex and affection. People in high-drama professions—emergency room physicians, for example, and cardiologists—thrive on the adrenalin charge of their professions. Secret rendezvous meetings associated with illicit affairs provide that same kind of adrenalin jag that comes from the dangers of "being found out" by spouse or colleagues.

Sexual Infidelity versus Emotional Infidelity. There are some gender differences in the way men and women regard affairs. Men feel more betrayed by their wives engaging in the physical act of sex with someone else. Women feel more betrayed by their husbands being *emotionally* involved with someone else. Most women believe that if you love your partner, you wouldn't even be interested in an affair. Since men often separate love and sex, many men believe that a one-night stand or even a long-standing affair has nothing to do with their love for their wives. Even men who do love their partners and enjoy good sex at home, may still never turn down an opportunity for extramarital sex. In fact, 56 percent of the men who had extramarital affairs said that their marriages were happy. Some studies suggest that marital satisfaction is higher for men in long-term relationships when they have had affairs (Glass, 1998). Well, of course. These men are having their cake and eating it, too. They are enjoying the romantic passion they no longer have for their wives, which they interpret as adding a "little spice to their life." Then they come home to the "little lady" who provides them with both domestic service and emotional comfort—until the betrayed wife discovers the affair (Greer & Rosen, 1997).

Outcomes of Discovery. Discovery can lead to a number of different outcomes. The Betrayer may be so entangled with the Other Person as to decide to leave the committed relationship. Surprisingly, however, only about ten percent actually end up with the Other Person (Glass, 1998). The committed couple might decide to work to repair their relationship. Or they can agree to separate until the affair is concluded, and most affairs eventually do dissolve. Unfortunately, the affair may last a long time. Why so? Because affairs are glamorous. The two persons are experiencing the thrilling "Being-in-Love" romantic stage, discussed in Chapter 7, which is not being spoiled by children bickering with each other, repairing the toilet plumbing, or cleaning up after the dog has made a mess.

If the marriage is still in an early stage or when there are no children, an affair is more likely to end in divorce because there still isn't a lot of investment in keeping the marriage together. Even yet, the couple may decide to stay together "for the sake of the children," remaining two strangers living under the same roof. If the divorce would result in significant financial loss for one or both persons, the marriage may remain intact, at least on the surface. The affluent and wealthy tend to avoid divorce because of the financial aspects involved. In these situations, the partners remain married in name only, and lead what is called "separate lives," a euphemism for having extramarital relationships or even having a live-in relationship with someone else.

Relationships may withstand infidelity, but not all relationships can be fixed. Unfaithful partners who fail to show empathy for the pain they have caused to their betrayed spouses results in more disillusion, and the betrayed person concludes that nothing can repair their marriage. The unfaithful partner must be willing to be patient when the betrayed partner becomes suspicious occasionally, hypervigilant about what is going on when the person is late coming home, and needing continual assurance of love and affection. If the unfaithful partner takes responsibility for the affair instead of blaming it on problems in the marriage, the attempt to heal the relationship may work. People are more willing to survive affairs these days, but without a good deal of marriage counseling, it is hard to get over the pain and humiliation (see Box 8.6). If the problems of the affair are worked through, the couple can recommit to each

---

BOX 8.6 Defining an Affair, Avoiding an Affair, and Repairing the Relationship

Defining an Affair: Danger Signs and Signals of an Affair

1. **Keeping secrets.** Even if two people regularly eat lunch together in a public place but don't tell their partners, it is deception.
2. **Being emotionally intimate.** If a person confides things to someone that they do not confide with their partner, it is a danger sign, especially if the confidence is about negative aspects of their marriage.
3. **Sexual chemistry is present.** An affair can exist without consummation. For example, people can have affairs without touching at all as on the Internet. If they let each other know they are attracted, the sexual tension increases.
4. **Any kind of touching or kissing.** Such actions indicate the two people know they have crossed the line from friendship to affair.
5. **Lying is involved.** Whether by commission (a total lie) or omission (not telling the whole truth), it is lying.
6. **Having the opportunity.** For example, being together in the work place for long hours. In this environment we usually look our best and are energetic. It's much sexier than having to come home to a flooded toilet and a disheveled spouse. Women in the workforce are increasingly having more affairs than in the past. There is simply more opportunity to meet men and to look glamorous in their dress and style.

Avoiding an Affair: Protecting Yourself from Falling Into an Affair

1. **Being careful of your own curiosity.** If you are "invited to lunch" without a substantial reason (such as a business lunch or working on a mutual charity, etc.) and want to accept just out of curiosity, it may be the first step to an affair.
2. **Avoiding emotional intimacy.** If someone comes to you in distress, don't become the confessor and confident. Recommend a good therapist. Be

BOX **8.6** Defining an Affair, Avoiding an Affair, and Repairing the Relationship (continued)

careful, yourself, with whom you share your deepest feelings. Don't discuss a fight with your spouse with a potential partner.

3. **Be suspicious when someone lets you know he/she admires you.** Your Significant Other has known you a long time, long before all of your present achievements. If someone new comes along and perceives you in your present high status or glamorous role, it is ego-enhancing and seductive.

4. **Getting bored with your marriage.** People in long-term relationships tend to take each other for granted. Getting bored is an early warning sign that the relationship needs more leisure time, fun, and excitement.

5. **Actively engage in more couple-centered activities.** The best gift you can give your children is your own happy marriage. You can't have a happy marriage if you never spend time together alone. The affair is exciting partly because the two people are finding time to be alone with each other. Very busy couples have to work with their calendars and find time to spend with each other.

6. **If you travel with someone else, never invite that someone for a drink in the room.** Similarly, do not accept an invitation for a drink in the other person's hotel room.

Repairing the Relationship: Difficult But It Can Be Done

1. **Rebuild security and trust for your Significant Other by ceasing all contact with the affair partner.** The affair must be broken off absolutely. If the

Other Person works in the same work area, keep the communication polite but distant.

2. **No matter how painful the process may be, answer all questions put to you from the betrayed partner.** In the beginning the Betrayed Partner wants the gory details: *Where, what, and when.* For example: *Did you tell the affair partner you loved him/her?* Be prepared to answer all the factual questions about where you went, the sexual activities, and gifts and other monies spent. Answering these questions may be painful, but take heart, for these questions and their truthful answers are crucial to rebuilding trust.

3. **Both parties need to be more realistic in their perceptions of the Other Person.** The Betrayed Person needs to stop seeing the Other Person as "evil incarnate" and the Betrayer needs to stop seeing the "Other Person" as the idealized angel and lover.

4. **The Betrayer needs to put more effort into the relationship.** The popular notion is that the person who is having the affair wasn't *getting enough* at home. In actuality, the Betrayer wasn't *giving enough* at home.

5. **Both partners need to cooperate by sharing together what they think went wrong and how to remedy these problems.** Repair of the relationship does not depend solely on the Betrayer. It may be that the Betrayed Person had been neglectful or irritable or no longer generally supportive of the other person.

Sources: Glass, 1998; Greer & Rosen, 1997; Pittman, 1989.

---

other. But the relationship may never be the same again. Neither are the persons the same as they were before the discovery of the affair and the commitment to their marriage. Paradoxically, it may end up stronger. Why? Because the two people are learning to relate to each other in new, scary, strange, exciting ways as they have not done in a long time (Glass, 1998; Greer & Rosen, 1997; Pittman, 1989).

When Divorce Is Inevitable

Divorce as a Modern Institution. This chapter has been devoted to the building of a marriage-and-family partnership, but we would be remiss if we did not discuss divorce as an ever present possibility and to provide some guidelines for living through the divorce procedure and subsequent "singlehood" status. It is axiomatic now that about one out of every two marriages is currently ending in divorce. That does not mean that one out of every two persons will go through divorce because this "average" statistic includes those who get married two, three, four, and more times. But what it does mean is that divorce is no longer rare or even as shameful as it was once considered. Divorce has become almost as much of an institution as marriage.

The factors that used to hold marriages together no longer do so today. Women were once shackled to abusive marriages because of economic necessity. With women entering the workforce in larger and larger numbers, the economic factor no longer holds. Men who used to be willing to remain in a loveless marriage "for the sake of the children" are no longer willing to do so. They do not believe that it is better for children to be subjected to years of verbal bickering, insults, and screaming arguments. With the shadow of AIDS ever present, neither men nor women are as forgiving of adultery. To reiterate the opening theme of this chapter, modern persons expect much more from the marriage contract than in previous eras. They want fidelity. They want responsible life-partners. They want to come home to a safe harbor of loving companionship and an expectation of continued growthful interaction. When that is no longer possible, they want out (Jones, 1990).

Divorce may be a quick end to the most painful aspects of a conflict-habituated marriage that may include verbal and physical abuse, philandering and incessant lies to cover up, gross neglect of the family unit, etc.—but divorce brings other problems for which the man and woman are usually quite unprepared (see Box 8.7).

BOX **8.7**) **Dimensions and Tasks Involved in the Process of Divorce**

Understanding the many transitions involved in divorce may help us make sense out of the chaos that occurs during the divorce.

- **The Legal Dimension.** This dimension is what is worked out between the attorneys and the divorce courts. It consists of the date of termination of the marriage, agreements about property, finances, child custody, and visitation rights. The divorcing couple think that is what divorce is all about, but they soon discover that divorce and its aftermath have other dimensions.
- **The Emotional Dimension.** This dimension involves the heartfelt emotions of sadness over the loss of what has been that is no more. The divorcing partners experience the loss of intimacy; the absence of the other person who used to do some of the household and children-raising tasks. Not only have they lost their identity as one of the partners in a marriage, they may even experience a loss of self-identity.
- **The Co-Parenting Dimension.** This dimension involves agreements about child care and upbringing; dealing with the children's reactions to the divorce; and unanticipated problems that cannot be set down in a legal bill of divorce. *You're never on time and I wait and wait for you to pick up the children.* Or *You spoil them and then they think I'm mean.* Or *You forgot Jeff's birthday and he was so disappointed.*

- **The Economic Dimension.** Although both partners anticipate a financial decrease in their budgets, they seldom anticipate many of the bills and debts they will incur. Additionally, they will have to deal with a myriad of unexpected expenses of both children and stepchildren. Men normally recover in better economic status than women, since women are generally less prepared for earning income than men, and most women have lower-paying jobs. In 1984, 60 percent of all female-headed families lived in poverty (Sidel, 1986).
- **The Community Dimension.** One of the most painful tasks that divorcing couples face is telling their families and friends. These announcements are generally met with surprise (sometimes even shock), protests, and painful questions. Mutual friends cannot easily maintain an intimate contact with both divorced partners so they generally decide to be friends of him or her, not both. If they have attended church together, they may now have to go to different churches to avoid embarrassing questions.
- **The Psychic Dimension.** This dimension has to do with evolving a new and autonomous identity as a single person or a single person-with-children. This is perhaps the most difficult dimension for a woman but men also have problems being a bachelor-with-children. Deeper still are the remnants of attachment that persist even when love has been shattered.

A Kind of Dying. When a person dies, we process the loss of the person we have loved through the *rites of passage* we call funerals. We grieve, we mourn, and then we let go of the person so we can begin to heal (vanGennep, 1908/1960). Death is final. The person is no longer on this plane of existence.

No matter how brutal the marriage, or how deep the feelings of betrayal, divorce is also experienced as a kind of "dying." The divorce may come as a relief to years of agony, but nevertheless both partners will experience the loss. The loss may not be that of losing someone we love, but it is the loss of the someone and something that was once the central focus of our lives. Not only are we divorced from our spouse, we may also go through divorce from our children, from our neighbors, and from friends that we shared in common.

Furthermore, there are no cultural **rites of passage** by which to process our change in status from married to single/divorced. We suffer the pain of divorce mostly by ourselves. After all, who wants to listen to the woes of a person in a failed marriage? If the divorce proceedings are dragged out, the suffering can be extended over months and years. Just as we are beginning to heal, wounds are unintentionally reopened when old friends, unaware of the divorce, ask, "How are Annie and the kids?" or "What is Charlie doing now?" It is then the divorced person has to reiterate the painful disclosure that they are "no longer together" before leaving hurriedly to escape from detailed explanations of "what went wrong." Even when the heaviest responsibility for the splitting up of the family falls on the "other," even the most "innocent" of the partners will still feel a sense of guilt and shame for the "failure of the marriage."

When Custody Is Shared, a Divorce Is Never Final. The courts once generally gave custodial custody of the children to the mother—unless there were very extenuating circumstances, such as a charge of "unfit mother." Today, there has been considerable modification of this tradition. In most states, the custody of the child and child support is now awarded to both parents—although how much time the child spends with each parent depends on the state laws and the particular family situation. As long as the parents share the custody of the children, the divorce has put an end to the marriage only on paper. The necessity of talking to each other on the phone to arrange visits or to keep the other informed about illness or school problems, and so on, continue to connect the divorced couple to each other. To make matters worse, the divorced spouses and their children are not the only characters in this drama. There are generally a lot of people off-stage who are coaching the main characters and stirring the pot.

> *He has some nerve not calling you if he was going to be late picking up the kids.*
> *You tell that no good ex-wife of yours to teach your children better manners.*
> *Don't you let him/her dictate the rules of the visitation. You insist on your rights.*

Sometimes these off-stage coaches involve the children by asking them questions about what goes on in their other house.

Problems of the Custodial Parent. Even when the divorcing spouses have made an attempt "to be civil" and have promised "not to involve the children"—a promise born of good intentions but unrealistic in actuality—they will have problems they did not anticipate. For example, the children of shared custody often have to spend weekends and holidays such as Thanksgiving or Christmas or the summer vacation with the noncustodial parent. The custodial parent, bereft of losing the child at (say) Christmas, may react by having a second "Christmas morning" complete with gifts. The noncustodial parent may try to woo the child's affection and loyalty with costly gift-giving or by treating the child to "Disneyworld" or other theme parks and by generally having fun with them. The custodial parent, while happy to hear of the wonderful places the child was taken, may feel somewhat wistful that the child seems to have "lots of fun" with the divorced spouse. The custodial parent is the one who has to take care of the everyday raising of the child, which includes supervision of homework and consultations with the school, nagging to brush teeth and take baths, disciplining the children in instances of misbehavior, and so on.

Problems of the Noncustodial Parent. But noncustodial parents also have their fair share of problems. In the beginning it was fun to take the child to the zoo or the park or the movies or go shopping. Eventually, however, noncustodial parents may begin to wonder if the child really has a genuine affection for them or are the child's shows of affection the result of "buying the child's love." Furthermore, the visiting child is also divorced— divorced from playmates and friends, divorced from familiar toys and objects of interest, divorced from the child's own room, which is the child's "homeplace" of safety and trust. No matter how well the noncustodial parent and child get on, the child is a "guest" in someone else's house.

Parenting Education Programs. Effective on January 1, 1994, Public Act 93-319 went into action. This act requires that all court systems establish parenting education programs for people involved in issues concerning divorce and children. The primary goal of this legislation is to make sure that parents are aware of the effects of divorce on children, when the divorce is final and the family structure is changed. The programs are designed to prepare the divorcing couple (and any interested relatives) for the way the divorce may affect the children and also to help the children adjust to the situation. The programs specifically focus on how to provide cooperative planning, parental dispute resolution and conflict management, and guidelines for visitation. An interesting part of the program provides for educating the divorcing parents about how to reduce the stress in their relationship and also how to reduce the stress on the children. The parents are also instructed on how the issues change according to the age of the children. The charge for the program is minimal and can be accomplished in about six hours. Finally, the judge has the option to excuse the parents from the program if he or she deems it unnecessary based upon parental attitudes and behaviors (McKnight, 1999). Whether these programs are proving effective is being studied.

Alternatives to Divorce Court Battles: Mediation, Prenuptial, and Living Together Contracts

One of the disheartening aspects of the divorce procedure is the bitterness that arises during divorce litigation—bitterness over character assault, unfair property settlements, and custody of the children. Such bitterness cannot help but affect the children, even if both parties agree never to talk badly about the other. The bitterness and the heartache inevitably leaks out in nonverbal ways when the other parent is referred to—a stiffening of the body, a tone of voice that is unmistakable, or a grim set to the jaw. Moreover, if the divorce proceedings are dragged out month after month, the only winners become the divorce lawyers who are charging by the hour. In an effort to avoid the negative fallout of divorce proceedings, an alternative method of ending a marriage has emerged in a process called **mediation**.

The assumptions and process of mediation differ from traditional divorce in several significant ways. The assumption that underlies divorce is that the marital partners are in an irreconcilable battle that requires representation by attorneys and refereeing by the court. The assumption underlying mediation is that the marital partners are committed to cooperative resolution of the failed marriage. Instead of two warring attorneys presided over by a judge, mediation involves the two marital partners and a single mediator who has training in counseling and other types of "people skills." Third, the marital partners do not leave the decisions up to a third-party judge but make all the divorce settlements and custodial decisions themselves. The mediator's job is solely one of facilitating communication between the spouses (Emery & Wyer, 1987; Folberg & Taylor, 1984). The chief advantage of mediated divorce is that the control is in the hands of the two persons and not in the hands of attorneys, court judges, and biased witnesses in the courtroom procedure.

Mediation would seem to be a superior route to the dissolution of marriage, but has mediation worked out in practice? Well, yes and no. Follow-up studies of mediated proceedings reveal more satisfaction generally by the women than the men. Children seem to make better adjustments. Women report more satisfactory financial settlements. But fathers often feel that they have been given the bad end of the financial stick (Emery & Wyer, 1987). Nor should mediation be considered for everyone. If the couple are already engaged in revengeful warfare, no amount of mediation seems to cool their feelings of hatred and resentment. If there has been any physical or sexual abuse of one of the partners or of the children, legal action must be taken to prevent further damage. Finally, if one of the partners is submissive and the other dominant, then the submissive partner may indeed need the protection of a strong attorney (Schulman & Woods, 1983).

Another approach has been gaining some popularity, particularly among the more affluent classes—the **prenuptial agreement**. Before the marriage ceremony, each partner lists his and her financial contributions to the marriage along with the personal possessions each of them brings. After that, the partners agree on what each divorcing spouse should get if divorce becomes inevitable. For example, suppose one partner brings very few financial assets to the marriage but agrees to work in order to put the other one through graduate school. The working partner would expect to get some compensation for his or her contributions to the increased financial potential of the educated spouse. This list becomes a legal contract so that there is no question about the material division should the marriage need to be dissolved. Although many young people tend to view prenuptial agreements as demonstrating a lack of faith in their forthcoming marital career, it has more to do with the kind of memory loss that happens over the course of months and years and when divorce emotions are running high. What belongs to whom can be a cause of furious resentment. A small vase of little financial worth but of significant emotional value can lead to furious battling. Who gets the family pet—while it might seem trifling to others—has not infrequently become a court issue.

More popular than prenuptial agreements is the contract that has become increasingly more popular since the 1960s; namely, living together agreements. **Cohabitation** may sound like a realistic way of discovering how compatible two people are, but recent studies on living together before marriage does not guarantee "marital satisfaction." In fact, some studies show more couples divorce after living together than those who did not live together until marriage. But there are also unexpected results from this kind of arrangement—even more legal trouble for separating after cohabitation than there is from the dissolution of a marriage.

Since the laws affecting cohabitation are different from state to state and are swiftly changing, we can discuss the personal and legal issues of cohabitation only in very general terms. First, let it be clearly understood that separating unmarried couples have the same loss of memory as do divorcing couples—what belongs to whom? What if (as has happened in more than one case) one partner takes off with all the money in the joint account or all the furniture the couple possess? Obviously, the other partner cannot resort to the courts if cohabitation is illegal. Or try this: In some states, there may be an underlying assumption that all possessions belong equally to both even if one party came into the living together situation with nothing. Despite the recent **palimony** rulings, in many states, unmarried partners still do not have the same rights as spouses to share property or to receive alimony or child support. Of course, if one partner wishes to pursue their "rights" or their possessions in those states that do officially recognize cohabitation, the litigation may end up in civil court with a jury trial that may entail weeks and months. Unless there is some kind of written agreement, courts generally do not give much credence to "verbal agreements" between a couple, since that kind of testimony comes down to "your word against your partner's word." If you are thinking about living with another person or are already doing so fairly comfortably, it is wise to draw up a **living-together agreement** (LTA). There are books and inexpensive "kits" on the market that can be used to detail property division. Roughly, however, the procedure is as follows:

1. To decide if either partner has rights to the property or income of the other.
2. To decide which assets belong to which partner.
3. To make a list of debts and decide whose debts belong to whom.
4. To decide how your assets will be divided if you make an investment in both your names.
5. To declare yourselves a common-law marriage if you so choose (where legal).
6. To make arrangements for possession of the home and custody of children in the event of separation.
7. To decide the circumstances under which one or the other would be justified in ending the relationship (infidelity, spouse or child abuse, etc.)

Investment counselors also advise making up a will if you want the other to inherit. Otherwise, the inheritance may go to the deceased's family—even if you have been living together for forty years.

Reintegrating Oneself into Society. Unless the person has another partner to go to, life after marriage or cohabitation may be freer, but it is not necessarily easier. Unlike marriage, there are no *rites of passage* to reintegrate the person back into society—although it is somewhat easier for the man than for the woman in the case. In our society, divorced and widowed women have an ambiguous social status even today as we acknowledge the legitimacy of single career women. Formally married women complain that while they are interested in real companionship, the men who make an approach are more interested in a casual sex relationship. If the woman moves too quickly toward a more committed relationship, she may discover that the man has made a fast get-away. A divorced woman's complaint: "I'm good enough to go to bed with, but I'm not good enough to marry."

But lest it be thought that the formerly married man is having an idyllic bachelor's existence, let it be understood that he too has his problems—of a somewhat different kind. Divorced men are besieged with invitations to "fill in" at a party and pressured by friends to be introduced to another woman. Furthermore, the newly single man gets the impression he should be an aggressive "Lothario" at all times. The formerly married man may enjoy his new sexual freedom in the beginning and may even "play the field" as he never did when he was younger. But as men get older, the excitement "of the chase" becomes very old very quickly, particularly after the mid-life transition—when more transcendent values (such as the companionship of another mature adult and children) come to the fore.

The Effects of Divorce on Children

The effects of divorce on children is a highly controversial subject. On one side are those who believe that children without a two-parent home are part of the "moral decay" of society. On the other side are those who believe that the real issue is not whether children can survive divorce but whether they can survive an atmosphere of screaming arguments and abuse. There are a few fairly consistent findings, but they do not enlighten us as to whether or not it is better for a hostile or abusing couple to stay together "for the sake of the children" or to divorce. They only enlighten us about what to expect in terms of the children's consequent responses and behaviors.

There is no doubt that the children miss and mourn the loss of one parent or the other—even ten years later (Wallerstein & Kelly, 1980). Boys in particular were not only "unhappy and lonely" and felt they had "missed a lot" by not having a father, they found it difficult to relate to girls. A British study found that girls from divorced homes were more apt to leave home immediately upon their eighteenth birthday, more apt to have babies out of wedlock, and much less apt to go on for post-secondary education. Obviously, the splitting of their own families by divorce did not instill in them much confidence or respect for the institution of marriage (Jones, 1990; Furr, 1998).

Children Do Feel Guilty and They Resent Stepparents. Unless divorcing couples are very quick-witted, children can very easily work one parent against the other to get what they want. When parents are divorced, children can become even more skillful in manipulative tactics. But, probably the single most overwhelming effect on children is guilt. While they may not voice their anxiety, children of divorcing parents tend to believe it is their fault that their parents are splitting up. Perhaps they have heard their parents screaming how the other one coddles or brutalizes the child. Because children believe they have been the cause of the split, they also believe it is up to them to bring the parents back together, and so they will resent any other person in the life of their parents. They will try to undermine the divorced parent's new relationship. What can you do when children feel "to blame"? Listen attentively to what they are saying and what they are not saying. Make sure you tell them they are not to blame. And tell them that over and over again. Gently, without probing, ask them why they think they are to blame. When the reason comes out (such as a misdeed or something someone said), let them know otherwise. And tell them that over and over again. Long-held guilt is not easy to overcome. Divorce counselors often advise open communication with the children, and, if possible, with the other parent (Krantzler, 1999).

So What Is a Poor Stepparent to Do? Tips for the Novice Stepparent. Read everything you can about stepfamilies. Libraries have many books with advice and suggestions about relating to stepchildren. We have provided many guidelines and tips for adult–child interaction in previous chapters, and we have more to say in the later chapters one devoted to parenting. But since stepfamilies are such a special situation, we are inserting here just a few of our favorite tips for the novice stepparent or stepparent-soon-to-be.

1. Be friendly, but don't try to "make friends" too soon. Stepchildren or children of "your friend" are suspicious of anyone "usurping" the place of the biological parent. If you try to smother the child with affection before the child wants it, you will only raise the child's resentment even more.

2. Allow the child to make the first real bonding approach. Eventually, the child will become used to your presence and your general friendly demeanor and will begin to accept you. Let the child make the first approach. Be on the alert for this approach as it may come in very disguised form. For example, the child will ask you what to call you. If that happens, ask the child what he or she would like to call you. Or the child may ask you some personal (and sometimes embarrassing) questions about yourself. It's not just curiosity but a way of getting to know you.

3. Don't be the disciplinarian—just be the friend. Remember that the child will always be more resentful of any discipline you administer than if the biological parent administers it. If the child engages in an undesirable behavior, let the biological parent take care of it. Your job is to be the child's friend. If the child asks permission to go someplace (where you feel he or she should not go), refer it always to the child's biological parent: "Oh, that's something you better ask your father (or mother) about. I'm unsure of that." If the child is "acting up" inappropriately, you can say, "Hey, I don't think your mother/father would want you to do that." If that does not suffice, you can say in a friendly (and confidential way), "You don't want me to have to tell your mother/father, do you? I sure don't want to tell her/him, but I'll have to if you keep it up. Why not . . . " (and then suggest another behavior or activity he can do).

4. Make sure you carve out some quality time for your stepchild alone. When the time is right and the child is exhibiting more acceptance, take the child (by yourself) for special things to do, such as buying clothes, having a lunch out together—without your own children or without the other biological parent. Those kinds of experiences will produce a sharing/bonding/cementing of your relationship because it doesn't include other people.

5. Discuss all these questions with your intended even before the wedding. Before you enter into a committed relationship with the biological parent, have many discussions about your relationship to the child beforehand, including some of the tips we have just mentioned.

Intimacy: The Keystone of Building and Maintaining a Supportive Family Environment

So here we are, having described the problems involved in modern marriage in today's society. The question now becomes: *What can we do toward building and maintaining a supportive relationship with our committed partner?* Before we suggest guidelines, let's recap what we have learned (from this chapter and from the previous chapter) about what makes for romantic love, courtship, and the honeymoon stage of early marriage, as well as how romance fades and the relationship begins to deteriorate. When we were blissfully involved in the stage of being in love, we couldn't seem to get enough of each other. We talked all the time, sharing confidences with each other, confidences that we never revealed to another living soul. We dropped out of the social whirl of parties and even avoided friends. We made room for each other and we cherished and protected those precious moments of intimacy.

Then when we got married and settled down together in a joint residence, we began to discover the realities of everyday existence: doing household chores, appliance repair, lawn maintenance, paying bills, having those obligatory dinners with relatives (now with two sets of families), buying birthday gifts and Christmas cards and presents (now for two sets of families) and working and going to classes and . . . and . . . and . . . so on. Our moments of intimacy begin to dissolve one by one . . . until they have almost disappeared. But we still managed to eke out some time for ourselves . . . until children came along.

Despite the time and energy required to take care of each child that arrives, we took pride in our children and derived a lot of joy from them. But with all the care they need, the few moments of intimacy we still hung onto came under siege. No more quiet Sunday morning brunches and reading the newspaper. No more romantic candle-lit dinners with champagne for "just the two of us."

Anyway, most parents these days are so tired after working, doing the household maintenance, and carting their children here and there during the week, they find themselves just not "in the mood" at night anyway. *Maybe on Saturday or Sunday morning when they don't have to get up and go to work?* Ha! Just let the parents close the bedroom door and some child starts pounding on it: *What are you doing in there? Can I come in?* So much for those intimate moments we used to have. No wonder affairs are so attractive—nothing interferes with being with each other, not household tasks, not the sudden arrival of a friend or relative, and not children who demand so much attention from us.

If a major part of the problem of modern marriage is lack of intimacy, then at least a major part of the solution is to build moments of intimacy with each other and protect them at all costs. With rare exceptions, intimacy is achieved only in one-on-one moments with each other, not just in marriage, but in our relationships with our parents, our children, and our friends. We cannot say the same things in groups of three or more that we can say when we are alone with our Significant Other, or with a close friend, or with a colleague whom we trust. In today's pressure cooker of a society with the hundreds of people we intertwine with in the course of a week, we need those moments of intimacy with the people we hold dear more than ever before. If intimacy is a keystone of building and maintaining a firm and secure relationship, the question now becomes: *How do we establish these moments of intimacy and protect them?* Each relationship is unique of course, but the following guidelines apply to almost every situation.

Make Time to Be Together, Just the Two of You Alone. Notice that we said "make time." If you wait for private time to happen, it just isn't going to happen. You have to work hard at *creating* that time to be together. You have to learn to say "no" to invitations from friends, and working colleagues. It is difficult to say "no" when an invitation is unexpected. So you have to have a standard reply ready: *That would be wonderful but we have a previous commitment.* That is not a lie; your previous commitment is with your Significant Other.

With children, it is going to be especially difficult to make time, but it can be done. Send them off to summer camp. Even teenagers would like to go to soccer camp or basketball camp. You may just enjoy having the house to yourself (for a change) where you can relax, do a few interesting things, and make love when you want to (after that romantic candle-lit dinner). If that doesn't work for you, take a trip. Away from the house, you are also away from the phone, away from the mailbox full of bills and junk mail, away from a computer brimming with e-mail that needs to be answered, and away from the family member who sometimes shows up at the door unexpectedly.

Continue Talking to Each Other. As strange as this may sound, married people talk less and less the longer they are married. The average time that the average couple spends talking to each other after ten years of marriage has been estimated as no more than 11 minutes every 24 hours. There are many reasons for this paradoxical fact. One reason is that we tend to assume that we know what the other person would say. If we have always spent Thanksgiving with one set of parents and Christmas with the other set, we assume we shall continue to do so. No need to check it out with the other person. But maybe the other person wants to do something different? Too late, we have already confirmed it with the parents or parent-in-laws. Moral: *Don't assume anything.* Make a habit of checking things out about everything, especially about those activities you have done year after year. Suggest something different. Even if the suggestion is not met with a resounding agreement this year, it may give our Significant Other something to consider in the future. *And you are talking to each other.*

Stop Talking Through the Children. Sometimes, parents begin talking to each other through the children. *Sister, tell Daddy what we did today.* (It would be a lot more interesting if you told him all the activities of the day.) *Bubba, ask your mother when she'll be ready to leave.* (Aw, come on, tell her yourself. She may have some questions she wants answered before she can make a decision.) If you stop talking through the children, *you will be talking more to each other.*

Don't Avoid Areas of Conflict. Worse still is the desire to avoid problems. Little by little, as we get to know what upsets the other person, we avoid topics that might lead to a quarrel. We want to keep the peace, so to say. Eventually there are so many topics to avoid, there is not much to talk about. Attempts to communicate with each other without causing disruption feels like finding our way through a landscape full of landmines. What takes the place of talk is silence. In a committed relationship, silence is not golden. It is deadly. Our answer: So what if a landmine is triggered and leads to a quarrel? Follow the guidelines for constructive quarreling, and you at least get things out in the open. *At least, you are talking.*

It may take a while to quit hurting at what has been said, but at least you are talking. If she is feeling lonely and like the family drudge, make a time when you are both recovered from the argument, to brainstorm suggestions for bringing some rest, relaxation, and excitement into her life. It may be any of the suggestions we made above or as simple as going out to dinner, just the two of you occasionally. Or helping out with vacuum cleaning. (Thoughtfulness and helping her with her chores occasionally often turns a woman on!) If he is feeling like a displaced person just living in the house, brainstorm what causes him to feel like that and what can be done to help him feel more like a real "man of the house" (Faludi, 1999). It may be painful. It may even be brutally emotional for the two of you. *But you are talking.*

Have we made the point clear enough?

Important Terms and Concepts to Know

• abuse	• custody	• man of the house	• shouting
• accusations	• disciplinarian	• mediation	• stepchildren
• adolescence	• divorce	• moral	• Super Mom
• apologies	• emotional	• nuclear	• talking
• battered children	• equality	• pandemic	• time
• children	• extended	• prenuptial	• unhappiness
• cohabiting	• future	• secret	• win-win
• communication	• intimacy	• separate lives	
• cultures	• literate	• sexual	

Make Your Own Chapter Summary by Filling in the Blanks

Use the "Important Terms and Concepts to Know" to fill in the blanks.

Sweeping societal changes. Today as never before, society is undergoing tremendous changes, causing people to experience _____ shock. Traditionalists view the high rate of divorce as symptomatic of _____ decay. Nontraditionalists view it as the unwillingness to accept infidelity and physical or sexual _____ any longer.

The evolution of the American family. The American colonies were founded by women who were capable and _____, and men who treated women with more _____. The _____ rural family, with more than two generations under one roof, provided physical and emotional support for the members of the family. Today the _____ family couple is burdened by having so many multiroles to perform.

Problems of modern marriage. Today's husband and father often feels that he is no longer the "_____" because so much running of the homeplace is done by "_____." Because we want to give our children "every advantage," parenting today results in a huge drain on our finances, _____, and energy. Marital dissatisfaction is highest when children reach _____. Domestic violence is _____ around the world. The _____ wife often doesn't leave for many reasons, two of which are that she believes she cannot survive on her own, and also because the abusing male makes _____ and then romances her so the cycle of violence continues.

Developing better communication. Men and women have different communication styles because they come from two different _____. For a man, _____ is merely a matter of "blowing off steam," but women have been raised to be soft-spoken and they are hurt by it. The couple needs to develop a common _____ style to improve their relationship. The two partners need to avoid _____ that start with the pronoun "you" and "yours." If a quarrel breaks out, we can quarrel intelligently for _____ solutions.

When vows are broken.   Infidelity is defined as a _____ relationship outside of the committed relationship. Predictors of extramarital affairs include marital _____, and a workplace where there is a permissive attitude toward office affairs. Men are more distressed by _____ infidelity while women are more distressed by _____ infidelity. _____ is more likely when there are no children and the financial investment in the marriage is less. If the financial loss would be too great, affluent couples may not divorce but lead "_____."

Divorce and alternatives.   Divorce is never final when _____ are involved and _____ is shared. As an alternative to divorce, the couple may decide on _____, which has the assumption of cooperation rather than a divorce with two warring attorneys. More frequent these days is _____ agreements in which the two partners agree to take away the financial assets that each came with. It is advised that couples who are _____ make a list of possessions that belong to each person before they decide to live together so there is less of a problem of *who* gets *what* if they decide to separate.

After divorce.   Second marriages have problems of having _____ who are negative toward the stepparent. The advice to the stepparent includes waiting for the child to make the first approach and being a friend rather than the _____.

Building a supportive family environment.   If a major problem of marriage is lack of _____, then the major solution is to find time to be alone together and protecting it. A supportive family environment can also be achieved by encouraging intimacy of each family member with every other. Most important of all, keep _____ to each other.

9

Conditioning and Learning

How We Have Been Conditioned and How We Can Use Conditioning to Build Constructive Habits

BOX 9.1 SCENARIO

Eduardo Reports on How He Is Learning to Stop His Smoking

Eduardo: I've made a discovery, a very important discovery! I know why it is so hard to stop smoking! Smoking is not one habit. It's a hundred habits.

Martha: Oh, come on, you're going to tell us that's why you can't quit—because it's a hundred habits?

Eduardo: Oh, I'm quitting all right. I've made my mind up to that! But I'm quitting them one at a time.

Jill Smith: Tell us about it.

Eduardo: Well, you know how you told us to keep a journal of the target behavior for a week or two? Well, I did that. Here's what I discovered. I smoke when I drink coffee. I smoke when I have a beer. I smoke when I begin to play the guitar. I light up when I start the car. I smoke after every meal. I light up when I open my books to study. See what I mean?

Jill Smith: So how are you quitting?

Eduardo: Well, you said to avoid places I smoke. So I don't go to the bar and have a beer any more. Good for me anyway, not to drink beer. I was getting a beer belly.

Jill Smith: Any other habits broken yet?

Eduardo: Yeah, I used to smoke first thing getting up in the morning. Isn't that terrible—to put all that poison in your system first thing! Whew! Now I say to myself I will not smoke until after breakfast. Pretty soon, I will stop that habit too. I'm just doing one at a time. But I've broken two more habits.

Jill Smith: They are?

Eduardo: Well, I stopped smoking in the car completely. That's one. And I stopped using a cigarette to start my guitar playing. I love playing my guitar. I don't need a "starter." I think my hardest ones to

Eduardo's List: Smoking Is Made Up of Many Habits

1. Waking up
2. After breakfast
3. With coffee
4. Starting car
5. With beer
6. With coffee
7. Playing guitar
8. Begin studying
9. In-between classes
10. After last class
11. With Roger (a friend)
12. Watching TV
13. After lunch
14. After dinner
15. On the telephone
16. As a study break
17. Decision making
18. Offer one to girls

break will be not smoking after a meal. That's my most enjoyable time to smoke. But I know I'll succeed. I'm determined.

Jill Smith: Eduardo has discovered something called behavior modification, which is discussed in this chapter. Eduardo, do you reward yourself when you stop one of your smoking habits?

Eduardo: After I break a habit, I let myself go to the movies. If I find myself lighting up a cigarette with coffee, I make myself run around the building three times. I'm out of breath then and I don't feel much like smoking. It's a good way to keep myself in shape too.

CONDITIONING AND THE SCIENCE OF LEARNING

Conditioning is being applied everywhere in our society: in education, in medicine and dentistry, in the military, in business, and in many other organizations. You can also apply the facts of conditioning to your own personal life. In this chapter, you will learn not only how you have been conditioned to be the way you are, but also how you can use conditioning in your college studies, in your work environment, and in your personal life toward a more creative life style (see Tip 9.1). For example, by applying what you learn in this chapter, you will be able to acquire the following skills:

- How to improve your spelling;
- How to get better grades by more effective studying;
- How to deal with disruptive children in the classroom situation;
- How to foster more desirable social behaviors in your own child (without yelling);
- How to eliminate unhealthy habits and replace them with more constructive ones.

In order to understand how conditioning works, we start our discussion with one of the most famous psychologists of all time, Ivan Pavlov.

Ivan Pavlov: A Dog Is Conditioned to Salivate to a Bell

We made the point in earlier chapters that any new area of investigation seems to need an intellectual giant to make a foothold in an unknown scientific area. The intellectual giant who got us started on the scientific investigation of how we learn was a Russian physiologist by the name of Ivan Pavlov. He was a superb scientist and so dedicated to science that he was willing to work in unheated laboratories in the freezing winters of Russia, protected from the cold only by wearing his overcoat, fur-lined Russian hat, and gloves. Before his monumental work in conditioning, he had already received the Nobel Prize in 1904 for his work on the physiology of dogs. Today we revere him as one of the great pioneers of psychology. Yet, ironically, until his dying day, Pavlov insisted he wasn't a psychologist—he was a physiologist. He said he didn't even *like* the discipline of psychology because of its lack of scientific rigor (Fancher, 1979). Nevertheless, Pavlov contributed to psychology its first rigorous scientific methodology, which he called *conditioning*.

What Pavlov discovered came about in this way. His original research objective was to study the amount of salivation produced by a dog within a given period of time on the presentation of meat powder. To do this, he harnessed a dog so it could not move very far. Pavlov had invented a device very similar to the dentist's implement for removing saliva from your mouth. But instead of having the saliva washed away, the saliva was collected in a beaker so it could be measured. But a major problem began to arise. The problem involved a curious time factor. In the beginning, the dog began to salivate immediately upon the bowl of meat powder being placed in front of him. But in very short order, the dog began to salivate at the mere

---

Tip 9.1 Maturational versus Learned. From time to time in this or other textbooks, you will come across other terms that mean the same thing as *maturation* and *learning*. It's a good idea to make note of these other terms as follows: *Maturational:* Inherited, genetic, biological, inborn, innate, and even reflexive (a term fallen out of favor). *Learned:* Environmental, experience, conditioned, upbringing, sociocultural variables, situational influences.

sight of the bowl, and then to the sight of the lab assistant carrying in the bowl. A few more days, and the dog began to salivate at the sound of the door opening and even earlier than that—to the sound of the footsteps coming down the hall. The lab researchers just could not keep the timing at a fixed point. Now another lesser intellect might have given up on the experiment as impossible to carry out. But Pavlov realized that they had stumbled on a very significant phenomenon. What they had stumbled on was conditioning (Pavlov, 1927).

Unconditioned Means "Unlearned." In a typical experiment, Pavlov would place some meat powder in front of the dog. The dog would, of course, salivate to it. Because the dog does not need to learn to salivate to meat powder, Pavlov called the meat powder an **unconditioned stimulus** (**UCS**). The dog's behavioral *response* of salivating to the **UCS** is now called an **unconditioned response** (**UCR**) because the dog didn't have to learn to salivate (*memory jog: for unconditioned, think unlearned*). The next step was to establish the fact that the dog did not salivate to a bell. When we ring a bell in the hearing of a dog who has never heard a bell before, does the dog salivate? No, of course not. At the sound of a bell, a dog might cock his ears, orient his head toward the sound, might cock his head, or even paw the bell but the dog will not salivate. For that reason, Pavlov called the bell a *neutral stimulus* (NS) for salivation.

Conditioned Means "Learned." The third step in Pavlov's procedure was to *pair* the meat powder (the UCS) with the bell (the neutral stimulus) several times; that is, every time the meat powder was presented to the dog, the bell was sounded. After several *pairings* of bell (NS) and meat powder (UCS), what happened when the bell was sounded by itself? If you say that the dog now salivated, you are right. Pavlov called this salivating behavior a conditioned response (CR). Very simply, a **conditioned response** (**CR**) is a *learned* response. The fact that the dog is now salivating to the bell means that the bell is no longer a *neutral* stimulus for salivation. The bell has become a **conditioned stimulus** (**CS**) for salivation (see Tip 9.2). Pavlov further discovered that a conditioned stimulus **generalizes** (transfers) to other stimuli within the same *sensory modality*. He called this transfer **stimulus generalization**. The dog would also salivate to other *auditory* stimuli, such as bells with a higher or lower pitch or even to buzzers, which Pavlov called **generalized stimuli** (see Figure 9.1).

Experimental Extinction Means "Forgotten/Deconditioned." What will happen to the conditioned response of salivation if we keep ringing the bell over and over *without the presentation of meat powder*? If you reply that the dog will stop salivating, you are again quite right. But Pavlov used a more *empirical* term. He said that **experimental extinction** had been achieved, which simply means that the dog no longer salivated to the bell. So the bell was put away for a while and the researchers turned their attention to other projects. Then one day

---

Tip 9.2 You May Have Conditioned Your Pet! If you have ever had a pet, you may have observed this example of conditioning in your own home. Just pick up the leash and your dog instantly becomes excited. The leash is now a **conditional stimulus** for the **conditioned response** of anticipating a walk. Or perhaps you have a cat that you feed with a can of cat food. The moment you use the electric can opener to open the can, your cat comes running, tail up, at the sound of the buzzing. The buzzing of the electric can opener was originally a neutral stimulus but after a few pairings of buzzing and the smell of food, the buzzing became a **conditioned stimulus** (CS) for the **conditioned response** (CR) of running-to-the-kitchen. The cat may also come running at the buzzing of the alarm clock, which would be **generalized responding**.

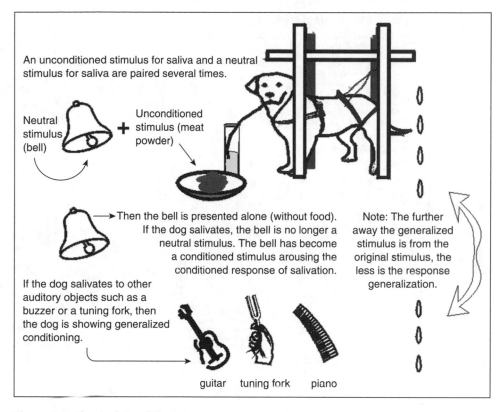

An unconditioned stimulus for saliva and a neutral stimulus for saliva are paired several times.

Neutral stimulus (bell) **+** Unconditioned stimulus (meat powder)

Then the bell is presented alone (without food). If the dog salivates, the bell is no longer a neutral stimulus. The bell has become a conditioned stimulus arousing the conditioned response of salivation.

Note: The further away the generalized stimulus is from the original stimulus, the less is the response generalization.

If the dog salivates to other auditory objects such as a buzzer or a tuning fork, then the dog is showing generalized conditioning.

guitar   tuning fork   piano

Figure 9.1 Classical Conditioning.

someone rang the bell accidentally and, to the astonishment of everyone in the laboratory, the dog was salivating again. This sudden reappearance of the conditioned response of salivation had occurred *by the simple passage of time*. Pavlov called this sudden reappearance of the salivating behavior **spontaneous recovery**.

      Higher-Order Conditioning. After Pavlov had conditioned the dog to salivate to a bell, he discovered he could use the bell in place of the unconditioned stimulus (meat powder). In other words, Pavlov could use the conditioned stimulus of the bell to condition the dog to salivate to an electric light or to the whirring of a fan, etc. In fact, Pavlov managed to achieve four levels of higher-order conditioning in this way (see Table 9.1). It was because of the phenomenon of higher-order conditioning that Pavlov concluded that conditioning is the basis for all human learning and human personality.

John Watson Applies Conditioning to a Human Baby

Pavlov worked only with dogs. It was an American psychologist, John Watson, who first applied conditioning to a human being. Watson had been an engineering student before studying psychology. When he got into psychology, he became disgusted with the lack of scientific rigor in the young science. Upon hearing of Pavlov's work on the conditioning of dogs, Watson was seized with excitement: Here at last was an empirical method worthy of being called scientific.

Table 9.1   Higher-Order Conditioning

Pavlov suggested that higher-order conditioning is how simple conditioning leads to the complexities of human cognition.	Unconditioned Stimulus	Neutral Stimulus	Becomes a Conditioned Stimulus	Conditioned Response of Salivation
STEP ONE The meat powder is paired with a bell until the bell elicits the conditioned response of salivation.				
STEP TWO The bell is now used in place of the unconditioned stimulus and paired with the sound of a buzzer, which elicits salivation (although not as much as the original conditioned salivation).				
STEP THREE The buzzer is now paired with an electric light until salivation. The response is quite weak now.				
STEP FOUR The electric light is paired with the whirring of a fan, and a very weak conditioned response is elicited.				

Pavlov suggested that higher-order conditioning is how simple conditioning leads to the complexities of human cognition.

Every higher stage of conditioning elicits a weaker and weaker response of salivation as symbolized by the lessening of salivary drops. Pavlov was unable to go beyond fourth-order conditioning in dogs.

He decided to apply it to a baby, known to us only as "Baby Albert." Watson and his assistant, Rosalie Raynor, performed the following experiment (Watson & Raynor, 1920).

They selected a nine-month-old baby in a foundling home who seemed to exude good physical health and a happy, cheerful nature. They put into Baby Albert's crib several white, furry objects, such as a white Santa Claus beard, a white muff, a real white rabbit, and a real little white laboratory rat. Albert showed no signs of fear to any of these objects, including the little white rat. In fact, he tried to grasp all the white, furry objects, including the little white rat, and—as babies are wont to do—to put them in his mouth.

Having established the fact that Albert did not fear any of these white furry objects, the next part of the experiment was carried out three months later (Watson didn't tell us why he waited three months) when Albert was twelve months old. Watson and Raynor put the white rat into the baby's cage, er, crib, but this time they made a loud noise every time Baby Albert tried to reach for the little white rat. Now all babies have a natural reaction (a reflex or unconditioned response) to loud noises. They cry, or fall over on their faces, and show other signs of distress. That's exactly what Baby Albert did. The experimenters now stopped making loud noises, but continued to put the white rat into Albert's crib to see what Albert would do. If the readers have already guessed that Albert cried and showed other signs of distress, they are right. Clearly, Albert had been conditioned to fear the little white rat via Pavlov's **classical conditioning**. Furthermore, Albert's *conditioned* fear of the little white rat *generalized* to anything that was white and furry such as the Santa Claus beard, the white rabbit, and the white muff. Upon putting these other objects into the crib, Baby Albert cried, fell over on this face and showed other types of distress (see Figure 9.2).

What Happened to Baby Albert?   Students generally ask what happened to little Albert? Did he remain scared of white furry objects? We simply don't know since Watson

Figure 9.2 Baby Albert. The baby that was the first human being upon whom conditioning was experimentally demonstrated.

never published anything further. Was there any attempt to help Albert get over his fear of white furry objects? Alas!—no, so far as we know. This experiment could not be performed on a human subject today because of the establishment of *ethical procedures* by psychology and other professions. As for Baby Albert, his name has gone down as one of the "famous children" of psychology, along with others the reader has encountered in previous chapters: Helen Keller and Piaget's three children.

What we have been describing is called **aversive conditioning**, which means conditioning that results from painful stimuli. An example of using aversive conditioning for therapy is the drug *antabuse*. This is a therapy treatment that individuals in some states may choose following guilty sentencing for driving-while-intoxicated. Someone who takes this drug and drinks becomes extremely nauseous to the point of vomiting. After a couple of times of drinking alcohol and then throwing up, individuals stop drinking. For some people this is a successful method that helps them quit drinking. Others, however, react differently. Aware that at the end of the drug treatment they will no longer experience vomiting when they drink alcohol, they may choose to drink again.

The Russians and Ferdinand Lamaze Adapt Classical Conditioning for Natural Birthing

A practical application of classical conditioning comes from Russian medicine. Philosophically, the Communist regime was committed (at least in theory) to a policy of equality and education for all peoples. (This didn't work out in practice considering its treatment of their minorities.) This official position of equality included equal opportunities for all women. Consequently, many Russian women became physicians and, for many years now, most Russian physicians are women (Haavio-Mannila, 1995). The preponderance of women in the medical profession doubtless led to a deep concern for women having a difficult labor. After intensive study, the Soviet physicians decided that a significant reason for women having so much pain during labor is that they have been *conditioned* to fear the birth process. They reasoned as follows: Young women often had to listen to terrible tales about women having difficult labor (like Aunt Olga) or even dying in childbirth (like Cousin Tatiana). These stories so scared the young woman having her first baby that she worked against the birth process by being "uptight" and by clenching her hands and bracing her entire body, instead of relaxing her body and "letting go."

The Soviet physicians decided to **decondition** the negative emotional mind-set of the pregnant women and to **condition** a new mind-set about the birth process, not as an illness but as a phenomenon of health. First, they taught the young women about the physiology of their bodies and the process of birth, in order to enable them to understand what goes on during birth. Then they taught the pregnant women how to breathe during labor, how to press down in rhythm to the contractions, and so on. This training was so successful, anesthesia was no longer used in 90 percent of the births. The Russians called their natural birthing the *psychoprophylactic method* (*PPM*). So why do we call it the Lamaze method? When the French physician Ferdinand Lamaze heard about the astounding results the Russians were reporting,

BOX **9.2** STUDENTS VERBATIM
How I've Been Conditioned

Female (24 years): Whenever the phone rings in my apartment, I have an urge to say "Financial Aid" because I worked in that department for three years.

Male (26 years): Once when I ate 11 hot dogs in a row (just to win a bet), I got sick and upchucked for hours. Now I can't touch a hot dog.

Male (18 years): When I was a kid and my mother called me by my first and middle names, I knew I was in trouble.

Female (26 years): My father used to beat me with a belt with brass studs on it. To this day, the sound of someone clicking their notebook shut makes me nervous.

Male (32 years): I think all guys are conditioned like this. I check my zipper three or four times when I leave a men's room. I was once embarrassed when some kids in grade school made fun of me because I had forgotten to zip it up.

Female (19 years): When I was in grade school, I had to come in from playing at five in the afternoon because that was when we kids had to eat without fail. Now I get hungry when it's five o'clock even if I've just eaten.

Female (23 years): Has anyone noticed that just walking into a movie theater makes you yearn for popcorn? It gets to me every time, even after just eating.

Male (41 years): When I was young, I used to visit my grandfather at the farm. He used to have me come in the barn and he'd help me learn how to whittle or make things or just help him. That's how I got to be so handy. But the barn was filled with wood chips and sawdust. It was a wonderful place. Now whenever I smell wood or sawdust, I get a very pleasant sensation.

Female (40 years): I've been conditioned to associate food with love and prosperity and good times and all the good things of life. If someone gets engaged, my family would celebrate by eating. If the wedding is called off, we celebrate by eating. As long as there is food on the table, why should we worry? I eat to cheer myself up, when I'm lonely, or if I'm nervous. I am comforted by eating because it represents good times and love.

Male (19 years): This is hard to talk about, but I've been conditioned to be prejudiced. I live near my grandparents and they grew up in the 1930s and I guess lots of people were prejudiced then. I know it's wrong, and I'm working on deconditioning all the prejudices they instilled in all of us grandkids. Some of us are almost free of it but my older brother is so prejudiced that we can hardly have a friendly conversation.

Female (24 years): I realize that my drinking may be conditioned. I noticed that while I've tried to cut down on how much I drink, it's harder at some places and with some people. Every week when my friends and I go out to our favorite restaurant, it seems natural to order a drink. We've been eating there every Thursday night for the last couple of years and drinking is part of the event. Recently, we went to a new restaurant and I had no problem ordering soda.

Reflective Writing: Reflect on some feeling or behavior that has been conditioned in you or someone else.

---

he went to the Soviet Union to learn their techniques and brought them back to the West. Besides, it was the era of the "cold war" and we were not about to admit that anything good could come out of the U.S.S.R. Today, the Lamaze method of birthing or modifications of it are used all over the world (Lamaze, 1956).

B. F. Skinner's Operant Conditioning

We Also Learn Through Our Own Exploratory Behaviors. For many years, it was assumed that classical conditioning accounted for all human learning. Then a young man from Harvard, B. F. Skinner, introduced the psychological world to another approach to conditioning, an approach he called **operant conditioning** (Skinner, 1938). Skinner agreed that classical conditioning was scientifically sound, but he pointed out that it is a very unnatural way to learn. Under normal circumstances, bells and food do not occur simultaneously very often. Classical conditioning, he pointed out, *depends on someone artificially putting two dissimilar stimuli together*. The bell and the meat powder were put together in a scientific laboratory. And, many times, we do the same thing. We teach dogs to bark by offering the dog a treat (unconditioned stimulus) and urging them to "Speak!" (neutral stimulus). We sometimes teach children to be polite by putting a cookie in front of them and prompting them with the word "please."

But, said Skinner, in everyday life, people learn (are conditioned) through their own voluntary behavior, and they discover for themselves positive or negative consequences (reinforced, nonreinforced, or punished). For example, when a two-year-old toddler accidentally puts his hand on a hot stove, chances are that he will not put his hand on that stove again. No one paired the *unconditioned stimulus* (pain) with the *neutral stimulus* (hot stove) together. The child was exploring his environment and discovered, on his own, that if he puts his hand on a hot stove, it hurts! Skinner would call that *one-trial conditioning*. The child will not do *that* again. No one had to teach him that. He learned it on his own. Skinner boldly asserted that most of our learning happens through just this kind of operant conditioning. Learning as the result of avoiding pain is called **aversive learning**.

A Typical Operant Conditioning Experiment. Analyzing a typical operant conditioning process will illustrate Skinner's basic approach. A rat is put into a so-called "Skinner box." A typical *Skinner box* is simply a cage and a container filled with food pellets. The container of food pellets is attached electrically to a very delicately balanced level inside the cage so that when the lever is touched, even slightly, it releases a pellet of food (see Figure 9.3). When a rat is put into a Skinner box for the first time, it will run around all over the box sniffing and

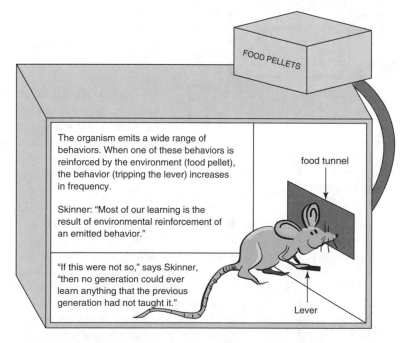

FOOD PELLETS

The organism emits a wide range of behaviors. When one of these behaviors is reinforced by the environment (food pellet), the behavior (tripping the lever) increases in frequency.

Skinner: "Most of our learning is the result of environmental reinforcement of an emitted behavior."

"If this were not so," says Skinner, "then no generation could ever learn anything that the previous generation had not taught it."

food tunnel

Lever

Figure 9.3 Operant Conditioning. A model of a "Skinner box."

crawling in the corners and trying to climb the wall (presumably looking for a way out). As the result of this exploratory behavior, the rat will hit (accidentally) the delicately balanced lever with its nose, or its tail or haunches and out comes a pellet of food.

Of course the rat will eat the pellet of food and search for more pellets and again it will hit the lever (accidentally) and down will come another pellet of food. When this spontaneous *emitted behavior* becomes *purposeful* behavior is hard to say, but very quickly (in a matter of minutes) the rat is hitting the lever and eating the food, perhaps up to 20 times a minute until it is satiated. Notice! Nobody paired the food and the lever. In the course of the rat's exploratory behavior, one of the behaviors (pressing the lever) was reinforced (food pellets) and that behavior increased in frequency.

The World as a Giant Skinner Box. Skinner believed that the world is a giant "Skinner box" in which we human beings are being reinforced or nonreinforced continuously. One of Skinner's basic assumptions concerning human nature is that we have no such thing as free will. Concepts such as *freedom* and *free will* are simply illusions. Why we do what we do (our learned behaviors) is because we have been reinforced by somebody or a group of somebod-

ies in our society. Skinner categorized reinforcers into two kinds: primary reinforcers and secondary reinforcers. Animals respond mainly to **primary reinforcers**, such as water and food and escape from pain. Humans respond to these kinds of primary reinforcers, too, but we respond also to **secondary reinforcers** such as smiles, money, prizes, honors, applause, and phrases such as "Thank you" or "How thoughtful your present was." Parents, teachers, scout leaders, our peer groups, athletic coaches, our employers—all of these people are constantly reinforcing or extinguishing our behaviors in one way or another all the time (see Figure 9.4).

Figure 9.4 Skinner's World. Skinner believed that the world is a giant Skinner box, which is continually shaping our behavior with reinforcements we value. Can you identify these reinforcers?

What We Think of as "Punishment" May Actually Be Positively Reinforcing. Skinner made the point that the most effective way to extinguish a child's behavior is through **nonreinforcement** (ignoring the behavior). Why? Because if we punish a child for an undesirable behavior, what we may really be doing is reinforcing it—*simply by giving attention to it.* Let's analyze an example from real-life.

Can you remember back in your grade school of some child who was the class clown or class cutup? He was usually a child who was not doing very well in his school work and he took out his frustrations by acting up in class or challenging the teacher with "sassy" remarks. Of course, the child was yelled at constantly by the teacher or sent to the office. You may recall how the other pupils giggled and egged the boy on to talk back and misbehave. (They didn't dare get in trouble by acting up, but they got much vicarious enjoyment out of his misbehavior.) The class clown was getting a lot of positive reinforcement from his classmates. Realizing this, the teacher usually instructed the other students not to giggle when he misbehaved. But of course her admonitions did no good, and they continued to giggle.

BOX **9.3** RESEARCH METHODOLOGY
Experimental Conditioning

On the Plus Side

1. **Experimental conditioning turned the study of psychology into a genuine science.** With the discovery of both classical and operant conditioning, psychology "came of age" as a science in its own right. Psychology finally had developed a rigorous scientific methodology for measuring the psychological variable we call learning.

2. **Experimental conditioning can be done under rigorous laboratory conditions.** As a method of research, conditioning is the example par excellence for how we learn, and its conclusions are unassailable for the laboratory situation. In contrast to naturalistic observation, survey, case study, etc., laboratory conditioning can control all the relevant variables. By controlling all the variables we can finally make a statement about cause-and-effect. Only experimental research under laboratory conditions can isolate the determining factor or factors. With all other methods, we can make a statement about "probable cause," but this probable cause is always based on inference, which means we *think* we know what is going on. But until the "probable cause" is supported by experimental research, the hypothesis must always remain tentative.

3. **The experimental observations are empirical.** *Classical* and *operant conditioning* have both derived terms that do not depend on inference. Terms such as *unconditioned response* and *extinction* and *spontaneous recovery* do not infer what's going on inside the "mind" of the rat, or the dog, or the person. Two independent observers can agree that the subject in question is demonstrating this behavior, called empirical observations. The behavior can be turned into numerical data and graphed.

4. **Animal subjects can be used.** Since many laboratory experiments cannot be done on human beings, animals are used in this type of experimental research.

On the Minus Side

1. **The artificiality of the laboratory situation.** The laboratory situation is least like real life. The very fact that the conditioning takes place in a laboratory makes the environment artificial. Under real life circumstances, there may be not just one or even two variables influencing the behavior of the person. Most human behaviors are determined by a multitude of influences.

2. **Generalizing research on animals to humans.** The big problem is applying the results of laboratory conditions from animals to human beings who are much more complex in nature and subject to many more environmental influences of real life.

What the teacher may *not* have realized was that her own behavior of yelling and scolding him was also positively reinforcing to the child and actually *increasing* his misbehavior. As Skinner pointed out, any attention, even punishing attention, can be reinforcing. So how do we tell if we are extinguishing the behavior or positively reinforcing the behavior? Skinner said: *Simply look at the consequences.* If the undesirable behavior decreases or extinguishes, your actions have been **nonreinforcing**. If the undesirable behavior increases, then your actions (no matter how negative or punishing you thought them to be) were actually **positively reinforcing**.

Behavior Modification: Reinforcing the Desirable Behaviors Through Environmental Engineering

Fortunately, most of a child's undesirable behaviors (such as thumb sucking) will decrease in frequency and eventually drop out (*be extinguished*) simply by being ignored. Unfortunately, we can't always ignore a child's behavior. If the child is screaming insults in a classroom with 30 other children, a teacher is unwise to ignore it since the other children may follow suit! So what can the teacher do instead? For such situations, Skinner suggests that we devise a behavior modification program with techniques he called **environmental engineering**, such as **immediate feedback, time out** and **shaping of behavior**.

Immediate Feedback. A very important aspect of environmental engineering is **feedback** to the child about how the behavior is being perceived, whether the response is correct or incorrect, appropriate or inappropriate. *To be effective, the feedback must be immediate and clear.* The faster and clearer the feedback to animal, child, or adult, the faster the learning.

For example, let's take a child who is not doing well in arithmetic. The teacher is too busy to help her. She sits there helplessly while all the other children are doing their "independent seat work." What this child needs is a tutor to sit right down beside her, one-on-one, and to provide her with immediate feedback about what she is doing right and where she has gotten off the track. The tutor can correct any errors—then and there! As stated in Chapter 5, earlier one-on-one tutoring is the best instruction anyone can have—not just the little girl who is failing her arithmetic, but all of us—whether it is music lessons, basketball, or computer skills.

Time Out. Now to get back to that poor teacher with the child screaming insults at her in the class. For this situation, Skinner devised the technique of *time out*. **Time out** means putting the child in an environment that is nonreinforcing. If he is sent to sit in an office where other problem children are sitting, they will soon be giggling at each other, making faces, and if they are creative (as most children are), they will soon be inventing a sign language to communicate silently. The company of other children in the office turns out to be *positively* reinforcing. So what kind of an environment is nonreinforcing? How about a room that has nothing in it but a desk and chair! We are talking boredom here. There's not much that is reinforcing about boredom. (See Tip 9.3.)

The child must be told that he can go back to the classroom whenever he demonstrates appropriate classroom behavior. Don't tell him what that behavior is—let him tell you. Most children know how they are supposed to behave. If he says he doesn't know, you reply (in the kindest and most reinforcing way imaginable) that you know how smart he is and you feel sure he can figure it out on his own. He may pout some now because this particular gambit isn't working as it has in the past. But eventually he will get so-o-o-o bored that he will tell you how he should behave. "Wonderful," you respond, "Do you think you can do that in the classroom?" He growls a grudging "Yeah," and you tell him that when he goes back, he must repeat his answer to the teacher. You feel sure she will let him return to his seat. No yelling here! No screaming! No lecturing! Just positive reinforcement when he makes the correct response. More boring time out when he doesn't!

The Many Applications of Behavior Modification. Behavior modification has proved to be a highly reliable way to change behavior and its spin-offs have been many and varied. For example, cigarette smoking is a very difficult habit to stop and it amounts to a virtual addiction. Smokers want to quit the habit but have a very hard time doing so. In fact, in a survey conducted by the American Lung Association (Gemignani, 1998), seven smokers in ten said they hoped to quit and had tried repeatedly to give up tobacco. The most frequently

---

Tip 9.3 For Test-Taking. Notice that Skinner never uses the word *stimulus*. He said that he did not know what the stimulus is. Is it the food? Or the rat's own hunger pangs? Or the delicately balanced lever? Skinner would simply not theorize about it. Skinner only uses the word *reinforcer*. Therefore if you come across a test item that has the word stimulus in it, the item cannot be referring to Skinnerian conditioning.

used method to stop was "cold turkey," which turns out to be the least effective way, amounting to a mere 5 percent success rate. Pharmacological aids, nicotine replacement products, and antismoking medications (patches and gum) have been loudly touted by TV advertisement and have a higher success rate. Even antidepressants and tranquilizers have only a modicum of success. However, when these treatments are combined with a behavior modification program that has been devised by the smokers and therapists, the success rate is much higher.

Behavior modification is the basis of training animals, such as the porpoises in the shows at Marine Land. It is often used to help parents deal with defiant and unruly children or to build the self-esteem of educationally disadvantaged children. It is being employed also with patients with Alzheimer's disease, with children who have enuresis, and with adolescents who have eating disorders.

Whereas operant conditioning and environmental engineering certainly have their positive aspects, there may be a downside. Environmental engineering is an effective way to induce desirable change but it is not necessarily a creative act in that it does not foster original thinking. Environmental engineering may also lead to undemocratic usage since it is essentially a way of controlling a person's behavior. We are manipulating the person just as we manipulate robots or animals we want to train. In that respect, it is contrary to our democratic belief in the worth and dignity of our constitutionally given freedoms. Nevertheless, behavior modification programs are extremely valuable in enabling the institutions of education, health, and the law to carry out their mission of rehabilitation when nothing else seems to work.

BOX 9.4 My Son Sucks His Whole Hand? It's Driving Me Crazy!

Martha: My ten-year-old son sucks his whole hand. It's driving me crazy! (*Class laughter.*) Well, at least four fingers. He puts all four fingers in his mouth. There I am vacuuming, and he begins his hand sucking and he's driving me crazy with it. I yell at him every time he does it, and what Skinner says is that my yelling at him is reinforcing that behavior? (*Jill Smith nods.*)

Martha: But I don't want him to suck his fingers in school.

Eduardo: I'll give you odds he's not sucking his fingers in school.

Martha: How do you know that?

Eduardo: Cause the other guys would make fun of him.

Jill Smith: Does your son know he gets a rise out of you every time he does it?

Martha: He knows I can't stand it!

Jonnimae: He's jerking your collar, baby! My brother used to do that to my mother. She couldn't stand anyone sniffling. Whenever she got on his case about something, he'd start sniffling. She'd say, "Stop that sniffling. I can't stand it. Go blow your nose." He got out of a lot of bad situations like that.

Jill Smith: It probably entertains him to see you fly off the handle. Children are very smart, a lot cannier

and foxier than their parents. I'm not saying they are wiser than we are. Wisdom comes with years of living on this earth and learning from many life experiences. But children in this age group like to see if they can outfox their parents.

Martha: So I shouldn't say anything at all? Can I at least turn away so I don't have to watch it?

Jill Smith: That's a good idea. Your back is not very reinforcing. Just calmly turn your attention to something else so he doesn't know he's "jerked your collar" again.

Martha: (*A few weeks later.*): It's working! I wasn't sure I could hold my temper because I still seethe inside. I don't show it though. He's not sucking his hand as much any more. I know it will take more time, but I'm wise to it now. (*The class reinforces her new behavior and success with a lot of handclapping and expressions of congratulations.*)

Reflective Writing: Reflect on some behavior on your part by which you unwittingly reinforced undesirable behavior in someone else. Record your insight. Then devise a strategy by which you no longer reinforce that behavior.

DEVELOPING BETTER STUDY HABITS USING THE FACTS OF LEARNING, CONDITIONING, AND MEMORY

Three Types of Memory: Sensory, Short-Term, Long-Term

The prevailing theory today is that we have at least three kinds of memory: *sensory* (or *trace*) *memory*; *short-term* (or *working*) *memory*; and *long-term memory*. The purpose of discussing these three kinds of memory is to understand that we need methods by which to move information from our sensory memory through to our short-term memory and finally into our long-term memory (see Figure 9.5). Our **sensory** or *trace memory* lasts for a very brief period—milliseconds, in fact. It is composed of all the thousands of stimuli that impinge on us from moment to moment: auditory sounds, stray thoughts, colors and forms, momentary bodily feelings, the dynamic whirlwind of passing emotions, unconnected bits of memory, smells, tastes, changes of temperature, etc. We are hardly aware of most of them, so quickly do they pass through our millisecond trace memory. A minute percentage, a very minute percentage, lasts long enough to pass on to our short-term memory.

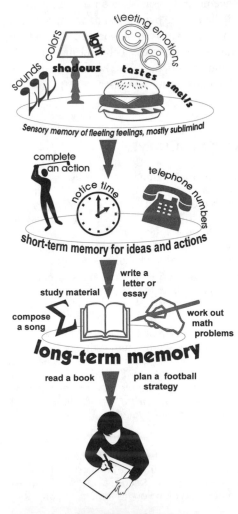

Our **short-term** (or *working*) **memory** is very busy. It functions for many everyday purposes, such as looking up and dialing a telephone number. We remember the number just long enough to dial it, and then we forget it. Another example of our short-term memory is when we scan newspapers for an item that might interest us. Unless we have a photographic memory, we probably couldn't tell you what most of the articles were about since our lack of interest lets them fade right out of our short-term memory. It really is very convenient to have a short-term memory. If we had to remember everything that ever happened in our lives, the clutter in our minds would interfere with our everyday functioning. The Russian psychologist, Alexander Luria, studied a person with a remarkable photographic memory. He could scan a newspaper quickly and remember every article and every word he had read. What Luria discovered was that this kind of photographic memory is not a blessing at all, but a curse. When asked to summarize an article, the man was unable to do so. Every word he read would release a flood of visual images and associations, which actually incapacitated his ability to isolate the essential points of the article (Luria, 1982).

Storing Material into Our Long-Term Memory: How to Study Less and Remember More. A famous early German psychologist discovered that once something gets into our **long-term memory**, it has a good chance of lasting forever (Ebbinghaus, 1913). What makes something proceed to our long-term memory? Meaningfulness, clarity, and how compelling it is in terms of size, color, sound, etc. If it attracts our attention with much compelling force (like a car accident), we

Figure 9.5 Three Types of Memory.

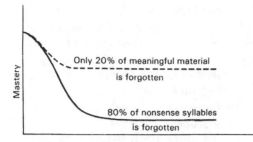

Figure 9.6 The Ebbinghaus Curve. If we can get something into our long-term memory, it may last forever.

will likely store it somewhere in our memory to be recalled many times (see Figure 9.6). There are a variety of techniques for getting material into our long-term memories and the reader may already have developed many of them, but some of them will be new. Furthermore, most of these techniques are based on validated research studies so they are not just good ideas, but based on the scientific facts about how we learn, forget, and remember.

 1. Become a proactive learner. The most basic element to improving your memory as you study is to realize that learning (putting something into your long-term memory) is not a passive process of simple absorption, as if our memory was a sponge. Most of us have had a similar experience to this first grader. The teacher called on him to read orally, which he did in very fine fashion. "Very good," said the teacher, "Now can you put what you read in your own words?" The little boy shook his head. "No, ma'am, I can't." Surprised, the teacher said, "But you read the material so well." "Yes, ma'am," replied the little boy, "only I wasn't listening." Sometimes, when we think we are reading, we realize after a couple of paragraphs that we haven't been paying attention (all those words we scanned dropped right out of our short-term memory). Getting something through to our long-term memory is an act of will, a very active process involving a mind-set to remember and determination to do so.

 2. Make the material meaningful: Avoid rote memory. Don't fall into the trap of learning facts or memorizing names without knowing what they mean. That is called rote memory. Yes, you can memorize a formula or a series of names but they fade very quickly from memory. In fact, what you learned may not even last until you take the exam. Every time you commit something to memory, understand what it means. Lock the new material into something you already know.

 3. If you do have to memorize, concentrate on the nonsalient features. If you do have to memorize a list like the twelve cranial nerves, you need to be aware of the **serial position effect**. In a list, the two salient aspects are the beginning and the end of the list. The terms in the middle of the list do not stand out (are not salient) and will fade fast. Advice: Overmemorize the middle part of the list.

 4. Use mnemonic devices that are meaningful. Everyone uses mnemonic devices, and they are very useful. But make sure the mnemonic device relates to what you are trying to remember. Graduate students in medicine are asked to learn the twelve cranial nerves, that start with the *ophthalmic* nerve, the *occulo-motor* nerve, the *optic* nerve, and then go on to the last nerve, the *hypo-glysseal* nerve. There is a traditional sentence that students sometimes use to remember the order that goes like this: *On old Olympic's towering tops, a Finn and German vaulted a hedge.* Each of the beginning letters is the same as the beginning letter of a cranial nerve. There are two problems with this mnemonic device. The first is the sentence we are memorizing has little to do with neurology. The second problem is that if we accidentally skip one of the words, we've lost all the rest of the nerves that come after. Two much better mnemonic devices are the ones we had to learn in the early grades to help us with our reading and spelling. They are both related to the material we are trying to remember, and they both employ rhythm and rhyme, which make them much easier to store in our long-term memory.

To distinguish when we use *ei* or *ie*:	To remember how to pronounce words *boat, read, raid, etc.*:
I before e	*When two vowels go walking,*
Except after c	*The first does the talking.*
Or when sounded like A	(In each of the words above, the first vowel
As in neighbor or weigh.	is spoken while the second vowel is silent.)

5. Use distributed and massed practice appropriately. Some students insist they do their best studying under pressure, meaning that they wait until the last minute to crash-study for exams. That is an example of **massed practice**. (We generally agree with them since that is usually the only time they really study.) **Distributed practice** means to study or practice some each day (usually for a much briefer period of time). Well, if you are practicing the piano, or studying for a psychology exam, or learning Spanish, or working out on the football field or in the gym, then definitely distributed practice is the most efficient. Seven hours of practice on Sunday is not nearly as good as one hour of practice each day of the week. There are situations, however, when massed practice is better, for example, when the material you are working on demands much thinking or organization, such as a physics problem or a term paper. That doesn't mean you should wait until the night before to write a term paper. Actually, you should write the paper sometime before the due date and then redraft in the week or so before it is due!

6. Use motor learning: It is highly resistant to extinction. One of the best-known facts of learning and forgetting is this: Any activity that has been learned with some kind of muscular involvement (motor learning) is highly resistant to extinction. Those of you who have done a lot of swimming and diving know that even if you haven't been in the water for several years, you do not forget your diving or swimming techniques. You may have lost some of your stamina or polish, but you won't have forgotten how to stroke or dive. The same is true of music. Ask a musician if she remembers how to play a certain song, and she may screw up her face as she tries to remember the melody. In short order, however, her fingers will be reaching for all those old familiar chords even though she may not have played the piece in several years. So how can you use motor learning to become a better student? The answer: Take notes. When you write, you use your muscles. As a matter of fact, if you're the type who likes to write lists, you may have already discovered that once you have written your list, you may not even have to refer to it. Writing the items helps you remember. So take notes. Take notes in class. Take notes when the teacher is lecturing. Take notes as you read the text. Incidentally, this technique does not work as well on a computer keyboard. Why? Because computer typing does not require much muscle effort.

7. Use a multisensory approach. If using motor learning is an effective way to remember what you are studying, think how much more effective it is when you use more than just your muscle memory. We have many kinds of memory that involve our senses. We have several kinds of visual memory: a memory for faces, a memory for geometric designs, a memory for color, etc. We have many kinds of auditory memory: a memory for names, a memory for music, a memory for speech. We also have memory for scent, for feeling and touch, and for taste, etc. (see Figure 9.7). How do we know we have different kinds of memories? From the area of neurological pathology. A lesion to one part of the brain may result in loss of the memory for faces. A lesion to another part of the brain may result in the loss of memory for color, etc. The more of these sensory memories we use in our learning, the more connections we make in our brain—and the more opportunity to get the material into our long-term memory. Use both sides of your brain when studying: For example, on Monday and Wednesday nights, study math (left brain) and your art course (right brain). On Tuesdays and Thursdays, study your English course (left brain) and your music course (right brain).

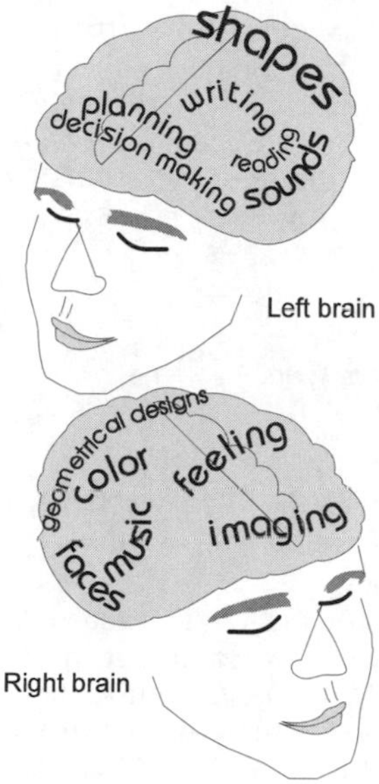

8. Provide yourself with immediate feedback. If you can make flash cards with questions and answers on possible exam items (as has been done commercially with language vocabulary cards), you are providing yourself with *immediate feedback.*

9. Make yourself specific study objectives. If you just go home and say to yourself, "I will study for two hours," your study objective is a matter of clock-watching. You will pay more attention to the clock than to what you are studying. *Gosh! Only forty-five minutes. I've still got an hour and fifteen minutes to go.* (*Sigh.*) Make your study objective the material you are learning. *OK, I'll take notes on Chapter 6 of my history* (left brain) *and do the first part of my art assignment* (right brain). Then when you are finished with your two objectives, you have a feeling of satisfaction for having accomplished your study objectives. Now *reinforce* your studying behavior by whatever is good for you: Call a friend, turn on TV, go to the movies, do whatever is fun and rewarding.

10. Set the material by reviewing, reviewing, reviewing. You've heard this many times before so we won't elaborate except to say that reviewing solidifies your learning in your long-term memory.

Figure 9.7 We Have Many Kinds of Memory. By using a multisensory approach and both our left and right brain, we establish more neural connections between the different memories.

BOX **9.5**   SCENARIO REVISITED
Jonnimae Learns How to Study Efficiently

Jill Smith: Now let's bring all these facts of conditioning and learning to a practical every day level. Jonnimae, do you remember how you described your studying problem when we first began our unit on conditioning?

Jonnimae: Sure, I said I get sleepy the minute I start to study in my bedroom.

Jill Smith: But where in your bedroom? (*Jonnimae looks puzzled. Then a look of understanding spreads over her face.*)

Jonnimae: Oh my gosh! I see what you mean! I study on my bed!

Jill Smith: Good! You've discovered something. Can you put it in Pavlov's empirical language?

Jonnimae: I'm conditioned to sleep on my bed. So when I try to study on my bed, I get sleepy instead.

Annamaria: *Mama mia!* I use the kitchen table to study and nibble and nibble and nibble.

Jonnimae: Does that mean I can't study in my bedroom? I don't have much privacy.

Jill Smith: Well, at least not on your bed. What you need to do is to make a place that you don't do anything else but study. It can be a desk or simply

BOX **9.5** SCENARIO REVISITED (continued)
Jonnimae Learns How to Study Efficiently

a chair in the corner of the room, even your bedroom. What you will be doing is conditioning yourself to study there. The minute you sit down in that chair or at that desk, it will arouse the conditioned response to study.

Jonnimae: Well, I'm going to get myself a desk and chair. No more studying on the bed.

Annamaria: And no studying on the table for me! That's where I eat and eat!

Jonnimae: I think I've got a good memory for figures, but how do you use color memory or music memory for studying?

Shannon: I think I know how a little. I call them my "study tricks." For example, I make diagrams and charts and I color them. I love to make models of molecules for chemistry. All it takes is a few cotton balls for the atoms and some toothpicks to hold them together to make molecules. I guess you could use clay or plastic styrofoam, too.

Eduardo: I sometimes put names and dates and facts to music. I got that idea from my humanities course. The teacher gave us this one to help us remember who wrote it: (Sings the opening bars of Schubert's "8th Symphony.")

This is the symphony that Schubert wrote and never finished.
This is the theme in G. . . .

I make up words to songs that help me remember things. English is a hard language to learn how to spell. In Spanish, everything is spelled the way it looks. But not English. So I put hard English words to music. Here's one to La Cucaracha. *Ought* is a hard word. It has all those silent letters: *u* and *g* and *h*. So I hum in my head (*sings to La Cucaracha*)

O-U-G-H-T   O-U-G-H-T
That's the way to spell the word.

(*Laughter from the other students.*)

Martha: Is there any truth to the idea we have a left-brain and a right-brain and they do different things?

Jill Smith: The jury is still out on that but there seem to be definite differences. Even daydreaming seems to function more on the right. But of course both brains are involved in everything we do and the more we use both parts of the brain, as many areas of the brain as we can, the more fixed becomes the concept in our memory banks. Got some ideas you can use now, Jonnimae?

Jonnimae: I think so. Kind of makes studying less of a chore and more fun.

Important Terms and Concepts to Know

• Albert	• freedom	• meat powder	• short-term
• classical	• free will	• mnemonic	• smiles
• conditioned	• generalization	• multisensory	• stimulus
• empirical	• genetics	• neutral	• time out
• environmental	• higher-order	• noise	• unconditioned
• extinction	• learned	• operant	• white
• extinguished	• long-term	• rat	
• forget	• loud sound	• reinforced	

Make Your Own Chapter Summary by Filling in the Blanks

Use the "Important Terms and Concepts to Know" to fill in the blanks.

Etiology of behavior.   Generally speaking, there are two types of behavior, _____ and maturational. Maturation has to with our _____, while learned behavior has to do with environmental factors.

Ivan Pavlov.   A Russian physiologist by the name of Ivan Pavlov introduced the world to the process of _____ conditioning. What Pavlov discovered was that any _____ stimulus (such as a bell) can be made to be a conditioned stimulus by pairing it with an unconditioned stimulus, such as _____. The dog's salivation can also be _____ by sounding the bell many times without the _____ stimulus of meat powder. If the dog also salivates to a musical instrument or tuning fork, we know that stimulus _____ has taken place. Pavlov came to the conclusion that _____ conditioning was the sum-and-substance of human learning and personality.

John Watson.   Since Pavlov worked only with dogs, it wasn't until Watson conditioned a little baby called _____ that we could say, for sure, that conditioning was also the way human beings learned. What Watson did was to condition a baby to fear a little white _____, by pairing it with the unconditioned stimulus of a _____. The baby also responded with fear to anything that was _____ and furry, such as a rabbit, a Santa Claus beard, and a muff.

B. F. Skinner.   Skinner introduced another type of conditioning, called _____ conditioning. Skinner explained that we also learn through our own exploration behaviors, which are then _____ by the environment. Skinner never used the term, _____, because he preferred _____ terms rather than inferring what was causing the conditioned behavior. It was Skinner's belief that the world is a giant Skinner box in which certain of our behaviors are being reinforced by awards, honors, and _____. For Skinner, the concepts of _____ and _____ are illusionary and that our behavior is completely determined by our conditioning. Skinner devised learning methods, which he called _____ engineering, using such techniques as immediate feedback and _____.

Guidelines for effective studying.   The chapter then described the prevailing theory that we have three types of memory: sensory memory, _____ memory, and long-term memory. Effective studying involves techniques whereby terms and concepts are encoded in our _____ memory. _____ devices that help us remember facts, figures, and concepts. Motor learning is highly resistant to _____, which means that we are less liable to _____ it. Since we do not have one memory but, in fact, have many different kinds of memory, using a _____ approach connects these memory banks for more effective learning.

10 The Psychotherapies
Many Approaches, Many Applications

BOX **10.1** SCENARIO
How Do We Know If We Need Therapy? Or What Kind?

Eduardo: Professor, if all of us live with anxiety most of the time, like you've been telling us, how do you know when our problems are serious enough that we need psychotherapy?

Dr. Weitzman: There are many ways to answer that question but perhaps the most direct is simply to ask ourselves: How are we feeling most of the time? Are we usually optimistic and cheerful despite the problems we are having? Or are we generally depressed and anxious and feeling that life is a misery? A good psychotherapist can help you assess what is going on in your life and provide options for you to think about or help you develop coping strategies for working through problem areas.

Martha: But you can't get the same results by discussing a problem with a good friend?

Jonnimae: I tried that once! I thought I had a friend who would keep a confidence I gave her. Never again! I don't trust her with anything I don't want published in the newspaper.

Dr. Weitzman: If what you told her was very serious and traumatic, she may not have been capable of keeping it to herself. It was too much for her. A therapist is legally and ethically bound to maintain the person's confidentiality. Another problem is that friendship is supposed to be mutual give-and-take. Eventually your friend may get tired of listening to your problems.

Alec: I have this friend who's in therapy with a counselor and she raves how it has helped her so much. I admit I see a real change in her—for the better. She talks like it's the answer to all of life's problems. But it can't keep a person from dying of AIDS.

Dr. Weitzman: Alec, that's a very good point. There are some things psychotherapy cannot do. It can't keep a person from dying of AIDS. But a therapist with expertise in AIDS counseling can provide information about alternate courses of action. The counselor can also help the family members deal with their concerns, their anxieties, or their guilt feelings if the afflicted person deteriorates to the point of needing institutional placement.

Alec: Can it help with the hatred in our society? I'm on a personal crusade to work against all these hate groups in our nation—even the world.

Dr. Weitzman: That's a wide-open question and one that social scientists all over the world are discussing. We know, for example, that people who are angry and hostile and who have low self-esteem are more likely to externalize their unhappiness onto others. If these people can get some insight into their unhappiness, they become more open to new ideas and cultures. They are less likely to go in for the destructive defense mechanisms of physical violence, projective identification, scapegoating, and so on. They become more respectful of the rich diversity in our country.

Eduardo: There's a joke that if I am thinking about going to a "shrink," I ought to have my head examined.

Dr. Weitzman: (*smiling*) I've heard that joke, too. Actually, if a person has lost touch with reality and is in the midst of an acute psychotic episode, psychotherapy is not going to help. The person needs medical treatment first. Once the person has been stabilized with medication, psychotherapy can be provided for the person. Therapy is more suitable for people who are not psychotic.

Eduardo: So getting back to my original question: What I want to know is how do you know what kind of therapy a person needs?

Dr. Weitzman: So glad you asked! That's what we are about to discuss right now.

THE NEED TO BE THERAPY LITERATE

Therapy means healing, and **psychotherapy** means healing of the mind. We tend to think that psychotherapy started with Sigmund Freud's technique of psychoanalysis, and in one sense that is true. He helped us to understand that expressing our negative emotions through the "talking cure" can alleviate our anxiety and problems. But historically there have been many kinds of therapies. Consider, for example, the story of King Saul of the Hebrews. His episodes of depression were remediated by the soothing music of the young shepherd boy, David, who played to him on his harp. Today, we would call that music therapy. Long before the Christian Era, India was developing several kinds of yoga designed to bring about inner peace and enlightenment. The early Christian Church instituted the rite of confession and today we still say "confession is good for the soul"—an assumption that is not too dissimilar from the insight therapies of today. One hundred years before Freud, Franz Mesmer introduced his method of **mesmerism**, which today we would call **hypnotherapy**. In 1875, Mary Baker Eddy formulated a Protestant sect she called Christian Science, which advocated basic spiritual principles in order to achieve good mental and physical health. At the present time, many churches encourage spiritual retreats in which both clergy and parishioners can get away from the maddening crowd and enter into self-contemplation and meditative prayers. In fact, all the major religions have advocated prayer and meditation as paths to the healing of the mind/spirit/soul. (We must mention, however, that some practices were not very healing, such as the "snake pit" of the medieval era, or the tortuous practices of the Inquisition and the New England Puritans.) Furthermore, it has long been known that people who write about the negative events of their lives experience a cathartic emotional release. Today, we have several types of therapies that would fall under the heading of writing therapy. In fact, the reflective writing activities in this text can be categorized as writing therapy. Psychotherapy, then, has a long history, but the scientific approach began just a little over one hundred years ago with Sigmund Freud.

Because there are so many approaches to the healing of the mind/body/spirit, it is wise for everyone to become therapy literate. A good place to start becoming therapy literate is to recognize the three basic categories of psychotherapy: *Insight* therapies, *behavior* therapies, and *cognitive* therapies.

THE INSIGHT THERAPIES

Freud and the Psychoanalytic Approach

The assumption underlying the **insight therapies** is that when we gain insight into ourselves and our problem, we will experience relief of our symptoms and change our behavior. It was Sigmund Freud who opened up the field of insight therapy with his development of **psychoanalysis**.

Freud began his therapeutic work with patients by using hypnosis. In the hypnotic state, the patient would recall unconscious traumatic events and bring them into conscious awareness. Over the course of time, however, Freud discovered that simply encouraging the person to talk, a technique he called **free association**, would bring up the repressed material as easily as hypnosis (Freud, 1900). The patient was told simply to lie back on the couch and say anything that came to mind, any thoughts or feelings, or whatever. Nor did these associations have to "make sense." The patient could ramble on disjointedly about past events, present guilts, or future fears, etc. He also encouraged his patients to discuss their dreams, which Freud called "the royal road" to the unconscious—by which he meant the swiftest way to uncover unconscious conflicts.

The Aim of Psychoanalysis: To Catharsize Traumatic Events. Psychoanalysis was based on the assumptions that most of our behavior is motivated by unconscious conflict, generally as the result of repressed childhood memories. Freud explained that repressed memories require psychic energy to stay in the unconscious. If people have too many repressed memories, explained Freud, so much psychic energy is being drained away from everyday functioning that they become emotional and/or physical cripples for the rest of their lives. Freud called this emotional and physical crippling by the term **neurosis** (see Tip 3.2). Freud also said that traumatic memories do not have to be "real." They can also be a child's misinterpretation of events. For example, a child may witness his parents having sexual intercourse and misinterpret that as an act of violence of his father against his mother. By recalling this event and understanding its real significance, the adult no longer has to hate his father because of his childhood misinterpretation—that his father was hurting his mother.

As Freud formulated psychoanalysis, it was a long and involved process, consisting of one hour a day, three to five times a week. It often required three to five years to alleviate the person's symptoms. Clearly, the only people who could take advantage of psychoanalysis were those who could afford the time and money involved. "Classical psychoanalysis" was introduced to this side of the Atlantic after World War I and is still practiced today in large urban centers. But as a therapeutic approach, it was out of the reach of most North Americans with modest incomes. What was needed was a more practical and less expensive approach, an approach that was called *counseling*.

Carl Rogers and the Client-Centered Counseling Approach

The counseling approach began in the 1930s as a task-oriented situation, such as vocational counseling, marital counseling, academic counseling, etc. This type of counseling was usually a one hour, once-a-week situation for a limited period of time. Sometimes, as in the case of academic counseling, the task might even be accomplished in one session. Over the course of time, however, counseling also became involved with the individual's entire life and career. Finally in the early 1950s, the counseling approach was molded into a psychotherapeutic model that was significantly different from Freud's psychoanalytic model. The person responsible for this evolutionary development was a therapist by the name of Carl Rogers (1950).

Since Freud had been a physician and a neurologist, it was natural for him to develop a psychotherapy that reflected his medical worldview. Psychoanalysis was a doctor-patient relationship. When Freud's patients entered his office, they listed their symptoms, which Freud then diagnosed and treated. Eventually he pronounced his patients "cured" or "incurable." In other words, psychoanalysis was a **medical model**. Carl Rogers, almost singlehandedly, introduced a **nonmedical model**

Figure 10.1 Carl Rogers. Rogers introduced the nonmedical, client-centered approach.

Table 10.1   Assumptions of the Medical Model versus Rogers' Nonmedical (Counseling) Model

Assumption	Medical Model	Nonmedical (Rogerian) Model
Person seeking help	Is a "patient."	Is a "client."
Therapist	Is a "physician."	Is a "counselor."
Person describes	"Symptoms."	"Has problems."
Therapist's role	To make diagnosis and prescribe treatment.	To listen empathetically and to reflect empathetically. To enable the "client" to get in touch with center-of-growth.
Worldview	Some people are healthy and some people are sick.	We all have problems since "life is problematic."
Therapist–person relationship	The doctor is the authority. "Tell me, Doctor."	Therapist is a consultant. Therapist is a facilitator of client's self-discovery.

with the publication of his now classic book *Client-Centered Therapy* (1950). These two models, medical and nonmedical, are built on entirely different assumptions (see Table 10.1).

A Humanistic Self-Fulfillment Model.   Carl Rogers had been a minister before becoming a counselor. His previous ministerial career provided him with a different worldview that had different assumptions. As Rogers put it, he was not a physician; therefore, he did not have patients. He had clients. Rogers' clients, then, could not have "symptoms." They simply had "problems." In fact, said Rogers, we all have problems. As the French philosopher Herbert Marcuse once wrote, "Life is problematic" (Marcuse, 1974). Since Rogers was not a physician, his job was not to diagnose or treat. Rogers did not view himself as a physician whose job it was to heal patients. His job was to facilitate his clients' self-healing. Clients were people who needed improvement in communicating with themselves and with others. As far as Rogers was concerned, he was simply an expert in interpersonal and intrapersonal relationships.

Rogers' nonmedical personality model also differed significantly from Freud's medical model of human personality. Freud's medical model portrays human consciousness (the ego) as a beleaguered battleground on which the id and the superego wage war. It is a conflict model. Rogers' theory, on the other hand, is a **self-fulfillment theory**; namely, that our conscious and unconscious processes are not antagonistic. What is going on, said Rogers, is the attempt of our entire personality complex to harmonize and evolve to higher levels of consciousness. Rogers' theory is that we have a Self and that this Self is seeking to grow into more creative levels of expression. Rogers' model is called a **humanistic model** of personality.

Aim of Therapy: To Harmonize and Expand the Self.   Rogers' self-fulfillment model of personality has a direct bearing on his model of therapy. All our early lives are spent trying to live up to what *others* (parents, teachers, adolescent peers) think we should do. If we have tried to conform too much to the expectations of other people, we lose touch with our own **center-of-growth**. Said Rogers, we all have a center-of-growth—even the most depressed patients on the psychiatric ward of a state hospital. If they did not, said Rogers, they would be dead. The task of the Rogerian therapist is to enable the client to get in touch with that center-of-growth. That means that the Rogerian therapist does not lecture to the clients, tell them what to do, offer advice, or in any way try to direct the person's life. Well, if the therapist doesn't do any of these things, what does the therapist do? The therapist listens with empathy (without the judgment) and reflects back to the clients what they seem to be expressing. In this way, the client hears his/her own thoughts reflected back. Little by little, the clients begin to listen to themselves, and to trust their own feelings and intuitions. They become self-directing.

Empathy versus Sympathy. Rogers distinguished empathy from sympathy. When we are engaging in **sympathy**, we are feeling superior to that person. One clue that we are being sympathetic is a remark such as "Oh you poor thing, I feel so sorry for you," which really means "How much better off I am than you." **Empathy** has more equality to it. We are looking at the world through the eyes of the client and we can identify some of the same emotions in ourselves. We are not feeling sorry for the person. Nor are we judging the person. We are understanding the person's **phenomenology**. We may say something like, "I've been in a similar situation myself." Or "I think I understand a little of what you are going through." At that moment we truly understand the Native American saying mentioned in an earlier chapter: *Never judge a person until you have walked a mile in his moccasins.*

In order for the clients to reveal their "true Self," Rogerian therapists must create a special environment in which the clients feel safe enough to communicate all those emotions they have bottled up for so long. The clients must believe that the therapist likes them, and accepts them for what they are. Rogers called this acceptance of the client in totality **unconditional positive regard**. The task of the client-centered therapist, therefore, is to create a **warm environmental climate** of mutual respect and liking where clients can feel safe enough to be self-revealing. When the therapist accepts the clients in this manner, they can begin to accept themselves (see Box 10.2 for a transcript of a Rogerian-type therapeutic session). Rogers'

BOX **10.2** TRANSCRIPT
Client-Centered (Rogerian) Therapy

The following is an actual transcript of the therapeutic situation. Notice how the therapist reflects Mr. Smith's feelings and thoughts to him and, in doing so, Mr. Smith's mood changes from depression and guilt to one of amusement.

Mr. Smith: I feel depressed. . . I can't get over being ashamed of myself.

Therapist: You feel really badly about yourself.

Mr. Smith: Sure I do. I must really hate my wife if I wanted to smash her face in! If I feel that violently about her, I can't really feel very loving toward her.

Therapist: You believe that you can't have feelings of love and hate toward the same person.

Mr. Smith: Can I?

Therapist: Can't you?

Mr. Smith: (*after some silence*) Well, maybe I can. I remember times when I hated my father when he

disciplined me, but I also loved him. But I was a child then.

Therapist: You think only children can have ambivalent feelings toward someone?

Mr. Smith: I like to think of myself as a rational adult.

Therapist: And rational adults never have irrational feelings.

Mr. Smith: (*smiling at this*) I guess none of us are rational all the time.

Therapist: I'm certainly not rational all the time. In fact I don't know anyone who is rational every single moment. Do you?

Mr. Smith: No one's perfect! . . . (*after a few more moments of silence*) . . . What's irrational is to think I can be perfect. Good Heavens! What an absurdity! I'm only human just like everybody else.

theories have found their way into marriage counseling, education, child-raising, interacting with adolescents, and juvenile delinquents.

Frederick Perls' Gestalt Therapy

Freud's psychoanalysis and Rogers' client-centered counseling are both time-consuming, There are other approaches, however, that are much more direct and economical in time and money. One approach was developed by Frederick Perls, who left his native Germany during the Nazi regime and eventually arrived in the United States, where he developed an insight therapy that was quite different from both Freud and Rogers. Like Freud, it was Perls' contention that we do not function as a complete person. But whereas Freud divided human personality into the three component parts of id, superego, and ego, Perls divided human personality into two component parts. He called these two component parts Top Dog and Underdog (Perls, 1967, 1969).

Top Dog and Underdog represent our two parents, who vied with each other for control and dominance in the family unit. As we grew up, we introjected the personality characteristics of each of our parents, including their struggle for dominance. When we interact with others, especially in personal and intimate relationships, we sometimes take the Top Dog roles and sometimes take the Underdog role. Make no mistake, however, Top Dog is not always the victor. While Top Dog is the louder, more aggressive part of our personality, Underdog has powerful manipulative devices to get its own way—devices such as martyrdom, weakness, and coyness—that frequently topple Top Dog. For example, if boyfriend or husband is acting in his Top Dog role, he may yell at his girlfriend or wife who (in this situation) is poor little Underdog. He stomps off feeling victorious in this interaction. *Man, did he tell her off!* Later the same day, he approaches the lady in question only to find her cool and quiet and not very responsive in her Underdog role. She may even be tearful. He does not want her in this nonresponsive state. He wants to resume his happy relationship with her so he ends up apologizing for his previous behavior until she smiles and warms up to him. According to Perl, Underdog has won again! Although we have depicted Top Dog as the male in this case and Underdog as the female, the relationship can be just the opposite—the man as Underdog and the woman in Top Dog position.

Aim of Therapy: To Resolve Unfinished Situations from the Past and Learn to Live in the Here-and-Now. The aim of gestalt therapy is to live in the here-and-now. We do this by resolving the Top Dog/Underdog conflicts of our past. To do so, Perls developed some dramatic and lightning-swift techniques to dramatize our conflicts by imaging the person in a chair and having a dialog with that person, later called the "hot seat" technique. (It might be added that Perls' direct technique is not for the timid or shy person who could be easily daunted by being put on the "hot seat.") But by dramatizing our interpersonal conflicts and exaggerating them, we do gain insight into our unconscious resentments. It does not matter whether our resentments are "real," exaggerated, distorted, or complete fabrications. It was Perls' contention that all our perceptions of the world are products of our own imagination. His worldview was this: *How we perceive others is simply a reflection of ourselves. We are looking into a mirror.* If we perceive the world as hostile, we are perceiving our own prevailing hostility—products of past unresolved situations. All that mattered is that we resolve the unfinished situations in our own minds, which could be done very quickly in the course of a therapeutic hour.

Figure 10.2 The Figure-Ground Relationship. Perls used this illusion as a metaphor for our inability to distinguish past conflicts and present events in the here-and-now. The vase represents the figure or present focus. The two faces represent the ground (or background or previous history). People sometimes confuse the ground with the figure. Now read Box 10.3 and identify the ground and the figure.

What Perls often wrote and talked about was that most of us are living out resentments from the past or haunted by specters of the future that usually never come about. In either case we are not really living in the present. We are living as deadened bodies unable to feel alive to the present moment. Perls urged us to live in the **here-and-now**. Looking at Figure 10.2 we see a familiar illusion. If we focus on the black, we see a vase, but if we focus on the white, we see two faces. The black is the figure and the white is the ground (background). The significance of the **figure-ground** relationship for Perls was that we often confuse the past (the ground or background) with the present figure (the figure). The transcript in Box 10.3 provides an example of just such distortion. As you read the transcript, note how Mr. X confuses the present situation (the figure) with events of his personal background (the ground).

Group Insight Therapies

Transactional Analysis (TA). Group psychotherapy became popular for several reasons. First, the cost is much less, the fee being shared among the group members. Second, the therapeutic session does not have the rarefied atmosphere of a patient-client relationship but more of a realistic everyday atmosphere of adults discussing mutual problems in an atmosphere of trust. Third, the group members develop close emotional/social relationships, similar in some ways to those of a family. Unlike family members, however, the group members do not have a long knotty history of parent-child conflicts,

---

BOX **10.3** TRANSCRIPT
A Gestalt Therapy Session with Frederich ("Fritz") Perls

In this group was a pert and attractive young woman (Miss Y), who came into the group with a smile and a hello for each of the other members, all of whom were men. The therapeutic session had not officially started. Mr. X, one of the group members, made a seemingly joking remark to Miss Y, that went something like: "I see you are being your usual flirtatious self." The attention of most of us was immediately riveted on Miss Y, but Perls turned his attention to Mr. X.

Perls: Mr. X, what do you "see" when you look at Miss Y?

Mr. X: (*startled by Perls's question*) I was just making a joke.

Perls: Let us examine your "joke." What do you "see" when you look at Miss Y?

Mr. X: I didn't really mean anything by the remark—it was just a remark.

Perls: Would you direct your attention to Miss Y now?

Mr. X: Sure.

Perls: What do you see?

Mr. X: I see a pretty, kind of flirtatious girl, that's all.

Perls: Would you direct your remarks to her? (*Perls always asked the group members to talk to a person, not talk about the person, which he called gossiping.*)

Mr. X: She heard me.

Perls: We don't allow "gossip." Please direct your remarks to Miss Y.

Mr. X: All right, if you say so. Miss Y, I see you as being a very flirtatious person.

Perls: What are you experiencing now?

Mr. X: I'm looking at Miss Y, that's all.

Perls: By experiencing, we mean what is going on in your body.

BOX 10.3 TRANSCRIPT (continued)
A Gestalt Therapy Session with Frederich ("Fritz") Perls

Mr. X: You mean inside me?

Perls: Ja!

Mr. X: Well, my heart is pounding. You've made me nervous.

Perls: (*after some silence*) Go on . . . what else do you experience?

Mr. X: I'm feeling angry.

Perls: Could you act out your anger? Could you say what is making you angry at Miss Y?

Mr. X: I don't know.

Perls: Would you be willing to try?

Mr. X: I don't know . . . maybe.

Perls: Let us "see" your "maybe."

Mr. X: Maybe I will; maybe I won't . . . Yeah, I guess I will. (*to Miss Y*) You make me mad!

Perls: Could you tell her more how mad she makes you?

Mr. X: I don't know. (*to Miss Y*) I get mad at women who flirt around with men.

Perls: Could you tell Miss Y that you would like her to flirt with you?

Mr. X: (*suddenly very loud and obviously angry*) Why should I? I resent her flirtatiousness. It's manipulative.

Perls: Would you play Miss Y being manipulative?

Mr. X: You mean act like Miss Y? (*Perls nods.*) I don't know if I can. . . All right, I will. (*He imitates a "female" voice and smiles to various persons in the room, saying "Good morning, dear" to each person. His voice is strangely authentically female.*)

Perls: Could you tell us who says "Good morning, dear" like that?

Mr. X: Miss Y, whenever she comes in the room.

Perls: You didn't hear me. Who says, "Good morning, dear" to you?

Mr. X: I don't know what you mean. (*The rest of us realize that Miss Y has never used the word "dear."*)

Perls: Could you exaggerate "Good morning, dear"?

Mr. X: Good morning, dear. Good morning, DEAR! GOOD MORNING, DEAR! (*He is talking very loudly now, almost screaming. His face has become very red. The room has become very quiet now.*)

Perls: What is going on now?

Mr. X: (*Visibly shaken, it takes a few moments for him to respond.*) That was my mother talking. She always talked like that when she came into the room.

Perls: Go on.

Mr. X: I can see her now, the bitch! (*There follows here a rather involved session in which Perls requests Mr. X to act out each member of the family on one of these occasions: his mother, his father, his brother, and himself. Mr. X describes how his mother played each of them against the other. He seems to have two unresolved situations, an Oedipal conflict with his father, and an unresolved sibling rivalry with his brother. After almost twenty minutes of this roleplaying, Perls has Mr. X return his attention to Miss Y.*)

Perls: Can you look at Miss Y now?

Mr. X: Sure.

Perls: What are you seeing?

Mr. X: I see Miss Y . . . (*then after a few moments*). I also still see my mother. It's like a double image.

Perls: Ah! Can you put your mother into the chair in the corner of the room?

Mr. X: You mean in my imagination? (*Perls nods.*) . . . OK. She's over there in the brown chair.

Perls: Now regard, if you please, your mother in the brown chair. Can you see her clearly?

Mr. X: Yeah.

Perls: Now look at Miss Y, and see if you can see her clearly.

Mr. X: Not very. She looks a little fuzzy.

Perls: Ah! Now, try to shuttle between your mother in the brown chair and Miss Y until you can see them both very clearly.

Mr. X: OK. (*He spends a few minutes "shuttling" his gaze from the chair to Miss Y and back again.*) She's gone now.

Perls: Who?

Mr. X: My mother. She's faded out.

Perls: Now look at Miss Y, please.

Mr. X: Yeah, I can see her pretty good now. She's sitting there. (*Correcting himself by talking to Miss Y.*) You're just sitting there.

Perls: What is your experience?

Mr. X: (*to Miss Y*): I guess you're not as flirtatious as I thought. You're not my mother.

sibling rivalries, and smoldering resentments that lie just under the surface of many family relationships. The value of the group is that the individual members can work out many of their family difficulties in the safe climate of the therapeutic group. Finally, group therapies often take the form of professional training, such as human potential seminars, leadership training, and management workshops so this type of group membership is something the participants can be proud of and add to their education/vocational resume.

Transactional analysis was formulated by psychiatrist Eric Berne and psychologist Thomas Harris (Berne, 1978; Harris, 1969). Transactional analysis (TA) is based on this assumption that personality is composed of three ego states: the *child-ego state*, the *parent-ego state*, and the *adult-ego state*. Sometimes we are acting from our calm, logical **adult-ego state**, but at other times we are acting out our *child-ego state* (our inner child), or our *parent-ego state* (our introjected father, mother, or other significant figures). Thus when any two people are speaking to each other, six ego states can be operating. Transactional analysis (TA) got its name from its therapeutic approach; namely, to analyze any transaction between two people to determine which ego state is operating, as in the following hypothetical dialogue between a husband and wife:

> **Husband:** (*in his accusing parent-ego state*) What happened to my cuff links!
> **Wife:** (*in her defensive child-ego state*) How would I know where they are?
> **Husband:** (*still in his accusing parent-ego state*) Because you used them last.
> **Wife:** (*switching to her accusing parent-ego state*) Just like all men, you always blame things on women!
> **Husband:** (*switching to his emotional child-ego state*) I hate it when you get on your women's lib kick!
> **Wife:** (*switching to her logical adult-ego state*) Quarreling isn't going to help us find your cuff links.
> **Husband:** (*switching to his logical adult-ego state*) You're right. Maybe they're in the shirt I wore yesterday. Yes, here they are.

The **child-ego state** represents all the drives, needs, and impulses of the internal biological organism. It is the emotional aspect of the personality. It contains all our positive and negative feelings from our conception to the present time. This child-ego state within us has both its constructive and destructive elements. Its constructive element is our spontaneity (nobody is as spontaneous as a child) and our adventurous spirit (a child is naturally adventurous) and our creativity (a child delights in discovering what the world has to offer). Our child-ego state laughs, experiences joy and delight, is enthusiastic, and is bursting with energy. The negative aspect of our child-ego state occurs when our feelings dominate our personality (a child can pout or cry at any slight or rage with a temper tantrum), which interferes with our ability to keep a cool head on our shoulders.

The **parent-ego state** begins to develop, said Berne, at the moment of birth and consists of all the conscious and unconscious "recordings" of what our parents (or other caretakers) communicated to us and to each other. And what do these recordings consist of? All those commandments, rules and regulations of our parents, all the "shoulds" and "should nots" of our school teachers, etc. In short, our parent-ego state consists of all those admonitions of what we are "supposed to do," and are frequently couched as proverbs, sayings, epithets, and maxims. In addition, the parent-ego state has many nonverbal recordings: Frowns, finger wagging, angry tone-of-voice, hands-on-hips, etc. Parental recordings include the imperatives of "never" or "no" or "It can't be done," or the everlasting "Let me show you how to do it right!"

These prohibitions become part of us as we grow up, expressed through hands-on-the-hip postures, our finger-pointing gestures, and our disapproving frowns (see Tip 10.1).

The **adult-ego state** is the rational, logical part of the personality that can view a problem objectively and solve it with cool scientific reasoning. The alert reader may have already equated the child-ego state with Freud's id or the more modern metaphor of the "child within" us all, even the most sophisticated and mature personalities. The parent-ego state, then, can be equated with the superego. The adult-ego state, however, is quite different from Freud's ego state. Freud's ego is a beleaguered battleground, whereas TA's adult-ego state acts with logic and cool rationality.

Aim of Therapy: To Learn to Use Our Ego States Appropriately. We can never erase the recordings of our child-ego state or our parent-ego state. They are permanent recordings. Nor would we want to erase them, even if we could. The child-ego state represents our joyous, adventurous feelings and creativity ("Isn't it fun!"). Our parent-ego state consists of the admonitions of 5,000 years of civilization that enable us to survive ("Don't run out in the street") and to get along in society ("Mind your manners when you visit them"). Nor would we want to remain forever in our adult-ego state. While our adult-ego state is a rational thinking state, it is devoid of our feelings of joy and exuberance and love.

In the group situation, the group members will call attention to each other's ego states. If we are the mercy of our emotions and are always getting our feelings hurt, or if we get angry easily, a group member will say something like, "You sound hurt/angry. What's hooked your child-ego?" If we suddenly get a frown on our face or wag our finger while we are talking, a group member will say, "You're lecturing now. Will you get off your parent-ego state and stop lecturing her!" Verbal and nonverbal clues of the ego states are listed in Table 10.2.

Peer-Support Groups: No One Understands Like Someone Who's Been Through It! The first peer-support group was Alcoholics Anonymous (AA), organized in 1935 by two recovering alcoholics. The AA concept goes something as follows: No one can appreciate the problems of an alcoholic or how difficult it is to stay "on the wagon" as much as other alcoholics. The members come together for one or more meetings through the week to share their problems, to provide emotional support for each other, to be inspired by religious and other readings, and to formulate goals. The AA members become a kind of family that is willing to help the alcoholic when he "slips" and has "gone under" again.

There has been a lot of criticism of Alcoholics Anonymous for several reasons: because of its quasi-religious 12-step method, because it demands total abstinence (as compared to the method of controlled drinking), and because of its basic assumption that alcoholism is a disease. Evaluation of AA has been difficult because only about 25 percent of people who join AA remain with the organization after 12 months. Of those who do remain, praise for AA is very positive. Often the reclaimed alcoholics give testimony at the group meetings of the long list of psychiatrists, psychologists, pastors, and other counselors who were of little help—nothing was helpful, until they went to AA.

Tip 10.1 Comedians Act Out Our Ego States! One of the reasons we enjoy comedies is because the comedians are acting out our ego states. Comedy teams who acted out the parent-ego and child-ego state include Bud Abbott and Lou Costello; Jackie Gleason and Art Carney; Lucille Ball and Desi Arnaz; Jerry Lewis and Dean Martin; and the Smothers Brothers. We laugh because these comedians are holding "the mirror up to nature." In short, we are laughing at our own human frailties and foibles.

Table 10.2   Transactional Analysis: Clues to Our Three Ego States

	Child-Ego State	*Parent-Ego State*	*Adult-Ego State*
Permanent Data and Recordings	**Internal Events:** Bodily needs and feelings, sensations, emotions, curiosity, exploratory and experimental drives.	**External Events:** Do's and don'ts, shoulds, admonitions, rules and laws, and all the *how to's* and gestures, facial expressions of adults.	**Evaluation of Internal and External Events:** Information and data gathering, thinking, open-ended judgments, and planning.
When Overdominant	**Always in the grip of our feelings:** We remain childlike in our emotional repertory, easily hurt or always angry and desiring to strike back.	**Generally repressed and over-anxious:** Lack of spontaneity, inhibited, rigid, overly conforming, irrational fears, narrow-minded, and opinionated.	**Too controlled and sober:** Too studied and sober, lack of spontaneity and human responsiveness.
When Used Constructively	High motivation and energy, spontaneity, creativity, ability to enjoy life.	Productive habits, life-saving caution, time-saving knowledge, "common sense."	Able to reinterpret child "injustices" and able to forgive parents for their mistakes, able to deal with family conflicts nondefensively.
Physical Clues	Quivering lip, tears, temper, high-pitched voice, shrugging, rolling or downcast eyes, nose thumbing, teasing, squirming, giggling, feelings of delight, raising hand for permission.	Furrowed brow, pursed lips, pointing index finger, foot tapping, hands on hips, arms folded across chest, wringing hands, tongue clucking, clearing throat.	Listening attitude, thoughtful, interested in what person is saying, unperturbed, calm, focused on task, patient.
Verbal Clues	"I wish . . . " "I guess . . . " "I dunno . . . " "I hate . . . " "I don't care . . . " "You make me made . . . "	"Always . . . " "Never . . . " "How many times . . . " "That's wrong!" "Let me show you how to do it right!"	"Let me see if I understand this." "Who? What? Where? When?" "What are our options?" "How can we solve this?"

Source: Adapted from Thomas Harris, *I'm O.K.—You're O.K.* (New York: Harper & Row, 1969).

Multifaceted Peer-Support Group Spin-Offs. Negative criticism not withstanding, AA has been the inspiration for (literally) hundreds of spin-off peer-support groups. Peer-support groups were originally organized for women (or men) who have been raped, for adult survivors of incest, for victims of disaster, for parents of murdered children, for abused spouses . . . the list keeps getting longer and longer. Now there are peer-support groups not only for the victims, but also for the perpetrators—the rapists, the molesters, those convicted of murder, spouse abusers, etc. These kinds of groups, however, are generally led by one or more professionals in these areas. The peer-support group approach is the fastest growing therapeutic milieu at the present time (see Table 10.3).

Table 10.3 A Few of the Many Peer-Support Groups

Al-Anon (for families of alcoholics)	Parents Anonymous
Co-Dependents Anonymous	Partners of Survivors of Incest Anonymous
Codependents of Sex Addicts	Partners of Survivors of Sexual Abuse
DD-Anon Group One (Dissociative disorders)	Sex Addicts Anonymous
Incest Anonymous	Sex-Mutilators Anonymous
Men Overcoming Violence	Sexual Abuse Survivors Anonymous
Men in Recovery	Synanon (for drug addiction)
Mothers of Sexually Abused Infants and Children	Transcendental Meditation Ex-Members Support Group
Narcotics Anonymous	Victims Anonymous

The basic assumption of all these peer-support groups is that while professional intervention is helpful, *no one can be as helpful to a survivor-victim*, or to a perpetrator, as those who have had similar experiences. Group members gain insight and inspiration by listening and learning from each other. They help each other struggle with their sense of shame, guilt, their nightmares, and (sometimes) the overwhelming terror that the experience might be repeated. Generally, the peer-support groups follow certain guidelines established by a national organization that also provides materials, movies, cassettes, and other types of audio-visual aides. Sometimes, the peer-support groups function in as hospital setting, in a clinic, in a church, but sometimes, the meetings can take place in someone's home. (See Box 10.4 for a partial transcript of a peer-support group.)

BOX **10.4**) **Transcript of an Adult Incest Survivor Peer-Support Group**

The meeting has been in progress for about forty minutes.

Josie: I feel like I'm going crazy lately.

Marion: What about?

Josie: I have this kind of feeling . . . I know it's stupid . . . but I can't get it out of my head. I think about it all the time . . . I can't say it.

Marion: Sure you can. Try.

Josie: What keeps going around in my head is that the same thing that happened to me will happen to Missy (*her three-year-old daughter*). That she'll be raped or seduced by somebody.

Ellen: By whom?

Josie: Anybody. Everybody. Anybody.

Marion: That doesn't make any sense, Josie. The world isn't filled with men who all set out to seduce young girls. We just had hard luck.

Josie: I know that with one part of my mind. But the other part says you can't trust any man with a girl-child.

Marion: Josie, are you afraid of all men you know?

Josie: No, just . . . (*she stops suddenly*).

Ellen: Just who?

Josie: Nobody. It's just stupid.

Marion: Are you afraid of leaving her with your father? (*Josie's father was the perpetrator of Josie's incest experience.*)

Josie: Oh, no. He's too old now and crippled. I'm not even afraid of him anymore.

Marion: Well, who are you afraid of?

Ellen: You're afraid of your husband, aren't you? You're afraid of leaving Missy with your husband.

Josie: Yes, I know it's stupid . . . but every time he picks her up, I shudder.

Marion: Have you talked about this with him?

Josie: No, I'm scared to.

Ellen: Honey, there ain't a gal in this group has a baby daughter hasn't felt the same way.

Josie: Then I'm not going crazy.

Ellen: Lawd, no. It's natural. Just natural.

Peer-Support Operates in Many Situation on an Informal Basis. Peer-support has been found so efficacious in enabling people to cope with very real situations that hospitals now group their patients according to the disease or problem. For example, in one study, researchers found that bypass-surgery patients who share the same room do far better, by-and-large, than a control group of patients who had different health problems. The patients with the by-pass surgery who shared rooms with other by-pass patients were less anxious and more ambulatory immediately after surgery and their length of stay in the hospital was 25 percent shorter than the control group. Why would this be so? Well, let's try these possible explanations "for size." While professionals listen to their patients, they do not have that same empathetic listening that does another person with the same symptoms. Second, it simply helps to know that we're not alone in dealing with a life-threatening disease. Finally, another patient can provide supportive information that busy professionals might forget to say or not even know how to say.

> *Feeling queasy? So did I when the anesthetic wore off but it won't last long.*
> *Feeling dizzy? My doctor told me that often occurs. Happened to me too.*
> *You may feel weak now, Buddy, but they'll have you up and walking in 24 hours, like me.*

THE BEHAVIOR THERAPIES: INSIGHT ISN'T NECESSARY—JUST CHANGE THE BEHAVIOR

Skinner's Behavior Modification (Therapy)

A basic assumption that underlies the insight approach is that insight leads to behavioral change. This assumption has not proved to be correct in all situations. Therapists sometimes complain that despite gaining insight into their problems their insights did not necessarily motivate their clients to make productive changes in their lives. A case in point is that surely by now all smokers must know that smoking is hazardous to their health. Yet they continue to smoke. All their insight has not led them to change their smoking behavior. **Behavior therapy** aims directly for change in behavior with or without insight. Verbal interchange is minimal and insight into past behaviors is deemed unnecessary. We shall discuss three of them: behavior modification therapy, systematic desensitization training, and biofeedback training.

Behavior modification is based on B.F. Skinner's operant conditioning (1938). The basic assumption of this approach is that a destructive life style or pattern of "neurotic" symptoms is simply an inappropriate complex of *conditioned (learned) responses.* If that is so, it follows that what has been conditioned can be *deconditioned.* What has been learned can be unlearned. Behavioral therapy, say its advocates, is much more economical in terms of time, money, and professional staff simply because—when it works—it accomplishes its goals in a remarkably short period of time. There is no need for extensive case studies, months of searching for "causal factors" (that may never be discovered), or endless discussion of problems, which may only reinforce and magnify the symptoms. The behavior modification technique described next is called shaping of behavior.

Shaping of behavior is a step-by-step method of teaching a behavior you want a child to learn. The shaping of a child's behavior is done through a *series* of *small, successive, successful steps* (memory jog = think of 4 S's). The following classic example of behavior therapy was carried out in a nursery school (Harris, Johnston, & Wolfe, 1964). In this nursery school, teachers were devoting considerable time and attention to an apparently immature and withdrawn child who spent most of her time on the floor, playing by herself with her back to the other children. When the nursery school teachers failed to get the child adapted to the school routine, they called in a behavioral therapist as consultant for advice and help. The behavioral consultant observed the child in the nursery school for an entire day. Then he called the staff together and explained what the teachers were doing was actually reinforcing the very behaviors they didn't want. By coaxing her and calling her name and trying to get her to play with the other children, they were giving her more time and attention than all the other children put together. Why should she change her behavior?

When the nursery school teachers got over their astonishment, they asked her what it was they should do. The behavioral consultant outlined a behavior modification plan for them. The first step was to extinguish the child's isolated behavior by **nonreinforcement**: *Don't wave, talk, or call her by name when her back is turned.* Only **reinforce** her behavior when she is turned around toward the other children or when she is standing. In a few days, she was standing much of the time and watching the children play. The next step was to smile and call her by name only when she approached the other children. Within two weeks, she was playing with the other children so that an outside observer could not distinguish her from the others.

The nursery school staff wondered if perhaps she had just gotten over her shyness. To answer that objection, the consultant told them simply to reverse the procedure and reinforce her behavior only when she was turned away from the group and in only a few hours she was right back on the floor again. Quickly, they reversed again and—in only few hours—she was playing with the other children.

Applications. So successful are some kinds of behavioral therapies that these techniques have been adopted in many institutional milieus: classrooms, mental hospitals, physical therapy situations, juvenile delinquency programs, and special education. Despite its therapeutic advantages, however, behavior therapy is not a solution by which to create a perfectly Utopian world. Behavior modification can modify existing behavior; it does not necessarily foster creativity. Behavior therapy is simply a method by which to solve a single concrete situation. Nevertheless, when it works, it works very well indeed (Abramson, Seligman, & Teasdale, 1978).

Joseph Wolpe's Systematic Desensitization

One of the first persons to appreciate the behavioral approach was a physician, Joseph Wolpe, who developed a **counterconditioning** method for dealing with overt fears and phobias (Wolpe, 1958). This method is based on a powerful **assumption**: *The two emotional states of fear and relaxation cannot exist within us at the same time.* When we are anxious, our body is tense, our muscles are contracted, and we are in the **adrenalergic state**. When we are calm and relaxed, our muscles are not contracted, we are not fearful, and we are in the **cholinergic state**. Wolpe's approach is remarkable in its simplicity. All we have to do is to help the person stay calm in the presence of whatever is making the person fearful or phobic. It doesn't matter what the anxiety-provoking stimulus is. It can be the common phobia of snakes, claustrophobia, or a fear of heights. Wolpe's method enables the client to remain relaxed in the presence of the anxiety-provoking stimulus (snakes, cars, heights). He outlined the following three-step process by which to achieve this goal of relaxation.

Table 10.4   A Hierarchy of Fears. The level of anxiety is associated with each fear stimulus

Anxiety	Stimulus
5	Picture of a car
8	The word "car"
10	Planned honking
20	Unexpected honk
30	Imagining a car
40	Talking about driving
50	Hearing a siren
55	Screech of brake
60	Imagining being in a car
70	Seeing adult drive
75	Imagining self drive
80	Photo of car crash
85	Seeing TV car crash
90	Riding in a car
95	Sitting in driver's seat
100	Actually driving

1. The client constructs a hierarchy of fears. The therapist has the person identify as many anxiety-provoking stimuli as possible (at least 15 such associated stimuli). If the phobia is driving, the client may list all of the stimuli noted in the insert (Hierarchy of Fears) along with an assessment of the level of fear associated with each stimulus (see Table 10.4).

2. The client becomes very relaxed. The therapist trains the client in deep muscle relaxation, until the client can keep his body in a state of relaxation at will.

3. The therapist introduces the anxiety-provoking stimulus while the client remains relaxed. The client puts himself into a state of deep relaxation. The therapist then presents the least-anxiety provoking stimulus, for example, a picture of a car for those with driving phobias. If the client remains relaxed in the presence of the picture of the car, the therapist goes on to the next stimulus on the hierarchy, the word *car*. If the client gets fearful and tense, the therapist signals the client to put himself in a state of deep relaxation again. When the client is relaxed again, the therapist again says the word *car* again. If the client can stay relaxed in the presence of this anxiety-provoking word, the behavioral therapist goes on to the next stimulus on the hierarchy (*honking*) and so on up the hierarchy list of anxiety-provoking stimuli.

Using this method, therapists can sometimes dispel a fear or phobia in a few sessions. Obviously, this method would only be an exercise in futility unless the person can actually drive again. And they do! With this method, thousands of people with a driving phobia have been enabled to drive again. We know this because, for many years, driving on the California Freeway was the single most frequent phobia to be treated at Wolpian clinics. (That fact will not surprise anyone who has driven on that freeway.)

Biofeedback Training

It was once thought that basic bodily processes such as heart rate, circulation, and metabolism, were *autonomic*; that is, not under our own conscious control. Then a certain Yogi Swami Rama once astonished Western psychologists by proving that he could voluntarily slow down or speed up his pulse rate; stop his heart from pumping blood for 17 seconds; raise or lower the temperature in his hand; and alter his brain wave patterns (Kassin, 1995). What Swami Rama had demonstrated was that those bodily processes we had previously believed to be autonomic functions (beyond our conscious control) can be altered through our own conscious control. The power of will! Biofeedback training works on the assumption that we all can alter our bodily processes. Here's how the biofeedback procedure works.

Suppose you suffer from simple tension headaches. Tension headaches are most often caused by muscular tensions in the forehead, neck, and shoulders that constrict the arteries to the brain, which results in "headaches." Under supervision, you would make yourself comfortable in a sitting or reclining position. The biofeedback trainer would attach an EMG (electromyograph) to your head or finger. The EMG translates muscular tension or brain waves into an auditory or visual signal. The purpose of the auditory or visual signal is to enable you to become sensitive to your body functioning. During the first part of the training, you learn to associate, for example, a higher-pitched tone to increased muscle tension in your head and a lower-pitched tone to decreased muscle tension. In addition to recognizing the tension in your body, the trainer may accompany the biofeedback with verbal autosuggestions in a calm monotone to lower the temperature in your head as follows:

> I feel very quiet. I am beginning to feel relaxed . . . My head feels heavy and relaxed . . . My ankles, my knees, my hips, my shoulders are all feeling relaxed. My neck, my jaw, my forehead are all feeling relaxed . . . Relaxed as I am, the tension is flowing out of my head. My head is already getting cooler. The warmth of my head is flowing into my arms and hands. I can feel my hands becoming warmer . . . I can feel my head getting cooler and cooler.

Within a few sessions, you are able to decrease your muscular tension and reduce your headache strain under your own volition. Eventually, the trainer commits those relaxation phrases that seem to "work" for you on to a cassette tape which you take home and use by yourself when you feel a headache "coming on."

Aim of Therapy: Shift the Locus of Control (LOC) from External to Internal. Probably the most revolutionary aspect of biofeedback, say its advocates, is that it shifts the **locus of control (LOC)** from external to internal control. No longer does the client look to drugs to alleviate insomnia, migraine, cramps, hypertension. The client's worldview now includes the understanding that we are not just the victims of external forces. We are, in fact, the perpetrator of our bodily ills. That is good news! If we do indeed perpetrate our "dis-eased" bodies, it follows that we can do something about it. Research studies indicate that 50 percent of the patients who have tried biofeedback for their tension headaches have benefited permanently.

THE COGNITIVE THERAPIES: COMBINING INSIGHT AND BEHAVIOR THERAPIES

Albert Ellis' Rational-Emotive Therapy (RET): "Get Rid of Your Irrational Beliefs; They're Driving You Crazy!"

A third approach, called cognitive therapy, rests on another assumption; namely, that many of our conflicts are based on misperceptions and "errors" of thinking. The aim of cognitive therapy is to gain insight into these misperceptions and "errors" of thinking and to change the way clients process information. Knowing that our perceptual belief system motivates our actions and our interactions, the therapist is attempting to foster a whole new worldview in the client. In fact, he or she will use any method to help us change our ideas and self-image, by playing the many roles of therapist, teacher, coach, friend, and partner. Whatever it takes! To illustrate the cognitive approach, we begin with rational-emotive therapy.

Albert Ellis was originally trained in psychoanalysis (an insight therapy) but like other behavioral therapists, he became convinced that insight is not enough. If people want a better life, they must do something on their own behalf. The responsibility for our lives rests

Table 10.5   RET: Example of Irrational Beliefs

I have to be the kind of person everybody likes.	I have to be a perfect wife/husband.
It's my job to keep peace in the family.	I have to be a perfect parent.
What happened to me has ruined me for any kind of normal life.	I have to be a perfect adult child to my parents.
	I won't be able to go on if she/he leaves me.
I should not be selfish. I must keep everyone's needs ahead of my own.	Maybe it's just my lot in life to suffer.
	It's too late for me to change my life.
Nothing ever goes right for me.	Bad things aren't supposed to happen to good people.
I've made a failure of my life.	If I don't get approved of by everybody, I must be
I should live my life so that I don't make enemies.	dislikable.

squarely on our own shoulders. Also, he had become very impressed with one significant aspect of human discomfort: Our anxiety and depression (and general misery) are not necessarily caused by actual events but by how we respond to them. What drives us "crazy" are our irrational beliefs, which keep us in constant emotional turmoil. What are these irrational beliefs? Some examples can be found in Table 10.5.

A-B-Cs (and D-E-F-Gs) of RET. Ellis' underlying assumption is that it is not what actually happens to us that is so catastrophic but how we react to it. Case in point! In the opening scenario of Chapter 1, six people received the same letter but how they reacted to it was dramatically different. On person was jubilant, one was anxious and depressed, and one committed suicide. Ellis could easily cite this example as illustrative that the activating event (A) is not what hurts us but the beliefs (B) we have about what happened. If our beliefs are irrational, it will lead to self-defeating consequences (C). Ellis explains that all people are born with self-defeating tendencies. When something goes against their goals or values or desires (failures or rejections or whatever), they have a choice of responding fairly healthily with appropriate emotions (feeling sorry or disappointed) or making themselves miserable, terrified, panicked, self-pitying, or even suicidally depressed (Ellis & Dryden, 1987). To continue his A-B-C-D-E-F-G model (see Box 10.5), the person learns next to dispute (D); that is, to challenge the irrational belief system that is causing him so much anxiety. Behavioral techniques to dispute the person's belief system may result in any one of a host of activities: public speaking, going for the job interview they are afraid of, approaching members of the opposite gender, etc. If the disputation (D) is successful, the person experiences a new effect (E) of no longer feeling anxious and depressed. So he stops procrastinating, drinking, etc. The person now has a new feeling (F) of confidence about getting along in the world, and achieve the desired goal (G).

Aim of Therapy: Substitute Rational Cognitions for Irrational Beliefs. The demands we acquire as we grow up set us up for a life of continual misery. Furthermore, we can never succeed in living up to all these "shoulds." We are setting ourselves up for failure. When we experience failure, we get anxious, depressed, and suffer from low self-esteem. So how does the RET therapist shake these kinds of irrational beliefs out of us? By pointing them out to us—very bluntly if need be—using "sandpaper" questions and sarcasm:

Why must you always "should" on yourself?
You'd rather suffer than leave this abusive relationship? Do you like to suffer?

BOX **10.5** **Transcript of Rational-Emotive Therapy**

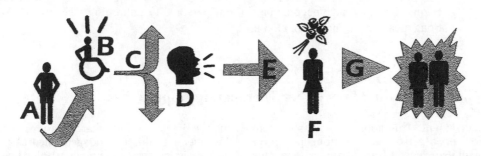

The client came into therapy with the goal (G) of becoming "dateable." When a classmate began to show an interest in her, which was the Activating event (A), her Behavior (B) reflected her anxiety with the Consequence (C) of wanting to drop the class. At this point, the RET therapist disputed (D) her belief she is "damaged goods." If the disputation is successful, the effect (E) will be a new feeling (F) about herself, which should help her attain her goal (G) of being dateable. Dana had been subjected to incest as a child from ages ten to fifteen. She has been dealing with this experience for several sessions.

Dana: I feel like it [the incest] ruined me for life.

Therapist: If it ruined your life, why come to therapy? Why don't you just grovel in your misery?

Dana: You could be more sympathetic.

Therapist: What would you like me to say . . . "Oh, you poor thing, you. I'm so sorry for you"?

Dana: Now you're being sarcastic. I just want to know that you know what I went through.

Therapist: I know what you went through. You've talked a lot about it. It's an obsession with you. Maybe you don't want to get over it. You seem to hang on to it, like a teddy bear. You need an attitude change.

Dana: That's not true.

Therapist: You aren't the only woman it has happened to. It has happened to maybe 30 percent of American women, maybe more. The estimates are getting higher all the time.

Dana: Thirty percent? That many?

Therapist: The only thing ruining your life is your irrational idea that it has ruined you.

Dana: It hasn't ruined everything. It hasn't ruined my ability to work. I'm a good worker.

Therapist: Well, congratulations, you have finally uttered a rational statement. So it hasn't ruined your whole life. What has it ruined?

Dana: Well, it's ruined how I react with men, emotionally.

Therapist: In what way?

Dana: I feel so ashamed. I feel like damaged goods.

Therapist: We are all damaged goods. That's part of growing up. No one has had a completely "happy childhood." That's one of our absurd modern fallacies.

Dana: No man really wants a woman who had sex with her father.

Therapist: How do you know, have you asked them?

Dana: No, only he made me feel like it was my fault. That I came on to him.

Therapist: All right, let's straighten this out before we go on. He was the adult and you were a child. He was the perpetrator. You were the victim. Say it!

Dana: He was the perpetrator. I was the victim.

Therapist: Again!

Dana: He was the perpetrator. I was the victim.

Therapist: AGAIN! LOUDER!

Dana: HE WAS THE PERPETRATOR. I WAS THE VICTIM! ALL RIGHT. IT WASN'T MY FAULT!

Therapist: You got that straight in your head?

Dana: *(quietly)* I think so.

Therapist: Furthermore, you survived. You are now an adult survivor. Congratulations!

What's ruining your life is not what happened to you. It's your attitude.
Does it make you happy to worry?
Whatever gave you the idea that life is fair?
You believe that life is always a happy situation? You must still believe in Santa Claus.

Sometimes the therapeutic treatment may seem cruel to an observer and Ellis has been criticized that his unconventional approach is extreme and could be humiliating and damaging. Ellis responds to these criticisms in this way: We have lived with these irrational beliefs so long that they have become part of our personality patterning (see Box 10.6). It takes strong measures to shake them loose.

BOX 10.6 A Few of the Many Other Therapeutic Approaches

Crisis Management. This approach is a short-term therapy to help a person recover from the serious events we all experience (death of a loved one, rape, or depression as the result of the loss of job.) It has also proved to be effective for persons who have functioned well throughout their lives.

Family Therapy Systems Approach. It used to be that when a family member was in serious trouble, the person was sent to a therapist to be "straightened out" as if the person functioned in a vacuum devoid of other people. Virginia Satir recognized that every family has a "personality," i.e., there are basic dynamics within a family. The problem may not be in any one individual, but in the way the whole family interacts. Thus the whole family is encouraged to come into the therapeutic situation and to make changes in the family dynamics. The aim of therapy then is to change the way family members communicate and interact with each other. Various forms of family therapy include parent-child therapy, couples therapy, and marriage counseling.

Humor. We may have the famous "Patch" Adams, M.D. to thank for the introduction of humor to the therapeutic situation. Just as Dr. Adams discovered that transforming the solemn atmosphere of a hospital to one of circus-like jollity (he himself frequently dons a clown costume on his hospital rounds), so too have psychotherapists been using humor as a way to avoid the continual grim quality of therapy sessions. They believe that emphasizing the negative side of living all the time may simply be reinforcing the client's depressive moods. This is not to say that the client's serious problems are avoided, only that it reminds both therapist and client that humor is one of the healthiest ways to deal with perplexity, suffering, and tragedy. The ability to see humor is one of the hallmarks of the truly healthy personality.

Logotherapy. Viktor Frankl, who went through the horrors of Nazi concentration camps and survived, believed that one of the main problems of modern humanity is that we have placed too much importance on material goods and other "pleasures of the flesh." We suffer, he said, from **noogenic neurosis**, a state of apathy, aimlessness, and boredom. A life lived without purpose must ultimately leave us with the taste of "bitter ashes." The aim of **logotherapy** is to develop a philosophy of life that has more transpersonal values, and to engage in suprapersonal activities (service to others and/or working for world peace, world brotherhood, and world ecology).

Stress Inoculation. The other therapies in this box focus on healing a traumatic event during or after an event. Stress inoculation, on the other hand, focuses on the prevention of emotional discomfort, and was originally developed for groups whose job it is to respond to emergencies: firefighters, highway patrol officers, medical personnel caring for burn victims, and "mop-up crews" who must deal with trying to identify body parts before putting them into a body bag. This approach involves videos taken on-site; experienced service personnel who relate some of their own early physical and emotional reactions; training sessions for ways to cope with what they may encounter, and open group discussions. The reader has already come across an example of stress inoculation at the end of Chapter 6, pages 161–162 where we discuss how parents can ask their adolescents what would they do if they were presented with various dilemmas under group pressure.

Therapy Online. Long distance phone therapeutic sessions have been in existence for some time when either therapist or clients must be out-of-town. This kind of at-a-distance consulting has been extended to the Internet. Still in its infancy, the American Psychological Association is concerned about certain inherent problems, such as security and type of client. For example, paranoid schizophrenics would probably not be good candidates. On the other hand, some beginning research indicates that children with AD/HD appear to be responding well since they are so often fascinated by television. It would seem to be suitable for people unable to consult a therapist because they are invalided or they live in isolated

BOX (10.6) **A Few of the Many Other Therapeutic Approaches (continued)**

areas. One interesting finding is that people seem more willing to reveal very personal information very quickly in this seemingly anonymous situation than is ordinarily the case in face-to-face situations. This willingness to reveal such confidential information could lead to exposure to unauthorized and unscrupulous predators. Another issue is how effective is the online therapeutic situation. In the online situation, the counselor lacks very valuable clinical observations so important to the therapeutic situation—the person's facial expressions, bodily posture, voice quality, rate of speech, spontaneity, pauses, etc. The APA is already working on organizing research into this extension of telehealth.

Writing Therapy. Ira Progoff is the therapist most associated with the therapeutic aspects of keeping a journal, but any literature teacher can relate the cathartic effect of autobiographical writing or fictionalized autobiographical writing. In fact, keeping a journal of one's hopes, wishes, fantasies, dreams, disappointments, etc. has become the "homework" aspect of many types of therapies. The reflective writing assignments in this text are designed for that purpose.

Aaron Beck's Cognitive Therapy

Like Ellis, Aaron Beck was trained in psychoanalysis. Like Ellis, he was impressed by the self-defeating worldview of depressed patients. They look at the world, he said, not through rose-colored glasses, but through dark-colored glasses. They magnify small events into catastrophic ones. When they have "butterflies in the stomach," they imagine they are having heart palpitations. The smallest social gaffe causes them to imagine they "can never show my face again to those people" (Beck, 1991).

Aim of Therapy: Change Negative Self-Talk. All cognitive therapists share the same objectives (to change behavior, to eliminate self-defeating beliefs, to adopt more rational attitudes, etc.) How they do this is a reflection of their own therapy style. In contrast to the sometimes harsh sounding RET therapists, Beck has a much more folksy, country-style approach. Therapists who use this approach ask Socratic-like questions. Beck particularly stresses learning to replace negative self-talk with more efficacious statements (see Table 10.6).

How did you come to that idea?
What's your evidence for that idea?
Are these the facts or your interpretation of them?

Table 10.6   Beck's Cognitive Therapy: Improving Self-Talk

Negative Statements	Positive Statements
I can't do it. There's no use trying.	If I get some help, I can master this situation.
I'm not getting anywhere.	My progress is slow, but I see definite progress.
It's too much for me.	This is going to take some concerted effort, but I'll do it.
I've never been able to do math.	I'll approach math in a more adult fashion.
He'll never give me the job.	I may not get the job but the interview will be good experience.
I'll make a fool of myself.	I'll practice until I feel confident and secure of myself.

Let's take a look at that situation from another angle.
What's the worst that can happen?
Where is it written that we have to put everybody else's needs in front of our own?

Albert Bandura's Social Learning Theory and Guided Mastery Technique

One significant way we learn is through what is sometimes called **social learning** and sometimes called **observational learning**. The psychologist who has done the most to conceptualize this type of learning is Albert Bandura. He has demonstrated, irrefutably, that we learn simply by watching what others do. Having established that we learn simply by observing, Bandura has sought ways to use it in working with people's emotional and physical problems (Bandura, 1986).

Aim of Therapy: Learning from a Role Model. Bandura points out that much of what we fear is not just the situation itself, but our presumed inability to cope with it. In that respect, Bandura is like other cognitive therapists. When people come to believe that they do not have the skill to handle a situation, that the situation is overwhelming for them, they begin to break down morally and physically. What is important to Bandura is to help them handle the overwhelming situation. What Bandura suggests is to introduce the person to experts in the area who can handle the feared object or situation. Suppose, for example, a person has a snake phobia and runs screaming from the presence of even the gentlest garter snake. Bandura has the client watch the snake expert handle the snake in a gentle manner. Step-by-step, the client approaches the snake and under the tutelage of the snake expert, is encouraged to pet the snake or even hold it. The client is learning how the snake expert handles the snake and, at the same time, is learning a different emotional response. Eventually, the person walks with the snake expert in the woods, while the snake expert teaches the client how to walk and look for snakes, how to dress for snake protection, and to enjoy the beauty and usefulness of snakes. Eventually, the client ventures out on his own to see if he can take a walk in the woods by himself. He rates himself on his fear reaction (say from 1 to 10) in all the steps we have outlined above, until his snake phobia is no more than his natural fear of any uncertain situation.

Eclecticism: Most Psychologists These Days Use a Multivariate Approach

In discussing the various therapeutic approaches in this chapter, it might seem that a psychotherapist is either a Rogerian therapist or a behavioral therapist or a cognitive therapist. And (truth to tell), some therapists do get enamored with a particular approach (particularly if they were the formulators of that approach). But most psychotherapists are **eclectic**; which is to say, that they get training in as many therapies as they can and use whatever approaches seem to be appropriate for a person's particular situation. That might sound a bit bewildering but a real-life example may clarify what eclecticism means.

Theodora (called Teddy for short) was a vibrant, pretty college student about 20 years of age, with very blue eyes, very blonde hair, and was seldom without a smile on her face. She had often been told she looked like the movie star, Goldie Hawn. Not only was she a bright student, she was also putting herself through school financially. She seemed to have it all

Group therapy

Play therapy

Family therapy

Humor

Art therapy

Since Freud's discovery of the "talking cure", there have been many different kinds of approaches developed for the integration of personality. Only a few of these many approaches are pictured here. This chapter discusses 12 of these approaches. Other approaches are discussed in other chapters.

Bibliotherapy

Hot lines and crisis management

Therapy on-line

Behavior Modification

Journal writing

Medication

Biofeedback

Figure 10.3 Some of the many types of therapies available.

together. She was pretty, popular, and had a cheerful personality that just didn't stop. But what most people didn't know was that Teddy had a severe phobia, a phobia that she had managed to keep hidden from others, and which sometimes even triggered an attack of asthma. She was scared to get into closed and crowded spaces, such as an airplane, or when she did not feel in control, such as riding in a car driven by others. She had to drive the car herself. Of course, this phobia limited her existence in many crucial ways. One of the most serious of these limitations was how it sometimes prevented her participation in many family celebrations.

Her immediate family lived in Orlando but the rest of her large Polish family still lived in Toronto, Canada. If one of those innumerable family events (engagements, marriages, christenings, or funerals) was going to take place up there, Teddy's family would take a plane and fly to Toronto, everyone except Teddy. If she wanted to go there, she had to drive herself in her car. So, many times, she had to miss out on these family celebrations. It limited her in other ways as well, such as being unable to sit in a movie theater or go for a "happy hour" with her friends in places where she could not see outside. We list next the eclectic combination of therapeutic approaches used for Teddy's claustrophobia.

Session 1: Intake and a little Rogerian therapy. The therapist could have used Wolpe's deconditioning therapy immediately but this therapist preferred getting to know Teddy on a personal basis and learning something about Teddy's life. What was revealed in this meeting was that Teddy was the oldest of three children, and was called upon by the parents to arbitrate in family quarrels. After her family uproars, she would be deluged with frantic telephone calls from one or more family members, after which she sometimes experienced asthma attacks. The therapist and Teddy soon agreed that she was being smothered psychologically by being pulled into the family arguments that had nothing to do with her. The feeling of being smothered was being expressed physically as asthma.

Session 2: Assertiveness training. Teddy wanted to tell her family to leave her out of their conflicts but she didn't want to hurt their feelings. So the therapist introduced Teddy to assertiveness training. After only one session of assertiveness training, Teddy was able to tell the various family members, in a nice but firm manner, that she did not want to mediate their quarrels any more. Another part of this assertiveness training was to tell her friends about her phobia. She learned how to say something as follows: *I sometimes get claustrophobia in movie theaters. So I need to sit at the end of a row of seats. Then if I get an asthma attack, I can get out quickly. If that's OK with you, I'd love to go.* What she discovered, to her surprise, was not only that they accepted her on that level, they admired her for being able to tell them. It came as a huge relief that she didn't have to hide her claustrophobia from other people. They even asked her to let them know how they could help.

Session 3: Hypnotherapy. When the therapist asked Teddy about how the phobia began, Teddy was unable to tell her. In order to find out about the etiology of the phobia, the therapist utilized hypnotherapy, and asked Teddy to go back to the earliest onset of the phobia that she could remember. Teddy was also told to bring back any important information that would help her understand her fear. The hypnotherapy session revealed that the onset of the phobia occurred in a Toronto hotel when she was ten years of age. Her family had flown to Toronto to attend a family wedding that was being held on the penthouse roof. She had been riding up and down in the elevator with her brother Joel (who was a year younger than herself) when Joel played a practical joke on her. He used one of the elevator buttons to stop the elevator between floors. Then he turned around and told her the elevator was stuck. Believing him, she flew into such a panic that he quickly started the elevator again. But the event that truly upset her was what happened when she ran to tell her mother what Joel had done. Her mother dismissed it as nothing to be upset about. As Teddy recounted this event after the session, she realized that, *at that moment*—at the tender age of ten—she had decided that she could never depend on her mother (or anybody else in the family, for that matter) to help her when she was in distress. With that insight, she understood her need to be always in control as, for example, always being in the driver's seat.

Sessions 4 and 5: Wolpian deconditioning therapy. On the fourth session, the therapist conducted Teddy through the first dozen of her listed hierarchy of anxieties (see Table 10.4). On the fifth session, Teddy was able to sustain all 12 of her anxiety-producing stimuli with calm at the same time. But now the deconditioning needed to be tested with a reality check.

Session 6: Some reality testing. The first reality test came when the therapist and Teddy went to a shopping mall where there was a glass elevator she could see out of. The therapist acted first as role model but, very quickly, Teddy was going in and out of the elevator and, as long as she herself could open and close the elevator doors, she remained calm. The next step was to take her to the university elevator that had no glass door to see out of. Teddy made the passage easily to riding up and down the three flights several times.

Sessions 7 and 8: Boarding a plane and taking off. The next step was for Teddy to try being in an actual plane. With the help of the airline, a program was worked out whereby Teddy and the therapist would board a DC-10. When they got on, they discovered half a dozen airline workers were on board and already seated. They greeted Teddy and invited her to inspect the cockpit with them, which she did and which she enjoyed. Then she sat down by one of the windows. But she wasn't ready for a flight that day. Instead, the therapist and Teddy returned another day. Teddy told them she thought she was ready to go up. The airline steward allowed her to close the cabin door herself, and to sit whenever she felt ready. Giving her control of the departure, the pilots and crew waited for her signal that she was ready to go up. When she gave the signal, the plane took off. It was a successful flight.

Postscript. By this time, it was nearing the Christmas holidays, and during this particular Christmas season, Teddy was able to fly to Toronto for a wedding along with the rest of her family. She has been flying ever since and she is doing just fine. The entire process took eight sessions. A strict Wolpian therapist might have taken just two days, but this eclectic therapist believes that with more information into her past and present relationships, Teddy gained much more understanding of her family and herself, such as when they try to entangle her in their family uproars.

Important Terms and Concepts to Remember

• anxiety-provoking	• empathy	• online	• shaping
• behavior	• gestalt	• peer	• symptoms
• biofeedback	• hierarchy of fears	• perpetrator	• TA
• catharsize	• inoculation	• psychotherapy	• therapy
• center-of-growth	• insight	• psychoanalysis	• unconditional
• client-centered	• irrational	• reinforcement	• unconscious
• eclectic	• locus-of-control	• role model	
• ego states	• nonreinforcement	• self-talk	

Make Your Own Chapter Summary by Filling in the Blanks

Use the "Important Terms and Concepts to Know" to fill in the blanks.

General background. _____ means healing and _____ means healing of the mind. Psychotherapy has a long history all the way back to ancient times, but it was Freud who started our modern understanding of it with his technique of _____. Today, we categorize the therapies in three groups: _____, behavioral, and cognitive.

Insight therapies. Freud's psychotherapeutic aim was to bring _____ conflicts into consciousness and to _____ them. In contrast to psychoanalysis,

Carl Rogers's _____ therapy is a nonmedical approach. Rogers's approach emphasized _____ positive regard. Rogers believed that the task of the therapist is to reconnect the client with his/her _____, which guides and directs our behavior. Rogers distinguished sympathy from _____, which does not judge the person or feel sorry for him or her. Frederick Perls's _____ therapy seeks to resolve unfinished situations. Transactional analysis identifies three _____: child, parent, adult. The aim of _____ is to learn to use the ego states appropriately. The fastest growing therapy today involves the many _____-support groups available for both the victim and the _____.

Behavior therapies. The assumption underlying the behavior therapies is that insight is not necessary; simply change the behavior and eliminate the _____. Skinner's behavior modification procedure involves _____ of the undesirable behavior and _____ of the desirable behavior. Skinner's _____ of behavior involves a series of small, successive, successful steps. Wolpe's systematic desensitization involves a _____ which introduces _____ stimuli under conditions of deep relaxation. _____ training involves teaching the client to monitor his/her bodily functioning through auditory or visual signals. One of the chief advantages of this training is that it changes the _____ from external to internal.

Cognitive therapies. Cognitive therapies seek to combine the insight and _____ therapies. Albert Ellis wants us to get rid of the _____ beliefs that are driving us crazy. Aaron Beck's therapy enables the client to exchange of negative _____ with more positive statements. Albert Bandura's social learning theory involves having the client observe a _____.

Other therapies. Today there are many kinds of therapeutic approaches including crisis management, family therapy, play therapy, writing therapy, stress _____ (which seeks to prevent rather than remediate), and _____ therapy on the Internet. Most therapists do not adhere to any one type of therapeutic approach but use an _____ approach.

11

Psychological Disorders
Trying to Function in Dysfunctional Ways

BOX 11.1 SCENARIO
Shannon Consults Her Psychology Professor

Dr. Weitzman is waiting quietly for the young person in his office to gather the courage to speak.

Shannon: I'm sorry it's taking me so long to talk. I asked for an appointment, and here I sit. When I do this at home, my mother says, "Cat got your tongue?"

Professor Weitzman: Take your time. It must be difficult to talk about it.

Shannon: But I know you're a busy man. OK, here goes. How do you know if someone is just moody or is really crazy or not? I mean really insane.

Professor Weitzman: Terms like "crazy" and "insane" are only used by the legal system. They don't have much meaning for mental health professionals. We prefer other terms, such as disorder or dysfunctional. And the answer to your question is that it isn't always easy to know whether someone has a serious emotional disorder or whether it's a temporary and normal reaction to something that is happening in his or her life.

Shannon: I'm not sure I know what you mean by "normal" reaction.

Professor Weitzman: Let's suppose a person has just suffered the loss of a child after a long and terrible illness, and suppose that the cost of the battle to save the child's life has resulted in an enormous number of bills not covered by health insurance, so that the family is staggering under increasing debt and on top of all that, the man of the family loses his job . . . wouldn't it be normal for him or his wife to suffer a king-size depression? We can all be dysfunctional at times.

Shannon: Sure.

Professor Weitzman: In fact I would be much more concerned if he didn't experience a hefty depression.

Shannon: But I'm not talking about getting depressed once in a while. I know how that is. I used to get depressed sometimes when I had to go to school. I'm talking about really . . . I don't know how to put it—doing really strange things.

Professor Weitzman: Even then we would have to have a lot more information than a description of some of the person's behaviors. Let me give you an example. Delusions and hallucinations are symptoms of schizophrenia. Yet, all those same symptoms can be observed in a person with a very high fever or who has a brain tumor or who is suffering from a bad drug "trip." Before we can say that a person has a serious emotional disorder, we need to know many things; such as the person's health history; the circumstances of the person's life from infancy; and the person's present situation. Whom are you concerned about?

Shannon: My mother.

Professor Weitzman: Why don't you tell me about your mother? I'm not a psychotherapist but if I know a little more about what you are concerned about, I would be in a better position to make some suggestions.

Shannon: Until your lecture on bipolar mood disorder, I never thought anything about my mother's behavior. We just always considered her as being "moody" or "high-strung." At least, that's what my dad always says when she has one of her "spells." Sometimes she will cry for hours. It's even worse when she doesn't cry, just sits on the bed all hunched up and saying it would be better for everybody if she would just die. We all tell her that it isn't true. And it isn't true! When she's feeling good, she's just the cheeriest person and takes us all out shopping and gets us clothes. And she'll sew new curtains for the house and make dresses for Gram (that's my grandmother) and me. Wow! We can hardly keep up with her. Dad says she's got more energy than a barrel full of monkeys. Then Dad thinks everything is OK again.

Professor Weitzman: And isn't it?

Shannon: He says he just has to watch how she spends money. But that isn't the half of it. When she gets into one of these happy moods, she does strange things, like writing checks that bounce. And sometimes she comes home with things I'm sure she didn't pay for. Once they caught her shoplifting.

BOX **11.1** SCENARIO (continued)
Shannon Consults Her Psychology Professor

Later, she told me she doesn't even remember doing it. Then suddenly she turns quiet . . . just like that! For days. And for no reason that we can see. Has she got a bipolar mood disorder?

Professor Weitzman: How long have these mood cycles been going on? One of the determining factors is the length of time the behavior manifests.

Shannon: It's hard to say. I've mostly lived with my grandmother. But I think a long time. Ever since I can remember and realized that other people weren't like that.

Professor Weitzman: From how you have described her, it might just be the case. You might suggest to your father that he take your mother for a psychiatric

examination. If it is confirmed that she has a serious mood disorder, she could benefit by some medication. In the last 20 years, mental disorders have been much alleviated by drug therapy.

Shannon: (*sighing*) We're just country folk, and my parents are real suspicious about "shrinks." My dad and I are close though. I guess I could at least talk to him anyway when I go home. But I'll try.

Professor Weitzman: One thing you need to keep in mind, Shannon. Don't force her to go. It's best when the person goes for an evaluation under her own free will and motivation. You might convince her to go if you emphasize how much better she will feel with medication.

WHY STUDY DYSFUNCTIONAL (ABNORMAL) PSYCHOLOGY?

Sometime, in each of our lives, we will share the same concerns as Shannon did in the opening scenario. When is a problem serious enough to warrant professional help? In fact, the readers may have already asked themselves such questions as:

Is my spouse just a social drinker or does she have a serious alcohol problem?
Is my daughter losing weight because she's on a diet or does she have bulimia?
Has my son become addicted to drugs? Should I hospitalize him?
My brother has been so depressed lately; is he "at risk" for suicide?
One of my employees is acting strangely lately; is he having a "nervous breakdown"?
My son's teacher says he is seriously hyperactive. How can I tell?
I get so anxious I feel like I'm going to burst out of my skin. Am I losing my mind?

A few years ago, a survey resulted in an astonishing conclusion by the investigators. Almost half (48 percent) of the American population could qualify for a mental disorder diagnosis at sometime in their lives, and 27 percent could qualify for two or more different mental disorders at some time in their lives (Kessler et al, 1994). That doesn't mean that all of these people have ever spent time on a mental ward, not at all. Many people who have suffered serious problems may have gone to work every day throughout their emotional crisis and may never have seen a mental health professional. But it does mean that occasional dysfunctionality is part of "the human condition." And if that isn't enough—our worries today are not just personal and social but global—we wonder each day if some small tribal warfare halfway across the world will be the beginning of World War III (see Table 11.1). Small wonder that so many of us will experience some kind of emotional problem during the course of our lives.

So when are symptoms and behaviors serious enough to warrant consulting a mental health professional? For many reasons, it is not at all an easy task to diagnose a "mental disorder." First, unlike most physical diseases, a "psychological illness" cannot be determined by

Table 11.1   Sources of Our Personal, Social, and Global Anxieties

Personal Anxieties
Pressures to be successful and to climb the social and vocational "success" ladder.
The rising cost of living, and difficulties understanding taxes and paying bills on time, including credit cards.
The obligation to raise happy children and to prepare them for responsible citizenship.
The fear that social security and retirement funds will collapse after a lifetime of working to fund them.
The need to stay healthy, slim, young, and beautiful, as portrayed by advertising.
Fear we cannot keep up our present frantic pace of life.

Social and Vocational Activities
Disillusionment with the American Dream of financial success and happiness for all.
The plight of our cities with their increasing problems of ghettos, riots, and crime.
The need to be well informed and to stay abreast of social and financial developments.
Our sense of "rootlessness," as 20 percent of our population move away from home every year.
The need to support equal civil rights for all and to support multicultural diversity.
Our hopes to help the poor, the homeless, the aged, and the infirm.
Fear of being laid off as the result of downsizing.
Pressures to keep abreast of computer technology.

Global Anxieties
Recognition of our "rape of the planet" and the fear that we have poisoned it irreversibly.
A desperate search to find new energy sources as the world's fossil fuels run out.
The shadow of World War III always hovering on the horizon as the result of tribal disputes and wars.
Since 9/11, the ever-constant threat of terrorism.

a single test (such as a blood test or an X-ray). It is more a matter of **differential diagnosis** (a process of eliminating what the condition is *not*). Many factors must be taken into consideration; for example:

> *Are the symptoms or behavior seriously out of the statistical "average range"?*
> *How long have the symptoms or behavior existed?*
> *What is going on presently that might account for such a dysfunctional reaction?*
> *Is the person reporting feeling "out of control"?*
> *Are the symptoms so bizarre that they are causing discomfort in the onlookers?*
>
> *Is the person unable to function in the everyday world of work and interpersonal events?*
> *Does the person's behavior suggest he/she might do harm to self or others?*
> *Could the dysfunctional behavior be caused by a physical problem—such as a severe reaction to a drug or a brain tumor or the leftover ravages of drug addiction?*

Difficulties of Defining and Diagnosing "Mental Disorders"

Depending on how we define "mental disorder," estimates of the number of Americans who could be labeled as having had a "mental disorder" some time in their lives varies considerably, anywhere from 25 to 50 percent (Robins & Reiger, 1991). Mark the beginning of the previous sentence: *depending on how we define "mental disorder."* What it depends on is what we are willing to classify as "mental disorders." For example, is a child who hates his teacher and who consequently acts up in class really having a mental disorder now classified as Oppositional Defiant Disorder? Another problem is that these estimates are based on **self-report** surveys, and not through psychological or psychiatric evaluations, which is a necessary factor in diagnosis. In a self-report survey, some people may exaggerate their concerns and anxieties just because they are trying to be conscientious or because they misinterpret the items on the self-report. Nevertheless, while we need to be somewhat cautious about accepting these statistics, they do help us understand that mental disorders are far more common than most people realize. Generally speaking, however, the present definition of **abnormal behavior** includes the three factors listed below. It should be noted, however, that not all three of these factors are necessary. Just one of these factors is sufficient for a diagnosis of mental disorder.

1. The behavior is significantly and negatively deviant from the general population;
2. The behavior is so maladaptive as to render the person incapable of functioning in everyday society;
3. The behavior is distressful to the person or to others in the person's vicinity.

One of the problems of diagnosing a mental disorder is that some symptoms are **comorbid** (appearing along with) other mental disorders or even physical problems. It means that a person may be diagnosed as having a "mental disorder," when they really have another problem. Two examples will clarify.

The first example has to do with one of the tragedies of the musical world. George Gershwin was the genius who composed *Rhapsody in Blue, An American in Paris*, and *Porgy and Bess*. A few of his remarkable individual compositions include *Fascinatin' Rhythm, Someone to Watch Over Me*, and *I Got Rhythm*. Gershwin was suffering from migraine headaches and bouts of depression, and for two years was being treated by a psychoanalyst in the Hollywood area for what we now would call Major Depression Disorder, when he unexpectedly died. A postmortem examination revealed that Gershwin had a brain tumor that was undoubtedly the cause of his migraine headaches and perhaps even his depressions. He was only 38 years of age when he died. Had he been diagnosed correctly, he might have lived to write more remarkable compositions. Gratefully, that probably would never happen today as psychiatrists would get the patient checked out medically first via every possible medical exam. But misdiagnoses of other kinds are still happening.

Our second example is of a young lad of our own knowledge, 15 years of age, who was just refusing to go to school. No matter what his mother did to urge him to go to school, he simply stayed at home reading or watching television. The high school he was supposed to attend finally sent him for a psychological evaluation. When asked why he refused to go to school, the young lad said *he just didn't feel like it*. He was subsequently diagnosed as **Oppositional Defiant Disorder**. The school district was just about to take the young man into court, along with his mother, when he was discovered unconscious in his bed. He was rushed to the hospital where he remained unconscious until his blood and urine tests came back: He was in a diabetic coma. Nobody had suspected anything physical was wrong with him. In retrospect, we realize that when the young lad had said, "I just don't feel like it," he really meant it. It didn't occur to anyone (not even to him) that he was just feeling too tired and too weak to go to class.

Another problem is that there are sociocultural influences associated with the appearance of certain symptoms and disorders. Individuals who come from low-income, minority neighborhoods have the highest rates of mental disorders. When this population is studied *[handwritten margin notes: "ethnic min. are more susceptible / but due to race / distress of poverty / near poverty circums. / defense system breaks down (abnormal) / talks abt DSM-IV-TR (APA) also called psychiatric Bible"]*

more precisely, however, the findings reveal it is not so much the ethnic minority that is the major predictor, but the person's poverty or near-poverty existence (Nolan-Hoeksema, 2001). When the living conditions of poverty create overwhelming distress, the person's defense system breaks down in behaviors that are defined as "abnormal." Gender also contributes to mental illness. It is now well-known that women tend to *internalize* their distress; i.e., turn their bad feelings in on themselves. As a consequence, they are more apt to be diagnosed with anxiety disorders and depression. Men, on the other hand, *externalize* their bad feelings, by verbal and physical aggression, by blaming others, and by anesthetizing their anxiety through substance abuse. As you read the various disorders, note the other factors concerning the etiology, the prevalence, and appropriate treatments. **Etiology** refers to beginning or cause. **Prevalence** has to do with the estimated percentage in any given people. **Treatments** include both medications and psychotherapies.

The DSM-IV-TR Multiaxial Evaluation. Popularly known as the **DSM**, the **Diagnostic and Statistical Manual of Mental Disorders** is to the mental health professions what the **Physicians Desk Reference (PDR)** is to the medical professions. The present edition, published by the American Psychiatric Association (APA) in 2000, is called the *DSM-IV-TR*, which means that the *DSM* is now in a text revision of the fourth edition. The *DSM* is often referred to as the "Psychiatric Bible." To respond to criticisms leveled at previous editions of the *DSM*, the American Psychiatric Association introduced a multiaxial evaluation. The **multiaxial evaluation** includes some valuable information about the person's physical health, social and environmental support, occupation and financial resources, problems related to the criminal activities and the legal system, etc. Why is this information so valuable? Simply this: A person, who has a good family support system, who has a secure financial base, and has been a self-supporting citizen, is generally more open to therapeutic treatment, has less need for hospitalization, and has a better chance for recovery than, for instance, a person with a life-long problem with substance abuse and who has been involved in criminal activities. Thus the multiaxial evaluation aids the diagnostician with information as to the severity of the disorder, the probable prognosis, and the treatments that might be best for any particular person. The present *DSM-IV-TR*, also states very clearly that the classifications of mental disorders does not mean to classify people. It is only classifying the disorders that people have, in the same way that the *Physicians Desk Reference* (*PDR*) classifies physical illnesses. The text states (p. xxxi),

> *For this reason, the text of DSM-IV-TR avoids the use of such expressions as "a schizophrenic" or "an alcoholic" and instead uses the more accurate, but admittedly more cumbersome, "an individual with Schizophrenia" or "an individual with Alcohol Dependence."*

As well, the *DSM-IV-R* has also given considerably more attention to statistics on the variables of gender, age of onset, general ethnic background and culture, prevalence, course of the disorder, and familial patterns.

The *DSM* has always engendered considerable debate and controversy and probably always will (see Box 11.2). That is as it should be, for scientific knowledge advances through debate and criticism. In a few years, there will be another edition of the *DSM*. Nevertheless, the *DSM* has become the reference for classifying and diagnosing mental disorders around the world. It has, at last, become the *common language* of the many mental health professions in our country and in other countries as well.

BOX 11.2 EVALUATING THE DSM

Nothing Is Perfect—Certainly Not the *DSM* or Our Understanding of What Is Normal or Abnormal

Professor Weitzman: It should be understood that this chapter only covered a few of the most common mental disorders of the over 300 disorders described in the *DSM-IV*.

Li Ho: What about all those other disorders we do not cover?

Professor Weitzman: We'll cover the most statistically frequent. And remember that many of the disorders listed in the *DSM* are not disorders in themselves. Many are the side effects of physical disease. Let's take substance-related disorders as an example. The side effects of substance abuse can produce symptoms much like the mental disorders we have been studying.

Dan: You mean like alcoholism? When I was drinking heavily, the people who took me to the emergency room said they thought I was crazy. I was hallucinating like mad. I wasn't seeing pink elephants, but I kept telling people to get the insects off me.

Professor Weitzman: Alcohol is a good example. Incidentally, it may be the most serious legal drug. It is implicated in 70 percent of fatal auto accidents, 65 percent of murders, 88 percent of knifings, 65 percent of spouse batteries, 55 percent of violent child abuses, and 60 percent of burglaries, according to a 1990 report by the National Commission on the Causes and Prevention of Violence. And, yes, alcoholism can result in hallucinations, paranoia, and many other mental symptoms. But there are many substances that can have the same toxic effects, such as nicotine, marijuana and cocaine, and even the medications your physician prescribes.

Martha: Medications!

Professor Weitzman: Why is that so surprising? You all must know somebody who has had an allergic reaction to an antibiotic.

Shannon: Oh, I know what you mean! My brothers and I all came down with flu and the doctor prescribed an antibiotic for all of us. The boys did fine but I had a terrible reaction to it. The doctor had to change my prescription.

Jill Smith: Shannon, I hope you carry a card with that notation. Should you ever be taken to the hospital unconscious, the emergency medical team would need to know that!

Shannon: You mean like diabetic people carry? (*Jill nods.*) I haven't but I will from now on.

Jill Smith: Some people even have a negative reaction to caffeine which means they have to limit their coffee, tea, and cola. Cheese and chocolate and coffee can bring on migraines in some people. And those of you who take over-the-counter diet pills had better check the list of ingredients. Many of these pills contain amphetamines—"uppers." And you can have allergic reactions to one or more of them.

Martha: Gosh! I'm always trying one new diet pill after another.

Professor Weitzman: Back to Li's original question which had to do with all those other "mental disorders." Don't forget some were discussed in earlier chapters. In Chapter 6, for example, we discussed anorexia nervosa and bulimia. AD/HD in children was discussed in Chapter 5, and autism was discussed in Chapter 4.

Natasha: (*raising her hand timidly*) Professor, this chapter frightened me a little.

Professor Weitzman: How is that?

Natasha: My parents have often told me in the country I came from . . . that there was a time . . . people were often . . . put into mental hospitals . . . if they spoke out against the political leaders. . . . Does that ever happen here?

Professor Weitzman: You are talking about what they called "dissident thinking." We have to be on guard against that always. Critics of *DSM* have pointed out that labeling a person as having a "mental disorder" may actually be the same thing in the end. And that can lead to other abuses. Living in a democracy means that all of us participate by being "watch dogs" of societal institutions.

Martha: I heard that a long time ago if a woman was disagreeable to her husband he could have her put away in a mental institution. Is this true?

Professor Weitzman: It is true, even in our democracy, these types of atrocities occurred at a time when women did not have rights equal to men. Furthermore, individuals with a physical handicap, such as blindness, deafness, or muteness were also sometimes institutionalized under the category of mental retardation. We've come a long way in our classifications, therapies, and theories about what is abnormal and what is normal. But we still need to alleviate the stigma associated with mental illness. Another criticism is that diagnosis and treatment are being influenced by insurance companies.

The *DSM-IV-TR* lists more than 300 "mental disorders." It is an encyclopedia. Obviously, you cannot be expected to become acquainted with all these disorders in the course of one short term. Indeed, mental health professionals out in the field will be studying and working with the *DSM-IV-TR* for several years before they feel proficient in it—and by that time there may be a *DSM-V*. But the reader needs to become familiar with the most frequent of these disorders, familiar enough at least to recognize that you or someone you know may need help. We are fortunate today to have derived some effective treatments for many of these disorders. Unlike previous eras, an afflicted person can be helped to live again in society and to find a compatible work.

A Word of Warning: The "Intern's Disease." Medical students sometimes come down with what is called the "intern's disease"; namely, the tendency to believe they have contracted whatever disease is being presently studied. A headache may arouse a concern of having a tumor of the brain. A blister on the foot may arouse the thought: *Ohmygod! I've got leprosy!* Occasionally, interns are known to slip down to the lab in the wee hours of the morning to take a look at their own blood sample under a microscope. This tendency to become somewhat **hypochondriacal** (imagining we have symptoms and diseases we don't have) is also noticeable in beginning psychology students. It is quite a normal reaction when studying abnormal psychology. What the readers need to keep in mind always is that we all have experienced symptoms associated with the various emotional disorders. Experiencing a few of the symptoms does not mean that the reader actually has the disorder being discussed. What makes for a serious disorder is whether the symptoms have existed for a long time, are intense in quality, and are interfering in the individual's personal, educational, or vocational arenas. If the reader believes that these criteria are being fulfilled, the next step is to consult a mental health professional. But before you rush off, remember that all of us experience all kinds of symptoms from time to time, but they are generally transient in nature.

The Anxiety Disorders

We begin with the anxiety disorders because they are the most statistically frequent disorders. Estimates vary, but, in any given year, between 15 and 30 percent of the adult population is afflicted with a severe anxiety disorder. All of us probably have experienced depression of some sort at some time in our lives. While there is some genetic component to the anxiety disorders, as it seems "to run in families," we also know environmental stress plays a major part in its etiology. We know because the **World Health Organization (WHO)** reports that the frequency of anxiety disorders (as a group) has been increasing steadily in the past 50 years (World Health Organization, 1997). Anxiety disorders are the most expensive in terms of economic cost to the nation. Fortunately, they are also the most treatable.

Generalized Anxiety Disorder. People who have this disorder have such pervasive fear that it is described as **free-floating anxiety**. These people complain that they "worry about everything under the sun," that they are tired and excessively fatigued all the time, and that they can't seem to do their work because they can't concentrate. They may suffer from insomnia night after night, and this lack of sleep intensifies their problem. They may be afraid they are "losing their minds" or "going crazy." Friends and relatives will accuse the person of "wanting to worry," of "looking for things to worry about," of "being happy only when they are worried about something." Now most of us have probably experienced these symptoms

etiology = the study of why things occur
reasons behind the way that things act
prevalence = measurement of all individuals affected by the disease within a particular amt of time

from time to time in our lives, particularly if we are doing too much or if we are having trouble coping with all our responsibilities. That doesn't mean we have an anxiety disorder. In order to qualify as an **anxiety disorder**, the symptoms must be ongoing and of at least six months in duration.

STRESS being overwhelmed

Etiology, Prevalence, and Therapies. Life in society has become stressful. We are more fearful now about terrorism, about child abuse and kidnapping, about more nuclear accidents, and about safety in our schools. Older workers are awed by the new technologies. Educationally disadvantaged people are feeling overwhelmed by the computer age. Fortunately, advances in medication have been extremely helpful, particularly the tranquilizers and mood elevators. Estimated prevalence is about 4 percent of the population, much more frequent in women than men.

if put into situation individual will panic to an extreme - exclaustophobia - agoraphobia (prisoners)

Specific Phobic Disorders. Phobia comes from the Greek word for "fear." A phobia is a persistent, exaggerated, and unreasonable fear about a person, an object, or a situation (see Table 11.2). We all have minor fears of one sort or another. Most of us have a fear of snakes, and a lot of us feel fearful of climbing ladders, some of us are a little afraid of heights. So the question becomes: *When does a fear become a phobia?* An example should clarify. People with **claustrophobia** are so fearful that they will manifest a panic reaction, dizziness, palpitations, diarrhea, or nausea. Then the phobia will generalize and they will avoid any place where they cannot escape. An extreme case of **agoraphobia** (fear of open spaces) is the recluse who does not dare venture out of the house, but remains forever inside with locks on the door. They are prisoners of their own homes by their own choosing.

PHOBIAS - have a lot to do w/ the tendency to go in accordance w/ phases of life i.e. children → young adults → heights → snakes older → broken bones etc.

Etiology, Prevalence, and Treatment. The etiology is often age-related. Small children often develop school phobia, which is generally remedied with understanding and gentle handling by parents and teachers. Young adults are often quite phobic about heights. The fear of snakes already mentioned is (interestingly enough) most frequent around the age of 20 years. As we get older, we may become phobic about being in crowds or in subways where there is a danger of being mugged. Older people are afraid of falling and breaking a bone or hip. They can also be phobic about an incapacitating illness and death. All of these phobias, by the way, may even be "the norm" for their age groups (Agras, 1985). Because they manifest so differently and are age-related, it is difficult to get precise statistics on the frequency of phobias. We do know that phobias tend to be two times as frequent in women than men. Fortunately, the behavior therapies and cognitive therapies have proved quite successful in dealing with specific phobias such as those listed in Table 11.2, particularly Wolpe's desensitization training and Bandura's guided mastery technique.

Table 11.2 Some Specific Phobias

Acrophobia	Heights	Mysophobia	Dirt, Germs
Agoraphobia	Open spaces	Nyctophobia	The Dark
Astaphobia	Thunderstorms	Ophidiophobia	Snakes
Claustrophobia	Closed Spaces	Pyrophobia	Fire
Hematophobia	Blood	Zoophobia	Animals
Melanophobia	Bees		

Panic Disorder. One day a friend of your keels over, his face grimacing with pain. As you go to help your friend, he describes pain in his chest and down his left arm plus all the classic symptoms of a heart attack. You rush him to the hospital and (lo! and behold!) his EKG (electrocardiogram) reveals normal heart rhythms. What your friend has suffered is not a heart attack but a panic disorder. Panic attack is characterized by such overwhelming anxiety it can produce all the symptoms of a major disease, including heart disease, an acute diabetic episode, or even a severe occurrence of asthma. The person will describe themselves as "being out of control," of wanting to "scream for help," or sure they are "about to die with nobody around for help." One of the side effects of panic attack is the tendency for the victim to avoid any situation that might trigger another episode—leading eventually to the *comorbid* (two or more diseases or disorders) condition of panic disorder with agoraphobia (described previously).

Etiology, Prevalence, and Treatment. Many explanations have been offered to account for why certain people are "at risk" for panic attacks. The present estimate of the frequency of panic disorder is between one and three percent of the general population. It affects twice as many women as men and typically begins in the late teens or twenties. It also appears to have a genetic component, but while it may have biological underpinnings, it is often triggered by traumatic stress—death of a loved one, divorce, or by a serious physical illness. Sometimes, however, it seems to appear for "no reason at all." A physical explanation has to do with an imbalance of a brain **neurotransmitter**, norepinephrine (Papp & Gorman, 1993). A psychological explanation has to do with the person's over-sensitivity to and misinterpretation of bodily sensations and pain. For example, suppose a person's anxiety is manifesting as "butterflies in the stomach" or even heart-pounding. Most of us will recognize these symptoms as anxiety. The person with panic disorder, however, is convinced that he has ulcers or is undergoing a heart attack. They have become so anxiety-sensitive that any insignificant event may trigger exactly what they are trying to stave off.

Fortunately, **antidepressant drugs** and **tranquilizers** (particularly the benzodiazepines) seem to be highly effective for panic disorder, particularly those that restore neurotransmitter balance. But many victims are also helped immensely just by being informed of the diagnosis. Most people seeking help for their symptoms resist the idea that some or much of their distress is "psychological." Their concept of the psychological aspect of a disease is that it indicates some weakness in their character. Not so with most panic attack victims. It's usually a big relief for panic sufferers to find out they aren't gravely ill and that the problem is treatable. Some are downright happy about it. The good news is that alleviation of symptoms is about 80 percent at the present and getting higher all the time. The bad news is that 50 percent of the patients experience a recurrence. What is also needed then is the inclusion of cognitive/behavioral therapy in the treatment plan. The cognitive aspect involves helping the patient identify the anxiety-provoking symptoms, and then helping the patients reprogram their cognitive schemas so they know a serious heart attack (or whatever) is not coming on. They then realize they are in control and they can stop their panic attack. The behavioral component is to teach the person how to handle the anxiety-provoking symptoms: relaxation and breathing techniques, desensitization training, stress inoculation, the use of cue words such as "stop" or "cancel," and other coping strategies (Meichanbaum, 1993).

Acute Stress Disorders, Including Posttraumatic Stress Disorder (PTSD). Attention was first drawn to acute stress disorders when social scientists were doing their best to help Holocaust survivors get reestablished physically and psychologically. But sometimes

Figure 11.1 PTSD. PTSD is the latest in a series of terms for the symptoms that occur as an aftermath of war and other trauma. In World War II, it was called "battle fatigue" and in World War I it was called "shell shock." We know now that it also occurs in victims of abuse, earthquake, devastating floods, tornadoes, and hurricanes.

nothing seemed to help the survivors recover from the nightmare of the concentration camps. In one comprehensive study, it was discovered that 97 percent of the Holocaust survivors were still suffering from severe anxiety symptoms many years after their release. Even worse, the suicide rate was considerably higher than in the general population even though they were now "in safe hands." The Holocaust survivors worried their family might be in danger if they were out of the house. Many had nightmares recalling their captivity and dreamed that their children (who had been born after liberation) were imprisoned with them. Eighty percent of the survivors felt guilty that they had survived when so many of their relatives and friends had died (Kuch & Cox, 1992). So acute are the symptoms that mark the Holocaust survivors, that the anxiety and despair is known now to affect not only the children but the grandchildren of the survivors (Fox, 1996).

Then the mental health professions began to focus their attention on a similar **syndrome** (symptoms that occur together) appearing in returning Vietnam veterans. Americans are very familiar now with **posttraumatic stress disorder** (**PTSD**), but it took some time to be defined. The medical services had been used to "shell shock" and "battle trauma" that occurred during or right after a battle (see Figure 11.1). But the Vietnam veterans were showing symptoms long after coming back stateside. After more than 25 percent of the returning Vietnam veterans began to have serious and long-lasting symptoms of anxiety similar to the Holocaust victims, PTSD became a new mental health disorder. Appetite or sleep may be disturbed and frightening dreams may be frequent, and these symptoms may last anywhere from six months to, unfortunately, a lifetime (APA, 1994). In Hawaii, for example, the Veterans Administration has reported a surprising number of PTSD veterans are survivors of the Japanese surprise attack on Pearl Harbor. Also needing treatment are many of the Nisei 442nd Regiment, the Japanese-American soldiers who became the most decorated combat unit in American history. They returned from war to find their homes gone, the family business dismantled, and sometimes their family members interned in prison camps. While these World War II veterans claim they never had these symptoms, it is likely they were simply overlooked as just "being grumpy" or "needing to be alone for a while." Today, we might use other terms for their emotional states, such as having *high anxiety* or *social isolation*. But since they kept working and seemed mostly all right, nobody took notice.

Etiology, Prevalence, and Treatment. We are becoming aware also that PTSD has occurred as the result of many other situations. Women who have been raped may develop an aversion to sex and display other symptoms such as pounding heart, shortness of breath, or dizziness. High risk for PTSD are parents who have suffered the loss of a child through illness or accident. Not only are they bereaved by the loss, they may also be suffering guilt that they could somehow have prevented the child's death—even when it was clearly no fault of theirs. Posttraumatic stress disorders may also follow natural or accidental disasters such as earthquakes, floods, tornadoes, fires, airplane crashes, and serious car accidents. There seem to be some factors that make for "high risk" for PTSD. Prevalence is high, as much as eight percent of the adult population in the United States. Three factors have been identified in those persons who suffer the most severe anxiety disorders. First, they have had a history of traumatic events, such as divorce and death of parents in childhood, or a history of physical abuse. Second, they do not have a sense of control of their own lives. They tend to feel they have always been at the mercy of a cruel Fate. Third, they do not have a strong social/emotional support system whereby they can share their anxieties or experiences (Kobasa, 1979). But it is also true that many victims of PTSD have been functioning very well at work and are contributing members of their society. What is immediately necessary is the alleviation of the symptoms, which generally means the use of tranquilizers and other medications. Once the anxiety has been somewhat diminished, other treatments are highly recommended, such as behavior modification and cognitive modeling. In addition, all the anxiety disorders are amenable to insight therapies such as counseling or a peer-support group. For example, women who have been brutally raped recover from their trauma much more quickly if they have a strong support system and can share their experiences with receptive listeners (Kushner, Riggs, Foa, & Miller, 1992).

The Mood Disorders

Major Depressive Disorder. Depression has become a household word. Even children in middle school are able to describe themselves as "being depressed." A deep and profound depression or *dysphoric* (unpleasant) mood state is the single most obvious symptom of major depressive disorder. We all have experienced being depressed for a day or so, or even for a week or two (or longer), but to be diagnosed as having a major mood disorder, the depression must be of at least two months duration. As well, the depression must not be related to a physical disease or other mental disorder, although the onset can manifest as "postpartum blues." Another feature associated with this disorder is **catatonia** (extreme lack of energy and highly limited ability to move, even stupor). The person may sit or stand for hours in a rigid posture and cannot be induced to move or change position (see Figure 11.2). In addition to sleeping 12, 14, even 18 hours a day, the person's appetite is reduced and the person may suffer a serious weight loss. (Occasionally, the exact opposite may happen: Appetite may be gigantic and the person will put on excessive weight.) The person also may be hyperactive and not be able to sleep. But most students, who have been asked to describe what their depressions feel like, have given the following kinds of answers.

It's hard to get up in the morning and drag one foot in front of the other to get to school.
I just want to dig a hole in the earth, get into it, and cover it up above me and stay there.
Being depressed is hopelessness. Nothing is ever going to get better ever.
Utter Dejection. Gloom. Despair. I think about death. Death is better than this.

Figure 11.2 Major Mood Disorder. This disorder is twice as frequent in women than in men.

The last statement is not an exaggeration. Up to 15 percent of people suffering from this disorder die by suicide, if not immediately, then later on when another episode occurs. Furthermore, life is perceived as so miserable that a mother may kill her children, as did the lady in Texas who drowned her five children, so that her children may not suffer as she had been suffering.

Etiology, Prevalence, and Treatment. So common is major mood disorder, that it has been called the "common cold" of the mental disorders. While statistics vary, surveys of community samples indicate that perhaps as many as 15 to 37 percent of the people surveyed report having suffered a major mood disorder sometime in their lives, with women having twice the frequency of men. So far, this disorder has not been found to be related to any of the other usual demographic variables, such as *ethnicity, education, income, or marital status.* Onset may begin at any age, even in adolescence but, on the average, the onset occurs in the middle twenties. The disorder has a somewhat moderate relationship to genetics and it can also occur after a severe trauma, such as loss of a spouse.

There are many drugs that can help alleviate the symptoms of depression, some of which are called mood elevators and antidepressants. When the person's depressive state has been lifted, therapeutic treatment is highly advised so that the person can be better able to deal with the environmental events which seem to trigger the patient's depression. It is important that the person get help as soon as possible because the longer the person is depressed, the more it is likely for the depression to reoccur, even more seriously the next time around. Occasionally, a patient will report suddenly feeling better without any medication or psychotherapy, called **spontaneous remission**. What is the reason for spontaneous remission? At this point, it is anybody's guess, although we may have a clue from the following written report by an older student in our class.

> When the family knew I was having a depression, they laid off me for a while. I was always the one everybody came to with their problems. I was always the "strong one." It just got too much for me. And I sank into a depression. Suddenly, no one was bothering me with the problems. I didn't have to answer the telephone. Other people did the jobs they all thought I should do. I stayed in bed and slept and rested. It was such a relief to have a little rest from everybody's demands and some peace in my life, I began to feel better.

In severely depressed people who do not respond to antidepressants, and have either attempted suicide or expressed strong wishes to commit suicide, **electro-convulsive therapy** (**ECT**) (formerly known as shock therapy)—as barbaric as it may seem to some—does lift the depression for some patients for whom no other approach has proven beneficial (Fink, 1992).

Dysthymic (Minor) Mood Disorder. *Dysthymia* has gained recognition as a mood disorder only in the last three decades. The reason for such a long delay is that the symptoms are not as dramatic as they are in major mood depression or schizophrenia. People so afflicted were simply characterized as an underachiever, as lazy, as chronically irritable, or just as always feeling "plain miserable." Because of the nonspecific aspects of the symptoms, statistics are still tentative, perhaps around 5 percent of the population are afflicted. We expect to see an increasing gain in reported cases as the general population becomes more aware of this disorder.

Dysthymic victims, unlike victims of major mood depression, can often continue to go to work each day, support themselves, and appear to be doing a satisfactory job. But their unruffled external appearance is a camouflage for their internal unhappiness and despair. They manage to get through the workday, but at home they may just seem to "fall apart." They may drink or use drugs to cover their misery. Their families sometimes say they "just aren't

BOX **11.3** STUDENTS VERBATIM
The Mood Disorders

a. On Major Mood Disorder: Male Caucasian, (47 years). When my wife died, I thought I couldn't go on living. Everything that mattered to me seemed gone. Sometimes I felt like there was a ton of weight on my chest holding me down. I had trouble breathing. My arms ached. I felt like I couldn't get up on my feet, that they wouldn't hold me. It was hard to go to sleep. It was even harder to wake up to face another dreaded day. Eventually breathing became easier and the terrible weight on my chest got lighter. Then one day it was gone, the whole sad melancholia I had been feeling was gone. I knew it was over and I could live again. Thank God for antidepressants.

b. On Dysthymia (Minor Mood Disorder): Older Professional Woman. I have worked hard all my professional life. I thought I was all right, at least as all right as most people. Then I woke up one day and realized that I had been depressed for ten years. Ten years! I had a feeling of happiness! Actual happiness! When people used to talk about "feeling happy," I really didn't know what they were talking about. I thought I did. But what I assumed was "happiness" were those occasional times when I felt "less bad." At my best, I was living a kind of dull gray existence. I was at my best in my job because I knew how to do my job, but I didn't like social relationships. People expected things I couldn't give them. Then I woke up one morning, and the whole world had become brighter overnight. What caused me to have a ten-year depression, I have no idea. I didn't even know I was having one. I thought

everyone felt like me. It was like a "numbness." In comparison, now I actually wake up most mornings glad to see the sun shining and hear the birds singing.

c. On Bipolar Mood Disorder: Male College Student. My mother was diagnosed with bipolar mood disorder. I don't know which was worse, her bad moods or her good moods. When she was in her bad mood state, she would cry a lot and say that she didn't deserve to live, that nobody loved her, and . . . threaten to commit suicide . . . Then all of a sudden, she would switch for no apparent reason and be full of life and happy, but I can't really say happy exactly . . . it was more like racing, racing, racing, and giggling like she was a little tipsy. One time, she got us redecorating the house and ran up thousands of dollars just to do it. Another time, she said we all needed a vacation. The next thing we knew we were all in the car going out West. It was no use saying that we couldn't leave school, she'd just say we were too conventional. We didn't even have time to pack the things we needed, so when we got to the mountains, it was cold and we had to buy clothes to keep warm . . . Finally, our father couldn't take it anymore and he left, leaving the rest of us with her. I don't think we ever had a real childhood . . . we were always struggling to keep our mother's condition from getting out of hand . . . . When she was in her bad mood state, she would cry and say she was no good and go to church and get very religious. I'm very bitter at my father for having left us with her. That was no kind of childhood for us kids.

there" most of the time—they isolate themselves from family involvement and often ask to just be "let alone." They often describe themselves as "a phony" or "an empty shell." A professional friend of the authors is a good example. She is a speech therapist in a local hospital and is highly regarded by the members of the medical team. She has even been called "a wonder worker." Yet in a conversation about the ability of some people with dysthymia to keep functioning in a limited capacity, she responded that she herself had been such a person—for more than ten years (see Box 11.3b).

Etiology, Prevalence, and Treatment. Worldwide studies indicate that the major and minor mood disorders are on the rise in the technological societies and have been increasing since 1915 (APA, 2000). Are the mood disorders, then, a disease of our pressure-cooker society with its emphasis on personal achievement, "getting ahead," and dog-eat-dog competition? Is the rise of the mood disorders a fallout consequence of having to acquire more and more knowledge and skills to compete in the job market? Surely, the increasingly fierce competition for college grades, the pressure to achieve academic and athletic honors, the increasing academic standards being demanded by all the professions and paraprofessions are intensifying the problems of adolescence and adulthood. We may literally be working our-selves into major and minor depressions (at least in part) in our desire to achieve the American Dream of material wealth and of climbing the "success" ladder.

Bipolar Mood Disorder (Formerly Called Manic-Depressive Psychosis). People afflicted with **bipolar mood disorder** also suffer periods of depressions, but their depressions alternate with periods of *mania*. In the **manic state**, the person experiences a hyperactive and optimistic **euphoria**, which is to say that they feel elated and energetic. They become exuber-ant, full of ideas to improve their situation at work or at home. Their physical energy can astonish other people who may even complain they cannot keep up. They may decide to remodel their homes, to add a swimming pool, to build a racing car, to start a new business, etc. (see Box 11.3c). If they are gifted and creative artists and writers, they may produce remarkable works of art in an extraordinarily short time. In fact, there seems to be a relation-ship between some types of creativity and bipolar mood disorder. George Frederick Handel, who has been described as having a bipolar mood disorder, may have written *The Messiah* during one of his manic states. As soon as he conceived the idea for this celebrated oratorio, he locked himself in his room for three weeks, saw no one, ate little, and emerged with most of it in finished form. It should be noted, however, that the creative juices flow only when the person is in the euphoric manic stage and not in the depressed stage. One suggestion as to why the creativity seems to flow during the manic phase is that the speeded up cognitive processes heighten the person's natural flexibility and fluidity of thinking: quick associations, energy, confidence, and a general sense of well-being (Goodwin & Jamison, 1990).

Unfortunately, not all is auspicious in the manic phase of bipolar mood disorder. For one thing, the mania also includes a grandiose self-esteem—even a sense of omnipotence. Persons in the manic phase may believe they are capable of anything even when they have lit-tle skill in an area. Their self-confidence often borders on recklessness. Once they conceive an idea, they refuse to "listen to reason" no matter how many people tell them they are being "foolhardy" and taking dangerous and stupid risks. They may go on shopping sprees, buy things for which they have no need, run up their credit card debt, write checks that bounce, and give large sums of money away to strangers. If someone tries to restrict their activities, they may become irritable, angry, and turn on anyone who pleads with them to slow down and think about what they are doing. Their incessant talking will now become a tirade of com-plaints and angry criticism of the people around them who are "stupid idiots who can't see opportunities being handed to them." Their attempts at wisecracking humor turns to fury. Their remarkable physical energy may even become destructive to themselves or to others.

Then, just as suddenly as it began, the manic episode will come to a dead stop. But, gen-erally, these people do not just return to "normal." The sudden end of the manic phase gener-ally marks the beginning of the depressive phase. All that creative flow drains away, and the person feels life has no meaning any more, and may even become suicidal.

Etiology, Prevalence, and Treatment. While the unipolar mood disorders (major and minor depression) have some genetic component to them, the evidence of a genetic compo-nent for the bipolar mood disorder is undeniable. The World Health Organization (1997) has reported a consistent 1 percent of the population as having bipolar mood disorder over the last 50 years around the world. "Twin studies" also support the genetic etiology of this disorder.

A twin study in Denmark, for example, revealed a concordance rate for bipolar mood disorder of almost 70 percent for identical twins as compared to fraternal twins who show a concordance rate of only 20 percent. But the fact that the twin studies do not show a 100 percent concordance means that environmental factors must also play a part. Serious emotional trauma, the person's early life history, living at a distance from family and friends, drug abuse, and a lack of a social/emotional support system all affect the chances of bipolar mood disorder (Kendler & Diehl, 1993).

The specific "cause" of bipolar mood disorder seems to be an imbalance of certain neurotransmitters in the brain. Research has revealed that people suffering from mood disorders have abnormal levels of norepinephrine and serotonin. That sounds like bad news, but actually it is also good news. When diabetes was discovered to be a deficiency of insulin, it followed that injections of synthetic insulin would counteract the symptoms of diabetes. In like manner, if the mood disorders are the result of chemical imbalance, it follows that appropriate chemicals will restore the normal chemical balance. And so they do! Antidepressants and mood elevators such as Lithium, Prozac, Elavil, Zanax, and other drugs contain the necessary counterbalancing brain chemicals.

Seasonal Affective Disorder (SAD): Seasonal Pattern Specifier. In the 1980s, there came to light (both metaphorically and literally) a disorder that had to do with the fact that some people can experience major depression in the winter months. All of us can get a little "high-strung" or "nervous" or complain we have "cabin fever" if we can't get out for days on end because of inclement weather. The moment blue skies break out and we can feel the warmth of the sun, we find ourselves cheered up. That kind of reaction is normal. But some persons are so sensitive to the low levels of light during the long winter months that they get seriously depressed. The person's whole physiology seems to slow down. The research suggests that the person's circadian rhythms have been seriously disturbed. **Circadian rhythms** have to do with those seasonal cycles of the universe that affect all life on earth. Examples of circadian rhythms include the migration of birds, animal mating seasons, and a woman's menstrual cycle. Persons afflicted with SAD have melatonin levels that are "out of sync" or desynchronized. In terms of duration, the depressed phases show a repetitive cycle that can vary as much as months on end to several in a day. That's the bad news, but good news follows.

Etiology, Prevalence, and Treatment. If lack of sunlight is the cause of this depressive state, the researchers decided to see if flooding the depressed person with light, called phototherapy, would lift the depression. And it did—in the majority of patients. Perhaps this is why citizens of the northern latitudes (Canada, Great Britain, and Scandinavia) take winter holidays to Greece, Italy, Mexico, Bermuda, and other places south. The researchers even have advice for people who work indoors all day. Instead of the common variety fluorescent light, get what is called full-spectrum lighting, which most closely resembles natural daylight. (See Tip 11.1.)

Tip 11.1 HINT on SAD. We have described this mood disorder under the rubric of Seasonal Affective Disorder (SAD) as if it is a separate category because so many journal articles still refer to it in this manner. It should be noted, however, that the *DSM-IV-RT* does not label it as a separate disorder but simply as a **seasonal pattern specifier** for any of the other mood disorders. In other words, it is one of the diagnostic symptoms for people who are suffering from any of the mood depressions during the darker of the months of the year or in the northern latitudes.

The Schizophrenias

Schizophrenia is the professional term for what lay people think of as "crazy" and "insane" because of the seemingly strange behaviors these people display. The term schizophrenia comes from two Greek words meaning a "split mind." But the split is not the same as a person who has split into several "personalities." The patient's **affective** functioning (emotional reactions) seem to be split off from the **cognitive** (intellectual understanding) aspect. This "split" appears as inappropriate responses to what is going on in the environment. For example, the schizophrenic patient may giggle inanely during a funeral. Christmas and other festive occasions may trigger tears, anger, depression, and other bizarre or embarrassing behaviors.

Positive Symptoms. There are two types of schizophrenic symptoms: positive symptoms and negative symptoms. The positive symptoms are fairly easy to identify. Normally clean and well-dressed, he may become slovenly and stop taking baths or wear a strange and outlandish costume (perhaps wearing several overcoats, one on top of the other). She may leave the safety and security of her home and become a "bag lady." Delusions, hallucinations, and disorganized speech are also examples of **positive symptoms**. **Delusions** are grossly erroneous beliefs that have little to do with reality. Patients who exhibit persecutory delusions may be convinced that people are spying on them; that they are being followed; that their telephones have been tapped; that people are lying to them; or that they are being subjected to ridicule. These **persecutory delusions** may indicate a very serious and very dangerous personality pattern—the **paranoid personality disorder**.

Patients who exhibit **referential delusions** may believe that comments on television or certain gestures people make or articles in a newspaper have to do with them personally (see Box 11.4). **Bizarre delusions** could be scenes out of our worst nightmares. A person may believe somebody has destroyed all his internal organs. Or that "somebody" has control of her

---

BOX **11.4** **Examples of the Positive Symptoms of Schizophrenia**

a. Delusion. A colleague of ours was sinking deeper and deeper into a delusional state. He was convinced that his salary check contained a message that said that he had only so many more days before he was going to be fired and then die. What he was referring to was a notation that appeared monthly on that portion of the paycheck we tear off and keep for our records. The notation was simply an update on the number of sick leave hours that the employee had left in the fiscal year and it appeared monthly on all our checks. His update read: You have 192 hours of sick leave time still available. He had figured out that 192 hours was approximately four working weeks and that at the end of that time he was going to be fired and die. Although a few of us tried to break through this delusion by showing him that we had similar messages on our paychecks, it availed us nothing. When he got back into contact with reality, he told us that what triggered his delusion was the word *sick*. He knew he

was sick, so he believed the notation was meant for him personally.

b. Auditory hallucination. I'm 24 years old now. Ever since I was seventeen years old, I have always heard voices. I may have heard them before that, I'm not sure. They used to be very loud, and I could never get away from them. No matter where I was, they were always in my head and drowning out what other people were saying to me. I tried all kinds of things to keep from hearing them, like playing the piano or turning the TV up loud or humming to myself, but they always managed to be heard anyway. Sometimes they became quite obscene, or they would curse me and tell me how terrible I was. Sometimes they told me about the other people and how evil they were. I began to think they were the angels that live in Hell and I was their sole victim. Finally, my parents began to believe me about the voices. They took me to a

BOX **11.4** **Examples of the Postive Symptoms of Schizophrenia (continued)**

psychiatrist, and he diagnosed me as a paranoid schizophrenic. Thank God for that. Since I've been taking his medication, the voices became much quieter and there are even times I don't hear them at all. But I know they are always there, waiting around the corner for a chance to take control.

c. Disorganized Thinking and Speech. A psychiatrist reported this unexpected phone call:

> Hello, I'm a paranoid schizophrenic from Tampa. Are you the Dr. Maxim [sic] who wrote the book *The New Psychiatry?* [Yes.] Well, I'm 75 years old, but I grew up in the home of the very famous Dr. Zuckerman . . . the Dr. Obsessive-Compulsive Neurosis psychiatrist, who was a brilliant cardiologist, and I was his only psychiatric patient, and he never said he was my father, but my mother was a borderline butch-lesbian personality, and Dr. Zuckerman was the first to take me to the Metropolitan Museum of Art because I have a tooth on the right side that's too big just as in that Picasso painting, and I have a malformed skull and a right leg also longer than my left, and my daughter Infanta Marguarita Pequina lives in Chicago, but Dr. Zuckerman didn't rescue me from a terrible marriage from 1948 to 1966 in which a man beat me and raped me in the Jewish community . . . My brain waves flash too fast, just as you said in the book, which I'm taking to my clinical psychologist, where I go three times a week, although Dr. Zuckerman studied with A. A. Brill and Dr. Freud . . . but that can't help my skull which was

genetically deformed and made worse by my sadist husband in the Jewish community. Do you see patients?

Source: J. S. Maxmen, & N. G. Ward, *Essential Psychopathology and Its Treatment,* 2nd ed. (New York: Norton, 1995), p. 178.

d. Visual Hallucinations. The following was written by a French woman who described her first acute episode of schizophrenia at the age of six during the school recess period. (Notice that the constancies of size and shape are disappearing.):

> I remember the day it happened . . . a strange feeling came over me . . . I no longer recognized the school, it had become as large as a barracks; the singing children were prisoners, compelled to sing . . . My friend approached me . . . the nearer she approached, the taller she grew, the more she swelled in size . . . I cried out, "Stop, Alice you look like a lion. You're frightening me!" . . . The other pupils looked to me like ants under bright light. The school buildings became immense, smooth, unreal . . . I fancied that the people watching us from the street thought all of us were prisoners, just as I was a prisoner . . . when one of my schoolmates came toward me I saw her grow larger and larger, like the haystacks . . . all the children had a tiny crow's head on their heads.

Source: Renee (pseudonym). (1951). *The Autobiography of a Schizophrenic Girl.* New York: Grune & Stratton.

mind and body. Patients with **grandiose delusions** may believe they are superior beings and have superior powers; for example, they may believe they are the President of the United States or God or Jesus Christ.

Hallucinations refer to sensory perceptions that are not shared by anyone else in the vicinity and can occur in any of the five classic senses: seeing, hearing, tasting, smelling, and feeling. The most common hallucinations take the form of voices in the head, which make it difficult to communicate with the afflicted person. As any mental health professional can testify, it is very difficult to interview a patient whose voices are screaming in the patient's head that the mental health professional is a satanic demon (see Box 11.4c). Tactile sensations can manifest as insects crawling over the skin or electric shocks or tingling or burning. Visual hallucinations will distort colors or shapes or the size of objects. Hallucinations of taste can convince the person his food is being poisoned. Hallucinations of smell may lead him to the conviction that the sulfuric fumes of hell are present.

Negative Symptoms. Negative symptoms are not so easy to pinpoint because they are nonspecific and are recognized only as a diminution of certain faculties and behaviors. They involve such characteristics as affective flattening. **Affective flattening** means a low level of emotional response or disinterest in communicating with other people. The person avoids eye contact, responds to questions in brief and laconic and noninformative answers. They may smile occasionally and even seem to have moments of cheerfulness but they vanish almost as soon as they appear. Their energy level remains at a very low level. They do not have an organized life plan or the ability to sustain a job unless it is very undemanding and repetitive. Many of our "homeless" population or "street people" exhibit this kind of affective flattening. Because of their confused cognitive skills, they often end up in jail for vagrancy, stealing food, trespassing, urinating in public, and "disturbing the peace" (*Harvard Mental Health Letter*, July 2003).

Etiology, Prevalence, and Treatment. The prevailing theory about schizophrenia at the present time is that several factors may be involved: genetic, environmental, and interactive. For some cases of schizophrenia, genetic factors seem to be the primary etiology, which means that these people will develop schizophrenia no matter what kind of environment they grow up in. The evidence for genetic etiology is mounting from the many twin and adoption studies both in the United States and Europe. In a second group of cases, a traumatic childhood may result in a lifelong schizophrenic disorder. Finally, many persons may be born with a genetic predisposition toward schizophrenia, but whether this genetic disposition actually develops depends on environmental factors. For example, studies show that schizophrenic patients also have had a higher incidence of birth complications, such as prolonged labor resulting in oxygen deprivation. And from Holland comes another statistic. During the winter of 1944–1945, the Germans tried to starve the Dutch into compliance. Babies conceived during that time of famine have been studied ever since. One of the findings: As adults, they had double the risk of hospitalization for schizophrenia as a comparison group in nearby countries that did not suffer the same starvation.

Finally, there is the effect the child has on its parent, which may alter the parent's **interaction** with the child (*Harvard Mental Health Letter*, June 1999). An example of this kind of interaction comes from the authors' own close family. In a letter written in her eighties, the mother of a schizophrenic daughter (now in her fifties) made a humble confession. We have changed the name of the daughter (of course), otherwise, the following is the mother's verbatim written words.

> *People have always asked me why I treated my two children so differently. For a long time, I denied it. But it has come to me lately that they were right. There was always something different about Louise that made me nervous. I didn't like having her near me. I don't know what it was that made me feel this way. I just had this uncomfortable feeling. When Tommy came along, I felt so much closer to him.*

This may be a very good example of an interaction effect. Let us suppose that there was "something different" about Louise from the day she was born. Let us suppose also that this "something different" caused her mother to avoid holding her and caressing her and playing with her. We can then further surmise that this lack of physical contact between Louise and her mother affected Louise still further, manifesting as **shallow affect** (diminished emotional response). Thus the cycle continued to escalate.

Schizophrenia is reported to be in the range of 0.5 and 1.5 percent worldwide, but the figures can be higher for displaced persons, for immigrants to a new country, for people born and raised in urban cities as compared to rural areas. The onset for men and women differs somewhat: early to mid-20s for men and in the late 20s for women, but for both men and women schizophrenia can occur much earlier in late adolescence and even in childhood. Even with medication, the person will probably always have reoccurrences of the positive symptoms. There is no precise treatment for any one individual. What may work well with one patient may have little or no effect on another. To be frank, many practitioners admit they use "whatever seems to work," but most practitioners also agree that at least three types of treatments are necessary. The first is to alleviate the positive symptoms with medication. The second is to develop a support plan with the patient's family and friends. The third is to develop a long-term psychotherapeutic treatment plan with the patient.

The Dissociative Disorders

Dissociative Amnesia and Fugue. Dissociative disorders, which include *amnesia*, the *fugue state*, and *dissociative identity disorder* (formerly called *multiple personality*) have gained a lot of publicity in the media because of their dramatic qualities. The dissociative disorders affect the person's memory to such an extent that whole aspects of the person's personality or history can be lost to the patient's awareness. Many factors can affect our memories including disease (such as Alzheimer's disease) or chemical addiction (drug and alcohol abuse) or physical trauma (such as an accident or brain disease). To qualify as a dissociative disorder, the memory loss must be profound and psychogenic (the result of psychological stress and not as a secondary symptom of a physical disease).

Etiology, Prevalence, and Treatment. The media tends to exaggerate the intensity and duration of most amnesia. Most cases of **dissociative amnesia** are of short duration lasting for a few hours or a few days at the most. **Global amnesia** involves the person's entire identity. In some cases, the afflicted person may age regress to (say) five years old and be unable to add two plus two. Dissociative amnesia generally follows extreme anxiety resulting from environmental stress at home, in the military, or as the result of earthquakes, or personal victimization, such as rape.

In the **dissociative fugue state**, the afflicted person not only runs from the memory of who they are, but they also run from their physical home place—where they lived and work. They just disappear one day. Sometimes they assume another identity in another location and find a job similar to the one they had before. Most fugue states last only a few hours, but some cases of fugue state have lasted for many years. Strangely, if the person's original memory returns, the memory of what they were doing while they were in the fugue state may be lost. The fugue state is rare, perhaps affecting only 0.2 percent of the general population. We mention this disorder because it is sometimes associated with the next disorder we discuss, Dissociative Identity Disorder.

Dissociative Identity Disorder (DID): Formerly Multiple Personality Disorder. No other subject electrifies a college class more than a discussion of this disorder, which used to be called multiple personality disorder. It first came to the attention of the public in 1957 when two health professionals wrote *The Three Faces of Eve* (Thigpen & Cleckly, 1957). At the end of the book, the authors believed that the three personalities had coalesced into a single overall identity. That did not prove to be true. The woman in question later wrote her own account and revealed that after the original therapy had been terminated with the authors of the book, she developed many more personalities—in fact, 21 different alter identities (Sizemore, 1973). A more recent book, *Sybil*, narrated the sad story of a woman who had been horribly abused—psychologically and sexually—by her own psychotic mother. Over the course of her life, she developed many personalities, each quite different from all the others (Schreiber, 1989).

Generally, the victims are unaware of their altered identities. They come into therapy because they know they have lapses of memory. They may have headaches—sometimes severe migraines. They do not understand why they find clothes in their closet they don't remember buying. Or why they find canned goods in their kitchen that they would not ordinarily buy. Or why they have the burns or scratches and cuts they find on their bodies. They come because they are scared. It generally takes many months, generally years, for the *alters* (short for "alter identity") to appear. Why so? The alter identities have been in hiding for so much of the person's life, it generally takes a long time for alters to develop trust in the therapist and to feel "safe" enough to come out of hiding. Are these altered identities really different from each other? Yes, that much we know. They may differ in their memories, in their likes and dislikes, in their attitudes, in their learning ability and knowledge, and in their gender, sexual orientation, age, and rate of speech. Moreover, they may even differ in their autonomic nervous responses (blood pressure, brain rhythms, visual acuity, etc.).

Etiology, Prevalence, and Treatment. The remarkable stories of Eve and Sybil made headlines because at that time it was thought that dissociative identity was so rare as to be "one in a million." However, in the past three decades reported cases of DID have been increasing. It is difficult to make an estimate of the number of DID cases in the general population because diagnosis is so difficult. One estimate puts it at perhaps as high as 1 percent of the population.

Any explanation of etiology at the present time is strictly hypothetical, but one explanation may be that we know that perhaps as many as 95 percent of people afflicted with DID were, like Sybil, victims of terrible physical and sexual abuse. And if that was not terrible enough, the child's response to the brutality brought on more mistreatment. However the child behaved (defying the abuse, screaming, crying, hiding) only increased the abuse. The child thereby learned to exhibit as little emotional reaction as possible. The consequence was that the surface identity develops a very constricted range of emotions and behaviors to deal with the horror and pain of the abuse. The child escapes conscious awareness of the torture by dissociating from it—she is simply not present through the repeated ordeals.

But we already know that repressed emotions seek to be expressed. The child's repressed emotions coalesce as altered identities. So, for example, denied anger may become an alter that is masculine, aggressive, and maybe even sadistic to others. Or the child who has never been allowed to have toys or to play with other children develops an alter identity that is as spontaneous and playful as a toddler and just as irresponsible. A child who was punished severely for masturbating developed only one alter who could enjoy sex. The alter identities may have full-blown personality characteristics, but they may also simply be "fragments" of behavior. For example, one alter first appeared to the therapist when the patient and therapist were walking across a busy street. When the surprised therapist asked the "alter" for a name, the patient could only reply, "I'm the one who crosses the street." Sure enough, that was the only time this alter ever appeared.

Once the therapist and patient become aware of the alter identities, the presently prescribed treatment for DID is hypnosis and/or free association to uncover the repressed memories and thus to catharsize them within the safe climate of the psychotherapeutic situation. Besides hypnotherapy, the psychotherapies that have been found successful are psychodynamic therapy and cognitive therapy. But it is a slow process. The average time of therapeutic involvement has been set at about four years, with some cases lasting up to a decade. In terms of medication, antidepressants and tranquilizers have been found helpful, not in terms of "curing" the person, but in terms of enabling the person to cope with the confusing situations (Putnam, 1989).

Is a "cure" possible for persons with alter personalities? It depends on what is meant by "cure." If by "cure" we mean the ultimate consolidation of all the fragmented parts of the personality into one unifying "presentation of self," then we may have to respond with the medical prognosis of "guarded." However, if by "cure" we mean the ability for the afflicted person to be able to function in society and to be financially self-supportive, the answer is— many times—yes.

A Controversial Issue: Recovery of Repressed Material or False Memories? At the present time, there is no more heated psychological debate going on than the discussion over whether some recovered memories are actually fabricated, either intentionally or unintentionally. So heated has been this issue for the last two decades, sometimes with bitterness on both sides of the controversy, that the American Psychological Association (APA) finally called for a "voice of reason" and a cool-headed investigation, rather than the contentious dialogue often dominated by the televised polemics of accusers and accused and their attorneys. A working committee was created to find some common ground and some suggestions for validating actual recovered memories and for the protection of those falsely accused.

Although it has been acknowledged that repressed memories can emerge in the course of simply getting older or during the therapeutic situation, we need to mention that some recovered memories have been empirically substantiated. Others may indeed be false. The abuse may not actually take place but was, perhaps, the consequence of hypnotic or therapeutic suggestion. For example, in 1993, Steven Cook, a young man of age 34, filed a lawsuit claiming he had been sexually abused by Cardinal Joseph Bernardin. Later, however, he stated that the memory had been "assisted" under hypnosis, and the case was dismissed. On the other hand, one woman's repressed memory was so clearly described that the police were able to find the body of the woman's childhood playmate, who had been murdered by the woman's own father. This issue has been the source of lawsuits, and the whole issue of false memories has become not just a very "touchy" subject, it has become the grist of legal battles played out in the public media as well as in the courts of law.

The Personality Disorders: Let the Reader Take Warning!

Personality disorders differ from all the other disorders discussed so far in several very significant ways. First of all, people with personality disorders generally do not often recognize there is anything wrong with them. They attribute the discomfort or problems they are suffering to other people or to society in general. Second, because they have very little insight into how they are contributing to their own problems, they do not often enter the therapeutic situation voluntarily. Third, they are probably the most problematic disorder to work with. Although people with personality disorders may never land in a hospital, they often have a long police record that can include prostitution, drug addiction or drug dealing, eccentric and histrionic and even bizarre behavior, and violent or "white-collar" crime. That leads to the fourth difference—they are the people most likely to cause discomfort, pain, and suffering to others—even more than to themselves.

The incidence of these disorders is quite high. Depending on which disorder we are talking about, the statistics range from between 4 and 15 percent of the adult population (APA, 2000). This means that it is highly probable that the reader will discover that a painful relationship with a relative, a "friend," or a co-worker is because that person has one of the personality disorders described in this section. The *DSM-IV* groups the personality disorders under the three categories called Cluster A, Cluster B, and Cluster C. Cluster A involves disorders characterized as having odd or eccentric behaviors. Cluster B involves disorders characterized as potentially dangerous. Cluster C involves disorders characterized by anxious and fearful behavior. We discuss only the disorders that are most frequent and/or the most difficult for others.

Paranoid Personality Disorder. If you have ever had a relative or coworker who is very hard, if not impossible, to get along with no matter how hard you try, you may be dealing with a person who has a paranoid personality disorder. This person is described in the literature as being cold, hostile, suspicious, and distrustful of others. Compliments are almost always misinterpreted. If you admire a new acquisition of theirs, it is interpreted as an accusation of being selfish and stingy (and indeed they are). If someone offers to help them in some way, they interpret it as a criticism they are not doing well enough on their own. They are so unforgiving that these imagined slights will become life-long grudges. They retaliate in overt aggressive ways or through more devious ways, through gossip or lies. They can be pathologically jealous of spouses, relatives, or anyone who seems to have more than they do in some way. They gather trivial evidence for their jealousy and accusations to justify their retaliation against others. Because of their distrust of others, they have a strong need to be in control of their environment. They set up rigid routines for themselves and for their spouses and children. Any deviation from these rigid routines is met with anger and, if excessively stressed, they may have brief psychotic episodes.

Students often ask: *Why aren't these people diagnosed with paranoid schizophrenia?* That's a good question but it is not easily answered. Mental health workers struggle to differentiate paranoid personality disorder from paranoid schizophrenia disorder. Ultimately, the answer lies in the ability of the paranoid personality to keep working at their jobs and maintaining control of their home life. While they cause considerable problems for others in their home or work vicinity, their personality disorder does not disrupt their ability to maintain themselves (however unsociably) in everyday life.

Etiology, Prevalence, and Treatment. Prevalence is reported as .05 to 2.5 percent in the general population. Onset is often observed in childhood or adolescence when their general solitariness, poor peer relationships, underachievement in school, and other idiosyncratic traits cause other children to view them as "odd" or "eccentric" and attract their teasing. There is some strong indication that this disorder is genetic, as they tend to have relatives who have the same disorder or one of the schizophrenias, particularly paranoid schizophrenia. The following is a good example of a paranoid personality disorder. It was written by a mature woman in her late forties.

> *After reading about the paranoid personality disorder, I realized that I had an aunt who was just like that. After my parents died, I was put in her care (along with her husband, my uncle). They had three children. The oldest, Marion, was six months older than I was and somehow it was ordained that I was to be "a friend to Marion" because none of the children in the neighborhood*

liked her because of her "babyish" ways. Unfortunately, we were both in the same class at school. Marion would have failed every subject if it weren't for her mother (my aunt) who tutored her every afternoon after school. School was easy for me. I never had to study and I made good grades all the time. That was the problem. My aunt turned against me in every way. She never hit me. She never hit anybody. (In fact, she didn't even like touching anyone or being touched.) But she never tired of accusing me of everything under the sun. She turned around every attempt I made to be "good" and obey her as being sly, cunning, tricky, and trying to get on her "right side." She began to treat me so badly that even the neighbors and school teachers noticed that I was coming to school in rags compared to Marion who was always well dressed (although my aunt and uncle were being paid insurance money to keep me). But she always had a reason for her ill treatment of me. The reason Marion was so well dressed was because Marion sewed her clothes (I wasn't good at sewing). Looking back, I remember that she was always at odds with our neighbors, had no real intimate friends, and interpreted what anyone said in the worst way possible. It was seven years of hell until I was rescued by a wonderful couple who took me in. My aunt and uncle let me go when this couple told them they could keep the insurance money they had been getting for me.

Histrionic Personality Disorder (Cluster B). These people are characterized by their flamboyant personality styles and attention-seeking behaviors. They often don outlandish clothes and assume theatrical postures or gestures. If female, they wear sexually enticing costumes. If male, they may don exaggerated "macho" attire and wear dark glasses as if they don't want to be seen, but, of course, the dark glasses succeed in drawing more attention to them. They often give the impression of being larger than life in their appearance and emotional expressiveness. They may be movie stars or opera stars who storm off the stage in a temper. They can be athletes who consider themselves the "star" of their particular teams and insist on special treatment. They can be overtly smiling, enthusiastic, and friendly and (sometimes) wonderful to have at a party since they will get things going—and how! Even on short acquaintance, they will call you by terms that indicate intimacy, such as Cutie, Lover, Sweet Thing, etc. But don't be fooled by these terms. They are like movie stars who call everyone "Darling"—even strangers on the street.

Borderline Personality Disorder (Cluster B). The "border" indicated here is the borderline between what can be considered as psychotic or nonpsychotic. The personality structure is so unstable as to be marked by violent moodiness, sudden reversals of emotions, regression to very primitive defense mechanisms, and extreme impulsiveness. Because of their erratic acting-out behaviors, they can be very dangerous at times, pulling knives on people, reaching for broken bottles to bring down on someone's head, or throwing dangerous objects at people. They can be extremely dangerous individuals. The serial killer who murdered five college students in Gainesville, Florida, was diagnosed as a "borderline personality." The woman who picked up men by hitchhiking and then murdered them was also diagnosed the same way. So why are they not considered psychotic? While their understanding of reality suffers from major distortion, they do not have the obvious psychotic symptoms of hallucinations, delusions, and thought disturbance. Other examples may include the woman who plotted the attack on Nancy Kerrigan, the American medal-winning Olympic ice-skater, and the society woman who killed her husband and his new wife. But their violence can also be directed toward themselves, and they may try to hang themselves when locked up, engage in reckless driving, and attempt to show themselves as fearless by reckless acts of self-mutilation. In fact, a high percentage of patients that arrive at the hospital emergency room (particularly after midnight) are either borderline personalities or are the victims of this type of personality disorder (Gibson, 1990).

Etiology, Prevalence, and Treatment. Clinical case studies of borderline personalities reveal a marked fear of being abandoned. So striking is this fear that it has led to the hypothesis that disturbed child/parental relationships may be a root cause of many borderline histories. This disturbed relationship may have been an abusive one, but research indicates a high percentage of the physical loss of parents. This loss can involve being orphaned, being placed in a foster home, or simply suffering the neglect of noncaring parents (Ludolph et al., 1990). There are also discernible biological differences such as disturbance of sleep patterns, a genetic involvement, and abnormal levels of certain neurotransmitters in the brain. Prevalence is about 2 percent in the general population.

Therapeutic treatment is difficult with these people because if their ongoing underlying anger and resentment of any kind of authority and because they continue to blame others for their difficulties. If the therapist can manage to walk a very careful line between a caring person and avoiding the parent role, there is a moderate chance for improvement. Group therapy composed of "like people" has proved to have some beneficial results since the other group members can spot the "blaming game" very quickly and call attention to each others' irrational thinking and behaviors. In contrast to other emotional disorders, therapy with personality disorders may have to involve eliciting an element of guilt and anxiety since they seem to have very little of either. Rapists may be faced with a video of people expressing their hate for the rapist and what it did to them. Child molesters may have to come face-to-face with the victim-survivors who tell them what the molestation did to them. Sometimes, these confrontations develop a minimal "superego" in these people where they had none before. The destructive acts and impulses of borderline personalities peak in their early adult years. If they can survive until their thirties and forties, there is some evidence that they can reach a more stable integration and gain confidence in what they can do—particularly with some therapeutic help.

Narcissistic Personality Disorder (Cluster B). The most apparent character trait of these personality types is their utter self-absorption, like the Greek character they are named for, Narcissus. In the Greek legend, Narcissus was a beautiful young man who fell in love with his own image in the water and pined away for love of his own reflection. The outstanding characteristics of narcissistic personalities are the (seeming) grandiose opinion they have of themselves, their need for admiration, and their lack of empathy for others. They fantasize about having all the social rewards due gifted people (like themselves), vocational and financial awards, and a privileged status wherever they are. They exaggerate their achievements and talents, and have an arrogant attitude when dealing with friends and acquaintances. Their manipulative skills in getting people to work for them are remarkable. As a consequence, they may actually get a promotion on the backs of other people. For an up-close view of the narcissistic personality, we quote directly now from the *DSM-IV* (pp. 658–659), while pointing out to the reader that few *DSM-IV* disorders are as graphically described, probably because therapists have found personality disorders so infuriating to work with.

> *Individuals with this disorder generally require excessive admiration. This often takes the form of a need for constant attention and admiration. They may expect their arrival to be greeted with great fanfare. They may consciously fish for compliments. They expect to be catered to and are puzzled or furious when this does not happen. For example, they may assume that they do not*

have to wait in line and that their priorities are so important that others should defer to them. They expect to be given whatever they want no matter what it might mean to others and may over-work [their employees] without regard for the impact on their lives. They tend to form friendships or romantic relationships only if the other person seems likely to advance their purposes or otherwise enhance their self-esteem. They often display snobbish, disdainful, or patronizing attitudes. For example, [they] may complain about a clumsy waiter's "rudeness" or "stupidity" or conclude a medical evaluation with a condescending evaluation of the physician.

Etiology, Prevalence, and Treatment. What causes narcissistic personality disorder? Theories range from loss of parental care to being treated too positively in childhood. Some theorists believe that the super-macho exterior is a cover-up for an extremely low self-esteem underneath, similar to Adler's overcompensation theory. The "too positive" theory receives support from the higher incidence of this disorder among firstborns and only children, whose parents often do treat them as having special talents or intelligence. Unfortunately, when these children go to school, they discover they are not accorded the same reverential treatment they receive at home. Their self-esteem crumbles. They bolster their lagging self-esteem by developing a grandiose exterior "Persona." Another theory is that they are afraid they cannot live up to other people's expectations. They may come from a brilliant family with many outstanding relatives but they feel unable to follow in their footsteps. So they invent a personality that seems (at least to them) to be also outstanding (Curtis & Cowell, 1993). Estimated prevalence is about 1.0 percent in the general population.

Generally, narcissistic personalities do not go voluntarily into the therapeutic situation. Many therapeutic approaches have been used, from confronting their grandiose opinion with a mirror of themselves from family members to a more gentle approach such as Rogerian therapy, where the person can feel safe enough to take off the mask of superiority and reveal the frightened and vulnerable child underneath (Masterson, 1990).

Antisocial Personality Disorder (Cluster B). Other than the paranoid schizophrenia discussed earlier, the antisocial personality disorder is the one for which you need to be most on your guard. What characterizes these people is their disregard of the rights of others or for societal norms. Their antisocial behaviors may range from vandalism to harassing others; to employing tactics to cheat people out of their money; to actual illegal acts such as stealing, physical aggression against others (spouse or child abuse is common); to stalking, rape, and even homicide. They have little (if any) kind of feeling, respect, or empathy for others. For example, not only do they seem fearless, recent studies have revealed peculiar differences from other people. They don't seem to have the same startle reactions for dangerous or violent stimuli. They don't sweat as much. They don't blink as much at a loud sound, and some don't even blink at all. They do not show evidence of any bad feelings when shown pictures of victims of violent beatings or murders. The conclusion that was reached by a team of investigators is that they simply do not have the same emotional reactions as other people, and that they have a predisposition to violence (*Harvard Mental Health Letter*, February, 2002). They are sexually exploitive, are often irresponsible as parents, and may do illegal things just to see if they "can get away with it," as if outwitting the forces of law and justice is a game. Other behaviors include impulsivity, irresponsible work behavior, risk-taking "for the fun of it," and drinking-and-driving. They take little if any responsibility for their victims and express no remorse for having hurt them; in fact, they often blame their victims and describe them as "stupid" and that "they had it coming to them" (see Box 11.5).

BOX 11.5 ANTISOCIAL PERSONALITY DISORDERS
Only the "Mask" of Sanity

Harvey Cleckley (1976), who made it his life work to study antisocial personality disorders, described them as having only the "mask of sanity." While they do not have overt hallucinations, delusions, etc., their mask of sanity covers an extremely aberrant personality patterning. He listed 16 traits that are characteristic of their personality patterning. While Cleckley's research was published more than 30 years ago, his description of antisocial personalities is still valid today in a way that students have an easy time identifying such a person of their own knowledge. Their relationships, of course, had highly negative events, such as the person who wrote her experience at the end of the box.

1. Superficial charm and intelligence
2. Irrational thinking
3. Absence of symptoms of anxiety; smooth and calm exterior, although may be fast-talking
4. Unreliable, does not live up to promises
5. Untruthful, insincere, lives by fabrications, the proverbial "pathological liars"
6. Lack of remorse or shame
7. Antisocial behavior, treats others as "marks"
8. Egocentric, incapable of real caring for others
9. Sex life impersonal, trivial, and casual
10. Poverty of affect/shallowness of emotions
11. Little if any insight into self, blames others for problems

12. Unresponsiveness and lack of responsibility to others in social situations, out to get what they can
13. Alcohol stimulates obscene and other undesirable behaviors
14. Suicide threatened but rarely carried out
15. Poor judgment and failure to learn by experience
16. Failure to follow any organized life plan

On reading the sixteen characteristics of personality disorders listed above, a college student, aged 22 years wrote the following about her ex-boyfriend.

He showed almost all of the characteristics described in Cleckley's list. He abused me verbally. He lied. He checked on me. He accused me of all the things he was doing. He used drugs and got me on them. Then he disappeared for several weeks and left me on my own. Oh, but before he left, he took all the cash he could find in the house, emptied our joint bank account (Boy! What a fool I was not to have my own bank account!). Sex? He was a great woman chaser but Cleckley is right—sex was trivial and shallow. He really didn't make love—just "quick fixes." I tried to leave several times before I finally did but he would, get this, threaten suicide if I left. He'd worm money out of his mother by sweet-talking her. But if he got mad at her for some reason—like when she would say she didn't have any money right then—he'd turn around and tell her how stupid she was and what a slob. I think back about him and wonder how I could have been taken in by him. Grrrrrrr!

Etiology, Prevalence, and Treatment. Although by definition antisocial personality cannot be labeled as such until the person is 18 years or older, the antisocial characteristics are often evident in childhood. The three main diagnostic behaviors that show up in case studies again and again include 1) a tendency toward physical aggression and bullying; 2) pyromania (a fascination with fire), and 3) cruelty to animals. It is estimated that about 3 percent of men are so diagnosed and 1 percent of women. Again, reader, this is the person to watch out for in terms of your wallet, your spouse, your daughter, and your entire household. Prognosis is guarded, which means in plain English that it is very difficult to treat these people since they have little insight into themselves and they externalize their problems (blame others). There are some medications that reduce their impulsivity and lower their risk-taking tendencies. Group psychotherapy composed of other antisocial personalities has been used and these groups prove helpful because "you can't con a con" and an individual's glib alibis, lies, and excuses are detected and exposed by the other group members.

Obsessive-Compulsive Disorder (Cluster C). *Obsessions* are thoughts, feelings, ideas, or impulses that repeat and repeat and repeat (get the idea?) in a person's consciousness. If the reader has never had such an experience, just remember when a song ran through your mind over and over and over again and you couldn't get rid of it. *Compulsions* are actions that the person feels driven to repeat and repeat and repeat (got it?). All of us have ritualistic compulsions that allay our anxiety: finger-tapping, foot-wagging, tie-stroking, mustache-twirling, and hair-twirling. Minor obsessions, such as most of us have experienced, are sometimes life-saving, as when we check a second or third time to see if we have turned off the stove or locked all the doors. But when the ritual is repeated many times over to the point of incapacitating the person, it is categorized as an **obsessive-compulsive disorder**. Freud was the first to describe and diagnose this condition. Frightened of any kind of disorder or the slightest suggestion of dirt or dust, obsessive-compulsive personalities have a nagging drive to dust, vacuum, and clean their homes, offices, cars, etc. One student told us that she may spend up to 20 minutes turning a light switch off and on because she is not sure the switch will remain in the "off" position when she leaves the room. Once she did it so long that her finger got bruised. They have a constant, nagging anxiety that whatever they are doing is not good enough. Nothing must be left to chance. Everything must be arranged carefully to preclude mistakes and inadequacies, even holidays and vacations, down to the last minute. This utter lack of spontaneity and nagging doubts deprives them from the everyday joys of living. But nothing they ever do will meet their perfectionist standards. Nor can anyone else live up to their standards. Their rigidity can also be reflected in their limited ability to express affection. Members of their families describe them as "unloving" or "mean" or "picayune" or "always criticizing."

Etiology, Prevalence, and Treatment.   Since obsessive-compulsive personalities believe they are simply doing the best possible job they can, they find it difficult to see what's wrong with their need for cleanliness, orderliness, and incessant attention to detail. What is wrong is that they are driving their family, co-workers, and subordinates "crazy." What is wrong is that their need to go over and over the same material is making them inefficient at work. What is wrong is that there is not much joy, freedom, or creativity in their lives. Estimated prevalence in the general population ranges between .05 and 2.5 percent. Drug therapy may help them alleviate their anxieties. Psychotherapy will help them get in touch with their basic feelings of insecurity. Behavior therapy will enable them to take risks. The cognitive therapies are sometimes useful in breaking through their worldview that they must supervise and control everything and everybody in their environment or things will break down. The "letting go" of control will allow their families more freedom to be spontaneous and expressive with each other and their subordinates to make more independent decisions and escape continual and nagging supervision.

Important Terms and Concepts to Know

• affect	• delusions	• language	• posttraumatic
• age-related	• differential	• manic	• psychiatric bible
• amnesia	• free-floating	• mood	• SAD
• bipolar	• fugue	• narcissistic	• spontaneous
• borderline	• hallucinations	• panic attack	• therapy
• circadian	• histrionic	• paranoid	
• common cold	• identity	• phobias	

Make Your Own Chapter Summary by Filling in the Blanks

Use the "Important Terms and Concepts to Know" to fill in the blanks.

The Diagnostic and Statistical Manual. The *DSM* popularly known as the "_____" and now in its DSM-IV-TR edition, has been established as a "common _____" for the mental health professions, but categorizing a "mental disorder" is not at all simple and generally depends on _____ diagnosis (diagnosing through a process of elimination).

Anxiety disorders. _____ are differentiated from ordinary anxiety in that the former incapacitates the person in everyday life. They are often _____, since fear of school is common in young children and fear of being mugged on the streets is common in older adults. Anxiety that is pervasive and spreads to whatever the person is thinking about is described as _____ anxiety. _____ disorder often imitates physical diseases such as heart attack and asthma. _____ stress disorder is the aftermath of severely painful or tragic experiences (such as war, earthquake, rape, etc.), in which the person suffers from anxiety, guilt, flashbacks, etc.

Mood disorders. Major _____ disorder is so pervasive in our society that it is sometimes called the "_____" of the mental disorders but, fortunately, it is one of the easiest disorders to treat. In fact, sometimes it is alleviated without any specific treatment, which is called _____ remission. _____ mood disorder was formerly called manic-depressive psychosis. In the _____ phase, the person feels euphoric and

has high energy, but unfortunately may act out with severely dysfunctional behaviors as shoplifting. _____ refers to the disorder that results from lack of sunlight for too long a period of time, which seems to interrupt our natural _____ rhythms.

The schizophrenias. These disorders involve positive symptoms that include: _____ (irrational beliefs), _____, involving the five senses; and confusion of thought and language. Negative symptoms include a flattened _____ and lack of an organized life plan.

Dissociative disorders. These disorders include _____ (repression of all or partial memory); and the _____ state, in which the afflicted person flees from the home environment. What used to be called multiple personality is now called dissociative _____ disorder.

Personality disorders. People who have these disorders do not often enter into _____ voluntarily, since they blame others for their problems. People who are described as being cold, hostile, and pervasively suspicious of others are categorized as having _____ personality disorders. The _____ personality is theatrical, seductive, and attention-getting. They use whatever means they have to involve others in the dramatic and ongoing sagas of their lives. _____ personalities can be extremely dangerous because of their acting-out behaviors. The _____ personality is characterized by their total self-absorption and grandiose self-esteem.

12

Strategies for Staying Healthy
Coping with the Stresses and Strains of Modern Life

BOX **12.1** SCENARIO
Dan Westwind Visits the Infirmary

The physician has finished reading the file and turns to Dan Westwind.

Dr. Ling: Good news and bad news. The bad news first. Your blood pressure is sky-high.

Dan: I have high blood pressure? Is that the cause of my headaches?

Dr. Ling: Well, yes and no. "Cause" is not a very definitive word in health science. While your blood pressure may be responsible for triggering your headaches, there are many possible causative factors, such as diet. Westerners eat far too much fat, too much red meat—in fact, too much protein entirely. Another factor is stress. Pressure in your environment.

Dan: That fits. I'm taking a lot of courses. I have a part-time job at the garage in town. I don't have much time to study, and every time I turn around, there's another test I have to study for! I'm up at dawn, and I don't get to bed till after midnight. This school business is too much for a man of my age.

Dr. Ling: Do you drink?

Dan: I used to drink. I was an alcoholic. I guess I'm still an alcoholic who just happens not to be drinking. At least that's what they say at my AA meetings.

Dr. Ling: So how do you handle your anger?

Dan: What?

Dr. Ling: Well, you used to cover your anger with alcohol. You aren't using that to handle your stress now. So the anger may be coming out in other ways—like migraines.

Dan: Thank you Dr. Freud! I didn't come here to get my head shrunk!

Dr. Ling: *(calmly)* We also know that anger and hostility are factors. I detect a lot of anger and hostility in you. What you need is an "attitude adjustment."

Dan: O.K. So I don't like the white man's school. I'm a second-class citizen here.

Dr. Ling: So am I.

Dan: You! You've got it made. You're a physician. You've got a secure job.

Dr. Ling: I am also a Chinese-American. And a woman physician in a male-dominated profession.

Dan: But your people weren't victims of genocide by the whites.

Dr. Ling: Oh, weren't they, though! Have you ever read about the building of the railroads? Or the history of mining? Chinese coolies were imported by the thousands and died by the thousands. Hatred only hurts yourself.

Dan: You're giving me all the bad news. What's the good news?

Dr. Ling: Hypertension is treatable with medication and with some alternative health measures—a change in your diet, a program of daily exercise. Also, do you pray or meditate?

Dan: I thought science was opposed to religion.

Dr. Ling: I think you'll be a little surprised by recent research in health science. How about getting some counseling? It might help defuse some of your anger and hostility.

Dan: You mean counseling would help my headaches and blood pressure?

Dr. Ling: Isn't it worth a try, just as exercise and a change in diet is worth a try? We can set you up to meet with one of our health counselors. Are you willing?

Dan: At this point, I am willing to try anything.

Dr. Ling: I'm also recommending a psychophysical program to help you develop some coping strategies for your anger. It's called stress inoculation training.

BOX **12.1** SCENARIO (continued)
Dan Westwind Visits the Infirmary

Dan: Is that some kind of sissy therapy stuff?

Dr. Ling: Not exactly "sissy stuff." SIT has been developed to help deal with maladaptive anger—in law enforcement officers, prison guards, and athletes—to name just a few of the populations. You're in

good company. What it does is to give you some training about how to recognize warning signs of anger, and how to defuse your anger in future stress situations.

Dan: I know my temper gets out-of-hand so lead on.

A BRIEF HISTORY OF DISEASE THEORY

Primitive persons had an *animistic* view of disease. They believed that when a person was sick, it was because they had offended some malevolent demon or god. Or that some human enemy had voodooed them. In the twelfth to fourteenth centuries, the Church laid the blame for the bubonic plagues that devastated Europe on the sins of humanity. Priests urged their parishioners to repent of their sins, and many church members even flagellated (whipped) themselves in the hope of forestalling the spread of the contagion. Even today some persons believe that AIDS is the punishment for evil-doing.

"Mind Over Matter." Over the centuries, there have been some hints about other explanations about why we get diseases. For example, an American woman by the name of Mary Baker Eddy (1821–1915) founded a religious sect, Christian Science, based on positive mental attitudes. Perfect faith and love, she declared, produces perfect physical health. In the area of medicine, Franz Anton Mesmer (1734–1850), a French physician, seems to have "cured" many persons by his methods of "mesmerism," now known as *hypnosis*. Unfortunately, he began to get more and more theatrical in his methods and a couple of his patients died in convulsions. He was condemned by the European medical profession and "mesmerism" fell into disrepute. For many years, no honorable physician would have anything to do with the "black art" of hypnosis. Nevertheless, a French pharmacist by the name of Emile Coué (1857–1926) began to practice a kind of autohypnosis in free clinics all over Europe. A major part of his therapeutic approach was to have the patients repeat to themselves over and over again, "Every day in every way, I am getting better and better."

Charcot's Hypnotism: Physical Symptoms Can Have Psychological Etiology

About the same time as Coué, a renowned French physician, Jean-Martin Charcot (1825–1923), began demonstrating what hypnotism could do in front of audiences of European physicians. To a male patient with a severe stutter, Charcot gave the hypnotic command to talk without his usual stammering and, lo!, the man could speak. Charcot gave a hypnotic suggestion to person who could not walk that she *could* walk—and she did. It seemed miraculous, a fulfillment of the promise that the mute would speak and the lame would walk. Alas! The two patients were "cured" only so long as they were in hypnotic trance. As soon as they were out of their trance states, their physical symptoms reoccurred. What was significant, however, was that Charcot demonstrated that physical illness can have psychological **etiology** (causation).

Sigmund Freud: Conversion Hysteria

One of the persons sitting in the audiences of Charcot was a fledgling physician, Sigmund Freud by name. Freud was deeply impressed by what he observed, but was hesitant to use hypnosis until he met another physician who would become his mentor, Joseph Breuer. To use hypnosis was a courageous step since "mesmerism" was still classified as one of the "dark arts," and in some quarters, a practitioner was even considered as "being in league with the devil." Breuer had been using hypnosis to treat a young woman with many physical and emotional problems. In his writings, Freud called her by a pseudonym—"Anna O." Among her physical symptoms were semiblindness, the inability to swallow, and the inability to walk. She also suffered from bad dreams at night and frightening fantasies during the day. Breuer would put her into a hypnotic trance and have her recall repressed memories. Over time, some of her symptoms seemed to be alleviated. When the young Anna O. began to express romantic feelings toward Dr. Breuer, he turned her over to Freud. Freud continued with hypnotic treatment for some months until he developed his psychoanalytic method instead. It was through his work with Anna O. that Freud evolved his theory of conversion hysteria.

Freud came to believe that one of the ways people deal with overwhelming anxiety is through what he called conversion hysteria (Freud, 1900). In **conversion hysteria**, the person transforms anxiety into physical symptoms (see Box 12.2). People with conversion hysteria behave quite differently from those the lay public calls hysterical. Hysterical people display a wide range of emotions: crying, laughing, screaming, etc. By contrast, the people who have a hysterical conversion have a calm, even tranquil exterior—even when they are victims of a fatal disease. The French psychiatrists, who were awed by the peacefulness of these patients, called this phenomenon *la belle indifference* ("beautiful indifference"). What gives rise to this surface tranquillity is that the patients no longer feel anxiety; they have successfully converted all their anxiety into physical symptoms.

BOX 12.2 CASE STUDY
Mr. Smith's Conversion Disorder

Mr. Smith (the same Mr. Smith from Box 10.2, p. 242), was a man of exceptionally high moral character, and his conduct in business was ethical to an extreme. Mr. Smith treated his employees with unusual diplomacy and dignity, and they in turn were loyal to the firm. Being a friendly and genial person, he had many friends. His home life seemed to him to be satisfying. His wife was intelligent and his college-age children were doing well in school. But one morning he woke up with a paralyzed right arm. He had made the rounds of physicians and neurologists who could find nothing physically wrong. One neurologist suggested that his difficulty might be psychological. He said there was nothing in his life that could account for "psychological paralysis." The idea that the paralysis of his arm might be psychological seemed to amuse Mr. Smith as he sat in our office. But he was willing "to try anything—even psychotherapy!"

After a few therapeutic sessions, however, some deeply repressed emotions began to surface. He became aware that all was not as "ideal" as he had believed. His wife—whom he deeply respected—tended to be demanding, and sometimes her nagging "got" to him. In the fourth session, he reported remembering a morning when his wife's nagging had been so disagreeable to him that he felt like punching her in the jaw. Raised as a "Southern gentleman" who does not hit women, Mr. Smith was horrified by his own impulse. The next time he came to the office, he showed off his right arm, which he could now move. After forgiving himself for his "ungentlemanly thoughts," his paralysis disappeared. He himself was utterly amazed. "The strange thing," he said with a smile, "was that I had forgotten both the disagreement with my wife and my impulsive urge to hit her."

The Era of Psychosomatic Medicine

Eventually, Freud's theory of conversion hysteria began to attract attention both in Europe and America. In the 1920s, a new field of medicine evolved, called **psychosomatic** (meaning mind–body) research. Psychosomatic research revealed a strong correlation between psychological problems and diseases of respiration: hay fever, asthma, and many allergies (Alexander, 1950). Clinicians began to notice that after a family "blow-up" or an on-the-job slight, for example, their patients' respiratory illness would also "blow-up."

Even the "Common Cold"? Even the common cold came under scrutiny. Clinicians reported that their patients would verbally dismiss the family blow-up or slight as unimportant, but two or three days later, the patients found themselves in the grip of a miserable cold. Their patients had resisted the temptation to cry at the time of the negatively charged event, but their eyes were now watering with tears. They were not crying, but the cold was causing them to sniffle. They were not crying, but they were now breathing with gulping sobs. Their eyes became red and puffy, and they had a general feeling of self-pity. Psychosomatic clinicians became convinced that when people do not allow themselves the release of crying that the "common cold" allows them that release (Dunbar, 1955). There is some experimental evidence that crying may decrease our vulnerability to contagion (Cohen & Williamson, 1991). Moreover, it appears that strong social ties may reduce the risk of catching a cold. People who have fewer social relationships may be more susceptible to colds (Gilbert, 1999).

Heart Disease and the Type A Personality

The psychosomatic research of the 1920s and 1930s relied on clinical studies. There is nothing wrong with clinical studies, per se, but scientists always feel more comfortable if they can find statistical evidence. This kind of statistical evidence began to pour in after World War II. By the 1970s, a number of statistical studies related stress to cardiovascular diseases. A book entitled *Type A Behavior and Your Heart* (Friedman & Rosenman, 1974) called attention to a personality type that is at "high risk" for a coronary attack. In addition to being overweight from lack of exercise and having a poor eating regimen, Type A personalities are also fiercely competitive, have a continual sense of pressure, and the feeling that there is never enough time to accomplish their job tasks. They are aggressive, impatient, highly competitive, and the master of the "hard sell." They hate to wait in line at checkout counters, talk far too fast, and often interrupt others in the middle of a sentence. As managers they "get things done," often at the cost of those under their supervision.

Type A personalities almost always use the singular personal pronouns: "I," "me," "my," "mine." Type B personalities, on the other hand, use the first person pronoun in the plural: "we," "us," "ours" (Fischman, 1987).

The medical profession has put the final imprimatur on the detrimental effects of anger on heart disease and also the risk of having a cerebral vascular accident—what the lay person calls "stroke" (*Johns Hopkins Medical Letter*, 1999). Part of the susceptibility may be what is called a "hot reactor." Given the same stimulus as the rest of us, **hot reactors** respond with racing hearts, fast breathing, and tense muscles—all of which may be precursors of heart disease (Siegman & Dembroski, 1989).

Heart Disease and Loneliness. Physicians have long been fascinated by the phenomenon called death by **conjugal bereavement**; that is, the death of a widow or widower soon after the death of the spouse. Mortality rates suggest that there is a high incidence of just such deaths, particularly in the first six months of bereavement. Is it too great a leap to suggest that the death is caused by grief? A noted cardiologist, Robert Lynch (Lynch, 1977), wrote a book entitled *The Broken Heart: The Medical Consequences of Loneliness*. Lynch frankly asserted that what is happening to many heart disease patients is that they are really dying from . . . (well, let's just say it) loneliness! He noted the high rate of heart fatalities among the single and divorced population of Nevada. But Lynch warned us that it is not simply a matter of being unattached. Many people are married in name only. They are really strangers or hostile antagonists living under the same roof. Not only do they experience loneliness, they are also undergoing the pain of never feeling they can come home to a "safe haven" and to a place where they can feel love and a sense of belonging—so necessary to our feeling of well-being (Maslow, 1954).

Warning for Women! The public still seems to make the assumption that heart disease is primarily a man's disease. That may have been true once but the facts are otherwise now. At the present time, heart disease kills six times more women annually (500,000 every year) than breast cancer. Moreover, heart disease is a much stealthier killer in women than in men. Instead of announcing itself with crushing chest pains, says Christina Northrup (1997), a specialist in women's diseases, there are few warning signs in women. Furthermore, she continues, women are much more likely than men to fall victim to depression. The significance of that statistic is that depressed patients are four times more likely to die of heart attack than nondepressed women.

Too Many Life Changes—Even "Happy" Changes— Can Affect Our Health

Another advance in health psychology was the recognition that too many changes in our lives, even happy changes, can have the cumulative effect of "excessive stress." A team of researchers developed a measurement for change that they called **life crisis units** (**LCUs**). After the development of a scale, called the *Social Readjustment Rating Scale*, they followed the health records of their subjects for several years. Some life events are obviously hurtful: death of a family member, illness, or being fired from a job. But, too many *positive* changes— marriage, birth of a baby, advancement, buying a house—could have as detrimental an effect on health as the negative changes. Death of a spouse, of course, has the highest emotional consequence, with a score of 100. Death of a spouse not only causes grief, but also many changes in sleeping, eating, recreation, get-togethers with friends and relatives, etc.

Whether sad events or happy events, the research data indicated a very high **correlation** between a high LCU score and what they called "a psychological or physical depression." In short, too much change within 18 months resulted in a severe physical or emotional problem. If the LCUs measured 300 in that time frame, 50 percent of the subjects came down with physical or emotional illness. If the LCUs measured 400 in that time frame, 80 percent came down with physical or emotional illness.

With this in mind, consider your present circumstances. Becoming a college student brought about significant changes in your life. It probably included most of the following changes: your residence, your eating habits, your study habits, your social habits, your relationships with your family and friends, your church, and your financial status (see Box 12.3).

BOX **12.3** SELF-EXPLORATION
How Is Your College Stress Rating Today?

Rate yourself on your stress factor by checking off the event that has occurred, multiplied by the number of times the event occurred in the last eighteen months. For example, if you broke up with your intimate friend three times, your score would be 150 (see asterisked item).

Changes in educational situation	Your Score
Began college	(60)___
Changed major field of study	(45)___
Transferred from another college	(55)___
Failure in course	(45)___
Hassles with school administration	(20)___

Moved residence

From one country to another	(75)___
From one state to another	(63)___
From one city to another within state	(45)___
Within city	(35)___
Vacation away from home residence	(13)___

Changes in family situation

Got married	(50)___
Got engaged	(45)___
Got divorced	(73)___
Planned pregnancy	(40)___
Unplanned/unwanted pregnancy	(85)___
Gained a new family member	(39)___
Extramarital affair	(56)___
Increase in arguments with partner	(52)___
Broke up with intimate friend*	(50)___
Reconciliation with spouse/friend	(35)___
Concern for children cared for by others	(42)___
Sexual difficulties	(40)___
Serious problems with parents	(39)___
Trouble with in-laws	(29)___

Changes in work

Held a job while attending school	(38)___
Had a problem with employer	(39)___
Fired or laid off from full-time job	(47)___
Fired or laid off from part-time job	(35)___
Changed to a different line of work	(50)___
Promoted with new responsibilities	(29)___
Changed hours or location of job	(29)___

Change in personal habits

Major change in eating habits (New diet/switch to vegetarian)	(15)___
Changes in sleeping habits	(24)___
Changed church or church activities	(19)___
Changes in family get-togethers (number and type)	(19)___

Changes in recreational activities (dating, hobbies, sports)	(19)___

Personal achievement

Hard studying brought high G.P.A.	(22)___
Earned award in some activity (athletics, speech contest, etc.)	(45)___

Change in financial status

Lost significant income	(40)___
Assumed mortgage over $10,000	(31)___
Retired from life work (Ex: army career)	(45)___
Spouse began or ended job	(26)___

Personal trauma

Death of spouse	(100)___
Death of a close relative or friend	(70)___
Close family friend commits suicide	(66)___
Serious drug addiction	(60)___
Personal injury	(60)___
Abortion	(63)___
Recovery from drug addiction	(55)___
Major illness of close relative or friend	(55)___
Infidelity of spouse	(49)___
Major problems with child	(49)___
Jail term (over a year)	(65)___
Prison term of close family member	(56)___
License suspended or revoked	(45)___
Trouble with neighbors	(23)___
Found guilty of minor violations of law	(15)___
Foreclosure of property	(30)___

Total Score _____

SCORING

0–299	Mild	500–799	Substantial
300–499	Moderate	Over 800	Excessive

Reflective Writing: What is your reaction to your stress level?

How does your stress level relate to your physical health over the last 18 months?

If your stress level is high, think of three ways you could reduce your stress overload.

Source: Adapted from M. B. Mark et al., "The influence of recent life experiences on the health of college freshmen," *Journal of Psychosomatic Research 11* (1975), 341–345; A. O'Connell & V. O'Connell, "How much change in your life?" in *Choosing and Changing.* (Englewood Cliffs, NJ: Prentice Hall, 1974), pp. 26–35.

You may be trying to support a family, earn extra money by one or even two part-time jobs, etc. Is it any wonder that you feel tired a lot of the time? Or come down with frequent colds, or worse—the flu? Or have you had a lot of back pain lately? Or how about that popular college disease, mononucleosis? Or how about that "new" illness called **chronic fatigue syndrome (CFS)**? In this generally nonfatal but utterly debilitating disease, the victims demonstrate all those factors that make for career success: high achievement motivation, successful accomplishment of career objectives, upwardly mobile aspirations, and, finally, the tendency toward workaholism. So many of the diseases of modern day are being attributed to stress, that many health professions are calling stress the number one health problem today.

Our Significantly Overweight and Obese Population

An Increasing Problem in Affluent Countries. If stress is the Number One health problem today, the second most serious health problem is the population of significantly overweight and obese children and adults. So prevalent is this problem that it has become a major focus of many professions in terms of etiology, demographics, and treatment. In fact, so severe has the problem of obesity become that in 2002, the Internal Revenue Service announced a new policy (IRS Ruling 202-19), that "Obesity is medically accepted to be a disease in its own right." For taxpayers, this means that treatment specifically for obesity can now be claimed as a medical deduction, provided the expenses have not been already paid for by a third-party insurance provider. It also means the ruling will encourage Medicare, Medicaid, and private insurance providers to consider including treatment for obesity in their coverage.

Significant overweight and obesity are major deterrents to positive self-esteem. Moreover, people so afflicted are vulnerable to discrimination. Employers are loathe to hire them for a variety of reasons, no matter how good their professional skills and academic credentials. First of all, persons suffering from obesity may be upsetting coworkers who are intolerant of obesity. Another reason is that obese persons suffer from many chronic diseases of respiration, circulation, and gastrointestinal problems, so absenteeism is a frequent problem. A third reason is that, because obese persons suffer so many physical ills, the company's health insurance payment may increase considerably. There are now federal laws against the discrimination of obese persons, but there are ways to get around these laws. Your authors are well acquainted with such an example.

A friend of ours, a very competent bookkeeper, finally got a job with a local building firm. The employer believed that hiring her for this position would be an ideal situation because she would be somewhat isolated from the view of the general public. There was, however, a common eating area that was the only area in which the employees were permitted to eat lunch or have coffee and a snack now and then. Because our friend was a frequent visitor to the eating area, the other workers began to complain that they did not want to eat lunch with her or be around her. They started leaving the office to eat lunch elsewhere, which (because the company was in a fairly isolated area) took at least 20 minutes to get to. Given that it took another 20 minutes to get back and 40 minutes or so to get waited on and eat before they finally got settled back into the routine of work, it added up to a severe loss of time, creating a backlog of work. The employer, a man of great compassion for our friend's physical problem, knew he could not keep her on the payroll without suffering financial loss. But how could he let her go without incurring a law suit for discrimination? What he did to resolve his dilemma was to close down her bookkeeping department on the premise that it was cheaper to contract an outside bookkeeping firm. Our friend and two others were forced to leave.

Etiology, Prevalence, and Treatment. Recent statistics report that more than 64 percent of the American population are overweight or obese causing severe problems, not only on the person's health, early mortality, and personal financial base, but it is also a drain on the national economy. Not able to find companies who will hire them, obese persons are often on welfare rolls. So alarmed has the health profession become concerning "the fat American," research into what we can do for severely overweight people has become a major mission of the health and social science professions. Federal agencies are now allocating funds for research into the cause of the increasing overweight problem, effective treatments, and methods of educating the populace on prevention.

In Medieval times, the Church assigned the cause of obesity to one of the *seven cardinal sins*: gluttony. Some people still hold that view. Today, however, the health and social sciences are discovering other possible etiologies, including genetic factors and prenatal disturbance of many of the internal organs. Although the obese person does eat more than the average person, dieting doesn't seem to help very much. What the dieting may actually do is to cause the overweight body to lower its metabolism rate to compensate for the decrease in carbohydrates and fat. In fact, the less food the obese person eats, the lower does his metabolism become. To overweight persons, then, it seems nothing they do helps them lose weight. They give up and go back to their overeating.

Consider, also, that overweight persons are being continually subjected to environmental stimuli that trigger the desire to eat. The American populace is being bombarded at every turn with billboards, magazine advertisements, and TV commercials of appetizing food. Another problem is that both fast-food places and restaurants serve ever-larger portions of food, much larger than the same portions served by eating places in Europe. Not that Europeans are not also experiencing an increase in overweight and obese persons. They are. But according to The World Health Organization (2000), which collects data on many health problems from all over the globe, Americans are leading the world population in being overweight and obese.

So what can be done for the significantly overweight and obese person? Many treatments are in the offing. Oral medications include pills that limit the desire for food; pills that bloat the stomach so the person feels full; and pills that are supposed to block fat-producing foods, etc. Some physicians assert that most of the infomercials on TV exaggerate their claims. Few persons may benefit but the average overweight person doesn't achieve the results shown on TV. There is also an increase in the number of bypass surgeries that cut out portions of the intestines and/or stomach and limits the amount of food the person can eat and digest at any one time. With bypass surgery, rapid weight loss can amount to hundreds of pounds, producing a psychological increase of self-esteem when the person is able to fit into smaller and smaller size clothes. There is a downside, however, in this radical approach. Gastric surgery is irreversible, which means that side effects may persist throughout the person's life. These side effects can include bothersome (and sometimes painful) complications of the gastrointestinal system. The other problem is that this kind of major surgery can cause other kinds of internal injuries and even death.

Clearly, the most effective approach to the problem of overweight is prevention. Obese babies and children tend to become obese adolescents and adults. The estimate of obese children and adolescents is about 15 percent of the population. It is especially prevalent among those sections of the population that have had a history of poverty and regard a table full of food as a sign of coming up in the world and the way they can show love to their children. Another causative factor is that children and adolescents are spending more and more time at sedentary occupations doing their homework, sitting at their home computers, and watching TV. Health and social science professionals are also protesting the fact that schools across the country are eliminating recess in order to give more class time to academic subject matter, adding to the problem of lack of exercise of our children. (See Box 12.4 for specific strategies for prevention and dealing with the increasing problem of overweight.)

BOX **12.4** **Guidelines for a Weight-Loss Program**

For Everyone

1. **Start prevention and treatment programs as early as possible.** The earlier a program is started, the easier it is for the child or adult to lose weight.

2. **Initiate and maintain an adequate exercise program, depending on the age of the person.**

3. **Involve the whole family in building healthy eating and physical activity habits.** It benefits everyone and does not single out any one child.

4. **Eat home as much as possible.** Do less eating out in restaurants, particularly fast-food eating places, because their meals contain many more carbohydrates and fat.

5. **Engage in physical activities that the whole family can enjoy.** Except for the most densely populated areas, most cities have places that the family can enjoy biking together. You can join a marathon walk for charity and so can those children who are old enough.

6. **Create a special "family chores" time weekly.** On Saturday morning, the whole family can take part in washing the family car or cars, even the littlest children. With several people working on the inside and outside of the car, the task is finished quickly and is enjoyable. On another day, it can be "spring cleaning" the living room or cleaning out the garage.

7. **Make sure everyone eats breakfast.** Studies show that children do better in school with breakfast under their belts. If adults skip breakfast, they may get hungry by mid-morning and be tempted to partake of the jelly donuts someone has brought in to work.

For Children

1. **If you are worried that your child is overweight, check with your health care provider.** Sometimes a baby or toddler is simply going through a "fat stage," which she will grow out of, but do check with your pediatrician.

2. **Don't use food as a reward.** If the child doesn't want to eat the vegetables, don't bribe with the offer of a special dessert. As children grow up, their sweet taste buds diminish and eventually they will have a more adult taste and will probably try out the vegetables. Don't force them.

3. **Discourage inactive pastimes.** Children are spending too much time these days doing homework, sitting at the home computer, and watching TV. To make matters worse, recess has been canceled out in many schools to provide more time for subject matter. Therefore limit the amount all of the children watch TV and encourage more playtime.

4. **Encourage physical activity.** Children need about 60 minutes of play and other exercise per day, although it can be broken up in ten or fifteen minute time zones.

5. **Be supportive of your child.** Let your child feel esteemed, special, and loved, no matter what weight the child is.

6. **Provide healthy snacks out in the open.** For children who like to munch when they get home from school, maintain a fruit bowl on the counter and another one for nuts and dried fruit. Do not keep candy or cookies in the house except ones that you know are nutritious and low in calories.

7. **Let your child talk about his or her weight.** Overweight children are embarrassed about their weight and they are probably being teased about it at school by being called "Fatso" or "Roly-Poly." If you yourself are overweight, speak about it openly in front of the child, and invite your child for a walk or bicycle ride with you. It's a good way, anyway, to get that private intimate time with the child (discussed in Chapter 5 and elsewhere).

8. **Encourage the child to engage in physical activities of the child's own choosing.** Boys can take their choice of softball, baseball, football, or basketball. Girls may enjoy learning to dance, learning one of the martial arts, and playing tennis.

For Adults

1. **Avoid eating out in public with others.** We tend to eat more when we are in a crowd of people. If you can't avoid eating out with others, choose food from those items on the menu that are advertised as "low calorie" or "low fat," etc. Don't feel

BOX **12.4** **Guidelines for a Weight-Loss Program (continued)**

embarrassed to tell other people you are on a "strict eating regime." It sounds so much more important than the word "diet."

2. **Spouses and friends can work out together.** You and your Significant Other, and/or your teenager can enroll in a health club. You can round out an early evening workout with a healthy meal afterwards.

3. **Avoid drinking in public.** There is something about wine or other alcohol that invites snacking at the same time. If you need to have a drink after work, don't join a "happy hour" group, unless you can resist the snacks everyone else is having. Have a drink at home instead.

4. **Do count your calories.** Find out what weight you should be and use a weight book to determine how many calories you can eat and still lose weight.

5. **If you have a sedentary work situation, find ways to have some physical activity.** Climb stairs instead of taking the elevator up two or three flights. Take a walk at lunch time; it need be only 15 to 20 minutes long and it will do your body good. If you shop at a mall, don't look for a parking space close by. Park further away so you can get some walking in.

6. **Lose weight slowly.** If you lose weight slowly (one to two pounds weekly is enough), it will stay off a lot longer than when you go on a crash weight diet. Those kinds of diets result in the yo-yo weight rebound. Remember you are losing weight for the long haul.

7. **Learn to drink less calorie-loaded fluids.** Some people mistake their need for fluid for the need for food. Keep low-calorie drinks on hand and take them to work with you. But many soft drinks are higher in calories than you realize. Labels are misleading. They may say the drink has only 120 calories per serving but the soft drink container may have $2\frac{1}{2}$ servings, making the soft drink 300 calories. Three such soft drinks on a hot day and you have drunk 900 calories. Not much free space for real food.

8. **Take up an interest that is not sedentary.** Apart from the physical exercises noted, find an interest that requires outside activity. Older folks may have the time for bird watching with community groups. Younger adults may develop an interest in photographing some interesting nature sites of city scapes. Become your neighborhood crime watch organizer. Take up gardening.

Source: The American Obesity Association. http://obesity.org 2/6/2004.

BUT JUST HOW DOES THE BODY–MIND CONNECTION WORK?

So far in this chapter, we have focused on the correlational evidence of the stress factors in a person's life and obvious ill health. But health scientists have always endeavored to discover the actual physiology of the mind–body complex. What they want to know can be phrased as: *What are the actual physiological processes involved? How can our emotions affect our bodies in such a direct way?* The first inroad was made by Walter B. Cannon in the 1920s with his model of the flight-or-fight syndrome, which later was extended as the fight-flight-freeze response (discussed already in Chapter 6, pages 158–160). What we need to discuss here, however, is Cannon's theory of homeostasis, which is the body's two states of energy, and how they function for our well-being. These two states are the adrenalergic state and the cholinergic state.

Homeostasis

What Cannon discovered was that human life must stay within certain tolerance limits of chemical and fluid balance in order to stay healthy. He called perfect bodily balance **homeostasis** (meaning "stable state") but, of course, no such perfect state really exists in any of us. In reality, the body is continually going through many internal physiological changes to meet the constantly changing external environment. For example, when the body gets too cold, we shiver. Shivering actually raises the body's temperature. When the body gets too hot we perspire, which lowers the body's temperature. If we lose too much fluid (as the result of perspiring), our bodies have a need to replenish the fluid loss—we experience the drive state of thirst, and we drink. If we lack air, we yawn, which allows us to take in more oxygen in one huge gulp (and so on and so forth). These changes are what Cannon called the body's *inner wisdom* by which it adapts to everyday situations (Cannon, 1929). We have come to call this "inner wisdom" of the body by the term **need-drive state**. The body experiences a *need* (lack of water and consequent thirst) and goes in search of water, which is a *drive*. When the person quenches the thirst, the need is satisfied and *homeostasis* (optimum fluid content) is restored.

But every so often, said Cannon, we are faced with more than the usual everyday situations. We are faced with emergencies that require more than the normal amount of energy. When walking down a dark street at night, we may hear footsteps in the dark that seem to be following us. Or we may have to jump out of a window three stories up because of fire.

The Adrenalergic State versus the Cholinergic State. In the adrenalergic state, adrenalin races through our blood stream energizing every part of our body. The pupils of the eyes dilate which improves our vision. The nostrils expand to let in more air and therefore more oxygen. Respiration and heart rate increase in rate with a corresponding increase in metabolism. The blood withdraws from the surface of the body so that we do not bruise and bleed as much if we are hurt. Blood salts and sugars rise to higher levels. The higher salt level increases the blood's clotting ability. The higher sugar level increases the metabolic rate. These are only a few of the bodily changes. In fact, our whole physiological system is fired up and racing with literally hundreds of neural, hormonal, muscular, and other bodily changes! When we are in this adrenalergic state, we are capable of so-called superhuman feats. Newspapers report stories of people who have reacted with just this kind of strength in times of crisis. A woman lifts up the front end of her minivan to pull out her child pinned beneath it. The football player grabs the ball, dodges eleven other men, and runs the whole length of the football field before he realizes that he has been severely injured. All of us are capable of this kind of adrenalergic energy—for a short while.

But we cannot sustain this kind of energy for very long since eventually our fluids and bodily chemicals are used up and we simply burn out and get ill. At some point, we have to stop so that our bodily reserves can get replenished and the tissue damage repaired. As we rest or sleep, our bodies change over to the **cholinergic state** in which the toxins are drained out of the body, the chemical and fluid balance restored to normal levels, and damaged tissue is healed (see Figure 12.1).

The General Adaptation Syndrome: The Effects of Ongoing Stress. A famous physiologist, Hans Selye, wanted to know *What would happen if the body was always reacting to an emergency and had to remain in an adrenalergic state? What if the body did not get the opportunity to be in the cholinergic state for the benefit of draining the bodily toxins and replenishing its needed reserves? In other words, what if an animal does not get enough time for rest, relaxation, and sleep?* To find out, what Selye did was to subject healthy laboratory rats to stressors that would not kill the rats but were definitely traumatic. The stressors he used were varied: electric shock (which Selye used to induce emotional trauma), sublethal doses of

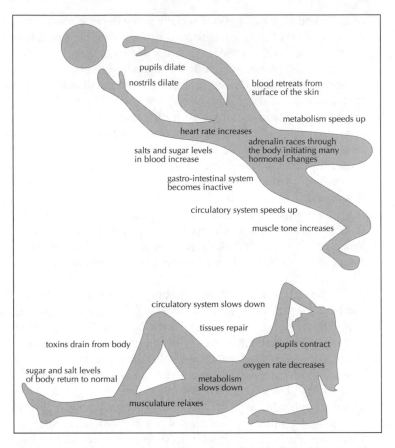

pupils dilate

nostrils dilate

blood retreats from
surface of the skin

metabolism speeds up

heart rate increases

salts and sugar levels
in blood increase

adrenalin races through
the body initiating many
hormonal changes

gastro-intestinal system
becomes inactive

circulatory system speeds up

muscle tone increases

circulatory system slows down

tissues repair

toxins drain from body

pupils contract

oxygen rate decreases

sugar and salt levels
of body return to normal

metabolism
slows down

musculature relaxes

Figure 12.1 The Adrenalergic State versus the Cholingeric State. The
adrenalergic state is engaged when we are active and expending
energy. The cholinergic state is engaged when we are relaxed and rest-
ing and the body is repairing tissues and draining toxins.

poison, extreme cold, and semistarvation diets. Whatever the stressor, the results were the
same. The animals went through three predictable stages:

1. Stage of alarm reaction. After the healthy animals had been subjected to stress for
a period of time, they began to look and act sick. When animals are ill, they stop eating, drinking, and copulating, huddling by themselves in a corner. An autopsy on a few of these rats
revealed the ravages of disease; bleeding ulcers, diseased adrenal glands, a withered thymus,
abnormally high levels of blood salts and sugars, and a high white-blood-cell count.

2. Stage of resistance. If the stressor was not too severe, many animals seemed to
recover. They began to eat, drink, run around, and copulate. Were they really better? Autopsies
revealed all the diseased tissues had healed and the bodily fluids returned to normal—but only
for a while.

3. Stage of exhaustion. If the stressor was not removed, the animals again became
sick and died. Autopsies revealed the same bodily ravages as in the stage of alarm. Selye also

noted that the animals could resist one stressor for a time, but when another was added, and yet another, death could come instantly.

How Does the General Adaptation Syndrome Apply to Our Health? Selye postulated that if we live and work in an environment where the pressure is constant or the environment is hostile, our bodies deteriorate with what he called the "diseases of civilization"—arthritis, the heart diseases, the cancers, etc. In further work, he differentiated stress from *eustress, hypostress* and *distress*.There is no way to avoid **stress** since it is normal "wear and tear" on the body that comes from everyday living. Nor would we want to avoid stress for if we did nothing all day long, the boredom of doing nothing would be stressful, which Selye termed **hypostress**. On the other hand, if the stress becomes overwhelming, we are then in a state of **distress**, which has serious consequences on the body (see Box 12.5). He then defined **eustress** as the excitement and joy that comes of happily challenging situations. His recipe for maximizing eustress is to develop optimistic and altruistic attitudes toward others and toward life in general (Selye, 1991).

BOX **12.5** STUDENTS VERBATIM
The Stressors in My Life

My roommates. Female (18 years): My friends all tell me this is an old, old story. I came to the university with three of my high school friends. Being such good friends, we thought it would be wonderful to become roommates. Wow! Did that prove to be wrong. First of all, one of my roommates turns out to be a slob. I don't think she has ever washed a dish in her life. Another roommate has her boyfriend over all the time so we really have five people in the apartment instead of four. The other roommate and I suffer in silence until we can't stand it anymore. Then one of us explodes and all hell breaks loose! Everybody is fighting. We have four months till the lease is up. In the meantime, I must be at the next-to-lowest level of Maslow's hierarchy of existence—safety.

Credit card debt. Male (20 years): I grew up last year when I got into debt over my ears. I got a credit card in the mail with my name on it, and I thought "Wow! What a neat thing." I was getting an apartment with a computer and a computer desk and a few pieces of furniture. I just figured somehow I would be able to make the payments when the time came. (Talk about a denial system—that was me!) Anyway, you can guess what happened next. When my first credit card bill came, I couldn't believe it. Whew! Had I really run up that much? I made the first payment OK, but I couldn't make the second one, so I took another credit card out and started on that one! Of course I was only making matters worse. I began to lie in bed at night trying to figure out how to get out of the hole I had dug for myself. I was scared to tell my parents . . . I got a part-time job. Then I got two part-time jobs. Then my grades began to slip . . . I

got put on academic suspension. Then wham! I got the flu. I mean, I got really sick. When my parents came, they were so sympathetic about how ill I was that I confessed what I had done. They just brought me home. My father said I could work off the debt at his place of business (he's a landscape gardener), and so I did. I worked for "nothing" except for board and room and twenty dollars a week. . . . I was really grateful to my Dad for letting me do that. Anyway, I'm back in school and I'm not going to get myself into financial debt any more! The stress is too great.

Too much moving from place-to-place. Female (26 years): My whole life has been stressful. My father was a career army officer. We moved around the world—Germany, the Philippines, Canada, and a lot of places in the United States. I've heard "army brats" like myself say they loved going from place to place, and my parents are always saying it was a wonderful education. I suppose it was, but all I can remember was the anxiety I always felt when I had to leave all my friends in one place and I was scared I wouldn't make any friends in the next place. Plus moving and moving and moving. It's awful. One year my father got transferred three times, don't ask me why! Talk about changes in eating and dressing and local customs. Change! Change! Change! No wonder I began to have "acid indigestion" and stomach aches and diarrhea all the time. My whole gastro-intestinal system had gone wacky. I thought that I just couldn't get used to the new food all the time. Now I bet all these changes would be way over 2000! I'm not kidding. I'm better now, even with all the pressure of school. At least I am staying in one place.

BOX **12.5** STUDENTS VERBATIM (continued)
The Stressors in My Life

My manhood is being threatened. Male (44 years):
My greatest stress level was just after I was released
from the Air Force. I had always loved flying and got
myself a job as a pilot with a commercial airline. I
had all the confidence in the world as a pilot for the
Air Force, but I began to lose it with the commercial
airline. They had stringent exams every six months.
Also the FAA official could get aboard our flights at
any time (generally three times a year) and give the
entire crew a check while en route on our duty trips.
The pressure for success was overwhelming. I was
older now, and I was getting nervous about whether
I would be able to pass the physical tests or the
instrument check rides. The stress level is extreme.

If you don't pass these tests, you may be looking for
a new job. I had a wife and two sons in college, and
I was scared of losing my job. I had serious "check-
itis." I was anxious all the time. I had insomnia. I
had bouts of "acid stomach." I finally had to resign
when my blood pressure got so high they didn't
dare let me fly. So here I am back in school. There's
a lot of stress of course with exams and working and
all that, but nothing like the constant fear I had at
the commercial airline.

Reflective Writing: Describe a particularly stressful
situation in your life, past or present, and how it
affected your physical health.

The Placebo Effect and Its Applications

The placebo effect is a phenomenon long known to the medical community. The term **placebo**
(Latin for "I please") was originally applied to sugar pills, that could not, in themselves, have
any effect on a patient's symptoms or the illness. Yet patients who get placebo pills seem to get
better more often than patients who do not receive any pills at all. What can be the explanation?
Even if pills will not have any effect on flu, we would probably be disappointed if the physician
did not give us a prescription and say, "Take two of these and call me in the morning." We feel
powerfully reassured by taking medication, and it is that reassurance that seems to be the real
healer. So powerful are the effects of placebo that when testing for a new drug, it is necessary
to have a placebo control group, a group of subjects who do not take the real drug but take a
placebo pill instead (see Box 12.6). There have even been cases of placebo surgeries, where the
patient was wheeled into the operating room, given an anesthetic, a simple scalpel incision, and
then sewn up. These patients actually did as well as those who received antibiotics or actual
surgeries (Beecher, 1961; Frank, 1964). (This kind of research, like the Baby Albert research,
may not be done again since it violates more recent standards of ethics for research.)

Until a few decades ago, the placebo effect was regarded simply as an intervening variable, something that interfered with the "real" treatment of the disease or experimental data.
Now the health professions have come to recognize that the placebo effect is not something to
be eliminated from the treatment program. Instead, medical teams are incorporating the
"placebo effect" into the patient's ongoing treatment plan. The placebo treatment can come in
the form of a pill or a hypodermic needle. But it may come also in the form of "laying on of
hands" or prayer or the incantation of a shaman or medicine man. The effect of these "placebo
treatments" may even seem miraculous, such as the powerful healings that happen sometimes
at Lourdes in France or St. Anne de Beauprés in Quebec. Such healings may be a demonstration of the power of the patient's "expectant faith" (Frank, 1964). One explanation for the
placebo effect is that it encourages the patient to energize the body's ability toward self-
healing. Or it may be that the patient is receiving visible affirmation of love and caring and
concern—all of which have proved to be efficacious in the healing process.

BOX **12.6** RESEARCH METHODOLOGY
The Placebo Control Experiment

Ordinarily, experimental research uses two groups or two treatments. The *experimental group* is the group that receives the new and different treatment. The results of the experimental treatment are then compared to the *control group*, which does not receive the experimental treatment. If the experimental treatment proves to be superior, then the results of the two groups are compared to determine if there is a statistically significant difference. The experimental model is fairly simple as follows:

Control Group	Experimental Group
No difference in treatment	Given experimental treatment

However, when human subjects know they are being given experimental treatment (whether it be a different diet or exercise regimen or a new medication), they react differently just because of that awareness (an intervening variable). In terms of medication, the placebo effect is so powerful that the experimental subjects who are given a placebo sugar pill will (on the average) get better faster than a control group who did not receive a similar pill.

Consequently, when pharmaceutical companies develop a new drug, they must use a third group, called a *placebo group* in which the subjects are given a placebo medication (pill, topical ointment, hypodermic injection) so that they can determine whether the alleviation of symptoms is the result of their new drug or simply the placebo effect. When the subjects do not know whether they are being given experimental treatment, it is called the *single blind technique.*

Sometimes even the experimenters also keep themselves "blind" as to which subjects got the placebo, and that method is called the *double blind technique* (subjects and researchers both "blind"). Why would the researchers want to keep themselves blind? Because sometimes the treatment involves the researchers themselves. For example, if the researcher is the physician prescribing the new drug to his patients with ulcers, he does not want to bias his later examinations of them by knowing which patient had the new

drug, no change in treatment, or the placebo. So he tells his assistants to administer all the medications, including the drug he was previously using, the new drug, and a placebo drug—without his knowledge, but they are to keep records as to which patient received which treatment. Since he doesn't know which patients are in which group, his later determination of the results is free of bias. Such an experimental model is more complex, with at least three groups as follows:

Control Group	Experimental Group	Placebo Group
No difference in treatment	Given experimental treatment	Placebo treatment

The data from the three groups are statistically compared. If the results show that there is a statistical difference between the placebo and experimental groups, then we can be more confident about the efficacy of the treatment.

Does this account for the power of faith healers? We simply do not know as yet, but some physicians believe that all the medications before the twentieth century were useless, by and large. They believe that what healed the patients was the powerful effect of the physician's comforting and reassuring bedside manner or the nurse's loving kindness—"the power of expectant faith." It may even be the knowledge that someone cared enough for them to nurse them through illness (Jaffe, 1974). Consider, for example, what some gerontologists (scientists who specialize in the psychology and health of older people) have been observing for a long time. When we place our older relatives in a nursing home (because we believe we can no longer care for them adequately) without their consent or input, we are literally "consigning them to death" (Butler, 1980). Like the tribal member that has a voodoo curse placed on him and is then shunned by the whole tribe, it is likely that the old person feels cast out and unwanted by their families. Conversely, when older people are given some decision-making power in what should happen to them and take part in choosing the nursing home, the mortality rate is much lower.

Psychoneuroimmunology: An Interdisciplinary Science of Health and Disease

The foregoing discussion brings us finally to the topic introduced at the beginning of this chapter and which is one of the exciting frontiers of health psychology; namely, psychoneuroimmunology—the research and theory about how people get ill or stay healthy. Psychoneuroimmunologists

BOX **12.7** PSYCHONEUROIMMUNOLOGY
Factors Affecting Our Immune System

1. Toxins in the environment. Contaminated water supply (caused by the runoff of fertilizers, garbage, and other poisons), poisoned food; and air pollution, including smog.

2. Poor health practices. Smoking; not getting enough rest; inadequate nutrition; overuse of alcohol; and drug abuse. Even prescribed medications can inhibit the immune system.

3. Overwhelming life events and change. Traumatic events can overwhelm the immune system's ability to cope; even too many positive changes may be stressful.

4. Naturalistic stressors. Even expected stress events (such as taking exams, or working extra shifts) can substantially reduce the body's ability to sustain its usual immune defense.

5. Chronic stress. Stressful events that last for a longer term, say months or even years (such as caring for a patient with cancer or Alzheimer's disease) have the potential of weakening the immune system. Even more interesting is the fact that the depressed immune state can last for years after the stressful event has ceased. For example, the residents of Three Mile Island suffered depressed immune systems for more than ten years after the nuclear accident that happened there in 1979.

6. Seriously depressed emotional disorders. A meta-analysis of over 40 studies suggests that there is relatively strong correlation between severely depressed patients and a lowered immune system.

7. Day-by-day mood states. Even transient negative mood states lasting only a few hours in a day reveal that the antibodies that fight disease and foreign substances are at higher levels during good days than during depressed mood days in the same person.

8. Day-by-day family stress events. Even small negative upsets in the family system can increase the vulnerability to colds and other respiratory distress.

9. Lack of good interpersonal relationships and/or support systems. People who report feeling isolated and lonely have lower levels of immune antibodies than people who report less loneliness. There is substantial evidence also that poor marital relations or marital interruptions (separation, divorce, widowhood, etc.) also affect the immune system negatively, making the person more likely to succumb to flu and other contagious diseases.

10. Personality. While the findings have not been consistent, there is some indication that repression and a pessimistic personality style contribute to a lowered cellular immune function. Particularly important is the role of depression as a contributing factor to earlier mortality in cancer.

Source: From a review of the literature by Cohen & Herbert, 1996.

are not as much interested in whether or not our emotional states affect our physical states. All the research we have been describing has established that by now. What psychoneuroimmunologists are more concerned with, at the present time, is *how* it happens—the physiological processes whereby our immune system is either enhanced or inhibited by our response to environmental stress. What these researchers have discovered has significantly altered our understanding of what we have considered as belonging to "the mind" and what we have considered as "the body." In fact, their discoveries are leading to a surprising implication; namely, that we are not made up of a "body" and a "mind." We are a unity of physiological processes of body/mind/spirit striving to harmonize ourselves with the environment. (See Box 12.7.)

Antigens versus Antibodies. The body is vulnerable to many and varied invading microorganisms called **antigens**, such as bacteria, virus, fungi, and parasites. Other antigens include dust, pollen, bee stings, poisons, free radicals (unattached oxygen molecules), and cancerous growths. Fortunately, the body has many built-in protective devices to combat these antigens. If it did not, our life spans would be very short indeed. One such protective device is the immune system. The **immune system** is composed of many organs throughout the body and includes the thymus, the tonsils, the thalamus, the lymph system, the spleen, and the white blood cells. Of particular interest to us here are the antibodies produced by the lymph system. These **antibodies**, known as T-cells, B-cells, and NK cells (for "natural killer" cells) hunt down the toxic antigens, destroy them, and get rid of the waste. These antibodies wait in the spleen and elsewhere until they are alerted that there are invading microorganisms or other antigens somewhere in the body. They then race to the infected area and surround and attack the antigens. If the invading antigens are bacteria or virus, they literally kill them. Other antibodies, called **phagocytes**, engulf and gobble up foreign substances, such as dust or pollen, and act like the garbage disposals of the immune system. The immune system is a wonderfully intelligent complex of many kinds of antibodies that do many different kinds of things to protect us. The immune system, as a whole organ system, is a floating, roving body of cells that "seek out and destroy" dangerous invading antigens.

It is important to remember that all of the information describing the immune system had been known for some time to **immunologists** (scientists who study the immune system). But the immunologists wanted to get deeper down into the actual physiology of the body-to-mind connection. What are the precise mechanisms by which our thoughts and moods can raise or lower the immune cells? What they discovered is this: *When we are elated and joyful, the brain's neurotransmitters stimulate the immune system to produce more of the antibodies that protect us from the invasive antigens. When we are depressed or anxious or have other negative emotions, fewer antibodies are produced. It is almost as simple as that.* While these connections may seem obvious to us now, these discoveries completely upset the medical assumption that we have a "mind" and a "body" that may influence each other but that are basically separate systems. Psychoneuroimmunologists are now suggesting that we do not have a "body" and a "mind" but rather a seamless integrity of bodymind. This integrity of bodymind has been a position advocated by the "holistic" health professions for a number of years now. Indeed, holistic health professionals have gone even farther and speak of a bodymindspirit integrity. For that perspective, we turn now to the area of holistic health.

The Personality Style of Psychophysically Hardy People. We have already learned that the more changes in our lives—and the more stress—the more liable we are to come down with a serious physical or psychological depression. Even day-by-day changes in our moods can contribute to relatively minor ailments such as colds and other respiratory problems. But not everybody! There seem to be a number of people who do not seem as vulnerable to illness as the rest of us, so health professionals began to study these *psychophysically hardy people*. The questions they were asking were as follows:

What keeps these people physically and emotionally healthy?
What health regimen do they follow that enables them to survive so much change?
Do they have distinct personality characteristics that foster health?
Can we foster these personality traits in other people?
If these traits can be developed, what methods are most efficacious for doing so?

What was discovered should not surprise the reader by now for, in one way or another, most of the characteristics of psychophysically hardy people have already been discussed in previous chapters. Nevertheless, a complete listing of them is not only a good summation of what we have learned thus far but also focuses our attention to their importance in our lives.

Ten Characteristics of Psychophysically Hardy People

1. Positive self-esteem. When people have low self-esteem, they tend to think that they deserve ill health and that it is their punishment for their sins or their inadequacies as a person. In contrast, psychophysically hardy people have high self-esteem and do not blame themselves for their illness but take it in their stride as happening to everyone on occasion.

2. Internal locus of control. Many people still have an animistic perception of disease, as if some external and terrible fate has attacked them which is an *external* locus-of-control. Psychophysically hardy persons are characterized by a strong internal locus of control. They believe they can monitor their own health. To understand their disease, they engage in deep self-observation of their symptoms in terms of their possible meaning.

3. Aggressive pursuit of health. Psychophysically healthy persons are highly motivated to engage in effective preventative health measures. They exercise daily, eat nutritiously, do not smoke, and drink only on occasion.

4. Believe they engage in useful and creative work. They do not "work to live" but "live to work," which is to say they enjoy what they do. They may even have a tendency toward workaholism just because they get so much satisfaction from what they work at.

5. Have a strong emotional/social support system. Many have strong family ties and take pleasure from family gatherings. Others may not have personal ties, but they are engaged in activities that bring them into contact with persons of similar interests and ideas.

6. Regard problematic situations as a challenge. They may have stresses in their lives (as do we all), but they work at solving problems in a logical and motivated effort.

7. They investigate alternative health approaches. Among the many approaches are deep relaxation measures, biofeedback training, meditation and meditational prayer, visualization methods, and any of the therapeutic approaches discussed in Chapter 10.

8. Able to discuss their life problems with openness. Since they do not feel guilty about problematic situations in their lives, they are able to use their friends as a sounding board for actively seeking opinions and advice. They are willing to consult counselors for aid and assistance for specific problems or in crisis situations.

9. Have a purpose and meaning to their lives. They believe that life is worthwhile. They may have a strong religious belief and attend church. Or they may simply have a spiritual sense that life is purposeful and that they are contributing, in some measure, to that purpose. They are often oriented to supra-personal goals.

10. Proactive participation in their own self-healing. They are not "pill poppers." When they occasionally do experience pain, they do not "pop" pills for instant relief of symptoms. They understand pain to be symptoms that need to be understood by themselves and to be reported to their health-team professionals. At the same time, they know themselves to be

Table 12.1   Shifting Assumptions of the Health/Disease Paradigm

Assumptions of the Traditional Medical Approach	Assumptions of the Holistic Health Approach
1. Disease is the focus.	1. Health is the focus.
2. Emphasis on specific organ or area.	2. Emphasis on the whole person: physical, emotional, cognitive, and spiritual—a unity.
3. Origin of illness viewed as an external invasive force.	3. Origin of illness viewed as a complex of forces: genetics, past history, present stresses, and future expectations.
4. Disease viewed as an entity (germs, virus, etc.).	4. Disease viewed as changes the body goes through in its process of reestablishing health.
5. Physician diagnoses, prescribes, and treats.	5. Physician, patient, and adjunct health professionals are a team working together toward patient's well-being.
6. Placebo effect is evidence of power of superstition and suggestion.	6. Placebo effect is evidence of mindbody's ability to employ powerful symbols of self-healing.
7. Primary therapy is chemical or surgical.	7. Alternative forms of holistic healing are investigated and used appropriately.
8. Physician makes final decision for treatment.	8. Patients make final decisions for treatment based on their values and belief systems.

the most important person in their own "health team." As well, they understand that we have different reactions to different medications and they record side effects of their prescriptions. If they do need surgery, they take care to get as much information as they can concerning the operation, possible after effects, and what they can do to aid their own process of recovery. They work with their physician and other health team staff to determine how to prepare themselves for the surgery and to decide what needs to be done afterward, concerning the immediate effects of the operation and long-term recuperative and rehabilitation needs. As well, they discuss these matters with their support system and community resource agents (see Table 12.1).

BOX **12.8** **The Famous Case of Norman Cousins**

The use of humor in the treatment plan of illness was given a jump-start by the publication of a noteworthy autobiographical account by Norman Cousins about his bout with cancer (1979). Cousins was an internationally famous correspondent for several magazines and newspapers. While on assignment in Russia, he collapsed with pain and had to return to the United States, where he was diagnosed with collagen disease, a progressive and deadly form of cancer.

Cousins refused to accept the prognosis of "terminal" and took a hand in his own treatment. First, he decided that "a hospital is no place for a person who is seriously ill." He was particularly angry about the food, convinced that the hospital's most serious failure was in the area of nutrition. He also concluded that he was being toxified by the painkillers, and he decided to redefine his role as patient. He set himself up in an apartment near the hospital where he could cook his own food. He reasoned that if stress has negative effects upon the body, then perhaps positive emotions, such as love, and hope, and faith, and laughter, and the will to live, would have a therapeutic effect. He rented films that were funny and would make him laugh, such as the "Candid Camera" series and films of

BOX **12.8** **The Famous Case of Norman Cousins (continued)**

the Marx Brothers. He found that joyous laughter enabled him to have at least two hours of pain-free sleep. He initiated a vitamin program and after months of slow recuperation was able to resume his work.

Upon his recovery, he emphasized the three most important healing factors for him were (1) the will to live; (2) his medical team's holistic approach and support; and (3) refusal to participate in the gloom, fear, depression, and panic that so often accompanies a verdict of cancer.

Cousins was eventually invited to join a California hospital (at UCLA) as adjunct professor so that he might introduce the medical staff and students to the healing value of laughter, good nutrition, and the holistic approach to health and recovery from disease. He died ten years after his ordeal with illness, not from cancer, but from heart disease.

Hospitals everywhere are introducing holistic health concepts. Hospitals were once solemn places where noise (including conversation) and visitors were kept to a minimum. That scenario is changing rapidly. Whatever raises the patient's morale is not only permitted but encouraged. Where the number of visitors to hospital patients were strictly limited (only two at a time and only for 20 minutes), hospital staffs now encourage visiting, phone calls, spiritual healers and "laying on of hands," or whatever might raise the patient's "expectant faith." Walking through a hospital corridor these days is an enlightening experience. Some hospital rooms may seem like a small party with colorful balloons and wonderful laughter. The medical professions are shifting their assumptions about the health/disease paradigms (see Table 12.1) and are endeavoring to enhance the patient's self-healing by whatever physical, emotional, social, or spiritual avenues are significant and meaningful to the patient.

Shifting Assumptions of Medical Treatment. So impressed are the health professions of the power of placebo treatments that the health professions are incorporating the placebo effect in their treatment plans. Visitors to hospital patients were once strictly limited (only two at a time and only for 20 minutes). Now hospital staffs encourage visiting, phone calls, spiritual healers and "laying on of hands," or whatever might raise the patients' "expectant faith." Walking through a hospital corridor these days is an enlightening experience. Some hospital rooms may seem like a small party with gay balloons and wonderful laughter. The medical professions are shifting their assumptions about the health/disease paradigms (see Table 12.1) and are endeavoring to enhance the patient's self-healing by whatever physical, emotional, social, or spiritual avenues are significant and meaningful to the patient.

The Holistic Approach to Psychophysical Health

The Patient As Part of the Medical Team: In Fact, The Most Important Member. All of these converging lines of research—from the clinical studies of ill patients to psychosomatic research to the discoveries of the "placebo effect" and the psychophysically hardy people, and finally to the research of psychoneuroimmunology—have led to a new direction in the study of health and disease. This new direction is called the **holistic health movement**. The holistic health movement is not a discipline in itself but an approach that not only views the person as a *bodymind* or *mindbody* but as a unity of *bodymindspirit* (see Table 12.1). Moreover, say these holistic health professionals, we must understand the person within his/her total complexity of environments of home, school, neighborhood, work, church, and recreational leisure. That last term, *recreational leisure*, is interpreted as the time to re-create (renew) our physical, emotional, mental, and spiritual energies. One of the first well-known examples of this approach is the famous case of Norman Cousins who, with the aid and support of his physicians and medical team, recovered from a particularly fast-raging and venomous form of cancer (Cousins, 1979) (see Box 12.8).

The Therapeutic Value of Humor. In Chapter 3 we learned that humor is considered one of the highest level defense mechanisms. But in fact, the ability to laugh may be more than a defense mechanism. It may be one of the most transcending of all the gifts of nature, as valuable perhaps as what has been called "the miracle of language." Including laughter in the treatment plan of patients has proved beneficial in a number of studies (Dean, 1997). The famous Mayo Health Institute has already legitimized the use of humor not so much as a cure in itself but as a complement to the body's natural ability to heal itself. They explain the use of humor as having a beneficial influence on the respiration system by increasing the amount of oxygen in the blood, by providing an increase in blood circulation, which sends nutrients to your tissues faster; and by increasing the concentration of immunoglobulin A in saliva. Immunoglobulin A is known to fight off colds, flu, and sinus infections. Studies have already demonstrated that humor helps patients cope with pain. Because of the efficacious healing effects of laughter, the Mayo Clinic encourages their physicians to expose patients to humorous experiences (*Mayo Clinic Health Letter*, 1993).

  The Famous Gesundheit! Institute of Patch Adams, M.D. Perhaps no one exemplifies this approach better than Dr. Patch Adams, whose work at his famous Gesundheit! Institute was even made into a movie, starring Robin Williams. The German *gesundheit!* means "Good health!" And that is what this now almost-legendary physician named his first clinic/hospital in an economically depressed area in rural West Virginia. Dr. Adams wants to move our society away from needing Xanax and Prozac. With a firm belief in the healing power of laughter and joy, he has created an institute that celebrates laughter rather than sadness, good spirits rather than depression, and life rather than death. He walks around in a clown's uniform and encourages his staff to try out whatever funny faces, comic clothes, and masks may appeal to them. He employs all the healing arts available, which include comic theatrical presentations, art therapy, dance therapy, peer support groups, and all the alternative therapies noted in Box 12.9.

BOX 12.9 Alternative Holistic Health Approaches

Important Note: When these methods are used as treatment, all of these alternative holistic approaches are to be used in conjunction with the person's medical team. They can also be used by the individual as preventative disease measures.

Jacobson's Deep Relaxation Method. In 1938, an American physician by the name of Edmund Jacobson published his method of "deep relaxation," in which he taught his patients to relax large groups of muscles from the legs up to the head. He was convinced that his patients were living such tense lives that it was producing various kinds of disease.

His patients were taught to alternately *tighten* and *relax* the large muscle groups, at the end of which they were able to experience a kind of relaxation that few had ever known before. He reported his patients as having significant reduction of both their physical and psychological symptoms. Jacobson's methods have stood the "test of time." Jacobson's deep relaxation methods are now used in the treatment of migraine, insomnia, hypertension, test anxiety, phobias of all kinds, and Raynaud's disease. It is also used as a way to induce hypnotic trance and is one of the techniques employed in *desensitization training* and *biofeedback* (see below).

Weight Control, Nutrition, and Exercise. Nearly 80 percent of all Americans are overweight. Excessive weight and poor eating habits contribute to many diseases including diabetes, the heart diseases, chronic respiratory and gastrointestinal problems, and the

BOX 12.9 **Alternative Holistic Health Approaches (continued)**

cancers. Nutrition researchers have launched a successful campaign in alerting Americans to the dangers of fad diets, which eliminate all but one type of food or suggest excessive amounts of one food element. In addition, we need to avoid fast foods or foods that are heavy with preservatives. We need also to avoid saturated fats and excessive protein and red meat in our everyday eating habits. Summarizing the latest research, protein should make up no more than 20 percent of our diet and fat no more than 30 percent. Fruits, vegetables, and complex carbohydrates should make up the other 50 percent. This eating regimen should be supplemented with a daily routine of exercise and more pure water than we ordinarily drink.

Stress Management through Self-Discipline Regimens: Yoga, Karate, Aerobic Exercises, Tai-Chi. Hatha yoga

is a series of slow stretching postures performed with a calm state of mind. Although yoga may seem to be an esoteric eastern practice, it is actually a very systematic method of toning the body muscles under slight stress. While yoga tones the body muscles, the major objective is to achieve "peace of mind." By remaining calm and relaxed while practicing the physical stress of the asanic stretching, the person is learning to react calmly when encountering psychological stress during the rest of the day. If the person does experience stress during a moment in the daily routine, all that is needed is to stretch the body slightly once again to restore body-mind calm. Other types of body control approaches include karate, aerobic exercises, and tai-chi.

Massage. The skin is the body's largest and heaviest organ, weighing about nine pounds (the brain weighs only three pounds) and is our most basic sense. Long before infants can see well or hear well, they respond to the slightest touching of their cheeks and lips. Cuddling and rocking a baby is the traditional human technique to soothe the child into sleep. As a therapeutic holistic approach, massage is a technique for relaxing the bodymind. Massage techniques have been developed for wrestlers and boxers and other athletes. The Indian technique of gently rubbing their babies all over with an oil preparation has the effect of comforting and quieting the crying child (Leboyer, 1976).

Hot Baths. Public hot baths have been used for centuries in both western and nonwestern cultures long before the days of the Pharaohs of Egypt. The "Turkish baths" and the hot springs of Europe (such as those at Marianbad, Germany) have been part of European health programs for centuries. Finnish businessmen often take saunas together with their international business associates before undertaking their formal business interactions. (Is it their intention to foster complete and naked honesty in their business partners?) The Japanese have long used family bathing as a way of being together psychologically as well as a way of cleansing the body. The popularity of the hot bath can be discerned in the rising popularity of the Jacuzzi industry.

Biofeedback. The type of holistic technique that has received the most rigorous experimental research is biofeedback. Biofeedback is a process by which the client learns to use his own biological signals to regulate his physiological activities. During the training, certain physiological functions (for example, heart rate, finger temperature, or blood pressure) are translated into a visual or auditory signal. The client then learns to associate the signal and the stress symptom. For example, if a patient suffers from a tension-produced headache, the biofeedback trainer helps the patient associate the occurrence of migraine with muscle tension in the neck and shoulders. The client then learns to release the auditory signal by releasing the tension in the neck.

Meditation and Meditational Prayer. For centuries, in both eastern and western traditions, contemplative prayer and meditation have been considered a transcending path to peace of mind and elevated states of consciousness. Some meditations concentrate on a visual symbol such as the Catholic Stations of the Cross or the Eastern mandala. Other meditations focus on an auditory sound such as the *Schema* of Judaism, the long drawn out OM mantra of Tibetan practice, or the chanting of the Catholic Rosary. Meditation

BOX 12.9 Alternative Holistic Health Approaches (continued)

can also take the form of deep concentration on themes of love or peace or universal harmony. Zen Buddhist meditation aims at achieving a mindless state, as compared to the everyday noise that goes on inside our minds. What all these meditations and meditative prayers have in common is the person's withdrawal from the everyday hurly-burly to a place of interior quiet and calm. At its most exalted level, it seems to correspond with what psychologist Abraham Maslow (1954) called a "peak experience" and psychologist Carl Rogers (1950) called the "center-of-growth." The Christian tradition has described it as the "mystic experience" and the "Grace of God." Other traditions have called it *enlightenment, zazen, satori, at-one-ness with the universe.* Such experiences allow the person to "forgive and forget" the trivialities of anger, resentment, and irritation, and remember what is really important: to live our lives as creatively as possible within the framework of love and service for others and for the world in which we live and hope to pass on to future generations.

Research studies on meditational practices have been concentrated on transcendental meditation (TM). A metastudy of subjects who meditate with subjects who practice daily deep relaxation indicate certain similarities. These similarities include the mind-body responses of lowered blood pressure and

hypertension; less anxiety; deeper, slower, and more rhythmic respiration; the ability to relax; and slower brain patterns.

Visualization Methods: The Simonton Technique. Carl Simonton, a physician who specializes in the treatment of cancer, encourages his patients to use visualization methods toward their own self-healing. He believes that patients can use their own "bodily wisdom" to eliminate cancerous growth toward complete remission. Several steps are involved in Simonton's methods. The first  is to enable the patient to lower his overwhelming fear of cancer and to replace that fear with the conviction that the cancer can be controlled. The second step is to foster the patient's proactive participation in the treatment process through open communication with the oncology team. The next step is to have the patient engage in visualizing the tumor or cancer cells in a symbolic way and then to create a visual symbol for the healthy cells that will destroy the cancer symbol. One patient visualized the tumor as a serpent and the healthy cells as a dragon that destroys the serpent. Simonton also wants the patient to discover the secondary gain that their illness will provide. Is it increased attention from loved ones? Does it allow the person to lead a less achievement-oriented life? Does it give him permission to finally retire from the active world of work?

Carl Simonton: The Metaphoric Meanings of Illness.   Carl Simonton is an **oncologist** (a physician who specializes in the treatment of cancer). Simonton believes that the first step in recovery from illness is to discover the meaning of it. It is his belief that cancer and many other illnesses afford the person with some secondary gain (Simonton, 1995). The secondary gain can be the need to resign from a work that has become toxic to the patient. Instead of experiencing "burn out," which may seem a sign of "weakness," the patient develops an illness that provides him with the "right" to leave work. Or it may be that the cancer provides a way out from a family situation that is overdemanding to the point of exhaustion. Or it may be the person's only way to be the recipient of more attention from loved ones. It is not easy to recognize the secondary gain we get from our illness, said Simonton. It takes absolute honesty with oneself and a willingness to discover other ways to deal with the underlying difficulty. A lady of our acquaintance analyzed her incapacitating chronic fatigue syndrome (CFS) in this manner:

> I was a chronic workaholic. When I was growing up, nothing I ever did pleased the adults I lived with. Nothing! I was always at fault, always wrong, always lacking in some way. I struggled harder and harder and harder "to do right" and to get approval—to no avail. Since I was never sure that what I was doing was enough, I overdid everything. I had a work style of doing more

than I was asked to do. I didn't go the whole nine yards. I went the whole ten yards, and eleven yards—and not for my own gain!—but for the gain of my bosses or the company I worked for. I exhausted myself at home and at work, until finally I came down with CFS. After the worst of the CFS symptoms diminished, I was able to return to work. I did not tell my bosses the nature of my illness—only that I had a chronic muscle disease and had to regulate my life with a little more attention to my physical health. My bosses did not want to lose such a good worker (which I had never realized before) and were only too happy to accommodate to my need to "throttle back" just a little. I could have throttled back years ago if I had just understood I was working far harder than anyone else in my department. I could have taken more time for rest and recreation—just to enjoy myself. I have come to regard the CFS as my body's way of slowing me down and letting me have some rest and relaxation in my life—a blessing in disguise.

Simonton and other holistic health professionals suggest that we need to learn to read our own bodily symptoms. If we have a headache, we can ask ourselves who or what is giving us the headache. Is it that office party we dread going to? Is it our boss who is always nagging us to get things done faster? Or the income tax form that doesn't seem to make sense to us? If we have a backache, we can ask ourselves "what burdens are we carrying that are becoming too heavy for us? Or the pile of work that is getting larger and larger by the day?" No one can tell you what the symptom might mean. You and you alone have the clue to your body's state of being ill-at-ease; i.e., diseased. Or does a sudden cold suggest that you need to have "a good cry"? (see Box 12.10). This may seem outrageous at first, but many health professionals take it very seriously. As Robert Lynch noted, body language is embedded deeply within our language: Does common sense recognize something that scientists and physicians cannot see? Why do we continue to use phrases such as *broken heart*, *heartless*, *sweetheart*? Why do we persist in the notion that people die of broken hearts when no such diagnoses ever appear on twentieth-century death certificates? (Lynch, 1977).

BOX **12.10** CARL SIMONTON
Learning to Read Our Bodily Symptoms

The following are only a few examples of body metaphors. Each person needs to analyze what the meaning of his or her symptoms might be.

Headache? Who or what is giving you a headache?

The common cold? What situation would you like to cry about? What happened within the last forty-eight hours that hurt your feelings or wounded your pride—only you refused to admit it. After all, you figured, you're above such petty feelings.

Stomach problems? Knot in your stomach? Queasy stomach? Nausea? What has you so tensed up, your stomach can't relax? What is it that you can't "stomach"? Nausea? What is making you "sick to your stomach"?

Lump in your throat? What piece of news can you "not swallow"?

Insomnia? What worries are keeping you awake?

Abdominal cramps? Is there something going on in your life that is "cramping your style?" Are you feeling squeezed into doing something you don't want to do? Do you feel like you are caught in the middle of an argument not of your choosing and being squeezed dry by both parties?

Sensitive shoulders? Have you taken on too much responsibility and, like Atlas, feel you are carrying too many burdens on your shoulders?

Constipation? Are you holding on "for dear life" in your job or at home? It could be you are just so busy you are not taking time out for much needed relaxation.

Arthritic fingers? Are you trying to control people or events beyond your control? Does your "reach exceed your grasp?"

Reflective Writing: Describe one of your chronic bodily ills. What might be the significance of the symptoms?

Toward a Definition of Health: Harmony of BodyMindSpirit

Health professionals are working on deriving a definition of health. Strange as this may seem, it is a lot harder to create a definition of health than a definition of disease. Traditionally, health has been defined as an "absence of disease or disease symptoms," but that definition is no longer acceptable to holistic health professionals. Health is not the mere absence of disease or other pathologies, it is something more. But before we can begin to evolve that "something more," we need to make some quantum leaps in our understanding of what disease actually is and what our disease symptoms mean.

The first quantum leap is to understand the difference between the *disease* and the *symptoms of disease*. The symptoms you are feeling, such as fatigue, fever, aches and pains, etc., are not necessarily the disease itself but the body's response in getting us well again. Let us take, for example, a cold or viral flu. The cold or flu is running rampant through your system. You feel sick with all the usual symptoms of headache, fever, muscular aches and pains, drowsiness, and the desire just to go to bed and stay there. These symptoms are the result of your body's reaction to the invading bacteria or flu. The fever will burn off the bacteria or flu. The headache and muscular aches and pains are the result of the fever—not the bacteria or virus. All of these symptoms, along with the drowsiness and desire to nod off, are the way your body is urging you to go to bed and sleep.

When you go to sleep, your body shifts out of the *adrenalergic state* to the *cholinergic state*. Now you will remember that it is when we are in the cholinergic state that our bodies can drain built-up toxins, heal damaged tissue, conserve the body's energy, and speed up the process of healing. You probably should have gone to bed earlier but you told yourself you had too much work to do. So eventually, the fever and the aches and pains and the drowsiness have gotten so great that you now have no choice but to go to bed. You call whomever you need to call and tell them that you won't be able to work or go to class or do those other things on your "to do" list. What we need to understand then is that the discomfort and the pain of the symptoms are not the way Fate in the form of the disease is punishing us, but the body working hard to heal us. *The symptoms we feel (the fever, the aches and pains, the headache, and the drowsiness) are the changes the body is undergoing to combat the disease and restore health.*

Deriving a Definition of Health. Now let's proceed toward deriving another definition—that of health. Health professionals are working toward a holistic definition. We have said that health is not merely the absence of disease: It is a matter of our entire psychophysical well-being. Any valid definition of health must include more than freedom from disease and disease symptoms. It must include the concepts of energy, vitality, enjoyment, zest, and exuberance for life plus a sense of fulfillment in living a creative life, and a sense we are living up to our highest potential at the moment. It must include the ecological freedom to grow, adapt, and change—and the willingness to allow others to grow, adapt, and change. **Psychophysical health** must include such terms as peace, joy, and—yes—the concepts of love and loving relationships. *We must consider health as a harmonious ecological unity of bodymind—and even bodymindspirit.* Think about a time in your life when you felt your very best, when you were bursting with energy, and brimming over with happiness. That approaches the definition of health. Health must be considered as a total experience of living peacefully, joyfully, creatively, and with purpose and meaning. (See Box 12.11 to evaluate your own psychophysical health.)

BOX 12.11 SELF-EXPLORATION
Toward Your Own Psychophysical Health

Devise a proactive program for yourself that will increase your psychophysical health. The goals of this plan may be accomplished tomorrow or next week or next month or even next year or over an entire lifetime.

1. **Improving the bodymind.** Think of goals that have to do with:
   a. Nutrition _____
   b. Exercise _____
   c. Weight _____
   d. Rest and sleep _____
2. **Improving the mindbody.** Think of goals that have to do with:
   a. More leisure time _____

b. Recreation ("just having fun") _____
c. Self-observation _____
d. Locus of control _____
e. Social/emotional relationships _____
f. Life-career _____

3. **Improving the bodymindspirit.** Think of goals that have to do with:
   a. Mending a relationship _____
   b. Reaching out to another person _____
   c. Spiritual orientation (purpose and meaning to your life) _____
   d. Meditation and meditational prayer _____
   e. Thanking others who have helped you get where you are today via phone, letter, or personal visit_____

Important Terms and Concepts to Know

- adrenalergic
- alternative
- animistic
- antibodies
- antigens
- change

- cholinergic
- conversion
- etiology
- esteem
- eustress
- freeze

- hypnosis
- loneliness
- patient
- placebo
- psychophysically
- psychosomatic

- stress
- symptoms
- Type A

Make Your Own Summary by Filling in the Blanks

Use the "Important Terms and Concepts to Know" to fill in the blanks.

The history of disease theory has undergone many transformations from _____ theories (caused by malevolent entities or punishment for evil-doing. The effect of our mental states to our physical health began with the work of Franz Mesmer, who demonstrated cures for physical disease through what we would today call _____. Jean-Marc Charcot demonstrated that physical symptoms could have psychological _____. Sigmund Freud described _____ hysteria, in which the patient's symptoms of anxiety are converted to physical ailments. All of these clinical observations led to the era of _____ disease, which means that the physical symptoms have at least some correlation with social/emotional problems. Certain diseases have been correlated with personality. For example, _____ personality has been associated with heart diseases. Robert Lynch believes that many people die simply from _____ caused by physical or emotional separation from friends and family.

The effects of stress. An early correlational study revealed that simply the amount of _____, including happy events, can have an effect on our physical and mental health. Hans Selye investigated the effects of chronic _____ on our bodies. He later differentiated _____, hypostress, and distress. When we sense a threat, our bodies go into the _____ state, which causes many physical changes and increases our energy levels. We cannot remain in this state for too long or we would "burn out." We need time for relaxation and sleep so we can restore our bodily energies, which occurs during the _____ state. When the body is under threat, our bodies react with the fight-flight-_____ response. Other evidence of the effects of our emotional state on our health comes from the studies of the _____ effect, that includes not only nonmedicinal pills but also the laying on of hands, prayer, laughter, and other mood-elevating factors.

Psychoneuroimmunology is a relatively new field of science that has discovered a direct relationship between the neurotransmitters of the brain and the _____ of the immune system. What has been discovered is that our emotions and mood states affect the number of T-cells, B-cells, and NK-cells, all of which are needed to protect us from invasive _____.

The holistic health approach. Psychologists have discovered that _____ hardy people have personality characteristics in common, including positive self _____, a strong social/emotional network, challenging work, have a strong moral/ethical system, and are proactive in their own health. The medical approach today is to consider the _____ as part of the health team. Holistic professionals now view health as a unity of mindbodyspirit and encourage the patient to use _____ health measures including nutrition, exercise, prayer or meditation, biofeedback, etc. In their view, the definition of health can no longer be limited to the absence of _____. We must also include such elements as joyous energy, vitality, and harmonious life with others.

13

Consciousness and Variations

Sleep and Dreaming, Hypnosis, Meditation and Meditational Prayer, Drug-Induced and Peak Experiences

---

BOX **13.1** SCENARIO

"Altered States" May Simply Be Varieties of Consciousness

Professor Weitzman: Eduardo, when was the last time you experienced an "altered state of consciousness" (ASC)?

Eduardo: Hey, Professor, you got me wrong! I don't do drugs. Oh, when I was a kid I had to try out some grass like kids do, but that was a long time ago.

Professor Weitzman: I didn't say anything about drugs. I said "an altered state of consciousness." They don't only come by way of drugs, illegal or legal. They are happening to us all the time. Anybody have an ASC in the last 24 hours?

Jonniemae: I had a really vivid dream last night. When I woke up, I wasn't sure if I was awake or still dreaming. How's that for an ASC?

Professor Weitzman: Exactly. Anybody had a day-dream today? Maybe of a pretty girl?

Eduardo: I have those all the time. Wow! I have a lot of ASCs! (*class laughter*)

Shannon: When I am in a special deep kind of praying, I sometimes feel carried away. Would that be an ASC?

Professor Weitzman: Sounds like it to me.

Li Ho: What about hypnosis?

Professor Weitzman: There's another one.

Eduardo: Sometimes when I play my guitar, I feel . . . well kind of . . . you know . . . gone. Not here any more. Somewhere else. Like real inspired. I guess that would be an ASC.

Martha Vining: ASCs are beginning to sound pretty common.

Professor Weitzman: Exactly! We used to discuss all ASCs as if they were the result of some esoteric Eastern meditation or illegal drug-induced states.

Now we know that in the course of a day, we are continually undergoing changes in our level of consciousness. In fact, psychologists are beginning to let go of the term "altered states of consciousness" altogether. We're beginning to use other kinds of terms like "levels of consciousness." Freud started us off with several levels of awareness, which he called the conscious, preconscious, and unconscious. You all just added many levels of consciousness. There are other experiences we can add to the list of ASCs, too; for example, when we have just imbibed some alcohol, or when we have taken painkillers, or when we are watching a movie or reading a book that is so engrossing that it feels like an actual experience we are having. And so on. We are continually flowing from one level of consciousness to the next every day and night of our lives.

Alec: So what you are saying is that ASCs are very common indeed.

Professor Weitzman: Exactly!

Dan: Hold on, Professor. I have to challenge that statement. We have a man in our village—white men would call him a "medicine man"— who goes into a trance state every so often. It's awesome to watch. When he comes out of the trance, he says very wise things. I don't think that's very common.

Professor Weitzman: Granted! And psychology is very interested in what is happening in those uncommon levels. Psychologists the world over are presently pursuing studies of yogis, sufi dancing, meditation and prayer, and what many religions call the "mystic experience." But to begin our discussion, let's start with those experiences that are more common—which all of us have had all our lives.

DEFINING THE MANY VARIATIONS OF CONSCIOUSNESS

Let us define **consciousness** as our everyday perception of the world as we go about our usual routines of getting up in the morning, eating breakfast, going to school or work, interacting with our classmates and coworkers, driving home, having dinner, etc. Unless something grabs our attention, we are operating "on automatic," in which we are hardly aware of what we are doing. Strange to say, much of what we experience as normal consciousness is largely unconscious and conditioned by our previous life events. No wonder some personality theorists consider us as not much more than mindless robots or trained monkeys.

Then every so often, something jolts us out of our conditioned consciousness. It may be an event so startling that from thence forth our whole worldview has been altered, which is why these events have been called *altered states of consciousness (ASCs)*. ASCs have been described as taking us "out of ourselves" or as the sudden widening of "the doors of perception" (Huxley, 1963). We look at the world with "new eyes" and listen with "new ears." Maslow described one type—what he called a "peak experience"—as one in which the person feels "at-one-ment" with the universe.

But they can also be quite common experiences, as for example, when we are tipsy and not quite ourselves. We can be driving for miles and not even realize that the hours have flown by. Where have we been? Obviously, in some state of consciousness. Maybe we've been daydreaming or thinking about a problem. Maybe we've been taking a mental trip into the past. That's another variation of consciousness. What kind of consciousness is it when we have had such a traumatic experience that we feel numb or frozen, unable to speak? Or when a death of someone we love causes us to "break down," as it is said, and weep copiously? Or when we pray so deeply that we feel wonderfully "uplifted"? In contrast to the nervousness psychologists had about researching "inner experience" in the first half of the twentieth century, psychologists have become vastly interested in all our "inner experiences." We will be discussing some of the more dramatic of these experiences in this chapter, but let's start with the most common experience of all, that of sleeping and, after that, what we have learned about the dreaming state.

SLEEP AND DREAMING

Sleep: We Just Aren't Getting Enough

Sufficient sleep is one of the keys to long life. As young people, we seem to get by on less sleep, but if we keep living a hectic lifestyle and thinking we can get away with a lack of sufficient sleep forever, we are wrong. It has now been demonstrated that people who do not get their share of good sleep have a shorter life span than those who get their full eight hours of solid sleep. Shakespeare could not have been more accurate with his description of sleep "that knits up the raveled sleeve of care." So basic is the need for sleep that when we do not get enough the consequence is a lowered immune system, which of course can lead to illness. If the sleep deprivation becomes severe, we can experience delusions, hallucinations and confused thinking, quite similar to schizophrenia. What happens during sleep is that the body, including the entire nervous system, is able to drain the toxins that have built up in the muscles and restore the needed salt, sugar, and other metabolic reserves. When we are habitually sleep deprived, we are running on empty.

So How Much Sleep Do We Need? Much more than you might think. We tend to think that if we get eight hours of sleep at night, we are doing well. But there is some evidence that people feel more alert, are more accurate in their work, and have a better sense of well-being when they sleep longer, up to ten hours at a time. Consider previous eras when working people got up with the sun and went to bed with the sun. Now consider modern life: The electric light has turned night into day. With night-time television keeping people glued to the screen, and computers keeping people glued to the monitor until the wee, small hours, people are simply staying up longer and longer and missing more and more sleep. Sleep is particularly vital for babies, children, and adolescents since their whole nervous system, including their brain, is still developing. Unfortunately, adolescents are getting even less sleep than their parents, making them more vulnerable to peer pressure and poor decision making (Carskadon, Acebo, & Selzer, 2001).

Consequences of Lack of Sleep. Lack of sleep can also cause major interference with our circadian rhythms. **Circadian rhythms** are the natural cycles of our body's wake-and-sleep patterns, menstrual flows, and other metabolic functions. When these natural cycles are interrupted temporarily as in *jet lag*, the effects are generally mild. But continual interruption of our circadian rhythms can have serious consequences, as in shift work. When employees have to change their shift every few days or few weeks, their circadian rhythms can be so disrupted as to become desynchronized. This desynchronization has been associated with a number of near accidents with pilots who were subjected to a new shift and had not yet gotten acclimated to the new time change. There is evidence that some of the major technological accidents of the last 30 years occurred between midnight and morning: the Union Carbide chemical accident in Bhopal, India; the nuclear power plant disaster in Chernobyl; and the Alaskan oil spill of the Exxon ship, *Valdez* (Charland, 1992). It is also quite likely that the causal factor of the nuclear accident of Three Mile Island in 1979 was because the team of workers at the time had been on a six-week period of constant shift rotation and now placed on the night shift. Such constant shifting of work schedules impairs focused attention, alertness, and decision making, particularly in reacting to emergencies and other unexpected situations. The workers are simply not functioning at their best (Moore-Erde, Sulzman, & Fuller, 1982). College students, in particular, who are working part- or full-time jobs, in addition to their studies, need to become more conscious of their sleep needs. Sleeping late and taking naps on their days off makes up for some of the lost sleep time, but not entirely. Nothing really takes the place of a sound night's rest of eight hours or more.

REM Sleep and the Dreaming State

In the normal course of sleeping, most individuals go through several reoccurring stages of sleep. Most college students are aware that what we call dreams is associated with **rapid eye movements** (**REMs**) and a stage of sleep, sometimes called Ascending Stage 4 or Stage 5 sleep. This stage of sleep occurs every 90 minutes and has a brain wave pattern resembling relaxed wakefulness. Because of the work of the sleep-lab research, we now have the answer to an age-old question: *Are dreams instantaneous or do they exist over time?* The answer is that *a dream can vary in length from a "flash dream" to one that takes up to 20 minutes.* These longer dreams generally contain several scenes and more characters (Takeuchi, Miyasia, Inugami, & Yamamoto, 2001; Webb, 2000).

THE ALTERED STATE OF DREAMING

Dreams have fascinated humanity since the beginning of time. In dreams, we do not seem to have to obey the physical laws of time and space as we do during the day. We can go forward and back in time. We can put people together who never knew each other. We can fly through the air. And a nightmare can haunt us for days. It is obvious that the dreaming state is a quite different reality than our waking state.

A Brief History of Dreams and Dreaming

Today it is difficult for us to realize that dreams were considered so much "stuff and nonsense" by the educated elite of the nineteenth century. For them, dreams were simply a bodily response to physical distress. If someone dreamed of being guillotined, it was because the dreamer was being choked by bedclothes. If someone dreamed of drowning in a sinking boat, the explanation was that he needed to urinate. Ebenezer Scrooge, in Charles Dickens' *A Christmas Carol*, was relying on this *physicalist* theory of dreaming when he reacted to his "night visitor" as nothing more than "a bit of undigested food."

The physicalist approach to dreaming came as a relief to the educated elite of the nineteenth century and was a step in the right direction since previously, in medieval times, bad dreams were believed to be caused by night monsters (in Old English, *nicht mares*). During the medieval witch hunts, erotic dreams were seen as the work of devils (*incubi* and *succubi*) that invaded the souls of innocent men and women. Many an unfortunate young woman was burned to death as a witch because a man had had an erotic dream about her (Huxley, 1986). It was comforting for the educated elite of the nineteenth century to dismiss their embarrassing dreams and frightening nightmares as simply physical discomfort.

Dreams in Ancient Times

It was disturbing, then, for Sigmund Freud to announce to the world that our dreams are far from meaningless—that, in fact, they come from a very deep part of our personality which lies hidden below the conscious mind. According to Freud, dreams are the "royal road" to our unconscious wishes, urges, desires, angers, etc., which we cannot consciously admit to ourselves. Dreams, said Freud, reveal the savage, infantile, uncivilized aspects of the self we prefer to ignore. Furthermore, Freud insisted that the lusty, exhibitionistic, violent, childlike dream self is just as valid (if not more so) than the polite, civilized self of the waking state. And most extraordinary of all, Freud said that while this new understanding of dreams might seem revolutionary, he was taking his stand with "the Ancients"—with the prophets of the Bible, with the scribes of Egypt's Pharaohs, and with the seers of other ancient religions who believed that dreams are very significant messages for human beings.

The *Old Testament* is not only a source of ancient dreams, it is also one of the first handbooks on dream interpretation. Joseph (he of the coat of many colors) gained such a good reputation as an interpreter of dreams that eventually it gained him a high position in the Court of Pharaoh. The Hebrews had long believed that dreams were one of the ways men and Jahveh communicated. The famous dialog between Jahveh and Solomon takes place in a dream dialog. The fall of Jericho to Gideon is predicted in a dream of a soldier of Canaan. All the way through the Old Testament and into the New Testament, dreams continued to play a very

BOX **13.2** **Dreams in the Bible**

Solomon's Dream. It must have come as a surprise to Solomon to be anointed as the heir to David's kingdom. He was one of the youngest of David's sons, and the Bible records his true humility in becoming King of all Israel. He retreats to a "high place" and prays to the Lord God for guidance. He then falls asleep and has a dream in which God speaks to him, "Ask what you would like me to give you?" Solomon replies:

> My God, you have made your servant king in succession to David, my father. But I am a very young man, unskilled in leadership. Your servant finds himself in the midst of this people of yours that you have chosen, a people so many that its number cannot be counted or reckoned. Give your servant a heart to understand how to discern between good and evil, for who could govern this people of yours that is so great?

Pleased, the Lord God answers:

> Since you have asked for this and not asked for long life for yourself or riches or the lives of your enemies, but have asked for a discerning judgment for yourself here and now, I do what you ask. I give you a heart wise and shrewd as none before you has had and none will have after you. What you have not asked I shall give you also; such as riches and glory as no other king ever had. And I will give you a long life, if you follow my laws and commandments as your father David followed them.

To remind us again that this dialogue between the Lord God and Solomon has come by way of dreaming, the scribe writes, "Then Solomon awoke; it was a dream" (Kings 1:3).

Dreams in the Book of Matthew. When Joseph discovers his bride-to-be, Mary, is pregnant, he is very distressed. But being a man of honor, he does not want to expose her publicly. Instead, he decides to divorce her quietly. The Lord's angel, however, Matthew tells us, appears to Joseph in a dream and tells him not to refrain from taking Mary as his wife, for her conception is by "the Holy Spirit" (Matthew 1:20).

After making adoration of the "new king" of Israel, the Magi are instructed "in a dream" not to go back to Herod and inform him of the whereabouts of the Babe, but to return instead to their own country "by another route" (Matthew 2:12).

The Angel of the Lord appears twice again to Joseph in his dreams: first, to tell him to flee with Mary and the Child to Egypt, and the second time, to tell him that it was safe to return to Israel with his family (Matthew 2:12–13 and Matthew 2:19–20).

In the last hours of Jesus' life, at the moment in which he is standing before Pontius Pilate and the crowd, Pontius receives a message from his wife. She is not named in the Bible (although tradition has it that she is called Claudia). The message is a plea of mercy.

> Now as he was seated in the chair of judgment, his wife sent him a message, "Have nothing to do with that man; I have been upset all day by a dream I had about him" (Matthew 27:6).

important role in the Judaic-Christian tradition. The Book of Matthew highlights the birth, childhood, and death of Jesus with dream messages (Box 13.2).

Mohammed, the prophet of Islam, made a practice of relating his dreams each morning to his top lieutenants, and he had them relate theirs as well. Mohammed considered dream interpretation as an important study of philosophic science. Our Native Americans had a practice of isolating themselves in the wilderness and fasting until they had a "big dream." Today, most psychologists would agree with the first century rabbi who said, "A dream uninterpreted is like a letter that is not read" (see Figure 13.1). The fact that so many ancient religions believed that dreams were of special significance was the meaning of Freud's statement, "I stand with the Ancients."

Freud: Dreams as Catharsis and Wish-Fulfillment

To Freud, dreams were neither divine revelation nor prophecy. While he believed dreams were significant, he believed the significance was of a different kind. According to Freud, dreams are unconscious thoughts and feelings that surface at night in our dreams. Freud discussed two kinds of dreams: Repressed impulses that our consciousness finds unacceptable and **wish-fulfillment** of what we would like in the future. While we are asleep these impulses and wishes come to the fore, but in disguised symbolic form. Why in disguised symbolic form? Freud's answer was that if these unacceptable wishes were to appear in undisguised form, we would wake up in horror—as we often do with nightmares. For example, suppose a man dreamt that he wanted to kill his father. He would be as horrified as Oedipus was at the Oracle's prophecy. Instead he simply dreams that he throws a wheel at a snowman, and the snowman melts away. It just so happens that the snowman is wearing a hat like his father has, smoking a pipe similar to his father, and is sporting a red plaid scarf such as his father wears. And why a wheel? Because it revolves—and the word suggests the gun we call "a revolver." By camouflaging his desire to kill his father with dream symbols, the dreamer's unacceptable thoughts and feelings are catharsized and he is permitted to continue sleeping. For Freud, dreams were the "guardians of sleep."

According to Freud, we dream whatever we repress in our everyday life. Since the society of his times was so sexually repressive, it follows that his patients had dreams that were highly sexual in nature. Elongated objects such as knives, sticks, spears, rifles, and even bananas were representative symbols for the penis. Hollow containers such as boxes, chests, cupboards, even ovens, could represent the vagina and uterus. A train going through a tunnel could be a symbolic representation of intercourse. But sexual symbols are not the only kind of symbols in dreams, said Freud. Conflicts of all kinds can emerge in disguised symbolic form. Dreams can be the repository for our anger, our hurts, our jealousies, our desire for revenge, etc. Whatever emotions or thoughts that we repress or do not want to deal with are the substance for our dreams.

Figure 13.1 Rabbi Chisdau. "A dream uninterpreted is like a letter that is not read."

The Jungian Approach: Dreams as Inspiration, Creativity, and Prediction

Freud's student and colleague, Carl Jung, developed another approach to dreaming, one that differed significantly from Freud's in many ways. While agreeing with Freud that dreams can use nonsexual symbols to disguise sexual phenomena, Jung came to believe that the reverse is also true. A sexual symbol can have nonsexual meaning, even a spiritual meaning. For Jung, dreams were a source of inspiration and creativity. For example, suppose a man dreams that he is pregnant and about to have a baby. A strictly sexual interpretation might result in the hypothesis that the man has "female envy." In a Jungian interpretation, the symbols of pregnancy and birth of a baby could be metaphors for something else. What kind of metaphor? Well, suppose the man is a businessman or a scientist who has been working for months and months on a project. The dream then could be a metaphor that after many months of "being

BOX **13.3** DREAM TRANSCRIPT
I'm Being Kidnapped!

The following are excerpts from an actual dream. Ginny, an 18-year-old freshman, has had a dream that has disturbed her greatly. (The ellipses mean that a few sentences have been omitted.)

Ginny: In my dream, I am in my car and I am going to my boyfriend's house. Only I can't see anything around me like houses and cars because it is all gray and dark . . . I come to my boyfriend's house—only it's a garage. I pull up in my car and he puts gas in it. Then suddenly I am not there at all, but sitting in a room in a house, and it seems as if he has kidnapped me, which I can't understand because my boyfriend is very nice.

Therapist: Try playing the grayness and darkness in your dream.

Ginny: Well, I'm the grayness in Ginny's dream. It's foggy and the fog is covering everything up. I make it hard to see . . . Hey, does that mean I feel like . . . I don't know where I'm going? I'm kind of confused?

Therapist: Sound right to you?

Ginny: Yeah . . . So when I get to my boyfriend's house . . . he comes over and pumps gas in my car, I guess that means something sexual. I guess it means I want to sleep with him.

Therapist: Let's find out . . . Become Tim [her boyfriend] in the dream and let's see what he is doing. Talk like you're Tim.

Ginny: . . . I'm Tim putting gas in Ginny's car . . . (*smiling*) That's really funny. That's what he does. Every time I get moody, he kind of fills me up . . . He's so enthusiastic about everything . . . He kind of straightens out all my problems . . . and he's always cheerful and good humored.

Therapist: OK. Getting back to your dream.

Ginny: Then I'm at my Tim's house, only . . . I'm crying . . . and the strange thing is Tim is sitting there and laughing at me . . . and so are my father and brother. It seems like I've been taken there against my will . . .

Therapist: . . . Play your father laughing at Ginny.

Ginny: I'm Ginny's father and I'm laughing at her . . . Only Ginny's not laughing. That's strange. I guess I'm not taking her crying seriously.

Therapist: So in some way, your father is not taking you seriously. Is that the same for Tim and your brother? What might that be in your waking life?

Ginny: They think I worry about foolish things.

Therapist: Such as?

Ginny: Like getting married or not. I keep trying to tell them that maybe I'm too young to get married. But they all just tell me I'm being silly. I really feel as if I haven't lived yet!

Therapist: . . . Do you feel like a "child bride"?

Ginny: Oh, Boy! I sure do!

Therapist: . . . Ginny, do you feel a bit as if you're being kidnapped into marriage?

Ginny: Wow! That's just how I feel. Oh, wow!

Later we asked Ginny to translate her dream symbols into everyday language.

Ginny: I guess I feel lost and confused about getting married and I don't know if I should or not. I am pretty young, I guess. Anyway, every time I tell Tim how I feel, he just tells me not to worry about it . . . I'm not really sure if it's the right thing to do because he makes it sound so exciting. But I guess I'm not really sure. I feel like a kid and I'm being kidnapped. And no one is taking me seriously.

Reflective Writing: If this dream had been interpreted along strictly Freudian lines, how might it have been interpreted?

---

pregnant with an idea," he may now be on the verge of a breakthrough (finally), symbolized as "giving birth." Another example is provided in Box 13.3.

Dreams as Spiritual Guidance and Intuitions of the Future. Freud believed that dreams had to do with the past, that we dream at night of our unconscious conflicts. Jung believed that dreams could predict the future. He provided examples of such dreams from his own clinical practice.

Here's an example of a predictive dream. A man who confessed himself to be a workaholic had the following dream. He is bicycling along a road going uphill all the way and struggling to get to the top. All along the road there are signposts that read: STOP, SLOW DOWN, DON'T EXCEED THE SPEED LIMIT, 180 MPH. The dreamer insisted he could not fathom what the dream might mean since he was a very careful driver and never exceeded the speed limit. Others who were present in the dream workshop were nonplused by the man's inability to penetrate his dream symbols. They proposed that his dream was a warning that if he didn't slow down and take it easier, he was headed for a serious illness. At that, the man admitted that his last blood pressure reading had been 180 over 130!

Synchronicity. The idea of *synchronicity* has struck such a deep chord in the hearts of some artists and writers that it has become an accepted word in our everyday vocabulary. The reader may even know a song entitled "Synchronicity," written and played by the rock group, "The Police." Jung had come from a long line of Calvinist ministers. Although rejecting the orthodoxy of formal religion, he came to believe that there are forces beyond human understanding that are sometimes glimpsed through our intuitions, our art and artifacts, and our dreams. He believed that what other people call coincidence is not coincidence at all, but evidence of our psychic connectedness. Have you ever had the experience of thinking of someone when, all of a sudden, the phone rings and it is the person you have been thinking about? Or have you ever received a letter from a person you have just written to? Jung said these are not coincidental events, but evidence of our connectedness to each other, which he called **synchronicity**.

In his search for universal spiritual themes, Jung studied many philosophical systems and their symbols: the Chinese Tao; the Tibetan mandala; Kali, the Hindu goddess of destruction; even medieval alchemy. While Freud viewed Jung's interest in mysticism as so much superstition, Jung believed the symbols of these ancient ethical/philosophic systems held great wisdom for modern humanity—if we can but discover their meanings. American psychologists, too, were skeptical about Jung's forays into esoteric symbolism until the post–World War II decades of the 1960s and 1970s. Young people, the world over began using the ancient Egyptian ankh as a universal symbol for peace. American psychologists began to take Jung's explorations into other cultural paradigms more seriously.

The Key to Jungian Dream Symbols: The Polarities of Human Existence. From his study of other cultural systems, Jung formulated a personality theory based on his study of *The Tao*—a traditional Chinese philosophic system of knowledge. Jung came to view the yin/yang symbol as revealing a great truth about human nature. Human understanding, Jung believed, is a matter of distinguishing between opposites. We are able to sense cold because we also sense hot. Other polarities include up/down, light/dark, creation/destruction, male/female. In a similar vein, our understanding of our emotions comes about by way of contrast. Here is an example from everyday life: If we have grown up fairly happily with few problems, we tend to take what we have for granted. Then, somewhere over the course of time, our lives are overshadowed by ill health or financial stress. After a bout of illness, we appreciate good health as we never have before. If we have been buried in debt, we will be more sensitive to living within a budget. Having experienced the dark, we now appreciate the light.

Two Levels of the Unconscious: Personal and Collective. Like Freud, Jung (1955) believed that we have an unconscious aspect to human personality. But whereas Freud postulated only a personal unconscious, Jung postulated that we also have a collective unconscious.

This deeper level of unconsciousness has to do with the evolution of the human race and connects us to everyone on earth. (If the reader finds that difficult to accept, we can use the analogy of the DNA by which we are related not only to all other human beings but to all life on earth.) This collective unconscious connects us not only to all other living persons but also to all previous generations of humanity.

Persona and Shadow. Jung distinguished two aspects of our personality, the *Persona* and the *Shadow*. Notice that the word *Persona* is closely related to the word *personality*. Actually, the **Persona** is what we would like to think our personality to be. It is the "public image" we put on when we put our best foot forward. It is what T.S. Eliot meant when he wrote of putting on "a face to meet the faces that we meet." The Persona can also be thought of as the roles we take on in life as "the Doctor," "the Lawyer," "the Drill Sergeant." The Persona also contains those qualities we portray ourselves to be, such as "sexy" or "pure" or "noble" or "macho" or whatever.

If the Persona is everything we like to think that we are, then the **Shadow** is everything we reject about ourselves. The traits we reject coalesce in our unconscious as our Shadow. We can deny the shadow side of ourselves but we cannot get rid of it. Like our physical shadow, our psychological shadow is always with us. When disagreeable aspects threaten to emerge in our consciousness, we protect ourselves by projecting our bad feelings onto others, sometimes making others our scapegoats. Some of the classic scapegoats have been the Jews, African-Americans, Native Americans, the Gypsies, etc. Sadly, even at the present time, ethnic groups all over the world are killing each other in horrible ways. In our dreams, the Shadow is often that fearsome person or something that frightens or chases us. For a man, it may be a person with a knife or a gorilla, all of which are symbolic of the "beast within" that the man fears might be getting out of control. A woman's Shadow may appear as something opposite to her public image. If she is a conservative person, modest in dress and speech, her Shadow may appear as a fun-loving seductress. If she values herself as intelligent and mature, her Shadow may appear as a retarded child.

Our Shadows are not necessarily "evil"—they are simply parts of ourselves we want to deny, some trait perhaps that embarrasses us or we think of as "childish" or "foolish." An example is a businessman who prided himself on being pennywise once threw some dollar bills into the coffers of the traditional Christmas bell-ringers. That night he had a dream in which he was a beggar giving his last dollar away. In his own eyes, his bit of spontaneous charity was really a bit of foolishness. He would have done better to write them a check so as to have evidence for a tax credit!

Our Rejected "Male" and "Female" Aspects: Anima and Animus. Freud had shocked many of his readers when he wrote that we are all biologically double-sexed—a fact that modern readers take for granted. Now Jung extended this thesis. What he said was that every culture develops certain ideas about which personality traits are appropriate for males and which are appropriate for females. Every child growing up learns the appropriate behaviors for his or her gender and rejects all those traits his family or culture deem inappropriate. The denied "female" traits in the young boy coalesce as the **Anima**. The denied "male" traits in the young girl coalesce as the **Animus**. As long as all goes well, the man and the woman can hang on to their culturally accepted Personas and hide their Shadow, Anima, and Animus.

But there come those moments in life, when the man and the woman are jolted by the circumstances of their lives and, suddenly, the man's Anima takes over his personality and the

Figure 13.2 Three Aspects of the Anima: The Virgin, the Mother, and the Hag!

woman's Animus takes over hers. It is a confounding event to the man or woman involved (and fascinating to watch). Let us consider a young lad who is taught to feel ashamed of crying or tears of any sort. He grows up with a "macho" style personality, always tough, able "to take it on the chin" or "bite the bullet." Aggressive acts come easily to him. Other female traits, such as caring and tenderness, have been repressed and have coalesced as his Anima. For much of his life, he is able to hang on to his macho style until one day something happens that penetrates his toughness. His wife walks out on him or his son is in an accident—and suddenly he cannot "hold it together." His Anima breaks through and takes over his personality. Behaviors he has denied for a lifetime suddenly break through as tears, copious weeping, bewildering sadness, and utter loneliness. These strange emotions may make him feel that he is "losing his mind." Said Jung, he is not losing his mind but actually getting in touch with the part he has denied for so long, which is part of what happens to him in the midlife crisis.

According to Jung, this denied part of the man, the Anima, is a true wellspring of creativity. Those who are more in touch with their Anima, said Jung, become the artists, reformers, visionaries, and creative scientists. Indeed, said Jung, poets and composers and writers, for centuries, have talked about their Muse—the goddess to whom they pay homage as the source of their inspiration. And who is this goddess? She may be called Harpsichord or Diana or Aphrodite but whatever she is called, he is calling forth his own Anima, and reaching deep into that rich source of his creative unconscious (see Figure 13.2). Like the psychologically androgynous child, men who can call on both sides of their psyche have a much wider spectrum of cognitions and emotions available to them. Is that only Jung speaking? Not at all. American psychologists who have been studying truly creative individuals validate Jung's thesis (Barron, 1970; Kubie, 1967; MacKinnon, 1978).

Furthermore, said Jung, when he falls in love with a woman, a man is really falling in love with himself—a way of uniting that other part of himself he has denied for so long. In the presence of his lady-love, he is able to express his repressed emotions of tenderness and caring (see Tip 13.1). That is why love makes us feel so good—we are feeling and expressing more sides to our personality than we ever have before.

Tip 13.1 Three Aspects of the Anima. Jung was a friend to all of the women in the world when he explained male psychology in this way. There are three aspects to the Anima: the innocent *nymph* (or virgin), the gracious and loving *Madonna* (the gracious and loving mother), and the hideous *hag* (or witch). Man falls in love with the young and innocent *nymph* and captures her in marriage. When she becomes the mother of his children, she is transformed into the archetypal Madonna. As he gets older and disenchanted with married life, he begins to call her "the old lady," the "nag," the "ball-and-chain"—he has come to view her as the *hag*. Now has she changed over the course of time? Of course not. Only his perception of her has changed. Furthermore, his vision of her (whether nymph, Madonna, or hag) has never been based on reality. Each aspect of her is really an aspect of his own unconscious Anima, which he has thrust upon her (see Figure 13.2).

In cultures such as ours, where the girl-child has been taught to repress her intellectuality and independence, those aspects of her personality will go underground as her *Animus*. If she has been defining herself all her life only as the wife of her husband and the mother of her children, she will have no identity of her own when her husband is taken up with his work and her children are grown away. Or her denied Animus may take another route. Instead of subjugating herself, she may subjugate her husband and children in either martyrdom or subtle sabotage of her husband as a person worthy of respect. Thus she comes to dominate the house. The Animus may appear in a woman's fantasies and dreams as the ideal lover of her romantic hopes or romantic disillusionment. The Animus may appear as a father figure from her child-like desire to remain "Daddy's little girl." Or as the priest or savior of her unfulfilled life. The Animus may also emerge as a nameless, faceless ogre, the ruffian who brutalizes her. This ogre may seem a little far-fetched to the reader. Who would want to be so brutalized? We have only to point to the women who have offered themselves in marriage to convicted murderers—even serial killers—for the psychological truth of this form of the Animus Archetype.

The Polarities of Our Collective Unconscious: The Archetypes. The Persona/Shadow and Animus/Anima polarities reside in our personal unconscious. There are certain aspects of our personality, said Jung, that have their roots in a far deeper part of the unconscious—they are the Archetypes of our racial or collective unconscious. Jung devised the term Archetype to convey something very old, buried in the most archaic aspects of the personality. As the off-spring of previous generations of humanity, we still contain "psychic remnants" of our ancestral forebears. As personality traits, these Archetypes are "predispositions" to perceiving the world in certain ways and expressing ourselves. So potent are these Archetypes in our racial unconscious that they have appeared in the legends, the literature, the art and artifacts of previous cultures. They continue to appear today in our dreams, in our fantasies, in our art, and in our literature. They crop up even in the most modern of dress, in movies and television, and in cartoons and comics. Just as our personal unconscious is characterized by the polarities of Persona/Shadow and Anima/Animus, so too are the Archetypes polarized. The adult Archetypes are composed of the *Wise Old Man* and *Wise Old Woman*. The children Archetypes are represented by the *Wise Child* and the *Trickster*.

The Wise Old Man. The **Wise Old Man** is the personification of the tribal wisdom collected in one person. Over the course of centuries the Wise Old Man has appeared as the medicine man, the shaman, the witch doctor, the rabbi, the minister, the priest, and as a tribal elder. The Wise Old Man formulates principles of conduct for the individual, for the tribe, for the clan, or for society-at-large. Moses of the *Old Testament* is a perfect personification of the Wise Old Man since he was the leader who laid down the wisdom of the Ten Commandments. For Catholics, he may be represented by the Pope. Mythology, folklore, and literature have idealized the Wise Old Man as King Arthur, as Father Time, as Shakespeare's Prospero. In whatever form he appears, his wisdom is the wisdom of experience that comes from having lived many years on this earth, learning the cyclical laws of nature, and the psychological motivations of men and women. However he is represented, his society or culture looks to him for help and guidance. On TV today, he may be the Father who "knows best" or the Beverly Hillbilly who looks like a country bumpkin but who knows about what comes naturally to human psychology. He may appear as the genial, popular talk show host or the all-knowing newscast anchorman. In our dreams, the Wise Old Man Archetype may come in the form of a deceased relative such as a father or grandfather, who counseled us in his lifetime, and now comforts us in our dreams. He may even come in the form of the president of a corporation or even the President of the United States.

The Wise Old Woman.   This archetype is the female polarity of the Wise Old Man. Over the course of centuries, she has been personified as the oracle, the Gypsy, the fairy godmother and good witch, the Nordic rune-thrower, the vestal virgin, and the high priestess whose symbol is the writhing snake of wisdom. Her wisdom, however, is of a different kind from that of the Wise Old Man. Her wisdom is not of this earth at all. The wisdom of the **Wise Old Woman** is that of intuition, the intuition that can see around corners and into the future. This wisdom vexes the men in her family. They scoff at "woman's intuition" but are awed by it. In the past, women who were deeply in touch with this aspect of themselves learned to listen to it but to keep still about it—or risk being burned at the stake. Despite their suspiciousness, men of other ages consulted the Wise Old Woman in form of the oracle, sibyl, or the Gypsy fortune teller. Today, we legitimize the appearance of these Wise Old Women at certain times—at Halloween in the forms of witches and as "psychic readers." On TV, she appears as Samantha of *Bewitched*. In the movie *The Wizard of Oz*, she is the Good Witch of the North, Glinda.

The Wise Old Woman can take the form of a man—but a very special type of man, a man who is innocent of life's carnal pleasures. Merlin is a good example. As long as he remained chaste he retained his mystic powers and lost them only when he allowed himself to be seduced by the witch-woman called Vivian. In the TV series *M*A*S*H*, he is that mystical character "Radar" who seems to know what people want before they ask him and can hear the helicopters before they come into listening range. He, too, the series makes plain, is a virgin innocent of the pleasures of the flesh.

The Wise Child.   The **Wise Child** Archetype represents the wisdom of goodness and purity, innocence and sweetness, joy and radiance. This is the wisdom we all had as children when we were more trusting and loving and open to the world. It is the wisdom we lost (alas!) as we grew older and became more cynical. With his lack of worldliness, Francis of Assisi was a Wise Child of the Church. In literature, the Wise Child has been portrayed by Antoine de St. Exupery as the Little Prince and by Charles Dickens as Tiny Tim and David Copperfield and Oliver Twist. But the Wise Child has also been portrayed as a girl, as Heidi and Pollyana or the Little Mermaid. In more modern form, the Wise Child is represented by Woody, the naive and trusting bartender of *Cheers*. Sometimes the Wise Child comes in surprising form. Although outwardly tough and highlighting all his sentences with all the four-letter words of the English language, Holden Caulfield (from the novel by J. D. Salinger) can see through the hypocrisy of society and wants none of it. Huckleberry Finn is another such Wise Child. Both Huck and Holden see through the sham of "The Emperor's New Clothes" and know him to be naked. And who among us will ever forget the Wise Child who befriended "E.T." The supreme example of the Wise Child is, of course, the Christ Child whose message is "Peace on earth, good will to men." Perhaps that is why our favorite holiday is the Christmas season for it is at this time that we are able to renew our childhood wisdom of faith and hope and express our love to others through the sending of cards and the giving of gifts.

The Trickster.   If we believe that children are all sweetness and kindness and lovingness, we beguile ourselves. There is also in children a mischievous, fun-loving, and unsocialized side. Jung called this aspect of a child's personality the Trickster, and he is the humorous polarity of the Wise Child. The Trickster can be impish at times like Puck in Shakespeare's *A Midsummer's*

Night Dream or the Irish leprechaun or the Scandinavian troll. Tom Sawyer tricks his friends into whitewashing his fence for him and Dennis the Menace outwits all of us adults.

Like the other archetypes, the Trickster has a unique wisdom all his own. It is the wisdom of *comic relief*. We cannot always be "good" and "lady-like." There are times when we simply must strip off the conventional standards and prohibitions of society and allow some sheer animal exuberance and wild laughter into our lives. He is Charlie Chaplin's "Little Tramp" and the irrepressible Marx Brothers, and Jerry Lewis. Because of his opposition to the conventions of society, the Trickster is often portrayed as an outlaw, like the movie portrayal of the Sundance Kid or the Norse god Loki who stole the fire of heavens and gave it to humanity. For that, Loki was severely punished and was condemned as pariah! (Thank you, Loki.) The Trickster is frequently portrayed as the "beast within" us in the form of fox or beaver in Native American folktales or Br'er Rabbit of the Uncle Remus stories. The Trickster is a shape-shifter.

The Integration of Personality: Our Search for Soul! If our basic nature consists of these many polarities, it followed logically for Jung, that our basic task in life is to integrate these polarities within us. It was Jung's belief that for most adults this happens most often at the midlife crisis. It is then that we take stock of our lives. We reevaluate where we are and what we want to do with the rest of our lives. Men who have been workaholics until then may suddenly find themselves struggling to express tenderness, caring, and love—all those parts of his Anima he has repressed for so long. Women who have had the opportunity to express nurturing and love may now reach for their repressed Animus, the assertive and intellectual side of themselves. But the process of integrating these aspects of ourselves can begin at any time in our lives (see Box 13.4).

This uniting of neglected aspects of ourselves is what Jung called the integration of personality (Jung, 1955). We are reaching for our soul, he said. For example, the Anima may appear to a man in any one of her three aspects of innocent and beautiful nymph (or virgin), as the gracious and beautiful archetypal queen or fairy godmother, or as the ugly hag from whom he must escape. But how can a man know when a woman in his dreams is the embodiment of his own Anima and not a "real" woman? Jung's reply is that he awakens knowing that he has experienced something magical and numinous, even unearthly. Even if he has dreamt of sexual intercourse with her, says Jung, the physical intercourse is a metaphor for the integration of his rough-and-ready self with the emotional/spiritual aspects of himself. In short, he is awakening to his own Soul. He may not be able to put his experience into words; all he knows is that the dream has left him strangely uplifted and transformed in ways he cannot yet describe.

Stephen LaBerge: Lucid Dreaming

In 1981, Stephen LaBerge introduced lucid dreaming. Lucid dreams are a technique by which dreamers can become aware they are dreaming and can alter the outcome of the dream. As an example, LaBerge related a lucid dreaming experience of his own. He dreamed that he was in the middle of a classroom riot in which a mob of people was raging about, throwing objects here and there and actually fist-fighting. At the center of this dream was the dreamer himself, who was being pinned down by a large, pock-mocked "Goliath." At this point, LaBerge recognized he was dreaming and immediately stopped struggling. He realized, he writes, that the struggle was within himself. On awakening, he knew that the "odious barbarian" of his dream was some Shadow-Ogre aspect of himself and the best (and perhaps the only ultimately effective way) to end the conflict was "to love my enemy (the Shadow-Ogre) as myself."

BOX **13.4** APPLICATION
Interpreting a Dream According to Jungian Dream Theory

The following is an actual student dream. Read the text and try your hand at interpreting it according to Jung's Archetypes.

Jonathon was the most serious young man we had ever come across. He was barely 19 years old, quite introverted, and hardly spoke at all until, unexpectedly, he spoke up and said he wanted help with a recurring dream that was making him frantic, which he reported as follows:

> *I keep having nightmares about a clown who does outrageous things! I know that doesn't sound like a bad dream but this clown does terrible things, like throwing all my books around and scattering my papers all over, and generally making a mess of my apartment, particularly my desk.*

Such a dream would be more funny than nightmarish for most people, but for Jonathon it was a terrifying dream. What he revealed about himself went something as follows:

> Jonathon was born into a military family; in fact, his father had retired as a full colonel. Jonathan was a late-in-life child; his mother was around 42 years old at the time of his birth. As he was the only child born to the couple, Jonathon was their central focus. Unfortunately, however, Jonathon did not grow up to be the large, muscular type like his father, but remained thin and slight, never growing taller after he reached five foot, five inches in height.

With all good intentions, Jonathon's father lectured to him constantly. Since Jonathon could certainly never follow in his father's footsteps and become an officer in the service, or play football, or engage in "manly jobs" (like becoming a policeman), the Colonel told him many times that the only way Jonathon was going to have a secure and dignified future was to go into a profession, such as becoming a physician. The colonel even supervised his homework. Jonathan made straight A's all through high school and was getting a B+/A− GPA in college. But Jonathon admitted that all the studying he had to do sometimes depressed him and if he studied too late in the evening, he often ended up with a headache. He rarely left his apartment and had only one friend whom he saw occasionally at campus where they had lunch together. There was no time for dating either, Jonathon explained because all his energy had to be directed to getting a high GPA so he could get in medical school.

1. Of all the Archetypes discussed in the chapter, which Archetype might the clown represent? State the reasons for your choice. _____
2. If you were a member of Jonathon's dream group, what might you want to say to him? Phrase your answer in two or three sentences. _____
3. If you believe you have had an archetypal dream, describe the dream and the Archetype(s) in it. Then state why you think you had such a dream.

LaBerge goes on to say that lucid dreaming is not new with him. Tibetan Buddhists have been using this technique since the eighth century. Furthermore, he is sure that most of us have experienced lucid dreaming at least once in our lives, and that it is easy to learn. What advantages does lucid dreaming have? LaBerge believes it fosters our growth and evolution by light years. Furthermore, if we believe that life is all too brief, he suggests that we stop being unconscious of one-third of our lives by remaining ignorant of what is going on during our sleep. Do we want guidance about a problem? Or are we concerned about our relationship with someone? Then all we need to do is to tell ourselves ahead of time to "dream on it" (LaBerge, 1981).

DAYDREAMING

Not Just Wishful Thinking, But Practical Problem Solving

Another level of consciousness is daydreaming, which involves drifting off into fantasy. It used to be thought that daydreams are simply an "escape from reality" or fulfilling an erotic desire. In nineteenth-century books on parenting, authors frequently warned against allowing children to daydream lest they slide into a life style of idleness and shiftlessness! The psychologist who legitimized daydreams as an important human event was a man by the name of Jerome Singer. By having his subjects keep a diary on what they daydream about, Singer was surprised to discover that very few daydreams are erotic in nature—even the daydreams of healthy, red-blooded college males. Nor are they very often violent. In actuality, our daydreams cover every aspect of our daily lives: our work, our studies, our family conflicts, our emotional relationships, our plans for the future. Of course, more of our daydreams will occur at moments of boredom or leisure. Lifeguards and truck drivers daydream to ease their boredom. But daydreams can also help "psych us up" toward some threatening event. Soldiers daydream how they will act in battle. Employees going in to ask for a raise may spend considerable daydreaming time imagining the scene, going over it "in their heads," preparing themselves for the dialog. In a very important sense, daydreaming is a kind of "rehearsal of the mind" (Singer, 1975; Klinger, 1990).

Furthermore, daydreaming is a vital source for our creativity, although we may call it by other terms: imagination, intuition, drawing on our inner resources, etc. Daydreams enable us to know what directions we want to take in our lives. Singer gave an example from his own life. Like other adolescents, he had many daydreams. The most frequent were of Singer, the Great Lover; Singer, the Hall-of-Fame Athlete; Singer, the World-Famous Surgeon; and Singer, the Concert Violinist. But Singer early realized that his athletic career would end with his high school graduation. It took a little longer to realize that he would never be a first-rate violinist. But his surgeon daydream did eventually lead him to his studies in psychology and to his career in a university setting. Singer concluded that, for most of us, daydreams are often the lodestar for the possible directions we may want to travel someday.

But not for everyone! Singer discovered that our daydreams tend to reflect our personality style. Persons who achieve their goals and who have a positive attitude toward life have positive fantasies with happy endings. Persons who are depressed or suffer from severe emotional problems tend to have unhappy daydreams that end with a depressing resolution. Persons who have passive personalities have daydreams that are rather aimless and meandering.

We can't leave this discussion on daydreaming and fantasy without mentioning the classic work of Joseph Campbell, entitled *The Power of Myth* (1988). Campbell helped us to realize that we all have dreams of greatness, of being a hero or heroine. Call them dreams, call them daydreams, call them fantasies, or simply images or icons of what we would like to be. We may not achieve the height and grandeur of our idols, but they represent something that we yearn to be and motivates our behavior. In that respect, Campbell's thesis is not unlike that of Alfred Adler's theory of personality; namely, that we are all living out a great mythic theme (see pages 57–58). But back to Campbell, who presented us with another Archetype: *the Hero*.

Joseph Campbell: The Hero Archetype with a Thousand Faces

Like Freud and Jung, another scholar believes that our mythologies, ancient and modern, represent profound truths of the human experience. If folklore and fairytale have meaning for the child, the great mythic themes have meaning for adults. Each one of us, says Campbell, is not only the Hero (or Heroine) of our life story, each of us is living a mythic theme. For example, if we are a young man on the threshold of our adult life, we may be living out the traditional archetypal hero setting off to accomplish a great deed. We may be Jason pursuing the Golden Fleece or Saint George slaying the Dragon or Galahad in search of the Holy Grail. The Hero has "a thousand faces," said Campbell, but whatever his face, his Quest is always the same. The capture of the Golden Fleece and the slaying of the Dragon and the search for the Holy

Grail are all simply metaphors for the Quest. And what is that Quest? It is the same for all of us: To know ourselves completely (Campell, 1988).

Sometimes, the Hero may have to become an Outlaw to achieve his Quest. A rebellious teenager, in and out of jail for shoplifting, may be living out a Robin Hood myth since he may see himself as stealing from the rich (the stores) and giving to the poor (himself and his adolescent friends) and hiding out from the Sheriff of Nottingham's law (the police). In which case, we need to help him reinterpret the Robin Hood legend in a constructive way. Or consider the traditional interpretation of Lucifer's revolt against God. As a sacred myth, it relates the story of the rebellion of a light-giving angel (Lucifer means light) who fell from the heavens in defeat. Mythologically, it has to do with some of our most unconscious motivations to challenge authority and to become an outlaw, if necessary, in order to be heard. Everyone deserves to be heard, said the Medieval Church, even Lucifer. It was the Medieval Church that instituted this tradition that all persons, even those accused of heresy and witchcraft, had a right to be defended by the "Devil's Advocate." Today we accord the same privilege to all defendants, even those who have admitted to heinous crimes—representation by an attorney. If the defendant does not have an attorney, we will provide one for him. *Everyone has a right to a defense.*

Do not be put off by the quaintness of a myth. If we can discover what dominant myth we are living out, we can then decide if we want to continue to live that myth to its ending—or if we want to choose a Quest of another type. Or perhaps the mythic theme we have been living has come to a natural ending. For example, a woman who has been blessed by beauty and living the myth of a "love goddess" may need to come to terms with her increasing years and fading beauty. If she does not, she will become a tragic caricature of herself who puts more and more makeup on her face to hide her wrinkles and bleaches her hair until it is pink or purple. Discovery of our mythic theme is not always such a cause for despair. Our discovery can be joyous in fact. A lady of our knowledge told us of the discovery of her life-long mythic theme.

> I was orphaned early in my childhood, and for most of childhood and adolescence lived in a physically and psychologically abusive family. Being most of the time alone and isolated from others, I became almost a feral child. In my isolated ignorance, I used to wonder, many times, how people become adults; that is to say, how did a person gain enough knowledge to become grown-up and acquire the wisdom to make decisions? Being a reader, I used to wander through the shelves of the local library looking at all the books, wondering how I would be able to read them all. Having no one to talk to or ask questions of, I thought the only way I could learn to be an adult was by reading as much as I could. Reading and studying became my pastime and my obsession. Of course, it stood me in good stead because later, when I escaped from the abusive foster family, I was able to go to college and professional school with ease. One day, as I was reading a book on the goddess archetypes, I realized that my archetypal goddess was Athena. My life-long quest had been to become wise. I do not count myself as any "great shakes" of intellect, but my students sometimes tell me that I seem wise to them. My life has been one of great upheaval of traumatic events—including the death of three of my five children. But now at the twilight of my life, I think that my Quest has been at least a little successful.

So popular has the mythic theme become in the last decade that many such books have appeared on the publishing market. Some deal with female goddess archetypes; some deal with male god archetypes. Some deal with mother/daughter archetypal themes, while others deal with sister themes.

MEDITATION AND MEDITATIONAL PRAYER

Meditation tends to be associated with esoteric Eastern philosophies. Actually all major religions, including the Judaic/Christian, have developed specific techniques to attain other states of consciousness. These techniques may utilize visual symbols such as the **mandala** of Tibetan Buddhism, the cross of Christianity, and the Jewish Star of David. Other techniques use auditory techniques to induce the meditational and prayerful states, such as the Buddhist **mantra**, which can be a long, drawn-out OHHHhhhmmmm, or the intonation of the Tibetan phrase OH MANI PADME HUM. The Catholics intone the familiar *Hail, Mary* fingering bead after bead of the Rosary. All Christians repeat the *Our Father* as a preamble to the prayerful state. The Jews intone the ancient Judaic prayer, the *Shema*, the most fundamental and ancient of Hebraic prayers. Auditory symbols can involve the beating of drums, the ringing of bells, and the sound of chanting. Incense and other scents may be used to alter the person's state of consciousness. Nor are the paths to altered meditational and prayerful states limited to the classic five senses. Some traditions utilize physical postures not ordinarily used by people in their everyday routine. Catholics and Protestants kneel. Orthodox Jews bend their heads and torsos repeatedly in front of the famous Wailing Wall of Jerusalem. Hindus and Buddhists use various yoga positions. The Sufis of Persia are renowned for the spinning dance technique they use, going round and round, to induce a trance state.

Results of Meditation and Meditational Prayer

But what do meditation and meditational prayer accomplish? When well practiced, they remove us from our ordinary mind-sets and conditioned responses of everyday life, and allow us to perceive larger universal paradigms. We are withdrawing from the usual hurly-burley to a place of interior calm. Some have described prayer as "interior talking" and meditation as "interior listening." In religious terms, people have described the difference as "talking to God" "listening to God." However they are described, they are methods by which people are reaching for higher levels of consciousness.

Advocates of meditation assert that it can enhance learning, creativity, cognitive development, energy level, and happiness while reducing tension and anxiety caused by stress and thereby increasing longevity. Are the claims of meditators borne out by research? Studies of long-term meditators do show actual physiological changes. There is a change of brain wave patterns from predominantly beta waves (our usual waking brain wave activity) to alpha waves and theta waves, which are slower and deeper. Most studies also show changes in heart rate, respiration rate, oxygen consumption, skin resistance, and a decrease in blood lactates (which are built-up toxins after activity). All of these physiological changes are similar to the changes that occur after deep relaxation. In fact, one investigator (who has been studying transcendental meditation for several decades) believes that meditation is a kind of **relaxation response** (Benson, 1987). While some of the claims for meditation and meditational prayer may be somewhat "hyped up," there seems to be no doubt that faithful practice of prayer and meditation is good for body and soul. Recently, we asked some persons to tell us what meditation means to them. Although varied in expression, their answers suggest the attainment of joy, of loving compassion for the whole world, and for what has been called the *peace that passeth all understanding*. At its most basic level, meditation is a way of getting in touch with one's **center-of-growth** (Rogers, 1961, 1970). At its most exalted level, it partakes of what

Abraham Maslow called the **peak experience**, a feeling of exultation, peace, and at-one-ment with the universe (Maslow, 1954, 1976).

HYPNOSIS: ITS HISTORY AND APPLICATIONS

As a healing art, hypnosis has had a curiously roller-coaster experience. The reader will remember that hypnosis got its start when a physician by the name of Anton Mesmer discovered he could cure some of his patients' symptoms by putting them into a trance and altering their "animal magnetism." Unfortunately, after a few mishaps in which his patients had convulsions and a few actually died, he was literally run out of town and denounced as a charlatan. "Mesmerism" remained a "black art" until a Scottish physician, by the name of James Braid, gave it the name of hypnotism in 1843 (Hypnos was the Greek god of sleep). Braid tried using it for minor surgeries and apparently it seemed to work, but since trance induction takes a fair amount of time, it was not appropriate for an emergency situation.

Freud began his practice using hypnosis to uncover repressed memories but later dropped its use when he discovered that unconscious material could be brought to consciousness by the simpler method of free association. In the first half of the twentieth century, hypnosis was treated as a kind of "parlor game" and taken no more seriously than a seance or a Ouija Board. Today, however, it is being explored as a valid healing art in many areas. Dentists are using it to allay the anxieties of "apprehensive patients." Psychologists are using it to catharsize the stressful events of posttraumatic stress disorders. Although inadmissible in court, hypnosis is sometimes used in law enforcement to enable a victim or witness to recall significant details of a crime. Health professionals are using it to induce more rapid healing for surgery. As a self-improvement method, autohypnosis is used as a way to enable people to become more confident in themselves, more self-directed, and more self-assertive. As a healing art, research is being conducted worldwide on the many possible applications of hypnosis (Gibson & Heap, 1991).

But What Is Hypnosis?

The irony is that though we are finding many uses for hypnosis, we still don't know what it is. Theories abound! In fact, there are almost as many theories about what it is as there are scientists studying it. *It is a state of narrowly focused attention. It is a state of deep relaxation. It is a state of creative fantasy. It is conditioned susceptibility to suggestion. It is split-consciousness. It isn't even an altered state of consciousness, it's simply role-playing.* Finally, *it is a puzzlement.*

Characteristics of Hypnotizable Subjects. But some of the pieces of the puzzle are emerging (Hilgard, 1986; Kihlstrom, 1985; Meyer, 1992). The following findings are fairly well established.

1. *Subjects differ in their responsiveness to hypnosis.* Not everyone can be hypnotized. About 10 percent of the population cannot be hypnotized at all. About 10 percent are exceptionally good at allowing themselves to be hypnotized. In fact, the more studies being undertaken and the more subjects being tested, the more the ability to be hypnotized approaches the "normal curve."

2. *Exceptionally good subjects are also rich in "inner resources."* Subjects who are "exceptionally good" in responding to hypnotic suggestion are also people who have a vivid imagination and a strong ability to use daydreaming creatively. In other words, they have outstanding inner resources. They are not afraid of new experiences. They can focus their attention easily. They are good at using self-hypnosis toward their own holistic healing and growth. There is also a suggestion that people who experienced severe punishment in childhood tend to show good hypnotic responsiveness. It may be that under severe stress, these children coped by retreating from the external environment to their inner environment. As a consequence, they developed their "exceptionally good" inner resources (Nash, Lynn, & Givens, 1984).

3. *Subjects can be led to sensory distortions and hallucinations.* The trance inducer can lead the subjects to changes in their perception—even to the point of hallucinating objects that are not visible and hearing sounds that are not in the environment. Other sensory hallucinations can also be induced. A person can be made to smell the sweet scent of a rose or the odious scent of decaying matter. They can be led to feel warm or cold. This sensory-perceptual distortion has become a serious subject for induced "false memories" of child incest and rape.

4. *Subjects become more disinhibited in what they are willing to do.* Very conventional people can be led to behave in "silly" ways they would normally be unable to do, such as "crow like a rooster" or "squat like a chimpanzee." One person was even induced to rob a bank (Deyoub, 1984). Normally, however, even the most responsive subjects will not perform acts that go against their moral grain. It may be that the subject who robbed the bank had always wanted to try his hand at it in much the same way that adolescents go in for shoplifting just to see if they "can get away with it."

5. *Subjects can be given post-hypnotic suggestion.* It is true that hypnotized subjects can be given post-hypnotic suggestions. In fact, some hypnotherapists use post-hypnotic suggestions to enable their subjects to reduce their cigarette or food addictions. Other psychotherapists, however, will only use hypnosis in conjunction with counseling sessions— and with good reason! If a person is smoking in order to cope with extreme anxiety or other "mental" symptoms, what happens to that anxiety if we give the subject a post-hypnotic command to "stop smoking." The anxiety may come out in other, more serious symptoms, such as a panic attack or obsessive-compulsive behavior. Hypnotherapists, therefore, generally approach the addiction on two fronts: post-hypnotic suggestion *and* psychotherapeutic counseling.

6. *Subjects can remember their hypnotic experience or not—as the trance inducer commands.* Whether a person can recall the hypnotic experience or not is a matter of a simple post-hypnotic command. Generally speaking most ethical hypnotherapists do not want to elicit material without the subject's post-hypnotic awareness. They simply do not want to intrude on a person's privacy without the subject's consent and knowledge. Of course, there may be times when a subject does not want to bring back full awareness of the experience, as in the case of rape or a brutal beating.

What can we say, then, about hypnosis? Perhaps the best summary statement we can make at the present time is to say that *hypnosis is a very special and intense kind of communication* between the trance inducer and the hypnotized subject (Meyer, 1992). Within this intense communication, people can be helped to catharsize past trauma, to cope with present problems, and to become more self-directing in the future (see Box 13.5).

BOX **13.5** TRANSCRIPT
A Hypnosis Session

The subject was to have an operation. She was experiencing severe panic, not because of the operation but because of her extreme fear of anesthesia, so severe it bordered on phobia. Before the hypnotherapeutic session began, she related the following:

Subject: My parents died before I was eight . . . and I was raised by an aunt and uncle . . . who received a weekly sum of money from the insurance money that came from my father's death . . . My aunt and uncle had three children of their own . . . and they did not like me, since I was half Jewish, and they were very anti-Semitic. It was a horrible situation, and I was a scapegoat for their anti-Semitism. When I was eleven, I had a severe attack of appendicitis . . . I lay on the couch for a long time in pain. Finally, I was taken in a taxi to the hospital and put under anesthesia. I remember being very scared and wanting to tell someone, but when I started to say something, they simply clamped the anesthetic mask over my face, and I remember feeling like I was choking to death. When I woke up, people came in and out of my room, but no one ever seemed to talk to me . . . I was in a room by myself and never saw anyone else, except my aunt. For ten days I was visited by my aunt and one or two nurses and the doctor. I never had other visitors. I never even saw the other patients in the hospital . . . the only gift or toy that I received was, one day, a bunch of letters came written by my classmates, I suppose written under the direction of the teacher. Ever since that experience, I have had deathly fears of doctors, hospitals, and particularly any kind of anesthesia. I hated our family physician after that and all doctors ever since. He made such a big gash in my abdomen that I have had a scar ever since.

We have reproduced excerpts from the transcript. The subject has been trance-induced and has had the suggestion of awakening in the hospital room.

Hypnotherapist: How are you feeling?
Subject: All right. No pain. Glad of that . . .
Hypnotherapist: Can you see your hospital room?

Subject: Yes.
Hypnotherapist: Can you describe the room?
Subject: Yes.
Hypnotherapist: What color are the walls?
Subject: Kind of brown. Light brown. More like beige. Curtains. Kind of lacy. Arm chair brown. Dresser is brown, just brown wood. Everything brown wood . . .
Hypnotherapist: Can you hear [anybody] moving?
Subject: No. I can't hear anything. I'm supposed to call them but I don't know how. They don't seem to hear me.
Hypnotherapist: Can you hear anything at all?
Subject: No, everything is so quiet. I seem to be by myself. I can see trees out the window. The tops of trees.
Hypnotherapist: You said "house."
Subject: This seems like a house.
Hypnotherapist: It doesn't seem like a hospital?
Subject: No, just a house . . . (*The hypnotherapist told us later he proceeded extremely carefully now because of what this might mean and he didn't want to lead the subject or induce false memories.*)
Hypnotherapist: What is happening now?
Subject: Someone came in the room. I am telling them I have to pee. They say they will bring a bedpan.
Hypnotherapist: Male or female?
Subject: Female.
Hypnotherapist: How is she dressed?
Subject: Dress with flowers on it. Yellow flowers. Pink flowers. Different colors.
Hypnotherapist: She is not in a uniform?
Subject: No one in this house wears a uniform.

The hypnotherapist had the subject move forward in time to when she was going home. She is helped to walk by her aunt and someone else, not in uniform.

Hypnotherapist: Where are you?
Subject: Holding onto stairs.
Hypnotherapist: Can you see anything else?

BOX **13.5** TRANSCRIPT (continued)
A Hypnosis Session

Subject: People . . . old people . . . yes, very old people . . . Wait a minute . . . I think this is not a hospital.

Hypnotherapist: You think it is not a hospital?

Subject: No . . . more like . . . more like . . . just a house with upstairs and downstairs . . .

The hypnotherapist instructed the subject to return to her usual consciousness and to retain the memory. The following is an interview held immediately afterwards.

Hypnotherapist: How are you feeling?

Subject: Strange. It's like I understand something I never understood before. It wasn't a hospital at all. It was just a house. I don't know how to fathom that. How could I have had an operation in a house? It was more like an old folks' home.

Hypnotherapist: An old folks' home?

Subject: My God! That would explain a lot, . . . wouldn't it? . . . Why I never saw anybody or heard anything . . . like other children. It was . . . always quiet. They had me tucked away from the other patients. . . . There really weren't any nurses. More like attendants.

Hypnotherapist: How do you explain all this?

Subject: I think my aunt was trying to save money. They were poor. I think now that explains why I was there. A hospital would have cost too much.

Hypnotherapist: But you said there was insurance money for you being there.

Subject: Yes, but my aunt was so stingy. I guess from being poor. That would account for why there was no ambulance either. I went in a taxi. I remember that. I went home in a taxi. We didn't even have a car. There was no hospital in our town. Oh my! I just remembered. There was an old folks' home there. There really was. That's where I was!

HOW DRUGS WORK ON OUR PSYCHOPHYSICAL MINDBODY

To understand how drugs work, we need to understand about neurology. We will do our best to explain the structure of the nervous system in as few words as possible. With just a little bit of basic neurology, we can then understand how drugs alter its functioning.

Within our bodies are (perhaps) 10,000,000 neurons (lay people call them nerves), which do many, many things. They transmit information from all our senses (eyes, ears, nose, mouth, and skin) to our brains so that we can see, hear, smell, taste, and feel. They activate our muscles so we can walk, write, talk, and even breathe. They deliver messages from our internal organs so that we experience hunger, or the need to urinate, or sexual stimulation. They also deliver pain signals to let us know that all is not well within us. All of this is done in "nanoseconds." Neurons differ in size and shape depending on where they are in the body, but they all communicate with each other in the same way. This communication of one neuron to another throughout our body is called **neuronal firing**.

When early neuroanatomists were mapping out the nervous system, they made a discovery that astonished them. Despite the millions of neurons that are involved in the action described, not a single neuron ever touches another neuron. They are separated by tiny spaces called **synaptic gaps**. So the question they asked themselves was, "If no neuron touches any other neuron, how do they fire each other across the synaptic gaps?" The answer was not long in coming. *Neurons fire each other by the release of chemical compounds called **neuro-transmitters** that communicate the synaptic gap and fire the neighboring neurons.* Or they may tell the neighboring neurons to STOP firing. Or they may tell the neighboring neurons to speed up their firing. Or they may tell the neighboring neurons to slow down their firing.

Whether in our eyes and ears or muscles, heart, liver, or bladder—or in the brain itself—the significant functioning of our nervous system is taking place at the synaptic gap with the action of the neurotransmitters. To use an analogy, the synaptic gap can be thought of as the "playing field" where the neurotransmitters are acting and reacting with each other.

How they interact with each other depends on their chemical structure. There are over 200 known to us at the present time and, undoubtedly, many more will be discovered in the coming decades. The reader may even be familiar with the names of some of the better known transmitters, such as *choline, acetylcholine, dopamine, epinephrine, norepinephrine,* or *serotonin.* Now anything that alters the firing of these neurotransmitters will alter how we perceive our external and internal environments. Of course, we are reacting all the time to slight changes in our vision, our hearing, our feelings moment-by-moment. We suddenly sense a cool breeze on our face or hear someone blowing a horn. Or we notice a banana skin on our front steps and realize we had better pick it up so that no one will get hurt.

Now if the neural communication is greatly altered, we will experience significant and sometimes astonishing changes of how we see or hear or feel, etc. These significantly altered perceptions of our internal and external environments have been called **altered states of consciousness**. That is exactly what drugs do—they change the usual functioning of the transmitters. These drugs are generally classified as depressants, stimulants, and hallucinogens.

Depressants. All substances (including all legal or illegal drugs) are categorized according to how they alter the transmission of the neurotransmitters. If the substance slows down the firing of the transmitters, they are called **depressants**. Examples of depressants are anesthetics and all those drugs we call "pain killers" or (to use the professional term) **analgesics** such as aspirin or ibuprofen. Other depressants include tranquilizers, barbiturates, and sedatives. One of the effects of alcohol is to act as a depressant. Obviously, the more depressants we take to allay our anxieties or to cover up pain or to soothe our jangled nerves, the less "awake" we are. Eventually, we can become drowsy, fall asleep, lose consciousness, go into coma—and die. From being fully alert to being drowsy, to falling asleep, to lapsing into coma and death is simply a continuum. The death of Marilyn Monroe was a combination of depressants—alcohol, "pain pills," and tranquilizers—all within a few short hours.

Alcohol is our most dangerous legal drug. When we drink, we are slowing down the action of the neural transmitters. With every ounce of alcohol, neural firing becomes slower and slower. Our vision gets clouded. Our perceptions become distorted and our general motor coordination becomes sluggish. Using any machine while under the influence of alcohol becomes extremely dangerous. Carpenters have lopped off fingers with a skill saw. Hunters have mistaken other hunters for the animals they are hunting. And it has been estimated that driving "under the influence" is responsible for perhaps 10,000 automobile accidents every year. Drinking and driving is a lethal combination.

Stimulants. Certain substances seem to "buoy us up" and get us energized. These substances are called **stimulants**. Their action on our neurons is to tell them to fire more or to fire faster! Included in this category are caffeine (in our coffee, in our tea, in our hot chocolate), nicotine, sugar, amphetamines ("pep" pills). College students have used all of these to crash study. Truck drivers use them to keep awake on long, solitary routes. If used over a prolonged time, stimulants can eventually interfere with REM sleep and our other circadian rhythms. What follows will be insomnia, night terrors, and **sleep apnea** (cessation of breathing for 15 to 60 seconds). Extended interference with REM sleep results in irritability and drowsiness during the day. But even short-term usage will have an effect on us. For example, "diet pills" (some of which contain high-powered stimulants) may keep us "jittery" and feeling as if we "can't sit still." Furthermore, there is some increasing evidence that how "high" we get will determine how deeply we crash. The more extended the "high" the more extended will be the resulting period of psychological depression and low physical energy.

Hallucinogens. Depressants and stimulants work on our **peripheral nervous system**, which includes the muscles, the organs, our respiratory system, etc. What about the substances that target the **central nervous system**, which is made up of our brain and spinal cord? These substances include LSD, mescaline, and psilocybin (from mushrooms), marijuana, and the manufactured "designer drugs" such as ecstasy. The moment we alter the functioning of the neuronal transmitters in our brains, we are going to perceive things quite differently. How we see colors may change. Our sense of time may seem to slow down or even stop. Our senses of taste and smell may be sharpened. The perceptual constancies of shape and size may crumble, and we may again experience the world as unconnected events as we did as infants and children. We may have a wonderful time wandering through a new and exotic environment. We may experience a euphoria that arouses our desire to express it in music or art. These were the kinds of experiences that were the quest of the many entertainers who died from overdoses. On the other hand, we may have a "bad trip" and be unable to awaken from a brutal nightmare that goes on and on for hours. A "bad trip" may even leave after-effects similar to posttraumatic stress syndrome involving paranoid episodes, confused thought processes, and "flashbacks."

We are not debating here the legality of drugs nor even the mind-altering insights that can come from hallucinogenic drugs. What we are concerned about are the negative effects that can decimate even the most successful personality structure. We have enough examples now of famous men and women in the arts and entertainment fields who used drugs to stimulate their creativity, only to fall victim to drug use later. We are saddened by the loss of these wonderfully talented people: John Belushi, Janis Joplin, Jimi Hendrix, Marilyn Monroe. Before their brilliant careers became a trajectory toward death, they endured many physical and psychological difficulties, including loss of memory (difficulty in remembering lines, appointments, time of day), physical depletion, frequent insomnia, loss of self-confidence, the inability to make decisions, heightened sensitivity to painful stimuli, sexual impotence, anxiety to the point of panic attack, catatonic reactions, and so on.

Peak Experiences

Our Perceptions of "Reality" Differ Tremendously. When it comes right down to it, we each know very little about what we call *reality*. What we think of as "reality" is the result of a complex of our genetics, our gender, our culture, our conditioning and past experiences, our age or stage in life, and so on. This total complex of personality variables results in vastly different reactions to any given situation; as, for example, how the six people described in the opening scenario of this book (Box 1.1) responded to the same event in vastly different ways. Just as no two people have exactly the same fingerprints, no two people have the same perceptions of reality. We don't realize that our perception of reality is limited or different from other people's perceptions. To use Plato's famous analogy of prisoners chained in a cave: There is a world of light outside the cave, but all the prisoners can see are their own shadows. The moral of Plato's analogy is that we think we know reality, but what we are really perceiving are simply our own shadows.

To use another analogy, it's as if each of us is walking around in a glass bubble (something like an astronaut's helmet) through which we perceive the world and all the people in it (our worldview). Some people may have a glass bubble that is dark and shadowy, making the world seem a frightening place to be with danger always just around the corner. Some people are looking through glass bubbles like those mirrors in a carnival that make everybody (including themselves) as ugly as the monsters in our nightmares. Still others are looking through rose-colored bubbles and reality seems as lovely as a rose window. It seldom occurs to us that our perception of reality is actually a reflection of ourselves (our worldview) rather than what is really "out there."

Then Every So Often Our Perceptions of Reality Are Suddenly Shattered. Some event comes along that causes a crack in our glass bubble. This event can be triggered by any number of experiences, but whether positive or negative, it jolts our complacency. Sometimes it happens through hallucinogenic drugs that alter our sense of the constancies of space, color, and time. It can come about as a severe bout of alcoholism, which may result in seeing pink elephants or cockroaches on the wall. High fevers, medications, and sleep deprivation can also dramatically change our sensory perceptions. Sometimes, the perceptions can be quite positive, even inspirational.

Positive experiences were described by the philosopher, Aldous Huxley, in a book entitled, *The Door of Perception,* (1963). Huxley was almost blind, but under the influence of mescaline (still legal at the time), he was able to see rich details of color and fabric he had never before been able to make out. Later, while he was dying, he was given LSD (lysegic acid diethylamide) by his wife who was a physician. She reported that as the drug began to take effect, the dying man turned to her and said that he understood now that *what mattered most in life was love*. This was a revelation for that man who had placed such importance on his philosophic writings and essays. We are not advising the reader, in any way, to experiment with controlled substances. There are much healthier (and legal) ways to heighten consciousness.

Cracks in our bubbles can also come about by psychosocial events. One of these events happens quite frequently in our midlife (or earlier) when a parent dies. Men often report that the death of their father brings about the realization that their own existence on this planet will not go on forever (Levinson, et al., 1978). They can no longer deny their own mortality. Earlier, Carl Jung (1955) had described the midlife passage around 40 years of age as the time that men must acknowledge that more than half of their biblical "three score years and ten" has come and gone. The issue they must now address is: *How shall I spend the second half of my life?* This acknowledgment sometimes causes them to make an about-turn in their goals and direction. Where "success" was perceived in terms of money, status, and power, "success" may now be experienced as reconnecting to their families once again, being inspired by the forces of nature, and partaking of intimate moments with friends and colleagues.

Other more positive events can trigger cracks in our day-to-day established perceptions of the world. Consider, for example, the woman described in Chapter 11, page 275, who suffered from dysthymia (moderate depression) for years and then woke up one day to realize how blue was the sky and how lovely the sound of birds singing. Consider, for example, the change in a person's perception when he or she "falls in love." The whole world seems to have changed. Of course the world has not changed. It is the person in love who has changed (Brown & Amatea, 2000). Or consider the reactions of students who have been in the vicinity of a terrorist event. They report that they realize, for the first time in their lives, how fragile life really is, and that they are determined never again to take existence for granted but to value every moment of every day. They also have a drastic reversal in their perceptions of parental "nagging" and "over-protection." They now understand their parents' concerns and to express more love to them whenever possible (O'Connell & Grunder, 2003).

Maslow's "Peak" Experiences. The cracks in our perceptions of reality can also lead to what Abraham Maslow termed "peak experiences." In investigating his highly self-actualizing persons, Maslow came to the conclusion that one of their outstanding characteristics was the number of peak experiences they had had. Maslow was well versed in those extraordinary experiences described by different cultures in various ways: *satori* by Zen Buddhists, *enlightenment* by the Hindus, *at-one-ment* by the Hasidic Jews; *touched by Allah* by the Sufis; and the Christian experience of being *born again.* Mystic and transpersonal experiences have been described by saints and sages down through the centuries and across cultures. All of these experiences were categorized by Abraham Maslow (1954) as "peak experiences."

Maslow didn't want to use such terms as religious experience, or mystic experience or spiritual experience, so he devised this new term, *peak experience,* to cover these moments of illumination that people have reported. The reason for this was that, at the time of Maslow's ground-breaking "Third Force" humanistic thrust, the study of "inner experience" was still not considered a valid subject for psychological research. There didn't seem to be any scientific way to study such private and personal experiences (see Tip 13.2). By using the term "peak experience," Maslow hoped that he would avoid turning off psychologists who felt such topics were not appropriate for psychological research. Well, it is more than fifty years later, and psychologists are not as nervous about investigating such inner experiences as love, as sexual arousal, as dreams and daydreams, as the experience of dying, and (as we shall see) . . . even the phenomenon of "spirituality" (see Tip 13.2).

Spiritual Peak Experiences and the Role of Service. Nevertheless, "spiritual and religious experience" has been a difficult phenomenon to define because of the vastly different ways that people describe them. Some people even say it is impossible to describe. Social scientists have had to devise special research techniques to study the experience, as in the research we are about to describe. What the research team did was to have people who have reported such experiences to talk about them into a tape recorder or to write a description of them, whichever was most comfortable. Then other social scientists independently analyzed the content and extract, if they could, whatever common factors they could discover. The social scientists then came together as a team, to compare their results (Deikman, 2000). After allowing for variations of language and specific church dogma, there seemed to the researchers that they could identify some common elements as follows:

1. There was a sense of connectedness to something-larger-than-themselves;
2. This something-larger-than-themselves seemed to be much more immense than their small ego-selves. Some of the terms they used included something "out there in the

---

Tip 13.2 On the Problems of Defining Religiousness and Spirituality. This person may be a regular church-goer and contribute generously to the church, but does that mean he is religious? Perhaps his church membership is a route to making a connection to other prominent businessmen in the community. Alternatively, some people volunteer many hours in the nitty-gritty work of visiting prisoners who have no one else who comes to see them. Or medical teams who give of their time to people throughout the poorer countries of the world, particularly those that have a high frequency of AIDS. They may not necessarily go to some church but does that mean they are not spiritual people? One such organization, *Doctors Without Borders*, was recently awarded the Nobel prize for Humanitarianism.

universe—maybe the Universe itself," "some higher power," "some force that is supra-personal," something "infinite and beyond human understanding." Others even said that they felt they were part of this something-larger-than-themselves.

3. This connection to something-larger-than-themselves was sometimes so awesome that it could have been frightening except that the feelings of awe were also accompanied by feelings of joyfulness, of being intrinsically inspirational, and leading to good.

4. Finally, the experience of being connected to something-larger-than-themselves lead them to do something valuable in the world, sometimes expressed as being of service to others.

Sometimes the subjects' experiences came by way of study and deep moments of meditation. Sometimes, however, their experiences came quite by accident to people who did not call themselves religious by any means. To get a better idea of the experience, we are about to provide some actual quotations of people who have reported such moments. It is one thing to quote highly religious people who have a strong affiliation to a certain church or sect. It is quite another to quote mental health professionals who described themselves as not being particularly religious or who were scientific skeptics about "spiritual peak experiences"—until they also experienced one themselves—often much to their surprise. As we quote these experiences, note how they fulfill one or more of the four commonalities noted previously.

The first experience reported is that of C. P. Snow, the well-known English scientist and novelist, who described his experience in the following way:

> It was as though I'd looked for a truth outside myself and finding it [I had] become for a moment part of the truth I sought; as though the world, the atoms and the stars were wonderfully clear and close to me, and I to them, so that we were part of a lucidity more tremendous than any mystery. Since then I have never quite regained it. But one effect will stay with me as long as I live. . . . When I was young, I used to sneer at the mystics who have described the experience of being at one with God and part of the unity of things. After that afternoon, I did not want to laugh again; for though I [might] have interpreted the experience differently, I thought I knew what they meant.

Other people say that this sense of something-larger-than-themselves also involved the need to serve others. People who provide such service do not want to get credit for it or even to make public what they are doing. For example, the person who founded an organization to provide care for people with AIDS, described the task as follows:

> I'm not serving myself . . . or getting brownie points for Heaven. "Doing what needs to be done" is the way I used to say it to the [AIDS] volunteers. You're serving something greater and deeper than the person in front of you. . . .

Almost the same words are used by a physician who founded an organization to provide support for cancer patients. She says that she knows when something is really of service:

> It's a sense of connection . . . to something beyond the moment . . . It's like both of you are part of a much larger process that has no beginning and no end.

To these quotations from *The Harvard Mental Health Letter*, we add two others that also involve mental health professionals. The first report is that of a psychiatrist by the name of

Richard Maurice Bucke, a physician who was a friend of Walt Whitman, and who was eventually appointed as the Superintendent of The Asylum for the Insane in London, Canada. He was a remarkable scientist with a bent for philosophy and literature but was not particularly religious when he had a shattering experience at the age of 35 years. He was returning to his residence in London (England) after an enjoyable evening spent with friends. We quote now from the preface of his book, *Cosmic Consciousness* (1901). He described himself as being in a quiet and pleasant frame of mind as he was returning to his residence in a hansom cab when:

> All at once, without warning of any kind, he found himself wrapped around, as it were, by a flame-colored cloud. For an instant, he thought of fire—some sudden conflagration in the great city. The next (instant) he knew the fire was within himself.
>
> Directly after, there came upon him a sense of exultation, of immense joyousness, accompanied or immediately followed by an intellectual illumination quite impossible to describe. Into his brain streamed one momentary lightning flash of the Brahmic Splendor whichever since lightened his life. Upon his heart fell one drop of the Brahmic Bliss, leaving thenceforward for always an aftertaste of Heaven.

Finally, we quote from another mental health professional, a psychologist who prefers to remain anonymous. She reported that when she first read this account of Bucke's experience, she was astonished by the similarity between his account and her own experience. While there are some differences in the setting (such as the fact that Bucke's experience happened at night while hers happened in broad daylight), the sense of illumination, that it happened "in a flash," and that the experience was of such a joyful nature could hardly be more similar.

> I was going to the grocery store to pick up a few items. I still remember what I was going for: A loaf of bread, a quart of milk, and a package of cigarettes. It was a warm, sunny June day in Ohio, a bright blue sky above me, some large shady maples making shadows on the concrete sidewalk. I noticed how cracked the concrete sidewalk was, and that a squirrel was running right across in front of me, and somewhere a bird chirping away. Then, as I was stepping over a crack in the sidewalk, it happened . . .
>
> That bright June day suddenly became brighter, the blue sky became bluer, and Time seemed to stretch out to infinity. Or rather, Time just stopped. In that moment of Time, it seemed as if I was being given a glimpse of the Universe.
>
> Also that I was being given all the answers to those questions we all have on occasion, like *Why does God allow such terrible things, like war, to go on in the world? Is there any purpose to life? If so, what is that purpose? What are we doing here anyway?* Later, I realized that it wasn't so much that I had answers to these questions as they didn't matter anymore.
>
> What did matter at that moment was the awareness that the blue sky and the shady maple trees, and the squirrel running in front of me, and the cracked sidewalk and myself—we were all connected . . . all the same thing . . . all One . . . And the most remarkable thought came: that All Things Are Moving to the Ultimate Good. I didn't reflect at the Time on the paradox that war and other evils could be moving us to the Ultimate Good, only that they were a part of the All Things That Happen. The moment was, just as Bucke had described it, a moment of joyous and unbelievable rapture.
>
> And then, almost before I could realize the tremendous thing that had happened, Time began again. I had been stepping over a crack in the concrete sidewalk and now I was finishing that action. Almost in a trance, I continued walking to the convenience store. I must have picked up the bread and the milk, and asked for the cigarettes (which were generally just behind the

cashier), and paid for all the articles but I don't remember much about that. I was still engrossed in what had happened to me.

I did not say anything about my experience to anyone for three days, and for those three days, I was coexisting in two worlds, the one where I had to cook meals and make beds and play hostess, and this other world of the spirit, still feeling some of the leftover joy and peace from that extraordinary moment when Time stood still.

Sometimes, she adds, she has had many moments of joy but never one that was as intense or as glorious as that moment when Time stopped. She admits that occasionally she yearns for that experience again, and sometimes comes quite close to it when she realizes she has been of service to someone who has needed some soul-affirming experience. But this sense of having been of service to someone is an awareness only in retrospect, never at the time she is being of service. Her awareness is not that of pride but of gratitude to "the Universe" that it gave her that opportunity. She adds, however:

> Don't think I am a Saint or anything like that. I have faults and limitations a-plenty. I don't smoke any more but I cuss like a pirate in front of my friends and family which I am sure shocks them, and I'm still working on my judgmentalness (which is such a terrible beast to tame) and once in a while my temper flies (although I am proud of the gains I have made in that direction). I have had a truly strange and, at times, grim life, but those grim situations only made me more understanding and compassionate as I work with others in distress.

A recent edition of the *Monitor on Psychology* (December, 2003) devoted almost the whole edition on the values of incorporating a strong faith, spirituality, or firm religious values (call it what you will) for the psychophysical health of people—if the clients want to. A team of researchers at Bowling Green State University, under the direction of psychology professor, Kenneth Pargament, investigated the consequences of a spiritual approach in therapy, in medicine, and in marital satisfaction. One study that employed a spiritual approach in therapy was helpful for women coping with cancer. A second study found that marriages that incorporate a religious component was positively correlated with marital satisfaction. A large part of this study was attributed to the ability of the partners to solve problems cooperatively rather than antagonistically. A third study found that when parents and children discussed religious principles together that child-parent conflict was not nearly as great as in those families that did not hold open-ended discussions of the same sort (Kersting, 2003). Other studies have noted that clients who have a spiritual orientation to begin with are concerned with such questions as *Why is there evil in the world? How do I reconcile "turning the other cheek" when someone attacks my daughter? Where is the dividing line between being forgiving and not being a doormat?* In such situations, the therapist should not avoid discussing such topics, even if he or she has conflicted opinions about such questions. That the therapist may not have answers does not upset the client. On the contrary, it comes as a relief to know that other people, even counselors, have difficulty answering those types of questions (Richards & Bergin, 2003; Sharanske, 1996).

You Probably Have Had Peak Experiences Already: You Just Didn't Know It. We have been providing some extraordinary examples of peak experiences that may leave the impression that these kinds of intense peak experiences will never happen to you, that you are just not made of such stuff. That is what we *don't* want you to think. What we want you to realize is that you have probably already had peak experiences, maybe not quite as intense as the ones we have described, but you have had them. If you have ever had a truly loving moment with a parent, child, or lover, that no words can describe, you have had a peak experience. If you have achieved something that you really worked at and you feel a glow because it is good and worthwhile, you have had a peak experience. If, while observing the beauty of Nature, you experience a new and profound awe, you have had a peak experience. If, when consoling a grief-stricken friend, you suddenly felt an incredible closeness as if your souls had touched, you have had a peak experience.

And you will have more of them, sometimes when you least expect them. It may be that while in class, one day, someone will say something that is so startling, that your perceptions of the world will fall into a whole new pattern like the turning of a kaleidoscope. Or you may remember something from years ago when you were a child and now you realize what was going on and your feelings about your mother or father or sister or brother will undergo a dramatic change. You may have a counselor or therapist say something so insightful, you will be jolted into rethinking your perceptions about yourself and your life. You may simply be walking in the country and get an idea that never occurred to you before, an idea so exciting that you are transformed. On becoming a parent and looking into the face of your newborn child, your self-identity may be forever altered. Whatever the event that does provide you with a peak experience, *you will have a deeper appreciation for who you are and the possibilities that lie before you*. Finally, the more of these peak experiences you have, the more frequent they will become, and the more intense they will be (see Box 13.6).

Finally, Any Original and Creative Achievement is the Result of a Breakthrough of Consciousness. We need to add that any truly original and creative insight or work of art or scientific discovery is a peak experience because you have broken through to something new and previously undiscovered. Watch for peak experiences in your own life. In fact you can prepare the way for them. Do something that you have never done before. Do something you love doing but don't give yourself the opportunity because of all the things you "have to do." Do something for someone who is unhappy. Do something for someone anonymously. Make a private time for yourself to think about what you want. And most of all, take up something that has value for others as well as for yourself. It doesn't matter if it is working for a charitable organization, or for a political organization, or for a relative that needs your help, or for the street people who are homeless. The joy you will get back from this service will truly be a peak experience.

BOX **13.6** **Achieving Inner Peace and Joy**

Alec: OK, so altered states of consciousness are common experiences which we just have not recognized. Have I got that straight, Professor?

Professor Weitzman: More or less.

Alec: Earlier we learned that highly self-actualized people consciously pursue these experiences. What if I wanted to become more self-actualized, how could I go about it?

Li Ho: Well, we can get in touch with our dreams. I'm kind of interested in the lucid dreaming that the chapter described.

Martha: I'll tell you something that happened to me. When we decided to go on a health plan, back toward the beginning of this course, I decided it was time for me to learn to eat better and take off some of these pounds I've been complaining about for years. Hasn't anyone noticed how much thinner I am? I'm not so blubbery.

Jonnimae: I have. You look wonderful, years younger. Congratulations!

Martha: Well, not only did I lose weight but when I stopped eating sugar, I became much more sensitive to the natural sweetness in things—I can smell an apple now on the other side of the room. And it tastes wonderful. Isn't that an altered level of consciousness, Professor?

BOX **13.6** **Achieving Inner Peace and Joy (continued)**

Professor Weitzman: I certainly would say so!

Dan: I know what I need more of—more physical activity but not just physical activity—activity out there in the natural world. With all my studies and working a full-time job, I miss that part of my life a lot. I seem to be more in touch with who I am when I'm not stuck in buildings all the time.

Professor Weitzman: Mother nature is a source of harmony we lose touch with if we spend all our time in the concrete jungles of the city. Dan, I would say for you, Nature is crucial.

Jill Smith: If we can't garden or take an occasional walk in the woods, we can grow our own small jungle of indoor plants. Industrial psychologists are urging people who work in windowless offices to bring plants into their work place since it has been found that a "touch of Nature" in our environment is therapeutic. I think that's what I'm going to do this very week—buy some plants for my office space.

Professor Weitzman: I've been working late into the wee small hours for several weeks. I'm getting dull from all work and no play. I'm planning to take some afternoons off for a few rounds of golf.

Alec: OK, I get the point. What you're saying is that each of us must find out what is missing or needed in our lives and that would be different from person to person. Dan misses his outdoor life so he should get more of that. Martha needed to lose weight and when she did, she enhanced her self-esteem and I guess brought about an altered level of awareness for her. And I need to get in touch with my center-of-growth (as Carl Rogers) would put it . . . and maybe I could quiet down and not be so worried about hate groups.

Shannon: I love my quiet times. I'm sort of an introvert and while I like all the friends I've found in this class, I find I need more quiet time to myself. I can't get it at home with everything that is happening there. The twins are so noisy—they're teenage boys and that's natural for them. I'll have to find more time for myself. Sometimes I sneak into the chapel for—what did the book call it—meditational prayer? I think that's what I do when I want to get back to my center.

Natasha: Yes, more quiet time would be good for me too. Just being a good wife and going to school and being with my small children at night—I think I have no time for me. I don't complain about that because my husband is working so hard too.

Professor Weitzman: Haven't heard from you, Eduardo. What's going on? A class discussion without your input seems lacking somehow.

Eduardo: I've been thinking. When everybody started to talk about more quiet time, I thought maybe this is what I need too. I'm such an extrovert, I'm always with people. But then I remembered that I get a lot of happiness being with people. So I discarded that idea. It's like what Alec just said—we all have to discover what's missing in our lives. And then it came to me. What's been missing for me is more time with my guitar. I used to play regularly—every chance I could. That's what I've been needing.

Shannon: That's one of the places you're so creative, Eduardo. You should hear him, Professor.

Professor Weitzman: I would like to—very much. Music is Eduardo's way of centering himself. We all have our own unique ways of getting in touch with our center of growth. They help us to catharsize our anxieties. Only in those quiet moments of reflection or authentic self-expression can we inaugurate more centered ways of being in the world.

Important Terms and Concepts to Know

• adolescents	• hallucinogens	• peak	• spiritual
• Anima	• Hero	• Persona	• stimulants
• Animus	• hypnotic	• problem solving	• Testaments
• Archetypes	• inner	• relaxation	• Trickster
• circadian	• lucid	• REM	• theme(s)
• depressants	• mandala	• service	• valuable
• dreaming	• mantra	• Shadow	• wisdom
• erotic	• neurotransmitters	• shift	

Make Your Own Chapter Summary by Filling in the Blanks

Use the "Important Terms and Concepts to Know" to fill in the blanks.

Sleep. While some variations of consciousness are infrequent, such as _____ trance and drug-related reactions, other variations are everyday experiences, such as sleeping, daydreaming, and night _____. In terms of sleep, we are just not getting enough, particularly children, _____, and college students, which can lead to illness and disruption of our _____ rhythms. What is particularly stressful (and the cause of serious accidents and near accidents) is night work and _____ work. The sleeping state has recurring cycles, one of which is _____ sleep associated with intense dreaming.

History of dream interpretation. Ancient peoples believed dreams could foretell the future and both the *Old* and *New* _____ include many such examples. Freud believed that dreams were the result of repressed conflict and _____ impulses. Jung, on the other hand, viewed dreams as potential sources of inspiration, _____, and prediction. He described the _____ as the coalesced image we present to the public, and the _____ as the coalesced complex of traits we dislike and repress. Jung posited a deeper layer of the unconscious that contains symbols he called the _____, representing the polarities of human existence. The _____ represents the man's rejected "feminine" traits, while the _____ represents the woman's rejected "masculine" traits.

Other Archetypes include the Wise Old Man, the Wise Old Woman, the Wise Child, and the _____. Another approach to dreaming is _____ dreaming, in which the person is dreaming consciously.

Daydreaming. Sometimes called fantasy, daydreaming is no longer considered wish-fulfillment of erotic desires but as practical _____. Joseph Campbell enabled us to understand another Archetype in fairytales and mythology, the _____, which represents each of us as we play out the mythic _____ of our life story.

Meditation and meditational prayer. All cultures have devised special techniques for achieving other states of consciousness, such as the _____, which is a visual symbol and the _____, which is an auditory symbol. Research into meditation and meditational prayer reveals bodily changes, similar to deep _____.

Drug induced variations of consciousness. These drugs affect the _____ that communicate with other neurons. Certain drugs are called _____ because they increase the firing of the neighboring neurons. Other drugs are called _____ because they slow down or block neural firing. _____ drugs affect our usual perceptions of color, shape, size, and even our usual perceptions of time.

Peak experiences. Fifty years ago, psychology avoided any kind of "_____ experience" as inappropriate for valid scientific investigation, so Abraham

Maslow devised the term _____ experience, which he hoped might encourage research. Psychologists today are no longer embarrassed to investigate what some people describe as _____ experiences. Commonalities among these self-reports include a sense of connection to something larger than the small ego self, as something intrinsically _____ and joyful, and is often associated with _____ to others.

14 Building a Life-Career
Your Educational, Vocational, and Personal Future

Education and Work in the Informational Society

Professor Weitzman: You all know that our society has changed radically in the last hundred years. Two centuries ago, we were an agricultural society. In the 19th century, we became an industrial society. In the 20th century we became a technological society, and now we are fast becoming an informational society. All of this change has affected our understanding of work and education.

Eduardo: I've heard the term *informational society*, but I don't really know what it means.

Professor Weitzman: Information is what most of your professional careers will consist of. If you go into scientific careers; you will be observing, analyzing, and sharing data. The same is true in business and government. Local governments have to gather information on traffic control, usage of utilities, and housing. State governments need information on industry trends and setting standards of vocational areas like plumbing, heating and air conditioning, and auto mechanics. National governments have to keep in touch with global markets, population trends, employment and unemployment figures, and other economic issues. The World Health Organization (WHO) collects information on the prevalence and spread of disease such as AIDS, SARS, and the West Nile virus.

Jonnimae: And we're going to learn all that now?

Professor Weitzman: (Laughing) Not quite. Most of that is beyond the scope of this one course. Your entire college career is involved in getting you ready for the information society whether you are going to be a doctor, lawyer—or (looking at Dan)—Indian Chief.

Dan: You make it sound as if college is nothing but a vocational school.

Professor Weitzman: Well, in one respect college is. But a college education is supposed to do many things. We hope also to foster good citizenship, which means a sense of responsibility toward your family, your neighbors, and all the citizens of our global society. We presume you are learning how to lead healthier, more creative lives. We hope we are preparing you for the leadership roles not only at your place of work

but also in your community. The information age requires people working together, sharing knowledge, learning to be a team—even if members of that team are separated by thousands of miles and communicating over the "information highway" via the Web.

Li Ho: Wait a minute, Professor. I understand about scientists having to work together these days. But I'm thinking of becoming a surgeon.

Martha: And you don't think a surgeon has to interact with his surgical team?

Li Ho: I see what you mean! A surgeon needs all the input he can get from the anesthesiologist and the other techs.

Professor Weitzman: The informational society has changed in another way. We used to think of education as something that ended with high school or college or graduate school. Now we know that if we are to stay abreast of the developments in this information age education has to be a life-long process.

Alec: A life-long process!

Professor Weitzman: Exactly. We may not be registered formally as a college student but we will have to be upgrading our knowledge and our skills all the time. For example, sometimes several times a year I attend psychological conferences where I listen to lectures and discussions of new developments.

Jonnimae: I've been told by my accounting professors that CPAs (certified public accountants) have to gain dozens and dozens of CEUs every year just to keep up with the tax changes every year.

Professor Weitzman: That's right. We call them *conferences* or *workshops* or *in-service training*, but they are all basically educational avenues to upgrade our knowledge and skills.

Eduardo: Professor, I'd like to know how to get a good job. Do you have some tips on how to get a job?

Professor Weitzman: We sure do. And also how to write a resume that will get you your first interview. And how to make a success of your first job. So let's begin.

WORK AS ESSENTIAL FOR OUR NATIONAL AND PERSONAL WELL-BEING

In all studies of healthy and creative people, one of the essential ingredients has been the inclusion of a satisfying and productive work. When asked what constitutes a healthy personality, Freud's famous answer was, "To work and to love." One of the characteristics of highly integrated, creative, and self-actualizing persons is that they have a work that provides them with both economic and psychological satisfaction (Maslow, 1954). A work we can be proud of is not just a means to an end an end in itself. In contrast to those who "work to live" (working at any job to get money), they "live to work" (look forward to each new day and getting back to work). Working is a process by which we grow, mature, and evolve. When we are happy at our jobs, we feel good and we are healthier. In contrast, when we have trouble in our jobs or when we are out of work, our personal health suffers. So does our self-esteem and general morale (McGourty, 1988).

Furthermore, a good job can also sustain us through the darker moments of life. We may experience physical suffering through a debilitating disease or an accident. We may feel betrayed by those we love. We may lose those that are nearest and dearest to us. In fact, the longer we live, the more liable are we to experience the problems and crises of living. Those who have come through those kinds of losses successfully have often said that they were grateful to have a work that sustained them and kept them "centered."

A good job also provides us with an avenue for contributing to the growth of others. As we get older and we become skilled and knowledgeable in our work, there comes a time when we want to share that skill or knowledge with others. We gain a joy by mentoring another person who is just beginning on his or her life-career or who may be having difficulty in their work. There is a special satisfaction that comes from helping someone else become successful and self-sustaining. *If I give a man a fish to eat, he will not be hungry for a day. If I teach him how to fish, he will not go hungry for the rest of his life.*

If You Don't Know What You Want to Do When You "Grow Up," Take Heart!

Some of you reading these pages may know exactly where you are going. You enjoyed math or science in high school, and you decided early on that you would obtain an engineering or mathematics degree. Congratulations, but you are in the minority. Most students who come to college are really not sure what they should major in. Or because they can't make up their minds, they change their majors frequently. Some of you may not be sure that you should even be in college. We have good news for you. That's what you are here in college to do: to discover what it is that you would like to do. That is why educators insist on a "liberal education." By experiencing a wide spectrum of educational disciplines, you may find yourself attracted to an area you didn't know about before. Moreover, you will rub shoulders with other students who will talk about their majors. Listen to what they have to say about their courses and career possibilities. You can take advantage of all the **career days** your college offers. If you become interested in a certain area, ask your college counselors for an opportunity to gain firsthand experience by **shadowing** a person working in that area for a day or two. Shadowing has become a popular method of introducing people to possible career areas.

Furthermore, vocational choice is not a target—it's a direction. Whatever major or minor you choose in college is not so much a permanent work choice as a direction. In our swiftly changing society, the work place is also changing constantly. People who have been employed in one job will discover, five years later, that their job description has very little similarity to what they are actually doing. Job specialties will appear that weren't even on the job market when you entered college as a freshman. Actually, not being sure of what you want to do may even be an advantage in such a swiftly changing job market, because you will be more open to new career possibilities.

What Organizations Are Looking for in Prospective Employees

If you have been reading the newspaper or just scanning the headlines, you must be aware that corporations are "downsizing" their companies. During previous recessions, the "unskilled worker" has been hit the hardest. Today layoffs are happening across the employment strata: skilled and unskilled, blue- and white-collar workers, middle and top management. What does that mean in terms of your career hopes? Will you be able to find a job in your vocational interest? Yes, you can—if you know what corporations are looking for.

They Are Looking for People Who Are "Team Players."   In the last several decades, management has been slowly moving from authoritarian leadership to democratic participation. Until the twentieth century, most employers held the *traditional authoritarian style of leadership*; that is to say, the employer gave orders and the employees followed them, no ifs, ands, or buts! But research in business management reveals that when we treat people as mindless robots, they behave as mindless robots. They are not acting as thinking human beings in the jobs they are given to do. The result of this robotization are employees who care about collecting a paycheck but not much else. They shrug their shoulders if there are mistakes occurring on the assembly line. Their attitude is "You can take this job and shove it!" They treat clients, customers, and the general public in cursory fashion. The results of this kind of employee workforce are automobiles and appliances with many defective parts, poor customer relations, and a negative public image for the company—all of which are destructive to an organization's success. Furthermore, as an organization gets larger and larger, these problems increase substantially.

Recognizing the problems of the traditional authoritarian leadership styles, business schools began to teach team leadership, an approach that fosters the maturity and creativity of every employee at every level (Homans, 1950; McGregor, 1960). The employee is no longer to be considered as a cog-in-the-wheel worker carrying out orders from above but as a thinking, rational human being willing and wanting to do the best possible job. This type of organizational leadership needs managers who view the people in their departments not as employees but as members of a team all working together. That means the wise manager and professional does not see themselves as "boss." A more apt metaphor would be a *coach* or a *captain* inspiring his team to think creatively toward their job tasks, encouraging them to assume responsibility, and providing them with the trust and the authority to act autonomously.

They Want People Who Have a Well-Rounded Education and a Variety of Skills and Talents.   Students sometimes get irritated by having to take courses that do not seem to have direct relevance to their chosen job, vocation, or professional specialty. That is a shortsighted viewpoint. The day of "the specialist" is receding into history. We used to need specialists who had a deep knowledge of specific areas but we have computers now to store gigabytes of data. The computer has taken the place of the specialist. We simply no longer need people who have a depth of knowledge of a single topic. We need people who can connect with and exchange information across many departments, many technologies, and many professions.

They Don't Want Just "A-Getting Grinds"; They Want Multidimensional People. Work organizations want people who have a lot of "know how" and are "problem solvers." They are not looking for the "grind" who is an "A"-getter and not much else. They are looking for "doers" as well as "thinkers." In your curriculum vitae or résumé, they want to see what else you've done besides "study." They like to see that you have been active in extracurricular activities. They like to see that you took on an important project and completed it, whether it was designing and constructing the Homecoming float or working for Habitat for Humanity (community-based projects for building or restoring houses for the poverty-stricken of our nation). If you have been an officer of a club, they know you are willing to take on the problems and responsibilities of leadership. If you have been a member of a dance troupe, or choral group, or in the cast or crew of a play, they know you have had experience being a team member. If you have collected funds for a charitable organization or put on a benefit performance, they know you have compassion and a concern for those less fortunate than yourself. These activities and events on your résumé glow like jewels in a crown.

They Value College Students Who Have Held Full- or Part-Time Jobs. If you have had previous work experience before coming back to school, that is of interest to future employers since they know then that you are a person willing to continue your life-career education. If you held one or a few part-time jobs while attending college, so much the better for you. Your willingness to take some financial responsibility for your life looks good on a résumé. Prospective employers know you have gained much knowledge and experience even in the most menial jobs. They know that you have learned the importance of good public relations. They know that you have learned to juggle work and school, and some of you are juggling work, school, marriage, and parenting. These responsibilities have enlarged your worldview and your judgment has become more mature. Prospective employers know that you have experience now in working with other employees and (presumably) have developed a realistic view of the work world (see Tip 14.1).

They Want People Who Have Good People Skills. To become a participative and democratic manager or leader requires good "people skills"—all those constructive verbal and nonverbal communications discussed in earlier chapters. For example, they want supervisors and managers who are able to listen actively. They want people who understand the differences in the communication styles of both genders. So important are "people skills" considered that business schools from Harvard to Berkeley have required courses in psychology and interpersonal

---

Tip 14.1 To the Mature Student. *For those making a midlife change at 30 or 40 or so: You are more employable than you realize!* People who come back to school after many years and are making a midlife career change may worry that they will have more trouble than the young college graduate in getting a job they want. Actually, the reverse is true. If you have a previous good work record, they know that you are not only mature in years, you are also mature in experience and (yes, we'll say it) mature in wisdom. They know that coming back to college was an expensive proposition for you, so they know that your commitment to this discipline (whatever it is) must be based on a heart-felt desire to do this kind of work. They will actually value your previous work experience as bringing a hard-won specialty to your new career. It may even make you doubly employable since employers are looking for those generalists we discussed earlier.

Figure 14.1 The Informational Society. In this information age with its emphasis on teamwork and the need for good "people skills," the ability to communicate with others is a major key to a successful career.

communication (see Figure 14.1). Good people skills are considered so important, we need to explain how this emphasis came about.

Douglas Macgregor: Theory X and Theory Y (and Now Theory Z)

In 1960, a man by the name of Douglas Macgregor wrote a book that substantively changed the managerial theories of business organization. Macgregor had once been the president of Antioch College but he was not just a professional educator. He had been associated with the corporate world for many years and was disturbed by the lack of insight that management at every level had into the psychology of their workers. It was his philosophy that workers were a lot more responsible and creative than management gave them credit for. In fact, Macgregor was convinced that the business world was mismanaging most of their workers. He did not believe that the way to get things done was to shout orders, treat workers like mindless robots, and watch them so they didn't stop working—a management style he called the **Theory X**. It was his belief that the way to achieve the goals and objectives of management was by treating the workers as intelligent human beings who want to work and who are responsible and creative if given the chance. He called his approach to management **Theory Y**. The title of Macgregor's book was *The Human Side of Enterprise*, and it swept Corporate America like wildfire. Workshops on the new organizational philosophy were organized and literally thousands of business leaders all over the nation were trained in the Macgregor's approach to management (see Box 14.2).

To carry out the new management style of Theory Y, Macgregor knew that organizations had to change the atmosphere of the work place. Carl Rogers (1950) had written about the need to develop a warm climate of trust in the counseling situation. Macgregor now wrote about the need to develop a warm **climate of work**. The manager was no longer to stay locked up in an office but to adopt an "open door" policy and make it a friendly place to enter. Punitive managerial policies, such as pay-docking for lateness and the ever-present threat of

BOX **14.2** DOUGLAS MACGREGOR
Assumptions of Theory X and Theory Y

Theory X Assumptions

1. Workers are inherently lazy and shun work whenever possible.
2. Workers must be directed, controlled, and motivated by fear of punishment or deprivation to impel them to work as the company requires.
3. Workers have little ambition and work solely for money.
4. Workers cannot be trusted because they avoid responsibility.
5. Workers have little imagination and creativity.

Theory Y Assumptions

1. Work is as natural to human nature as play and rest.
2. Workers do not always need to be directed and controlled by management; workers can be self-directing and are happy to be given responsibility.
3. Workers want to work in order to fulfill their highest potential.
4. Workers don't avoid responsibility; they seek responsibility.
5. Workers are capable of creativity when given the opportunity.

being fired were replaced with invitations to suggest innovative problem-solving and with some control by the workers over their work situation, encouraging them to participate in the decision-making process.

Macgregor then applied Maslow's **hierarchy of needs** (see Table 1.1) to the work situation. A paycheck provides the basic (*physiological needs*) needs of *safety and security*. Having co-workers provides people with a sense of *belonging*. Being able to contribute something valuable to the organization provides for the need of *self-esteem*. And there is probably no more direct route to *self-actualizing*, said Macgregor, than through the world of work. Macgregor urged managers not to think of workers as irresponsible employees always looking for ways to avoid working. Think of employees, he wrote, as workers wanting to be useful and productive. Macgregor concluded that people do not always work to live, they also live to work—if we can help them find work that makes them feel good about themselves.

Eventually, **Theory Z** would be added to Macgregor's theories X and Y (Ouchi, 1981). Theory Z acknowledges that we must continue to have a participative management style for workers. But there will always be some workers (let's call them goldbrickers) that call for a more direct and authoritative approach. So Theory Z is also called a contingency approach to management, meaning the management style we use should be appropriate to the situation. Let it be clearly understood, however, that Theory Z still calls for giving every worker the benefit of every doubt, and wherever and whenever possible treating them with every courtesy and all due respect. And what that means is that not only do we apply all the listening skills we have been discussing but also that we adopt a speaking style that is different from directing, ordering, threatening, etc. We don't treat people as naughty children who have to be scolded. We treat them with dignity and give them every due courtesy. And what that means is that we have to learn a facilitative speaking style.

Six Strategies for Landing Your First Real Job!

By the time you graduate, over 1 million students will begin the process of "job-hunting." You may find yourself asking the same questions that most other graduates will be asking themselves: *How does a person land a first real job? Will I even be able to find a job?* Some vocational and professional departments actually run workshops and mini-courses on how to go about job-hunting, how to write a résumé, how to dress, how to be interviewed. A few pages of a text cannot take the place of these learning opportunities, but we can provide you with a few of their tips and guidelines. Some of these tips and strategies will already be familiar to you. Skip over them. But some of these tips and strategies may surprise you.

1. Take your time finding a job. It pays to be patient. If you are having to take some time to get that first real job, don't panic by grabbing the first job that comes along. It may take you three to nine months to find that special job just made for you. What do you do for money in the meantime? Well, if there isn't someone supporting you while you job hunt, you have two other options. You can get a part-time job to put food on the table and keep your car running while you job hunt on your off-time. You say you also have other hungry mouths to feed and you can't ask your spouse to continue supporting you? In that case, you can get a full-time job in the evening, and during the day do your job-hunting (when you aren't sleeping). What you need to do is to explain to your family that the first job is an important one, and it takes time to find it. Hasten to assure them that you are not avoiding a job; in fact, a few months of patient job hunting will result in a financial pay off eventually. You might even want to let them read these pages so they can see you are getting this information from "a reliable source."

An important note: You do not have to wait for graduation before job-hunting. It can begin while you are still a student. Your college probably has a list of job opportunities. If you want to speed up the process of landing your first job, avail yourself of the Internet job listings in your vocational interest area. Private employment agencies are also expert in matching a person's interests and competencies with the needs of local firms. They not only have a variety of better-paying jobs in your locale, they are often able to interest an organization in a person of your qualifications. If you don't mind moving away from your college area, make sure to go to state and national professional conferences in your field of work. In addition to the latest updates in your professional field, they usually have a room devoted to job market opportunities. Finally, don't be hesitant in asking a professor or instructor to keep you in mind for information on jobs that may pass their desks. Instructors are always happy to help their students locate employment.

2. Create a résumé that is distinctive. Once you have some leads on a job, the next step is to secure an interview. Employers and personnel departments are flooded with job applications. To secure an interview, create a résumé that (1) is distinctive enough to catch their eyes and (2) indicates that of all those applicants, you are definitely a person worth interviewing. Start by putting together a concise but comprehensive résumé form. There are many paperback books on the market that show you how. That is only the first step, however. After you have put together a conventional but comprehensive résumé, spend some time making it distinctive. We are not saying to make it bizarre or so radical that you scare off the prospective employer. But prospective employers get so many résumés that look alike, nothing sets them apart. You want something that gets their attention (see Figure 14.2). What can get their attention that won't look bizarre? Well, a modest photograph in the upper right-hand corner will turn an impersonal résumé into something more personal. After you have put together a fairly conventional

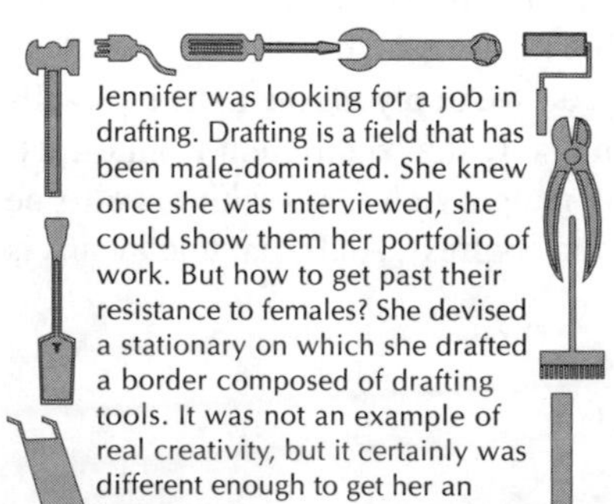

Jennifer was looking for a job in drafting. Drafting is a field that has been male-dominated. She knew once she was interviewed, she could show them her portfolio of work. But how to get past their resistance to females? She devised a stationary on which she drafted a border composed of drafting tools. It was not an example of real creativity, but it certainly was different enough to get her an interview.

Figure 14.2 Jennifer's Résumé.

résumé, think about how you can make it just a little more distinctive from others in your field (Corewen, 1988). We'll give you a few examples.

- Don wanted a job working with computers. With his résumé, he enclosed three disks containing programs he had devised himself, along with user-friendly instructions for their immediate use.
- Deidre wanted to break into the children's literature field. Publishing houses are besieged by manuscripts. Since Deidre has an artistic talent, she used her talent even on the brown paper she wrapped the manuscript in. When the first editor saw a brightly illustrated package on his desk, he was immediately attracted to it and opened it before he opened anything else in the mail. Her book was published.
- Jason was applying for a high-paying oil job in the Middle East. He was smart enough to realize that knowing even a little Arabic would be a valuable asset. In his last year at the University, he took an independent study course in Arabic. Although he added that skill to his résumé, he wanted to be sure it was noticed. In the place marked "Special Skills and Abilities" he wrote: "I am learning to read and write in Arabic." That grabbed their attention!

3. Prepare ahead of time for your interview.   Until you have been interviewed a few times, the interview situation may be anxiety arousing: *How should I act? What should I say? What will the interviewer ask me? What should I wear?*

Finding out what to wear is probably the easiest question so we'll start with that one. You probably know that you need to look well-dressed but not garish. If the location of the interview is not too far away, it might be wise to visit the job site or company before your interview day. Take a walk around inside and out and get an idea of what clothing styles are being worn by both management and workers. If you want them to know you are their "kind of person," wear something within the range of their clothing styles. Take your best friend with you if you are going to buy that special "interview" outfit. In this situation, two critical heads are definitely better than one. If you do buy an "interview outfit," wear it before your interview until you feel comfortable and natural in it and until it looks and "feels right." If you are not used to a collar and tie, get used to wearing them long before the interview situation.

The next step is to go through some dry runs of the interview situation. Wear your "interview outfit." Get some of your friends or an instructor to act as an interviewer. You might want to tape record the sessions. Make a note of some of the questions they ask. Prepare answers for the questions they ask you. Prepare good answers that are not phony but that represent who you genuinely are. "To thine own self be true." Ask different people to act as interviewers because each of them will have different ideas and questions. Tell them not to be afraid of being critical. (Tell them you will do the same for them if they so choose.) The more interview situations you enact, the less anxiety you will experience. Familiarity diminishes the anxiety of the unknown. Then practice again and again until you feel comfortable and can speak fluently and naturally.

4. Prepare some questions that you would like answered by the interviewer. Interviewers also like prospective employees to ask questions. Give some consideration to the following items and choose ones that seem important to you as you plan your life-career:

What are the chances for advancement?
How are salary increases decided?

Are there possibilities for flex-time so you can continue your education?

Does the organization foster education through full- or part-time tuition payment?

How does the organization react to necessary or emergency needs that must be done during company hours, such as taking a child to the hospital or meetings with teachers?

How does the organization see itself in terms of contributing to the community?

Who would you be working directly under?

Which other areas would you be relating to?

Who else besides your immediate superior will you be interviewed by?

5. When you have obtained an actual interview, read up on the history and goals of the organization. Nothing will impress an interviewer more than to realize you have been reading the history of the organization and have become familiar with its short-term and long-term goals. Don't show off about it. As the interview continues, your responses, both verbal and nonverbal, will make apparent your knowledge of the organization. Eventually, the interviewer may say something like, "You seem to be familiar with this" at which point you modestly reply, "Well, I've been familiarizing myself with the organization's history and goals." Spoken without any sense of self-aggrandizement, it will be very impressive!

6. If you really want a job with the organization, don't take a "no" as a permanent answer. Some people get discouraged by getting turned down for a job. They simply walk away and never go back. That's because they don't know human psychology. If you like the organization and the people who interviewed you, don't give up. It pays to be persistent. If you are told that someone else got the job, ask the interviewers what you lacked. Find out what qualifications were deemed important. If it was a special skill, acquire it. If it was experience in a certain area of work, go about getting it. Then, when a position opens up again, get another interview with them. Do you have to be embarrassed? Not at all. They will be impressed by your dedicated and sincere desire to work for them. They will be impressed by your willingness to acquire more qualifications. They will be impressed by your persistence. They will be impressed by your patience and determination. All of these attributes are what employers are looking for.

TEN PRINCIPLES FOR SUCCESS IN YOUR JOB: APPLYING ALL THE PRINCIPLES OF PSYCHOLOGY YOU HAVE BEEN LEARNING

Let us suppose now that you have been hired. How do you go about doing your job not just well but in a way that leads to salary raises and promotions? Will you be surprised if we call your attention again to your communication and "people skills"? We hope not because they are the key to success in every area of your life—with your spouse, with your children, with your employment, and with just about every situation that involves people.

1. Effective managers are not expected to act like the "boss" anymore; they act more like team captains. We have already learned that the chief reason for firing someone is not because they didn't do their job. It is because they didn't know how to work with other people. What that definition implies is that the effective manager has to be sensitive to other people's needs. He or she has to be receptive to other people's concerns, always being friendly and approachable. There is an axiom in organizational life that effective managers do not wall themselves up in their offices but maintain an "open door" policy for anyone, including workers, to discuss what they are doing or to ask some advice. But no one is going to walk into the manager's office if the manager finds fault with everyone—no matter how wide open the door to his office. If a manager is known to say, "I am surrounded by fools," that manager needs an attitude change. If a manager gets exasperated by "mistakes" other people make, that manager needs an attitude change. If a manager begins to delegate responsibility and ends by saying, "Oh, never mind, I'll do it myself," that manager needs an attitude change. The attitude they need to adopt is the understanding that things only get done when everybody works together in a cooperative and friendly manner.

Effective managers understand themselves as the head of an organizational family. The position of a manager is not dissimilar to the position of the head of a family. Whether you are the night manager of a fast-food franchise or the department head of a large university, you may be astonished how often the people who work for you and even your colleagues will behave like a family. Coworkers will behave like sibling rivals. Collaborative colleagues may behave like divorcing couples if their conflicts become too volatile. Perfectly competent workers may revert into their child-ego states (see Chapter 10, pp. 246). Eventually, you will witness most of the defense mechanisms being enacted out where you work. Your job as manager will be to keep your organizational family as functional as possible. How? By using all the psychological techniques you have been reading about in previous chapters. Effective managers have been using them for several decades now.

2. Provide positive feedback. The most effective way of bringing out the best in your workers is to find something good they have done and tell them so. Better still, write it on a note that not only goes to them directly but gets put into their employment file. It is so easy to point out mistakes. Mistakes are glaring. It is less easy to note what people are doing right. An axiom of effective management goes: *Catch them doing something right!* (Blanchard & Johnson, 1982). In Skinnerian language, it is reinforcing the desirable behavior. Good jobs are deserving of words of praise and concrete actions, such as good performance appraisals, and approval of salary raises or promotions. Ask her, by way of compliment, if she would like to take on added responsibility. In the place of salary increase or promotion, such a question certainly will meet some of her esteem needs. It will also convey to her that you are appreciative of her talents and efforts. The positive feedback needs to be sincere, concrete, and objective. It is not enough to say, "Mary, you're doing a great job!" or "Joe, your sales are looking good!" or "Eddie, thanks for your help on the project!" Be more specific. "Mary, your accounting report was very helpful to me in the meeting." Or "Joe, you're the high scorer this month for sales!" Or "Eddie, your assistance on the project was so valuable that I had occasion to tell the president that you were mostly responsible for its success."

3. For workers who are having difficulties meeting their job responsibilities, assume an attitude of helpfulness. If someone is consistently late or frequently absent or not doing the job to satisfaction, don't make the assumptions that the employee is simply being irresponsible or shiftless. Try to discover what is wrong. It may be simply a very concrete problem requiring a simple solution. The worker who is always late may be having transportation problems. See if you can find ways to help that worker by finding a car pool. The employee who is not doing the job well enough may lack a simple skill such as faster typing, or they may need tutoring on the computer. The person who has had considerable absenteeism may have a chronically sick child, and there may be some kind of baby-sitting solution that can be worked out. They may be going through a divorce with all the heartache that it entails. Their spouses or children (or even themselves) may have landed in jail, and they may be overwhelmed by the legal aspects of what is going on. Everyone needs a hand now and then. What these workers need is not to be fired or blamed for their predicament. They need a little help. As a manager, it is not your job to loan them money, but perhaps you can get them financial assistance. As a manager, it is not your job to act as social worker, legal counsel, or physician. But you can become a referral source. Experienced employees who are having problems are not people to get rid of. They are people who need help through the occasional hardtimes we all go through.

4. Good news may travel up and bad news may travel down, but the effective manager keeps all lines of communication open. You have learned this axiom many times, and you will probably hear it many times again: *When things go awry, nine times out of ten, there's been a breakdown in communication.* It is not just a truism, it is a truth. As organizations get larger and larger and the number of workers increase, the more there is a chance for communication breakdown. Most of the time, miscommunications are accidental. But when the work climate has become hostile, much miscommunication may be deliberate. Another organizational maxim then goes: *Good news travels up; bad news travels down.* What that maxim means is that in an organization in which workers are treated on the assumptions of old Theory X (see Box 14.2), employees will not want to report problems to the upper echelon. They will tend to cover up mistakes. Or shrug their shoulders when they read instructions that seem incorrect. Things may be going wrong up and down on the production line and no one is informing the management.

On the other side of the ledger, bad news travels down. Management may discover a costly mistake and seek to find blame among the employees, following the centuries old phenomenon of **attribution bias**. Blaming a person (or even a whole group of people such as an entire department) may make us feel better but casting blame impedes the open communication we want.

5. The effective manager knows how to resolve conflict: Assumptions and guidelines of conflict resolution. Conflict and conflict resolution is one of the chief "people skills" of the effective manager. If you become known as a person who can resolve difficulties between people or departments, you will be targeted as a person who can handle greater responsibilities. Before we begin discussing how to handle conflict, we need to make note of the assumptions of conflict resolution: First, conflict is inevitable. We noted in our chapter on marriage that conflict is inevitable in any area where people are living in close proximity for a period of time. It is also true of the work arena. Today, as in every era and culture, we have many legitimate areas of conflict: labor/management, minorities, conservative/liberal, environmental/nuclear, right-to-life/right-to-choose, and so on. The second assumption of conflict resolution is that if the conflict is not legitimately recognized, it will go underground and emerge in costly and dangerous ways, such as in interdepartmental warfare, worker–management disputes, and organizational sabotage. The third assumption is that conflict is not necessarily destructive. In fact, conflict prevents stagnation and promotes new and creative ideas. The scientific professions actually promote conflict by inviting opposing points of view.

Wherever there are different departments or work sites, there will always be differences in perspective and points-of-view. The effective manager knows how to legitimize these opposing points-of-view and resolve them. Nothing will be more esteemed by the top echelon of your workplace as the ability to resolve conflict, and, in Box 14.3 we have listed some of the general principles of conflict resolution formulated by experts in the field.

6. The effective manager must be sensitive to issues of sexual harassment. Legally, sexual harassment has been defined as unwelcome advances or requests for sexual favors or any other verbal or physical behavior of a sexual nature. Although sexual harassment has been discussed in various organizations in both the private and public sectors, it was not until 1991 that sexual harassment in the workplace became such a large issue. It was in that year that Supreme Court nominee Clarence Thompson was accused of sexual harassment of law professor Anita Hill. Although Thompson was ultimately appointed to the Supreme Court, the hearings instigated corporate America to investigate their policies of sexual harassment and to institute policies against such practices. While sexual harassment is difficult to define precisely, organizations are making it clear that many behaviors are no longer acceptable in this country. These behaviors include unwanted touching and verbal sexual advances, and veiled threats that a woman can lose her job if she is unwilling to comply with an employer's sexual requests. But what constitutes sexual harassment does not stop with these behaviors. Sexual harassment also includes off-color jokes or comments by coworkers, sexual artifacts placed around the workplace (such as pictures of nudes), and power tactics based on gender (expecting women workers to make coffee, arrange parties, or do other stereotypic female activities, if the woman does not perceive that as being a normal part of her job description).

It also includes unwelcome female behaviors toward men. Sexual harassment is not limited to unwelcome male behaviors toward women. Sexual harassment also includes hostile anti-gay jokes and comments. In the largest possible sense, sexual harassment includes any behavior that makes the work environment a hostile climate for anyone. This a particularly sensitive area for the effective manager to deal with if there are no other witnesses but the two persons involved. As well, there may be accusations of sexual harassment where none exist. Yet the manager must deal with any and all such complaints. To that end, institutions and organizations have inaugurated workshops, forums, in-service training, and computer-based programs to sensitize managers and executives to sexual harassment issues and how to deal with them both here and abroad (Carrie, 1999).

7. The effective manager is sensitive to gender and ethnic differences in working with others. The workforce has changed radically in the last two decades and it is continuing to change. One major difference is the increasing numbers of women joining the workforce. Although men are still heading most of the higher echelon corporate positions, women are more and more reaching managerial and executive ranks. Given the increasing number of women at all levels of professional and business organizations, men are going to have to communicate with women in a different style. Men tend to shout and argue with each other, which women find offensive and rude. Women managers generally use a more cooperative and friendly style of communication with coworkers and those for whom they are responsible. Managers may expect women workers to be more absent than their male counterparts (generally because of illness or problems with children), but this fact notwithstanding, women will be as productive (if not more productive) than men in most organizations (Beebe, Beebe, & Redmond, 1996).

8. Choose a mentor and a few role models. When you first get hired, you're a new-comer. Your résumé may be loaded with certifications, licenses, and degrees, but you are still the new kid on the block. Even if you have majored in business administration, remember that every company has its unique approach to management and problem solving. Every company has its unique history, its special mission, its official flowchart and protocol, and its unofficial (and sometimes highly accurate) grapevine. Before you start making waves, do a lot of listening to other people. Get yourself a **mentor**, someone you can confide in with perfect trust, someone you can consult when you are not sure how to approach a situation. People who have had mentors report that it was a rewarding experience but surveys reveal that only a very small percentage of workers ever take advantage of the mentoring experience. We recommend not asking the person directly to be a mentor. Instead, simply consult that person from time-to-time when you could use a bit of advice, build a good reputation as a conscientious worker, and you and the person of your choice will ease into a mentor-mentee relationship quite naturally.

In addition to your mentor, observe other managers and administrators. Notice which of these persons work effectively with others and whom others like to work with and admire. Choose two or three of these people as **role models**. One person may be particularly expert in chairing problem-solving committees. Another person may be especially skilled in public relations. A third person may be outstanding in making presentations. Study these people for their leadership styles—how they do what they do so well.

9. Build your reputation as honest and trustworthy. In the last two decades of the 20th century, America has been shocked again and again by the revelations of **corporate criminality**. If the 19th century had its "robber barons," the 20th century has had its "robber CEOs" (Corporate Executive Officers) who removed billions of dollars for their own private fortunes before their corporations applied for bankruptcy. (Because of these scandalous thieves, corporations are going to be on guard against dishonest managers, supervisors, and executives.) In contrast to these robber CEOs, departments of business administration have urged its graduates to be honest, ethical and, in every way, above board. Furthermore, studies have shown that effective supervisors and managers are those who are respected and liked, not only because they are warm or charismatic, but because they are trustworthy in what they say and what they do. They will not lie or evade the truth. They don't pretend to know all the answers. If they don't know an answer to a question, they will frankly admit they do not, and promise to find out the answer, if possible. Their coworkers may grouse a little occasionally about these managers and supervisors at times but end by saying something like: *We don't see eye-to-eye but he'll never knife you in the back.* Or *she isn't always right but she'll admit it when she's wrong.* Employees are quick to detect phoniness and lies, and when they do detect it, they will pass it along the grapevine. Moreover, workers who do not trust their managers and supervisors will not go to them with problems or concerns. Instead, they will go around, under, and behind their supervisors whenever possible—a most unhealthy situation for the firm, and especially, for the supervisors when it becomes known. Build your reputation as a manager they can confide in and who is straight with you.

Our vastly different ethnic populations will have different communication styles. Workers with a Mediterranean and Arabic background will tend to huddle together while talking loudly in their common language, but what may look like arguing from the outside may in fact be their directness in working out a problem. Asian immigrants or Asian-American citizens will, on the other hand, seem to agree with everything that is being said because to be too direct or argumentative is, in their cultural background, appalling rudeness. Finally, there are many initiatives across the nation to provide jobs for people with many kinds of disabilities, including physical, emotional, and mental disabilities. We have gone a long way in providing both jobs and services for the physically disabled—according to a recent report about 70 percent are now employed. But we still have a long way to go for the emotionally and cognitively disabled (Rabasca, 1999).

10. Finally and above all, use the following words, phrases, and sentences frequently:

> *I appreciate what you did/contributed/achieved.*
> *What do you think?*
> *Thank you.*
> *Please.*

BOX **14.3** **Principles of Conflict Resolution**

Concentrate on the issue, not on personalities. To resolve any conflict, do everything you can to depersonalize the issue. Never allow it to become a matter of this person versus that person. If personality conflict becomes the focus of the problem, the only solution may be to get rid of one or the other of the persons. Getting rid of someone is never a good thing to do because of the fear and distrust it sets up in the rest of the organization. Successful managers, therefore, do everything they can to veer the problem away from being a personality conflict. Your job is to get everyone concerned to focus on the issue or issues, not on each other.

Ask to interview each person in the conflict separately. When people are fighting with each other, especially in front of other people, their disagreements get larger and their arguing gets louder. What is needed is to separate the disputants from each other by asking them to go back to their jobs and you will speak personally with each of them later. In the individual interviews, your first job is to defuse their emotions. When people are angry or hurt or feel an unjust accusation has been made, their emotions cloud reality. When people are steamed up or suffering in other ways, they cannot think logically or from any other viewpoint than their own. There is a professional

maxim about people who are brought to a treatment center for alcoholism: *Let them dry out first. There is no use speaking to the alcohol.* The same holds for hot feelings or hurt feelings. So encourage them to speak about how they feel. Use the technique of active listening. Once their negative feelings have been defused, they will be more open to logic and reason and more able to discuss the matter more objectively.

Maintain a calm, smooth, and interested exterior. No matter how emotional the situation has become, your job is to remain calm and collected. Don't allow yourself to feel insulted or shocked or irritated by the person as he or she is throwing accusations all around. It is part of the person's emotional baggage that is draining off. Communicate the feeling that you are not blaming them in any way for the conflict. As a matter of fact, you might even add the idea that you are glad that the problem has surfaced so it can be brought out into the open and resolved.

Look for win-win solutions. Ask all the participants individually for their suggestions on how to resolve the problem. When you have heard everyone's suggestions, put them together and formulate several alternative plans of action. Present your plan and alternate

BOX 14.3 Principles of Conflict Resolution (continued)

courses of action toward win-win solutions (everybody wins in the end). Win-lose solutions mean there will be losers, and losers never feel good about losing. They may actually turn their negative feelings against you instead of the people or departments they are losing to. Encourage every member present to voice opinions or to make additions, deletions, and modifications. Rather than vote on alternative plans, keep the discussion going until everyone (or almost everyone) seems to favor one of the plans. Then concentrate on implementing that one plan.

Negotiate real differences. Although your objective always is to find win-win solutions, sometimes that just doesn't happen. Don't cover up that fact. Admit it openly and honestly to the party or parties concerned, but with a sense of humor, with remarks such as: "Well, Bob, there's nothing I can do for you in this instance. Your people will just have to bite the bullet this time. But we'll owe you a big one! And I won't forget that!" Or "Janet, we can't do what you need done

at this time. Let's see how this is going to work. If we still have the same problems, you have the right to convene this committee again."

Give the team plenty of time to work out the bugs. Don't think conflict resolution can always be done immediately or that solutions can be thought through on the spot. It requires time. Your conflict resolutions group may have to meet several times before some viable and creative solution is worked out. If finally everyone concludes that the plan is not working, find out why it isn't working, and work out another plan.

Make the pronouns of "we," "us," and "ours" a habitual part of your language. There are many books on the market that give you "do's and don'ts" for conflict resolution. Study them. But for a quick overall tip on how to resolve a conflict, exchange the pronouns "I" and "you" for "we" and "us"—for all the reasons discussed in Chapter 8.

REBUILDING A COMMUNITY-BASED FAMILY

The Early American Community-Based Family

In the chapter on marriage and family (Chapter 8), we compared the extended family of rural America with the nuclear family of today. We noted that the advantage of the extended family (with its several adults living in the same household) was the physical and emotional support the adults provided for each other. If Mother was ill, Grandmother could cook and take care of the children. If Father broke his leg, it was a serious situation but Grandfather and Son could still work the farm chores. The situation for modern nuclear parents is very different. In times of stress, today's nuclear parents simply do not have that same kind of physical support for all the multiroles they have to perform. Suppose, for example, Mother becomes seriously ill or breaks a leg. Unless Father has the kind of job that permits him to take off as much time as he needs, he cannot be absent too many days from work. In the first 60 or 70 years of the 20th century, Grandmother might have been able to help out, but today she either lives too far away to help or she herself is working at a full-time job.

At the same time, we must take care not to romanticize farm life. Work was hard and farm life does not permit "days off." Privacy was virtually nonexistent. Education was sporadic since planting and harvest times require all hands (except those of the very youngest children). Too, inclement weather often prevented walking the miles-long trek to the one-room schoolhouse. But what the early homesteads did do was to foster a community-based family in which everyone helped each other and contributed to the common good. They had to, if they were to survive.

The Move to the City. As the American population kept increasing, larger and larger urban centers developed. Young people began leaving the farm for the city where there was more opportunity for paid employment, and survival was not threatened by drought in summer or freezing storms in winter. Not only did the city provide more economic stability for the young couple, it also provided a place they could call their own and longed-for privacy. The city had other advantages, such as nearby and better schools. Physicians and hospitals, too, were not far away. Many churches were in walking distance. City stores had a larger variety of goods than what was available at the country general store. Mother did not have to order clothes from a catalog; she could buy them at a ladies' dress shop. Dad could actually try on a pair of shoes at the shoemaker's before buying them. Too, city life has always provided many kinds of entertainment that rural areas cannot: theaters and movie houses (with the Saturday matinee for the kids), beaches and boardwalks, Fourth of July fireworks and marching bands, and plenty of excitement when the circus comes to town. But cities have always had their down side, too. With the great numbers of immigrants coming to these shores from other lands, the cities developed ethnic ghettos. Eventually, most ghettos eventually lead to slums, slums lead to ethnic gangs fighting each other, and to more crimes of violence (Shaw, 2004).

Flight to the Suburbs. In the second half of the 20th century, then, those who could afford it began fleeing the cities to Suburban America, hoping to get away from overcrowding, from the ever-increasing smog, from public schools where their children were being exposed to alcohol and drugs, and where adolescents were being introduced to sex at earlier and earlier ages. The nuclear parents wanted to find a "good place to raise the children." To provide their families with the advantages of living the American Suburban Dream, the men of the family were willing to add two to four hours of commuting time to their work day (Gutfreund, 2004). These suburbanites truly believed that their model of a working husband-and-father, two or three children, and the stay-at-home "Super Mom" was the ideal environment to produce absolutely happy, healthy, and well-adjusted children. They were wrong.

Disillusion with the American Suburban Dream. What these suburban families discovered was that they had not necessarily escaped the evils of the city. What they found, instead, was that drugs could be bought just as easily in suburban schools as in city schools and that sexual exploration, even sexual exploitation, was happening just as early in the so-called "better" neighborhoods. They discovered that rapes, even gang rapes, were not uncommon at the social gatherings of their teenagers. Then in the 1990s, Americans were shocked by the high school shootings that were occurring, not in the city schools, not in the slums and ghettos, not by ethnic minorities, but in Suburban America, by the adolescent children of white affluent families. Americans began asking themselves *What has gone wrong with these adolescents whose families gave them "every advantage money can buy"?* Deeply troubled, Americans began to look for who or what was to blame. They have come up with a lot of answers.

- *American families are drifting apart.*
- *It's the working wife who isn't staying home to take care of the kids.*
- *It's because of the absentee father.*
- *Parents don't know what their adolescents are doing.*
- *It's evidence of the general moral decay of our society.*
- *It's because of the high rate of divorce.*

> • It's because the schools aren't doing their job to prevent violence.
> • It's because the government isn't doing anything about all the sex and violence on TV.
> And . . . and . . . and . . .

Do these assertions have any truth to them? Well, yes, a few of them do have some measure of truth. But we need to remind ourselves that pointing the finger and assigning blame doesn't do anyone much good except to make ourselves feel better. Rather than cast blame, what we need to do involves several things. First, we need to remember that every society in history has had its strengths and problems, and ours is no exception. The second thing we need to do is to gain more understanding of what has really been going on under the veneer of the ideal model of the American family. Third, we need to review the sweeping sociological changes that have been occurring for the last five decades. Then we'll see if we can find ways to rebuild a community-based family within the framework of an increasingly technological society.

Yes, American Families *Are* Drifting Apart—Quite Literally

Commentators of the social scene have been writing articles to this effect for the last fifty years (LeBey, 2003). The sheer size of our country is a major factor. In this country, when a man or woman gets a promotion, it may require a move to another state far from kinfolk and friends. Now contrast this with European families. In Europe, if adult children move away from where their parents live, they almost always live within a few hours by train, car, or bus. In Ireland, for example (where one of the coauthors of this text was born and raised), a person never lives more than 70 miles from the sea. In France, it is less than a day's ride by car from Paris to the Riviera. Smaller countries, such as Denmark, Switzerland, the Netherlands, and Austria, are only a few hours ride from border to border. By contrast, in this country it is 3000 miles "from sea to shining sea"; not a very easy situation for staying in close touch with the family and friends we grew up with.

Moreover, we are moving around at a great rate. On the average, 20 percent of Americans make a move each year. Granted that some of these moves are from one part of a city to another, but every relocation requires getting used to a new neighborhood, new stores, new schools, new routes to get places, etc.

Moving Around Is Particularly Painful for Children in Middle School and High School. While relocation is not easy for any member of the family, it is particularly painful on children, especially adolescents. They know they may have to run the gamut of suspicion and rejection from their classmates before they find friends. And it scares them. Children in this age group are so needful of friends that some will do anything to get in with a crowd. They will tend to cave in to peer pressure to do something they know to be illegal, immoral, or dangerous. But desperate as they are not to be subjected to ridicule and jeers, they are now operating with the primitive emotions of their midbrain rather than from their more mature decision-making frontal cortex (see Figure 6.3, p. 159).

More Than Ever, Parents No Longer Really Know What Their Adolescents Are Doing. Early in the 20th century, the psychologist who first described adolescence, G. Stanley Hall (1904), noted that teenagers had a secret life of their own that excludes or even offends their parents. The situation is even more acute today. The parents of the present generation are bewildered and appalled by their adolescents' punk clothes, pink and purple hair, the tattoos and bells and rings attached to their tongues, and bellies, and pubic areas. And one more factor is beginning to frighten them—what their adolescents are really surfing for on the Internet (LeBey, 2003; Leland, 2003).

In a *Newsweek* survey, reported in May 2001, 47 percent of the parents admitted they really know very little about what their teens are doing on the computer. Even more (60 percent) believe the government needs to be more active in controlling what is permitted on the Internet. With computers situated in the high schooler's bedroom, what the teenager is doing on his computer may have nothing to do with his schoolwork. One clinical psychologist says that the adolescent's superior knowledge of the computer has turned the power structure of the family upside down (Mayhew, 1999). While surfing the Information Highway, the adolescent may be logging on to pornography, to step-by-step instructions on how to make home-made bombs and semi-automatic rifles, or to the many hate groups now on the Internet. It may be exciting to communicate all over the world with e-mail, but adolescents are not aware of the dangers of communicating with persons unknown, possibly even sexual predators.

Violence in the Movies and on TV. Another answer given for what is going wrong is the prevalence of violence on the media, particularly the movies and TV. When we sit down and watch the latest "action film," we are actually condoning the gangster who gets "respect" from his underlings, the men who violate women, and the outlaw-heros who seem to be successful in thumbing their noses at law enforcement agencies. It has long been known that children do emulate their parents. It has long been known that adolescents want to be like the hero-outlaws they see in movies. It has long been known that children will ape what they see, called "social learning" (Bandura, 1986). Still, there we all sit, the whole family, watching these violent films and munching popcorn. Can we prevent our children from being exposed to such anti-heros? Probably not very successfully. But we can provide something of an antidote. After the family has seen the movie, we can provide an opportunity to have the family discuss the reality of the gangster-hero, what that person is really like (a rapist, a thief, and a murderer), what it would be like to be involved with such a person, and the consequences of his or her actions.

The Working Wife and Mother Has Always Been with Us. Much has been written on the consequences of the working wife and mother and absentee father. They have been castigated as a principal reason for the problems of their adolescents. Before we go any further in castigating the woman, we need to gain a realistic picture of what has really been going on under the veneer of "polite society." The working wife and mother is not a new phenomenon. *The working wife and mother has always been with us.* We may have called her a teacher, a nurse, a governess, the town seamstress, a cook, a housemaid, a day laborer, a sweat shop worker, a migrant field hand, or a laundress. But whatever she was called, she was working outside the home to help support the family. The working wife and mother is still doing exactly that today. The point we are making is that the stay-at-home "wife and mother" was a model that only a small percentage of American families have ever been able to afford. It was a model that did not represent the large majority of families in the United States.

The Working Woman Has Been a Factor in the Economic Stability of the Country. Furthermore, during the last several decades, the economists tell us, it is the working woman that has been a major factor in keeping the economy stabilized in times of a nervous Wall

Street. The official recognition of the woman as independent wage-earner seems to have come during the "Great Depression." At its lowest ebb, 25 percent of American working men were laid off and out-of-work for long periods of time. The families of these men would have lost everything saved for the fact that their women could go to work as telephone operators just coming into existence or as sales clerks for the five-and-dime stores spreading across the country. Typewriters, too, were being introduced as the *sine qua non* of a respectable business, so women who learned to type were vastly employable (see Tip 14.2). With the advent of the five-and-ten cent stores during the depression, single women and wives found employment as sales girls. Even adolescents could contribute to the family income by earning money through paper routes and selling subscriptions to magazines (Smiley, 2002).

A More Realistic Understanding of the Present American Family. Clearly, we have to face the fact that the working wife and the working mother is here to stay. We have to recognize that many nontraditional households (single parents, single persons living alone, teenage mothers, divorced couples, gay and lesbian couples, and so on) are increasing rapidly. The 2000 census estimated these nontraditional groups as making up perhaps 25 percent of the American households. We have to discover more workable models of the dual-income family grouping. One such emerging model is what is called the peer marriage.

Introducing the Peer Marriage. Peer marriage is defined as an equal status partnership of "peers" in every aspect of the marriage (Schwartz, 1998). It sounds easy, but it is far easier to define than to accomplish. In fact, many married couples may believe they have a peer marriage when, in actuality, they have only taken some steps toward it. A peer marriage is not just a marriage in which both partners are earning an income. A peer marriage is one in which both partners share *all* responsibilities that are entailed in their life-careers together.

A fairly easy shared peer responsibility is taking turns at preparing meals, even if it simply means that husband or wife has the responsibility of picking up the pizza on the way home while the other makes the salad. Another fairly easy shared peer responsibility is making financial decisions together. What is *not* easy, is joint responsibility for child-rearing, because of the many emotional and social obstacles in the way. Traditionally, women have been the parent responsible for care of the children, at least up until the boys reach adolescence. These traditional role divisions of wife and husband have been transmitted from one generation to the next for centuries, and are not easily overcome. Emotionally, it takes a man with a good deal of **ego strength** (which can be interpreted as being a person of high self-esteem and who is highly individuated). Many men still today would feel that he has lost status if he assumes equal partnership for the care of their small children. A societal problem is that men, much more than women, have jobs requiring them to be away for days or even weeks at a time. Being away for any length of time means that, on their return to their home, so many events have occurred while he was gone, that he feels like an "outsider" until he has caught up with family history.

Finally, when we expect more from our peer partner than our peer partner can manage, we may feel such emotional disappointment and discouragement, that we will decide to abandon the whole idea of a real peer marriage. Just as in more traditional marriages, here is where

---

Tip 14.2 On the Beginning of the Typist. James M. Barrie, the author of *Peter Pan*, wrote a famous play, called "The Twelve Pound Note," about a wife who left her husband after she bought a typewriter and could earn her own living.

both parties have to sit down and figure out what went wrong and what to do about it. Then they try again. And again. And yet again. As yet, only a very small percentage of working couples are trying out the peer-marriage model. If in fact it catches on, your generation will be the pioneers of the peer-marriage movement. But those who have been successful in their peer-marriage relationship report positive consequences.

Positive Consequences of Peer Marriage. The hardest part of peer marriage—that of equality of the child-rearing aspects—proves also to be the chief strength of the marriage. What happens when a couple shares the responsibilities of child raising is increased intimacy, which we already know is a major keystone in a successful long-term relationship. Fathers no longer feel displaced as the "man-of-the-house." Mothers no longer feel that she has all the responsibility (and therefore all the blame) when the children have problems in the neighborhood, at school, or even with law enforcement agencies. The growing children have less of an opportunity to manipulate their parents by tricky translations of what one parent says to the other parent, which means they have less opportunity to play parents off each other. Most importantly, they are being given a role model of what a really supportive relationship is like.

Other interesting results of peer marriages include more effective fathering, which is so necessary for boys becoming men. Furthermore, the more men participate in the child-rearing details, the more attached they are to their children. The stronger the father–child attachment, the less child abuse, the less likely the susceptibility to extramarital affairs, and the lower the likelihood of divorce. The stronger the child–father attachment, the less burdened the wife feels. Her gratitude becomes a source of sexual passion that is too often lost when she feels overburdened. In a long-term relationship, women are less turned on sexually by physical attraction and are more turned on by thoughtfulness on the part of their men (Brown & Amatea, 2002). All in all, successful peer marriages result in increased satisfaction of both partners and the durability of the marriage itself.

Fostering Community-Based Attitudes in Our Children. It is the opinion of more than a few social commentators that we are breeding a generation of adolescents who lack empathy and are aggressively self-serving. For example, one psychologist (Glass, 2003) says that while empathy appears to be innate, we can stunt its development in three ways. First, we can overindulge our children with too much permissiveness. By not setting limits, children come to feel entitled, with that entitlement focused on themselves. Second, we can smother the child by being over-sympathetic when the child is hurting. We tend to try to fix the child's bad feelings whenever we can. What we need to do, occasionally, is to allow a hurting child to retreat and work through feelings of fear, anger, guilt, and shame. We will not always "be there" for the child as he grows up. If children are to learn *resilience* (the second of the "New Three R's"), we need sometimes to let them work through negative feelings on their own. We need also to put less emphasis on superior achievement (winning out over others) and more emphasis on such personality traits as generosity, altruism, and compassion for others. These kinds of personality traits can be fostered within the community-based family in three steps. First, the children are encouraged to help all members of the family, including parents and siblings. When the children show evidence of being kind and generous to their siblings (sibling rivalry and jealousy are not easily overcome), they are encouraged to direct these same qualities to their friends and classmates. As they get older, the children are then encouraged to engage in community projects. In these ways, we are fostering responsibility (the third of the "New Three R's").

Participating in Family Projects. How children learn to participate in a community-based family comes about by helping out the inside or outside tasks for the benefit of all. If all we do is try to provide our children with "all the advantages that money can buy," we may be teaching them that having a lot of money is the most important value in life. In addition to such personal tasks as keeping their rooms clean, as children grow and mature, we need to foster the understanding that sometimes we do things for "the common good," particularly, when both parents are working, or a single parent is working hard to support them. For example, Saturday morning can be declared as "household task" time. It need not be for more than an hour or two, but with everybody working for that hour or two, it can result in a car washed inside and out, or the garage cleaned out, or the living room swept, dusted, vacuumed, and windows washed. One or two hours a week is not much time out of a week, and by all children sharing these tasks, they also acquire neater habits. After all, if they are going to have to engage in washing the car inside and out, in a week or so, they will be less likely to dirty it up.

Another major participation activity is making sure that all adults and children are involved in the planning of a family get-together, whether it be a picnic, a birthday celebration, or a religious or national holiday. From organizational psychology, we have learned that when committee members and work teams are engaged in the planning of a project, they are more cooperative in carrying out the project and more satisfied when it is accomplished. So it is with children in the family. The more they are involved in planning of an outing, the more they will look forward to it and help in the preparation. They can decide what food to bring, and what to take along, such as softball or badminton sets, fishing rods, perhaps some reading materials (comics, children's books, magazines), and (oh, yes!) let's not forget blankets or those famous Girl Scout "sit-upons."

Two Important Qualities of Resilience: Patience and Perseverance. One of the negative traits that mark people who get in trouble with the law or who are unable to make a constructive life-career for themselves is the inability to tolerate not having their heart's desire immediately, sometimes called the need for **immediate gratification**. They want things NOW. They don't want to have to wait for it or to work for it. By contrast, successful people are able to work long and hard at what they want to achieve, whether it be in business, in becoming an athletic or singing star, or staying in school to get those necessary academic credentials for the job they want. They have acquired the two virtues of *patience* and *perseverance*. We can foster these traits in our children by not always giving into their demands. Instead, we can help them develop the means whereby they can earn their heart's desire.

Just as there should be shared household tasks, so should there be shared financial responsibility. First, there needs to be more openness about family finances, including expenses and budgeting. Then when a child expresses a need or desire for something, that need or desire can be put on a list shared by the whole family. Examples: Dad is saving for new car seat covers. Mom is saving for a special outfit (dress, shoes, pocketbook, and hat) for an upcoming wedding of a relative. The oldest boy, John, is saving for new hockey gear and a uniform. Middle-school-aged Dana is saving for a trip to Washington, D.C., with her school glee club. Now young Davy gets to put up his heart's desire which happens to be his own fishing rod. The children are helped to earn money toward it through baby-sitting and odd jobs at home or in the neighborhood. As they get older, they may earn money cutting grass for other people or through a newspaper route. For teenage girls (and boys as well), there is always a need for baby-sitters. Young Davy observes each person saving money and getting their heart's desire. He is learning patience and perseverance by what is called **observational learning** (Bandura, 1986).

Since we are working toward a peer marriage, we can also work toward eliminating gender-based jobs for the boys and girls in the family. Older children of both genders can help prepare the food, including cooking the casserole and preparing the coleslaw and sandwiches the night before. Teenagers, again both girls and boys, can help Dad clean out the garage and, in the meantime, learn about tools. It may be that the two genders will trade jobs: "I'll do the dishes tomorrow night if you will do them tonight. I've got to finish a school assignment and it's long." That's OK. They are learning the politics of cooperation, bartering, and time management.

Fostering Multicultural Understanding in the Community. We can foster the children's development of empathy and compassion for others in several ways. When a friend is sick, we encourage the child to send a card or call the friend on the telephone. If the friend is not suffering from a contagious disease and is well enough for visitors, we encourage the child to visit the sick friend. The child does not have to buy a gift. Bringing a game that both can play serves very well. We can encourage children to volunteer to bring homework assignments to the sick child. The child's parents, too, will be especially grateful for these contributions.

In terms of the larger community, we can foster the child's understanding of our multicultural diversity in several ways (see Tip 14.3). We can socialize with families that come from ethnic backgrounds different from our own. If our children and their children seem to get along, we can ask them to come along on our picnics and other activities, and invite them to birthday parties. As the children become fast friends, sleep-overs or even camping out will be fun (the first camp out can be in the backyard).

When the children come home with tales of bullying or nasty things said about other ethnic groups, we can discuss the fact that they are not respecting our large and wonderful multicultural population, and what our country's motto, *E Pluribus Unum* (Out of the Many— One), really means. We can encourage our schools to initiate knowledge of traditions and foods of Hispanics, Mid-Easterners, Chinese, Japanese, and Filipinos, along with those of European nationalities. At the same time, we need to emphasize that these ethnic groups in our country are all part of our identity as Americans. Very importantly, we can urge our schools to promote antibullying campaigns. The more emphasis on the evils of bullying, the more willing will the children be to report such incidents. Together, teachers and children and parents can promote antibullying by designing bulletin boards in the classroom and posters for the corridors.

Eventually, as our children learn the value of empathy and compassion for others less fortunate, we can begin to include them in our own adult endeavors. We know one family who spends their winter holidays working in their church's "Feasts for Indigent" programs. One of our own students, some years ago, was one of the four daughters of a well-known and respected Ohio senator. Our student related that whenever her family took family vacations, the senator always made it a point to include a visit to a well-known historical site, such as the Washington and Lincoln Memorials, to remind them of what this country stands for.

Tip 14.3 On Fostering Acceptance of Our Multicultural Diversity. The suggestions given here are taken from an educational journal entitled *Teaching Tolerance Magazine,* published by the Southern Poverty Law Center. For more suggestions, you may contact them as follows: Phone: (334) 956-8486 and Fax (334) 956-8486. The magazine is mailed to teachers twice a year at no charge.

Important Terms and Concepts to Know

- abuse
- authoritarian
- blaming
- career
- climate of work
- computers
- crime
- direction

- divorce
- esteem
- extracurricular
- father
- generalists
- ills
- jobs
- national

- patience
- peer
- people skills
- personality
- positive
- practice
- problem
- résumé

- right
- shadowing
- tasks
- tenacity
- we
- win-win
- working

Make Your Own Summary by Filling in the Blanks

Use the "Important Terms and Concepts to Know" to fill in the blanks.

Importance of work.   Work is essential to our _____ and personal well-being. When there is high unemployment, there is more spouse and child _____, more suicide, homicide, and street _____. A satisfying and creative work contributes greatly to our self-_____.

Vocational choice.   It is wise to take advantage of vocational _____ days offered by your college. A good way to get a realistic view of a career is by _____ someone already in the field throughout the work day. Do not be overly concerned, however, if you are not sure what you want to do. Career choice today is less a target than a _____.

Career success.   The day of the _____ "boss" is over. Organizations want employees with "_____" and who know how to communicate and motivate their coworkers and employees. They do not want people who are just "A-getting grinds." They are looking for people who have taken part in _____

activities and who have learned how to be _____ solvers. They value people who have had full or part time _____. They need people who are _____ and can relate to many departments and areas. The specialist is no longer as necessary because _____ can store gigabytes of specialized information.

Securing your first real job.   To land your first real job, create a _____ that is attention-getting without being bizarre. To prepare yourself for the interview, _____ with your friends by going through several dry-runs. Don't necessarily take "no" as an answer. Don't be afraid to return time after time. They will admire your _____.

Career success.   Effective managers build a warm _____. Effective managers catch their employees doing something "_____" and provide for _____ feedback. Do not allow arguments to assume a "_____ problem." Instead, focus on issues. Effective managers are skilled in conflict resolution because they seek _____ solutions. The reader is reminded to use first person plural pronoun "_____" when problems arise.

Building a community-based family once again. Commentators of the present social scene protest always blaming the working mother and wife as responsible for the present _____ of society, such as juvenile delinquency and the high rate of divorce. The _____ game is a dead end. As well, the _____ wife has not only contributed to the national economy, she has been with us since the beginning of our history. One emerging model is the _____ marriage, which is difficult to achieve, but when successful, the advantages are more parental intimacy, stronger _____-child attachment, fewer extramarital affairs, and a lower rate of _____. For a true community-based family, it is advised to include children and adolescents in common household _____ and planning family get-togethers. As well, they will learn _____ and perseverance by working for their needs and wants.

Glossary

Note: This glossary gives brief definitions of important terms and concepts in the text. For a fuller explanation of a term, look in the index.

abnormal behavior: Behavior that deviates markedly from the average range of behavior, which is painful to the person, destructive to self, or disturbing to others.

abuse: Any kind of physical, sexual, emotional, or neglectful treatment.

AIDS (acquired immune deficiency syndrome): A retroviral disease which breaks down the body's natural ability to resist illness.

adipose tissue: Fatty tissue that is added to a girl's figure during puberty.

adolescence: The sweeping psychosocial changes of personality that accompany *puberty*.

adolescent egocentricity: Elkind's term for the adolescent's self-absorption and inability to consider another person's point-of-view.

adrenalergic state: The many physical changes that occur when the body expends energy.

adult-ego state: That part of the personality that mediates between the *child-ego state* and the *parent-ego state*.

affect: The professional term for emotions or feelings. A person who is emotionally cold and unresponsive to others' feelings is said to have a flat affect.

age/stage theory: The theory that human beings change *qualitatively* at certain ages throughout the life span in all dimensions: physically, intellectually, emotionally, and spiritually.

aggression: The *defense mechanism* by which we attack others physically or verbally.

alarm stage: The first stage of Selye's *general adaptation syndrome* in which the organism exhibits external and internal symptoms of disease.

altruism: A high-level *defense mechanism* by which the person deals with trauma by helping others.

amenorrhea: Cessation of the menstrual period.

amnesia: Memory loss generally following physical or emotional trauma.

amniotic fluid: The watery environment in which the unborn child floats.

anal stage: The second stage of Freud's *psychosexual development* in which the *libido* is centered on the anal area and during which the superego develops.

androgeny: A mixture of masculine and feminine traits.

Anima: The personification of a man's neglected "feminine" traits.

animism: The belief that natural events have supernatural causation.

animistic thinking: The belief that inanimate objects have human feelings and thoughts, characteristic of Piaget's preoperative stage of *cognitive development*.

Animus: The personification of a woman's neglected "masculine" traits.

antigens: Any substance that is toxic to human beings, including bacteria, virus, pollen, dander, etc.

anorexia nervosa: A disorder in which the person manages not to eat and becomes dangerously thin, prevalent among adolescent girls.

anxiety: Mental or emotional pain that can be experienced variously as apprehension, dread, or general uneasiness.

Archetypes: Jung's concepts of the images and symbols that personify and express the deeply imbedded values and experiences of previous generations of humankind.

attachment: The degree to which the baby or young child feels emotionally bonded with the chief caretaker.

attention deficit/hyperactive disorder (AD/HD): A mental disorder marked by the inability to stay focused and quiet and associated with learning disabilities.

attribution bias: The tendency for people to ascribe their good fortune to their own positive characteristics but to ascribe another's good fortune to external (situational) factors. The reverse is also true, that we tend to ascribe our bad fortune to the situation but ascribe the bad fortune of others to negative personality traits.

authoritarian parenting: Parenting that assumes that "parents know best," uses power and force, and values obedience.

authoritarian personality: People who blindly follow authority, demand obedience from subordinates, and whose cognitions are dogmatic, prejudicial, rigid, and stereotypic.

authoritative parenting: Parenting that is "family based" and respects individual differences and rights of all family members.

autism: A congenital disorder characterized by lack of language and lack of attachment to caregivers.

autonomy: Erikson's Stage 2 characterized by learning the basic functions of eating, walking, and controlling bladder and bowels.

aversive conditioning: A learned response by which painful stimuli is avoided.

basic trust: The life task to be learned in Erikson's Stage 1 in which the baby develops healthy physical and emotional responses.

battered woman: The woman who has been subjected to physical and emotional abuse until she has lost confidence that she can survive on her own.

batterer: A person who physically abuses another.

behavior modification: Therapy which focuses on the non-reinforcement of undesirable behavior and the reinforcement of desirable behavior in small, successful, successive steps.

behavior therapy: Therapy which focuses on the elimination of symptoms.

biofeedback: Bodymind therapy by which the person learns to gain control of his/her biological functioning.

bipolar mood disorder: The *DSM* term for a person who suffers from extreme mood swings, formerly called "manic-depressive psychosis."

bulemia: An eating disorder characterized by alternating binge-eating and vomiting.

bystander effect: The key factor that affects a person's willingness to aid another person; namely, the number of people already in the vicinity and presumably able to lend aid.

caregiver: The term used instead of "mothering" in order to acknowledge the father's ability to care for infants and children.

castration complex: Freud's term for a little boy's fear that something negative will happen to his penis.

catatonia: A signifier of certain kinds of mental disorders, generally characterized by extreme immobility.

center-of-growth: Carl Roger's term for the inner knowledge or intuition by which a person is guided to make life choices.

centrated: A child's *cognitive* focus.

child-centered home: Permissive parenting in which there are few rules and children are allowed to explore and discover their environment on their own.

child-ego state: That part of the personality which expresses feelings.

circadian rhythms: The rhythms of nature, which includes the tides, the mating seasons of animals, and human biological sleep and waking states, menstrual cycles, etc.

cholinergic state: Opposite to the *adrenalergic state*, the body is at rest, and able to drain built-up toxins, repair tissues, and restore depleted metabolic reserves.

classical conditioning: *Learning* acquired when a *neutral stimulus* becomes a *conditioned stimulus* by pairing it with an *unconditioned stimulus*.

claustrophobia: Fear of closed spaces.

client-centered therapy: Rogers therapy that focuses on empathy, reflective listening, and feedback.

climate of work: The friendliness (or lack of it) among workers and administration.

comorbidity: Two or more symptoms, diseases, or mental disorders that are manifesting at the same time.

cognition(s): Professional term for thought processes (as distinct from *affect* or emotions).

cognitive development: How we develop our ability to think.

cognitive shortcuts: The way we clump events so as to cope with the myriad sensations and perceptions that impinge on us from moment-to-moment. When we clump people according to their ethnic background, gender, age-group, etc., we are perceiving them as *stereotypes*.

cognitive therapies: Therapies which combine *insight* and *behavior therapy*, and are particularly focused on replacing irrational beliefs and destructive self-talk with more constructive and healthier cognitions.

cohabitation: Living with another person without a legal marriage contract.

collective unconscious: Jung's theory that our deepest unconscious memories contain *Archetypes* of previous generations, and by virtue of these profoundest layers of memory, we are psychically connected to all other members of humankind, and which may explain the phenomenon of *synchronicity*.

compassionate love: Love which values the other person's welfare, characterized by an enduring sense of well-being in the company of that person, and emotional support of each other during times of crises, painful events, and conflict.

compensation: The *defense mechanism* in which the person performs well in one area to make up for a limitation in another area.

compulsion: Repetitive behavior over which the person seems to have no conscious control.

concordance rate: The degree to which a personality variable is shared by close relatives.

concrete operations: The third stage of Piaget's theory of *cognitive development*.

concrete thinking: The inability to comprehend abstractions, typical of Piaget's preoperative stage.

conditioned response (CR): A response aroused by a *conditioned stimulus*.

conditional stimulus (CS): A previously *neutral stimulus* that when paired with an *unconditioned stimulus* eventually arouses a *conditioned response*.

conflict resolution: The process by which disputes are settled.

conformity: The tendency to go along with others rather than acting from one's belief and values.

consciousness: Our moment-by-moment awareness.

constancies: Achievement of the cognitions of color, shape, and size during infancy.

conventional morality: The second stage of Kohlberg's theory of moral/ethical development characteristic of the majority of American males.

conversion disorder: Converting anxiety into physical symptoms.

coping techniques: The manner in which a person deals with problematic or *traumatic* events.

correlation: The relationship of two or more variables.

counter-conditioning: Another term for Wolpe's systematic desensitization.

crisis: 1. A troublesome situation; 2. A turning point.

critical time: The specific time zones during which a physical or personality trait develops. If this time is missed or interfered with, the trait does not develop as it should. Examples: mother-baby bonding, vision, and language.

culture: The complex of shared attitudes, values, and behaviors of any given population.

culture reduced tests: Psychological tests (generally "IQ" tests) that attempt to narrow the effects of poverty and ethnic background.

daydreaming: 1. Fantasy as a defense mechanism; 2. A variation of consciousness; 3. Imagining as a method of creativity and problem solving.

decentration: Piaget's term for the ability to consider a previous perception along with the present perception, allowing us to mediate two ideas at the same time. This ability develops in the concrete stage of cognitive development.

defense mechanisms: Unconscious processes by which the person copes with negative emotions.

deindividuation: Personal identity and standards of behavior drop away as the person identifies with group standards of behavior.

delusions: Irrational beliefs, as in believing that we are Jesus Christ or Napoleon.

denial: The *defense mechanism* by which we block out unacceptable perceptions.

depressants: Drugs that slow down the functioning of the nervous system.

depression: Feelings of hopelessness, helplessness, and apathy.

desensitization training: Deconditioning a person's anxiety-provoking stimulus, often used to treat simple phobias.

devaluation: Speaking negatively of a person to salvage self-esteem.

differential diagnosis: Diagnosing a physical or mental disorder through a process of elimination.

discrimination: Treating persons or groups in a negative way.

displacement: The defense mechanism of venting negative emotions against a person or group of people who generally cannot retaliate.

dissociative disorders: 1. Feelings of unreality; 2. Splitting off of the personality as in *amnesia* and *dissociative identity disorder*.

dissociative fugue state: Loss of personal identity (amnesia) and flight from place of residence.

distress: Stress that results in negative physical reactions, and which can lead to severe physical or emotional illness.

distributed practice: Spreading study or skill building over many sessions.

dogmatism: Narrow and uncritical belief systems.

double standard: The attitude that what is appropriate for one group is not appropriate for another group.

DSM: Initials standing for the *Diagnostic and Statistical Manual for Mental Disorders.*

dysfunctional behavior: 1. Abnormal behavior; 2. Behaviors that seriously interfere with one's ability to sustain mind-body well-being.

dyslexia: Disorder related to difficulty in learning to read.

eclectic: Using two or more psychotherapeutic techniques.

ego: Freud's term for the conscious part of the personality, which mediates between the id and the superego.

ego states: Berne's term for the three "recordings" of the personality that equate to the child, parent, and adult aspects of each person.

ego strength: The amount of psychic energy a person has in order to cope with and work through the problems and crises of living.

egocentric thinking: The inability of children to perceive the world from any other view than their own.

either-or thinking: The tendency to perceive people and events in absolute categories, as in good-or-bad and right-or-wrong.

electroconvulsive therapy (ECT): Commonly called "shock treatment."

Elektra complex: The strong attachment of the daughter for her father.

embryo: The unborn child from conception to the end of the third month.

emotional intelligence: One of the multiple intelligences that focuses on a person's empathetic sensitivity for others, ability to make good judgments in times of pressure and crisis; and compassionate aid for others in need.

empathy: Ability to see a person's problem as the person perceives it without judgment or blame.

empirical: Evidence obtained through the senses agreed upon by two or more independent observers.

environmental engineering: Creating better learning situations through techniques of time out, and other psychoeducational techniques.

etiology: Beginning(s) or cause(s).

euphoria: An extremely "high" mood state often associated with bipolar mood disorder.

eustress: Selye's term for *good* stress.

evolutionary psychology: The theory that many human traits derive from our evolution, retained because of their survival benefits.

experimental extinction: The elimination of *conditioned* behaviors through nonreinforcement.

extended family: The family constellation in which at least three generations live under one roof, sometimes with other related kin or hired hands.

extinction: The *conditioning* term for "forgetting."

extroversion: Orientation is outgoing toward others, friendly, and energized by many relationships.

F-Scale: A psychological test for measuring authoritarianism.

feedback: Immediate knowledge of results and the most efficient method of learning.

feeling function: The function in which emotions predominate.

fetus: The developing child in the uterus from four months to birth.

fight-flight-freeze response: The primitive emotions that stem from the midbrain.

figure-ground relationship: Perls' term to indicate the influence of past experience on *here-and-now* perception.

fixation: 1. Neurosis; 2. Stuck at a primitive level of emotional development.

formal operations: The fourth and highest (adult) level of Piaget's theory of cognitive development.

free association: Therapeutic technique in which the person is encouraged to say whatever thoughts or emotions come to mind without having to feel guilt, shame, or remorse.

free-floating anxiety: Anxiety that attaches to whatever the person thinks about.

Freudian slips: Slips-of-the-tongue and slips-of-the-pen presumed to be discharges from the unconscious.

frontal neocortex: The uppermost 1/4 inch layer of the cerebrum just over the forehead where we make mature and rational decisions.

functional thinking: Piaget's term for how preoperative children understand objects and events in ways that make sense to them.

gemeinschaftsgefühl: Adler's term for one's compassion and service to all humankind.

gender stereotyping: Making assumptions about someone based on whether the person is male or female.

general adaptation syndrome: Selye's term for the changes that occur as the result of prolonged *stress* and which ultimately produce disease.

generalized responses: Behaviors that are similar to *conditioned responses* and aroused by *generalized stimuli.*

generalized stimuli: Stimuli that are similar to *conditioned stimuli*.

generativity: The *life task* of Erikson's seventh age/stage development.

genetics: What we inherit from our parents.

genital stage: (Freudian theory). The final (adult) stage of *Freud's psychosexual growth*, or adult stage.

Genovese effect: The tendency to avoid "getting involved" in unpleasant or dangerous situations.

gentle birth: Leboyer's term for his nonviolent birthing methods.

gestalt: 1. The German word meaning the whole pattern or configuration; 2. Techniques formulated by Frederich Perls.

gestalt therapy: The therapeutic techniques formulated by Frederich Perls.

hallucinations: The acceptance of certain phenomena as external reality when, in fact, the phenomena are private and autistic experiences.

happiness: As defined by positive psychologists (and contrasted with pleasure), an enduring feeling of well-being.

hatha yoga: An Indian discipline that seeks bodymind integration via physical development.

hedonism: The philosophy of life that emphasizes the pursuit of secular pleasures.

here-and-now: Perls' term to indicate our focused attention at the present moment.

Hero Archetype: Campbell's term for the person's personal fable, in which he or she is the hero or heroine.

hierarchy of needs: Maslow's seven-stage theory of motivation.

high risk: Vulnerable to a particular disease or defect.

holistic health approach: Treatment of the entire person, including the physical, cognitive, social, emotional, and spiritual dimensions.

homeostasis: An ideal state of chemical balance within the body.

homophobia: An exaggerated fear of homosexuality.

homosexuality: A preference for a same-gender person as a sexual partner.

hot reactors: People who have extreme reactions to mild stress.

human becoming: Allport's term to indicate that we are continually growing, maturing, and evolving.

human relations approach: The *management theory* devised by McGregor and based on *Theory Y* assumptions.

humanistic psychology: "Third Force" psychology, which focuses on healthy personality and assumes that we are capable of *free will, choice and change*.

hypochondria: A continual fear that we are about to succumb to some dreadful disease.

hypostress: The lack of stress (challenge) in our life, which, in turn, becomes stressful.

id: Freud's term for the *unsocialized* aspect of the personality dominated by the *pleasure–pain principle*.

imaginary audience: The adolescent's belief that he/she is the center of attention wherever he/she may be.

individual differences: The variations between human beings that make us uniquely ourselves.

individuation: Jung's term for the evolution of personality when we act from inner convictions.

industry: Erikson's theory of the *crisis* and *life task* of the school-age child.

inferiority-superiority complex: Jung's theory for the need to find ways in which to be superior to compensate for feelings of inferiority.

information society: The technological society in which research, data, and other demographic information is shared by other institutions or persons through various media, particularly over the Internet.

initiative: Eriksonian's term for the *crisis* and *life task* of his Stage 3.

innate: Inborn, genetic, nativist, inherited.

insight therapies: Therapeutic approaches that focus on self-understanding, etiology and catharsis of psychological problems.

intimacy: Erikson's term for the *crisis* and *life task* of the young adult stage.

introspection: The process of self-examination and self-analysis.

introversion: Our need to withdraw from society and center ourselves in the process of integration.

intuition function: Jung's term for the way we take in information but cannot say what processes are involved.

latency stage: The fourth stage of Freud's *psychosexual development*, in which the libidinal drive is quiescent.

latent dream: Freud's theory that the real meaning of a dream lies beneath the facade of the manifest dream.

learning: Behavior that is the result of environmental factors.

libido/libidinal drive: (Freudian theory). 1. In its narrowest sense, the sexual drive; 2. in its wildest sense, the drive toward pleasure.

life crisis: Erikson's formulation of the challenge that confronts us as we transit from one age/stage to the next.

life crisis units (LCUs): The units of measurement for the amount of change in one's living, even happy change.

life lie: Adler's term for living in a way that is not in harmony with one's life style and theme.

life style: Adler's term to describe the direction, flow, and meaning of a person's life.

life tasks: Erikson's term for the competencies that people must achieve during the various age/stages so as to continue their personality integration.

locus of control (LOC): A person's worldview of whether one's fate is externally controlled by outside forces or internal, under one's own control.

logotherapy: The therapy devised by Viktor Frankl that focuses on the need for meaning in one's life.

long-term memory: Our more-or-less permanent memory.

lucid dreaming: Conscious dreaming.

mandala: A visual symbol that enables the person to focus on wholeness, health, and *personality integration*.

manic state: The mood state in which we experience a high degree of energy.

manifest dream: Freud's term for the surface dream that disguises the real meaning of the dream.

massed practice: Studying a given amount of material in long periods as opposed to *distributed practice*.

maturation: Growth as the result of the unraveling of our genetic programming as contrasted with learning (environmental factors).

mechanistic theory: See reductionist theory.

mediation: 1. Piaget's term for the cognitive process; 2. An alternative to divorce with an assumptive base of cooperation.

menarche: The woman's first menstrual cycle.

mentor: A person who is an advisor and consultant.

metastudy: A research methodology that analyzes and summarizes many other pieces of research in a particular area.

midlife crisis: Jung's theory of the upheaval that comes around age 40 as the result of spiritual bankruptcy.

mnemonic devices: Memory techniques.

mood disorders: Personality disorders that include major depression and bipolar mood disorders.

moratorium: 1. An authorized postponement; 2. Erikson's theory that the college experience is an opportunity for the person to avoid adult responsibilities.

mores: Strong ideas of right and wrong.

motor learning: Learning with use of muscles and highly resistant to extinction.

multisensory approach: Using two or more sense modalities to get material into the long-term memory.

myth: A story, tale, fable, or epic that attempts to explain the reasons for why things are as they are.

nature/nurture controversy: One of the basic issues of psychology, having to do with how much of human nature is due to genetics and how much is due to environment.

need-drive state: The psychophysical motivation to restore homeostasis.

negative role model: A person we do not want to emulate.

neoFreudians: Psychoanalysts trained in Freudian theory and methods but who include other factors of personality such as age/stages and cultural determinants.

neurosis: Freud's term for the fixation of emotional development at a primitive level, no longer included in the *DSM*.

neurotransmitter: Nerve cell chemicals released at the synapse, which affect other neurons.

neutral stimulus: A stimulus that does not arouse a specific conditioned response.

"New Three R's": Theory of intelligence that includes reasoning, resilience, and responsibility.

nocturnal emissions: Orgasms or emissions of semen while asleep, generally during erotic dreams.

noogenic neurosis: Frankl's theory that the psychological illness of our times is lack of meaning in our lives.

nuclear family: The modern type of family, which consists of parents and children as contrasted with the *extended family*.

nurture: The influence of the environment on human personality.

obedience experiments: Milgrim's studies of the tendency of people to obey authority without question.

object permanence: The infant's understanding that objects exist even if they are not visible.

observational learning: Learning that comes about simply by watching and imitating other people.

obsessive-compulsive disorder: Persons who are characterized by the need to repeat ritualistic actions, who are excessively tidy, and who equate money and cleanliness with goodness.

Oedipus complex: Freud's term for the strong mother-son attachment.

omnipotence: A defense mechanism in which the person assumes superior personality traits, found frequently among adolescents.

oncologist: A physician who specializes in cancer diseases.

open marriage: A type of marriage in which the partners have agreed to live independent lives, which includes sexual relationships with other people.

operant conditioning: Skinner's approach to conditioning, which emphasizes learning by the *reinforcement* of emitted behaviors.

oral personality: Freud's term for a person fixated at the *oral stage* of *psychosexual development*.

organizations of mind: Piaget's term for the four different cognitive stages.

overcompensation: Adler's term for the human tendency to exaggerate one aspect of their psychophysical development in order to be superior to others.

panic attack: Severe anxiety that can mimic heart trouble, asthma, etc.

paradigm: An analysis of a situation that describes and explains aspects of reality.

paralanguage: The nonverbal and physical aspects that accompany verbal language.

paranoid personality disorder: A person whose basic personality patterning is cold, suspicious, hostile, and grudge-carrying.

parent-ego state: Berne's term for all the admonitions and expressiveness of our parents including gestures, postures, and facial expressions that we have introjected.

parenting styles: Three common styles of parenting that have been identified are the *authoritarian*, the *authoritative*, and the *permissive*.

passive-dependent personality: Freud's term for the fixation of the personality at the *oral stage of psychosexual development*.

peak experiences: Maslow's term for the experience that has been variously labeled as the mystic experience, satori, Zen, enlightenment, at-one-ment, attunement, and cosmic consciousness.

peer marriage: An emerging model of marriage in which both partners have equal responsibility for every aspect of the marriage, including child care.

peer support groups: A therapeutic group situation whose members come together for the purpose of processing a common problematic life situation.

penetrance factors: Environmental toxins which can disrupt the development of the unborn child.

people skills: The ability of a leader to foster communication between individuals and groups.

perceiving function: Delaying decision-making until alternate options have been investigated.

perception: The meaning we attach to sensory experience.

permissive parenting: The parenting style that has few rules and fosters self-discovery.

Persona: Jung's term for the public face or mask we wear (our public image) and which we believe ourselves to be, as contrasted with the *Shadow* aspects of our personality.

personal fable: Elkind's term for the adolescent's belief in his/her own special uniqueness.

personality: A person's characteristic but dynamic way of responding to people and events and influenced by factors of age, gender, health, heredity, intelligence, socioeconomic and cultural factors, etc.

personality integration: The process or processes by which persons assimilate and synthesize their physical, cognitive, and social/emotional life experiences.

personality theorists: Social scientists who construct models of personality development over the total lifespan.

phallic stage: The third stage of Freud's *psychosexual development*.

phenomenology: The person's inner experience and worldview.

phobia: An unreasonable and exaggerated fear.

***Physician's Desk Reference* (PDR):** A medical book that lists the diagnosis, onset, etiology, possible treatments, and prognosis of a disease.

placebo control group: A group used for the purpose of measuring the effect of an experimental treatment, through the administration of a drug which does not contain a medication.

placebo effect: Healing as the result of a belief in an object, person, or event.

pleasure: As defined by the positive psychologists, a temporary state of feeling good.

pleasure/pain principle: The drive to seek pleasure and avoid pain, the chief characteristic of the id.

polarities: Jung's theory of *personality* based on oppositional forces, as *introversion/extraversion; sensing/feeling; Persona/Shadow*, etc.

population pool: The genetic probabilities of a racial or ethnic group that has remained stable for centuries.

positive psychology: The thrust toward studying human nature at its highest, most creative, and noble aspects.

positive reinforcement: Any event that increases the probability of a response.

postconventional morality: The third and highest level of Kohlberg's theory of moral/ethical development.

preconventional morality: The first level of Kohlberg's theory of moral/ethical development.

prejudice: 1. Prejudgment; 2. Making judgments about a person or group without personal knowledge of the person or group.

preoperational stage: The second stage of Piaget's theory of *cognitive development*.

primary group: The family we are born or adopted into.

primary reinforcers: Reinforcers based on *need/drive states* such as food, water, etc.

pro bono: Performing jobs without salary, simply "for the good" of the poor, the institutionalized, and anyone who otherwise might not get the service.

prognosis: Anticipating the course and outcome of an illness or treatment.

projective identification: Assigning blame of one's behavior to another person.

proxemics: The distances at which people communicate.

psychoanalysis: Freud's specific therapeutic approach, which seeks to reveal the person's psychodynamics.

psychodynamics: Unconscious conflicts from which much of human motivation is derived.

psychophysical hardiness: Persons who have an unusually strong and healthy body-mind sturdiness despite excessive stress.

psychosexual development: Freud's five stage theory of human emotional development.

psychosis: The acute stage of schizophrenia.

psychosocial development: Erikson's theory of social/emotional maturation through eight life stages.

psychosomatic disease: Emotional and/or physical problems as the result of stress.

psychosomatic medicine: Research that investigates the psychological correlates of illness.

psychotherapy: Healing of the mind/body/spirit.

puberty: The physical changes that occur sometime between 10 and 15 years of age as the result of maturation.

qualitative changes: Changes that are not simply quantitative or additive but are changes in kind or form. Example: the changes that come about by way of puberty.

quantitative changes: Changes of additive type, as contrasted with *qualitative* changes. Gaining an inch or pound are examples of quantitative changes.

rational-emotive therapy (RET): Albert Ellis' form of therapy which focuses on irrational and self-destructive beliefs.

rationalization: The defense mechanism by which we deny the real problem by constructing a face-saving excuse.

reaction formation: The *defense mechanism* by which we deny our unacceptable thoughts and feelings by expressing opposite behaviors.

reality principle: As a result of the socialization process, the acquisition of principles of behavior that warn us to be careful about our behaviors because of their possible consequences.

rebound effect: In trying to eliminate one's prejudicial cognition, the prejudicial thought comes back, sometimes even stronger than before.

reductionist theory: Theories that ascribe human behavior to simple laws of survival and adaptation, similar to other species. (Also known as mechanistic theory.)

referent group: Not one's primary group but the group one identifies with or would like to belong to.

replication: To repeat a study or experiment.

repression: Freud's term for the basic defense mechanism by which we "forget" unacceptable or painful conscious material.

resilience: One of the "New Three R's," the ability to rebound after emotional or physical trauma.

respondent conditioning: Classical conditioning formulated by Pavlov.

responsibility: One of the "New Three R's," the willingness to be of service where needed and to work toward bettering one's society.

ritualistic behaviors: Repetitive behaviors characteristic of the obsessive-compulsive personality.

role model: A person who seems to us to exemplify the kind of person we would like to emulate.

rote memorization: Memorizing without understanding the meaning, and highly vulnerable to forgetting.

rule making: Piaget's term for the need of ten- to twelve-year-olds to establish what is "fair" and "not fair" in their games, and which ushers in the second stage of moral/ethical development.

scapegoating: Aggressing on others unlike ourselves, generally on others who cannot retaliate.

schizophrenia: The personality disorder marked by delusions, hallucinations, and thought disorders.

second half of life: Jung's theory that the years that follow the midlife crisis are qualitatively different in values from the first half.

secondary sexual characteristics: Changes of the general body structure as the result of *puberty*, excluding the genital organs, which are the primary sexual organs.

secondary reinforcers: Reinforcers that are learned, such as smiles, honors, applause.

self-actualizing: Maslow's term for the highest level of human personality development.

self-concept: How we think about ourselves in terms of demographic variables, such as gender, race, age, political affiliation, sibling rank, etc.

self-disclosure: Letting others know about ourselves as we develop intimacy.

self-esteem: How we feel about ourselves, particularly when we compare ourselves to others.

self-report: The person's own response to questionnaires.

sensing function: How we absorb information through the senses.

sensory memory: The memory that connects our moment-by-moment neural firing, composed of momentary and fleeting sensations, thoughts, emotions, etc.

sensory-motor stage: The first stage of Piaget's theory of cognitive growth and organization of mind.

separation anxiety: The behaviors exhibited by a child with strong attachment when the main caregiver leaves.

Shadow: Jung's term for that part of personality that we disown and that coalesces in our personal unconscious.

shaping of behavior: Reinforcing of desired behaviors through small, successful, successive steps.

short-term memory: The second stage of memory that makes it possible for us to retain small chunks of information for a brief time (such as a telephone number).

sibling: Sister, brother, or litter mates.

sibling rivalry: The competition of children for their parents' attention and affection.

significant other: A fairly recent term that indicates the special person in our life with whom we have a committed relationship.

similarity filter: Mate selection influenced by similar age, socioeconomic level, education, even intelligence and personality.

simple forgetting: Forgetting as the result of decay of nonmeaningful material.

slow-to-warm child: The child who is shy and irritable in new situations but who eventually adapts to the environment.

social conformity: Agreeing with others rather than revealing our own inner opinion.

social Darwinism: A popular belief during the 19th century that people on top of the social-economic strata were there because of their natural superiority.

socialization: The process by which we are molded in certain ways by our culture, our parents, teachers, peer group, colleagues, etc.

social sanctions: The positive and negative responses of society toward certain behaviors.

social learning theory: Bandura's theory for how we learn by observation and imitation.

social loafing: Tendency for persons in a group to let others do the work.

spiritual bankruptcy: Jung's term for persons who have neglected the spiritual dimension in the first half of their lives.

spontaneous recovery: The reappearance of the conditioned response as a function of time.

spontaneous remission: The disappearance of symptoms without treatment.

stereotypes: Value judgments of a person or group of persons without personal knowledge.

stress: The problems and challenges that produce wear and tear of the body.

stimulants: Any ingredient (drugs, food, caffeine, etc.) which increases the rate of neural firing.

subculture: Over and above the culture we were born into, any affiliation that influences our cognitions and behaviors, such as our peer group, our political affiliations, and our professional associations.

subjective well-being (SWB): Self-reports of people as to their level of happiness.

sublimation: The defense mechanism by which we transform unacceptable behaviors into acceptable behaviors.

superego: Freud's term for that part of the personality by which we introject societal values, and which Freud equated with the conscience.

suppression: Consciously controlling an impulse to act.

synchronicity: Jung's term for what may appear as coincidence but is actually a sign of our psychic connectedness to each other.

systematic desensitization: Wolpe's therapy that seeks to eliminate simple phobias.

Theory X: McGregor's term for the authoritarian approach to management.

Theory Y: McGregor's term for the human relations approach to management.

Theory Z: Ouchi's term for a combination of Theory X and Theory Y approaches.

therapy: Healing methods.

thinking function: Jung's term for the process whereby we come to rational decisions as opposed to decisions made by feelings.

time out: One of the techniques of environmental engineering to improve a child's behavior in a social situation by removing the child from the scene of the disturbance.

transactional analysis (TA): A therapeutic situation based on analyzing our communication according to ego states.

transcending personalities: 1. Those who go beyond material gratification to higher, more universal values and service to others; 2. Those who are able to continue their self-actualizing growth despite physical disabilities or social limitations.

Trickster Archetype: The representation of the mischievous, spontaneous, and creative aspects of human personality.

twin studies: Studies of identical twins separated at birth and brought up in different environments to measure the influence of environment.

Type-A behavior: Behavior characterized by a fierce competitive drive and correlated with heart attack.

Type psychology: Personality theory based on innate characteristics of human functioning.

unconditional positive regard: Rogers' term for the therapist's empathetic attitude toward his client so that the client is able to reveal his inner self and thereby can grow and evolve.

unconditioned response (UCR): Any unlearned (reflexive) behavior.

unconditioned stimulus (UCS): Any event that arouses an unlearned (reflexive) response.

unconscious: Those memories, thoughts, and feelings driven out of our conscious awareness.

unfinished situations: Perls' term for the unresolved conflicts of our past life.

Universal Unconscious: Jung's term to indicate the relatedness and purposefulness of all phenomena.

visualization technique: Simonton's term for his holistic health approach to illness.

win-win solutions: Solutions to conflict that benefit everyone involved to some extent.

Wise Child Archetype: The representation of our innocent and trusting love of the universe and all creatures within it.

Wise Old Man Archetype: The representation of the knowledge that comes from years of experience.

Wise Old Woman Archetype: The representation of our intuitive knowledge.

wish-fulfillment: Freud's term for the symbolic meaning of many dream symbols.

worldview: The translation of the German word *Weltanschaung*, indicating the unconscious total fabric of one's beliefs and assumptions about the world.

References

Abel, M. H. (1997). Low birth weight and interactions between traditional risk factors. *The Journal of Genetic Psychology, 158*, 443–456.

Abramson, L. Y., Seligman, M. E. P., & Teasdale, J. (1978). Learned helplessness in humans: Critique and reformulation. *Journal of Abnormal Psychology, 87*, 32–48.

Adler, A. (1929). *The practice and theory of individual psychology*. New York: Harcourt Brace Jovanovich.

Adler, A. (1954). *Understanding human nature*. New York: Fawcett.

Adorno, T. W. (1973). *The jargon of authenticity*. Evanston, IL: Northwestern University Press.

Agras, W. S. (1985). Panic: Facing fears, phobias, and anxiety. New York: W. H. Freeman.

Ainsworth, M. D. (1979). The development of infant-mother attachment. In J. Belsky (Ed.), *In the beginning: Readings in infancy* (pp. 135–143). New York: Columbia University Press.

Alba, R. D. (1990). *Ethnic identity*. London: Yale University Press.

Alexander, F. (1950). *Psychosomatic medicine*. New York: Norton.

Allport, G. W. (1954). *The nature of prejudice*. Reading, MA: Addison-Wesley.

Allport, G. (1955). *Becoming: Basic considerations for a psychology of personality*. New Haven: Yale University Press.

Altemeyer, B. (1996). *The authoritarian specter*. Cambridge, MA: Harvard University Press.

Amato, P. R. (1981). Urban-rural differences in helping field studies based on a taxonomic organization of helping episodes. *Journal of Personality and Social Psychology, 114*, 289–290.

American Psychiatric Association (APA). (1994). *Diagnostic and statistical manual of mental disorders, 4th ed. (DSM-IV)*. Washington, DC: Author.

American Psychiatric Association (APA). (2000). *Diagnostic and statistical manual of mental disorders, 4th ed. revised (DSM-IV-TR)*. Washington, DC: Author.

Arendt, H. (1970). *The human condition*. Chicago: University of Chicago Press.

Arken, R., & Chang, LinChait. (2002, October). In B. Murray, Those who doubt themselves buy the most, study finds. *Monitor on Psychology*, 13.

Asch, S. (1951). Effects of group pressure upon the modification and distortion of judgments. In H. Guetzkow (Ed.), *Groups, leadership, and men: Research in human reactions* (pp. 177–190). Pittsburgh, PA: Carnegie Press.

Axinn, W. G., Barber, J. S., & Thornton, A. (1998, November). The long-term impact of parents' childbearing decisions on children's self-esteem. *Demography, 35*(4), 435–443.

Axline, V. (1964). *Dibs in search of self*. Boston: Houghton-Mifflin.

Bailey, G. R., Jr. (1996, Spring). Treatment of domestic violence in gay and lesbian relationships. *Journal of Psychological Practice, 2*(2), 1–8.

Bandura, A. (1986). *Social foundations of thought and action: A social-cognitive theory*. Englewood Cliffs, NJ: Prentice Hall.

Barron, F. (1970). *The shaping of behavior: Conflict, choice and growth*. New York: Harper & Row.

Baumeister, R. (1991). *Escaping the self*. New York: Basic Books.

Baumrind, D. (1973). Childcare practices anteceding three patterns of preschool behavior. *Genetic Psychological Monographs, 75*, 43–88.

Baxter, L. A. (1984). Trajectories of relationship disengagement. *Journal of Social and Personal Relationships, 1*, 29–48.

Baxter, L. A. (1986). Gender differences in the heterosexual relationship rules embedded in break-up accounts. *Journal of Social and Personal Relationships, 3*, 299–306.

Beane, J., & Lipka, R. P. (1986). *Self-esteem, self-concept, and the curriculum.* New York: Teacher's College Press.

Beaty, L. A. (1995, Winter). Effects of paternal absence on male adolescents, peer relations and self-image. *Adolescence*, 873–880.

Beck, A. T. (1991). Cognitive therapy: A 30-year retrospective. *American Psychologist, 46*, 368–375.

Beebe, S. A., Beebe, S. J., & Redmond, M. V. (1996). *Interpersonal communication: Relating to others.* Boston: Allyn & Bacon.

Beecher, H. K. (1961). Surgery as a placebo. *Journal of the American Medical Association, 176*, 1102.

Begley, S. (2003). Shaped by life in the womb. *Annual Editions: Human Development* (pp. 17–22). Guilford, CT: McGraw-Hill/Dushkin.

Bem, D. J. (1975). Sex role adaptability: One consequence of psychological androgyny. *Journal of Personality and Social Psychology, 31*, 634–643.

Bem, D. J. (1985). Androgyny and gender schema theory: A conceptual and empirical integration. In T. B. Sonderegger (Ed.), Nebraska symposium on motivation, 1984; *Psychology and Gender*, 32. Lincoln, NE: University of Nebraska Press.

Benson, H. (1975). *The relaxation response.* New York: Morrow.

Benson, H. (1975). *Your maximum mind.* New York: Times Books.

Berger, C. R., & Bradac, J. J. (1982). *Language and social knowledge: Uncertainty in interpersonal relations.* Baltimore, MD: Edward Arnold.

Berne, E. (1978). *Games people play.* Westminster, MD: Ballantine Books.

Bettelheim, B. (1987). *A good enough parent: A book on child rearing.* New York: Knopf.

Blanchard, K., & Johnson, S. (1982). *The one minute manager.* New York: Berkeley.

Blonigen, D. M., Carlson, S. R., Krueger, R. F., & Patrick, C. J. (2003). A twin study of self-reported psychopathic personality traits. *Personality and Individual Differences, 35a*(1), 179–198.

Bly, R. (1992). *A book about men.* New York: Random House.

Bohmer, C., & Parrot, A. (1993). *Sexual assault on campus.* New York: Lexington Books.

Bouchard, T. J. (1984). Twins reared apart and together: What they tell us about human diversity. In Fox, S. (Ed.), *The chemical and biological bases of individuality* (pp. 147–148). New York: Plenem.

Bouchard, Jr., T. J., Lykken, D. T., McGue, M., Segal, N. L., & Tellegen, A. (1990). Sources of human psychological differences: The Minnesota study of twins reared apart. *Science, 212*, 1055–1059.

Bowlby, J. (1969). *Attachment and loss.* New York: Basic Books.

Bowlby, J. (1980). *Attachment and loss: Vol. 3, Loss.* New York: Basic Books.

Brown, N. M., & Amatea, E. S. (2000). *Love and intimate relationships: Journeys of the heart.* London: Taylor and Francis.

Brownlee, S. (1999, Aug 9). Inside the teen brain. *U.S. News & World Report* (6), 45–50.

Bucke, R. M. (1901). *Cosmic consciousness.* New York: E. P. Dutton, p. 480.

Buss, D. M. (1994). *The evolution of desire.* New York: Basic Books.

Butler, R. N. (1980). *Why survive? Being old in America.* New York: Harper & Row.

Campbell, J. (1988). *The power of myth.* Garden City, NY: Doubleday.

Cannon, W. B. (1929). *Bodily changes in pain, hunger, fear and rage* (rev. ed.). New York: Appleton-Century-Crofts.

Capacchione, L. (1991). *Recovery of your inner child.* New York: Simon & Schuster.

Carrie, H. (1999). *Preventing sexual harassment at work.* Geneva: International Labour Office: Conditions of Work Branch.

Caron, S. L., & Carter, D. B. (1997, October). The relationships among sex role orientation, egalitarianism, attitudes toward sexuality, and attitudes toward violence against women. *The Journal of Social Psychology, 137*, 568–587.

Carskadon, M. A., Acebo, C., & Selzer, R. (2001). Extended nights, sleep loss and recovery sleep in adolescents. *Archives of Italian Biology, 139*, 301–302.

Charland, W. A. (1992, January). Nightshift narcosis. *The Rostarian, 160*, 16–19.

Chess, S., Thomas, A., & Birch, H. (1976). *Your child is a person: A psychological approach to parenthood without guilt.* New York: Penguin Books.

Cholst, S. (1991). *Finding love in a cold world.* New York: Beau Rivage.

Clark, H. H. (1991). Words, the world, and their possibilities. In G. R. Lockhead & J. R. Pomerantz (Eds.), *The perception of structure* (pp. 263–277). Washington, DC: American Psychological Association.

Clay, R. A. (2001, April). The greening of psychology. *American Psychological Association: Monitor of Psychology, 32*(4), 40–52.

Cleckley, H. M. (1976). *The mask of sanity*, 4th ed. St. Louis: Mosby.

Cochran, S. D., & Mays, V. M. (1990). Sex, lies and HIV. *New England Journal of Medicine, 322*, 774–775.

Cohen, S., & Herbert, T. B. (1996). Health psychology: Psychological factors and physical disease from the perspective of human psychoneuroimmunology. *Annual Review of Psychology, 47*, 113–142.

Cohen, S., & Williamson, G. M. (1991). Stress and infectious diseases in humans. *Psychological Bulletin, 109*(1), 5–24.

Coley, R. L. (2001). (In)visible men: Emerging research on low-income, unmarried, and minority fathers. *American Psychologist, 50*(9), 743–753.

Conn, J. H., & Kanner, L. (1947). Children's awareness of sex differences. *Journal of Child Psychiatry, 1*, 3–57.

Corewen, L. (1988). *Your resume: Key to a better job* (3rd ed.). Englewood Cliffs, N.J.

Cousins, N. (1979). *Anatomy of an illness as perceived by the patient: Reflections on healing and regeneration.* New York: Norton.

Csikszentmihalyi, M. (1997). Happiness and creativity. *The Futurist, 31,* 34–38. Bethesda, MD: World Future Society.

Curtis, J. M., & Cowell, D. R. (1993). Relation of birth order and scores on measures of pathological narcissism. *Psychological Report, 72,* 311–315.

Dahl, R. E. (2001). The consequences of insufficient sleep for adolescents: Links between sleep and emotional regulation. *Annual Editions: Adolescent Psychology, 01/02.* Guilford, CT: McGraw-Hill/Dushkin.

Darley, J., & Latané, B. (1986). Thy brother's keeper, Classic experiment 11: Diffusion of responsibility. In S. Schwartz (Ed.). *Classic studies in psychology* (pp. 122–142). Mountainview, CA: Mayfield Publishing.

Davidson, J. (1995). Overworked Americans or overwhelmed Americans? *Annual editions: Sociology* (pp. 22–25). Guilford, CT: Dushkin.

Dean, A. R. (1997, Spring). Humor and laughter in palliative care. *Journal of Palliative Care, 13*(1), 34–39.

DeAngelis, T. (2003, October). It's more than reading, writing and 'rithmetic. *Monitor on Psychology, 34*(9), 46–47.

Deikman, A. (2000). Service as a way of knowing. In Hart, T., Nelson, P. L., & Puhakka, K. (Eds.), *Transpersonal knowing: Exploring the horizons of consciousness* (pp. 303–318). Albany, NY: University of New York Press.

deTocqueville, A. (1830). *Democracy in America.* New York: Knopf.

Deveny, K. (June 30, 2003). We're not in the mood. *Newsweek, CXLI* (26), 41–46.

Diener, E. (2000). Subjective well-being: The science of happiness and a proposal for a national index. *American Psychologist, 55*(1), 34–43.

Dorman (1999). *The killing of Kitty Genovese* [WWW document]. http://www.lihistory.com/8/hs818a.htm.

Duck, S. (1994). Steady as (s)he goes: Relational maintenance as a shared meaning system. In D. J. Canary & L. Stafford (Eds.), *Communication and relational maintenance* (pp. 45–60). San Diego: Academic Press.

Duncan, L. E., Peterson, B. E., & Winter, D. G. (1997). Authoritarianism and gender roles: Toward a psychological analysis of hegemonic relationships. *Personality and Social Psychology Bulletin, 23,* 41–49.

Dunbar, F. (1955). *Mind and body: Psychosomatic medicine* (rev. ed.) New York: Random House.

Dunn, J. (1988). *The beginnings of social understanding.* Cambridge, MA: Harvard University Press.

Durkheim, E. (1984). *Suicide.* New York: Free Press.

Ebbinghouse, H. (1913). *Memory: A contribution to experimental psychology* (H. Ruger & C. Bussenius, Trans.). New York: Teachers College Press. (Original work published 1885.)

Elkind, D. (1984). *All grown up and no place to go: Teenagers in crisis.* Redding, MA: Addison-Wesley.

Ellis, A., & Dryden, W. (1987). *The practice of rational emotive therapy.* New York: Springer-Verlag.

Emery, R. E., & Laumann-Billings, L. (1998). An overview of the nature, causes, and consequences of abusive family relationships: Toward differentiating maltreatment and violence. *American Psychologist, 53*(2), 121–135.

Emery, R. E., & Wyer, M. M. (1987). Divorce mediation. *American Psychologist, 42,* 472–480.

Erikson, E. (1950). *Childhood and society.* New York: W. W. Norton.

Faludi, S. (1999). *Stiffed: The betrayal of the American man.* New York: Random House.

Fancher, R. (1979). *Pioneers of psychology.* New York: W. W. Norton.

Fink, M. (1992). Electroconvulsive therapy. In E. S. Paykel (Ed.), *Handbook of affective disorders.* New York: Guilford.

Fishbein, H. D. (1996). *Prejudice and discrimination: Evolutionary, cultural, and developmental dynamics.* Boulder, CO: Westview.

Fisher, H. E. (1998). Lust, attraction, and attachment in mammalian reproduction. *Human Nature, 9*(1), 23–52.

Fischman, J. (1987). Type A on trial. *Psychology Today, 21,* 42–50.

Fitzpatrick, K. M. (1999). Violent victimization among America's school children. *Journal of Interpersonal Violence, 14*(10), 1055–1069.

Flynn, J. R. (1999). Searching for justice: The discovery of IQ gains over time. *American Psychologist, 54*(1), 5–20.

Folberg, J., & Taylor, A. (1984). *Mediation: A comprehensive guide to resolve conflicts without litigation.* San Francisco: Jossey-Bass.

Forsyth, D. R. (1983). *An introduction to group dynamics.* Monterey, CA: Brooks-Cole.

Fox, S. I. (1966). *Human physiology* (5th ed.). New York: McGraw-Hill.

Frank, J. (1964). The faith that heals. *Johns Hopkins University Medical Journal, 137,* 127–131.

Frankl, V. (1962). *Man's search for meaning: An introduction to logotherapy.* Boston: Beacon Press.

Freedman, D. G. (1974). *Human infancy: An evolutionary perspective.* New York: Halstead Press.

Freud, A. (1926). *The psychoanalytic treatment of children.* New York: Halstead Press.

Freud, S. (1900). *The interpretation of dreams.* London: Hogarth Press.

Friedman, H. S., & Rosenman, R. H. (1974). *Type-A behavior and your heart.* New York: Fawcett.

Furr, L. A. (1998, Fall). Father's characteristics and their children's scores on college entrance exams: A comparison of intact and divorced families. *Adolescence, 33,* 533–542.

Galbraith, K. (1985). *The affluent society,* rev. ed. New York: New American Library.

Gardner, H. (1983). *Frames of mind: The theory of multiple intelligences.* New York: Basic Books.

Gelles, R. J., & Straus, M. A. (1988). *Intimate violence.* New York: Simon & Schuster.

Gemignani, J. (1998, November). Curbing the tobacco craving. *Business & Health, 16*:45–46.

Gibson, H. B., & Heap, M. (1991). *Hypnosis in therapy.* Hillsdale, NJ: Erlbaum.

Gibson, D. (1990). *Interpersonal personal perception.* New York: W. W. Freeman.

Gilbert, S. (1999). Social ties reduce the risk of a cold. In *Annual Editions 99/00: Social Psychology,* 3rd. ed. (pp. 114–115). Guilford, CT: Dushkin/McGraw-Hill.

Gilligan, C. (1982). *In a different voice.* Cambridge, MA: Harvard University Press.

Glass, J. (2003). Nurturing empathy. *Annual Editions: Personal Growth and Behavior* (pp. 108–111). Guilford, CT: Dushkin.

Glass, S. (1998, July/August). Shattered vows. *Psychology Today,* 34–42, 68–79.

Goedert, L. W. (1991). *The troubled teens: Too old for the pediatrician, too young for the gynecologist.* New York: Vantage.

Goldberg, L. R. (1993). The structure of phenotypic personality traits. *American Psychologist, 48,* 26–34.

Goleman, D. (1995). *Emotional intelligence.* NY: Bantam Books.

Goodwin, F. K., & Jamison, K. R., (Eds.) (1990). *Manic-depressive illness.* New York: Oxford University Press.

Gray, J. (1992). *Men are from Mars, women are from Venus.* New York: Harper & Collins.

Greer, J., & Rosen, M. R. (1997). *How could you do this to me? Learning to trust after betrayal.* NY: Doubleday.

Haavio-Mannila, E. (1995). Family, work, and gender equality: A policy comparison of Scandinavia, the United States, and the former Soviet Union. *Annual Editions: Human Sexuality* (pp. 17–21). Guilford, CT: Dushkin.

Hall, G. S. (1904). *Adolescence.* New York: Appleton-Century-Crofts.

Hall, E. T. (1959). *The silent language.* Garden City, New York: Doubleday.

Hall, S. S. (1999, August 22). The bully in the mirror. *New York Times Magazine,* 30–35.

Harris, F. R., Johnston, M. K., & Wolfe, M. M. (1964). Effects of positive social reinforcement of child behavior on regressed crawling of a nursery school child. *Journal of Educational Psychology, 55,* 35–41.

Harris, P. R., & Moran, R. T. (1991). *Managing cultural differences*, 3rd ed. Houston, TX: Gulf.

Harris, T. (1969). *I'm O.K., you're O.K.* New York: Harper & Row.

Hartshorne, H., & May, M. A. (1930). *Studies in the nature of character.* New York: Macmillan.

Harvard Mental Health Letter. (1997, August). Hearts and mind: Part II. *The Harvard Mental Health Letter, 14*(2), 1–4.

Haugaard, J. J. (2000). The challenge of defining child sexual abuse. *American Psychologist, 55*(9), 1036–1039.

Heart, T. (2003). This crazy online world: Your online safety guide. http://mogenic.com/advice/crazy_online_world.asp. Accessed August 2003.

Hilgard, E. R. (1986). *Hypnotic susceptibility.* New York: Harcourt, Brace & World.

Hine, T. (2002). The rise and decline of the teenager. *Annual Editions: Adolescent Psychology* (pp. 8–17). Guilford, CT: McGraw-Hill/Dushkin.

Hoffler, M. L. (1991). Empathy, social cognition, and moral action. In K. Kurtines & J. Gewirtz (Eds.)., *Handbook of moral behavior and development, Vol. 1: Theory.* Hillside, NH: Lawrence Erlbaum.

Homans, G. C. (1950). *The human group.* New York: Harcourt Brace & World.

Horney, K. (1942). *The collected works of Karen Horney, Vol. 2.* New York: W. W. Norton & Co.

Hornyansky, M. (1969). The truth of fables. In S. Egoff, G. T. Stubbs, & L. F. Ashley (Eds.), *Only connect: Readings in children's literature* (pp. 121–132). Toronto: Oxford University Press.

Huxley, A. (1963). *The doors of perception.* New York: Harper & Row.

Huxley, A. (1986). *The devils of London.* Washington, DC.

Inglehart, R. (1990). *Modernization and postmodernization: Cultural, economic, and political change in societies.* Princeton, NJ: Princeton University Press.

Ivy, D., & Backlund, P. (1994). *Exploring gender speak: Personal effectiveness in gender communication.* New York: McGraw-Hill.

Jacobson, N. S., & Gottman, J. M. (1998). Anatomy of a violent relationship. *Psychology Today,* 60–65, 81, 84.

Jaffe, D. (1974). *Healing from within.* New York: Simon & Schuster.

Jimerson, S. R. (2001). Meta-analysis of grade retention research: Implications for practice in the 21st century. *The School Psychology Review, 30*(3), 420–437.

Johns Hopkins Medical Letter: Health After Fifty. (1999, July). *Taking anger to heart* (pp. 1–2). Baltimore, MD: Medletter Associates.

Jones, A. (1988). *Women who kill.* New York: Fawcett.

Jones, E. E. (1961). *The life and works of Sigmund Freud.* New York: Basic Books.

Jones, M. (2002). *Social psychology of prejudice.* Upper Saddle River, NJ: Prentice Hall.

Jourard, S. (1964). *The transparent self.* Princeton, NJ: Van Nostrand.

Jung, C. G. (1955). *Analytical psychology: Its theory and practice.* New York: Vintage.

Jung, C. G. (1955). *Modern man in search of a soul.* New York: Harcourt Brace Jovanovich.

Jung, C. G., & Aniela, J. (1964). *Man and his symbols.* Garden City, NY: Doubleday.

Jussim, L., Nelson, T. E., Manis, M., & Soffin, S. (1995). Prejudice, stereotypes, and labeling effects: Sources of bias in person perception. *Journal of Personality and Social Psychology, 68,* 228–246.

Kassin, S. (1995). *Psychology.* Boston: Houghton Mifflin.

Kellogg, R. (1970). *Analyzing children's art.* Palo Alto, CA: Mayfield.

Kendler, K. S., & Diehl, S. R. (1993). The genetics of schizophrenia: A current, genetic-epidemiologic perspective. *Schizophrenia Bulletin, 19,* 261–285.

Kersting, K. (2003, December). Religion and spirituality in the treatment room. *Monitor on Psychology, 34*(11), 41–42.

Kessler, R. C., McGonigle, K. A., & Zhao, S., *et al.* (1994). Lifetime and 12-month prevalence of DSM-IIIR psychiatric disorders in the United States. *Archives of Geneva Psychiatry, 51,* 8–19.

Kihlstrom, J. F. (1985). Hypnosis. *Annual Review of Psychology, 36,* 385–418.

Kipnis, A. R., & Heron, E. (1995). Ending the battle between the sexes. *Annual Editions: Sexuality* (pp. 229–234). Guilford, CT: Dushkin.

Klein, M. (1960). *The psychoanalysis of children.* NY: Grove Press.

Klinger, E. (1990). *Daydreaming.* Los Angeles: Tarcher.

Knox, D., & Wilson, K. (1983). Dating problems of university students. *College Student Journal, 17,* 225–258.

Kobasa, S. C. (1979). Stressful life events, personality and health: An inquiry into hardiness. *Journal of Personality and Social Psychology, 31*, 1B11.

Kohlberg, L. (1984). *The psychology of moral development: Essays on moral development.* New York: Harper & Row.

Krantzler, M. (1999). *The new creative divorce: How to create a happier, more rewarding life during, and after, your divorce.* Holbrook, MA: Adams.

Kravitz, D. A., & Martin, B. (1986). Ringelmann rediscovered: The original article. *Journal of Social Psychology, 50,* 936–941.

Kubie, L. S. (1969). Blocks to creativity. In R. L. Mooney & A. T. Raik (Eds.), *Explorations in creativity* (pp. 33–42). New York: Harper & Row.

Kubler-Ross, K. (1975). *Final stage of growth.* Englewood Cliffs, NJ: Prentice Hall.

Kushner, M. G., Riggs, D. S., Foa, E. B., & Miller, S. M. (1992). Perceived controllability of posttraumatic stress (PTSD) in crime victims. *Behavioral Research and Therapy, 31*(1), 105–110.

LaBerge, S. (1985). *Lucid dreaming: The power of being awake and aware in your dreams.* Los Angeles: Tarcher.

Lamaze, F. (1956). *Painless childbirth: Psychoprophylactic method.* Chicago: H. Regnery.

Latané, B., & Nida, S. (1981). Ten years of research on group size and helping. *Psychological Bulletin, 89,* 308–324.

Latané, B., Williams, K., & Harkins, S. (1979). Many hands make light the work: The causes and consequences of social loafing. *Journal of Personality and Social Psychology, 37,* 308–324.

LeBey, B. (2003). American families are drifting apart. *Annual Editions: Personal Growth and Behavior* (pp. 169–171). Guilford, CT: Dushkin.

LeBlanc, A. N. (1999, August, 22). The outsiders. *New York Times Magazine,* 36–41.

Leboyer, F. (1975). *Birth without violence.* New York: Knopf.

Leboyer, F. (1976). *Loving hands: The traditional Indian art of baby massaging.* New York: Random House.

Leland, J. (2002). The secret life of teens. *Annual Editions: Adolescent Psychology* (pp. 156–159). Guilford, CT: McGraw-Hill/Dushkin.

Leung, K., Lau, S., & Lam, W. (1998, April). Parenting styles and academic achievement: A cross-cultural study. *Merill-Palmer Quarterly, 44*(2), 157–172.

Levinson, D., Darrow, C. N., Klein, E. B., Levinson, M. H., & McKee, B. (1978). *The seasons of a man's life.* New York: Knopf.

Lillard, A., & Curenton, S. (2003). Do young children understand what others feel, want, and know? *Annual Editions: Child Growth and Development,* 45–50.

Lim, J. K. (2000). *Male mid-life crisis: Psychological dynamics, theological issues, and pastoral interventions.* Lanham, MD: University Press of America.

Little, S. G., Sterling, R. C., & Tingstrom, D. H. (1996, June). The influence of geographic and racial cues on evaluation of blame. *Journal of Social Psychology, 136,* 373–379.

Loyer-Carlson, V. L. (1989). *Causal attributions and the dissolution of casual-dating relationships.* Doctoral dissertation, Oregon State University. Cited in Brown & Amatea, 2000.

Ludolph, P. S., Westen, D., Misle, B., & Jackson, A. (1990). The borderline diagnosis in adolescents: Symptoms and developmental history. *American Journal of Psychiatry, 147*(4), 470–476.

Luria, A. R. (1982). *Language and cognition.* New York: Wiley.

Lynch, R. (1977). *The broken heart: The medical consequences of loneliness.* New York: Basic Books.

Mackie, D. M., & Smith, E. R. (1998). Intergroup relations: Insights from a theoretically integrative approach. *Psychological Review, 105,* 499–529.

MacKinnon, D. W. (1978). *In search of human effectiveness.* Buffalo, NY: Creative Education Foundation.

MacLean, P. D. (1993). Cerebral evolution of emotion. In M. Sewis & J. M. Haviland (Eds.), *Handbook of emotions.* New York: Guilford Press.

Macrae, C. N., Bodenhausen, G. V., & Milne, A. B. (1998). Saying no to unwanted thoughts: Self-focus and the regulation of mental life. *Journal of Personality and Social Psychology, 74,* 578–589.

Marcuse, H. (1974). *Eros and civilization: A philosophic inquiry into Freud.* Boston: Beacon Press.

Marken, K. E. (2002). Normal and abnormal personality traits: Evidence for genetic and environmental relationships in the Minnesota study of twins reared apart. *Journal of Personality, 70*(5), 661–669.

Maslow, A. (1954). *Motivation and personality* (2nd ed.). New York: Harper & Row.

Maslow, A. (1976). *The farther reaches of human nature.* New York: Penguin Books.

Masterson, J. F. (1990). Psychotherapy of borderline and narcissistic disorders: Establishing a therapeutic alliance. *Journal of Personality Disorders, 4,* 182–191.

Mayhew, M. (1999, May 10). *Newsweek,* 158.

Mayo Clinic Health Letter. (1993, March). Laughter. *MDA Health Digest, 11*(3), 6. Baltimore, MD: Medletter Associates.

McAdams, D. P., & deSt. Aubin (1998). *Generativity and adult development: Why we care for the next generation.* Washington, DC: APA.

McGourty, C. (1988, September 22). Report cites unemployment as major health risk in Britain. *Nature, 335,* 290.

McGregor, D. (1960). *The human side of enterprise.* New York: McGraw-Hill.

McKnight, M. S. (1999). Mediating divorce: A step-by-step manual.

Meichenbaum, D. (1993). Changing conceptions of cognitive behavior modification: Retrospect and prospect. *Journal of Consulting and Clinical Psychology, 61,* 202–204.

Mencken, H. (1963). *History of the American language.* New York: Knopf.

Meyer, R. G. (1992). *Practical clinical hypnosis: Techniques and applications.* New York: Lexington.

Milgram, S. (1974). *Obedience to authority: An experimental view.* NY: Harper & Row.

Moore-Erde, M. C., Sulzman, F. M., & Fuller, C. A. (1982). *The clocks that time us.* Cambridge, MA: Harvard University Press.

Morris, D. (1970). *The human zoo.* New York: Dell.

Morris, H. J. (2003). Happiness explained. *Annual Editions: Personal Growth and Behavior, ed. 23.* Guilford, CT: McGraw-Hill/Dushkin, pp. 102–104, 203–208.

Murray, B. (2000, March). Sexual identity is far from fixed in women who aren't exclusively heterosexual. *Monitor on Psychology, 30*(3).

Nash, M. R., Lynn, S. J., & Givens, D. L. (1984). Adult susceptibility, childhood punishment and child abuse: A brief communication. *International Journal of Clinical and Experimental Hypnosis, 32*(1), 6–11.

National Association of School Psychologists (NASP). (1988). *Position statement.* Bethesda, MD: NASP.

Nelson, Toni (1996, July/August). Violence against women, *World Watch,* 33–38.

Neisser, U. (1998). Introduction: Rising test scores and what they mean. In U. Neisser (Ed). *The rising curve: Long-term gains in IQ and related measures* (pp. 3–22). Washington, DC: American Psychological Association.

Newell, S., & Jeffery, D. (2002). *Behaviour management in the classroom: Transactional analysis approach.* London: Taylor & Francis.

Nolan-Hoeksema, S. (2001). *Abnormal psychology* (2nd ed.). New York: McGraw-Hill.

Northrup, C. (1997). Your emotions and your heart: Learning to heed their messages could save your life. *Dr. Christiane Northrup's Health Wisdom for Women, 4*(8), 1–2.

O'Connell, A., & Grunder, P. (2003). The emotional, physical, and academic impact of living with terror. *Community College Journal, 75*(1), 25–29.

Ouchi, W. G. (1981). *Theory Z: How American business can meet the Japanese challenge.* Reading, MA: Addison-Wesley Publishing.

Panskepp, (2003). Cited in Kim, W., & Cole, W. Whatever happened to play? *Annual Editions: Child Growth and Development, ed. 23.* Guilford, CT: McGraw-Hill/Dushkin, pp. 79–81.

Papp, L. A., & Gorman, J. M. (1993). Pharmacological approach to the management of stress and anxiety disorders. In P. M. Lehrer & R. L. Woolfolk (Eds.), *Principle and practices of stress management* (2nd ed.). New York: Guilford.

Pavlov, I. P. (1927). *Conditioned reflexes: An investigation of physiological activity of the cerebral cortex.* London: Oxford University Press.

Pearman, R. R., & Fleenor, J. (1996). Differences in observed and self-reported qualities of psychological types. *Journal of Psychological Type, 39,* 3–17.

Pekkanen, J. (2001, September). The mystery of fetal life: Secrets of the womb. *Current,* 20–29.

Perls, F. S. (1967). *In and out of the garbage pail.* Lafayette, CA: Real People Press.

Perls, F. S. (1969). *Gestalt therapy verbatim.* J. O. Stevens (Ed.). Lafayette, CA: Real People Press.

Peterson, C. (2000). The future of optimism. *American Psychologist, 55*(1), 44–55.

Piaget, J. (1929). *The child's conception of the world.* New York: Harcourt Brace Jovanovich.

Piaget, J. (1932). *The moral judgment of the child.* Glencoe, IL: Free Press.

Piaget, J. (1962). *Play, dreams and imitation in childhood.* New York: Norton.

Piaget, J. (1970). *Genetic epistemology.* New York: Columbia University Press.

Piaget, J. (1973). *The child and reality: Problems of genetic psychology.* Brooklyn Heights, NY: Grossman.

Pittman, F. (1989). *Private lies: Infidelity and betrayal of intimacy.* New York: Norton.

Provence, S., & Lipton, R. C. (1963). *Infants in institutions.* New York: International University Press.

Putnam, F. W. (1989). *Diagnosis and treatment of multiple personality disorder.* New York: Guilford Press.

Rabasca, L. (1999, November). Knocking down societal barriers for people with disabilities. *APA Monitor, 30*(10), 14.

Reich, C. A. (1970). *The greening of America: How the youth revolution is trying to make America livable.* New York: Random House.

Remafedi, G., French S., & Story, M., *et al.* (1998). The relationship between suicide risk and sexual orientation: Results of a population-based study. *American Journal of Public Health, 88*(1), 57–60. Cited in *Harvard Mental Health Letter* (1998, December) 6.

Rice, F. P. (1989). *Adolescent development: Relationships and culture.* MA: Allyn.

Richards, P. S., & Bergin, A. E. (Eds.). (2003). *Casebook for spiritual strategy in counseling and psychotherapy.* Washington, DC: American Psychological Association.

Robins, L., & Regier, D. (Eds.). (1991). *Psychiatric disorders in America.* New York: Free Press.

Roberts, R. (2002). *Self-esteem and early learning.* London: Paul Chapman.

Rodier, P. M. (2003). The early origins of autism. *Annual Editions: Child Growth and Development,* 209–214.

Rogers, C. R. (1950). *Client-centered therapy.* Boston: Houghton Mifflin.

Rogers, C. R. (1961). *On becoming a person.* Boston: Houghton Mifflin.

Rogers, C. R. (1970). Toward a modern approach to values: The valuing process in the mature person. In C. R. Rogers & B. Stevens (Eds.), *Person to person: The problem of being human* (pp. 19–20). New York: Pocket Books.

Rogne, C. (1991). *Understanding and enhancing self-esteem.* Fargo, ND: Discovery Counseling & Educational Center.

Rotter, J. B. (1990). Internal versus external control of reinforcement: A case history of a variable. *American Psychologist, 45,* 489–493.

Sadler, W. A. (2000). *The third age: Six principles of growth & renewal after forty.* Cambridge, MA: Perseus Books.

Salovey, P., & Mayer, J. (1989). Emotional intelligence. *Imagination, Cognition, and Personality, 9*(3), 185–211.

Sakowicz, A. B. (1996). *The effect of retention, in grade one, on the slow reader,* M. A. Project. Kean College of New Jersey. ED 393 081.

Sanders, T. (1991). *Healing the wounded child: A 12-step recovery program for adult male survivors of child sexual abuse.* Freedom, CA: Crossing Press.

Santrock, J. W. (2001). *Adolescence.* Boston: McGraw-Hill.

Schulman, J., & Woods, L. (1983). Legal advocacy and mediation in family law. *Woman's Advocate, 4,* 3–4.

Schwartz, C. P. (1998, Summer). Peer marriage. *The Responsive Community,* 48–60.

Seligman, M. E. P., & Csikszentmihalyi, M. (2000). Positive psychologists: An introduction. *American Psychologist, 55*:1, 5–14.

Selye, H. (1991). History and the present states of the stress concept. In A. Monat & R. S. Lazarus (Eds.), *Handbook on stress and anxiety.* San Francisco, CA: Jossey-Bass.

Sevener, D. (1990, January). Retention: More malady than therapy. *Synthesis, 1*(1), 1–4.

Sharanske, E. (1996). (Ed.). *Religion and the clinical practice of psychotherapy.* Washington, DC: American Psychological Association.

Shaw, D. (2004). *City building on the eastern frontier: Sorting the new nineteenth-century city.* Baltimore: Johns Hopkins University Press.

Shulman, S., Elicker, J., & Stroufe, L. A. (1994). Stages of friendship growth in preadolescence as related to attachment history. *Journal of Social & Personal Relationships, 11,* 341–351.

Siegman, A. W., & Dembroski, S. A. (1989). *In search of coronary-prone behavior.* Hillsdale, NJ: Erlbaum.

Simonton, O. C. (1995, September 15). Mind-body essentials: How to use the power of the mind to beat diseases. *Bottom Line,* 9–10. Greenwich, CT: Boardroom.

Singer, J. L. (1975). *The inner world of daydreaming.* New York: Harper & Row.

Sizemore, C. (1974). *I'm Eve.* Garden City, NY: Doubleday.

Skinner, B. F. (1938). *The behavior of organisms.* New York: Appleton-Century-Crofts.

Slater, P. (1980). *Wealth addiction.* NY: Dutton, p. 25.

Sleek, S. (1999). Car wars: Taming drivers' aggression. *APA Monitor, 27*(9), 1.

Smiley, G. (2002). *Rethinking the great depression.* Chicago: I. R. Dee.

Solter, A. J. (1998). *Tears and tantrums: What to do when babies and children cry.* Goleta, CA: Shining Star Press.

Sommers, C. H. (2000, May/June). The war against boys, *Atlantic Monthly.*

Steinberg, L., & Silverberg, S. B. (1987). Influences on marital satisfaction during the middle stages of the family life cycle. *Journal of Marriage and the Family,* 751–760.

Sternberg, R. (2003, October). Enough of hate. *Monitor on Psychology, 34*(4), 5.

Sternberg, R. J. (1985, April). The measure of love. *Science Digest, 60,* 78–79.

Sternberg, R. J., & Barnes, M. L. (Eds.) (1988). *The psychology of love.* New Haven, CT: Yale University Press.

Sulloway, F. J. (1998). *Born to rebel: Birth order, family dynamics, and creative lives.* London: Abacus.

Sumerlin, J. R., & Bundrick, C. M. (1996, June). *Journal of Social Behavior and Personality, 11*(2), 253–271.

Takeuchi, T., Miyasia, A., Inugami, M., & Yamamoto, Y. (2001). Intrinsic dreams are not produced without REM sleep mechanisms. *Journal of Sleep Research, 10,* 45–52.

Teicher, M. H. (2002, March). Scars that won't heal: The neurobiology of child abuse. *Scientific American,* 68–75.

Terkel, S. (1970). *Hard times: An oral history of the great depression.* New York: Panton.

Thigpen, C. H., & Cleckley, H. M. (1957). *The three faces of Eve.* New York: McGraw-Hill.

Toffler, A. (1970). *Future shock.* New York: Random House.

Vaillant, G. E. (2000). Adaptive mental mechanisms: Their role in a positive psychology. *American Psychologist, 55*(1), 89–98.

vanGennep, A. (1908/1960). *The rites of passage.* Chicago: University of Chicago Press.

Walker, L. (1999, January). Psychology and domestic violence around the world. *American Psychologist, 54*(1), 21–29.

Wallach, L. B. (1995). Helping children cope with violence. *Annual Editions: Marriage and the Family,* (150–155). Guilford, CT: Dushkin.

Wallerstein, J. S., & Kelly, J. B. (1980). *Surviving the breakup: How children actually cope with divorce.* NY: Basic Books.

Wallis, C. (1985, December 9). Children having children. *Time,* 78–88.

Watson, J. B., & Raynor, R. (1920). Conditioned emotional reactions. *Journal of Experimental Psychology, 3,* 1–14.

Webb, W. B. (2000). Sleep. In A. Kazdin (Ed.), *Encyclopedia of psychology.* Washington, DC: American Psychological Association.

Weiss, R. S. (1986). Continuities and transformations in social relationships from childhood to adulthood. In W. W. Hartup & Z. Rubin (Eds.) *Relationships and development,* (95–110). New Jersey: Lawrence Erlbaum Associates.

Wolf, N. (1992). *The beauty myth: How images of beauty are used against women.* NY: Anchor Books/Doubleday.

Wolpe, J. (1958). *Psychotherapy by reciprocal inhibition.* Stanford, CA: Stanford University Press.

Woods, P. (1990). *The happiest days? How pupils cope with schools.* Bristol, PA: Falmer Press.

World Health Organization (1997/2000). *The World Health Report.* Geneva, Switzerland: World Health Organization, 364.

Zahn-Waxler, C., & Radke-Yarrow, M. (1986). The development of altruism. In N. Eisenberg-Berg (Ed.), *The development of prosocial behavior.* Academic Press.

Zimbardo, P. G. (1976). Pathology of imprisonment (277–279). *Readings in Psychology: Annual Editions 75/76.* Guilford, CO: Duskin Publishing Group.

Index